*f*P

ALSO BY JOHN FABIAN WITT

The Accidental Republic
Patriots and Cosmopolitans

Lincoln's Code

The Laws of War in American History

John Fabian Witt

FREE PRESS

New York London Toronto Sydney New Delhi

Free Press
A Division of Simon & Schuster, Inc.
1230 Avenue of the Americas
New York, NY 10020

First Free Press hardcover edition September 2012

FREE PRESS and colophon are trademarks of Simon & Schuster, Inc.

For information about special discounts for bulk purchases, please
contact Simon & Schuster Special Sales at 1-866-506-1949 or
business@simonandschuster.com

The Simon & Schuster Speakers Bureau can bring authors to your
live event. For more information or to book an event contact the
Simon & Schuster Speakers Bureau at 1-866-248-3049 or
visit our website at www.simonspeakers.com.

Book design by Ellen R. Sasahara

Manufactured in the United States of America

1 3 5 7 9 10 8 6 4 2

Library of Congress Cataloging-in-Publication Data

Witt, John Fabian.
Lincoln's code : the laws of war in American history / John Fabian Witt.
p.   cm.
1. Military law—United States—History.   2. War—United States—History.
3. War and emergency legislation—United States—History.   4. United
States—History—Civil War, 1861–1865.   5. Lincoln, Abraham,
1809–1865—Military leadership.   6. War (International law)—
History.   7. Lieber, Francis, 1800–1872.   I. Title.
KF7210.W58 2012
343.73'01—dc23   2012006187

ISBN 978-1-4165-6983-1
ISBN 978-1-4165-7012-7 (ebook)

For Gus and Teddy

and for

Private John C. Crowe
74th New York Infantry and
40th New York Infantry,
October 1861–June 1865

Contents

Lincoln's Code

Prologue

———⊱•⊰———

THIS IS A STORY about war in America. To be more specific, it is the story of an idea about war, an idea that Americans have sometimes nurtured and often scorned. The idea is that the conduct of war can be constrained by law.

A scene from the deadliest war in American history captures the puzzle that lies at the story's heart. The date is 1862, on Christmas Day. The setting is a modest room in a boardinghouse in Washington, D.C., tucked behind the perpetually unfinished Capitol building. At a small desk lit by an oil lamp, an aging professor works late into the night. From a distance, the man seems to be a serene oasis of calm amid the mud and the tumult of wartime Washington in winter. But if we look more closely, the illusion of peacefulness gives way to something unsettling. Below a shock of pewter hair, the man's eyes are dark hollows. His face is drawn into a perpetual scowl. A high white collar and black silk cravat cannot quite hide the old battle scars on his neck. The man's bearing betrays newer, less tangible wounds as well. In the past week, he has learned the gruesome details of the death of one son fighting for the Confederate Army in Virginia and sent another to fight for the Union in occupied New Orleans. A third son lost his right arm earlier in the year.

If we approach still closer, we can see in the dull glare of the lamp that he is working like a man possessed. He writes with a fierce intensity, pouring the furious energies of the war onto the pages before him, as if to vindicate the sacrifices of his sons by the force of his pen. At the request of President Abraham Lincoln's closest military advisers, he is drafting an order that will lay the foundations for the modern laws of war.

The man's name is Francis Lieber, and he is one of the forgotten figures from the American Civil War. As he works, the Civil War is in the darkest hour yet after almost two years of fighting. Chaos reigns in the Union war effort. In the past three months, the Army has suffered more than 25,000 casualties in two terrible battles, one at Antietam and another at Fredericksburg. President Lincoln has fired the commander of the Army of the Potomac, George B. McClellan. His replacement, Ambrose Burnside, is already failing and will be dismissed before another month goes by. In less than a week, on January 1, 1863, the Emancipation Proclamation will declare all slaves behind Confederate lines to be free. In one area after another, Lincoln has been compelled to abandon what he calls the "rose-water" approach to the conflict in favor of a far more aggressive strategy.

At this low moment of the Union's fortunes, Secretary of War Edwin Stanton and his general-in-chief Henry Halleck have turned to Lieber to draw up a code of laws for armies in battle. The project is breathtakingly ambitious. It aims not only to establish rules to govern the conduct of the Union Army but to set down in a short, usable form the accumulated customary rules binding all the armies of the extended European world. Nothing quite like it has ever existed. Lieber is its principal draftsman, and out of his pen flow prohibitions on poisons, on wanton destruction, on torture, and on cruelty. The code protects prisoners and forbids executions and assassinations. It announces a sharp distinction between men in arms and noncombatants. It disclaims tactics of bad faith and enjoins attacks motivated by revenge. It prohibits the infliction of suffering for its own sake. Lieber drafts the code in short epigrammatic articles, 157 in all, which not only set out rules for right conduct but provide the rationales and general principles that lie behind the rules. It is a working document for the soldier and the layman, not a treatise for the lawyer or the statesman.

When spring arrives and the season of active campaigning resumes, President Lincoln will issue Lieber's code as an order for the armies of the Union. He will deliver it to the armies of the Confederacy, too, and expect them to follow the rules he has set out. The code will be published in newspapers across the country and distributed to thousands of officers in the Union Army. It will endorse the new policy of Emancipation. And it will set the terms under which the Union expects the South to treat the thousands of black soldiers enrolling in the Union Army.

What starts as an American project will soon cross the Atlantic and become a global phenomenon. European international lawyers will translate it into French, German, and Spanish. In 1870, the Prussian army will adopt the American code as its own, and other European nations will quickly follow. At the beginning of the twentieth century, armies around the world will issue field manuals inspired by the American model, forerunners to the wallet cards that will one day instruct twentieth- and twenty-first-century soldiers on the laws governing such matters as the treatment of prisoners of war.

In 1899, diplomats and international lawyers will turn the American code into the first great treaty of the laws of war, signed at The Hague by nations from all over the world. Statesmen in Europe and America, along with generations of military men and lawyers, will pay homage to Lincoln and tout Lieber's code as a seminal document in the history of civilization. In the aftermath of World War II, its principles will provide part of the legal basis for trying Nazi leaders. Traces of the code will be visible in the Geneva Conventions of 1949, which will govern the law of war into the twenty-first century.

T HE STORY OF Lincoln and Lieber presents an enigma. The code Lincoln approved—the foundation of the modern laws of war—emerged amidst a war that was the harbinger of modern war in its mass destructive scale. Indeed, Lincoln approved Lieber's rules at the very moment in which he was working to transform the Union war effort. While Lieber wrote hurriedly in his Capitol Hill boardinghouse, Lincoln issued the Emancipation Proclamation and abandoned the limited war policies of the war's first year in favor of what William Tecumseh Sherman would later call the "hard hand of war."

The usual pattern of making the rules for war is very different. Laws of war typically come in the dismayed aftershock of conflict, not in the impassioned heat of battle. The first Geneva Convention went into force in 1864, shortly after a war between the Austrians and the French left Europe horrified at the carnage modern weaponry could inflict. The Franco–Prussian War of 1870–71 prompted an early effort in Brussels to draft rules for warfare in 1874. The Hague Conventions of 1907 followed hard on the Russo-Japanese War of 1905. A Geneva Protocol in 1925 prohibited asphyxiating gases and biological weapons soon after the poisonous clouds of World War I had lifted. The four Geneva Conventions of 1949 drew on the lessons of World War II. Humanitarians usually fight the last war when they make rules for the next one.

In December 1862, however, the United States was in the middle of a war in which it aimed to become more aggressive, not less. At such a moment, Francis Lieber was a striking choice. Lieber was no secret pacifist, no "simpering sentimentalist," as he liked to say scornfully. He was a passionate and sometimes even rash nationalist, a patriot who did not shy from war so much as he found himself powerfully attracted by it. He believed that nations had breathtakingly broad authority to use armed force. His hero was not the great philosopher of peace, Immanuel Kant, but the prophet of modern total warfare, Carl von Clausewitz, whose contempt for the law of war would later become legendary. In 1862, the man who helped create the modern laws of war urged blow after blow against the South and hoped fervently that the Union armies would strike the enemy with the greatest possible force. "The more vigorously wars are pursued," Lieber announced, "the better it is for humanity."

Looked at in a different light, Lieber's code seems not so constraining after all. It authorized the destruction of civilian property, the trapping and forced return of civilians to besieged cities, and the starving of noncombatants. It permitted executing prisoners in cases of necessity or in retaliation. It authorized the summary field execution of enemy guerrillas. And in its most open-ended provision, the code authorized any measure necessary to secure the ends of war and defend the country. "To save the country," Lieber wrote, "is paramount to all other considerations."

When the leaders of the Confederacy read the text the following spring, they spluttered in outrage. It was an "unrelenting and vindictive" code, they complained, one that gave "license for a man to be either a fiend or a gentleman." Jefferson Davis condemned the code as authorizing barbarous warfare. The basic rule of conduct in Lieber's code, Davis observed, was the test of military necessity. The code ruled out only four acts: torture, assassination, the use of poison, and perfidy in violation of truce flags or agreements between the warring parties. With these exceptions, armies could do virtually anything so long as it was necessary for "securing the ends of the war."

Here, then, is the beginning of an answer to the puzzle of Lincoln, Lieber, and the laws of war. The law of war Lincoln approved in early 1863 was not merely a constraint on the tactics of the Union. It was also a weapon for the achievement of Union war aims, like the Springfield rifle, the minié ball, and the ironclad ship. It is not just a humanitarian shield, though it was that. It was also a sword of justice, a way of advancing the Emancipation Proclamation and of arming the 200,000 black soldiers who would help to end slavery once and for all. As such, the code Lincoln sent into the world was the written embodiment of tensions that have been internal to the law of war in American history from the Revolution to the present. For many Americans, the law of war has been more than merely a set of constraints on the means available to armies in combat. It has been a tool for vindicating the destiny of the nation.

* * *

Human beings write history in the heat of political controversy, and in the fiery debates since September 11, 2001, Americans have begun to tell two competing stories about the law of war in U.S. history.

One story asserts that the actions of the United States after September 11, 2001, disrupted a long American tradition of respect for and participation in the international laws of war. Critics of the administration of President George W. Bush's war on terror tell this story with passionate energy. For them, acts such as the use of enhanced interrogation tactics, torture, kidnappings, and indefinite detentions, not to mention the disregard for the Geneva Conventions, betrayed a long-standing historical commitment to international law's code of conduct for war. We can see the aberration narrative in early accounts of the war on terror by journalists and lawyers like Jane Mayer and Philippe Sands, as well as in books published since 9/11 by leading historians on the military history of the founding generation. We can see it in historians' briefs to the U.S. Supreme Court in the hard-fought legal battles over military commissions. We can see glimpses of it in the Supreme Court's cautious holdings in post-9/11 terrorism cases.

Others, including many critics of international law, adopt a different story of historical rupture. For them, the novelty of our present moment is not American policy toward the laws of war. What is new, they say, is that international law has taken on a much more prominent role in American policymaking in the past few decades. Legal instruments such as the Geneva Conventions of 1949, a series of constraining statutes enacted by Congress in the 1970s and 1980s on topics such as torture and war crimes, and a controversial treaty promulgated through the United Nations in 1977 all seem (in this view) to signal a fundamentally changed regime of international law, one that has culminated in the International Criminal Court at The Hague and that for the first time seems to threaten U.S. policymakers with criminal prosecution for their wartime decisions.

Stories of great disruptions furnish the partisans on all sides of the contemporary debate with a usable past. They offer nostalgia-tinged golden ages for all concerned. But the cardboard stories we have told ourselves about the history of the laws of war in America are well-meaning myths at best. At worst they are dangerous fictions. If we look more closely at the history of American warfare, a pattern emerges, but it is not a pattern of sudden aberrations or ruptured traditions. Instead, it is the pattern captured by Lincoln and Lieber and by the startling juxtaposition of the hard hand of war and the laws of war in December 1862. From the Revolution forward, the United States' long history of leadership in creating the laws of war stands cheek by jowl with a destructive style of warfare that has come to be known among military historians as the "American way of war." Enlightenment rules stand alongside wars of extermination on the Indian frontier. Lincoln's code precedes Sherman's March to the Sea. The Hague Conferences of 1899 and 1907 bookend a terrible war in the Philippines. The American-made charter for the Nuremberg Tribunal is initialed in the same week the United States drops atomic bombs on Hiroshima and Nagasaki.

The failing of the stories told about American history on the left and the right is that they either discount the abiding significance of the law of war tradition in American history, or they offer a false idol of worship for the ideals of the law of nations, one that is so remote from our experience as to make it less likely (not more likely) that the laws of war will find traction in times of crisis. At their best, the laws of war have served as tools of practical moral judgment in moments of extreme pressure. If the law of war is to do this work, however, and not merely to be thrown overboard at the first sign of danger, it will have to rest on a better conception of the relationship between our ideals and our practices than the current historical conventions entail. Making better sense of American history—really taking account of it, in its ugly complexities instead of its airbrushed first drafts—will be indispensable if the laws of war are to survive as a useful source of moral engagement in the twenty-first century.

To MAKE SENSE of how the laws of war have functioned in American history, we will need to grapple with a third widely held view of war and law. It is one that tries to take account of the contradictions of that history, and it is perhaps the most commonly held view about the laws of war to be found in the world today. Its explanation of history is that the laws of war are hypocrisy through and through.

In the twentieth century, the hypocrisy critique animated the work of the formidable Nazi jurist Carl Schmitt, who viewed international law's pretenses of neutrality as thoroughly disingenuous. In the twenty-first century, hypocrisy is the explanation for the laws of war offered by critics of American military action, who claim that the so-called laws of war aim most of all to advance the authority of the world's most powerful states. (Hawks in the United States and Israel turn right around and level the same charge at weak states and insurgents in the developing world.) The hypocrisy claim can be found in conversations about American power today in every quarter of the globe.

Indeed, hypocrisy is the operative logic of what is undoubtedly the most influential work on the law and the morality of war in the past half century: the philosopher Michael Walzer's achingly beautiful book, *Just and Unjust Wars.* Written in the wake of the Vietnam War, Walzer's book identifies the moral aspirations of states and soldiers in war and contrasts those ideals with the acts of states and soldiers in combat. Walzer exposes the actions of states to the clear light of the moral and legal limits those same states claim to espouse. Walzer's account is radically different from Schmitt's. Where Schmitt sees power and hypocrisy all the way down, Walzer claims to identify humanitarian ideals in the moral engagement of states and warfare. Hypocrisy, Walzer tells us, is the tribute vice pays to virtue, and Walzer finds plenty of it in the actions of the United States.

It will not do to deny for a moment that hypocrisy abounds in the history of the United States at war, as it doubtless does in the history of other nations as well. The actions of nations time and again fail to live up to the standards they set for themselves. The United States is no exception. As we shall see, Thomas Jefferson engaged in wildly one-sided invocations of the laws of nations in the American Revolution. In the era of American expansion, Andrew Jackson raged against the British for their violations of the laws of civilized warfare, while at the same time treating the laws of combat with contempt. President Theodore Roosevelt and his secretary of war Elihu Root claimed to uphold the highest values of international law while whitewashing widespread torture by American forces in the Philippines. Today, there are many who view the startling influence of lawyers and legal rules in the conflicts of the twenty-first-century American military as a kind of moral cloak that disguises the brute exercise of American power.

Yet if we want to make sense of the law of war in American history, the hypocrisy answer is too easy.

The puzzle of December 1862 begins to come into focus once we see that two competing ideals have animated American behavior around the international law rules for war. The two ideals are the ideal of humanitarianism and the ideal of justice. We hold each of them so dear that it may seem like they should run together. What is peculiar about the laws of war is not merely that they sometimes do not. The peculiarity of the laws of war is that humanity and justice diverge by design. For 250 years, the laws of war have sought to minimize the horrors of war by inviting war's participants to temporarily set aside the conviction that their cause is right. Advocates of international law have aimed to create a parallel moral universe in which questions of justice are bracketed (even if temporarily) for the sake of reducing human suffering. Americans have been leading participants in the effort to elaborate these humanitarian rules. We have helped craft prohibitions on torture, on harming prisoners, and on violence against civilians. But when asked to abandon our deepest convictions of justice—even for a moment—Americans at war have been understandably reluctant to accept the invitation. The United States has thus undercut the humanitarian architecture of the laws of war even as Americans have often been some of its chief engineers.

THIS BOOK IS an account of the alternately troubled and triumphant history of the laws of war in the United States in the long century after independence. It follows the rise and fall of the project that culminated in Lincoln and Lieber, from the founding fathers, through slavery and Emancipation, to the launching of the American empire and the eve of World War I.

The book makes no claim that the paradoxes and tensions embedded in the idea of a law of war were unique to American history. Nations and peoples around the world have confronted the startling disjuncture between the law of war's humanitarian structure, on the one hand, and the pursuit of justice, on the other. Nonetheless, particular features of the United States experience have created distinctive patterns in the nation's history. In particular, the problem of slavery in wartime ran through the first century of American history from the founding onward. In 1862, it was the crisis of slavery and emancipation that called forth the Union's law of war instructions and thus helped produce the modern laws of war. Historians and international lawyers who discuss General Orders No. 100 usually call the order Lieber's code after its principal drafter. But once we see the Union's instructions as arising out of the crucible of slavery, the order is better thought of as Lincoln's. For it was Lincoln's Emancipation Proclamation that required its production and sent it out into the world.

Focusing on the history of the United States makes a good deal of sense for another reason as well. The United States is today the world's only military superpower. The United States accounts for almost half the defense spending in the world each year. Only the United States has the capacity to mount the sorts of military engagements that have become most familiar to Western observers. Grappling with the American history of the laws of war is therefore indispensable if we are to make sense of the law and morality of military force in the twenty-first century. Understanding this history is about coming to see that the idea of a law of war has contained inside itself two powerful but competing ideals for armed conflict. One is humanitarianism. The other is justice. We struggle to reconcile them today. Lincoln and Lieber wrestled with them a century and a half ago. And the founders sought to come to grips with them in the days of the Minutemen at Lexington and Concord.

PART I

You Have Brought Me into Hell!

A young Angel of Distinction being sent down to this World on some Business for the first time, had an old Courier-Spirit assign'd him as a Guide. They arriv'd over the Seas of Martinico in the middle of the long Day of obstinate Fights between the Fleets of Rodney & DeGrasse. When thro' the Clouds of Smoke he saw the Fire of the Guns, the Decks cover'd with mangled Limbs, & Bodies dead or dying, the Ships sinking, burning, or blown into the Air, and the Quantity of Pain, Misery, and Destruction the Crews yet alive were thus with so much Eagerness dealing round to one another; he turn'd angrily to his Guide, & said, You blundering Blockhead, you are ignorant of your Business; you undertook to conduct me to the Earth, and you have brought me into Hell!—No, Sir, says the Guide; I have made no Mistake; this is really the Earth, and these are Men. Devils never treat one another in this cruel manner; they have more Sense, and more of what Men (vainly) call Humanity!

—Benjamin Franklin to Joseph Priestley,
June 7, 1782

Chapter 1

The Rights of Humanity

⤜•◦•⤛

*The authorized maxims and practices of war
are the satire of human nature.*

—Alexander Hamilton, 1780

I N 1754, a rash young officer in the Virginia militia became for a short while the world's most notorious violator of the laws and usages of war. The officer, a twenty-two-year-old named George Washington, had come to public attention a year before when he made his way through a barely mapped wilderness to deliver a defiant message to the encroaching French. Now, as rumors flew of further French incursions along the Ohio River, Washington went once again into the woods, this time with 160 members of the Virginia militia and a party of Iroquois warriors. At a boulder-strewn glen between the Allegheny Mountains and the junction of the three rivers that form the Ohio Valley's eastern end, Washington encircled and attacked an unsuspecting French encampment. Firing the first shots of what would become the Seven Years' War, Washington and his men killed ten Frenchmen and took twenty-one prisoners in less than fifteen minutes. That much is clear, or as clear as such things can be. What happened next, however, has been obscured by controversy for two and a half centuries.

In his official report of the engagement Washington would later write that the French commander, Joseph Coulon de Jumonville, was killed in the initial shooting. But in French accounts, Jumonville was alive when the French company surrendered. According to the French, the entire attack was an outrage. Jumonville, they said, had not been a combatant but an ambassador delivering a message, much like Washington the year before. The French commander, they said, had not resisted the British attack, but had called for a cease-fire. And the French insisted that the attackers had murdered Jumonville in cold blood—that they had assassinated him after the fighting had stopped. In one version of the French story, the British executed Jumonville with a musket shot to the head. In another version, Washington's Indian ally, the Iroquois leader Tanacharison, did the deed. In full view of Washington and the British, Tanacharison said, "You are not yet dead, my father," whereupon he drove his tomahawk into the defenseless Frenchman's skull. Tanacharison's warriors fell upon the remaining wounded Frenchmen and killed them, too.

Washington's complicity in the Jumonville affair might have been left shrouded forever in the fog of war. But on a rainy night two months later, Washington committed an error that would haunt him for years to come. Rightly predicting that the main body of French troops would soon descend on them, Washington and his small band of Virginia militia had proceeded to construct makeshift fortifications, which Washington named Fort Necessity. But the wooden palisades proved no match for the larger French force. When the French attacked in early July, Washington's detachment was badly overmatched. With one third of his men killed or wounded, in a heavy downpour as darkness fell, Washington agreed to surrender the fort. But in the midst of the confusion and the soaking rain, with a Dutch translator who spoke French better than English, Washington hastily signed articles of capitulation that acknowledged the death of Jumonville as an "assassination," a treacherous killing abhorrent to the customs and usages of eighteenth-century warfare. Washington would later deny he had meant to sign any such acknowledgment. He would blame his interpreter. He would claim that the pouring rain had washed away the ink of the Articles. Regardless, the Articles of Capitulation from Fort Necessity were quickly circulated in Canada and France as a damning admission of British savagery. The French seized Washington's diary, and this also was published with supposedly incriminating passages in the Virginia officer's own hand. The case against Washington seemed open and shut. "There is nothing more unworthy and lower, and even blacker," wrote the governor of New France, "than the sentiments and the way of thinking of this Washington." George Washington had implicated himself in a violation of the laws of war.

For years afterward, Washington's reputation would be tarred by the affair of Jumonville Glen and its aftermath at Fort Necessity. He would spend the rest of his long and storied career as a soldier in a formal display of honor, seeking to ensure that war's chaos would never again damage his reputation.

Despite his original sin—or because of it—Washington would set out to show European soldiers that his military honor was a match for their own.

Washington and the Moral Logic of War

NO NATION IN the history of the world has made the law governing the conduct of armies in war more crucial to its founding self-image than the United States. The laws of civilized war are embedded in the Declaration of Independence, where Thomas Jefferson made the king's offenses against the rules of civilized warfare central to the Congress's brief for American independence. In the fiery peroration of the nation's founding document, Jefferson charged that George III had "plundered our Seas" and "ravaged our Coasts, burnt our Towns, and destroyed the Lives of our People." Foreign mercenaries had committed acts of death and desolation "scarcely paralleled in the most barbarous Ages," acts unworthy of civilized nations. British forces had taken Americans hostage and compelled them to bear arms against their own country. The king had incited slave insurrections and encouraged attacks by "merciless Indian Savages" whose approach to warfare was "an undistinguished Destruction, of all Ages, Sexes and Conditions."

The Declaration was only the most famous of an outpouring of professions by the men of the would-be republic declaring their faith in the laws of war. In June 1775, as the War of Independence got underway, the Continental Congress wrote the laws of war into George Washington's commission as commander in chief of the Continental Army. "You are to regulate your conduct in every respect," the Congress told Washington, "by the rules and discipline of war." A month later, the Congress explained its decision to take up arms against the British by denouncing General Thomas Gage in Boston for waging uncivilized warfare against the colonies. In the first days of 1776, the Congress addressed Major General William Howe, the commander in chief of British forces, to remind him that it was "the happiness of modern times that the evils of necessary war are softened by refinement of manners and sentiment"; in civilized warfare, Thomas Jefferson wrote for his colleagues, enemies were the "object of vengeance" only "in arms and in the field." The very same week, Congress rallied the colonies to the cause by calling their attention to the "execrable barbarity" of the British war effort. The British burned "defenceless towns and villages," Congress said. They murdered "without regard to sex or age," incited "domestic insurrections and murders," and bribed Indians "to desolate our frontiers." Congress instructed the colonies, by contrast, to "take care that no page in the annals of America be stained" by some act that "justice or Christianity may condemn."

The words of 1775 and 1776 put in place a pattern that would repeat itself time and again in the years to come. In the decades after the Declaration, the laws of war would be a staple of American politics. Angry charges of British wartime atrocities alternated with affirmations of the humanity of American forces. But for all the talk of American humanity, the revolutionary generation's embrace of the laws of war was considerably more complex than it seemed. Beneath the American celebration of the laws of war lay a deep ambivalence. The founding fathers invoked the protections of the law of war's terms. But it was not clear they agreed with its premises.

B Y THE TIME fighting started at Lexington and Concord in April 1775, a new way of thinking about war had been in the making in Europe for almost a century. Since at least the Middle Ages, long wars—often religious wars—among poorly organized armies had left broad swaths of the European Continent exhausted and depopulated. In the era of the European Enlightenment, however, the character of warfare seemed to change. War did not end. Far from it. But a combination of factors altered the way wars in Europe were fought. European wars no longer seemed to be desperate and destructive affairs, but elaborate (if deadly) games. Benjamin Franklin analogized war to chess. Others saw it as more like a gentleman's wager. Belligerents now played not for total victory but for limited purposes; in the metaphor of the gamble, the contestants had lowered the stakes.

A dashing Swiss-born diplomat named Emmerich de Vattel personified the new spirit of European warfare. Vattel, who lived from 1714 to 1767, fancied himself a poet, though his verses won him no acclaim. But as a stylish writer on the legal rules that governed the relationships among nations, he quickly became the most widely read authority in Europe and its colonies on questions relating to a body of rules known as the law of nations—the law governing states in their dealings with one another. Where many jurists still wrote in cumbersome Latin, Vattel wrote his *Le Droit des Gens* (published in 1758) in the vernacular: an accessible, even breezy French. Vattel took as his goal the persuasion of Europe's leaders to expand what he saw as the century's great humanitarian gains. "The humanity with which most nations in Europe carry on their wars at present," he wrote, could not be "too much commended." European princes of the eighteenth century, he told his readers, conducted warfare "with great moderation and generosity" and with an "extreme of politeness" unprecedented in world history. The tone of eighteenth-century warfare, he noted in one of his most frequently cited passages, was set by commanders who in the heat of battle sent food and drink to their enemy counterparts. For Vattel, the project of the laws of war was to capture the spirit of the limited wars of the eighteenth century and to encapsulate it into legal rules.

The idea of a law for warfare was not new to Vattel. For centuries, European thinking about war had proceeded along lines sketched out by Christian theorists of just and unjust war. In the medieval orthodoxy of St. Augustine and those who followed him, war was justified when waged by a commonwealth or prince to avenge an injury. Conduct in war, in turn, was justified when it was necessary to success in a just war. A sixteenth-century theologian named Francisco de Vitoria, writing in Salamanca in western Spain, put it this way: "A prince may do everything in a just war which is necessary to secure peace and security from attack." The trick, however, was that there could only be one just side in a war. The violent acts of the unjustified side were unlawful. Rather than legitimate acts of war, they were illegal acts of violence: assault and murder, trespass and theft. For the armies of the righteous, by contrast, necessity authorized terrible acts of violence. In just wars, armies could lawfully plunder the goods of the enemy and enslave them. It was permissible to sack entire cities, if necessity so dictated. It was permissible to execute prisoners taken in battle, and indeed men like Vitoria interpreted grave biblical passages in the book of Deuteronomy as authorizing the execution of all enemy combatants. The actions of a just warrior were constrained only by the requirements and necessities of victory.

When opposing armies were each equally convinced of their own righteousness, however, the medieval theory of just wars risked plunging warfare into uncontrollable cycles of destruction. Each new act by one army warranted escalation of the violence by the other. Each party to a war would be convinced that it represented the side of righteousness—or at least that if it won the war, it would be able to say it had.

For men like Vattel, the premises of Christian just war theory thus seemed badly flawed. Departing from the just war tradition, Vattel announced what he called "the first rule" of the modern law of nations. "Regular war," he wrote, "is to be accounted just on both sides." Wars would not *really* be just on both sides, to be sure. God would know which side was just. But in the fallen world of flawed and partial men, wars would be *accounted* that way in order to create a manageable way of policing the conduct of the contending armies. With justice set aside, Vattel hoped to bring an end to the otherwise endless and destructive contests over which of the belligerents—if any— fought on the side of the angels. "If people wish to introduce any order, any regularity, into so violent an operation as that of arms, or to set any bounds to the calamities of which it is productive, and leave a door constantly open for the return of peace," Vattel wrote, they would have to abandon their claims to justice.

At its heart, Vattel's conception of humanity introduced a way of separating means and ends, a way of preventing pursuit of war's purposes from obliterating regulation of its means. The moral neutrality of Vattel's approach allowed him to crystallize the limited war spirit of the age into legal rules. No longer would the bounds of permissible conduct be set by reference to the justice of the military objective in question. No longer would armies be restrained only by the loose standard of necessity.

Instead, Vattel's approach generated a dizzying array of rules. He insisted that "quarter is to be given to those who lay down their arms." Whole categories of people were to be exempt from the rigors of war. "Women, children, feeble old men, and sick persons" were to be protected. Soldiers were to spare men of the church, scholars, and "other persons whose mode of life is very remote from military affairs." Peasants no longer took any part in war and consequently no longer had anything "to fear from the sword of the enemy." All of these people were "protected, as far as possible, from the calamities of war." Military commanders and kings were sheltered from war's effects, too. Vattel's law of nations prohibited assassination, poisoning, and other forms of "treacherous murder." Even firing on an enemy's headquarters was condemned by Vattel's gentle rules. All of these were the voluntary conventions to which states at war submitted. "Humanity," Vattel summarized, obliged states "to prefer the gentlest methods" over the righteous pursuit of natural justice.

Enlightenment jurists were not the first to propose substitutes for the theory of the just war. For centuries, chivalric codes of combat had created reciprocal obligations of honor for knights in combat without regard to the merits of the underlying conflicts in which they were involved. In the sixteenth century, Francisco de Vitoria reasoned that soldiers fighting in unjust wars were not criminals if they had relied on the judgment of wise men who had pronounced them to be otherwise. A hundred years later, the Dutch-born jurist and statesman Hugo Grotius had responded to the Thirty Years' War by positing voluntary conventions of honor and equity that limited what soldiers and armies could do to those who fought for an unjust cause.

Vattel's move was to take these halting and partial starting points and turn them into the central animating principle of an Enlightenment law of war. Across Europe, in Scotland and France, the so-called publicists, as writers on the law of nations were known, embraced variations on the same idea. In Saxony, at the renowned university in Göttingen, the distinguished professor Georg Friedrich von Martens described Vattel's approach as the indispensable solution that the "civilized powers of Europe" had adopted to reduce "the horrors of war." Seven years later, the reclusive Prussian philosopher Immanuel Kant repeated the point, contending that a civilized law of war could not afford to declare either of the parties to a conflict to be "an unjust enemy." Attempts to impose unilateral resolutions for the ultimate questions of justice underlying armed conflicts, Kant observed grimly, would produce wars "of extermination" that could restore peace only at the cost of "a vast graveyard of the human race."

It was never as clear as publicists such as Vattel might have liked that the ideas of the eighteenth-century law of war were responsible for the limited wars between European states during the period. Military historians suggest that the limits on eighteenth-century European warfare were more directly connected to the balance of power among the states of Europe, to changes in military technology, to the expense of newly professionalizing armies, and to the reliance on victory in pitched battle as the arbiter of international disputes, than to the rules articulated by jurists. Nonetheless, for all this, the legal rules of the publicists captured the spirit of the age. And for a young republic—especially a weak one in a world of more powerful states—rules that might lower the toll of war held great appeal.

I N THE War of Independence, it was a chastened George Washington—twenty years removed from the Jumonville episode—who became the living embodiment of the Enlightenment way of war. Washington had never come to terms with his role in the bloody affair in the Ohio Valley. But after his first experience of battle he seems to have resolved not only to be an honorable soldier but to be seen as one as well. And as it turned out, rule-following came naturally to him. As a child, he copied by hand a short primer on "civility and decent behaviour." Later, as a commander in the years after the troubles of 1754, Washington had been a notoriously uncompromising disciplinarian of his own soldiers. ("I have a Gallows near 40 feet high erected," he once wrote, "and I am determined . . . to hang two or three on it, as an example to others.") As a wealthy planter in the Northern Neck of Virginia in the 1760s and 1770s, he became well known for his rigid insistence on contract terms and the laws of property in dealing with neighbors and business associates.

As skirmishers battled around Boston in August 1775, Washington displayed a perfect ear for the moral pitch of the eighteenth-century laws of war. The newly commissioned commander in chief wrote his British counterpart, General Thomas Gage, to demand humane treatment for the handful of captured American officers being held in the city. The American officers, Washington explained, had been acting "from the noblest of all Principles." Their cause was a just one; Washington even suggested with pride that it might be the most just cause ever. But he was adamant that the justice of their cause was irrelevant to the conduct of the armies. "Let your Opinion, Sir, be what it may," he wrote. The legal obligations of wartime arose not out of the merits of the controversy but out of what Washington called "the rights of humanity."

For the rest of the war, Washington's command recapitulated the moral structure of the Enlightenment laws of war. Even as he traded charges with the British over issues such as the treatment of prisoners of war, Washington ordered the distribution of the Articles of War to every soldier under his command, requiring that each man sign a copy of rules that included a number of provisions designed to limit the harm to civilians. When General Benedict Arnold began his ill-fated 1775 campaign into Canada, Washington ordered him to ensure that no inhabitant of the British province "be abused, or in any Manner injured" and to compensate any who were. He forbade pillage outside of Boston in March 1776, when the British had begun their evacuation of the city, and he did so again later that same year in the lower Hudson Valley in New Jersey and Westchester, constraining his own soldiers at a time when the British and their Hessian mercenaries were destroying large sections of the countryside. On New Year's Day 1777, days after the Continental Army's celebrated Christmas Day crossing of the Delaware and great victory at Trenton, Washington issued an order prohibiting the plunder of "any person whatsoever," Loyalist or revolutionary. "Humanity and tenderness to women and children," he told his men, would "distinguish brave Americans" from the "infamous mercenary ravagers" of the British forces.

*   *   *

ONE GREAT DIFFICULTY for Washington and the Continental Army was that the British viewed captured American soldiers as traitors, not prisoners of war. As such, they would not be protected by the customs of European warfare. In principle, American rebels would instead be subject to execution for treason, piracy, and other crimes against the laws of Great Britain. And though the British did not in the end pursue a plan of executions, their treatment of captured Americans was harsh enough. High-profile prisoners like Henry Laurens of South Carolina were imprisoned in the Tower of London. Ethan Allen of the Green Mountain Boys turned his own experience of two years' imprisonment, often in irons, into a book that found a ready American readership. As Allen's readers knew very well, death rates among ordinary prisoners were shockingly high. Historians' estimates suggest that 8,500 members of the Continental Army died in captivity during the war, which amounted to an astounding 47 percent of the 18,000 Continentals captured. The grim prison ships kept by the British in New York Harbor were especially notorious. The smallpox epidemic that raced through the armies of both the British and the Americans between 1775 and 1782 made the ships into virtual death traps.

The serious flaws in the British treatment of American prisoners were usually the result of logistical shortcomings and lack of preparation, not punitive policies or officially sanctioned abuse. British treatment of captured Americans stopped well short of treating the prisoners as simple criminals. Indeed, it was not as savage and cruel as many Americans suggested at the time (or as many patriotic historians have suggested in the years since). In practice, the actual treatment of such prisoners by the British was set not by the criminal laws but by the standards of eighteenth-century warfare. French prisoners were treated on mostly identical terms, though sometimes their rations were larger. Many wounded American soldiers were provided virtually the same medical attention in the aftermath of battle as British soldiers were. The British offered American prisoners food and shelter, usually in jails, old sugar warehouses, churches, and even in King's College (now Columbia University). British officers extended their American counterparts the courtesy of release on parole, and by early 1777, captured officers were living with few restraints in homes scattered throughout New York City and Long Island. In 1776 and then again in 1780, large numbers of American privates were released on parole as well, even though parole had traditionally been restricted to officers. From 1776 onward, American prisoners were exchanged on an ad hoc basis for British soldiers captured by the Continental Army and the state militias.

The problem was that the British were simply unprepared for the organizational challenges of holding thousands of prisoners in an unexpect-
edly long war of occupation 3,000 miles from London. No army in the
eighteenth-century world would have been prepared for such a task. The
formal exclusion of Americans from prisoner of war status only exacerbated
the situation.

From the very beginning of the war, Washington announced his intention to treat British prisoners by exactly the same "rule" the British adopted
for Americans in their hands. ("Painful as it may be to me," Washington
warned Gage, "your prisoners will feel its effects.") But he consistently drew
back from measures that might produce a downward spiral of reprisals and
retaliation. Washington usually decided to adopt unilaterally the standards
of the laws and usages of war without regard to British reciprocity. His disposition, he later claimed, did not allow him to follow what he called "the
unworthy Example" set by Gage. Stephen Moylan, an Irish-born aide to
Washington, suggested in 1775 that "his Excellency would rather err on the
side of mercy than that of strict Justice."

Of course, even in the early years of the war, Washington's army sometimes departed from the high standards of the eighteenth-century jurists.
Occasionally it did so egregiously. In the fall of 1777, in the chaos of the Battle of Germantown, an angry American contingent refused to grant quarter
to Redcoats even as the overwhelmed British company called for mercy; one
American recounted that "the rage and fury of the soldiers were not to be
restrained for some time, at least not until greater numbers of the enemy fell
by our bayonets." American behavior toward noncombatants in the first several years of the war also witnessed lapses. One reads Washington's repeated
orders prohibiting pillage and plunder with mounting respect for the army's
commitment to the laws of war—until it becomes clear that the orders were
given so often because of the frequency with which they were broken, especially in contested areas such as the lower Hudson Valley. (The Continental
Army court-martialed and convicted 194 soldiers for plundering civilians
during the war; typical punishments included 200 lashes and a fine of £50.)
And though Washington favored an official program of prisoner exchanges
with the British for what he called "motives of . . . humanity," the Congress undermined systematic exchanges early in 1778 when it realized that
exchanges would favor the British. Captured British soldiers would resume
their arms upon exchange, the Congress observed, but Americans held by
the British had often reached the end of their enlistments and might not
rejoin the Continental Army at all. By 1780, Washington, too, had come

to think that the strategic calculus of prisoner exchanges weighed heavily against moving forward with them, even if it meant subordinating humanity to "motives of policy."

Prisoner exchanges were the favored practice of civilized armies, but nothing in the Enlightenment laws of war required the Congress or Washington to enter into them. American treatment of the British soldiers captured in the victory at Saratoga in October 1777 was more problematic. The convention signed that month by American commander Horatio Gates and British general John Burgoyne guaranteed the return to Great Britain without delay of the nearly 5,000 prisoners on the condition that they not serve again in North America. Washington and the Congress, however, quickly realized that Gates had blundered. Releasing the Saratoga army to serve elsewhere in the British Empire or against France would free up an equal number of soldiers to come to North America. Accordingly, Washington and the Congress conspired to find trumped-up reasons to break the Saratoga agreement and delay the prisoners' return indefinitely. Virtually the entire Saratoga army remained in America for the next four years.

Despite all this, Washington made great efforts to display respect for the standards of eighteenth-century warfare. He returned to British lines American soldiers caught violating their paroles. He released vessels seized in violation of flags of truce. He ordered the humane treatment of prisoners of war held by the Continental Army. For the duration of the war, Washington remained reluctant to retaliate against the British prisoners in his power for attacks on noncombatants or indignities to prisoners. And when in the waning days of the war British forces in New Jersey committed one last atrocity, executing without trial a captured American officer named Joshua Huddy, Washington let it be known to the friendly citizens of New Jersey that it was now, of all times, that the laws of war were most important. "I shall hold myself," he wrote to New Jersey's patriot governor, "obliged to deliver up to the enemy or otherwise punish such of them as shall commit any act which is in the least contrary to the Laws of War."

TWO EPISODES FROM the War of American Independence captured the imagination of those who hoped that warfare might enter a new and humane phase. The first was a daring nighttime assault on British positions at Stony Point along the Hudson in the summer of 1779. Using only bayonets and swords so as to avoid alerting the British with the sound of musket fire, General Anthony Wayne stormed the fort. "Mercy! Mercy! Dear Americans, mercy!" cried the British, and this time the same men who had given no quarter to the British detachment at Germantown became exemplars of humanitarian restraint. In the hand-to-hand combat that seemed least susceptible to the restraining ethic of civilized warfare, Wayne and his men took 543 prisoners, killing only 63 and wounding 70 more. British commander George Collier, who had led the British assault on Stony Point just months before, praised Wayne for a "generosity and clemency which during the course of the rebellion has no parallel." Published accounts of Wayne's generosity and humanity spread across Europe. Wayne had behaved in a way that seemed to make American forces paragons of the eighteenth-century European law of nations. "You have established the national character of our country," gushed the leading Philadelphian Benjamin Rush to Wayne. "You have taught our enemies that bravery, humanity, and magnanimity are the virtues of the Americans."

A second episode showed that law did not remove war's sting. The trial and execution by hanging of Major John André, adjutant general of the British army, revealed that the moral logic of Enlightenment war could also be stern. André was, by all accounts, a man of great honor; Alexander Hamilton called him "a man of real merit." He was a European man of letters, an amateur artist, and a man of enlightened sensibilities. One acquaintance called him a man of "modesty and gentleness." André was the epitome of the civilized soldier of the latter half of the eighteenth century.

*The self-portrait of Major John André, sketched
as he awaited execution for spying in 1780.*

But in September 1780, André was drawn into a conspiracy with the treasonous American general Benedict Arnold to hand the American fortifications at West Point over to the British. The conspiracy itself was not a violation of the laws of war. Ruses and deception were permitted in wartime. But to execute the conspiracy, André arranged to meet with Arnold under false pretenses by a flag of truce. When the truce flag plan collapsed, André came secretly behind American lines along the Hudson to meet Arnold. Attempting to make his way back to British headquarters at New York on horseback and in disguise, André was captured by three members of the patriot militia near Tarrytown, New York. His captors found papers relating to the defense of West Point and implicating him in a plot. The trial that ensued became the most famous legal proceeding of the Revolution.

The laws of war, according to Vattel, offered no protections to spies. To be captured as a spy was to be subject to execution by hanging. In 1776, the British had executed the American hero Nathan Hale for spying against the British in New York. American forces had executed a number of British spies since then, but none of the stature and significance of André. Washington convened a Board of General Officers made up of thirteen generals (including Major General Nathanael Greene, the Marquis de Lafayette, and Baron von Steuben) to decide on André's fate. Observing that he had been caught in a disguise with papers containing intelligence for the enemy, the Board condemned him as a spy and sentenced him to death. Washington and Hamilton seem to have thought that André's real offense was not spying but intending to use a truce flag under false pretenses. Washington approved the death sentence nonetheless.

André's comrades among the British appealed for mercy. News of his fate traveled to England, to his friends and admirers, and to men of sensibility across Europe. André even captured the hearts and empathies of his captors. At the last moment, he appealed to Washington requesting that he be shot like a soldier rather than hanged as a common spy. But Washington determined that the "practice and usage of war" required that André be hanged. And so he was. "Never," Hamilton wrote to South Carolina's Henry Laurens, "did any man suffer death with more justice, or deserve it less." Washington later described him as "more unfortunate than criminal." Yet the laws of war had demanded that André be hanged, and though the equities of his case and the sympathies of mankind called out for a different result, the law had been followed.

The execution of André was a mirror image of the humane self-restraint exhibited by Wayne at Stony Point. Each episode gave Washington and the

Continental Army the opportunity to show that they lived by a code of warfare that imposed restraints on them that were not of their own making. Only altruism and kindness, Americans insisted, could explain the restraint of Wayne's men on the heights above the Hudson at Stony Point. And only the same selfless restraint could explain the execution by hanging of Major André, a man whose appeal had pulled so sharply at their heartstrings.

YEARS LATER, when the war was over, a cult of Washington would arise, celebrating Washington's humanity as evidence of the glorious cause to which the Revolution had been dedicated. Mason Weems, a minister who authored popular short biographies at the turn of the nineteenth century, was one of the chief architects of the Washington mythology. It was Weems who invented from whole cloth the story of young George Washington and the cherry tree. In Weems's hands, Washington's difficulties in the wilderness of the Ohio disappeared from the Washington hagiography. Weems and those who came after him substituted instead a Washington committed above all to humanity, a Washington who enjoined his soldiers to show civility and restraint in the Revolution.

Weems was right to praise Washington for his conduct during the Revolution. At critical moments of the war, Washington held off calls from his leading officers to adopt a more destructive way of war. The commander in chief had the foresight to see that American interests would be ill served by resorting to a style of war that might have left the farms and towns of British North America smoking hulks. He had the wisdom to grasp that so long as British naval superiority held hostage every seaboard town on the Atlantic coast, retaliation against British soldiers or prisoners was not just inhumane but foolish.

But the confluence of principle and interest in the American Revolution created a problem that Weems and the Washington mythmakers failed to appreciate. What Weems left out was that time and time again Washington had the good fortune of being able to cite his chief motives—considerations of "humanity, of zeal, interest and of honor," as he put it in 1777—without having to choose among them. American strategy in the War of Independence was served by Washington's adherence to the laws of war, not obstructed by it. The humane treatment of civilians, Washington reminded his officers, would secure the affections of the population. Likewise, the captured British soldiers whom the Congress looked after had American counterparts in British prisons. For all the American complaints about the treatment of their imprisoned soldiers, reprisals would have made their lives far worse. In any event, Washington observed, the "wanton Cruelty" of the British "injures, rather than benefits their cause." By contrast, Washington predicted, the forbearance of American forces "justly secured" to the patriot side "the attachment of all good men"; it might even, he hoped, "open the eyes" of the British to the merits of the American cause.

American interests in the laws of war were the flip side of the British resistance to them. The aim of the Revolution was to establish the membership of the United States in the club of civilized nations. The Congress and General Washington—not to mention Gage, Howe, and their successors—understood that by displaying respect for the club's bylaws Americans would move that much closer to an independent seat at the table of nations.

Ominously, however, some leaders of the new United States suggested that if interest and law came into conflict, interest would trump. "No fact can be clearer," wrote Francis Dana and Robert Morris for a committee of the Continental Congress, than that "interest alone (and not principles of justice or humanity) governs men." Alexander Hamilton described the actions of nations in war in much the same way. As a moral matter, Hamilton was one of the few members of the revolutionary generation to evince skepticism about the ethical achievements of the laws of war. On the occasion of André's execution, Hamilton complained that "the authorized maxims and practices of war" were "the satire of human nature." What kind of law was it, Hamilton wondered, that would permit widespread destruction and death while putting to death as honorable a man as André? Yet as a matter of the strategic interests of the fledgling United States, Hamilton thought, the laws of war had considerable appeal. In a world of powerful states, he would later write, a young republic was in a situation "little favourable to encountering hazards." And so Hamilton would encourage Washington to adhere closely to "the received maxims or usages of nations." Weak states, Hamilton thought, were well advised to promote the law of war as a matter of strategy regardless of its moral status.

Hamilton's view begged the question of what would happen if the interests of the American Revolution and the aspirations of humanity were somehow pried apart. What would happen if the interests of the United States diverged from the laws of humanity? Even after four years of war, no one knew the answer. The question had not even really begun to be posed. As the war moved into the South in 1780 and 1781, however, American leaders were hard-pressed to avoid it.

Jefferson's Savage Enlightenment

NO FOUNDING FATHER left a more enduring mark on American ideas about civilized warfare than Thomas Jefferson. Jefferson wrote eighteenth-century European standards for warfare into the Revolution's most famous document, the Declaration of Independence. He organized the Virginia state constitution's preamble around alleged British atrocities. He eloquently protested the treatment of captured American soldiers. But Jefferson also laid bare deep contradictions embedded in the revolutionary generation's ideas about the laws of war.

Jefferson was among the most learned students of the European laws of war in the North American colonies. In correspondence, he casually dropped references to the great authorities in the European law of war tradition. He quoted Grotius, whose three-volume work from the early seventeenth century formed the foundation of the modern treatment of the subject. He sprinkled his letters with references to the Swiss-born diplomat Vattel. (Vattel, Jefferson would later tell an aspiring young lawyer, should be read between noon and 2 p.m., sandwiched between Montesquieu's *Spirit of the Laws* or Adam Smith's *Wealth of Nations* in the morning and recreation in the afternoon.) Jefferson even read deeply in the lesser eighteenth-century authorities on the law of nations. He read Cornelius van Bynkershoek, a Dutch admiralty judge whose 1737 book set out a fierce conception of the laws of war but was nonetheless widely respected. He read the Swiss jurist Jean-Jacques Burlamaqui, who championed the "law of humanity" in warfare.

Jefferson brought the humanity of the European publicists to life. When 4,000 British prisoners of war—the remnants of the British army that had surrendered in October 1777 at Saratoga—were relocated to the area around Charlottesville, Virginia, Jefferson took the officers into his grand if perpetually unfinished home at Monticello. There he entertained his enemy with all the civility Vattel could have hoped for. As one of his most distinguished biographers puts it, Jefferson "opened his doors to them, entertained them, loaned them books, tried to make them comfortable." He played violin duets with a young English officer and assured another (in words that followed the Scottish philosopher Adam Ferguson) that for his part at least, the "great cause which divides our countries" would not be allowed to lead to "individual animosities."

The Enlightenment philosophers of war could not have said it better. War was to be fought without personal passions. "It is for the benefit of mankind," Jefferson wrote Patrick Henry, "to mitigate the horrors of war as much as possible." Modern nations' treatment of prisoners, Jefferson told Henry, was "delightful in contemplation" and of great value to "all the world, friends, foes and neutrals" alike. As secretary of state almost fifteen years later, Jefferson would hit upon as striking an image as any writer on the subject when he insisted that war ought not touch the lives of farmers, mechanics, or people of "other ordinary vocations." "For them," he wrote, it should be as if war "did not exist."

J EFFERSON BELIEVED THAT war should not exist for the slaveholder either. But with respect to slavery, Jefferson could not rely on the eighteenth-century laws of war. He had to rewrite them.

In April 1775, within days of the outbreak of war at Lexington and Concord, John Murray, the fourth Earl of Dunmore and the last royal governor of Virginia, threatened to free the slaves of rebellious colonists. In November, he carried out that threat in a proclamation that sent tremors through the colony's plantations. "All indentured Servants, Negroes, or others" belonging to rebels, Dunmore announced, would be freed if they were "able and willing to bear Arms." Four years later, in 1779, the commander of British armies in North America, General Henry Clinton, expanded Dunmore's proclamation to apply to all the rebellious colonies.

Over the course of the war, some 20,000 slaves made their way to British camps. Five thousand fled from plantations in Virginia alone, twenty-three of Jefferson's two hundred slaves among them. They served as laborers for the British army, they fought in arms as soldiers, and they served as pilots and guides for British raiding parties in the back waterways, byways, and swamps along the coast. Indeed, many of them proved more committed than the British royal army to combating the revolutionary cause. As late as 1786, a full three years after the British government officially gave up the war effort, encampments of former slaves along the Savannah River still fought a partisan war against their former masters.

A war of slaves against masters seemed like the kind of war that eighteenth-century publicists ought to have abhorred. Jefferson certainly did. As far back as antiquity, servile wars had seemed inevitably to entail the kinds of murderous behavior that the limited wars of the Enlightenment sought to disavow.

Yet if Jefferson searched the publicists' writings for arguments to marshal against the British wartime emancipation of American slaves, he came up empty-handed. References to slavery in the law of war literature were few and far between, and what references there were referred mostly to the ancient practice by which prisoners of war became the slaves of their captors. A passage in Vattel's *Le Droit des Gens* mentioned as an afterthought a Roman practice of restoring slaves to their masters at the end of a war. Perhaps that was some comfort to slaveholders such as Jefferson, who watched and worried as their slaves disappeared in alarming numbers. But Vattel's passage also implied that the seizure of slaves during wartime was permitted. In Grotius's work, the only passage that touched expressly on the status of slaves in wartime was even more discouraging. Grotius observed that according to the Greeks, the relationship between master and slave—even when it seemed to be peaceful—was actually a suppressed relationship of perpetual war. Writing along the same lines, English political theorist John Locke had described slavery as "nothing else but the state of war continued" between a conqueror and his captive. Slave insurrections, in this view, were the outward eruption of a suppressed state of war that already existed on plantations across the southern colonies. The Continental Congress seemed to have conceded as much in July 1775 when it complained that Britain was inciting insurrection among the "domestic enemies" of the colonies.

If anything, the eighteenth-century laws of war seemed to undermine slavery rather than offer it protections. To be sure, the European publicists were no abolitionists. Grotius had done nothing to destabilize the profits of the seventeenth-century Dutch slave-trading fleet. But a century later, the French writer Montesquieu turned the progressive humanity of the laws of war into a powerful critique of slavery. For centuries, Montesquieu pointed out, slavery had been justified as a happy alternative to death for prisoners of war. But a victor no longer had the right to kill his vanquished foe. How then could a captor justify his captive's enslavement?

Montesquieu's antislavery argument was familiar to virtually every American lawyer in the revolutionary generation thanks to Sir William Blackstone, Solicitor General to the Crown and Vinerian Professor of Law at Oxford. In his widely read *Commentaries on the Laws of England*, published in the 1760s, Blackstone followed Montesquieu almost to the point of plagiarism. The "right of making slaves by captivity," Blackstone wrote, depended on a "supposed right of slaughter." But the laws of war no longer permitted the execution of enemy captives. And once the right of slaughter was abandoned, the lesser-included power of enslavement collapsed as well.

Jefferson was well acquainted with the antislavery arguments of Montesquieu and Blackstone. Following the Scottish philosopher Lord Kames, Jefferson observed the evolution of European states' treatment of prisoners, from execution to enslavement to ransom. Jefferson famously expanded on the antislavery implications of the eighteenth-century laws of war in his initial draft of the Declaration of Independence. In that draft he accused the king not merely of unlawful acts of war against Americans but of crimes against Africans as well. "He has waged cruel war," Jefferson wrote, "against human nature itself, violating its most sacred rights of life and liberty in the persons of a distant people." The "piratical warfare" of the slave trade and its "execrable commerce," Jefferson exclaimed, epitomized the way of war of the man who claimed to be the Christian king of Great Britain.

These lines were soon cut from the Declaration at the insistence of the Congress's Georgia and South Carolina delegations. (Northern delegates concerned about slave-trading profits were also glad to see the language dropped.) Nonetheless, the passage offered powerful testimony both to Jefferson's thinking and to the capacity of the eighteenth-century laws of war to undermine the foundations of slavery.

Yet if there is anything that is now settled in debates over the founders, it is that Thomas Jefferson's views on slavery were deeply contradictory. At the very same time he was drafting the Declaration, Jefferson began to reverse the moral significance of the laws of war for the institution of slavery. Henceforth, he adjudged the law of war as civilized by the extent to which it protected slavery against the efforts of Dunmore and Clinton. In the Virginia constitution, written early in the summer of 1776, Jefferson penned what amounted to an indictment of the king for war crimes, observing in particular that the king had induced "our negroes to rise in arms among us." A month later, he wrote the same idea into the Declaration, and unlike his complaint about crimes against Africans, this protest would stick. In 1775 the Congress had called slaves "domestic enemies," tacitly reproducing the long-refuted argument that slavery was the right of the victor in war. The final draft of the Declaration complained that the king had "excited domestic insurrections amongst us."

Jefferson's contradictions on the question of slavery required extraordinary moral gymnastics. Five years after the war ended, he would tell an early historian of the Revolution that if Cornwallis had carried off slaves "to give them freedom *he would have done right*." But Jefferson quickly evaded the implications. The real reason Cornwallis had carried off slaves, Jefferson asserted implausibly, was "to consign them to inevitable death from the small pox and putrid fever then raging" in the British camp. The Virginian never paused to explain what would have motivated Cornwallis to do such a thing, though there is little doubt that slaveowners in Virginia in 1781 sought to persuade their slaves that this was just what the British had in store for them. Jefferson managed to recover at least five of his slaves. And when he did, he sent them right back into the slavery from which they had come so close to escaping.

With this one doubtful exception, Jefferson now wrote as if the stirring up of a slave population were one of the principal taboos of the eighteenth-century law of war. It was not. In developing and elaborating the rules of civilized warfare, the publicists had written for European wars, and in Europe there were hardly any slaves to speak of. But by inserting slavery into the law of war tradition, Jefferson set in motion a distinctively American departure in the laws of war, one that would persist in American law and statesmanship until the Civil War.

THE AUTHOR OF the Declaration worried as much about Indians as he did about slaves. The only "known rule" of war among the "merciless Indian savages," he wrote in the Declaration, was "an undistinguished destruction of all ages, sexes and conditions."

The phrase would soon become a favorite of Jefferson's. "The known rule of warfare with the Indian savages," he often wrote, "is an indiscriminate butchery of men women and children." Eighteenth-century European writers generally agreed. The European literature on the laws of war had given only slightly more attention to Indian wars than to slavery. But Indians seemed to observe no rules. Such nations gave "no quarter" and recognized no distinction between soldiers and noncombatants. Forceful tactics would therefore be permitted—and perhaps even required—in order "to force them to respect the laws of humanity." The savagery of an opponent (Vattel wrote) justified "coolly and deliberately putting to death a great number of prisoners" when necessary. Indeed, enemies who were sufficiently monstrous rendered "themselves the scourges and horror of the human race" and became "savage beasts, whom every brave man may justly exterminate from the face of the earth." Jefferson put it bluntly: "The same world," he wrote in 1777, "will scarcely do for them and us." The "end proposed," Jefferson said grimly, "should be their extermination."

*   *   *

JEFFERSON STIRRED ONE of the fiercest legal controversies of the war when he imprisoned the royal governor of Detroit for instigating Indian warfare against the revolutionary states.

Lieutenant Governor Henry Hamilton made for an unlikely Indian fighter. Hamilton was a cultured aristocrat of Scottish origins. He styled himself something of a ladies' man, if we can judge from his compulsively recorded observations of "well shaped" women during his travels through the British Empire. He was also a man of letters and the arts. Portrait sketches Hamilton made are among the best surviving likenesses of Indians in the Old Northwest. Hamilton was a soldier, too. But he had never been an especially good one. And that proved to be his undoing, for once the Revolution broke out, it fell to Hamilton to direct the Indians in the conflicts in the Ohio Valley.

For the first year and a half of Hamilton's tenure in Detroit, he did his best to keep Indian warriors out of the armed conflict between the Americans and the crown. Other royal officials such as General Gage in Boston had planned to involve Britain's Indian allies from as early as 1774. A year later, Lord Dartmouth and Governor Carleton of Canada instructed the Six Nations to "take up the hatchet" against the rebels. But Hamilton preached restraint. And when at last, in May and June of 1777, the British secretary of state for the American colonies ordered Hamilton to mobilize the western Indians for war, Hamilton instructed them to refrain from attacks on women and children. In September, he reported confidently that British officers were seeing to it that the Indians' conduct was marked by an "uncommon humanity."

Yet there was a contradiction in the professions of humanity in British policy toward the Indians. The rationale for enlisting Indians in the British cause was precisely to employ them in a campaign of terror. The Indians, as Lord George Germain put it to Hamilton, would excite "an alarm upon the frontiers of Virginia and Pennsylvania." (At least one report indicates that it may have been Hamilton who first urged mobilization of the Indians.) Already by September 1777, Hamilton was reporting that Indians were bringing back scalps to Detroit as evidence of their successes in combat. Soon outraged Americans on the western frontier were calling Hamilton "the Hair-Buyer General."

The war on the Virginia frontier took a dramatic turn in February 1779 when Major George Rogers Clark and 150 members of the Virginia militia captured Hamilton at Fort Vincennes on the present-day border between Illinois and Indiana. Clark was an Indian fighter in the frontier settlements of Virginia, in the same Ohio country that had almost swallowed up George Washington in the 1750s. Clark liked to say that he "expected shortly to see the whole race of Indians extirpated," and he wanted to be sure he took part in the event. He had "made a vow," he told a British prisoner, "never to spare woman or Child of the Indians."

The American victory at Vincennes quickly became one of the most celebrated stories of the Revolution. In a daring and brilliantly executed winter campaign, Clark took Hamilton's forces almost completely unawares. Laying siege to the palisade fort at Vincennes, he demanded that Hamilton and his Indian allies surrender. True to his nature, Clark refused to grant Hamilton generous surrender terms. "I told him," Clark wrote Virginian George Mason later that year, "that I wanted sufficient excuse to put all the Indians & partisans to death." But after a short siege, Hamilton had no choice but to surrender. Clark had captured the man who had become anathema all along the frontier, the dreaded lieutenant governor of Detroit, the notorious Hair-Buyer himself.

It took three months to transport Hamilton across Kentucky and Virginia to the state capital at Williamsburg, and when he arrived on June 16, 1779, Thomas Jefferson had just become governor. Two weeks into his tenure, the new governor decided to make an example of Hamilton. Meeting on the very day the exhausted prisoner arrived in Williamsburg, and without giving him the opportunity to tell his side of the story, the Virginia executive council concluded that Hamilton had violated the laws of civilized warfare. He had incited the Indians "to perpetrate their accustomed cruelties . . . without distinction of age, sex, or condition." Moreover, the council decided, he had done so eagerly and without compunction. Crediting Clark's accusations, the council found that Hamilton had given "standing rewards for scalps, but offered none for prisoners."

The Hamilton episode brought out Jefferson's barely suppressed rage at what he viewed as the outrage of the British uses of slaves and Indians alike. The "conduct of British officers, civil and military," Jefferson asserted for the Virginia executive council, had "been savage and unprecedented among civilized nations." Prison ships and dungeons were the destinations of American soldiers captured by the British, notwithstanding that (as the Virginia council insisted) captured British soldiers had "been treated with moderation and humanity." After four years of savage cruelty, Jefferson wrote, Americans had arrived at a "well founded despair that our moderation may ever lead them into the practice of humanity." And so the moderation would end with Henry Hamilton. Jefferson and the council ordered that Hamilton and two of his officers "be put into irons" and "confined in the dungeon of the publick jail," excluded from conversation with the outside world. Hamilton and the British officers of Detroit, Jefferson concluded, would be "fit subjects to begin on with the work of retaliation."

T HERE WAS a difficulty, however. The best reading of the events leading up to Hamilton's imprisonment in June 1779 suggests that the council—misled by unreliable witnesses and its own patriotic zeal—badly exaggerated Hamilton's complicity in Indian attacks. Moreover, Americans were doing the same things Jefferson accused Hamilton of doing. For every British entreaty to Indians to take up the hatchet against the Americans, there was an American request to Indians to do the same against the British. For every delivery of powder and shot to the Indians by the British, there was another by the Americans, and if the latter fell behind in the race to supply the Indians with weaponry, it was not for lack of trying. The Americans were simply not as well financed as the British.

Within days of sentencing Governor Hamilton, Jefferson happily reported to George Washington that the Virginia militia had killed a dozen Cherokee and burned eleven Indian towns, destroying the corn in the fields on which the Indians had planned to rely in the coming winter. Writing to John Jay the same week, Jefferson commented scathingly that the British war effort consisted of "ravages and enormities, unjustifiable by the usage of civilized nations." But with the next breath he celebrated the destruction of Indian villages and the burning of Indian crops. Clark's own mission to Vincennes, which Jefferson had supported from early on, had been particularly savage. At the outset of Clark's campaign, his men killed one woman prisoner, "ripping up her Belly & otherwise mangling her." During a pause in the assault on Vincennes itself, Clark dragged a French trader accused of assisting Hamilton into the clearing in front of the British fort. In full view of Hamilton and his men, Clark scalped the man. In quick succession, Clark's men then proceeded to dispatch four captured Indians allied with the British, killing them with tomahawk blows in the same clearing. Hamilton, who later claimed that Clark had tomahawked one of the Indians himself, watched the scene unfold from within the British palisades and described it in his journal:

> A young chief of the Ottawa nation called Macutté Mong . . . having received the fatal stroke of a Tomahawk in the head, took it out and gave it again into the hands of his executioner, who repeated the stroke a second and third time, after which the miserable being, not entirely deprived of life was dragged to the river and thrown in with the rope about his neck where he ended his life and tortures.

"The blood of the victims," Hamilton later wrote, "was still visible for days afterwards."

In the Revolution, neither side could make claims to a monopoly on virtue where frontier fighting was concerned. Even as he penned the Declaration's condemnation of Indian warfare, Jefferson had encouraged the use of Indian warriors in the conflict. Washington hoped that the use of Indians would "strike no small terror into the British and foreign troops, particularly the new comers." In 1779, he instructed General John Sullivan not merely to overrun Indian settlements but to destroy them, not listening "to any overture of peace" until the Indians' "total ruin" had been accomplished. A campaign of "terror" against the Indians might "inspire them" to abandon their British allies, Washington wrote.

As for the claims of scalp-buying, rewarding Indian allies for scalps was something that every European participant in the struggle for North American empires had done since at least the late seventeenth century. France had done it, England had done it. And in the Revolution, American states were doing it, too. Pennsylvania paid $1,000 for each Indian scalp. South Carolina offered £75 for male scalps. Men in Clark's militia were said to take scalps off of live Indians and to dig up Indian graves in order to augment their rewards.

In 1779 and 1780, however, Jefferson cast such facts aside. At the outset of the conflict, Jefferson had written to John Randolph that he would rather "lend my hand to sink the whole island in the ocean" than submit to the authority of the British Parliament. The cause for which Jefferson fought was what he would later describe as the "hallowed ark of human hope and happiness," a cause that held "everything dear to man." And now he was willing to take the dubious word of scoundrel witnesses seeking revenge against Hamilton for slights they had received during his governorship in Detroit. ("Interested men," said a captured British officer whom Jefferson had entertained just weeks before.) Fueled by his impassioned and righteous crusade, Jefferson lashed out with talk of atrocity and inhumanity.

The Enlightenment laws of war had been designed to remove such passions in order to prevent warfare from spiraling into bitter mutual recriminations. But as word spread of Jefferson's treatment of Hamilton, the dreaded cycle of reprisals commenced. British guards retaliated against Virginia officers held prisoner in New York. Jefferson responded by halting prisoner exchanges. If the British chose "to pervert this into a contest of cruelty and destruction," Jefferson grimly informed an understandably worried Virginia officer being held prisoner in New York, Americans would have no choice but to "measure out" and indeed "multiply" the misery of those British soldiers "in our power." Jefferson had brought the war to the edge of a perilous moral precipice. He would, he wrote to Washington, prepare "every engine" of violence that the enemy had "contrived for the destruction of our unhappy citizens." He would pray not to have to use them. But Jefferson was resigned to the "hard necessity" under which he would have to act.

Cooler heads soon prevailed. As the risks of retaliation and bitter mutual recriminations mounted, Washington urged caution. "On more mature consideration," he wrote, the case seemed to involve "greater difficulty" than he had initially grasped. Most of all, Washington urged Jefferson to avoid provoking a "competition in cruelty with the enemy." The Virginia executive council removed Hamilton's iron fetters in September 1779. Around Christmas, in the midst of a cold snap, Hamilton was moved from his basement dungeon to a warmer upstairs room in the Williamsburg jail. The next summer he was marched off to new, less severe confinement near Richmond. And in October 1780, he was paroled to British lines in New York. In March 1781, some two years after his capture at Vincennes in the Ohio country, Hamilton was exchanged for American officers and took passage back to England.

The exchange of Henry Hamilton resolved the immediate crisis. But it did little to address the dangerous undercurrents the episode had revealed. Deep convictions about the justice of the American cause had put enormous pressure on the laws of humanity in war. Cyrus Griffin, a Virginian in the Continental Congress, came to think of the Hamilton affair as an omen of things to come. "The bleeding Continent," he wrote to Jefferson, "must bleed still further." Jefferson agreed. In the fall of 1781, Griffin's grim prophecy seemed about to come true.

*   *   *

THE YEAR 1781 was one of destructive warfare in the American Revolution. After six years of fighting, tempers were growing short, especially in the southern states to which the war had turned since 1779. In South Carolina, General Nathanael Greene reported, contending bands of partisan militia fought each other "with as much relentless Fury as Beasts of Prey." The "whole Country," he warned the Congress, was "in danger of being laid Waste." British officers like the notorious Banastre Tarleton adopted slash-and-burn tactics and were rumored to deny quarter to their American opponents. Raids by British army forces into the interior of the southern states—some of them led by none other than Benedict Arnold, now a British brigadier general—burned patriot plantations and carried off thousands of slaves. In May 1781, forces under Tarleton just missed capturing Jefferson himself. (They had to settle for liberating some of his slaves.) In July, British general Alexander Leslie proposed returning 700 smallpox-infected slaves to their owners in order to set off a general epidemic. A month later, the British executed an officer in the South Carolina militia named Isaac Hayne for violating his parole, touching off a furious controversy. All the while, a steady drumbeat of Indian attacks on the western settlements kept the war at a fever pitch on the frontier.

In the escalating violence of the war, Americans resorted to startling brutality. In attacks on the Cherokee, the Virginia militia destroyed "upwards of one thousand houses" and "not less than fifty thousand Bushels of Corn." They put to the torch all the provisions stored by the Indians for a long winter season. In the Ohio country, Virginia militia killed a Cherokee man carrying a truce flag. At the Indian town of Coshocton, 300 Continental regulars under Colonel Daniel Brodhead executed and scalped their Indian prisoners. A year later, in the nearby Ohio Valley mission town of Gnadenhutten, a frontier militia coolly executed an entire band of eighty-six peaceful Indians who had been converted to the Moravian Church and whom Brodhead had relied on as allies. Men, women, and children were bound and systematically killed with a cooper's mallet and a scalping knife.

Further east, Nathanael Greene's campaign against Cornwallis and Tarleton rivaled the Indian conflict in sheer violence. As Greene raced to get his forces across the Dan River into Virginia to escape from Cornwallis's larger army, the cavalry officer Henry Lee (better known as "Light-Horse Harry Lee") conducted rearguard actions to give Greene more time. For most of the war, Lee had shown what his biographer calls an "uncommon degree of restraint." Lee himself spoke often of the importance of "a virtuous soldiery." But on the south side of the Dan, Lee ordered his men to give no quarter to the British. His men executed eighteen British dragoons from Tarleton's legion. A month later, as the skirmishing between Greene and Cornwallis continued, Lee and his men tortured a Loyalist militia member by burning the soles of his feet with a red-hot shovel in a futile attempt to extract information relating to the whereabouts of Cornwallis's forces. The behavior of the patriot militia was often even worse. Before his death by hanging at the hands of the British, Colonel Isaac Hayne of the South Carolina militia had apparently committed what one British witness called "extraordinary acts of brutality." Another partisan officer, Captain Patrick Carr, refused as a matter of policy to give quarter to Loyalists and instead "hunted them down like wild beasts."

As summer turned to fall, the combination of humanity and self-interest that had seemed to guide the American war effort at its outset looked like it might soon break apart. Eighteenth-century jurists warned that resorting to retaliation was fraught with danger. But retaliation was built into the laws of war, even in their Enlightenment recasting. It was the way armies enforced the rules and deterred violations. Now talk of terrible retaliations raced through the Congress. John Rutledge of South Carolina demanded that George Washington retaliate against British prisoners for what he claimed was the shocking treatment afforded Americans captured at Charleston. (For too long, Rutledge fumed, Congress had acted with "the milk of human kindness.") A month later, Congress approved tough reprisals by General Greene as he captured British outposts in the Deep South. At the same time, a committee of the Congress began preparations for using the inhospitable Simsbury copper mines in Connecticut as a vast and punitive dungeon for British prisoners of war. And in late September, after the British destruction of New London, Connecticut, Rutledge's fellow South Carolinian John Matthews introduced a motion in the Congress calling for widespread retaliation for British atrocities, a motion that gained momentum when it was seconded by former brigadier general James Varnum of Rhode Island. The danger, of course, was that counter-retaliation would follow. A vicious cycle of destruction would begin. Soon, it seemed, the rules might no longer apply.

T HE PASSIONS OF the Congress even caught up the cerebral James Madison, a brilliant thirty-year-old protégé of Thomas Jefferson. In 1779, Madison had served as the youngest member of the Virginia executive council. With Jefferson's encouragement, he had voted in favor of punishing the Hair-Buyer, Henry Hamilton. He had watched his senior Virginian reject prisoner of war privileges in favor of harsh detention.

Partly to manage his frail health, and partly by disposition, Madison usually kept himself aloof from the passions of the moment. Yet in 1781 the downward spiral of violence roused in Madison the same war emotions his mentor Jefferson had displayed two years before. As a member of the Continental Congress since 1780, Madison's ire was raised by British attacks on the towns of New London and Groton. With unsuppressed outrage, Madison excoriated the "barbarity with which the enemy have conducted the war in the southern states." The British, he exclaimed, had acted "like desperate bands of robbers" instead of like a nation at war. Rather than attacking "the standards and arms of their antagonists," the British burned private property and seized slaves, horses, and tobacco. They had, Madison spluttered, committed "every outrage which humanity could suffer."

In the fall of 1781, Madison decided to turn his considerable intelligence and his growing influence in the Congress toward accelerating a war of retaliation. Already in the previous weeks, the Congress had adopted a number of resolutions endorsing retaliation. John Matthews's motion had decried the burning of "defenceless towns" and the inhumane butchery of their inhabitants as "acts of barbarity" that were "contrary to all laws divine and human." Washington had long cautioned Americans to avoid destructive competitions in cruelty. But now Matthews called on the United States to respond by adopting tactics of breathtaking savagery. Matthews urged the Congress to "strictly charge" Washington to "put to death all persons found in arms" against the United States. He demanded that the small American naval force reduce coastal towns in England "to ashes." A week later, the committee report on Matthews's motion recommended even more extreme action. Appealing "to that God who searches the hearts of men for the rectitude of our intentions," the report declared that while "Justice has been delayed," now "invincible necessity" demanded retaliation. All soldiers captured while burning American towns, the report instructed, were "to be immediately consigned to the flames" they themselves had set.

Congress asked Madison to soften Matthews's harsh instructions. But in the passions of the moment, Madison barely modified the instructions at all. Madison did pull back from Matthews's threat to attack British towns. The "objects of our vengeance," Madison wrote, ought not to be the "remote and unoffending inhabitants" of British towns. (In any event, he observed, retaliation on British towns was not "immediately within our power.") But Madison was driven by the same energy that had possessed his South Carolina colleagues before him. He excoriated the British for the "scenes of barbarity by which the present war" had been characterized. He condemned what he called the "sanguinary and vindictive" war plans of British commanders. He accused the British of "burning our towns and villages, desolating our Country, and sporting with the lives of our captive citizens." The British, he fumed, had brought upon North America all the "severities and evils of war." The only way to demand respect for the "benevolent rules" civilized nations had adopted to "temper the severities and evils of war" was to wage a war of stark retaliation. Madison's conclusion was chilling. For every further attack on a defenseless town, he wrote, British officers held by American forces would be "put to instant death."

B Y EMBRACING RETALIATION when Vattel and the Enlightenment publicists warned against it, men like Jefferson and Madison showed that they were as comfortable playing just warriors as they were in the role of wartime statesmen of the Enlightenment. And they were not alone. In the pulpits, American ministers turned the Revolution into a millennial cause. The war, cried one fiery Long Island minister, was nothing less than "the cause of heaven against hell—of the kind Parent of the universe, against the prince of darkness, and the destroyer of the human race." New Haven minister and Continental Army chaplain Benjamin Trumbull told his soldier audiences in 1775 and 1776 that "the hand of God" was at work in the Americans' early victory at Ticonderoga. In Massachusetts, minister Jacob Cushing explained the logic of the cause in classic just war terms. "If this war be just and necessary on our part," Cushing announced to his congregation (and he was "past doubt" that it was), "then we are engaged in the work of the Lord." Cushing believed that the war's divine mandate obliged Americans to "use our swords as instruments of righteousness." Deists like Jefferson and Benjamin Franklin posited a more abstract connection between God and the rebellion. But they were just as impassioned. "Rebellion to tyrants," they urged, was "obedience to God." Even secular rationalists such as Tom Paine saw in American independence "a cause of greater worth" than had ever existed in history.

If a world-historical cause was at stake on the battlefield, and if perhaps even God fought alongside the American soldier, then a law of war built on the idea of the moral equivalency of warring armies would hold only modest appeal. As one historian of the Revolution has described it, a revolutionary millennialism broke out around British North America in the middle of the 1770s. Could such a people really embrace a system of laws that asked them to set aside their commitments about the righteousness of the war they fought? Merely to describe the moral neutrality of the eighteenth-century laws of war is to see how difficult it must have been for Americans of the revolutionary generation to adopt such a posture of detachment when locked in the grip of a belief in their country's world-historical importance.

In the War of Independence, the consequences of departing too far from the Enlightenment framework could have been horrific. Indeed, if the youthful Madison's retaliation manifesto had been adopted, the horrors that might have followed are readily imaginable. Thirty years before Americans took up arms against George III, an earlier King George—George II—had suppressed a different French-supported uprising, this one in Scotland, when the Duke of Cumberland put down a rebellion led by Charles Stuart, heir to the deposed Stuart line of monarchs. The violence of 1745 made the conflicts of the South Carolina upcountry look tame. In the aftermath of the rebellion's defeat at Culloden, widespread treason executions were accompanied by ritual disemboweling of the victims. Rebels caught with arms were shot upon capture. Prices were put on the heads of the Highland clan chiefs who had come to Charles's aid. Farms were burned, homes plundered and torched. The British government even adopted a policy of wholesale starvation, blocking all grain imports into Scotland.

The best historians' estimate is that most midlevel British officers in America (men like Banastre Tarleton) wanted to adopt a Scottish strategy in the American colonies, especially after the war had dragged on for years. George III certainly did not have to look far afield for the Scottish example. George II was his grandfather. The Duke of Cumberland was his uncle.

Franklin and the Mythology of the Revolution

IN THE FALL of 1781, the American Revolution seemed to be spiraling out of control. And then suddenly it ended.

Less than three weeks after Madison's retaliation manifesto, one of history's great accidents brought the war to an unexpected close. Strategic indecision by the British commander, Henry Clinton, and his best battlefield tactician, Charles Cornwallis, left a British army of over 7,000 soldiers exposed along the banks of the York River. Washington had preferred to attack Clinton's forces in New York City, but when the French navy under Admiral de Grasse arrived in the Chesapeake with twenty-nine warships and 3,000 men, Washington raced south to trap Cornwallis between the Continental Army and the French fleet. By October 1, even as Madison circulated angry retaliation plans in the Congress, the fate of the British army had been sealed. When word reached London of Cornwallis's surrender and the loss of his army, the prime minister Frederick Lord North is said to have cried out in despair, "Oh God! It is all over!" And for all intents and purposes it was.

For a year and a half, the war would limp on. There would be new atrocities and a few savage fights, especially in the no-man's-land between the patriot and Loyalist militias in the South and in the lower Hudson Valley. In the Indian country, some of the most horrific violence of the war had yet to take place. But the energies of the British army had been drained. By a great stroke of fortune, Washington had pulled the American War of Independence back from the brink of indiscriminate destruction.

I N MARCH 1782, Parliament enacted legislation announcing that the remaining American prisoners would be treated "according to the custom and usage of war, and the law of nations." For a young nation that had made the Enlightenment's legal standards for warfare central to its identity, Parliament's prisoner of war legislation marked an important recognition of independence. As an official legal matter, the war was now squarely on the civilized foundation of the Enlightenment laws of war.

It was on this basis that Benjamin Franklin began to craft a legacy for the American Revolution in the laws of war. Franklin's views on warfare were characteristically those of war's Enlightenment critics. Man's apparent proclivity for war made little sense to Franklin. Indeed, to the economical author of *Poor Richard's Almanack* war seemed a disastrous waste of human energies. Franklin was fond of saying, as he put it to his friend the British statesman David Hartley in 1780, that "there hardly ever existed such a thing as a bad Peace, or a good War." The costs of warfare, Franklin believed, almost always dwarfed the cost of achieving the same goals through more peaceful tactics. (The United States ought to buy Canada, he argued on more than one occasion, not conquer it.) The only conclusion Franklin could reach was that human beings were a "very badly constructed" species. Why otherwise, he wondered with his usual droll humor, did mankind seem to take "more pride" and pleasure "in killing than in begetting one another"? In war, men assembled in broad daylight to kill one another in massive public orgies of bloodletting. But "when they mean to beget," Franklin noted, men crept "into corners" and covered themselves "with the darkness of night" as if "ashamed of a virtuous Action."

Like Washington and Jefferson, Franklin espoused the eighteenth-century ethic of enlightened and civilized warfare. When his friend Charles Dumas, a Swiss-born man of letters living in Holland, published a new edition of Vattel's text on international law, Franklin passed the book around the Continental Congress. In one of his most widely distributed essays of the early 1780s Franklin wrote that it was "for the interest of humanity in general, that the occasions of war, and the inducements to it, should be diminished." "Motives of general humanity," he told Hartley in 1779, impelled nations "to obviate the evils men devilishly inflict" on one another "in time of war." To Edmund Burke, he wrote that "since the foolish part of mankind will make wars from time to time," it was the "wiser part" to "alleviate as much as possible the calamities attending them."

Franklin's chief contribution to the laws of war was his promotion of treaties between the young United States and the states of Europe: treaties that embraced the most civilized standards of eighteenth-century warfare. Franklin had begun to introduce the laws of war into American diplomacy in the busy summer of 1776 when the Congress asked him (along with John Adams, John Dickinson, and others) to prepare a model treaty to be proposed in the courts of Europe. Styled as guidelines for treaties of peace and friendship, the "plan of treaties" was principally a set of instructions to American ministers abroad regarding the commercial agreements American diplomats hoped to enter into with their European counterparts. But the plan also offered Franklin his first opportunity to articulate what one later commentator would call "the Ben Franklin program" in the rules of warfare—a program that quickly became the basic approach of U.S. diplomats for the next half century.

Franklin's model treaty sought in particular to protect maritime commerce from the ravages of war. It provided that neutral vessels and their cargo would be immune from seizure, even when some of the cargo was owned by nationals of the warring states; free ships, as the saying went, would make free goods. The only exception to the freedom of neutral shipping would be for so-called contraband goods, which the model treaty narrowly defined as arms and ammunition. The treaty prohibited privateering—the commissioning of private vessels as warships to attack an enemy's commercial shipping vessels. Article 23 of the treaty provided that if war were to break out between the parties, any merchant of one nation finding himself in the other would have a grace period in which to leave unmolested.

Such terms were not original to Franklin and his colleagues. Many of them had appeared in the commercial treaties accompanying the Peace of Utrecht in 1713 at the end of the War of the Spanish Succession. But if the terms were not original, they were successful. When the United States entered into a treaty of alliance with France in February 1778, Franklin's law of war program was adopted almost word for word into the young republic's first treaty.

Franklin's vision came to full fruition four years later as the war wound down. Franklin had spent almost the duration of the war serving as the United States' representative to France. He was far and away the most influential American representative in the courts of Europe. And in 1782, Congress asked Franklin and his fellow commissioners once again to try to draw the states of Europe into treaties of friendship and commerce. This time, Franklin would aim to expand still further the protections offered by the law of war to productive commerce. Armies, he wrote to Robert Morris in 1780, ought to fight only against professional soldiers and leave all others to work in peace for the "common benefit of mankind." A year later, he wrote to two Dutch merchants that the laws of war ought to protect "farmers, fishermen & merchants." The year after that he wrote to Benjamin Vaughan, an American living in London, citing the same humanizing progress that had captured the attention of Lord Kames and Thomas Jefferson. Wars of extirpation, he observed to Vaughan, had given way to wars of slavery, which in turn had evolved into civilized wars featuring the exchange of prisoners. As Franklin saw it, progress in warfare might accelerate, and if it did, then cultivators, fishermen, merchants, and artisans would all soon be eligible for protection from war's exigencies. "It is hardly necessary to add," Franklin continued, "that the hospitals of enemies should be unmolested" and that armies should pay property owners for the goods they took.

Franklin aimed to increase the costs of war by imposing new obligations on warring armies and to reduce war's upside gains by abolishing the rights of plunder and pillage. Franklin conjectured that these two steps might significantly diminish the frequency of war. In a bit of reasoning that was classic Franklin, he explained that the problem of war was essentially a competitive race to the bottom, a problem of pathological and ultimately fruitless competition among nations. At the beginning of every conflict, the privateers of one nation would take "a few rich ships." Success would encourage adventurers "to fit out more arm'd vessels" in hopes of repeating the early captures. An arms race would quickly ensue. Merchants would arm themselves "and the costs of privateering would go up" until "the expences overgo the gains."

Ultimately, there would be no profit in war at all. All that a war against commerce could accomplish was the "national loss of all the labour of so many men" diverted from more productive activities. Even worse, war might cause an entire nation to lose its "habits of industry" in a fit of "riot, drunkenness and debauchery." In a typically mordant bit of wit, Franklin suggested that "even the undertakers" made busy by war would ultimately come out the worse for the conflict. A seemingly endless stream of corpses would lure them into adopting expensive but unsustainable habits of luxurious living.

In 1784 and 1785, negotiations with Frederick the Great of Prussia produced the kind of treaty for which Franklin had long hoped. Frederick was perhaps the most respected Enlightenment sovereign on the European Continent. He cultivated French philosophes, promoted religious tolerance, and abolished torture. So large was his reputation that Immanuel Kant described the "age of enlightenment" and the "age of Frederick" as one and the same. Given such prestige, Jefferson said that a connection with Frederick would give the young United States increased stature on the European stage. And at American insistence, the treaty with Prussia embraced Franklin's Enlightenment program for the laws of war. As in the plan of treaties from 1776 and the treaty with the French of 1778, free ships made free goods, and the definition of contraband was sharply limited. In the event of war, enemy merchants had a grace period for wrapping up their affairs. But the treaty with Prussia added Franklin's favored protections for the productive classes as well. The treaty's Article 23 carved out protections for "all women and children, scholars of every faculty, cultivators of the earth, artisans, manufacturers, and fishermen." All those "whose occupations are for the common subsistence and benefit of mankind" were swept under the treaty's benevolent shield, their houses, farms, and goods made immune from destruction and waste. Article 24 added still another provision, apparently inspired by Jefferson, providing in fine detail for the wholesome treatment of prisoners. As John Adams saw it, the treaty's law of war provisions offered "a good Lesson to Mankind." A treaty between the world's new republic and Frederick the Great, Adams thought, would set an example far more powerful than the theoretical writings of European jurists.

P ieces of the Franklin program popped up in treaties executed by American diplomats for much of the next century. Law of war provisions first included in the plan of treaties from 1776 reappeared in agreements with the Netherlands and Sweden in 1782 and 1783, with Morocco, Great Britain, Spain, and Prussia in the 1790s, and with France in 1800. A treaty with Algiers adopted Franklin's provisions in 1815. More than a dozen treaties between 1824 and 1867 disseminated the Franklin program in Mexico and throughout Central and South America. Agreements with Russia in 1854 and Italy in 1871 reprised the language of 1776 for the second half of the nineteenth century. One of the few nineteenth-century American treaties of friendship and commerce not to include law of war provisions was a treaty with China in 1844. Otherwise, the treaties of the United States carried the Enlightenment laws of war into the treaty law of states from Europe to South America to North Africa. As John Adams had predicted, American diplomatic commitment to the dissemination of the laws of war had achieved sparkling results. The spread of the civilized laws of war, it seemed, would be one of the great legacies of the revolutionary generation.

Of course, it was not so simple. As a practical matter, the jewels of Franklin's law of war program were more like costume finery. During this entire period, the United States was almost completely unprepared to take up arms against the states with which it agreed to such enlightened rules of engagement. The agreement with Prussia was the most elaborate from a law of war perspective. Yet there was virtually no chance that Prussia and the United States would enter a war in 1785, let alone a war implicating the questions of naval warfare with which the treaty was primarily concerned. Where the prospect of war was more plausible, the rules Franklin announced virtually all put the United States at an advantage by restraining what nations with larger armies and bigger fleets could do. The treaties of Franklin and Jefferson and Adams announced happy ideas about humanity but never needed to confront the moral compromises those ideas might entail. They never grappled with the fierce underside of the Revolution's legacy. In a sense, the treaties of the early American republic never faced up to George Washington's original sin in the Ohio Valley in 1754.

WHEN WASHINGTON DELIVERED his resignation to the Congress on December 23, 1783, he brought to an end the first chapter of the United States' engagement with the laws of war. Washington told the Congress that he was "happy in the confirmation of our Independence and Sovereignty, and pleased with the opportunity afforded the United States of becoming a respectable Nation." Like Franklin, whose treaties were being put into place even as Washington stepped down, the retiring commander in chief saw the laws of war and the independent stature they conferred as signs of the Revolution's success. Washington never let on that there might be deep tensions between his attachment to the justice of the revolutionary cause, on one hand, and the laws of humanity, on the other. Good fortune had allowed much of the war for American independence to skirt the thorny moral questions raised by the Enlightenment laws of war. Many Americans had courageously championed the law of war's humanity. Others, however, had unleashed cycles of bitter destruction, dangerously escalating the violence of the war. At the close of the war, the American approach to the laws of war was mired in latent tensions and suppressed contradictions.

Beneath the surface of Washington's pronouncements and Franklin's enlightened treaties, the revolutionary generation's uneasy relationship to the laws of war laid out two very different paths into the future.

Chapter 2

The Rules of Civilized Warfare

---

*Our object was the restoration of all property,
including slaves, which, by the usages of war among
civilized nations, ought not to have been taken.*

 —John Quincy Adams, 1815

*It is among the evils of slavery that it taints
the very sources of moral principle.*

 —John Quincy Adams, 1820

O N T H E N I G H T of August 24, 1814, 1,500 British troops marched into Washington, D.C. The capital had been hastily abandoned. Hours earlier, First Lady Dolley Madison fled the White House with a portrait of Washington. President James Madison followed, fleeing to nearby Virginia. A motley assortment of inexperienced Maryland militia and badly led regulars from the army scattered in all directions.

At the head of the British force was Major General Robert Ross. Like the men he commanded, Ross was a battle-tested veteran, fresh from Britain's successful Peninsular Campaign against Napoleon in Spain. There Ross and his men had been witness to an exceptionally brutal war, one that historians have long treated as the beginnings of modern European warfare. Alongside the British veterans marched the Corps of Colonial Marines, some 200 strong. The Colonial Marines had not been witness to the horrors of the Peninsula. But they had reasons for engaging in a war of vengeance. All 200 of them were former slaves from the plantations of Maryland and Virginia who had taken up arms against their former masters.

Ross's men set fire to the Capitol building first. Soon the structure was up in flames. Next went the Library of Congress. With a smaller detachment of 150 soldiers, Ross marched up Pennsylvania Avenue to the White House, where they found the tables set for dinner. A few minutes before midnight, Ross and his men lifted glasses filled with the president's best wines and offered a toast to "Jemmy" Madison. Without further ceremony, they burned the president's abandoned mansion. The destruction continued on August 25. By the time Ross and his men were finished, virtually every public building in the city had been destroyed.

E VERY *PUBLIC BUILDING*—but not every building. And therein lies the striking feature of the British attack on the capital city. For all the horrors the British regulars had seen in the Peninsular Campaign, and for all the revenge the Colonial Marines might have desired, the British assault on Washington was in most respects disciplined and restrained. Only a handful of private buildings were damaged. As British officers and statesmen later pointed out, the destruction of the government buildings in the capital took place only after General Ross received no response to his repeated formal offers to negotiate. Instead, the British were greeted by a volley of muskets fired by 300 militiamen in the Capitol building and snipers in the private homes nearby, one of whom shot the horse out from under Ross himself.

These facts alone would have justified the destruction of the Capitol and of any houses that hid snipers. As British statesmen would later point out, the right of retaliation provided them a further justification for their actions. The U.S. Army, they said, had burned entire towns along the Canadian border. Even setting aside the right of retaliation, the European laws of war did not definitively prohibit attacks on an enemy capital. Emmerich de Vattel had concluded that the destruction of public buildings was permitted "when necessity or the maxims of war require it." A European precedent was readily at hand: just two years before, Napoleon had destroyed the Kremlin before his retreat from Moscow.

In the United States, however, the British march on Washington quickly became a symbol of perceived British barbarity in the war. Unable to mobilize an armed response, President Madison issued a stinging verbal denunciation of British conduct. From the smoldering ruins of the White House, he decried the depravity of British forces. For months, he said, British soldiers had destroyed and laid waste to towns along the coast. They had "wantonly destroyed the public edifices." They had burned "monuments of taste and of the arts" and the public archives. Their actions, Madison warned, exhibited "a deliberate disregard for the principles of humanity" and would lead to a war of "extended devastation and barbarism." The British burning of Washington, Madison concluded, was a gross violation of "the rules of civilized warfare."

Madison's proclamation from the ashes of the Capitol drew on two decades of American statesmanship around the laws of war. Since the founding, American statesmen and jurists had been arguing that if properly understood, the laws of civilized warfare put sharp restraints on the conduct of warring nations. With no standing army and with no navy to speak of, the young republic pioneered a vision for warfare that set unprecedented humanitarian limits on the destructive capacity of war, limits that anticipated the humanitarian law of the twentieth and twenty-first centuries. A distinctive tradition of restraints and limits had picked up where Benjamin Franklin's treaty program had left off.

Yet as Ross's troops headed back to the British vessels in the Chesapeake, leaving a burning Capitol behind them, a discerning observer might reasonably have wondered about the origins of the distinctively restrained American conception of the laws of civilized warfare. For as most American statesmen saw it, the 200 black Colonial Marines marching triumphantly away from Washington ought never to have been soldiers at all. In the American view, the marines were still slaves. By the standards of so-called civilized warfare, they were private property that had been unlawfully appropriated by the British army. And there was the tension. In early nineteenth-century America, the Enlightenment's humanitarian limits protected the slaveholder, not the slave.

The Art of Neutrality

IN 1793, congregational minister Jedidiah Morse of Cambridge, Massachusetts, published a book that quickly became (in the words of one historian) "the most widely read geographical book ever written in and about America." Morse's *The American Universal Geography* set out to map all of world history, all of its "remarkable events, discoveries, and inventions," compiling in one vast chronological table everything from "the creation of the world, and of Adam and Eve" in 4004 BC all the way to "the present Time." For Morse, history ended in April 1793 when George Washington issued a "Proclamation for the purposes of enjoining an impartial conduct on the part of the United States towards the belligerent powers, and of observing a strict neutrality." Washington's proclamation, Morse suggested, was a fitting historical bookend to the book of Genesis.

If Jedidiah Morse is remembered to history at all, it is as the father of Samuel Morse, the inventor of the telegraph and the namesake of its coded communication system. But in the 1790s the elder Morse understood that a different code, the code of neutrality, loomed large in American life. For more than two decades, from 1793 to 1815, the European world would be engulfed in war. The armies of France and Napoleon fought the armies of Austria, Great Britain, Prussia, Russia, and myriad smaller European principalities. The fledgling republic on the western side of the Atlantic aimed for a position that might hold Europe's wars at bay. Beginning with President George Washington, American statesmen aimed to be neutral.

But what exactly was neutrality? Alexander Hamilton explained the idea by likening it to the position of a married man. As a neutral nation in a world of war, he wrote, the United States "will regard his own country as a wife, to whom he is bound to be exclusively faithful and affectionate," watching "with a jealous attention every propensity of his heart to wander towards a foreign country, and mar his happiness."

Hamilton's explanation was colorful but not very helpful. His own extramarital adventure with the scandal-plagued Martha Reynolds suggested that the relationships of most husbands and wives were anything but simple. The ethics and obligations of neutral nations were almost as murky. And unlike marriage, the idea of neutrality was remarkably new.

In the medieval tradition, Christian theologians viewed neutrality as morally suspicious. Neutrality was tantamount to standing on the sidelines in the great battles between good and evil. In his epic medieval poem, *The Inferno*, Dante summed up the view of theologians and jurists when he described "the sorrowful state of souls unsure"—those "Who, neither rebellious to God nor faithful to Him, / Chose neither side, but kept themselves apart." For Dante, the neutral soul was "Repellant both to God and His enemies" alike. Heaven expelled them, to be sure, but Hell rejected them too.*

In the hands of seventeenth- and eighteenth-century jurists, however, neutrality came to seem virtuous. The same skepticism about men's capacity

---

*In the early 1960s, President John F. Kennedy attributed to Dante a line that captured the gist of the same idea: "The hottest places in Hell," Kennedy liked to say, "are reserved for those who in time of moral crisis preserve their neutrality." See Arthur M. Schlesinger, Jr., *A Thousand Days: John F. Kennedy in the White House* (Boston: Houghton Mifflin, 1965), 105.

to distinguish the just from the unjust in war that formed the basis for the Enlightenment's rules of armed conflict touched off a transformation in the moral status of neutrality. Vattel, for example, was willing to concede that if the justice of a war was clear, neutrality might be impermissible. (Obvious injustice, he wrote, was "not to be countenanced.") But Vattel thought that the clear case would be the rare case. In his view, the laws of war not only permitted neutrality, they encouraged it. Neutrality would prevent local wars from escalating into wider conflagrations.

In the Netherlands, the blunt jurist Bynkershoek was even more emphatic. With a stroke of his pen, the eighteenth-century Dutchman defined the new Enlightenment ethic of neutrality. "The enemy of my friend," Bynkershoek wrote, is "not my enemy."

IN THE REPUBLIC that aimed to stay on good terms with the enemies of its friends, the first crisis came just a few weeks after Washington's proclamation of impartiality. Edmond Charles Genet, the excitable minister from Revolutionary France, arrived in the capital in Philadelphia in May 1793 and began enlisting American vessels and men to serve as privateers against British shipping. The Washington administration demanded that he cease. Neither Jefferson, as secretary of state, nor Hamilton, as secretary of the Treasury, could believe the Frenchman's ignorance of the laws of war and neutrality. But Genet liked to thank God that he had forgotten what the books of the *ancien régime* jurists had to say. In Genet's view, the men who had written the laws of war were corrupt "jurisprudists" from the age of monarchs, men whose rules had no place in the age of revolutions. The United States was a revolutionary nation, too, of course. Its statesmen, however, sought not to reject the law of nations but to appropriate it in the service of independence from the European conflict.

Washington asked Chief Justice John Jay to advise him on the laws of war relating to France's rights to use American ports to attack British vessels. When Jay declined, citing the Constitution's separation of the judiciary from the executive branch, the cabinet issued through Jefferson a series of statements announcing bold positions on neutrality in the laws of war, positions designed to navigate between the contending claims of Britain and France. Jefferson's letters insisted that international law obliged neutral nations to prevent the arming of belligerent vessels in their ports and to prevent the capture of vessels by belligerents in their territorial waters. Many of the administration's positions were novel; Jefferson filled in specifics where the law of nations had remained content with generalities. But for the administration, Jefferson's letters served the purpose of articulating a broad conception of the rights of neutral nations in wartime. And in August, with its new positions securely in hand, the administration demanded Genet's recall. (A change in the winds in Paris meant that Revolutionary France was only too happy to comply.) The next year, Congress cemented the United States' commitment to keeping itself out of the wars of Europe by enacting a neutrality act that prohibited American nationals from assisting warring states when the United States was at peace.

I N THE YEARS after Genet's dismissal, much of the work of elaborating and defending American neutrality fell to John Marshall in his capacity as secretary of state and then chief justice of the United States. Marshall's experience and temperament prepared him well for the work of developing legal restraints on the conduct of nations at war. From 1775 to 1780, Marshall had served as a first lieutenant and captain in the Virginia militia and the Continental Army. In Virginia in 1775, he had helped kill virtually an entire column of British grenadiers in battle; the bloody aftermath, said one of his Virginia comrades, presented "the horrors of war in perfection." Early the next year, he watched his comrades burn Norfolk to prevent its falling into British hands. "Its destruction," Marshall later wrote, "was one of those ill-judged measures, of which the consequences are felt long after the motives are forgotten." During the course of the War of Independence, Marshall fought in the battles at Brandywine and Germantown. He wintered at Valley Forge, and fought again at the indecisive Battle of Monmouth in New Jersey.

Marshall's turn-of-the-twentieth-century biographer, Albert Beveridge, wrote that war was "strangely woven" into Marshall's life. A more recent biographer puts it crisply: psychologically speaking, Marshall was never mustered out of the Continental Army. Switching from muskets to diplomacy, he became one of the fiercest defenders of American neutrality. In 1797, President John Adams appointed Marshall to a crucial diplomatic mission to France, where he formed the moral backbone of an American delegation that resisted French demands of assistance and preserved the United States' hard-won neutrality in the European wars. Three years later, Adams appointed Marshall as secretary of state, where he issued instructions to American ministers abroad that became legendary for their acute statement of American impartiality.

If Marshall's experience helped him understand the dangers of destructive war and the strategic value of neutrality for U.S. interests, his personality and demeanor made him an ideal champion of the law of nations. To the uninitiated, the rules and principles of the law of nations could often seem obscure or unduly abstract. But Marshall brought arcane rules of international law down to earth. An awkwardly tall man, with a long mop of hair knotted by a ribbon at the back of his neck, Marshall had a personable style that one young lawyer described in the 1810s as "uncommonly mild, gentle, and conciliatory." Joseph Story, Marshall's junior colleague on the Supreme Court, remarked on his colleague's "unaffected modesty." Marshall was able to explain complex law of nations decisions with disarming simplicity. He was an intuitive and practical judge more than a scholar or learned jurist. Earlier justices such as the star-crossed James Wilson had drawn ridicule when they displayed erudition and showed off their book learning. Marshall, by contrast, had (as one historian has put it) "more use of his brains than of his bookshelves."

Early American diplomacy gave Marshall plenty to think about. The wars of Europe offered extraordinary commercial opportunities for neutral nations. ("The new world," Jefferson hoped, might be able to "fatten on the follies of the old.") The wars also presented the young republic with grave risks. The warring nations of Europe all sought to obstruct the trade of their enemies, and often that meant interfering with neutral shipping. In 1793 and 1794, British cruisers seized between 250 and 300 American merchant vessels carrying goods to or from the French West Indies. Not to be outdone, the French seized 316 American ships in 1795 and millions of dollars' worth of American goods in 1796 and 1797. Desperate for manpower, British naval officers impressed American seamen into service in the Royal Navy as alleged British subjects or deserters. Deserters abounded on American vessels, and the British and American governments disagreed on whether subjects of one state could abandon their obligations of loyalty for another. In any event, British commanders were none too careful about distinguishing deserters and British subjects from Americans. French cruisers were no more scrupulous. French commanders tortured American ship captains to obtain coerced admissions that the cargo aboard their vessels was British. Whether such admissions were true or not seemed less important than the pretext they offered for seizing the cargoes.

* * *

L ACKING THE MILITARY power to defend American shipping interests, American statesmen made the legal rights of neutral vessels central to the task of republican statecraft. Using little more than his wits, Marshall began to give content to the meaning of wartime neutrality in the very first case he heard as chief justice, a case called *Talbot v. Seeman.*

The *Talbot* case was Marshall's introduction to a fast-growing part of the Court's work, the adjudication of so-called prize cases. Today, the law of war often seems to be a law for the executive branch of the government—the president, the armed forces, and the diplomatic corps, rather than for the courts. But this allocation of authority was far less apparent when Marshall took the bench. In prize cases, the federal courts were asked to decide whether the crew and captain of an armed ship (usually an American warship or private vessel authorized by the U.S. government) were entitled to a captured vessel as a prize of war. That entitlement turned on whether the capture had been legal under the laws of war. And so in dozens of cases during the French Revolution and the Napoleonic Wars, the federal courts were called to interpret and apply the law of maritime warfare.

The story of the *Talbot* case began in 1799 amid the Quasi-War with France, a period when conflicts over neutral shipping had led to open hostilities. A French warship captured a Hamburg-based vessel called the *Amelia*, which had been carrying goods from the British colony of India back to Hamburg. The French seized the vessel on the basis of the controversial French policy of seizing any vessel (even neutrals such as the *Amelia*) carrying British goods. Before the French prize crew could get the *Amelia* into a French port, the American frigate *Constitution,* commanded by Captain Silas Talbot, seized the vessel from its captors and brought it to New York. The *Amelia* was not a legal prize to Talbot and the crew of the *Constitution* because the United States was not at war with Hamburg. The *Amelia* was a neutral ship. But Captain Talbot and his crew believed they were entitled to a reward—or "salvage"—for rescuing the *Amelia* from its French captors.

In deciding the case, Marshall blazed a trail for the prize cases that would follow. The United States had powerful interests in expansive neutral shipping rights. It had the world's leading neutral shipping fleet, and limits on what warring nations could do to neutral vessels seemed likely to redound to the United States' interest. But in *Talbot,* Marshall faced considerable obstacles to vindicating the policy of neutral rights. In particular, two acts of Congress seemed to cut against the Hamburg merchants. The first authorized vessels belonging to the United States to recapture any vessel such as the *Amelia* in the control of a French crew. The second authorized the collection of salvage fees by American prize crews from the owners of friendly vessels after their recapture by the U.S. Navy. The statute set the salvage fee at one half the value of the recaptured vessel.

The difficulty for Marshall was that the Congress (wittingly or otherwise) seemed to have impinged on the interests of neutral vessels in wartime. If the acts in question authorized American captors to collect one half the value of a recaptured neutral vessel, then the statute would exact a toll on the very neutral shipping that American statesmen were trying to expand and defend.

Less than a year removed from his post as secretary of state, Marshall turned in a classic (if little remembered) example of the brilliantly creative adjudication that would be the hallmark of his thirty-five years as chief justice. The meaning of the first statute, which authorized the seizure of armed French vessels, was too clear to be avoided. Captain Talbot had acted within the authorization of Congress in seizing the formerly neutral *Amelia*. But in the name of neutral shipping Marshall picked apart the second statute. The Congress, Marshall wrote for the Court, had provided salvage fees for vessels retaken from "the enemy." But "the enemy of whom"? If the Congress meant vessels retaken from an enemy of the United States, then the language swept in vessels from places like Hamburg, which were neutral in the conflict between the United States and France. But if the Congress had meant to affect only vessels retaken from a nation that was at war with both the United States *and* the nation from which the recaptured vessel hailed, then neutral shipping would not be implicated at all by the congressional salvage fee.

Marshall construed the statute as applying only to vessels retaken from an enemy of both the United States and the nation whose vessel was salvaged. In doing so, he interpreted the statute as saying what Congress could have said, but had not in fact said at all. Marshall swept aside all objections. "By this construction," he concluded, "the act of Congress will never violate those principles which we believe . . . the legislature of the United States will always hold sacred." The principles in question were expansive neutral rights in the laws of war on the high seas.

For three decades after *Talbot v. Seeman*, Marshall did his utmost to limit warfare's effects on neutral commerce in the Atlantic world. Whenever possible, he ruled that American policy in times of armed conflict was not "to be construed to violate neutral rights, or to affect neutral commerce, further than is warranted by the law of nations." Building case upon case, Marshall constructed a system of rules of engagement for naval warfare that placed sharp limits on warring nations' rights to attack neutral vessels and neutral goods in wartime. When neutral vessels were seized as blockade-runners, for example, Marshall undermined the long-standing rule banning trade with blockaded ports. The mere intention to go to a blockaded port, he determined, was not enough to turn a vessel into a blockade-runner. Nor, Marshall held in another case, did neutral vessels become blockade-runners merely by inquiring at a port to learn whether a blockade was in effect. Marshall construed acts of Congress narrowly to undo the capture of a neutral Dutch vessel leaving a French port during hostilities between the United States and France and to protect vessels with plausible but contested neutral status. He determined that neutral goods remained free from capture even when shipped in an armed enemy convoy. In all these cases and more, Marshall sought the rule that (as he put it in one of his most prominent pro-neutrality decisions, a case called *The Nereide*) "enlarges the sphere of neutral commerce."

Neutral shipping interests sometimes lost contested legal questions in Marshall's Court, of course. A case involving a vessel named the *Commercen* raised the issue of whether a neutral Swedish vessel was immune from American capture while delivering contraband military supplies to the British in Spain during the War of 1812. In a rare instance in which the chief justice was unable to persuade his colleagues that his own pro-neutral view was correct, the Court decided the case in favor of the American captor and against the Swedish vessel. (Marshall dissented.) Similarly, in the case of the *Schooner Exchange*, neutral shipping interests lost when the U.S. district attorney arguing the case told the Court that upholding neutral American merchants' claims to a vessel now serving as a warship of the Spanish government would be tantamount to a judicial declaration of war against Spain. This time even Marshall went along and rejected the neutral merchants' claims for restoration of the vessel. Where there was insufficient proof of neutral ownership, Marshall and his Court also routinely upheld the condemnation of goods. Nonetheless, the pattern in the Court's decisions was clear. Where the legal question at issue was close, neutral shipping interests almost always won. The policy advanced by Marshall's Court sought to uphold what the chief justice described as a "mitigated law of war." Marshall aimed to release neutral shipping from what one litigant before the Court called the "dark and even barbarous" acts that the European laws of war had all too often allowed.

The *Talbot* decision presaged Marshall's neutrality jurisprudence in a second sense as well. For in the *Talbot* case, Marshall decided in favor of neutrality and against the captain and crew of an American vessel. In case after case for the next thirty-five years, Marshall and the Court found in favor of foreign nationals and against American claimants. This was no easy thing to do. American claimants were often heroic naval officers such as Captain Silas Talbot who had risked their lives and their crews to make captures on the high seas. Yet in each such case Marshall took the long view. For Marshall, the real interests of the United States seemed to require a law of war that delimited as narrowly as possible the destructive authority of warring states, and increased as broadly as possible the rights of neutral nations.

A Path to War

P ERCEIVED SELF-INTEREST was not the only guide for American views of the legal limits on nations at war. Interest helped to motivate neutrality. But neutrality was an identity as well as an interest, and in American diplomacy the idea of neutral rights took on a life of its own, one that soon came to threaten the very interests American neutrality had been designed to defend. Indeed, within just a few short years, American statesmen's aggressive defense of neutrality put the entire republican project at risk.

The central rule in war at sea—one that all the relevant authorities agreed upon—was that neutral vessels were free to carry neutral goods in times of war. Since the days of Benjamin Franklin, American statesmen had contended for an even broader rule, a rule that would have made all goods carried on board neutral vessels (goods owned by neutrals or enemies alike) free from wartime confiscation. Free ships, under this principle, would make free goods.

Yet even if American diplomats could have persuaded the British to cede to the rule of free ships and free goods (and they could not), two potentially gaping exceptions to the rule of free neutral shipping posed obstacles to neutral rights in wartime. The first exception was that neutral vessels trying to run a blockade were subject to lawful capture. In the abstract, this seemed unproblematic. But the blockade exception—construed broadly enough—threatened to undo the first principle of neutral rights. Could a warring state simply declare a blockade on its enemy's ports? If so, all neutral shipping would be subject to confiscation. The second exception was that military supplies and arms were subject to confiscation. Such goods were "contraband" and thus seizable even when owned and carried by neutrals. Here the key question was the definition of military supplies. Could food be contraband? Perhaps even tobacco or coffee? If provisions counted as military supplies, then a broad interpretation of the contraband exception might eliminate most neutral trade.

The legal questions arising out of the rule and its exceptions quickly became pressing practical problems once British and French warships began scooping up American merchant vessels in the 1790s. From 1793 onward, the British took the position that provisions were contraband because they fed the massive armies of Revolutionary France. Later the British declared a broad blockade against Napoleon-dominated Continental Europe. American statesmen protested both policies vehemently. The American minister to London, Thomas Pinckney, argued that food could not possibly be contraband. James Madison insisted that ports could only be put under blockade if they were "actually besieged" by an enemy fleet. Jefferson complained that the British positions seemed "so manifestly contrary to the law of nations, that nothing more would seem necessary than to observe that it is so."

But as the controversies played out across the law of wartime neutrality, Jefferson's confidence in the clarity of the international laws of war seemed increasingly unwarranted. The general propositions contained in the old books on the laws of war failed to decide concrete controversies. For every American complaint, the British had a legal counterargument. By the conflict's end, the law of neutrality had become a vast diplomatic battlefield of its own. In the words of Henry Wheaton, a prominent American lawyer writing in 1815, the law of neutrality at sea was an internally inconsistent jumble, "a mass of contradictory decisions, usages, and conventions." As the diplomatic historian Samuel Bemis would later note, the texts of the traditional authorities on such questions possessed an "almost biblical elasticity."

As AMERICAN STATESMEN saw it, one rule adopted by the British seemed to transgress even the most flexible laws of naval war. The so-called Rule of 1756 had first been announced by the British at the outset of the Seven Years' War with France. It made neutral vessels attempting to trade with the French colonies in the West Indies subject to British capture. The theory of the rule was that neutral merchants did not have the right to engage in a trade that had ordinarily been closed to them in peacetime, but was then opened once a warring nation's own merchant vessels had become subject to capture. To engage in that trade was to breach the impartiality that neutrality required, turning ostensibly neutral merchants into the willing agents of France's end run around British naval power.

Upon the outbreak of war in 1793, the ministry of the youthful William

Pitt and his foreign secretary, Lord Grenville, reinstated the old Rule of '56. American statesmen immediately denounced it. James Madison complained that no ingenuity could possibly devise a plan "more unjust in itself" or "more disrespectful to neutral nations." It was, he insisted, a gross deviation from the laws of war, invented to serve expedient British interests.

Yet the argument that the Rule of '56 violated the laws of war at sea was not nearly as clear as Madison would have liked. During his term as secretary of state, Madison assembled a massive 200-page brief against the British rule. Madison confidently announced that nothing in the authorities on the laws of nations expressly authorized the British rule. But he could cite nothing in that literature that definitively ruled it out of bounds, either. In an embarrassing passage, Madison was forced to distinguish a contrary authority on the weak (though correct) grounds that it had been mistranslated from the French.

A decision by the British Lords Commissioners of Appeals in a case called the *Essex* in the spring of 1805 fueled the already heated disputes breaking out between the United States and Britain. For years, the British admiralty courts had allowed American vessels to circumvent the Rule of '56 by carrying goods from France's West Indian colonies to the Continent so long as the goods had first been imported to the United States. Vessels bound for the Continent from Martinique in the French West Indies would stop over briefly in the United States before departing again for Europe. They would pay import duties to U.S. customs officials, but thanks to congressionally enacted "drawbacks," they received refunds on all such payments. By 1805, the so-called re-export trade was booming.

Fed up with the ruses and fictions that had allowed American shipping interests to evade the Rule of '56, the Lords Commissioners of Appeals decided to bring an end to this open flouting of British policy. Neutral re-export vessels that merely touched at a neutral port as a pretext before continuing on to Europe or to European colonies in the West Indies—the Lords determined in the *Essex* case—would be treated as carrying on enemy commerce. As such, the vessels and their cargo would be subject to confiscation under the Rule of '56.

American merchants and statesmen reacted angrily to the *Essex* decision. An American war hawk exclaimed in 1811 that it was the "foundation" of the "system of vexation and injury" to which Britain had subjected the United States. Yet once again the laws of war shed little light on the merits of either the British or the American positions in the controversy. Nothing in the eighteenth-century authorities on the laws of war reached these sorts of questions. The legal status of the Rule of '56 was already murky. The *Essex* decision merely filled out the procedural details of how the British would apply this legally ambiguous British policy. In arguing about the *Essex* case, American and British statesmen were making arguments that were two levels removed from any concrete proposition to be found in authoritative sources for the laws of war.

B EFORE THE *ESSEX* controversy had a chance to settle down, another explosive episode presented even graver questions about the wartime rights of neutrals and aggravated still further the crisis in American-British relations. American reliance on thousands of former British seamen to keep its small fleet afloat was an open secret. One American vessel in particular, the frigate USS *Chesapeake*, was said to have as many as thirty-five British deserters among its crew. Deserters from the *Chesapeake* openly mocked their former officers as they walked about the streets of Norfolk, Virginia. And in the spring of 1807, Vice Admiral Sir George Cranfield Berkeley of the British fleet decided to act. Without consulting London, Berkeley issued an order to his fleet to stop the *Chesapeake* and search it for deserters.

It was one thing for British impressment crews to board neutral merchant vessels owned by American citizens. Such visitations and searches had been going on despite American protests since 1793. But boarding a vessel of the U.S. Navy, let alone one of the most heavily armed vessels in the service, was another matter altogether.

When the *Chesapeake* left Norfolk, it was soon hailed by a British warship, HMS *Leopard*. After fruitless requests to search the vessel for deserters, the *Leopard* fired on the unprepared American frigate. Within fifteen minutes, three Americans had been killed and eighteen (including the *Chesapeake*'s captain) injured. Firing only a single shot, the *Chesapeake* quickly offered its surrender. Captain Salusbury Pryce Humphreys of the *Leopard* imperiously refused to accept. But his boarding crew searched the vessel and seized four alleged British deserters.

Responses to the humiliating *Chesapeake* episode were virtually apoplectic. The Jefferson administration took the position that the attack was an outrage against American national dignity and against international law. American historians have tended to agree, in no small part because the British eventually returned two of the captured deserters (another they executed and the fourth died in British custody) and offered compensation for their injuries.

But did the law of war at sea really prohibit Berkeley's order or the *Leop-*

ard's actions? Even here the story turns out to have been far more complicated. There seems little doubt that Berkeley's order was unauthorized by the British government. As a matter of British law, the order may have been illegal. (The Foreign Ministry sorely wished Berkeley had sought advice from London before taking action that produced so much American outrage.) Yet as a matter of international law, there were once again legal arguments on both sides. Privately, leading British statesmen argued that the *Leopard* had not violated international law at all. Lord Bathurst, the president of the British Board of Trade and a former Lord of the Admiralty, argued that the United States had stripped itself of its neutrality by luring British seamen into deserting. In a widely circulated essay, the irascible English pamphleteer William Cobbett agreed. A onetime resident of Philadelphia, Cobbett insisted in high dudgeon that the law of neutrality did not authorize neutral nations to "inveigle away your troops." As Cobbett saw it, the United States had done just that and could hardly complain if British war vessels defended their rights. In the United States, Federalist critics of the Jefferson administration adopted the same view. Under the circumstances, wrote an author identified as "Old Soldier" in the *Providence Gazette*, "no impartial person" could doubt that the four deserters "ought to have been given up."

In the end, British foreign secretary George Canning offered a carefully hedged apology to Secretary of State James Monroe. Canning disavowed Admiral Berkeley and the *Leopard* to the extent their action against the *Chesapeake* rested "on no other grounds" than a general right to search for deserters. But of course, the *Leopard*'s actions did rest on "other grounds" over and above a generalized right of search. As Canning well knew, the legal arguments circulating in support of Vice Admiral Berkeley and the *Leopard* rested almost entirely upon the claim that the *Chesapeake* had encouraged and sheltered deserters. When Canning finally decided to disavow Berkeley's actions, it was (as the American historian Henry Adams later observed) "not because the lawyers were unable to prove whatever the government required." Canning disowned Berkeley and the *Leopard* "because the right of searching foreign ships-of-war was not worth asserting, and would cost more than it could ever bring in return."

A T THE HEART of many of the problems in the laws of war was continuing controversy over the issue that had preoccupied James Madison and the Continental Congress in the fall of 1781: the right of a nation to resort to retaliation.

No judge was capable of adjudicating disputes among nations. All the authorities agreed, therefore, that retaliation was a permissible response to the violation of the laws of war. The problem with retaliation, however, was that even if it was indispensable in enforcing the rules of the game, it also risked escalating cycles of retaliatory destruction. And that was exactly what seemed to be happening once again in the first decade of the nineteenth century. Retaliation seemed to be hindering cooperation, not promoting it.

After the *Essex* decision, Napoleon retaliated by barring the admission into French ports of any vessel that had previously called at a British port and by making all goods of British origin subject to confiscation, regardless of their present ownership. Napoleon's so-called Berlin Decree would have been a clear violation of American neutral trading rights if drafted on a blank slate. But once nations were retaliating for alleged violations of the rules by others, almost all bets were off. All too often, wartime rights at sea had proven to be a kind of legal quicksand. That was the lesson of the Rule of '56, the *Essex* case, and the *Chesapeake* controversy. But the right to retaliate threatened to render the laws of war almost completely indeterminate.

A year later, in a decree issued from Milan, Napoleon retaliated again, this time making vessels that had called at British ports not merely inadmissible in French ports but actually subject to seizure and confiscation by French cruisers. French retaliations touched off another round of reprisals. In the fall of 1807, the British instituted a draconian new licensing system requiring all vessels trading with the French to first purchase a license from the British. If drawn up in the abstract, the licensing scheme would have violated neutral rights. The celebrated British admiralty judge Sir William Scott thought so. But after France's Berlin and Milan decrees, the question was no longer (as Scott put it) "merely original and abstract." As a retaliatory measure, the British viewed the licensing arrangement as a reprisal, not a violation of neutral American shipping rights.

With each new turn in the vicious cycle of retaliations, American statesmen howled. American rights, they contended, were not contingent on British or French compliance with the laws of war at sea. Retaliation between the nations at war could not be aimed at an innocent third party such as the United States. But once again, there was nothing so specific as this in the law of war authorities. Beyond the general right to retaliate for violations of right, the authorities suggested weakly an obligation to exhaust peaceful avenues of resolution before resorting to arms. Even here, Vattel admitted that it was not always necessary to attempt peaceful reconciliation. So long as an aggrieved state had "reason to believe" the enemy would not enter into sincere negotiation, even this requirement could be abandoned.

M UCH OF LAW (to quote the lawyer and historian John Reid echoing the scoundrel founding father Aaron Burr) is made up of what can be "plausibly argued and forcibly maintained." In the laws of war at sea, the ambit of plausibility seemed extraordinarily wide and force was always at the ready. Often it seemed that what distinguished an effective legal argument from an ineffective one was a bit like the difference between a language and a dialect: one had a powerful navy and the other did not. In practice, this meant that what mattered most was that Britain's navy ruled the waves. Some wags said that this meant that Britain could waive the rules. But even this view seemed too hopeful about the legal regime in which war at sea took place. British naval power meant not merely that it could *waive* the rules but that it could *make* the rules, too. On the most hotly disputed questions of the day, rules barely existed.

From one point of view, the laws of war had simply been unable to shape the course of events. Power in the form of navies, ships-of-the-line, and the number of cannon in the British fleet had overwhelmed the hopeful rules of Enlightenment conflict. Yet there was another view, one that was still more daunting for those who hoped that law might tame the destructive violence of war. For it was plausible to think that the law had actually made things worse.

The acerbic William Cobbett argued that the laws of war had exacerbated the conflict between Britain and the United States, not ameliorated it. The "greatest curse of all," he wrote, were the "innumerable" pamphlets being produced by dueling propagandists sniping at one another from across the Atlantic. "What makes the thing more serious," he added, was that most of the propagandists were lawyers.

There was much evidence for Cobbett's dispiriting conclusion. A vitriolic language of injured national dignity had obscured the concrete issues at stake. Virginians swore pacts to defend the "sacred rights" purchased with the blood of their forefathers. A congressional committee spluttered that the assault on the *Chesapeake* had been "a flagrant violation of the jurisdiction of the United States." "Our rights are absolute," wrote the editors of the *National Intelligencer* in Washington, D.C. "We must strive for our rights," declared the *Richmond Enquirer*. Congressmen called the *Chesapeake* incident a "daring insult" and bemoaned the loss to the "dignity of the nation." Crowds marched in the streets of New York to denounce British outrages.

Claims of right and violated honor had made finding peaceful resolutions of the conflicts at sea harder, not easier. The United States was completely unprepared for the rigors of war. But talk of injured national dignity impelled American statesmen toward armed conflict nonetheless. After a decade of mutual recriminations and failed legal posturing, the Congress declared war against Britain in June 1812.

American War, American Slavery

THE COLLAPSE OF neutrality brought the United States back into armed conflict with Great Britain. For thirty years, the United States had managed to avoid armed conflict on land with powerful European states. For thirty years, American statesmen had developed a broad conception of the legal limits on warring nations. Now their ideas would be tested.

With the onset of fighting, recriminations that had been smoldering since the end of the War of Independence broke out anew. A massacre of wounded American soldiers by Indian allies of the British at the Raisin River on the western frontier produced angry accusations of British complicity. Along the

An American artist depicted British responsibility for the massacre of
American prisoners at Frenchtown along the Raisin River.
Note the British camp in the background at left.

Canadian border, British troops burned the American frontier towns of Niagara, Black Rock, Lewiston, and Buffalo. Accusation and counteraccusation led to the retaliatory imprisonment of dozens of officers on each side. A congressional committee launched inquiries into the British conduct of the war.

American behavior often matched that of the British. At York (now Toronto), undisciplined American sailors torched the Canadian Parliament building; as American forces left the city they deliberately set fire to the remaining public buildings. Forces under American brigadier general George McClure burned more than 100 dwellings in Newark, Upper Canada's first capital city. The British accused Americans in these and other incidents of looting and pillaging along the Canadian border. In Virginia, Americans were said to leave poisons in bottles of liquor to be drunk by unsuspecting and thirsty British raiding parties.

Writing from Belgium in the midst of the war, John Quincy Adams predicted that the laws of civilized warfare would likely collapse in the face of Anglo-American armed conflict. "No wars are so cruel and unrelenting as civil wars," he wrote to his wife, "and unfortunately every war between Britain and America must and will be a civil war."

H APPILY, John Quincy Adams was wrong, at least for the most part. It was a salutary feature of the War of 1812 that, despite moments of impassioned fury on both sides, the laws of war helped draw some of the passions from the conflict. The tradition powerfully shaped and limited the warfare that took place in the United States and Canada from the summer of 1812 to January of 1815.

As observers closer to the ground than Adams could hardly fail to notice, each warring side found room for acts of humane generosity toward the other. At the outset of the conflict, the Congress enacted a law authorizing the president to ensure "the safe keeping, support and exchange of prisoners of war." Congress and the president allowed British merchants in American ports a decent interval of six months to leave after war broke out. They provided the same opportunity to any enemy vessel that had left a British or Irish port prior to September 1, 1812, on the theory that such vessels might not have had notice of the onset of war. Both nations recognized flags of truce so as to allow the continuation of mail service between the two nations. Each nation recognized the other's agents in their own port towns as representatives of enemy prisoners. American agents were stationed in Canada, in the West Indies, and in Great Britain. British agents were stationed up and down the east coast of the United States. Agents on both sides had the power to visit the prisoners they represented on a regular basis. In the early stages of the war especially, the United States and Great Britain alike generally released captured prisoners on parole, leaving them to go free on a promise not to take up arms again until exchanged for prisoners on the other side.

In November 1812, American and British officials at Halifax agreed on a provisional plan for the exchange of all prisoners for the remainder of the conflict. The exchange agreement relied heavily on the general principles of the laws of war. Early the following year, American Commissary General of Prisoners John Mason and British Agent for Prisoners Thomas Barclay struck a more permanent deal on prisoner treatment and exchange, committing each side to treat prisoners taken from the other "with humanity conformable to the usage and practise of the most civilized nations during war." The agreement authorized warships to enter enemy ports under flags of truce from time to time for the release of prisoners. (The United States appointed an officer to handle such vessels as they came in.) And although as a formal matter the British government ultimately declined to sign on to the Mason-Barclay exchange cartel, the agreement and its incorporation of the laws of war set the terms for prisoner treatment and exchange for the duration of the conflict. In 1813 and 1814, each side exchanged more than 1,000 soldiers under the rules agreed on by Mason and Barclay.

Prisoners were less and less likely to be released promptly as the war dragged on. But even for those who were not paroled or exchanged, conditions of confinement were relatively humane. Prisoners held by the United States were allowed regular visits to nearby towns, where they bought and sold goods. Enlisted men hired themselves out to local employers. In Philadelphia, prisoners had the benefit of regular social visitors, gifts, and even visits by certain women of notoriety, discreetly registered in the prison log as "downtown Mrs. Smith and her elves." In 1814, Christmas dinner aboard the American prison ship *Aurora* was described by the *Salem Gazette* as a feast: the prisoners "sat down to tables loaded with roast turkeys, plum puddings, and other good things," reported the editors. Federal marshals charged with overseeing British prisoners ensured that the sick and the wounded received medical care.

The main complaint of British enlisted men held for any length of time was boredom. British statesmen complained mostly that American prison guards allowed captured British enlisted men to escape too easily. Given the expectation of exchange, escape into the American countryside was tantamount to desertion. The wide open spaces of the American interior called out to hundreds of British soldiers who chose simply to make their imprisonment the beginning of new American lives.

This is not to say that prisoners of war held by the United States in the War of 1812 did not face considerable hardship. In the winter of 1813–14, the British decision to send twenty-three Irish-born Americans to Great Britain for treason trials touched off a cycle of retaliation. Within weeks, both nations placed virtually every captured enemy officer in close confinement until at last the British announced that no such trials would held.

On balance, American soldiers taken prisoner by the British had it worse than their British counterparts. In fighting in the west and along the Canadian border, American soldiers worried with good reason about the prospect of being captured by Britain's Indian allies. Indian warfare did not offer the protections of the European laws of war to captured enemy combatants. Dozens—perhaps even hundreds—of American soldiers captured in the Great Lakes region paid a grave price.*

Yet we get a good sense of the treatment of prisoners by the British from one of the most famous episodes of the war. The lawyer and amateur poet Francis Scott Key came to know something about the relative restraint with which the War of 1812 was fought when he went aboard the HMS *Surprise* to request the release of a fellow Maryland citizen detained by the British in September 1814. Over dinner, Key spoke with the British commanders, Major General Ross and Vice Admiral Alexander Cochrane. He persuaded the two men to release his neighbor. Key was detained for a few days while the British prepared to assault Baltimore and then released to his own vessel. As the story has it, Key wrote "The Star-Spangled Banner" while on his way back to shore. Key's stanzas contained few kind words for the British; the lesser known ones castigated the "haughty hordes" and the "hirelings and slaves" of the enemy. But his lines were badly misleading. The circumstances in which Key wrote his verses made manifest the civilized limits of the conflict in which the British and the Americans were engaged.

* * *

---

*The next chapter discusses the clash between Euro-American rules of war and their Indian analogues in more detail.

ONE ISSUE PROVOKED bitter and protracted controversy throughout the conflict. That issue was the status of private property in war. The form of private property that received the most sustained attention was the very same private property that had preoccupied Thomas Jefferson more than thirty years before: property in slaves.

In the tomes written by leading European jurists, the rule for private property in wars on land seemed clear: enemy private property could be taken. To be sure, in civilized conflicts such seizures were discouraged. If it was necessary to feed one's army off the products of the enemy's land, Vattel encouraged armies to adopt an orderly system of requisitions rather than an undisciplined resort to looting and booty. (Good policy usually so dictated anyway.) But as to the legal question, even the relatively gentle Vattel left little room for doubt: "We have a right to deprive our enemy of his possessions," he wrote. "Whenever we have an opportunity, we seize on the enemy's property, and convert it to our own use." Such property was "booty" and belonged to the sovereign nation whose soldiers seized it. The Swiss jurist Jean-Jacques Burlamaqui had put it plainly a decade before Vattel: "Every man in a just war, acquires a property in what he takes from the enemy." Georg Friedrich von Martens agreed. "The conqueror has a right," Martens announced unambiguously, "to seize on all the property of the enemy that comes within his power."

From the days of the founding fathers onward, however, American statesmen departed from the harsh rule of European literature and embraced that literature's idealistic aspirations toward a much more protective rule for war on land. Benjamin Franklin's program for the laws of war advocated the immunity of all economically productive private property on land as well as at sea. Thomas Jefferson adopted the Franklin program in 1784 in a draft treaty that would have had the effect of "softening and diminishing the calamities of war" by protecting the goods, houses, and fields of farmers, artisans, manufacturers, and fishermen.

John Marshall helped to move the founders' view closer to realization in a leading case decided during the War of 1812. *Brown v. United States* involved American claims to enemy British property seized in Rhode Island. Faced with powerful authorities in the European laws of war, Marshall readily conceded that "war gives the right to confiscate" enemy property. But he then introduced a new distinction. Citing the "mitigations" of the old rules of warfare by the humane practices of modern armed conflicts, Marshall reasoned that the declaration of war by Congress did not by itself authorize confiscation. "The Constitution of the United States," he noted, had been written when a new and gentler law of war characterized by "moderation and humanity" had come to be "received throughout the civilized world." Congress could affirmatively authorize the seizure of enemy property, Marshall concluded, but a declaration of war did not automatically do so. Justice Joseph Story, practically spluttering in dissent, insisted that the law of war had always been understood to authorize "the subjects of hostile nations" to "lawfully seize each other's property wherever found." But the chief justice who had vindicated neutral rights now ingeniously extended the beginnings of similar protection to enemy private property.

A few short years later, the private property rule planted by the founders and nurtured by Marshall made its way into the first generation of American treatises on international law. James Kent's *Commentaries on American Law*, published in four volumes between 1826 and 1830, took Marshall's decision in *Brown v. United States* to its logical conclusion. Kent had retired as New York's widely respected chancellor, the state's most important judicial post. His book, which became the best-selling law book of the nineteenth century, asserted that "there are great limitations imposed upon the operations of war by land." Kent knew well that European writers like Vattel had reluctantly authorized the destruction and confiscation of private property. But he observed that, as a moral and ethical matter, Vattel had "condemned very strongly the spoliations of a country." In Kent's reading, Vattel had hoped for a more humane practice. That humane way of war, Kent asserted, had now become the general rule of civilized warfare in the greater European world. "The general usage" in the early nineteenth century, he insisted, was "not to touch private property on land, without making compensation."

Kent's book made him a rich man. It also fixed in American law the idea of rights to private property in wartime. Writing a decade after the publication of Kent's *Commentaries*, the diplomat, lawyer, and former publisher of Supreme Court decisions Henry Wheaton placed Kent's rule front and center in his own account of the rules of war. "Private property on land," Wheaton wrote, was "exempt from confiscation" by an enemy army. There were, he conceded, narrow exceptions to the protective rule for private property. An "extreme case" could "justify a resort to measures not warranted by the ordinary purposes of war." But Wheaton insisted that the "progress of civilization" had "slowly but constantly tended to soften the extreme severity of the operations of war by land."

In the first generations of American statesmen and jurists, only Alexander Hamilton loudly dissented from the distinctive emerging view of private property in wartime. In debates over the punishment of British Loyalists in the 1780s and then again in the Jay Treaty controversies of the 1790s, Hamilton defended the harsher European rule against its more restrained American critics. Enemy private property, Hamilton insisted, was subject to seizure under the laws of war. "Horses, cattle, and other movables" were "liable to become booty." The British army, he contended, had acted within its rights to carry away such property when it left American shores. Indeed, Hamilton went a step further, and in doing so he revealed one thing that was at stake in the private property rule. Hamilton argued that the British army had been within its rights in carrying off American slaves and setting them free.

E VER SINCE LORD DUNMORE threatened to upset slavery in the Chesapeake at the outset of the Revolution, the gentlemen slaveholders of the South had been arguing that the laws of war sharply separated the tobacco field from the battlefield. Henry Laurens of South Carolina, who had been released from captivity in the Tower of London in exchange for Lord Cornwallis after the Battle of Yorktown, inserted a provision protecting slave property into the peace treaty signed at Paris in 1783. The treaty required British armed forces to leave without "carrying away any Negroes or other property of the American inhabitants."

When British forces nevertheless took at least 3,000 slaves with them upon departing New York later that year, George Washington and the Continental Congress joined a loud chorus of bitter American complaints. For ten years, leading American statesmen including Thomas Jefferson as secretary of state pressed the British for a return of the slaves, or compensation for their seizure. Even a critic of slavery such as John Jay argued for compensation, though he failed to gain any credit with his southern brethren for doing so. The eponymous Jay Treaty of 1794 failed to extract any compensation from the British for slaves freed during the Revolution and essentially foreclosed the issue for good. Southern planters never forgave Jay for sacrificing their claims.*

---

* Decades later, in 1821, American slaveholders at last extracted some compensation for slaves freed during the Revolution when the beleaguered Creek Indians, chased and slaughtered by Andrew Jackson and the frontier militia, ceded lands to the United States. For all practical purposes, the Creeks had no choice but to abandon their lands in the face of the onslaught of white settlers. The treaty was a fait accompli. But in the terms of the treaty, part of the

*   *   *

THE RETURN OF British armed forces to the Chesapeake in the spring of 1813 raised the question of slavery in wartime once more. As early as April 1813, British forces under Rear Admiral George Cockburn began raiding American towns along the upper Chesapeake and Delaware Bay: first Frenchtown, then Havre de Grace, Fredericktown, and Georgetown. Orders from London initially warned Cockburn to avoid fomenting slave rebellion. But no one told the slaves. Everywhere Cockburn's raiding parties went, slaves escaped from their masters and ran off to British vessels waiting offshore. Cockburn and his men often quietly encouraged slaves to become British guides along the unmapped roads and backcountry creeks of the Chesapeake.

Newspapers in the South publicly denied the problem for fear of alerting more slaves to the possibility of freedom. Southern editors started false rumors on behalf of the planter class instead. According to the press, British officers were making off with American slaves to resell them in the West Indies, where the conditions of slavery were often far worse than in the United States. Such stories aimed to suppress black insurrection and flight by presenting American masters as the humanitarians. Historians have found no evidence to substantiate the slaveholder-sponsored rumors.

Privately, white planter families told a different story. Their correspondence practically trembled with anxiety about the possibility of a British-sponsored slave insurrection. Just outside the nation's capital, socialite Margaret Bayard Smith confided to her sister that she and her family were more worried about the "enemy at home" than about the British. Smith expected slaves to decamp for British ships at any time, but she could not exclude the possibility that they would simply rise up instead. Her husband had "procured pistols" and other weapons she hoped would be "sufficient for our defence" should such an uprising take place. A Virginia planter wrote that not only were slaves "flocking to the enemy from all quarters," they were also serving in the British forces against their former masters. "They leave us as spies upon our posts and our strength," complained the same planter, "and they return upon us as guides and soldiers and incendiaries." Former slaves directed British soldiers to Ameri-

---

land was nominally given to the United States as compensation for slaves the Creek allies of George III had captured and freed in the Revolution some forty years before—see Don E. Fehrenbacher and Ward M. McAfee, *The Slaveholding Republic: An Account of the United States Government's Relations to Slavery* (New York: Oxford University Press, 2001), 92.

can provisions and weapons stores. They helped British forces set up ambushes. Worse yet, some returned under false pretenses, pretending to reconcile themselves to their plantation lives while stirring up their fellow slaves for general insurrections and mass flight to British vessels awaiting in the Chesapeake. Even absent plots such as this, as one slaveholder put it, the "example" of those slaves who had escaped and come back in the company of British soldiers "must have a strong effect upon those blacks which have not as yet been able to escape." The "ruffian system" of British warfare, he worried, "will light up one universal conflagration throughout these counties."

White anxiety about a British-fomented slave insurrection was heightened by the recent memory of slave rebellion in Haiti in the 1790s. Even more recently, in 1800, an abortive slave insurrection near Richmond led by a slave named Gabriel had set the white South on edge. Now in 1813 and 1814, Virginians worried about rumors of a shadowy correspondence between British forces and the state's slaves. Slaveholder actions spoke as powerfully as their hushed words. The number of slave executions and deportations for insubordination in Virginia doubled from 1812 to 1813 and rose sharply again in 1814. Fear of slave insurrection caused the Virginia House of Delegates to write to President Madison seeking assistance against "external enemies" and "internal enemies" alike. In Maryland, Governor Levin Winder ordered that all small vessels be well-secured to prevent fugitives from making their way to British ships.

The planters' worst fears seemed to be realized in April 1814 when Vice Admiral Sir Alexander Cochrane announced that any American was welcome to come to British vessels, either to join British armed forces or to travel "as free settlers to the British possessions in North America or the West Indies." The proclamation never mentioned slaves or American blacks expressly. Perhaps Cochrane remembered how white Americans had reacted to Lord Dunmore forty years earlier. But everyone understood the order's intended audience. At Rear Admiral Cockburn's suggestion, Cochrane approved the creation of a Colonial Corps of Marines manned by escaped slaves who were paid a $20 bounty to join the British armed forces. The first of the Colonial Marines would march into Washington later that year. By the end of 1814, an estimated 3,000–5,000 slaves from Virginia and Maryland had escaped to British vessels and forts, never to return to their owners again.

* * *

T HE FEARED SLAVE insurrection never came to pass. But at the conclusion of the War of 1812, John Adams's son John Quincy Adams renewed the efforts of his father's generation to obtain compensation from the British for slaves freed during wartime.

John Quincy was an unlikely advocate for slavery. He had grown up with a deeply ingrained dislike for what his mother, Abigail, called the "iniquitous scheme" of slavery. He carried his opposition to slavery (that "great and foul stain upon the North American Union") throughout his adult life. Yet Adams was also an ambitious man. If he were to follow his father into the presidency, John Quincy would have to attract support from the South. And at the close of the War of 1812, he betrayed his antislavery principles and adopted the American view of private property in wartime on behalf of slaveholders.

As the lead member of the American peace commission in Ghent, Adams conditioned the peace on the return of all American slaves. The "seduction" and carrying off of slaves, he insisted, was a grievous offense against the laws of war. "Our object," he later explained, "was the restoration of all property, including slaves, which, by the usages of war among civilized nations, ought not to have been taken." In Adams's view, "all private property on shore was of that description." Slaves were private property, and it followed therefore that American slaveowners were "entitled by the laws of war to exemption" from the capture of their slaves.

The terms of the treaty seemed to vindicate the American view of the laws of war and private property. After much back-and-forth in the treaty-drafting process, the peace treaty signed at Ghent on Christmas Eve 1814 included an awkwardly drafted clause requiring restoration of possessions, including "Slaves or other private property," taken during the war.*

In fact, the saga of slavery and the Treaty of Ghent had only just begun. The British navy refused to return more than a handful of the thousands of men, women, and children who had fled American plantations. Instead, Admiral Cochrane took the position that the oddly written treaty clause had intended to cover only those slaves captured by the British inside American

---

*The convoluted provision of Article I of the Treaty of Ghent read as follows: "All territory, places, and possessions whatsoever taken by either party from the other during the war, or which may be taken after the signing of this Treaty, excepting only [certain] Islands hereinafter mentioned, shall be restored without delay and without causing any destruction or carrying away any of the Artillery or other public property originally captured in the said forts or places, and which shall remain therein upon the Exchange of the Ratifications of this Treaty, or any Slaves or other private property. . . ."

coastal fortifications who remained there at the time of the treaty's ratification. In the British view, all other captured and runaway slaves—especially those to whom the British had granted freedom—were outside of the treaty's terms.

Adams raged that Cochrane had adopted "a violent and unnatural construction of the article," one obviously designed "to avoid compliance" with the treaty's obligations. For ten years, he waged a legal-diplomatic campaign to force Britain to abandon its interpretation of the treaty and to pay for what Adams called its "dishonorable war" of "stealing and debauching" the slaves of the American South. In 1815, as the U.S. minister in Great Britain, Adams remonstrated with Lord Liverpool, the British prime minister. Seizures of private property on land in wartime, Adams insisted, were "deviations from the usages of war." Liverpool's answer brilliantly skewered Adams's antislavery pretensions. A "table or a chair," Liverpool reasoned, "might be taken" and then later "restored without changing its condition." But surely, Liverpool said, a "human being was entitled to other considerations."

Three years later, as secretary of state under President Monroe, Adams was still fighting for slaveholder compensation. In 1818, he persuaded the British to enter into arbitration to resolve the dispute. Two years after that, Adams prevailed upon the British to accept the Russian czar, Alexander I, as the arbitrator. ("There is something whimsical," Adams noted wryly, "in the idea that the United States and Great Britain, both speaking English, should go to the Slavonian Czar of Muscovy" to find the meaning of their own treaty.) Adams chose slaveholder Henry Middleton of South Carolina as the American commissioner to the arbitration panel to ensure aggressive pursuit of the American claims. Adams's instructions to Middleton carefully laid out the facts of the shameful British campaign of unlawfully stealing slaves. And thanks to Adams's unflagging efforts, the United States seemed to prevail at last. The czar—with whom Adams had become friendly years earlier when he served as the U.S. minister to Russia—ruled that the American construction of the treaty was the sound one.

The czar's interpretation of the treaty provision did not end Adams's work, however. When Great Britain and the United States established a mixed Anglo-American commission to determine the value and number of American slaves for which compensation was due, the commission deliberations stalemated and then collapsed. Finally, in 1826, in the middle of Adams's first and only term as president, he and his secretary of state, Henry Clay, instructed their envoy Albert Gallatin to negotiate with the British a lump sum payment in satisfaction of all American slaveowner claims. At the end of the year, the British agreed to deliver £250,000 sterling (or a little more than $1.2 million in 1826 dollars) to the government of the United States to end the slave controversy.

Even then, the story of compensating the slaveowners for wartime losses was not over. Slaveholders from Virginia, Maryland, Georgia, and Louisiana rushed pell-mell to make claims for compensation. Thousands of slaveholders across the South, from Georgia and Louisiana in the Southwest to Maryland and Virginia in the Upper South, now became righteous champions of the laws of war and their limits on the seizure of slaves. So many purported claimants rushed into the system that it quickly became clear that the available funds would be exhausted before all the claims were compensated. Claimants from Georgia and Louisiana began squabbling with those from Virginia and Maryland over what constituted proof of a valid claim under the Ghent Treaty. In 1828, funds ran out long before full payment of all the claims.

F OR MORE THAN four decades, leading statesmen in the early republic had defended slavery in the name of a humane and civilized law of war. American diplomatic efforts relating to slavery had helped to call forth a new proposition in the laws of war, one that European precedents had only hinted at. As John Quincy Adams put it to his British counterpart Lord Castlereagh in remonstrating for slave compensation in 1816, "private property is not the subject of lawful capture in war upon the land."

To be sure, the United States was not the only nation to adopt a view of the laws of war that was inspired by slavery. When Spain negotiated a treaty with Indian tribes in Florida in 1784 to establish humane limits in warfare, for example, it stipulated limits on enemy interference with slavery.

But the United States stood in a different posture with respect to slavery than European states, for the United States was a slave society in a way that no European state was outside of its colonial possessions. And therein lay the humanitarian paradox of the early American laws of warfare. American statesmen embraced tight limits on the destructive powers of warring armies; they embraced greater limits on war's destruction than European jurists had ever thought possible. But for many Americans, the preservation of private property in slaves counted as one of the law's chief humanitarian accomplishments.

*   *   *

YEARS LATER, long after he lost the election for what would have been his second term as president, after his hopes of vindicating his father's abbreviated one term in the White House had been dashed, an aging John Quincy Adams would change his mind about war and slavery. Twenty years after Czar Alexander's arbitration decision, Adams would decide that he had been wrong. Like Alexander Hamilton before him, he would decide that the laws of war gave armies and presidents and nations the power to emancipate slaves in wartime. Twenty years later still, in the presidency of Abraham Lincoln, this idea would end slavery and transform the United States.

But in the first decades of American history, all this was far off in the future. In the near term, the United States was fighting a new war, one that began before the dust had settled from the War of 1812. It was a war waged in significant part to protect the slaveholders of the Deep South. And when Andrew Jackson led the Tennessee militia into Florida to fight in this war, a new controversy about the laws of war captured the attention of Americans in the North, in the South, and—most important of all—in the Old Southwest.

Chapter 3

A False Feeling of Mercy

⟶•◦•⟵

The sovereign Editor cares not a lash,
But with goose quill and ink will eternally splash;
And higgledy, piggledy, will flourish his pen,
Disapproving good judgment, abusing brave men:
A qualified judge! he surely must be,
Who ne'er saw a battle, by land or by sea.

—John Hunter Waddell, 1819

I would barely remark that cases of necessity,
creates their own rule.

—Andrew Jackson to President James Monroe, 1817

ANDREW JACKSON FIRST encountered war's brutality as the War of Independence stretched into its sixth year. British dragoons captured the thirteen-year-old future president and his older brother near their home in the Carolina upcountry. The two boys had fallen into the hands of some of the most notorious British officers in the war.

As Jackson's authorized biography later told the story, one imperious British officer demanded that young Jackson clean the officer's boots. With extraordinary presence of mind, the youthful frontier American refused, insisting instead on the treatment "a prisoner of war had a right to expect." Jackson had invoked the protective shelter of the Enlightenment laws of war. But his appeal enraged his captor. The British officer drew his sword and swung it down toward Jackson's head. The boy managed to partially deflect it with his hand, but the blow nearly took off two of his fingers and left a deep wound on his scalp. Jackson would carry scars on his hand and head for the rest of his life.

Jackson's brother Robert refused the same demand. This time the officer's sword inflicted a more serious injury on the older boy's head. For days the wounded brothers languished in a South Carolina jail alongside 200 other prisoners from the patriot militia. Smallpox raced through the captive population. By the time their mother, Elizabeth, was able to liberate them, Andrew and Robert had each contracted the dreaded disease. Within two days of gaining his freedom, Robert was dead. Weeks later Elizabeth, too, would succumb to cholera contracted while tending to patriot prisoners held in the fetid prison ships lying in Charleston Harbor. Young Andrew Jackson would recover from his illness and from his wounds. But he would never fully recover from the experience of British cruelty. He had already lost his oldest brother to the war. He had never known his father. As Jackson later remembered it, British savagery had left him utterly alone.

The story of the British officer's boots may be apocryphal. It was first told publicly as an early salvo in Jackson's effort to become president of the United States. We will never really be sure whether it is true. But if Jackson artfully retouched the seminal moment of his youth, he described it as he wished the American electorate to remember it. In Jackson's story, he had appealed to the civilized laws of war only to see them violated by the savagery of America's enemies. Forever after, he viewed the laws of war with a combustible combination of awe and contempt. Jackson's worldview was as deeply bound up in the laws of war as that of any statesman who had come before him. Yet in Jackson's hands the laws of war had a dangerous significance. Jackson measured the savage atrocities of his enemies by reference to the laws of war. Their violation touched off his righteous fury.

Jackson embodied the outlook of the frontier and its militias, whose members were quickly moving to centerstage in the American experience. But not everyone thought of the laws of war as Jackson did. In the first four decades of the nineteenth century, Jackson became a lightning rod in a fast-emerging clash of cultures over the significance of the laws of war.

Lawyers, Soldiers, and Seamen

TWICE A YEAR, travelers along the road from Philadelphia to Washington at the turn of the nineteenth century came across a curious sight. At first glance, the well-outfitted carriage with its six well-dressed passengers looked like any of the fine coaches passing between the nation's new capital and its second most populous city. A French immigrant, Peter Stephen Du Ponceau, was one of the passengers. After abandoning a career in the French military, Du Ponceau had arrived in the United States just in time to help the Prussian baron Friedrich von Steuben reorganize the Continental Army at Valley Forge. He had gone on to be one of the early republic's most distinguished lawyers. Another passenger was Alexander Dallas, the Jamaican-born publisher of the first decisions by the U.S. Supreme Court. Jared Ingersoll, William Lewis, and Edward Tilghman were longtime Philadelphia residents and senior members of the city's legal profession. The last passenger, William Rawle, was the U.S. district attorney for Pennsylvania.

The distinguished group piled into Du Ponceau's coach to argue cases at the U.S. Supreme Court in Washington. Yet when traveling together, the close-knit band hardly seemed like an august group of the leading lawyers of the day. They were more like a congenial and sometimes even raucous fraternity. "We might have been taken for any thing," Du Ponceau recalled, "but the grave counselors of the celebrated bar of Philadelphia."

Few would have guessed it, but Du Ponceau's coach carried influential members of a fledgling group of American experts in the laws of war and especially the laws of war at sea. The law of armed conflict in the early nineteenth century dealt first and foremost with commercial rights and property rights in vessels and their cargoes. Large sums were at issue, and lawyers sprang forward to meet the demand for their services. Up and down the east coast of the United States, the steady stream of maritime prize cases in John Marshall's Supreme Court created a cadre of lawyers steeped in the rules of war. The six Philadelphia lawyers alone argued forty-four cases around the turn of the nineteenth century involving the laws of war at sea. And though Philadelphia lawyers dominated the early prize bar, every major city along the Atlantic had its share of lawyers who dedicated a large part of their practice to captures arising out of Europe's wars.

Charleston lawyer Robert Goodloe Harper argued more prize cases at the U.S. Supreme Court in the first two decades of the century than any other lawyer in the country. In Virginia, Charles Lee (the younger brother of Light-Horse Harry Lee) became an eminent maritime war advocate. Washington lawyer Walter Jones (who argued more cases in the Supreme Court than anyone before or since) had a significant share of the era's prize cases. In Maryland, Philip Barton Key, his son Francis Scott Key, and William Pinkney represented claimants and captors in dozens of prize cases. Pinkney argued additional prize cases in his capacity as attorney general of the United

States. In Baltimore, David Hoffman and William Henry Winder developed specialties in prize cases. Farther north, Thomas Emmet and Henry Wheaton in New York and Samuel Dexter of Massachusetts each took on substantial practices in prize cases before the U.S. Supreme Court.

All told, slightly more than two dozen men formed an elite corps of lawyers who argued law of war cases in the Supreme Court from the 1790s well into the nineteenth century. As Du Ponceau's friendly coach rides suggested, it was a highly collegial bunch. Opposing lawyers on one day found themselves acting as co-counsel the next. The group prized decorum and etiquette. When an excess of enthusiasm led Attorney General William Pinkney to criticize Thomas Emmet of New York in an 1815 prize case, he made up for it in a different prize case later the same year when he begged Emmet's forgiveness in open court, complimenting him on his "forbearance and urbanity," his "intellect and morals," and such "eloquence as few may hope to equal."

The influence of the prize lawyers reached beyond the courtroom. They were among the most prominent participants in the popular debate over American neutral shipping rights. Robert Goodloe Harper published a long vindication of American rights against the French in the Quasi-War of the late 1790s. William Pinkney's *Memorial of the Rule of the War of 1756* condemned British wartime policies toward neutral American shipping. Charles Jared Ingersoll's *A View of the Rights and Wrongs, Power and Policy of the United States of America* excoriated the British and championed the United States' legal position in the *Chesapeake* affair and in the controversy arising out of the *Essex* case in the British courts. Alexander Dallas's *An Exposition of the Causes of the Late War with Great Britain* reasserted the United States' legal position at the close of the War of 1812.

The prize lawyers established a fledgling professional literature in the international laws of war as well. In 1810, Du Ponceau published an English translation of Cornelius van Bynkershoek's *A Treatise on the Law of War*. The translation was immediately serialized in the *American Law Journal*, an influential early professional periodical. Five years later, Henry Wheaton's *Digest of the Law of Maritime Captures and Prizes* gathered together for the first time the collected wisdom of the Supreme Court prize bar. When David Hoffman of Maryland established a law school at the University of Maryland in 1817, his coursebook made the law of nations and the law of prize foundational elements of the curriculum. (Wheaton's *Digest* was required reading.) Two decades later, Wheaton published the first English-language treatise exclusively dedicated to international law, titled *Elements of Interna-*

tional Law. Almost half the book concerned the laws of war. The "progress of civilization," Wheaton wrote hopefully, had "slowly but constantly tended to soften the extreme severity of the operations of war." Wheaton's book was published simultaneously in Philadelphia and London; another edition came out in 1846. A French edition was published in 1848 and updated in 1853, and a sixth edition came out in Boston in 1855. By 1864, an edition translated into Chinese joined yet another American edition.

The careers of James Kent and Joseph Story put on display the prominence of the laws of war in the early American legal profession. Kent and Story were the two most influential writers on law in the first half of the nineteenth century. Kent held the post of chancellor in New York from 1814 to 1823. Upon his retirement, he published the most widely read law book of the century, his *Commentaries on American Law*. The book was modeled on William Blackstone's *Commentaries*. Unlike Blackstone, however, Kent made the law of nations and the laws of war central topics. When the first volume of his American *Commentaries* appeared in 1826, the law of nations was the first subject Kent took up. Across fourteen editions, stretching into the twentieth century, Kent described international law as a code of binding obligations, one to which the United States had appealed "as the common standard of right and duty" in times of war and peace alike.

Story was doubtless the most learned justice on the U.S. Supreme Court in law of war questions. While conducting an active practice in the first decade of the nineteenth century, he wrote a technical book for lawyers and edited American editions of two classic English law books, including one that dealt at length with the laws of war at sea. Appointed to the Supreme Court at the age of thirty-two by President James Madison, Story wrote some of the Court's most significant maritime war opinions. In 1829, after eighteen years on the bench, he was appointed Dane Professor of Law at Harvard Law School, where his teaching included international law questions dealing with war and peace. For a decade and a half, he served as a justice on the Court and a professor at Harvard while publishing a stunning number of books and articles, many of which took up topics such as the law of prize. Along with Kent, Wheaton, and Du Ponceau, Story made the laws of war part of the collective knowledge of the American legal profession. What could be "of more transcendent dignity," he asked the members of the bar, than the statesmanlike study of the "rights of peace and war, the limits of lawful hostility, [and] the mutual duties of belligerent and neutral powers"?

* * *

The early American military was slower than the legal profession to develop a sense of professional identity. It was slower still to develop a professional identity around the law of arms. But by the third and fourth decades of the nineteenth century, officers in the U.S. Army began to develop a culture of military professionalism that afforded considerable respect for international law and the laws of war.

The principal institution of the early military profession was the U.S. Military Academy at West Point. Thomas Jefferson founded the academy in 1802 as a school for military engineers, but it was when Sylvanus Thayer took over as superintendent in 1817 that the academy became a true professional training ground for officers. Thayer had studied in French military schools for two years after the War of 1812. His cadets studied the work of the finest French military engineers and strategists of the seventeenth and eighteenth centuries. They read the work of the seventeenth-century French engineer-general Sébastien Le Prestre de Vauban and the writings of Baron Antoine Henri de Jomini, a Swiss-born staff officer in Napoleon's armies who had become the most widely read tactical and strategic theorist of the period.

The French military theorists treated warfare as a rational science. For Vauban, war was a species of mathematics. The educated soldier, in Vauban's conception, was the man who mastered the geometric design of bastions and curtains, which were the flanks and faces of early modern defensive fortifications. Properly built, a Vauban-inspired fort would be made up of angles that left attackers no refuge from the surveillance of its defenders—or from the crossfire they would pour down from its ramparts. To build such a fort, a military man needed the basics of geometry. Vauban provided instructions on drawing right angles and parallel lines, squares and ovals, equilateral triangles and parallelograms. Eighteenth-century editions of Vauban's writings bundled a geometry textbook into the same binding in a two-for-the-price-of-one deal for the ambitious military reader.

Jomini's great contribution was to translate Vauban's rational science of fortifications into instructions for the open battlefield. The science of war, Jomini explained to his readers, required mastery of "a small number of fundamental principles of war." He listed "ten positive maxims" from which he claimed to be able to derive 200 discrete rules. Jomini cautioned that his principles and their associated maxims and rules were no substitutes for the "natural genius" of a Napoleon-like commanding general. But for many of his readers, Jomini's system resembled what he himself called "a mechanism of determined wheelworks" by which warfare might be reduced to a handful of calculable Newtonian laws. One American commentator insisted that Jomini's principles were so universal that they would not be shaken for 100 years.

As the Military Academy matured under Thayer and his successors, it modified French rationalism for American conditions. Dennis Hart Mahan, the most influential instructor at West Point from 1830 until his death in 1871, made his name with such books as *Complete Treatise on Field Fortification* (1836), *Elementary Course in Civil Engineering* (1837), *Advanced Guard, Outpost, and Detachment Service of Troops* (1847), and *Descriptive Geometry as Applied to the Drawing of Fortification* (1864). Each of Mahan's books adapted Vauban's geometry and Jomini's maxims to the smaller scale of American conflicts. The academy, wrote one early nineteenth-century officer, taught that battles were won by the "rule and compass" and by the accurate "measurement of angles."

Neither Vauban nor Jomini explicitly invoked the law of war tradition. Mahan did not either. But the strategic theory of Jomini and the geometry of Vauban adopted an implicit law and ethics of warfare. If war could be reduced to rational axioms and principles, it stood to reason that war could also be civilized, drained of the unreasoned passions and chaotic violence that had characterized it in the past. Conflicts that could be tamed by mathematics might also be constrained by the rule of law. Newtonian laws of belligerent motion went hand-in-hand with Vattelian conduct in arms. At the very least, the disciplined army envisioned by the professional officer class at West Point was one that would minimize the disorder and chaos that had proven conducive to atrocities in earlier eras of warfare.

In the 1820s, the Military Academy added training in international law and the laws of war as a finishing touch for its graduating students in the First Class, rendering explicit what had already been implicit in the rational geometry of its curriculum. As a text, Superintendent Thayer selected the standard writings of Vattel, the eighteenth century's master of genteel warfare. By 1826, the academy switched to Kent's *Commentaries on American Law*.

Strictly speaking, the roots of the law of war tradition in the professional military were still relatively shallow. Despite the influence of the academy, the military itself was tiny and barely professionalized. From the end of the War of 1812 until the 1830s, there were never more than 600 officers in the U.S. Army; by 1861, there were still only a little more than 1,000. The rest of the Army was made up of enlisted men, among whom there was little standard training until the Civil War. Among the small professional officer corps, the Army's Articles of War were far more important than the international law tradition in helping to establish an early code of professional ethics. The Articles were the U.S. Congress's general criminal code for the military. They had some small overlap with the rules of international law. They prohibited acts such as quitting one's post or one's colors to plunder. They authorized officers to punish abuses and disorderly behavior. They set out punishments for soldiers leaving camp without authorization. Such violations of the Articles could often lead to violations of the laws of war. But the Articles were rules of discipline, rules designed to promote the command and control of the Army, not restraints on what civilized armies could do as a matter of international law. Moreover, the short course at the Military Academy on the laws of war sometimes seemed to have little effect. During its entire print run from 1835 to 1844, the *Army and Navy Chronicle* magazine—an early effort to foster an ethic of professional learning among officers—published not a single article touching directly on the laws of land warfare. Some cadets remembered receiving "little exposure to history, ethics, government, and law." One later recalled that the ethics and law training he did receive had been a subject of ridicule and derision among his fellow students.

Yet for all this, Thayer's academy planted the seed of an important tradition. In 1821, Congress authorized and Secretary of War John Calhoun published *General Regulations for the Army*, which led off with a long epigraph from the ubiquitous Vattel. Compiled by Brigadier General Winfield Scott, the *General Regulations* put Vattel's influence on open display. Republished four times before the Civil War, the *General Regulations* set out instructions for treating prisoners of war (who were "under the safeguard of the national faith and honour") and for conducting sieges (which required "a strict observance of good order, and of the dictates of humanity"). The *General Regulations* were not a compendium of international law rules. But they repeatedly relied on and incorporated the "usages of war" as they had developed since the eighteenth century. Officers like Winfield Scott brought the outlook of the *General Regulations* to the Mexican War in 1846. Forty years after its initial publication, Scott and the professional officer class would bring the same principles to the Civil War.

THE U.S. NAVY lacked a formal institution of professional training for most of the first half of the nineteenth century. Yet by sheer necessity, naval men picked up a rough-and-ready knowledge of the laws of war rivaling that of the finest lawyers and best trained Army officers in the country.

For sea captains, the law of war at sea served as an indispensable guide to conduct. Communications with the government in Washington could take months when a vessel was out to sea. Captains thus needed to understand the rules governing the seizure of neutral and enemy shipping, not to mention the complexities arising when neutral ships held enemy goods and enemy vessels held neutral goods. Captains had to know the rules for belligerent vessels in neutral waters. Lawless pirates had to be distinguished from so-called privateers who were lawfully commissioned by warring nation-states to act as ersatz naval vessels. Contraband goods such as weapons and military supplies (which could be seized in wartime) had to be separated from free goods for civilian use (which could not). Effective blockades (which were recognized under the laws of maritime war) had to be distinguished from mere paper blockades (which were not).

President John Adams had recognized the significance of the laws of war for the Navy when he signed into law an act of Congress creating the Department of the Navy in 1798. Adams instructed officers to do whatever they could to protect American commerce, consistent with the "treaties, the laws of the United States, and the laws of nations." For decades, lawyers dominated the office of the Secretary of the Navy. Eight out of the twelve secretaries between 1801 and 1842 were lawyers. They included Robert Smith, who served for eight years under Jefferson; Samuel Southard, who served for six years under James Monroe and John Quincy Adams; and Mahlon Dickerson, who served for four years under Andrew Jackson and Martin Van Buren. Congress got into the act, too. In 1800, Congress invoked the international laws of maritime war governing captured prizes, pirates, and spies to fill out the regulation of naval officers. For decades thereafter, ship chaplains were required to instruct young midshipmen in an array of topics, including the law of naval warfare. Many chaplains knew little or nothing about the subject, of course. But after 1845, the new Naval Academy in Annapolis began to provide a modicum of formal instruction in the laws of nations to each graduating class of midshipmen. By a "judicious apprehension of the mutual rights and duties of the great family of States," the academy instructed its students, naval officers would be able to serve the honor and interests of their country. Like the academy at West Point, the Naval Academy adopted Kent's *Commentaries* as its text.

There were, of course, only a tiny number of naval officers. Fewer than 100 officers served in the Navy during the Jefferson administration. Twenty-five years later, the Navy consisted of barely 200 officers in the Jackson administration. Yet despite their small numbers, naval officers often knew as much about the laws of war and the rules of neutrality as anyone in the country. America's first great naval hero, John Paul Jones, followed his exploits against British vessels in the Revolution by touring the courts of Europe and debating the nuances of international law in a mostly unsuccessful attempt to win for himself and his crew the value of British ships he had seized during the Revolution. During the Latin American wars of independence, American naval commanders such as James Biddle skillfully navigated the shifting legal seascape of the Atlantic with its legally dubious blockades and its array of would-be privateers claiming commissions from new and untested Latin American republics. Commodore Matthew Perry, who would one day open up Japanese ports to U.S. vessels, urged his fellow naval officers to recognize that the "enlightened knowledge" of a naval commander on questions of international law was necessary to protect "the honor of his flag."

F OR ALL THE efforts made by lawyers, soldiers, and seamen, there was a startling mismatch between the expertise of the new professionals, on the one hand, and the kinds of armed conflict that took place in the United States after the War of 1812. A vast chasm divided the Military Academy's European-style training from the kinds of frontier conflicts most early American soldiers were likely to fight. From the end of the War of 1812 to the Mexican War in 1846, the armed conflict that mattered most for the United States took place neither among European states nor between the United States and European powers. It took place on the periphery of the Americas. War broke out in Spain's South American colonies, in the Caribbean, and along the Gulf of Mexico. Most importantly for the United States, bitter conflicts between settlers and Indians raged all along the western frontier.

The God of Scalps

T HE HOPI OF the North American Southwest believed in a god of war they called the Heart-of-the-Sky God, or Sotuqnangu. Pueblo societies had another god of war, a powerful eaglelike supernatural figure known as Knifewing. Many societies, of course, have had gods of war of one kind or another. Ares and Athena served the function for the Greeks, Mars and Minerva for the Romans. But Sotuqnangu and Knifewing were different. They were gods of scalping—the practice of cutting flesh and hair from the skulls of enemy warriors and keeping the mass of tissue as a trophy of war. Sotuqnangu was thought by the Hopi to have invented scalping. Knifewing was often pictured with a scalp hanging from his terrible wing.

Scalps were not the only war trophies taken by American Indians, but they were the easiest to take. They could be cut quickly from the head of a fallen enemy (usually after death, though not always). Scalps could be carried easily without slowing down a hasty retreat to safety. When conditions permitted, many Indians took other body parts from their conquered foes as well. In pre-contact California, virtually every identifiable tribe took severed heads as trophies. The Mohegans in what is today Connecticut cut the fingers and toes from their captive enemies' extremities. Among the Hopi, women took the heads of conquered enemies and fed their male children scraps of the flesh to invest them with supernatural bravery. The Apache, the Cheyenne, the Sioux, and the Ute made necklaces from the fingertips and hand bones of their captives, often setting the human remains alongside animal claws and teeth in a show of power and fearlessness. Iroquoian peoples between the Hudson River and the Great Lakes engaged in ritual cannibalism, eating the hearts of captives tortured to death after battle.

Anglo-American behavior was often just as startling, of course. The English had displayed the heads of rebels and heretics on London Bridge well into the seventeenth century. In 1798, Protestant Loyalists roasted the heads of live Irish rebels; courts sentenced leaders of the United Irishmen to death and ordered their heads impaled on spikes and displayed in town centers. A doctor in the U.S. Army in the 1830s cut off the head of a Seminole Indian chief, embalmed it, and hung it on his children's bed as a punishment for disobedience. As late as the 1860s, governors in the western United States paid bounties for Indian scalps. And in the 1870s, the U.S. Army shipped the heads of dead Indians to the Army Medical Museum in Washington, D.C.

Yet for the founding fathers and the European colonists who preceded them, Indian warfare seemed so savage as to have no law at all. Theirs were the atavistic customs of those whom Jefferson's Declaration had excoriated as the "merciless Indian Savages whose known rule of warfare, is an undistinguished destruction of all ages, sexes and conditions." At Ghent in 1814, John Quincy Adams repeated Jefferson's formulation from almost thirty years earlier, accusing the British of complicity with Indians whose "known rule of warfare is the indiscriminate torture and butchery of women, children, and prisoners." Adams's view was shared by virtually everyone in white America. The Indians, they believed, had no rules of war.

But white Americans were wrong. There *were* rules for Indian wars. In many ways, the Indians' rules were more effective at constraining war's violence than their European analogues. The difficulty was that Indian ways of ordering war were very different from the ones to which European colonists and their descendants were accustomed. For two centuries and more, Europeans had organized their ideas about the laws of war around a sharp distinction between crime and war. The European view was that killing soldiers in war was not murder and thus not subject to punishment. It was this immunity from punishment that underlay the rights of the prisoner of war. By the late eighteenth century, European jurists rooted the protection of noncombatants in the same distinction between war and crime; attacks on noncombatants were outside the immunity conferred on soldiers by the state of war.

American Indian groups made no such distinction. Among the Iroquoian peoples of the eastern woodlands, for example, a form of armed conflict known as "mourning war" was neither war nor criminal law enforcement, at least not as those concepts were understood by Europeans. In mourning wars, Indians sought to replenish spiritual losses caused by deaths in their own ranks. The principal aim was to take captives, who would either be adopted into the tribe as substitutes for the dead or tortured and killed in ritual satisfaction for lost members. Either adoption or execution could satisfy the spiritual needs of a warring Iroquoian village.

The mourning war had no room for the prisoner of war as the European tradition had developed it. Some prisoners—most often, though not exclusively, women and children—would be adopted into the capturing tribe. Others—usually male warriors—would be subject to excruciating forms of torture killing. Victims would be placed on a raised platform and cut with red-hot knives and firebrands. If they wilted too soon, they would be revived with food and rest before the torturers resumed their work. Victims' limbs would be cut off, their bodies disemboweled, and their genitals mutilated. Scraps of the victim's body would be ritually consumed. In the Iroquoian ritual, just prior to death the captive was scalped and hot sand poured into the wound on his skull before a warrior dispatched him with a knife to the chest.

Frontier conflicts engrained such images in the nightmares of white settlers for more than two centuries. Captured American soldiers such as Colonel William Crawford, who was ritually burned, tortured, scalped, and then killed by Delaware Indians in 1782, quickly became martyrs to what Americans saw as Indian savagery. Indeed, from the European-influenced view widely held among whites in the United States, the Indian way of organizing warfare was so horrific and foreign that it did not seem like a way of organizing armed conflict at all.

Yet Indian ritual torture was not arbitrary. It had social significance for the torturer and the tortured alike. For the captor, torturing captives served as a kind of spiritual replenishment and as a celebration of the supernatural. The captive, in turn, derived honor from the experience of being tortured. As one historian has put it, Indian warriors "earned posthumous esteem by bearing themselves stoically under the ordeal."

The logic of mourning war also imposed powerful restraints on the violence of Indian conflicts. Killing too many of the enemy would prompt a renewed cycle of warfare as the enemy sought to replace its own losses. In turn, deaths in battle always threatened to undercut the reason for going to war in the first place. Successful mourning wars required the maintenance of a fragile equilibrium, and when it worked properly the effect was to limit the destruction of native warfare. In seventeenth-century Rhode Island, Roger Williams observed that Indian war was "farre lesse bloudy, and devouring then the cruell Warres of Europe."

Indeed, many Indians seem to have experienced shock and revulsion when confronted with the destructiveness of European ways of warfare. In the Pequot War of 1637, observers reported that the Pequots "stamped and tore the Hair from their Heads" when they saw the extent of the colonists' devastation of their community. Even the colonists' Narragansett allies joined in the protest: "it is naught," they cried, "because it is too furious, and slays too many men."

The internal logic of Indian ways of war was usually lost on European settlers and their descendants, however. In conflicts between European settlers and white Americans on the one hand and Indians on the other, the coexistence of these two very different rule schemes produced a rapid descent into virtually unlimited violence. Indians quickly abandoned whatever compunction they may have had about the destruction of entire towns. The historian Patrick Malone has documented the abandonment of traditional limits on warfare by the Wampanoag of New England in King Philip's War in 1675, a development he traces to the effects of colonist behavior in the Pequot War four decades earlier. In the Wyoming Valley of northern Pennsylvania, Indian allies of the British during the Revolution burned and pillaged "hundreds of fields and farmhouses," turning the "beautiful valley into a wasteland."

Colonists and frontier settlers, in turn, set aside whatever norms they had about torture and dismemberment. Massachusetts Bay captain John

Mason ordered his men to torture and kill a Pequot Indian he encountered at Saybrook, Connecticut, in 1637. "The reason," he explained, "was, that they had tortured such of our men as they took alive." In the beginning of the eighteenth century, Solomon Stoddard of Massachusetts wrote that if the Indians would "manage their warr fairly after the manner of other nations," it would be "inhumane to persue them" in ways that were contrary to "Christian practice." But as Stoddard saw it, the Indians "act like wolves, and are to be dealt withal as wolves." In the 1760s, during Pontiac's War, American settlers near Pittsburgh used smallpox-infected blankets to try to destroy the Delawares. The revolutionary war hero George Rogers Clark reported about the Indians in the Ohio Valley that "he would never spare man woman or child of them on whom he could lay his hands." Colonel David Williamson's Pennsylvania militia brought Clark's dismaying vision to life in 1782 at Gnadenhutten when they herded nearly ninety Christianized Delaware Indians into two cabins and systematically beat them to death. By the 1830s such violence had become standard operating procedure in the regular army. The *Army and Navy Chronicle*—which was often at pains to emphasize the value of professional honor among the emerging officer corps—called for "nothing less than a war of extermination" against Indians in Florida and condemned the "mawkish philanthropy" of any who dared to suggest otherwise.

I N THE FORMAL literature of the laws of war, all of this frontier violence happened outside the law altogether. The humanitarian laws of armed conflict simply had no application to wars with those who seemed from the European view to act as savages.

Indians had not always been so treated by the law. The sixteenth-century Spanish jurist Francisco de Vitoria had argued that war with the Indians entailed "all the rights of war" in the European tradition. Hugo Grotius had little to say about American Indians, but his approach was similarly universal. In his view, the laws of nature and nations were derived from those axioms that "all men believe must be true."

A century after Grotius, however, jurists began to carve out hard-and-fast exceptions for Indians who did not follow the European laws of war. "When we are at war with a savage nation," Vattel wrote, "who observe no rules, and never give quarter, we may punish them in the persons of any of their people." American jurists took Vattel a step further. Vattel's approach treated

Indians on the basis of their alleged conduct, not on the basis of their status. But the early American literature excluded Indians from the protections of the laws of war on the basis of their race and religion. Kent's *Commentaries* explained that "the Christian nations of Europe, and their descendants on this side of the Atlantic" had "established a law of nations peculiar to themselves," one rooted in "the brighter light, more certain truths, and the more definite sanction, which Christianity has communicated." Continual and irregular war had (for Kent) left the American Indian in a "savage state" incapable of rising to the obligations required by the laws of war. Henry Wheaton's *Elements of International Law* made the same assertion. The law of nations, he contended, "can only spring up among nations of the same class or family, united by ties of similar origin, manners, and religion." As Wheaton understood them, the laws of nations had "entirely overlooked" the Indians.

On the frontier itself, however, the separation between the laws of war and Indian conflicts was never so neat. For the United States' frontier militia, Indian conduct in war was not something outside the laws of war, regardless what jurists like Kent and Wheaton wrote. To the contrary, the laws of war provided a moral language with which to describe and condemn the practices of Indians in armed conflict. For the militia, the laws of war were not alien to Indian wars. They were one more reason to engage in such wars with the passion and ferocity for which Andrew Jackson was quickly becoming famous.

Andrew Jackson and the Militia Tradition

ANDREW JACKSON OFTEN said that Indians were not entitled to the protections of the laws of war. "Why do we attempt to Treat with Savage Tribe[s]," he wondered in 1793, when they would "neither adhere to Treaties, nor [to] the law of Nations?" Twenty years later, he explained to President Monroe with his typical bluntness and characteristic grammatical indifference that in dealing with Indians, "cases of necessity, creates their own rule."

But this hardly meant the laws of war were insignificant in Jackson's Indian conflicts. Historians have been too quick to view Jackson's attitude toward the laws of war as one of utter contempt and rejection. Jackson's way of thinking about warfare was shaped deeply by the law of war tradition, though in an unusual fashion. Jackson gave life to a deep anxiety buried in the recesses of the Enlightenment laws of war.

Eighteenth-century European jurists and their early American followers had worked a dramatic change in the mechanics of international law in wartime. In the just war tradition of the Middle Ages and early modern period, legality in war was determined by a context-dependent inquiry into means and ends. Conduct was permissible if it satisfied the test of necessity: if it was necessary to advance legitimate ends. Eighteenth-century jurists, by contrast, aimed to substitute hard-and-fast legal rules, rules that would flatly permit or prohibit conduct regardless of context and regardless of the ends such conduct aimed to achieve. Vattel, in particular, insisted that the safety of mankind required "rules that shall be more certain and easy in the application" than the necessity standard of just war theory. In his treatment, "sure and easy" rules proliferated. Armies and soldiers could not use poisons or resort to assassination. They could not execute prisoners or attack the wounded. Noncombatants were protected, especially women and children. American writers working in Vattel's tradition followed suit. Kent and Wheaton reproduced Vattel's array of restraints and sometimes added new ones. Clear and certain rules would guide armies and allow them to reduce the carnage of war.

That was the happy rationale. But the proliferation of rules generated a danger of its own. As rules multiplied, the rules themselves created new occasions for angry recriminations. As Vattel put it, "continual accusations of outrageous excess in hostilities" would "only augment the number of complaints, and inflame the minds of the contending parties with increased animosity." If charges of inhumanity set off a destructive cycle of retaliation, Vattel worried, the sword "would never be sheathed til one of the parties be utterly destroyed."

ANDREW JACKSON'S MILITIA brought Vattel's nightmare to life. Jackson's first big step on the road to political success came in 1802, when he was elected major general of the Tennessee militia. For the next three decades, Jackson helped to build an American militia that self-consciously distinguished itself from the professional army.

The militia was deeply embedded in American democracy. The Second Amendment to the U.S. Constitution, ratified in 1791, embraced the militia and defended the right to bear arms in its name. ("A well regulated Militia, being necessary to the security of a free State," the amendment explained, "the right of the people to keep and bear Arms, shall not be infringed.") What was good for democracy and liberty, however, proved dangerous for humanitarianism in war. At the end of the eighteenth century, French military strategists had predicted that impassioned patriot armies would radically transform "the so-called laws of war." The structure of the American military threatened to vindicate their prediction. The American regular army was a tiny fraction of the size of its European counterparts. (In 1830, there were 200,000 soldiers in the armies of France, but barely more than 6,000 in the U.S. Army.*) And in the absence of a regular fighting force, the United States relied on the energies of its untrained citizen soldiers.

When the War of 1812 began, Jackson took up the righteous banner of the citizen soldier. Urging enlistment in the Tennessee militia, he issued ringing calls for the "free born sons of America" to fight for the vindication of the "national character" the British had insulted. "Your impatience," Jackson told the militia, "is no longer restrained." The "hour of national vengeance" had at last arrived.

The militia's passion often proved difficult to control, even for Jackson. In the War of 1812, Jackson's beloved militia was at the center of some of the most brutal episodes of the conflict. In the Old Northwest, the Kentucky militia destroyed Indian corn supplies and executed captured Indian combatants. In the Old Southwest, Jackson himself led the Tennessee militia in an atrocity-filled campaign against the Creek Indians. For months, white settlers and the Creeks had engaged in a series of raids, counterraids, and reprisals. At the end of August 1813, a party of Creeks managed to get inside the stockade at Fort Mims in Mississippi, where they killed some 250 whites. Rumors at the time put the number closer to 600.

In the fall of 1813 and the spring of 1814, Jackson led a ferocious counterattack on the Creeks. At Tallushatchee in Alabama, Jackson encircled a village of hostile Creeks. "We shot them like dogs," reported Davy Crockett of the Tennessee militia. Jackson's Tennesseans burned the village and took eighty-four women and children prisoner. "Half-consumed human bodies were seen amidst the smoking ruins," recalled one of Jackson's officers. "Dogs had torn and feasted on the mangled bodies of their masters." In a series of pitched battles, Jackson's militia killed close to 2,000 Creek Indi-

---

*European states spent between $3 and $6 per capita each year on their armed forces. The United States spent less than $1 per capita, amounting to less than 1 percent of the nation's annual economic production. See David M. Kennedy, "War and the American Character," *The Nation*, May 3, 1975, p. 522.

ans. At Horseshoe Bend on the Tallapoosa River alone, his men killed 900. The engagements burned Indian villages, destroyed Indian food supplies, and put the survivors on the verge of starvation. Jackson's men made bridle reins from the skin of their victims. They cut the tips off the noses of dead Creeks to keep a running tally of Indian dead. At the end of the conflict, Jackson forced the Creeks to sign away millions of acres of land in present-day Alabama and Georgia.

Jackson dictated the terms of the treaty (the "Treaty of Fort Jackson," as it came to be known). The treaty condemned the "unprovoked, inhuman, and sanguinary war" the Creeks had waged and praised the "honorable warfare" of Jackson's forces. It was difficult to imagine that either side had fought according to humane or honorable standards. At the very least, Jackson's militia had prosecuted a war with no resemblance to the rational conflicts that cadets studied in the Military Academy at West Point. Jackson did not believe in the geometric formulas of the new officer class. He had little faith in the learning of the Supreme Court bar or the intricate doctrines of John Marshall.

Yet Jackson was no monster, indifferent to questions of morality and charity. To the contrary, Jackson used the very injunctions that made up the Enlightenment's hard-and-fast laws of war to make sense of his enemies. Just as Vattel had feared, Jackson turned his enemies' violations of the rules into triggers for his formidable passions.

T HE END OF the War of 1812 did little to settle the simmering disputes among white settlers and hostile factions of Creek and Seminole Indians. The land concessions forced on the Creeks by the Treaty of Fort Jackson only made things worse. Attacks and counterattacks, retaliation and reprisals continued apace into 1816 and 1817. Raiding parties of American settlers and Creek Indians crisscrossed the treaty line between Indian country and white settlements to pillage and murder, to steal cattle, expand landholdings, and seize slaves. Families were massacred and prisoners executed.

In one especially gruesome episode, Seminoles seized an American military vessel that had unwisely moved upriver from the Gulf, killing more than forty men, women, and children inside. The few who escaped reported that the Indians had seized the children by their heels and smashed their skulls against the side of the vessel. In January 1818, Andrew Jackson headed back into the field.

SAVAGE BARBARITY.

Bitter fighting among settlers and Indians,
depicted here in a print from 1818, helped propel
Andrew Jackson into the First Seminole War.

Jackson's 1818 campaign against the Seminoles would become one of the most controversial episodes of his career. In West Tennessee, he called forth the volunteers once more. The great mistake of the Creek campaign, he told them without hesitation, had been that the United States had shown the Indians too much "mildness and humanity." But no more. Now the forces of the great American nation would set aside their "benevolent and humane" inclinations and act with "impunity" to achieve victory.

Sweeping down through Alabama at the head of a motley army of 800 regulars, hundreds of allied Creeks, and about 1,000 militia from Georgia, Tennessee, and Kentucky, Jackson plunged into Spanish Florida, destroying corn supplies, burning towns and killing men. Women and children were spared death but Jackson took them as prisoners. With each day, the fury of the American militia seemed to grow stronger. As Jackson's men moved through Indian towns, they discovered hundreds of scalps taken by Indian raiding parties, as well as the belongings of white settlers and American soldiers who had fallen victim in some of the most notorious Indian attacks over the previous year. In two villages they found red war poles festooned with the scalps of American dead.

Evidence of Indian atrocities encouraged Jackson to adopt retaliatory ruses that skirted the laws of war. The laws of war prohibited the use of false flags to take enemy prisoners. But in early April, Jackson captured two prominent Seminole leaders, Francis the Prophet and Homathlemico, by luring them aboard American vessels fitted out as British cruisers and flying the Union Jack. Once the Indians had clambered aboard the seemingly friendly ships, American sailors seized them and put them in irons. Jackson ordered them executed by hanging.

Inside the Spanish post at St. Marks (near what would become Tallahassee), Jackson captured a seventy-year-old Scottish trader named Alexander Arbuthnot. Ten days later Jackson captured Robert Ambrister, a swashbuckling former officer of the British army who was now assisting the Creeks in their campaign against white settlers. The presence of the two British men seemed to confirm Jackson's suspicion that a shadowy conspiracy existed among the British, the Spanish, and the Seminoles to expand European footholds along the Gulf Coast. With their arrest, however, Jackson believed he had brought a decisive end to the conflict. Their capture, he wrote to Secretary of War John Calhoun, "will end the Indian war for the present."

But even if the hostilities were over, Jackson was not finished. A week after writing to Calhoun, Jackson put Arbuthnot and Ambrister on trial before a tribunal of American officers at St. Marks. Jackson charged the two men with inciting the Creek Indians to war against the United States, with aiding, abetting, and comforting the enemy, and with supplying them with weapons of war. Arbuthnot was charged with spying. Ambrister was charged with commanding the Creeks in warfare against the United States.

For the next two days, an extraordinary trial took place at the small outpost in the wilds of Florida. Jackson's prosecuting officer put on evidence showing that Arbuthnot sympathized deeply with the Creeks. Letters seized from Arbuthnot's vessel made clear that Arbuthnot considered American settlers and the volunteer army that backed them cruel in the extreme. The U.S. government, Arbuthnot had written, would have to disown the acts of its citizens lest the country be known to posterity "as a nation more cruel and savage to the unfortunate aborigines of this country, than ever were the Spaniards." Witnesses with long-standing grudges against the aging Arbuthnot testified that he had incited Indian attacks on American settlers by urging the Creeks to resist the Treaty of Fort Jackson. The evidence of incitement was exceedingly weak. It was the worst kind of hearsay. Nonetheless, the special court of officers convicted Arbuthnot and sentenced him to death by hanging.

Ambrister chose to throw himself on the mercy of the tribunal. Though he denied that he had supplied the Creeks with weapons, he pleaded guilty to the charge of leading them in war against the United States. After initially sentencing Ambrister to be shot, the court reduced his sentence to fifty stripes on his bare back and twelve months hard labor with ball and chain. The next day, General Jackson reinstated Ambrister's death sentence and ordered both men executed immediately. It was, Jackson claimed, "an established principle of the laws of nations that any individual of a nation making war against the citizens of another nation, they being at peace, forfeits his allegiance, and becomes an outlaw and a pirate." In any event, Jackson added, "the laws of war did not apply to conflicts with savages." And so, he concluded, death was the appropriate sentence for both the British subjects he had encountered in the woods of Florida. On April 30, 1818, not two days after the end of Ambrister's short trial, the two men were executed at eight o'clock in the morning.

The great difficulty for Jackson, one that would haunt him for the rest of his career, was that his so-called established principle of the laws of war was no such thing. A citizen of one state participating in a war against another was neither a pirate nor an outlaw merely because his home state was not at war. In his outrage at the atrocities of the Seminoles, Jackson had become unmoored from the rules of war. Instead, he had lashed out at any who opposed the United States.

B Y 1818, Andrew Jackson was the United States' most popular war hero since George Washington and a strong candidate to succeed James Monroe as president. But more than most men, Andrew Jackson had political enemies, and as reports of his exploits in Florida seeped northward, those enemies began to plot a political attack to blunt the general's increasing national popularity. Jackson's political opponents charted a new path for the laws of war, one that made it a weapon of partisan politics.

The public process began in November 1818, in the annual address of President James Monroe to Congress. Monroe—the last (and today the least remembered) of the Virginia dynasty that had begun with Washington, Jefferson, and Madison—sought to defuse the potential political costs of Jackson's Florida adventures by assuring the Congress that his administration had speedily restored the post at St. Marks to the Spanish. But Monroe went further. Without comment, Monroe submitted to Congress the question of Jackson's actions in Florida for review.

Anti-Jackson forces in Congress smelled blood. In particular, Speaker of the House Henry Clay of Kentucky and Secretary of the Treasury William H. Crawford seized the opportunity to undermine a rival for the White House. On January 12, 1819, the House Committee on Military Affairs issued a report condemning the executions of Arbuthnot and Ambrister as unauthorized by any law of the United States and as illegal under the laws of war. Congressman Thomas Nelson of Virginia read the report on the House floor and called for a resolution disapproving of Jackson's actions. Jackson ally Richard Mentor Johnson of Kentucky followed immediately with a dissenting minority report twice as long as the committee's.

The dueling reports produced the longest debate ever to take place in the thirty-year history of the Congress. The debates unfolded in an incongruous setting. The Capitol building was still closed after its burning in 1814 by the British. Congress met in a quickly erected brick building near the Capitol on the site of an old boardinghouse. The justices of John Marshall's Supreme Court had sometimes stayed there during the heyday of the Court's Napoleonic-era prize cases. Now, for three weeks, the new building's narrow galleries were packed while the partisans of Jackson dueled with the supporters of Clay and Crawford on the topic of Andrew Jackson and the laws of war.

On the side of Jackson's critics, the case for censure seemed clear. Jackson had insisted that citizens of a nation not at war were liable to execution in the event of their capture. But that was simply not a rule of international law. As Thomas Nelson observed in the majority report for the Committee on Military Affairs, such a rule would have made an outlaw of the Marquis de Lafayette, the great French aide to General Washington in the Revolutionary War, who had joined the revolutionary cause in 1776, a year and a half before the French formally entered the conflict. Critics of Jackson such as Nelson were willing to concede that the formal rules of Enlightenment warfare might not apply in Indian campaigns. But if so, the real test of legality in warfare with Indians would be the test of necessity. By the general's own account, the war had come to an end ten days before he executed the two British subjects. "Where was the absolute necessity," Nelson demanded to know, to which Jackson could point to justify the executions?

Debate on the committee's condemnation of Jackson commenced on January 18. Thomas Cobb of Georgia (a close ally of Secretary Crawford) took the floor first. Brandishing an edition of Vattel's book, Cobb announced that he had searched through the authorities on the law of nations in hopes of finding some justification for the American general's actions. He had found none. "In one day," Cobb cried, "has the fair character of this nation been blasted! That character for justice and mercy in which we had thought ourselves pre-eminent, and of which we had so proudly boasted to the other nations of the earth, is now prostrated as low as theirs." Now, Cobb groaned, those nations would rejoice. "Boast no more," they would now say, for "you are not less cruel than other nations."

Speaker Henry Clay soon took the floor to throw his weight behind the attack on Jackson. For more than two hours, in what his biographer has called "one of the best speeches of his entire life," Clay methodically dismantled the purported justifications of Jackson's actions. Not content to focus on Arbuthnot and Ambrister, Clay extended his critique to the execution of the Indians Francis the Prophet and Homathlemico. Jackson had executed them, too. But their capture was not the result of "fair and open and honorable war." He had captured them by means of dubious deception and fraud. And in doing so, Jackson had revealed how far he threatened to take the United States from the path of humanity and honor in combat. Until now, Clay contended, the United States had scrupulously followed "the laws of civilized nations" in its dealings with the Indians. And while he would "most cheerfully" acquit Jackson of "any intention" to violate "the obligations of humanity," Clay insisted that Jackson's actions had done just that nonetheless. "The eyes of the whole world are in fixed attention upon us," Clay said, and Americans owed it to themselves to remember "our principles, our religion, our clemency, and our humanity."

By the end of Clay's performance, the partisans of Jackson "sat stony-faced" in their seats. But then one after another rose from their chairs to answer forcefully. Richard Mentor Johnson of Kentucky offered the strongest legal defense of Jackson's actions. In the War of 1812, Johnson was said to have killed the great Indian leader Tecumseh. Two and a half decades later he would become vice president under Jackson's successor in the White House, Martin Van Buren. Johnson insisted that it was a "clear principle" of the law of nations that individuals violating the laws of war "may be punished with death." The execution of the two Indian leaders, Francis and Homathlemico, was not seriously contestable, he insisted. Their race alone was "sufficient evidence" to support their execution. They were unlawful "banditti" or "pirates on land," men who had "no right to expect the treatment due to honorable prisoners of war." Did they meet white settlers in honorable combat? Of course they did not, and it followed that there could be no immorality in exterminating them. Johnson himself was, he admitted, "an advocate of mercy" in warfare, but only "of a mercy compatible with justice," for justice must not be overlooked in the pursuit of a "mistaken clemency." Johnson pledged to "let no false feeling of mercy in my bosom extinguish the obligations of duty to my country." What mattered was that Jackson had won a victory on behalf of the United States.

No fewer than eighteen members of the House stood to defend the general from Tennessee. Alexander Smyth of Virginia contended that "all the proceedings of Gen. Jackson . . . were justified by the law of nations." A "tribe of savages" like the Creeks or the Seminoles, Smyth insisted, was not a sovereign state but a band of robbers. It followed that in war with the Indians, "whatever degree of force, whatever destruction, whatever punishment for violating the usages of war" was permissible. Francis Jones of Tennessee, who had fought under Jackson in the War of 1812, concurred. Who, he wondered, could even pretend that "these vagrant savages," a "tri-colored party" of Indians, escaped slaves, and English incendiaries, were even "entitled to the rights of prisoners of war"? James Barbour of Virginia, who years later would become a Whig opponent of Jackson's, defended his future adversary on the ground that generosity could not be insisted on in war. Francis Johnson of Kentucky reminded his colleagues that "while we are searching our law books and libraries for our definitions," Jackson had been a general in the field, without the luxuries of time and hindsight. Henry Baldwin of Pennsylvania, whom Jackson would later appoint to the Supreme Court, took Johnson one step further and insisted that "General Jackson, in the wilds of Florida, better understood the laws of nations, and the constitution of his country, than gentlemen in this House." George Poindexter of Mississippi, a lawyer and veteran of the War of 1812, belittled Henry Clay's "inflated appeals to our humanity." The House debate, he said bitterly, was "great political theatre," but little more.

R ELISHING A POLITICAL fight as much as anyone, Jackson rushed from Tennessee to Washington to defend himself in the debate's early stages. Rumors quickly flew that he was threatening to assault congressmen who dared to speak out in favor of the House censure resolution. More than once in his career, Jackson had violently attacked his political opponents. (He still carried a bullet in his shoulder from a gunfight with his political rival Thomas Hart Benton.) Members of the Committee on Military

Affairs began to carry firearms with them through the streets of the city. Jackson thundered that he would cut off the ears of his political enemies. In the mouth of any other politician, it would have been easy to discount such vitriol as puffery. Coming from Andrew Jackson one could never be sure.

In the press, dueling pamphlets took up the great debate of the day. Even before the House debate began, the Monroe administration leaked to the press a powerful defense of Jackson's actions penned by Secretary of State John Quincy Adams. Privately, Adams had been stunned by the inhumanity of Jackson's Florida campaign. ("I was not prepared for that mode of warfare," wrote the secretary of state.) But in public Adams took the lead in defending Jackson's executions of Arbuthnot and Ambrister. The two British subjects, Adams said, were "firebrands" who had stirred up the savage Seminoles in a war of no quarter against the United States. Both men, Adams insisted, were therefore subject to lawful retaliation.

Adams's strong defense of Jackson's actions appeared in the administration organ, the *National Intelligencer,* in December 1818 and in dozens of newspapers around the country in the weeks thereafter. Jackson's Tennessee friend John Overton published a rousing defense of the popular general. Members of Congress printed their speeches for wide distribution. Jackson himself had a fifth edition of his memoirs rushed into print in 1819, describing him as having gone to battle against "a desperate clan of outlaws," and deriding his domestic critics as "fastidious civilians" with peculiar ideas on "abstract questions of international law."

As the debate progressed it grew more heated, not less. Jackson's supporters condemned his critics as offering arid and technical legalisms that evaded the real questions of justice and national interest. Francis Johnson of Kentucky mocked the "delicate fastidiousness of martial law when the enemy is knocking at the gate." Jackson supporter Rufus King condemned those who "for the first time in their lives" pretended to be "the champions of humanity, the teachers of the milder virtues, the accusers of the vindictive white warrior, and the protectors of the red men." James Tallmadge of New York addressed Henry Clay directly. "Sir," he said indignantly, "you are an American! Go, count the bleeding scalps of your murdered countrymen." Joseph Desha of Kentucky accused Jackson's detractors of seeking the approval of the European diplomatic corps at the expense of American citizens. Years later, when Jackson was president, his supporters would mock his critics as "learned Puffendorffs": men so taken with European jurists such as the German theorist Samuel Pufendorf that they had lost touch with the obligations of patriotism.

The aggressive posture of the Jackson faction put Clay on the defensive. "I, too," hate the "tomahawk and the scalping knife," he protested lamely. But the efforts of the Clay faction grew feeble. In a resounding series of votes in February 1819, the House voted down the Committee on Military Affairs' censure resolution, as well as a desperate series of substitutes offered by the supporters of Clay and Crawford. Andrew Jackson had won. He had prevailed over the self-appointed keepers of the laws of war.

TWO WEEKS AFTER the House finished its debate, a select committee of the Senate issued a new report criticizing Jackson's actions in Florida. The report's ostensible drafter was Senator Abner Lacock of Pennsylvania, a former brigadier general of the state's militia. ("I have passed [Jackson's] lodging every day, and still have my ears," Lacock quipped.) But its real author, everyone understood, was Jackson's rival, Secretary of the Treasury William Crawford.

Crawford and Jackson had been political enemies ever since 1816, when as secretary of state Crawford had ordered Jackson to adjust the boundaries set by his treaty with the Creeks at Fort Jackson. In private deliberations inside the Monroe cabinet, Crawford had proposed to order Jackson "to give no quarter to any white man found with the Indians." No such order had been issued (Adams, for one, had opposed it). But now Crawford sounded a very different note. The Senate report described the executions of Ambrister and Arbuthnot as "an unnecessary act of severity," as "a departure from that mild and humane system towards prisoners, which in all our conflicts with savage or civilized nations, has heretofore been considered not only honorable to the national character, but conformable to the dictates of sound policy." Crawford's Senate report also criticized Jackson for infringing on the neutrality of Spain. Once upon a time, explained the Crawford-Lacock report, the United States had been "a strong advocate for neutral rights." But now, thanks to Jackson, the United States had sent an army "to conquer and subdue a miserable and feeble, though neutral, colony." To support Jackson, the report concluded, would be to acquiesce in doctrines that were "in direct opposition" to the very principles for which the United States had gone to war in 1812. Jackson, the select committee of the Senate determined, had inflicted "a wound on the national character."

Yet even before the Senate took up the committee report, a diplomatic coup blunted the force of the new attack on Jackson. Two days before the select committee issued its report, Secretary of State John Quincy Adams and the Spanish foreign minister Luis de Onís put the ink on a deal that transformed the American landscape. The Transcontinental Treaty of 1819 cleared away Spain's objections to American claims in the territory that stretched all the way from the Arkansas River across the Rocky Mountains to the Pacific Ocean. It also achieved one of the most prized goals of Presidents Madison and Monroe: the acquisition of Spanish Florida, consisting of what is today the state of Florida, plus a strip of land along the Gulf Coast stretching all the way to the Mississippi River. The treaty granted the entire territory to the United States, and virtually everyone understood what had happened. Andrew Jackson's invasion had won Florida for the United States. It had revealed to Spain just how weak its hold on the colony was. As John Quincy Adams put it, Jackson's operations in Florida were "among the most immediate and prominent causes" of the treaty of 1819.

The Senate quietly buried the select committee's anti-Jackson report. By May, Jackson's friends could write confidently that he had survived the attacks on his character with the "gratitude" of the American people. State legislative assemblies in states as far away as New Hampshire resolved to thank Jackson for his great successes in the Florida campaign. Jackson's friend and military aide James Gadsden celebrated the Tennessee general's triumph. The American people, he wrote to Jackson, "have been with you and will always honor and reverence the man whose life has been devoted to the interests and glory of their country."

A final and decisive referendum on Jackson's actions in Florida came in the years after his vindication in the House and Senate. The presidential election of 1824 recapitulated the fierce debate of 1819. It pitted John Quincy Adams, Henry Clay, William Crawford, and Andrew Jackson against one another. Jackson won a plurality of the votes in the Electoral College but fell short of the majority required to win. Adams, who had defended Jackson at the crucial moment, was close behind. Jackson's critics Crawford and Clay came in a distant third and fourth. In the House of Representatives, Jackson's old political enemy Clay threw his support to Adams, who became the nation's sixth president. (Jackson's supporters said Clay did so on a promise that Adams would make him secretary of state.) But four years later, in the presidential election of 1828, Jackson decisively defeated the incumbent Adams. In both races, Jackson's opponents had tried to make his wartime atrocities a pivotal issue. But large numbers of American voters chose him anyway. They promoted to the presidency the executioner of Ambrister and Arbuthnot, of Francis and Homathlemico, the patriotic citizen soldier who had rampaged through Spanish Florida without the slightest concern for what French observers had long before predicted would become merely "the so-called rules of war."

T HE DEBATES OF 1819 had shown how the international laws of war could become a tool of partisan politics. Yet it took more than political infighting to sustain a month of debate on the floor of the House. The laws of war could only serve Clay's political purposes because they had considerable significance in the eyes of many Americans. Why else would the foes of Jackson (including consummate politicians Henry Clay and William Crawford) have thought they could use the laws of war to their partisan advantage? Powerful ideals lurked behind the political tactics. The debate over Jackson in 1819 was striking for another reason as well. Although Jackson's partisans sometimes expressed disdain for the law of war, they more often defended him in its terms. It was Jackson, they insisted, not his weak-kneed critics, who really understood the laws of war. It was Jackson, they said, who understood that the laws of war authorized ferocious responses to the savagery of Indian conflicts.

The great debate over Jackson and the laws of war had also produced a contest over the legacy of the founding fathers for humanity in war. At the heart of Henry Clay's case against Jackson was an idea that would be a recurrent theme in American law and politics for another 200 years. Clay contended that Jackson had interrupted a great American tradition of humanitarian respect for law, one that was rooted in the revolutionary legacy of the founders. Americans had always, Clay insisted, aspired to respect "the laws of civilized nations," even in their dealings with the Indians.

The partisans of Jackson saw the law of war tradition differently. James Tallmadge of New York, whose fierce attacks on Clay had already helped to turn the tide in Jackson's favor, took up the historian's role against Clay. He, too, remembered the prison ships of New York Harbor, the massacre at Paoli, and the American humanity at Stony Point. But he knew that the American tradition in the laws of war had been stern as well as humanitarian, that it had produced destructive passions even as it restrained wanton violence. The humanitarianism of the Revolution, Tallmadge insisted, had simply not extended to war with the Indians. In Indian war, Tallmadge reminded his colleagues, "our rule had been to burn and break up their towns." Joseph Desha of Kentucky raised the case of Major John André. General Washington had not indulged "technical niceties" based on "mere imaginary grounds" of humanity, Desha said. Washington had carried the stern logic of the law of war to its rigorous conclusion. What about Brigadier General John Sullivan and his destructive march through Iroquois country in the Wyoming Valley of Pennsylvania? What about George Rogers Clark and Henry Hamilton? John Floyd (a former brigadier general of the Virginia militia) called Clark "that great general and best of men," a soldier who had understood the savagery of Indian warfare and had put prisoners to death in full view of the British at Vincennes.

D URING THE SECOND term of Jackson's presidency, war broke out anew with the Seminoles in Florida. Under Major General Thomas Sidney Jesup, the U.S. Army issued orders reinstituting the medieval and early modern practice of booty and plunder, authorizing individual soldiers to keep hostile Indian property for their own account. In 1837 and 1838, American forces under Jesup repeatedly violated some of the most venerable rules of the laws of war by using flags of truce to lure in and capture the Seminole leadership.

Indian leaders protested Jesup's actions as an "unprecedented violation of that sacred rule which has ever been recognized by every nation, civilized or uncivilized." Dismayed American observers cringed at what they called "another breach of national honor." But moral recriminations were not the only effect of the American truce flag violations. When a young and influential Seminole named Coacoochee made a daring escape from imprisonment,

This triptych, titled "Massacre of the Whites by the Indians and Blacks in Florida," appeared in an 1836 account of atrocities in the Seminole Wars.

he quickly spread word of the American breaches of faith. Florida's Seminoles concluded that the United States could not be trusted and redoubled their commitment to resist deportation west across the Mississippi. Jesup's truce flag ruses had backfired.

The bitter violence of the Seminole Wars dragged on for decades. When the United States employed bloodhounds to track down Seminoles, a national debate broke out over the ethics and legality of such tactics. Some denounced the resort to bloodhounds as barbaric. Others condemned as overly sentimental any American who criticized his own nation's tactics, no matter how brutal. On a smaller scale, the debates that dominated the floor of the House in 1819 repeated themselves until 1858, when the conflict with the Seminoles finally came to a close, three years before the beginning of the Civil War.

I N THE FIRST HALF of the nineteenth century, new constituencies had developed for the laws of war. The lawyers and jurists of the eastern bar, the military officer corps at West Point, and the naval officer corps all developed professional investments in a legal tradition that American statesmen had begun to make their own. Yet at the very same time, it had become increasingly apparent that the laws of war were ill equipped for the kinds of Indian wars the United States was engaged in. To the contrary, in the hands of Jackson and his followers, the laws of war had helped to produce downward spirals of destructive violence.

In the years that followed, a number of Americans began to wonder whether the laws of war did more harm than good. Some began to reconsider the laws' basic moral compromise. The first thing the laws of war did was immunize the soldier from criminal prosecution when he killed in battle. This deep separation of war from crime had been what distinguished the legal tradition of European warfare from that of Indian wars. But was the European tradition sound? Why was killing in war different from killing in time of peace?

Chapter 4

Rules of Wrong

——≫•◦•≪——

What is war but organized murder?

—Charles Sumner, July 4, 1845

CRISP UNIFORMS STOOD OUT in brilliant sunshine on the morning of July 4, 1845, in Boston. More than 100 officers from the U.S. Army and Navy had gathered to celebrate Independence Day. Shoulder to shoulder, they marched from Boston City Hall down Tremont Street, toward Tremont Temple for the city's annual Independence Day address. In a show of respect, the city's political elite filed into the rows in the rear, leaving the front pews to the military men. Nearby, in Boston Harbor, the New England merchant fleet gave pride of place to the *Ohio*, a U.S. Navy ship-of-the-line. Bristling with more than 100 guns and decorated with patriotic banners to mark the day, the powerful vessel reminded all of Boston that independence had been won by force of American arms.

The appointed speaker seemed a natural choice to honor the armed forces. Charles Sumner was a rising star of Massachusetts politics. At the age of sixteen, he had planned to attend a local military academy. Though his father sent him to Harvard instead, Sumner often insisted he would have preferred to go to West Point. As a boy he loved the novels of Sir Walter Scott, novels like *Ivanhoe* that gloried in the chivalry of medieval knightly combat. Like countless youth of his generation, he had been infatuated with Napoleon, whose military successes seemed to make the French commander the great man of the age. Enrolling in law school at Harvard in 1831, he was captivated by the class in which his favorite professor, Supreme Court Justice Joseph Story, taught the laws of war. When Sumner was appointed as a lecturer at Harvard Law School in 1835, he took over Story's course while the justice was away, drilling his students on the rights and duties of nations in wartime. He taught the fine distinctions between enemy goods subject to capture and neutral goods that were not. He taught the fundamental difference between war and crime. Three years later, on a European tour, Sumner went out of his way to meet the Continent's most distinguished jurists in the international laws of war.

Yet the speech Sumner delivered was unlike anything the city's leaders or the military audience anticipated. Staring down from the Temple's raised platform, the orator who had taught the law of war at Harvard Law School now turned its logic upside down and indicted the uniformed men in the rows before him. Christians, he argued, could not justly resolve their disputes by combat. War was not a "trial of right." It was massacre and slaughter. Dueling among individuals had long been illegal, but war too had to "be ranked as crime." "Laws of war!" he thundered. "Law in that which is lawless! order in disorder! rules of wrong!" Sumner derided the very idea as an absurdity. As he saw it, there could "only be one law of war; that is the great law, which pronounces it unwise, unchristian and unjust." Any other view of the phrase "Laws or Rights of War" was merely "a contradictory combination of words." "Viewed in the unclouded light of Truth," he pronounced, war was "organized murder." The assembled military notables were the masterminds of war's criminal conspiracy.

For two hours, Sumner relentlessly attacked the sensibilities of his audience. With each new assault, the officers in the audience grew increasingly restless. But Sumner pressed on. What use, he demanded to know, was the standing army? What use was the Navy, whose proudest vessel floated like a hulk in the harbor? What use were the militia and the harbor fortifications that ran up and down the coast? The true Christian hero was not the uniformed soldier but the man who carried "comfort to wretchedness," who "dried the tear of sorrow," who fed the hungry and clothed the naked. Finally, Sumner turned directly to the military men before him as if to defendants in the dock. The lives they led, he accused, were "absorbed in feats of brute force." They had stained the pews of Boston's leading church, for their "vocation" was "blood" and wittingly or otherwise they had renounced "the great law of Christian brotherhood."

One angry observer later complained that Sumner had compared the military men in his audience to "so many lions, tigers, and other wild beasts." But Sumner had another more subversive comparison in mind. War was a "criminal and impious custom." Those who killed in times of war, he insisted, were no different from men who killed lawlessly in times of peace. As his speech wound down, Sumner ended where he began: "Our country cannot do what an individual cannot do." War among nations, like killing among individuals, was a crime.

S UMNER WAS NOT ALONE in thinking of war as murder. Beginning in 1815, a small but energetic group of pacifists came onto the American scene. The peace societies directly challenged orthodoxies in the laws of war. Moderates such as Noah Worcester in Massachusetts assailed the eighteenth-century moral compromise that accounted both sides in a war as just. Radicals like David Low Dodge of New York and the abolitionist William Lloyd Garrison insisted that the Gospels left no room for war at all. Taking pacifism to its extremes, the radicals argued that using force in any way was contrary to the Christian Gospel. Armies, state police forces, and criminal justice systems all violated the teachings of Christ. Even personal self-defense was impermissible.

The peace societies never counted more than a few thousand members in their ranks; a movement that flirted so aggressively with moral perfectionism had little hope of developing mass popular appeal. Nonetheless, charismatic and indefatigable apostles of peace such as Sumner, Worcester, and Dodge helped touch off a raucous and discordant debate in the United States about the difference between war and crime, a debate that ricocheted from Canada to Mexico and ultimately reached across the Atlantic.

Canada

T HE UNITED STATES nearly went to war with Great Britain in the late 1830s and early 1840s. Ironically, the conflict was almost triggered by one of the very ideas Sumner and the pacifists held dearest.

The episode began in late 1837, when a fierce but erratic former newspaper publisher and Toronto mayor named William Lyon Mackenzie collected hundreds of would-be freedom fighters at Navy Island on the Canadian side of the Niagara River near Niagara Falls. Mackenzie aimed to lead a revolution and establish a Republic of Canada independent of the British Empire.

As the British looked on with increasing alarm, Mackenzie hired an American steam vessel named the *Caroline* to ferry arms, supplies, and men to the island in preparation for their impending invasion of the Canadian mainland. The British reassured themselves that Mackenzie was slightly mad. But they found his efforts threatening nonetheless. And on December 29, the British commander in the Canadian town of Chippewa decided to destroy the *Caroline*. Under cover of night, a detachment of sixty British regulars and Canadian militia under Captain Andrew Drew of the Royal Navy rowed out into the river to burn the vessel. When Drew found that the *Caroline* had been moved to a berth on the American side of the river, he pressed onward and crossed into U.S. territory. With muskets charged and swords drawn, the British force took the unsuspecting crew and passengers by surprise. In a few chaotic minutes, the British gained control of the vessel. Putting the *Caroline* to the torch, they towed it into the main current and set it adrift, careering toward Niagara Falls. Some witnesses reported that it broke in half and sank before reaching the precipice. Others reported that the *Caroline* went over the falls as a spectacular fireball, extinguished by an awesome crash into the whirlpool below.

I N THE DIPLOMATIC exchanges that followed, Secretary of State Daniel Webster loudly protested the British incursion on U.S. soil. A country may use force in its defense, he insisted to Henry Fox, the British minister in Washington, only when there exists a "necessity of self-defence, instant, overwhelming, leaving no choice of means, and no moment for deliberation." More than 100 years later, when the United States emerged from World War II as the globe's great political and military power, Webster's formulation became the canonical test the world over for the legality of the use of force in national self-defense. In 1945, the Charter of the United Nations outlawed war but created an exception for self-defense, an exception that statesmen and lawyers around the world would construe by reference to Webster's *Caroline* standard. The next year, the International Military Tribunal at Nuremberg drew on Webster's formulation to conclude that Nazi Germany had waged a war of aggression, not one of self-defense. Nations have invoked Webster's *Caroline* dictum as the test of lawful self-defense ever since.*

---

*Shortly after President George W. Bush's June 2002 speech at West Point introduced the Bush Doctrine of preemptive self-defense, the Justice Department's Office of Legal Counsel issued a secret memorandum (since made public) that relied on and updated the *Caroline* standard, making it (according to the memo's authors Jay Bybee and John Yoo) "more nuanced than Secretary Webster's nineteenth-century formula."

The twentieth- and twenty-first-century triumph of Webster's *Caroline* formulation, however, has obscured the core of the controversy that produced his dictum. In its time, the elaboration of the *Caroline* rule for self-defense was a sideshow in a much more dangerous affair, one that raised the same dangerous and potentially destabilizing question that the peace societies had broached. Why was it that soldiers who killed in military engagements were not guilty of murder? What was it that made a soldier's violence different?

SOMETIME IN THE melee aboard the *Caroline*, a member of the British boarding party shot and killed an American passenger named Amos Durfee. Mackenzie's Canadian partisans and their American sympathizers quickly made Durfee a martyr to the cause of Upper Canadian independence. Three thousand people attended his funeral at the Buffalo city hall. Speakers called for revenge against the British and punishment of the wrongdoers.

Revenge was several years in coming, but in the fall of 1840 New York officials arrested a pugnacious Canadian named Alexander McLeod for Durfee's murder. McLeod was notorious for his fierce support of the British colonial regime. As a member of the Canadian militia, he had taken up arms to help suppress Mackenzie's uprising. Moreover, McLeod was widely disliked in the border region. After his arrest, a number of New Yorkers close to the Canadian patriot movement leapt at the chance to testify against him; some of the witnesses hoped to settle old grudges. On the basis of their testimony, a grand jury at Lockport in Niagara County indicted McLeod for arson and murder.

Now it was British minister Henry Fox's turn to protest. The problem with indicting McLeod, Fox warned, was that making soldiers individually responsible for the consequences of military action authorized by their home states undid a century's progress in the laws of armed conflict. Absent immunity, a soldier facing criminal prosecution and a possible death sentence might be willing to fight to the bitter end. Who would surrender if doing so meant execution as a criminal? Prosecuting men like McLeod, Fox contended, would thus "aggravate beyond measure the miseries" of war. It would mix "the ferocity of personal passions" with the resolution of national disputes. Fox argued that New York's prosecution threatened "to bring back into the practice of modern war, atrocities which civilization and Christianity have long since banished." McLeod's lawyer, Alvin C. Bradley, took the same position. "To hold the prisoner guilty of murder or any crime," he argued, would "produce in international law a revolution, the extent of which no human sagacity can foresee." What atrocities, Bradley asked, "would not creep into the practice of nations?"

New York officials and the New York courts disagreed. Judge Esek Cowen of the New York Supreme Judicial Court upheld McLeod's indictment on the ground that there had been no war between the United States and Britain in 1837, and that the law of war's immunity attached only when war commenced. Cowen therefore concluded that neither the United States nor New York was "under any obligation to observe . . . the rules of formal warfare" under which McLeod sought to claim immunity. But Cowen went further. It was "a mistake," he determined, "to suppose that a soldier is bound to do any act contrary to the law of nature, at the bidding of his prince." As Judge Cowen saw it, acting as a soldier on behalf of a sovereign might confer an immunity from prosecution, but only for those things the sovereign state might lawfully do.

New York's attorney general, Willis Hall, observed that even in wartime certain combatants were subject to execution if caught by the enemy. Spies, for example, were universally understood to be subject to hanging if discovered in the act. So were assassins. Foreign recruiters seeking enlistments were punishable by death, whether in peacetime or in war. In the Revolution, Washington had executed British agents caught trying to induce treason in the Continental Army. The Swiss jurist Vattel had also written that when soldiers undertook "informal and illegitimate war . . . without any right, without even an apparent cause," the laws of war provided them no shield against punishment for their acts.

As New York officials pressed forward with the prosecution of McLeod, tensions mounted. An irate Fox pointed out that McLeod was not an assassin. Nor was he a spy. Even assuming McLeod had been involved in the assault on the *Caroline*, he had taken (his lawyer pointedly observed) "the hazards of war" and "periled his life in the expedition." He had not recruited Americans to fight with the British against Mackenzie's patriots, let alone against the United States. And regardless of what one thought of the justice of the British incursion into New York to assault the *Caroline*, McLeod was not a soldier who had fought merely for the sake of killing and without any plausible claim of right.

British newspapers denounced the trial of McLeod as an "outrage of our rights." *The Times* of London demanded McLeod's release and vowed revenge. War with Great Britain came to seem more likely than at any time since the end of the War of 1812. The British foreign secretary Lord Palmerston instructed Fox to prepare for imminent hostilities. Palmerston wrote privately to his brother that "war would be the inevitable result" if McLeod were punished. By October 1841, Prime Minister Robert Peel was holding secret meetings with his cabinet to plan for armed conflict with the United States.

War fever raced through the United States, too. The pugnacious James Henry Hammond of South Carolina (soon to be governor of the state) urged his countrymen to take up arms against Great Britain. A convention of Ohio citizens called on the federal government to resort to war if necessary to sustain the country's honor. In Buffalo, a federal official reported that "the whole frontier" seemed to be "in motion." Andrew Stevenson, the American minister in London, advised American naval forces in the Mediterranean to prepare for the impending conflict.

I N THE WANING DAYS of his one term as president, Andrew Jackson's handpicked successor Martin Van Buren sided with the New York authorities. Van Buren was a New Yorker himself, which may explain his reaction. But after the inauguration of William Henry Harrison in March 1841, the United States reversed course. The new secretary of state, Daniel Webster, told Fox that the federal government now agreed with Britain's view of the law of combatant immunity. It was "a principle of public law sanctioned by the usages of all civilized nations," Webster wrote, that "an individual forming part of a public force, and acting under the authority of his Government, is not to be held answerable" for acts authorized by his sovereign. Like Fox, Webster believed that the immunity of combatants from the criminal law had laid the foundation of the modern laws of war. As Webster's allies at the *North American Review* wrote a few years later, a soldier faced with criminal prosecution if captured "would become a pirate and a scourge." He would wage not a rational war for his sovereign but an impassioned and all-out war "for his own revenge and his own safety."

The federal government lacked the formal authority to override New York's criminal justice system, but given the stakes, Webster did all that he could to prevent the punishment of McLeod. Within a month of taking office, Webster dispatched Attorney General John Crittenden and U.S. Army general Winfield Scott to western New York to stop American sympathizers from providing further aid to the Canadian rebels. He pressed New York's governor to abandon the prosecution and release McLeod. When New York officials refused to do so, Webster (in a highly unusual move) asked the U.S.

district attorney for northern New York to join McLeod's defense team. Webster himself gave advice to McLeod's lawyers on how best to defend their client against the New York charges.

W ITH EACH PASSING MONTH, the legal dispute grew more heated. Governor William Henry Seward of New York grasped the political gains to be made prosecuting a British national for crimes against Americans and insisted on going ahead with the trial. Webster's most scathing congressional critic, Senator Thomas Hart Benton of Missouri, linked the McLeod prosecution to Andrew Jackson's actions in Spanish Florida more than twenty years earlier. It was Benton whose bullet was still lodged in the former president's shoulder, but Benton had long since become one of Jackson's closest political allies. Now Benton declared that Jackson had needed "no musty volumes" on the laws of war "in the swamps of Florida." Benton thought it was "mournful to see gentlemen of eminent abilities consulting books to find passages to justify an outrage upon their own country." It would be better by far, he said, to do as Jackson had done, to "throw away the books, and go by the heart."

Ultimately, a jury averted the controversy without any resolution of the principles in dispute. After a long eight-day trial in the fall of 1841, the New York jury in McLeod's case took a half-hour to deliver a verdict of not guilty. The jury acquitted not because they agreed with Webster and Fox instead of Benton, Seward, and Cowen. They found McLeod not guilty, the jurors said, because they were not sure he had even participated in the attack on the *Caroline* in the first place.

H ISTORIANS HAVE LONG credited Webster with holding off war in the face of angry calls for retaliation. In August 1842, Webster and his British counterpart, Lord Ashburton, signed a treaty resolving controversies about the location of the U.S.-Canada border that had been simmering since 1783. In truth, however, it was not the Webster-Ashburton Treaty that saved the United States and Great Britain from going to war. Webster and Ashburton signed the treaty after the real crisis of the McLeod prosecution had already passed.

The treaty no more resolved the issue of soldiers' liabilities under the criminal law than the jury's verdict had. And when in March 1842 President Harrison's successor John Tyler learned that New York authorities had arrested another alleged participant in the assault on the *Caroline*, war seemed like it might be in the offing once again. Only now did Webster earn the credit for the peace that historians have given him for the treaty with Ashburton. At Webster's urging, the Congress passed a new law that gave federal courts the authority to stop state prosecutions of foreign citizens such as McLeod when their confinement violated the law of nations. The constitutionality of the legislation was unclear; many continued to think the federal government lacked the authority to interrupt state criminal proceedings. But Governor Seward's term in office was fast coming to a close and New York authorities no longer had the stomach to prosecute an already difficult case if it meant flying in the face of the federal statute. New York backed down.

Mexico

S O DECISIVE WAS Webster's success that when war finally did break out, it was not with Great Britain, but with the United States' neighbor to the south.

On May 11, 1846, President James Polk asked the U.S. Congress to declare war. "Mexico," he told the members of the House of Representatives and the Senate, "has passed the boundary of the United States, has invaded our territory, and shed American blood on American soil." Under Webster's famous *Caroline* formula, Polk had offered a clear self-defense basis for war. When Mexican forces under Colonel Anastasio Torrejón crossed over to the north bank of the Rio Grande to attack General Zachary Taylor's U.S. Army of Occupation, Polk reasoned, they had passed into and attacked the United States. The trouble, however, was that many in Mexico (and some in the United States) saw it differently. They believed the border was not at the Rio Grande but at the Nueces River, 150 miles to the north. Mexican officials insisted that Mexican blood had been spilled on Mexican soil. The commander of the Mexican Army of the North called Taylor's crossing of the Nueces "unjust, illegal, and anti-Christian."

Historians in Mexico and the United States ever since have carried on an inconclusive debate over the location of the U.S.-Mexico border and the legality of the United States' decision to go to war. What neither Polk nor his critics guessed—and what historians have usually overlooked—was that in a year's time the United States would be embroiled in a different controversy about the laws of war. Once again, the issue would be the difference between war and crime. And this time the American military would merge the two to create a forerunner to the modern idea of the war crime.

A T FIRST, the Mexican War followed the European conventions for regulating combat. Mexico and the United States each committed to follow the customs and usages of civilized war. Taylor and his Mexican counterpart Pedro de Ampudia agreed that "the laws and customs of war among civilized nations" would be "carefully observed" by the armed forces of both nations. The two generals communicated through white truce flags sanctioned by the laws of war. They entered into formal capitulation agreements allowing surrenders with honor. They followed the usages of war in their treatment of prisoners. Taylor readily exchanged prisoners and routinely paroled captured Mexican soldiers, officers and enlisted men alike, despite nagging worries that some paroled Mexicans were violating their oaths by taking up arms after their release. Mexican commanders likewise viewed captured Americans "as prisoners of war, to be treated with all the consideration to which such unfortunates are entitled by the rules of civilized warfare." Captive American officer Seth Thornton, for example, reported to Taylor that "kindness and attention" had been "lavished" upon him and his fellow prisoners. Within a short time, Thornton was back in the U.S. camp, exchanged along with all his men for the equivalent number of Mexican prisoners.

Taylor and his subordinates issued proclamations assuring the Mexican people that they, too, would be "protected in their rights, both civil and religious." As Taylor put it in June 1846, "We come to make no war upon the people of Mexico." When the war neared its end in January 1848, Secretary of War William Marcy boasted proudly to the Congress that the conflict had been conducted "within the rules of civilized warfare."

But if Marcy thought the Mexican conflict had not altered the laws of war profoundly, he was deeply mistaken. As the war dragged on, Marcy and his generals had made a critical change in how the laws of war worked.

In the war's second year, acute new problems began to develop for the American armies in Mexico. Most of the 73,000 volunteers who served in the Mexican War behaved honorably. But infamous companies such as the 1st Pennsylvania, made up of members of a Philadelphia gang known locally as the "Killers," had been stealing and robbing even before they crossed the Nueces and the Rio Grande. Once in Mexico, volunteers continued to commit the same kinds of depredations and worse. In June 1846, Taylor worried that the volunteers arriving daily in Mexico were proving to be "a lawless set." By 1847, he was condemning many of them as "G-d d——d" thieves and cowards. The volunteers, complained Lieutenant George Gordon Meade, acted like "Goths and Vandals"; using the conventional racial categories of the age, Meade wrote that they seemed more "like a body of hostile Indians than of civilized whites." According to General-in-Chief Winfield Scott, the atrocities were enough "to make Heaven weep" and to cause every American "of Christian morals" to "blush for his country."

Regular army officers were not the only observers shocked by the behavior of the raw recruits. A *Louisville Journal* correspondent remarked that Taylor's march from the Rio Grande toward Monterey "was everywhere marked by deeds of wanton violence and cruelty." At Marin, the same newspaper reporter observed "pillage, robbery, and devastation." Volunteers such as Henry Clay, Jr., son of the powerful Kentucky politician, were shocked at the "inhumanities" committed by some of their peers. George W. Kendall, a prominent New Orleans resident, expressed the same view in a manner common among white Southerners when he wrote in disgust that an American garrison near Punta Agua "had committed offenses that negroes in a state of insurrection would hardly be guilty of." The behavior of Zachary Taylor's troops left a lasting mark on his reputation, though not enough of one to prevent his election as president in 1848.

Mexicans committed atrocities, too. Throughout much of the war, Mexican authorities had a weak grasp on law and order. The Mexican presidency changed hands six times in less than two years. In the power vacuum, highway robbers preyed on American stragglers and Mexican civilians alike. Even before the onset of formal hostilities, bandits murdered Zachary Taylor's popular quartermaster Colonel Truman Cross when he wandered outside the U.S. camp. American observers wrote home of murderers run rampant. "The weapon used in most cases," George Kendall reported, was "a slim but exceedingly sharp sword-cane." "So expert are the cowardly miscreants in their murderous office," he wrote, "that but one stab is necessary to take life."

Most of the Mexican acts were not acts of war, strictly speaking. So far as anyone could tell, they were ordinarily committed by Mexican nationals, not Mexican soldiers. They were the acts of civilian criminals. In the second year of the war, however, that was about to change.

* * *

IN FEBRUARY 1847, Mexican authorities switched their tactics. For the better part of a year Mexican armies had fought and lost one pitched battle after another. Now, as Winfield Scott led 20,000 soldiers from Vera Cruz on the coast toward the capital city, Mexican commanders abandoned the set-piece battles in which they had been so badly overmatched and adopted the irregular tactics that had only recently come to be called "guerrilla war."

The new Mexican strategy modeled itself on the Spanish resistance to Napoleon some forty years before when peasants on the Iberian Peninsula had taken up arms to harass and demoralize the French-backed occupiers. Some Mexican military men had favored such tactics from the start. But the acting president of Mexico, Pedro Maria Anaya, made the turn to guerrilla tactics official in April 1847 when he called "for the establishment of a light corps to function as part of the National Guard." Anaya's proclamation went out to any "citizen having sufficient means and influence" to raise a unit of at least fifty men. The call echoed through Mexico. Wherever there were high concentrations of U.S. soldiers—in Puebla, Mexico, Vera Cruz, and Tamaulipas—guerrilla companies formed in great numbers.

Guerrilla detachments soon launched attacks on American wagon trains, especially those carrying goods along the critical supply line between Vera Cruz on the coast and Winfield Scott's army in the interior. Early in 1847, guerrillas led a stunning attack on a massive wagon train of 110 wagons and 300 pack mules on the road from Marin to Monterrey. Fifteen hundred guerrillas commanded by General José Urrea hid alongside the road until the wagons and their small escort were surrounded. Lieutenant William Barbour, the commander of the American force, had no choice but to surrender immediately. The guerrillas cut the canvas wagon covers into crude sacks and filled them with everything they could carry away. Having taken all they could, the guerrillas opened what an American medical officer later called "an indiscriminate slaughter" on the Mexican teamsters who drove the wagons for the U.S. Army. The Mexican command had issued a standing order that no quarter be granted to Mexican nationals working for the Americans. Many of them "were burned alive on their wagons." The bodies later recovered had been "most savagely mutilated."

Guerrillas often hid in the thick chaparral along the roads and picked off stragglers from the American lines. Men went missing from the camps, only to be found days later, dead in the heavy brush by the roadside. One victim was found with a lasso around his neck and tied to a prickly pear; he had been dragged 100 yards through the underbrush.

Guerrillas like a one-handed former highway robber named El Mocho ("The Maimed") quickly became infamous for their brutal treatment of American stragglers. When a young U.S. drummer was captured by El Mocho's men, for example, he was assaulted, "dreadfully wounded," and left naked "by the roadside to perish alone." Days later, El Mocho encountered the boy again and killed him outright, cutting the drummer's throat "from ear to ear." One American soldier wrote home in 1847 that the guerrillas "murder the soldiers who may, from fatigue, lag behind our army." Sometimes "they even cut our men's throat, heart and tongue out, hanging them on a limb of a tree right over their bodies."

To some Mexicans, the guerrillas were heroes. In the eyes of U.S. forces, however, they were villains. As guerrilla attacks mounted, American volunteers resorted to the same brutal and often counterproductive reprisals that Napoleon's forces had employed in Spain forty years earlier. When Mexican guerrillas killed a private in the Arkansas Volunteers, the victim's comrades chased a large group of Mexican men and boys into a cave at the Rancho Agua Nueva near Saltillo in northern Mexico and killed between twenty and thirty of them while they huddled inside. A month later, the Texas Rangers—already notorious for their rough treatment of Mexican civilians—retaliated for an attack on a wagon train by massacring twenty-four Mexicans at Rancho Guadalupe near the town of Ramos. In the suburbs of Mexico City in September 1847, the Texans avenged the death of one of their own by killing seventeen Mexicans. And when the popular cavalry officer Samuel H. Walker was killed later in the fall in an engagement with guerrillas near Huamantla, a "wave of vengeance" washed across the countryside. One historian has described the ensuing retaliatory violence as a "rampage of looting, destruction, murder, and rape." American soldiers on the ground described it the same way. "All around me," reported one Indiana soldier, "was desolation and ruin."

Guerrilla attacks and American reprisals touched off a downward spiral of violence. Attempts under Zachary Taylor's command to allow local Mexican officials to deal with criminal acts by guerrillas neither deterred guerrilla activity nor successfully stopped unauthorized American reprisals. As one Mexican observer remembered after the war, "desolation and death" had been "reduced to a system" along the roads of Mexico. Homes were left in ashes. Ranches stood deserted. "The dead bodies of men and the carcasses of mules lay unburied along with broken and plundered wagons."

* * *

WINFIELD SCOTT, who arrived in Mexico in February 1847 to lead the campaign to Mexico City, was as well positioned as any officer in the U.S. Army to deal with the problem of guerrilla war. Trained as a lawyer in Virginia, he had distinguished himself for more than thirty years as one of the leading professional officers of the age. In 1812, Scott had been captured by the British in a battle at Queenstown in Canada. (He almost certainly would have been executed by the British army's Indian allies if a heroic British officer had not intervened.) While serving as a prisoner himself, he had represented the United States in prisoner of war controversies for much of the rest of the war. In the decade thereafter Scott studied military operations in Europe, compiled the Army's new *General Regulations*, and wrote what became the drill manual for infantry in the U.S. Army. By 1847, he was general-in-chief of the U.S. Army, the Army's highest-ranking officer.

Scott was also among the most well read officers in the early U.S. Army, and like many of his fellow officers he made the Napoleonic Wars of Europe his principal study. As the Mexican War progressed, Scott began to pay particularly close attention to the military failures late in Napoleon's career. He read about Napoleon's disastrous invasion of Russia and his catastrophic retreat back to France. And he read about the campaign of the Spanish guerrillas on the Iberian Peninsula in 1808. From Sir William Napier's three-volume *History of the War in the Peninsula* and from Baron de Jomini's writings on the art of war, Scott learned that a population aroused to guerrilla warfare could undermine the efforts of even the most well trained army.

Drawing lessons from Napoleon's mistakes, Scott developed an innovative strategy for dealing with the twin problems of guerrilla attacks and indiscriminate retaliation by American volunteers. The first problem he took on was one he had been working on for decades: the discipline of his own soldiers. Zachary Taylor had long complained that he could not identify the perpetrators responsible for civilian deaths, even when they were his own soldiers. But if Taylor had been able to do so (and there was little reason to think he had tried very hard), he faced a seemingly insuperable problem: U.S. military authorities in Mexico lacked the authority to punish most crimes committed by American soldiers against Mexican noncombatants. The Articles of War, which traced back to the Continental Congress and which had not been significantly revised since 1806, left the authority to punish such crimes in the state and territorial courts of the United States. It had never occurred to the Congresses of the early republic that a U.S. army might fight a war of occupation in foreign territory. And so, when

Taylor asked Secretary of War William Marcy in the fall of 1846 what to do with an American soldier who had murdered a Mexican soldier after the end of combat at Monterey, Marcy instructed Taylor that military tribunals were probably incompetent "to take cognizance of such a case." Absent more authority from the Congress, Marcy advised Taylor simply to release the prisoner "from confinement and send him away from the army."

Taylor meekly complied, but Scott thought Marcy's advice absurd. Being discharged was exactly what disgruntled volunteers wanted most. American commanders in Mexico would never be able to maintain discipline over their men without the authority to punish those who committed crimes against the enemy.

Before he left for Mexico, Scott pressed the Polk administration to propose legislation to Congress authorizing military tribunals in Mexico to try such offenses. But neither the Congress nor the president was willing to act. Members of Congress claimed that there was no need for legislation because the president already had the power to try such crimes based on his authority under the laws of war. If he had such power, however, Polk failed to exercise it. As Scott later wrote, the question of an inherent executive power to enact a federal criminal code was "too explosive for safe handling." In Scott's homespun metaphor, Polk and Marcy handled the subject as gingerly as "the terrier mumbles a hedgehog."

Scott took matters into his own hands upon arriving in Mexico. By his own order he created a new martial law authority over crimes committed by U.S. soldiers on foreign soil. Scott's General Orders No. 20, issued at Tampico on February 19, 1847, authorized tribunals that he called "military commissions" for a wide array of acts deemed atrocities. He listed assassination and murder, malicious stabbing or maiming and rape, malicious assault, battery, robbery, theft, the wanton desecration of churches, and the destruction of public or private property. Military commissions were empowered to try any such offense committed by or upon a member of the United States' forces, including offenses committed by inhabitants of Mexico. Scott issued General Orders No. 20 anew at each major juncture in the campaign across central Mexico. He distributed the order widely in English and Spanish at Vera Cruz in April, at Puebla in June, and at Mexico City in September.

Scott's military commissions tried some 303 Americans during the Mexican War. As a mechanism for disciplining his own soldiers, his martial law innovation was a great success, a crucial piece of the widely praised campaign he waged from the sea to Mexico City. Indeed, Scott's martial law order quickly became part of an American national mythology of chivalry in the

Mexican campaign. It helped Americans view with pride the efforts of their army to bring order to the mounting chaos in Mexico. As one writer put it, the war had been fought with "chivalric generosity" and an "enlightened moderation" that connected the American armies in Mexico to "the best days of Knighthood." Shortly after the war ended, the best-selling author Emma Willard wrote proudly that the "Mexican capital was not conquered by the American republic, as Carthage and other cities were by the Roman." Mexico City had not been destroyed. It had not "become the sport of petty tyrants and a lawless soldiery." Even critics of the war came to think that "no war, in any age or country, was ever waged upon principles so humane, so civilized" or "so Christian" as the Mexican War. Scott's closest aides were positively effusive. "It would be a blessing to humanity," gushed Lieutenant Colonel Ethan Allen Hitchcock, "if General Scott's martial law order in Mexico could be recognized as an integral portion of the international law of the world."

D ESPITE HITCHCOCK'S PRAISE, one feature of Scott's military commissions was actually quite strange. It was one thing to punish American soldiers and Mexican civilians within U.S. lines. Such authority had long existed in the basic structure of European and American militaries. The much harder problem was to understand how Scott had the right to punish commissioned members of the Mexican army.

Scott initially declined to bring regular Mexican soldiers or commissioned guerrillas into his commissions. His 1846 proposal for the Congress and for Polk and Marcy proposed to punish "inhabitants of the hostile country" who committed murder or theft or any one of a number of other crimes. General Orders No. 20 at Tampico in February 1847 similarly established jurisdiction over "any inhabitant of Mexico." By "inhabitant," Scott almost certainly meant noncombatants, since the word had long been used in military law as a term of art that excluded soldiers. Two months later, Scott confirmed that he did not contemplate prosecuting enemy soldiers. In a proclamation to the people of Mexico, he announced that "injuries committed by individuals, or parties of Mexico, *not belonging to the public forces*," would be "punished with rigor." Those who did belong to the "public forces" of Mexico would not, or at least not by Scott's military commissions.

As late as October 1847, Secretary of War Marcy treated commissioned Mexican guerrillas not as criminals, but as soldiers entitled to prisoner of war status. Marcy excoriated guerrilla tactics, to be sure. They were "hardly recognized as a legitimate mode of warfare," he wrote to Scott, "and should be met with the utmost allowable severity." Guerrillas and their supporters were therefore not to be paroled or exchanged. But Marcy stopped short of suggesting that commissioned Mexican guerrillas were subject to criminal prosecution. Even guerrillas, he insisted, "should be seized and held as prisoners of war," not prosecuted as criminals.

Yet as the war ground on into its final months, American officials subtly but crucially altered the legal status of Mexican soldiers engaged in irregular war. Even as Marcy articulated the view that guerrillas were generally entitled to prisoner of war treatment, Taylor began to redescribe guerrilla attacks on his wagon trains as attacks by "robbers." The new description did not reflect a change in the underlying conduct of the Mexicans. Nor did it arise out of a change in the status of the Mexicans engaging in the conduct. Commissioned Mexican guerrilla parties were still assaulting wagon trains and killing the Mexican nationals they found acting as teamsters for the U.S. armed forces. Nonetheless, Taylor had begun to shift from the idiom of war to the language of crime.

The change in treatment moved slowly through the U.S. forces in Mexico. In the north, Brevet Major General John E. Wool decreed that "guerrilla parties" were "highway robbers under another name" and would be "executed wherever found." Further south, Major Walter Lane's Texas Rangers captured a guerrilla in late 1847 and executed him two days later after a hasty field tribunal. To ensure that word of the American attitude toward guerrillas would be spread far and wide, Lane ordered the guerrilla shot so that "as many Mexicans" as possible could "witness the execution." When Major General Joseph Lane (no relation to the Texas Ranger) led antiguerrilla forces on an engagement at Sequalteplan, he made plans to execute the enemy commander as a criminal.

At the same time, the U.S. Army began convening informal military tribunals styled as "councils of war" to prosecute Mexican military recruiters caught trying to lure away American soldiers. Mexican recruitment efforts posed a real problem. Some 6,825 American soldiers deserted during the course of the war, nearly 7 percent of the entire Army; several hundred of them formed the San Patricio Battalion, made up mostly of Irish and German Catholic immigrants who signed up to fight alongside their fellow Catholics in Mexico. The military commission scholar David Glazier has identified twenty-one accused recruiters tried by councils of war beginning in June 1847. Eleven were convicted, and the punishment was "almost always death."

In December, Winfield Scott drew on the councils of war for Mexican recruiters to formalize the treatment of guerrillas as criminals. General Orders No. 372, issued from Mexico City, announced that "atrocious bands called 'guerrilleros' and 'rancheros'" were violating "every rule of warfare observed by civilized nations." Many guerrillas acted under the commission and instruction of the Mexican authorities. But Scott no longer made such a distinction. "Whether serving under Mexican commissions or not," Scott ordered that such guerrillas were to be sent before a "council of war" for "summary trial" according to "the known laws of war." Councils of war, in turn, were to punish "any flagrant violation of the laws of war" by death or lashes, so long as there was "satisfactory proof that such prisoner, at the time of capture, actually belonged to any part of a gang of known robbers or murderers, or had actually committed murder or robbery upon any American officer or soldier or follower of the American Army."

Scott's councils of war were summary indeed, for there is almost no information in the historical record about the councils of war that tried guerrillas. No written transcripts were taken, at least none that survive. No general orders were published. As a result, we cannot be sure how many guerrillas were tried by council of war. Even the most thorough military commission scholars have found not a single surviving record of a council of war trying a Mexican guerrilla. But it seems clear that field tribunals in Mexico did exactly this. Colonel William Winthrop, who was the leading late nineteenth-century American authority on military law and who served in the Judge Advocate General's office during the Civil War, wrote in the 1880s that "guerrilla warfare" and "violation of the laws of war by guerrilleros" were among the "principal charges referred to and passed upon" by the councils of war in Mexico. Winthrop had not been in Mexico himself, but he was in a position to know what had taken place there. Moreover, Winthrop's report is corroborated by anecdotal evidence. Major General Joseph Lane's antiguerrilla detachment reported using precisely such a field tribunal to execute a guerrilla in late 1847. And at least one American officer was punished for executing a guerrilla "without the sanction of a council of war."

S COTT'S PROSECUTIONS OF Mexican guerrillas occasioned little fanfare at the time. But they marked a transformative moment in the laws of war. The U.S. military had never seen anything like it before. In the Revolution, Washington had tried Major John André as a spy. But spies were not criminals in the ordinary sense. They were loyal servants of their country whose clandestine (and often heroic) missions exposed them to a particularly severe sanction under the rules of the game called war. Though the spy might be forgiven for overlooking the distinction, spies were executed because doing so was simply (in Vattel's words) the only means "of guarding against the mischief they may do to us." That was why a spy who successfully made his way back to his own army's lines could no longer be executed, even if he was subsequently captured.

Nor were Andrew Jackson's executions of the British subjects Arbuthnot and Ambrister in Florida in 1818 comparable. Neither Arbuthnot nor Ambrister were members of the British armed forces; they were private agents working on their own account and thus not protected as prisoners of war. The closest thing the United States had ever seen to Scott's guerrilla prosecutions were the messy and ultimately inconclusive accusations leveled by Thomas Jefferson against Lieutenant Colonel Henry Hamilton ("the hair-buyer general") in 1779 for stirring up savage warfare on the early frontier and mistreating American prisoners. But even there, Jefferson had stopped short of formally treating Hamilton as a criminal. At Washington's urging, Jefferson had eventually relented and released Hamilton on parole as a prisoner of war.

Few precedents for Scott's councils existed in the history of modern European warfare. Centuries earlier, medieval chivalric courts had tried violations of the laws of arms by knights from around Europe. But the courts of chivalry had long since dwindled into insignificance. By the time of the wars of the French Revolution and Napoeleon's campaigns, controversial criminal punishments took place not between admitted enemy countries but in cases where one side denied that the other was entitled to the privileges of a sovereign state in wartime. When Napoleon arrested and executed the exiled French aristocrat the duc d'Enghien in 1804, for example, he charged him with treason, not war crimes. Napoleon's chief of police famously said the controversial execution was "worse than a crime, it was a blunder"; but no one at the time suggested that either Enghien's conduct or the execution itself amounted to war crimes. Napoleon's regime levied the same treason charges when it executed Don Giovanni Batista, the Marquis Rodio, in Calabria in southern Italy in 1807, and again when it executed guerrillas on the Spanish Peninsula in 1808. Napoleon claimed to exercise authority as the new sovereign (Spain) or as the military governor of territory occupied by the French army (Calabria). His victims were thus treated as traitors and rebels, not as soldiers. But the United States did not claim to be the new sovereign of Mexico, and its small army could not plausibly claim to occupy the vast landscape of Mexico.*

The absence of analogues in the recent history of warfare for Scott's treatment of the Mexican guerrillas reflected the basic structure of the orthodox laws of war as they had been handed down into the 1840s. For centuries, the law of war had been organized around separating soldiers from criminals, and for at least 100 years, jurists in Europe, Great Britain, and the United States had agreed that the key distinguishing feature—the very definition of a soldier—was holding a commission issued by a state. Those who held such a commission were privileged to commit violence in wartime. They were immune from punishment. Indeed, discussions of the laws and usages of war contained almost nothing about the punishment of crimes by men who carried such commissions.

To be sure, violations of the laws of war were met with forceful sanctions. But such sanctions were not conceived of as punishing an individual offender for an infraction against the rules of warfare. The notion of punishing individual members of the enemy's armies for violations of the laws of war was almost completely absent. William Blackstone, the English jurist with whom every American lawyer in the first half of the nineteenth century was familiar, wrote that when an individual violated a rule of the law of nations, it was the obligation of the violator's own government to see to it that he was punished. (As Blackstone put it, violators' home states were obliged "to animadvert upon them with a becoming severity, that the peace of the world may be maintained.") The victim government's recourse, by contrast, was not to the criminal law but to diplomacy and ultimately retaliation.

It was retaliation—not criminal punishment—that formed the eigh-

---

*Implausibility did not stop President Polk from trying to claim legitimacy as an occupying power. "By the laws of nations," he told the Congress, "a conquered country is subject to be governed by the conqueror during his military possession" (James D. Richardson, ed., *A Compilation of the Messages and Papers of the Presidents, 1789–1897* (Washington, DC: Government Printing Office, 1896–1899), 4: 494). But at no point in the war did American forces in Mexico exceed 30,000 soldiers in more than 1,000 square miles of territory containing some 7 million inhabitants. The guerrilla activity that Scott and his fellow American officers sought to control was testament to the meagerness of U.S. authority and the limits of Mexican submission. Even if the United States were understood as an occupier in the hinterland of Mexico where the guerrilla parties operated, the laws of war had not theretofore treated inhabitants rising up against an occupier as criminals per se. Action against an occupier (even by noncombatants) was neither "unjust" nor "contrary to the laws of war." The rising up was not a criminal act in itself. It was an act of patriotism. "Where is the man," Vattel asked, who would "dare to censure it?" (Emmerich de Vattel, *The Law of Nations*, trans. Joseph Chitty [Philadelphia: T. & J. W. Johnson, 1867], §228, p. 400).

teenth- and early nineteenth-century law of war's mechanism for responding to violations. Writers like the American Henry Wheaton and the Swiss Vattel set out elaborate taxonomies of retaliation, ranging from taking an eye for an eye ("retaliation"), to the suspension of privileges for enemy nationals ("retortion"), to the seizure of enemy property ("reprisals"). Wheaton wrote that when "the established usages of war are violated by an enemy," retaliation was the ordinary tool "to compel the enemy to return to the observance of the law which he has violated." As one leading international lawyer put it fifteen years after the Mexican War had ended, the law of war had not traditionally been "a Penal or Criminal Law." It was instead "a code of regulations in between sovereigns." A half century later, a U.S. Army officer would put the point more bluntly. The law of war, wrote Captain Elbridge Colby, was not a law of crime and punishment but a law enforced by "the cold steel of the bayonet," by "the cannon that speak the name of Krupp," and by "the typewriter rattle of automatic arms." These were the tools of "the litigation of nations under the laws of war."

There were stray exceptions. The eighteenth-century German jurist Georg Friedrich von Martens had noted as an afterthought that "soldiers who employ means which are contrary to the laws of war" could "be punished" by the enemy. Vattel similarly observed as an aside that if a prisoner of war were "personally guilty of some crime," the capturing army was "at liberty to punish" him. A few narrow categories of persons—foreign military recruiters and assassins in particular—were said to be subject to punishment. But with the exception of isolated references such as these, Enlightenment-era writers on the law of war had virtually nothing to say about punishing violators of those laws.

The reason why was articulated most forcefully by the French political theorist Jean-Jacques Rousseau. War, he wrote, was "not a relationship between one man and another, but a relationship between one state and another, in which individuals are enemies only by accident." A state, Rousseau explained, could only have "other States" as enemies because it was "impossible to fix a true relation between things of different natures." Here was the same idea Daniel Webster had expressed when he opposed criminal prosecution in the McLeod episode. The Mexican guerrillas were engaged in what no one doubted counted as a war. Their targets were usually U.S. combatants. Under Rousseau's reasoning, they were far better positioned than McLeod had been to argue for immunity from American criminal punishment.

*   *   *

YEARS LATER, Scott invoked the right of retaliation in defense of his military commissions. It was "a universal right of war," Scott observed, "not to give quarter to an enemy that puts to death all who fall into his hands." But Scott's military commissions and councils of war did not fit the concept of retaliation very well at all. Retaliation was not an individualized practice but a collective one. It was an act of one nation aimed at an enemy nation. It could entail taking measures against enemy prisoners and enemy property, or even (in extreme cases) enemy noncombatants.

In the century before the Mexican War, however, the law of retaliation had begun to change. James Kent of New York, writing in his wildly popular 1820s book on American law, explained that in modern warfare retaliation "ought to be confined to the guilty individuals, who may have committed some enormous violation of public law." It would be inconsistent with the spirit of the age to put "innocent prisoners, or hostages, to death" merely because "the community, of which he is a member," was guilty of some offense. Once retaliation was so limited, there was vanishingly little space remaining between criminal justice and retaliation. All that remained was for someone like Winfield Scott to push them together.

What Scott and the U.S. armed forces did in late 1847 was to assemble scattered pieces in the eighteenth-century laws of war—the military recruiter, the assassin and the spy, the Enlightenment preference for specific instead of general retaliation—and to build from them a general principle of individual criminal liability for violations of the laws of war. Neither Scott nor Marcy had any deep interest in the coherence of the laws of war for its own sake, or in the conceptual distinctions between retaliation and punishment, or between treating individuals or states as the subjects of the laws of war. Neither man was a jurist. Scott was a hardheaded general in command of thousands of soldiers occupying increasingly dangerous foreign territory. Marcy was a practical politician best remembered today as the man who had once defended party patronage in American government on the ground that he saw "nothing wrong in the rule that to the victors belong the spoils." But in a culture that for decades had challenged the difference between war and crime, theirs was a natural innovation. Without anyone quite understanding what was happening—without even using the phrase—Winfield Scott and the U.S. armies in Mexico had given life to the idea of the war crime.

* * *

No ONE IN the 1840s seems to have used the phrase "war crime." The practice of merging the laws of war with the law of crime was too new and too unself-conscious even to have been identified yet. But at least one man grasped the conceptual innovation taking place. He did not like what he saw.

William Jay, president of the American Peace Society and son of the founding father John Jay, objected that General Scott had dangerously reintroduced the idea of crime into the laws of war. What Scott called "murder," Jay said, was merely the killing of "any of the guard accompanying a baggage train." Scott had redescribed the "carrying away" of the property of the U.S. armed forces as "robbery," but Jay countered that this was precisely the kind

A Nathaniel Currier print from the 1848 presidential campaign.
Long thought to depict Zachary Taylor, whose volunteers committed
numerous atrocities in Mexico, it is more likely Winfield Scott,
whose military commissions in the Mexican War
were condemned by his critics.

of violence that the laws of war authorized. Scott claimed to have developed a new institutional mechanism for enforcing the laws of war. But as Jay saw it, Scott had set aside the laws of war, not vindicated them. (Indeed, in Jay's view, the Mexican guerrillas typically did "no more" than Americans of his father's generation had done in the Revolution.) Worse yet, Scott had done so, Jay implied, not out of humanitarian aims but to gain military advantage. By the middle of 1847, guerrilla tactics had become Mexico's most effective strategy, if not its only strategy. Guerrilla attacks had forced Scott to deploy more than a quarter of his troops—some 5,000 soldiers—to guard his supply lines. Executing guerrillas had allowed Scott to reallocate troops from the rear to the front.

Scott himself had nothing but scorn for Jay and the peace societies. War, Scott believed, was "the natural state of man." He called the peace societies "moral distempers," the "cankers of a long peace and a calm world," and listed them alongside anti-Masonry, constitutional nullification, and Mormonism as the United States' most glaring social disorders. In response to Jay's objections, the general observed contemptuously that armies had always put to death those who refused to give quarter to their enemies.

The difficulty for Scott was that as far as we can tell it was a bad exaggeration to say that all Mexican guerrilla parties executed U.S. soldiers. Guerrillas rarely spared Mexican wagon drivers. But that was because they treated Mexican nationals acting for the United States as traitors, not soldiers. And while many guerrillas were reported to adopt a policy of offering no quarter to U.S. soldiers, their attacks on stragglers and U.S. wagon trains were often perfectly legitimate (if particularly maddening) acts of war.

Yet if Scott dodged Jay's criticism, he also failed to own up to the innovative change his councils of war had made. In this sense, Jay understood something that Scott had not fully grasped about the significance of his own orders in Mexico. The councils of war marked a transformation in the orthodox laws of war. The immunity of soldiers on both sides of a war was a strange kind of moral bargain: one that immunized the enemy from the moral sanctions of the criminal law. Scott and his powerful army, however, chafed at the law of war's awkward covenant. And as it turned out, in this one respect Scott was making the same move Charles Sumner and the peace societies had made before him. Scott, like Sumner, saw crime in what many others deemed to be war.

Paris

A CROSS THE ATLANTIC, six years after peace in Mexico, fighting broke out in the Crimea on the northern coast of the Black Sea. Britain and France went to war with Russia to stop the czar's incursions on the declining Ottoman Empire.

William Marcy, now serving as secretary of state in the administration of President Franklin Pierce, took the occasion of the war to urge the belligerents to adopt the United States' long-favored rule of free ships and free goods. At last, American pressure seemed to make a difference. The British government agreed to the principle and exempted from capture all the goods on board neutral vessels, even enemy-owned goods, excepting contraband of war. France did the same, adopting what had long been the American view of neutral shipping in wartime.

Marcy and U.S. diplomats in the courts of Europe celebrated the triumph of America's cherished rule of free ships and free goods. A new day in the laws of war seemed to be dawning in Europe. From France, U.S. minister John Mason exclaimed that the circumstances suddenly seemed "most auspicious to the establishment of our cherished principles of neutral rights." Secretary of State Marcy wrote that at last there was "a fair prospect of getting" the free ships principle "incorporated into the international code." And at the war's close, the ministers of Europe agreed to do just that. At the Paris peace conference in the spring of 1856, the Concert of Europe codified the maritime war rules that the allied powers had adopted during the course of the war. The Declaration of Paris—signed by the plenipotentiaries of Austria, France, Great Britain, Prussia, Russia, Sardinia, and Turkey—pledged that neutral flags would cover enemy goods except for contraband. It reaffirmed that neutral goods were not liable to capture when found aboard an enemy vessel, and that blockades had to be "effective"— "that is to say, maintained by a force sufficient really to prevent access to the coast of the enemy." With the self-aggrandizing grandiosity characteristic of nineteenth-century European international law, the Declaration trumpeted that the principles it laid down would no doubt "be received with gratitude by the whole world." The neutral rights principles for which the United States went to war in 1812 seemed at last to have become the governing rules for war on the high seas.

*   *   *

B UT THERE WAS a problem. Great Britain had dealt a joker into the game. Articles 2, 3, and 4 of the Declaration of Paris reproduced the basic view advocated by the United States since the 1790s. They adopted the American principle of free ships and free goods and codified the requirement that blockades be effective. But the first article of the Declaration set forth a different principle. "Privateering," it announced with stentorian firmness, "is and remains abolished."

For centuries, private vessels carrying commissions from warring states had prowled the seas, seizing enemy merchant ships as prizes and keeping the proceeds for themselves. While the pirate was a criminal, the privateer attacked enemy vessels with a commission from a warring sovereign. The privateer's commission made him a soldier for legal purposes, entitled to the privileges of the laws of war and protected from punishment for his acts of war against an enemy. As one English commentator explained the distinction, privateers were "responsible to and punishable by the State alone from which their commission has issued."

Statesmen and jurists had been speaking out against privateering since at least the middle of the eighteenth century. In the United States, Benjamin Franklin argued that privateering was barbaric because it was principally aimed at an enemy's commerce, not its armed forces. The 1776 model treaty drafted by John Adams contained an article prohibiting privateering. The 1785 treaty between the United States and Frederick the Great's Prussia banned privateering, as did Jefferson's draft treaty with Austria the next year and a U.S. treaty with Spain ratified a decade later. Citizens' petitions from the peace societies and their allies had urged the Congress to promote "civilization and Christianity" by abolishing privateering. As secretary of state in the early 1820s, John Quincy Adams had advocated a treaty doing just this. Indeed, privateering reproduced many of the same problems Scott and Marcy had identified in guerrilla warfare in Mexico in the 1840s. It was a form of private violence that aimed at the enemy's commerce, not its military forces. The Declaration of Paris thus aimed to accomplish with privateering what Scott and Marcy had done with guerrilla warfare: place it outside the pale of civilized warfare, transforming it from a form of war into a form of crime.

The difficulty was that the Pierce administration believed that the United States could not afford to abandon privateering. In the most recent war with Great Britain, the War of 1812, some 517 American privateering vessels had seized around 1,350 British merchant ships and inflicted losses amounting to $45.5 million on British commerce. British ships going no farther than the Irish Sea saw their insurance rates rise by 13 percent. Now, four decades later, Marcy warned that the United States could not justifiably enter into a convention that would preclude it "from resorting to the merchant marine of the country" in the event of war. Even a cursory glance at the stunning disparities between the Royal Navy and the American naval fleet made abundantly apparent why Pierce and Marcy were so reluctant to abandon privateering. At the close of the Crimean War, the U.S. Navy consisted of barely forty vessels. The Royal Navy consisted of almost 1,000.

Given the privateering prohibition, Marcy viewed the Declaration of Paris not as a triumph of neutral rights but as a shrewd gambit by British statesmen to deprive the United States of the moral high ground. The Declaration appropriated for Britain the mantle of neutral rights and used it to criminalize a mode of warfare deemed indispensable by the United States. Writing from London, the new American minister to Great Britain, George Mifflin Dallas, seethed that the Declaration "was aimed exclusively at the great defensive weapon of the United States." The antiprivateering article of the Declaration seemed to Dallas "the groundwork of a coercive movement by a confederacy of European sovereigns against America." Signing the Declaration would abandon the long-standing American reliance on "voluntary action" by its citizens in wartime. At a "single stroke" it would double "the already resistless power of Great Britain's naval means of invasion and blockade."

Privately, British prime minister Lord Palmerston and his foreign secretary, Lord Clarendon, celebrated the Declaration as a diplomatic triumph over the upstart United States. The British, Clarendon wrote gleefully, had managed to "catch brother Jonathan in the trap which he had laid for us."

As it turned out, the government of the United States would never commission a privateer again, not because it signed on to the antiprivateering principles of the Declaration (the United States never did), but because commissioning private vessels to prey on enemy shipping was an increasingly less effective mode of making war. The Declaration of Paris prohibited privateering and adopted the rule of free ships and free goods at just the moment when improvements in naval technology—the rise of steam, the advent of the ironclad ship, and vast improvements in naval weaponry—had rendered converted merchant vessels unsuited for war service. Faster naval vessels with more powerful guns made effective blockades easier to construct. And in any event, merchants had learned to transfer goods to neutral owners in order to circumvent the rules under which privateers could seize enemy property at sea. ("The capacity of carrying on war in this fashion," one British editor wrote flatly, "has ceased.") Preserving the authority to commission privateers at the cost of the long-sought free ships principle would thus prove to be a bad strategic mistake.

In the meanwhile, however, the lessons of the Declaration of Paris for the laws of war seemed stark. Clarendon and Palmerston had managed to do what the British had rarely accomplished in the War of Independence or the War of 1812. They had split the professed ideals of American wartime policy from its perceived interests. When Marcy and Pierce seemed to choose interests over ideals, some thought that Americans had made plain the true character of their commitments. In the United States, by the same token, the experience of the Declaration served as a rude awakening to the midcentury politics of the laws of war. For many American observers and statesmen, the Declaration revealed the laws of war to be a creature of power, not of humanitarian ideals. The laws of war suddenly seemed a body of rules for strong European states to manipulate at the expense of the weaker military forces of the United States. Marcy complained to the French minister Eugène de Sartiges that the great naval powers of Europe were acting "to subserve their own interests and ambitious projects." George Mifflin Dallas in London accused the "combined potentates of Europe" of "forc[ing] their international code upon us." The United States' reliance on a volunteer military, he wrote in 1859, was at risk of being "diplomatized out of our power." Dallas warned his fellow American diplomats to be wary of the selfless language of humanity embraced by the powers of Europe; he had learned to be suspicious when European statesmen claimed to act out of "an excess of philanthropy."

Richard Cobden, a member of the British Parliament with pro-American sympathies, concurred in Marcy and Dallas's evaluation. "I am afraid," Cobden wrote in 1856, that "the law of nations has been hitherto little more than the will of the strongest." To be sure, he added, the will of the powerful was "modified and slightly controlled by civilization." But Cobden's bleak observation captured the disillusioning lesson of the Declaration for American statesmen.

———————

Five years after the Declaration of Paris, one southern state after another voted to secede from the United States of America. South Carolina did so in December 1860. Mississippi, Florida, and Alabama followed in quick succession on three consecutive days in January 1861. Before the month was out, Georgia and Louisiana had voted to secede as well. Texas did the same on the first day of February.

For eighty-five years, American soldiers, statesmen, and lawyers had expressed admiration for the laws of war, though to be sure their enthusiasm was leavened with frustration and even occasional disdain. Those who had spoken out in support of the international laws of war included men who now defended the Union as well as men who sided with the South.

Yet on the eve of the most destructive war in American history, there was reason to worry that the laws of war might fail to gain a foothold in the brothers' conflict between North and South. For one thing, the laws of armed conflict were made principally for conflicts between nation-states, not for civil wars and revolutions. To this day, international humanitarian law has many fewer rules for what is now called noninternational armed conflict. There were deeper and more intractable causes for concern, as well. For more than half a century, American statesmen had constructed a law of war that sheltered slaveholders in wartime. But now slavery was the very issue that had split the nation in two. The small regular army and its tiny officer corps trained at West Point embodied the law of war principles of the previous half century. But now those officers faced the daunting prospect of trying to govern mass volunteer armies of unprecedented size in a nation still powerfully influenced by the legacy of Andrew Jackson.

Moreover, for twenty years, through the activism of the peace societies, the border skirmishes with Canada, and a war with Mexico, Americans had argued about and debated with increasing controversy the difficult moral compromises the law of war entailed. They had even initiated an experiment to reintegrate the criminal law back into the laws of combat, a move that seemed to some a death knell for the effort to regulate war by law. As a final blow, the Declaration of Paris seemed to have revealed humanitarian doctrines as cover for the interests of the European states that created them.

Most of all, the Union leadership on the eve of the war was made up of men whose views of the law were up in the air. The powerful chairman of the Senate Foreign Relations Committee was the former pacifist Charles Sumner. Only fifteen years earlier, Sumner had denounced the laws of war as pernicious and absurd. Now, as he abandoned his pacifism to fight against slavery, his righteous fury seemed to admit few limits. In the spring of 1861, the new secretary of state was William Henry Seward, the former governor of New York who had fought tooth and nail with Daniel Webster to prosecute British soldier Alexander McLeod as a common criminal. Now Seward sat in Webster's seat in the State Department. Lieutenant General Winfield Scott was general-in-chief of the Union Army. He represented the highest aspirations of the small professional army of the antebellum United States. He was deeply versed in the laws and usages of war. But he had also set in motion a new and potentially dangerous experiment, one that had criminalized an entire class of Mexican combatants. Now in 1861 Scott would have to decide on the status of the white southerners who were taking up arms by the tens of thousands.

O N THE QUESTION of the laws of war, the new president of the United States was a blank slate. Unlike Sumner, Seward, and Scott, Abraham Lincoln had virtually no familiarity with war and even less experience with its laws. When the guns sounded in April 1861, Lincoln repeated the pattern that had been developing for a generation. The gathering armies of the South, he decided, were made up of criminals, not soldiers.

PART II

A Few Things Barbarous or Cruel

You dislike the emancipation proclamation; and, perhaps, would have it retracted. You say it is unconstitutional—I think differently. I think the constitution invests its commander-in-chief, with the law of war, in time of war. The most that can be said, if so much, is, that slaves are property. Is there—has there ever been—any question that by the law of war, property, both of enemies and friends, may be taken when needed? And is it not needed whenever taking it, helps us, or hurts the enemy? Armies, the world over, destroy enemies' property when they can not use it; and even destroy their own to keep it from the enemy. Civilized belligerents do all in their power to help themselves, or hurt the enemy, except a few things regarded as barbarous or cruel. Among the exceptions are the massacre of vanquished foes, and non-combatants, male and female.

—Abraham Lincoln to James C. Conkling,
August 26, 1863

Chapter 5

We Don't Practise the
Law of Nations

———◆◦◆———

I'm a good enough lawyer in a Western law court,
I suppose, but we don't practise the law of nations
up there . . . .

—Abraham Lincoln, April 1861

I T IS ONE of the most enduringly striking features of the United States' greatest wartime president that he came into office with virtually no prior experience of war. Of the fifteen men who served in the office before Abraham Lincoln, only two possessed wartime records as thin as his, and their records in office did not inspire confidence. Martin Van Buren led the country's bloody, ethically dubious, and indecisive campaign against the Seminoles in Florida in the late 1830s. Ten years later, James Polk leapt headlong into the Mexican War, a war that Lincoln himself bitterly opposed.

When compared to his Confederate counterpart, Jefferson Davis, Lincoln's meager wartime record seemed even weaker. Davis was a West Point graduate, a six-year veteran of the Army officer corps, and a former secretary of war in the administration of Franklin Pierce. In the Mexican War, he had proven himself a brilliant battlefield tactician. Lincoln's sole experience in armed conflict, by contrast, had occasioned more jokes than praise. In the short and sordid Black Hawk War of 1832, Lincoln had served as a captain of the Illinois militia. Historians have long speculated that Lincoln's leadership stint in the militia propelled him into politics. But no one disputes that Lincoln's actual role in the conflict was negligible. "I had a good many bloody struggles with the mosquitoes," he later quipped, "and although I never fainted from the loss of blood, I can truly say I was often very hungry."

Lincoln had no more experience with the laws of war than he did in the heat of combat. His own minister to Great Britain scoffed that the president "knew absolutely nothing" about foreign relations. His minister in Vienna worried that Lincoln did not even have the good sense to hide how little he knew. In the week before his inauguration, six weeks before the first shots of the Civil War, the president-to-be admitted to one European diplomat that he didn't "know anything about diplomacy." "I will be very apt," he confessed, "to make blunders." It was thus no small matter that one of the first problems Lincoln had to face after the firing on Fort Sumter on April 12, 1861, was a high-stakes and delicate decision about the laws of war.

A Strange Inconsistency

U P UNTIL THE middle of April, Lincoln had treated secessionists not as enemies but as criminals. "We must not be enemies," he had told the South at his inauguration. In one sense, his words were conciliatory. But the words had a double meaning that was not lost on his listeners. For if violence broke out and the secessionists were not enemies in war, then they were criminals subject to punishment for treason. "Acts of violence within any State or States against the authority of the United States," Lincoln had warned, were not acts of war but "insurrectionary or revolutionary" crimes.

This was no mere lawyer's game. If the violence that broke out in the second week of April was a crime, then the humanitarian limits on war's destructive powers had no application.

Many in the North took the logical next step. In Milwaukee, the *Daily Press & News* conceded that the laws of war required that nations "be hospitable to a foe," but observed that they said nothing about how to treat a treasonous brother. The editors of the *Buffalo Morning Express* wrote that the secessionists were not "entitled to the considerations belonging to a common humanity." In Missouri, the Unionist editors of the *Columbia Daily* concluded bluntly that if the limits of civilized war were inapplicable, then "no quarter should be shown to rebels." The *Elkhorn Independent* of Wisconsin called for a "war of extermination to all traitors." Elias B. Holmes, a former Whig member of Congress, urged Lincoln that all cities "refusing to lower the secession flag" should be "razed to the ground." The editors of the *New York Herald* foresaw a conflict "vindictive, fierce, bloody, and merciless

In the early summer of 1861, it was not yet clear whether captured
Confederates would be treated as prisoners of war or as criminals. Harper's
Weekly *artist Alfred Waud sketched a prisoner being interviewed by four*
Union soldiers and (at far left) a member of the local police force.

beyond parallel in ancient or modern history." Horace Greeley's *New York Tribune* predicted that "Jeff. Davis & Co. will be swinging from the battlements at Washington . . . by the 4th of July."

In the weeks after Lincoln's inauguration, however, a new problem called into doubt his treatment of secession as crime. A critical piece of the early Union strategy was to cut off the southern ports to foreign trade. The importation of weapons and supplies for the new Confederate Army would be vital to the southern capacity to fight a war. Cotton exports were the economic engine of the region. But the question of how to cut the South off from the world quickly caught the United States in a foreign policy predicament. The British and French economies relied heavily on southern cotton. When Secretary of State Seward floated the idea of closing southern ports at a dinner for European foreign ministers in late March, the group objected vociferously. The British minister, Lord Lyons, warned Seward ominously that "if the U.S. determined to stop by force so important a commerce as that of Great Britain with the cotton-growing states," he "could not answer for what might happen." Closing the ports, Lyons told Seward, would force the European powers to choose between "interruption of their Commerce" and "recognizing the Southern Confederation." Lyons left little doubt which choice he would prefer.

The greatest difficulty for the British, however, was not merely that closing the ports would stop the cotton trade. A bumper crop in 1860 had left British cotton markets with an excess of supply, and British cotton interests could survive virtually unscathed for another season, perhaps more, without imports from the American South. The bigger problem was that a port closure would subject vessels and crews of the British merchant fleet to the United States' criminal laws. Lord Lyons feared that British seamen caught trying to evade the port closure would provide a cause célèbre for British cotton interests, who in turn would be in a position to exert great pressure on the British government to recognize the South and reopen the cotton trade. Writing to the British foreign secretary Lord John Russell, Lyons observed that a port closure would make British vessels and their crews subject to American criminal prosecution, a sanction that Lyons thought would impose "vexations beyond bearing." "All kinds of new and doubtful questions will be raised," Lyons worried.

THERE WAS ANOTHER path open to the United States, however. What would happen, Seward wondered, if the United States declared a blockade against the southern states?

At first, the distinction between blockade and port closure seemed mere wordplay, the kind of distinction only a lawyer could love. But as Seward studied the administration's predicament, he began to understand that a blockade would be crucially different from closing the ports. Blockades were creatures of international law, not domestic U.S. law. A blockade would therefore operate according to rules that were shared on both sides of the Atlantic—rules that the British themselves had helped to forge in the wars against Napoleon a half century before. The international law of blockade would not be subject to change without notice by U.S. officials, which meant that British merchants would be able to guide their actions by reference to its known rules. Disputes would be determined by prize courts operating pursuant to the international law of prize, not by American criminal law and juries of impassioned American citizens. When Seward consulted with Lyons about the idea, the British minister conceded that "a regular blockade would be less objectionable" because the "rules of a blockade are to a great extent determined and known."

Most of all, turning to the blockade appealed to Britain's long-standing interests. It was Britain and its massive navy that had insisted on defending the international law power of blockades in the Napoleonic Wars. Now, fifty years later, Britain still leaned heavily on its navy as the guarantor of its far-flung empire. The blockade form thus appealed to Britain's aim of maintaining a broad power of blockades for use in any future war against the powers on the Continent. And so, at Seward's urging, the president issued a proclamation "to set on foot a blockade of the ports" along the coast from South Carolina to Texas. Eight days later, Lincoln extended the blockade order to the ports of North Carolina and Virginia.

The European ministers in Washington barely registered an objection. Partly this was because Lyons and other foreign ministers doubted that the tiny U.S. Navy could mount a blockade any time soon. Under international law, a blockade was only lawful if it involved a naval force sufficient to make it effective. But as Lincoln understood all too well, the size of the U.S. Navy meant that a good deal of cotton would get through for the foreseeable future. "Our ships," Lyons winked, "could at all events resort to any Ports before which the U.S. did not establish a regular effective blockade."

But American observers, especially many of Lincoln's closest allies, were furious. A majority of Lincoln's own cabinet feared that the president's inexperience had led him into a foolish and potentially disastrous blunder. "A nation cannot blockade its own port," spluttered a furious Attorney General Edward Bates. Postmaster General Montgomery Blair opposed a blockade in favor of "the legal and straightforward course" of closing the ports or setting up custom collection on ships stationed off the southern coast. Secretary of the Navy Gideon Welles would have to implement the blockade, but Welles was virtually apoplectic. The cabinet, he recorded in his diary, had "preferred an embargo or suspension of intercourse." The conflict with the South, he argued, was "a civil war, and not a foreign war." To blockade rebel territory would be to "raise the insurgents to the level of belligerents" and concede that "the Confederate organization" was "a quasi government" entitled to a position among nations. "If the interdiction is to be by Blockade," Welles said pointedly, then it followed that "the Confederate States must be considered and treated as a distinct nationality—their collectors, revenue officers, clearance, registers &c" would have to be "recognized as legitimate."

Lincoln seemed to have given away the game before it had even begun. Judah Benjamin, the Confederacy's attorney general, snickered that "the blockade of the Southern ports is illegal so long as the President claims them to be ports of the United States." Lincoln's own proclamation seemed to concede the independent status of the South by justifying the blockade not merely under the law of the nation (singular), but under "the law of Nations" (plural). Indeed, as many saw it, the blockade proclamation made no sense at all. Lincoln coupled his blockade with a declaration that private vessels commissioned into service by the so-called Confederacy would be treated as pirates (and thus subject to execution as criminals) rather than as privateers (and thus eligible for prisoner of war status). As Welles remarked acidly, this was a "strange inconsistency" in the proclamation. Lincoln had contradicted himself, treating the Confederacy as an independent country in one breath and as a criminal conspiracy in the next. An exasperated Welles blamed Lincoln's ignorance, the baleful influence of Seward, and an embarrassing submissiveness toward the European powers.

WHAT WELLES DID NOT grasp was that with a little push from Great Britain and France, Lincoln and Seward had stumbled into a distinctive way of thinking about the laws of war, one that would serve the nation well over the next four years and more. The blockade promised (in Seward's words) "to avoid complications" that both Lincoln and Seward believed "would be likely to involve us in a foreign war," and as Lincoln told his cabinet, the nation could not afford "to have two wars on our hands at once."

That the proclamation was incoherent as a matter of international law was less important to Lincoln than the fact that it helped smooth relations with the European neutral powers. Soon after the blockade proclamation, Lincoln ran into Congressman Thaddeus Stevens, a staunch abolitionist and chair of the powerful Ways and Means Committee in the House of Representatives. Stevens complained that Lincoln's proclamation had committed the United States "to conduct the war, not as if we were suppressing a revolt in our own States, but in accordance with the law of nations." The president, Stevens intimated, had misunderstood the principle at stake and had gotten the legal categories backwards. Lincoln replied with characteristically self-deprecating wit: "I see the point now, but I don't know anything about the law of nations, and I thought it was all right." With a bit of brilliant homespun banter, the president dismissed the self-righteous Stevens. "I'm a good enough lawyer in a Western law court, I suppose," Lincoln said, "but we don't practise the law of nations up there, and I supposed Seward knew all about it, and I left it to him. But it's done now and can't be helped, so we must get along as well as we can."

Lincoln knew far more than he let on. With a little help from the British, the president had developed a new appreciation for the laws of war, one that was grounded not in the abstract principles of Stevens and Welles but in a practical idea about what the laws of war could accomplish for the Union war effort.

T HE UNION BLOCKADING squadron's first capture came on May 12 off Charleston, South Carolina, when the steam frigate USS *Niagara* fired a shell across the bow of an inbound vessel called the *General Parkhill.* Captain William McKean of the *Niagara* seized the blockade-runner from its South Carolina owners and sent it to Philadelphia to be condemned along with its cargo by a federal prize court. The next week, off the coast of Virginia, Flag Officer S. H. Stringham of the Atlantic Blockading Squadron captured a dozen Virginia-owned vessels carrying cargoes of tobacco.

British vessels were soon caught up in the Union dragnet. On May 20, Stringham's 44-gun wooden steam frigate, the USS *Minnesota*, captured the English bark *Hiawatha* and sent it to New York for judicial investigation. The next day, Stringham captured another English vessel, the schooner *Tropic Wind*, off Hampton Roads and sent it to the federal district court in Washington, D.C. And these were just the first. Over the next four years, the Union blockade intercepted more than 1,200 vessels, most of them owned (at least nominally) by British merchants. When all was said and done, the federal district courts condemned more than 600 vessels as prizes of their U.S. Navy captors.

S IXTY-YEAR-OLD Secretary of State William Henry Seward was the unlikely architect of Lincoln's legal strategy for the blockade. Seward was his generation's consummate politician. A small, rail-thin, and slightly stooped man of incongruously prodigious appetites and a taste for Cuban cigars, Seward had served as governor of New York from 1839 to 1843 and then as a U.S. senator from New York from 1849 until his appointment as secretary of state. As a senator, Seward had become known for his outspoken opposition to slavery. But as a politician, his enemies viewed him as the corrupt puppet of the newspaper publisher Thurlow Weed, the powerful backstage manager of New York's Whig Party machine. Seward, it was said, would compromise on principle for the sake of Weed's partisan ends. So complete was Seward's association with Weed that even Seward joked about what others no doubt thought true: "Seward is Weed and Weed is Seward," he quipped. Together, the two men made a formidable political team. Thanks to Weed's influence behind the scenes and Seward's political charisma, Seward had been the favorite to win the 1860 Republican Party nomination for president until the nomination went to the relatively unknown Abraham Lincoln instead.

Seward was a lawyer, but like Lincoln his skills did not include mastery of the fine distinctions of the laws of maritime warfare or the law of nations. What Seward had going for him was an uncanny knack for appealing to judges and juries and getting them to see his client's side of the argument. Many worried that Seward's skills in the law would be unlikely to serve him as well in statecraft as they had at the New York bar and in the back rooms of New York politics. Contemporaries observed that Seward had "never given any particular attention" to international law. Charles Francis Adams, Jr., who knew Seward in the 1860s, later wrote that he "did not possess what is known as a legal mind, much less one of a judicial cast." Montgomery Blair stated plainly that Seward knew "less of public law than any man who ever held a seat in the Cabinet." Charles Sumner, chairman of the Senate Committee on Foreign Relations, believed that Seward knew nothing of international law. Attorney General Edward Bates announced that Seward was "no lawyer and no statesman."

Indeed, for two decades or more, Seward had been a well-known demagogue on questions of the laws of war. As governor of New York during the prosecution of the Canadian Alexander McLeod, Seward had managed the episode (with Thurlow Weed at his side) for maximum political gain. British statesmen remembered the episode very well. "His view of the relations between the United States and Great Britain," wrote Lord Lyons to Lord Russell, "has always been that they are good material to make political capital of."

I F SEWARD WAS the architect of the blockade, Secretary of the Navy Gideon Welles was its master builder. As an administrator, Welles did work that was nothing short of astounding. Beginning with a navy of merely sixty-seven ships, most of which were either out of service or on duty in far-flung posts around the world, Welles was asked to blockade some 2,000 miles of dense and intricate coastline. Only twelve vessels were ready for operation in U.S. waters when the war began. By the end of 1863, Welles had built a navy comprised of 588 seaworthy vessels. The blockade was never a perfectly tight fit. Historians estimate that three or four blockade-runners made it to their destination for every one the Union Navy captured. Yet the blockade deterred many of the largest vessels from even trying and dramatically reduced the tonnage of trade to southern ports. Without Welles's indefatigable efforts at the Navy Department, the blockade might never have made the kind of contribution it did.

For all his success, Welles had to be cajoled by Seward and Lincoln to comply with the administration's legal strategy for the blockade. An old newspaper man from Hartford, Welles had developed a well-earned reputation for self-righteousness. He was dogmatic and rigid where Seward was practical and savvy. From the beginning, Welles viewed Seward's invocation of the international laws of war as an unprincipled mistake and an embarrassing concession of weakness. The secretary of state, Welles later wrote, lacked "the bold and vigorous mind to assert and maintain a right principle, if fraught with doubt and difficulty, provided there was an easier path." An executive order closing the ports as a matter of U.S. law was the principled path. The ports of the seceded states were, after all, still U.S. ports. But the blockade had been the easier path, and the rash secretary of state had capitulated to European pressure. So upset was Welles that his first orders to the blockading squadron inadvertently recharacterized Lincoln's proclamation as a port closure instead of a blockade. "I am embarrassed," he confessed to the president, "as to the instructions I am to give our naval officers."

In Welles's view, turning to international law was certain to produce an endless series of crises and controversies. "Every capture," he warned the president, would be "resisted in the courts" by neutral foreign nations and the insurgent states alike on the ground that the United States could not legally blockade a region of its own country. Foreign merchants and the southern states, Welles worried, would forge a "common enmity" toward the United States because the blockade was nothing less than a limited "war against the commerce of the world."

Seward's intuition was precisely the opposite. In Seward's estimation, the existence of a common body of law governing the clash between Union vessels and neutral merchants on the seas—and especially a body of law in which the United States could appeal to rules in which Britain had a shared interest—would minimize the conflict on the seas between the United States and foreign nations. The quick-minded Seward enjoyed needling his ponderous cabinet colleague. On more than one occasion, Seward provoked Welles by admitting that he had never "looked in [a] book on international law"—not even once—since entering the office of secretary of state.

*   *   *

THE BLOCKADE CONTROVERSY soon sent lawyers and judges scurrying to the books Seward claimed to disdain.

As prize vessels arrived in the ports of the North, the argument between Seward and Welles now reappeared in the courts. What would happen there was anyone's guess. Roger Taney of Maryland, the author of the *Dred Scott* decision in 1857, was the increasingly frail but ardently anti-Lincoln chief justice of the United States. In 1861, he had issued an opinion denying Lincoln's authority to suspend the writ of habeas corpus.* Lincoln had evaded the chief justice's order, but adverse decisions in the prize cases would be much harder to ignore. Richard Henry Dana, Jr., the federal district attorney in Boston, worried that Taney "would end the war" by undoing the Union's capacity to stop imports to the South. "Where it would leave us with neutral powers," Dana wrote to the American minister in London, was "fearful to contemplate." In the worst-case scenario, the United States would be liable for millions of dollars in damages to Great Britain and France for prizes taken during the first two years of the war.

The administration did all that it could to delay a decision on the blockade by Taney's Court. William Evarts of New York, thought by some to be "the foremost trial lawyer of his day," urged Attorney General Bates not to let the cases reach the Supreme Court until the Lincoln administration had the chance to appoint some of its own justices to the Court. Bates agreed and did what he could to keep the cases percolating slowly through the lower federal courts. Congress got into the act as well. Even as the first prize cases were being argued at the Supreme Court in February 1863, Congress passed hurried twelfth-hour legislation adding a tenth seat to the Court and giving Lincoln the chance to swing the decision in his favor.

The additional seat on the Court proved unnecessary, but only by the thinnest of margins. On March 10, 1863, Justice Robert Grier of Pennsylvania wrote an opinion for the Court upholding the blockade by a bare 5–4 vote in four cases that came to be known together as the *Prize Cases*. Grier had long been a vociferous opponent of abolition and a loyal friend of the slaveholder class in controversial fugitive slave cases. In the *Dred Scott* case, Grier had voted with Taney and the majority. Grier had even colluded behind the scenes with his fellow Pennsylvanian, the president-elect James Buchanan, to shape the *Dred Scott* decision in a way that aimed to take the slavery question out of politics once and for all. With Grier's support,

---

*This was in the famous case of the Confederate sympathizer and Maryland militia leader John Merryman.

the decision had effectively declared the antislavery platform of Lincoln's Republican Party unconstitutional.

Six years later, however, Grier's opinion in the *Prize Cases* leaned hard in Lincoln's favor. Grier skewered the pretensions of citizens of the rebel states seeking to have their vessels restored. Counsel for the vessel owners had protested that "there must be war" before there could be a blockade that would give courts the jurisdiction over prizes. But Grier's decision rejected the formal distinction between war and crime that the petitioners urged on the Court. "The law of nations," Grier wrote for the Court's five-justice majority, was founded on "the common sense of the world." It contained no "anomalous doctrine" such as the one the vessel owners advocated. It simply was not true that the supporters of the Confederacy could not be "enemies" merely "because they are traitors." A belligerent party claiming to be sovereign in a civil war, Grier continued, "may exercise both belligerent and sovereign rights," not because of some arcane legal doctrine but because of good reasons based in practical common sense. Allowing the sovereign to mix war powers with sovereign powers would allow for application of the laws of civilized war; combat in civil wars would thus be regulated by "the milder modes of coercion which the law of nations has introduced to mitigate the rigors of war." But the law of war's shield came coupled with a sword. To allow the South to claim the protections of the laws of war without bearing the costs made no sense at all.

Some said Grier had embraced a theory advanced by Republicans on the floor of Congress the previous year. Charles Sumner, who had cast off his pacifism to make war against slavery, had made the point with characteristic panache: "Our case is double," Sumner announced in the Senate, "and you may call it Rebellion or War, as you please, or you may call it both." In fact, the theory advanced by Grier for the Court and articulated by Sumner in the Congress was none other than the mixed theory of the April 19 blockade proclamation itself. By establishing a blockade and declaring southern privateers to be pirates, Lincoln had insisted that the preservation of the Union could be a war and a criminal law enforcement action at the same time, that there was no need to choose either paradigm once and for all. With Seward's help, Lincoln had discovered that the laws of war did not so much restrict his power as augment it. International law offered a respectable power, one that promised to be appropriately restrained and responsible. But it was an awesome power nonetheless. And after the *Prize Cases*, Lincoln's mixed theory had the Supreme Court's endorsement.

*   *   *

No DECISION BY the Supreme Court could change a basic fact of life about the blockade: huge profits were available for those with the courage and skill to run past it. Merchant captains who had earned $150 per month before the war now made upwards of $5,000 a month as skilled blockade-runners. The price that cotton fetched in England and France increased. And the cost of goods imported to the South shot up dramatically. It was little wonder that the blockade-runners toasted the cotton growers, the blockade, and the British textile manufacturers. "To a long continuance of the war!" went the favorite cheer of the blockade-runners.

The flow of illicit commerce into the South ensured that the legal controversies over the blockade would continue beyond the *Prize Cases*. Legal loopholes threatened to undo the blockade's effectiveness, and nowhere were those loopholes more expansive than at the wide estuary where the Rio Grande emptied into the Gulf of Mexico. The sleepy town of Matamoros on the Mexican bank of the river was well known to residents of the United States as the site of the first engagement of the Mexican War in 1846. Fifteen years later, its location on neutral Mexican territory just across the river from Brownsville, Texas, made it a hub for merchants looking to make an end run around the Union blockade. Where a half-dozen vessels might have appeared in any given year, now dozens arrived every week with goods nominally headed for the neutral port but destined to be taken across the river into Texas and the South in return for cotton moving in the opposite direction. By early 1863, the commander of the U.S. Eastern Gulf Blockading Squadron, Captain Theodorus Bailey, reported a flotilla of 200 vessels anchored off the mouth of the Rio Grande. One Union naval officer at Key West concluded that "hope of crushing the rebellion" by blockade would be "utterly in vain" so long as "unlimited supplies" poured through the Rio Grande into Texas.

Secretary Welles determined to bring the Matamoros trade to a halt, but he soon learned how difficult that would be. In February 1862, Commander Samuel Swartout of the USS *Portsmouth* seized a British screw steamer called the *Labuan* found floating off the Rio Grande and sent it with a prize crew to report to Flag Officer William McKean, now commanding the Gulf Blockading Squadron. When McKean received the vessel, he was perplexed for there was nothing about it that proved its liability to capture. The *Labuan* was a neutral vessel in neutral Mexican waters. It was loaded not with contraband of war but with cotton. The traditional American rule that free ships made free goods protected the cargo unless the vessel carrying it had run the blockade. But the United States could not blockade the Mexican port of Matamoros without going to war against Mexico. In Washington, Lord Lyons demanded an explanation from Seward, who (hard-pressed to come up with one) deferred the question to the prize court in New York. In May, Judge Samuel Betts in New York—a district judge with thirty-five years experience on the bench—restored the vessel and its cargo to its owners, finding no legal basis for its capture.

Into 1863, the Western Gulf Blockading Squadron seized a parade of British vessels off the mouth of the Rio Grande. But the federal courts adjudged each and every such capture illegal and ordered restitution to the owners of the vessels and their cargo. The Union blockade had run headlong into one of the cardinal rules of the laws of war, a rule that the leading American statesmen of the early republic had done their best to promote and expand: Neutral vessels had a right to carry noncontraband cargo to neutral ports. In case after case out of Matamoros, the federal courts affirmed this principle and ruled against U.S. Navy captors.

I N THE EASTERN GULF, the Union Navy experimented with a new strategy for staunching the gaping hole in the blockade. This time the courts went along.

The British port of Nassau in the Bahamas lay only 180 miles east of Florida. By the fall of 1861, Secretary Welles had become convinced that "large quantities of arms and other articles contraband of war" were being "shipped to Nassau with the avowed object" of being sent from Nassau to "the rebellious ports" of the South. In November, Welles ordered the Navy to stop trade from the Bahamas to the southern coast of the United States. But doing so required that U.S. naval officers distinguish between vessels engaging in protected trade between Europe and the neutral port of Nassau, on the one hand, and those vessels covertly intending to run the blockade into Florida or another blockaded port on the southern coast, on the other. In some cases, the evidence was clear enough that a vessel claiming Nassau as its destination was really destined for a blockaded port. But in others, captured vessels had no ulterior destination beyond Nassau, even though their cargoes were likely to be "transshipped" (to use the maritime vernacular) by a separate vessel to a blockaded port.

The transshipment cases placed the United States in another awkward situation. Ever since the founding days of the republic, Americans had protested the British doctrine of continuous voyage, a doctrine that prevented neutral vessels from engaging in otherwise unlawful commerce by merely adding a pretextual intermediate port to their voyage. The rule had been laid down in the infamous *Essex* case in 1805 by the British Lords Commissioners of Appeal in order to stop the American merchant fleet from carrying goods between the European Continent and the West Indies. In the run-up to the War of 1812, American war hawks had decried the *Essex* decision's theory of continuous voyage as an outrageous imposition on the rights of neutral commerce.

Now, however, the United States took a different position. In February 1863, Commander Thomas H. Stevens of the USS *Sonoma* captured the English bark *Springbok* headed for Nassau and loaded with a cargo of contraband. The cargo included brass buttons marked "C.S.N." and "C.S.A.," presumably for the Confederate States Navy and Army respectively, along with hundreds of pairs of army boots, gray army blankets, and a small number of sabers and bayonets. The vessel was English-owned and had departed from London for a neutral port. But Stevens took the view that what mattered was the ultimate destination of the cargo. The courts agreed, at least when the cargo was contraband of war. Chief Justice Salmon Chase, whom Lincoln had appointed to replace Taney when Taney died in 1864, ruled that "the voyage from London to the blockaded port" was "one voyage" and that the cargo was thus liable to condemnation "during any part" of the extended voyage "from the time of sailing."

The United States pushed the doctrine of continuous voyage still further in a capture that brought Chase and the Court back to Matamoros. In late February 1863, the USS *Vanderbilt* captured the English steamer *Peterhoff* off St. Thomas in the Virgin Islands carrying a cargo of blankets, men's army bluchers, and artillery boots. The vessel was headed for Matamoros, and Chase observed (as all courts had observed in the earlier Matamoros cases) that neutral commerce with a neutral port was "entirely free." The *Springbok* decision meant that contraband cargo intended for transshipment to a blockaded port was subject to capture and condemnation. But the *Peterhoff* presented a different and still harder problem: not transshipment from Nassau by seafaring vessel to a blockaded port, but inland transportation from the neutral port of Matamoros to enemy territory in Brownsville. In 1801, Sir William Scott of the British Admiralty Court had ruled in the midst of the Napoleonic Wars that the prospect of overland transportation of goods from a neutral port to a blockaded port did not make otherwise free commerce subject to capture. The British, who had long pressed for restrictive interpretations of neutral rights, had thus declined to claim a right to capture goods using overland transportation to circumvent a blockade. But in 1863 Seward and Welles pushed for just such a right, and the courts recognized it. Chase and the Supreme Court ruled that where the cargo was made up of contraband of war, it was subject to capture "when destined to the hostile country, or to the actual military or naval use of the enemy, whether blockaded or not." As in the continuous voyage cases, all that mattered was the intended destination.

Had the United States betrayed its principles? Observers at the time certainly thought so. Lord Russell wrote to the American minister in London that he could hardly believe the United States was really altering its formerly "humane policy" of trying "to assuage and mitigate the horrors of war." The influential British international lawyer Montague Bernard charged that U.S. reversals of its long-standing positions "raised an inference that general rules of international conduct are practically useless" and merely "trampled underfoot in the heat of passion" or disregarded at the merest hint of a "temporary interest" to the contrary. And historians ever since have seen in Union actions evidence of a hypocrisy embedded deep in the DNA of international law. Frank Owsley, a historian who was a die-hard advocate of the South and president of the Southern Historical Association, put it harshly but essentially captured the views of less partisan historians before and after him. "Old Abe," Owsley insisted, had "sold America's birthright for a mess of pottage."

The problem is that these critiques fundamentally misunderstood the project on which Lincoln and Seward embarked in 1861. As the Court grasped in its *Prize Cases* opinion of 1863, Lincoln and Seward had adopted a mixed theory of the legal status of the Civil War. They had not invoked the laws of war at sea for the purposes of governing the relationship between the Union and the so-called Confederate States of America—at least not at first. Instead, they had invoked the laws at war for the far more limited project of managing the United States' relationship with neutral foreign powers, most importantly Great Britain. Lincoln had said just this in the initial draft of his first message to Congress in July 1861 when he wrote that it "scarcely needs to be considered" whether the blockade was "technically a blockade" or not, so long as foreign neutral nations agreed that "as between them and us, the strict law of blockade shall apply." For the purposes of regulating the relationship with Great Britain, the only important practical consideration was that British statesmen concur with the American interpretations of the laws of war at sea. But this hardly made the international laws of war a hypocritical cloak for underlying Union interests. By adopting the international laws of war at sea, Lincoln and Seward aimed simply to opt into a whole array of ready-made answers to questions arising between the United States and foreign neutrals.

Dozens of such questions appeared during the course of the conflict, and the laws of war supplied a host of useful answers. At various times in the war, the laws of war at sea facilitated the exit of foreign merchants who found themselves anchored in southern ports upon the declaration of the blockade. They governed the status of foreign nationals found aboard blockade-running vessels, ensuring that they were treated as neutral foreign nationals rather than prisoners of war or criminals. Law of war rules resolved thorny questions such as the proper disposition of a captured vessel whose crew had subsequently seized the vessel back from its U.S. Navy prize crew. The same laws of war provided standards to govern the compensation of foreign nationals for injuries they received in the war effort (something the Lincoln administration did repeatedly) and for denying such compensation when appropriate. In each of these controversies, and in myriad others, the law of war helped guide the U.S. and neutral powers down a path toward mutually acceptable resolutions to potentially explosive difficulties. That the United States had reversed its earlier positions on the doctrine of the continuous voyage was no matter, because the Lincoln administration had not committed itself (and never would commit itself) to treating the South as a belligerent entity entitled to all the rights and privileges of warfare. The administration had adopted the laws of war at sea for the much more limited purpose of smoothing its relations with Britain and France.

To be sure, Seward was playing a dangerous game. The usefulness of the law stemmed in no small part from the legitimacy it derived by seeming fixed and durable. If the United States' careful tailoring of the rules between it and Great Britain came to seem too much like playing fast and loose, the law's capacity to achieve practical ends such as coordinating conduct in times of crisis might be diminished.

It was a dicey strategy, and Secretary of the Navy Welles (among others) never quite grasped what Lincoln and Seward were up to. Until his death more than a decade after the end of the war, Welles would continue to criticize what he saw as Seward's blunders: errors of principle to which he thought Lincoln had all too readily consented. But Lincoln and Seward were engaged in something other than a careless abandonment of American principles. What distinguished Lincoln and Seward from Welles was that neither the president nor the secretary of state believed that the rules of war at sea were principles worth fighting for in and of themselves. For them, the rules were means, not ends.

Dog Eat Dog

I N THE FALL of 1861, the laws of war meant everything in the world to a thirty-eight-year-old South Carolina man named John P. Calvo.

On July 19, 1861, Calvo had sailed out of Charleston Harbor aboard the *Dixie*, a modest three-gun schooner. Calvo had a wife, Mary, and two children aged fourteen and twelve. He was a printer by trade, the publisher of the *Spartanburg Express* in the state's hilly upcountry. But in the summer of 1861, Calvo had embarked on a new enterprise. Along with thirty-four other men he had joined the crew of a Confederate privateer, a vessel commissioned by Jefferson Davis to capture Union vessels and their cargoes.

As Calvo and the *Dixie* slipped past the Union blockade and onto the high seas, they joined dozens of other crews taking part in what had become a craze in port cities across the South. For weeks the promise of huge profits from privateering had sent southern ports like Charleston and New Orleans into a frenzy as ship owners sought to refit their vessels and organize privateering companies. New Orleans observers enthusiastically predicted that nearly 1,000 private vessels would soon enlist in the cause.

The *Dixie*'s early days at sea seemed to vindicate the hopes of its investors and crew alike. After four days, the crew overhauled and captured the bark *Glen* of Portland, Maine, and sent it with its cargo of almost 400 tons of anthracite coal to Moorehead City, North Carolina, for adjudication. The *Dixie*'s owners and crew expected to net over $10,000 after the auction of their prize and its cargo of coal. Two days later the *Dixie* captured another vessel, the *Mary Alice*, bringing sugar from the West Indies to New York. The *Dixie*'s captain, Thomas Moore, assigned Calvo to the prize crew with orders to bring the *Mary Alice* into port for adjudication.

But Calvo and the skeletal prize crew of four other seamen from the *Dixie* never made it back into port. On August 3, at around 11 a.m., lookouts aboard the U.S. frigate *Wabash* spotted the *Mary Alice* off Wilmington, North Carolina. The *Wabash* gave chase, eventually capturing the *Mary Alice* and its crew of five from the *Dixie*. Captain Samuel Mercer of the Union Navy promptly sent the Confederate prize crew to New York, not as prisoners of war but as pirates. By the end of August, Calvo found himself imprisoned at Fort Hamilton in what is now Bay Ridge, Brooklyn. A month later he was transferred to the bowels of New York City's infamous prison, the Tombs, to await prosecution as a pirate. And a month after that he wrote a letter to Abraham Lincoln.

Calvo was not entirely honest with Lincoln. The canny newspaperman from South Carolina described himself as "a poor man," one who had not had the "chance to butt his head against a College wall." Calvo wrote disingenuously that it might be pointless for an uneducated man such as himself "to bandy words with you and others at the head of affairs." But if he hid his familiarity with language, his message was clear: he and his fellows were prisoners of war, not pirates. "You can no more make us out Pirates than you can the Army Prisoners of the Confederate States." His status was the same as that of men captured in "the Federal Navy and Federal Army," he noted, and indeed the same as "the Privateersmen" of the United States "when she was in her infancy and rebelled against England." But whether or not Lincoln would concede the point as a matter of principle, Calvo made a further and more disturbing observation. The character of the conflict now washing over the shores of the United Sates, Calvo insisted, turned on Lincoln's willingness to offer Calvo and his fellow privateers prisoner of war protections. If the Union refused to recognize privateers as soldiers, Calvo warned, the war would quickly become a "dog eat dog" fight. Calvo seemed for the moment to believe his description of himself as unlettered: "Steal my dog," he warned, and "I will steal your cat." However awkwardly he put it, Calvo had identified the logic of reciprocity in the laws of war. If the privateers of the South were "considered and treated as Pirates," then "those belonging to the Army and Navy" of the North would doubtless be "considered and treated the same."

L INCOLN'S APRIL 19 blockade order had promised to treat southern privateers not as legitimate combatants but as stateless pirates.

But southerners instantly objected that if Lincoln had invoked the laws of war by imposing a blockade, he could hardly reject the application of those same laws to Confederate privateers. In South Carolina, journalists reported "a good deal of joking"—and even derision—about the report that "Old Abe" had ordered Union cruisers "to treat the crews of Confederate privateers as 'pirates.'" Confederate attorney general Judah Benjamin warned grimly that the Confederacy had "an easy remedy for that." For any man

*The Union indicted Confederate privateers instead of treating them
as prisoners of war; here, the Union sinks a privateer called the* Petrel
outside Charleston Harbor in July 1861.

whom the United States dared to execute, Benjamin threatened, the Confederacy would "hang two of their people."

Once the Union began to pick up privateers and arrest them for piracy, the problem became more serious. Southern newspapers like the *Charleston Mercury* excoriated the "insane and blood-thirsty spirit ruling the Government of the North." "If the hair of the head of a single man of this crew is injured," wrote the *Mercury*'s editors, "South Carolina will demand that the outrage be atoned for—an eye for an eye—a tooth for a tooth—a life for a life."

Jefferson Davis himself responded to Lincoln on July 6 in a letter delivered personally to the president by Winfield Scott, now in his final days as the Army's general-in-chief. The Confederate president sounded the same note struck by George Washington writing to the British general Thomas Gage outside Boston in 1775. "A just regard to humanity and to the honor of this government," Davis told Lincoln, required that the Confederacy "deal out to the prisoners held by it the same treatment" given by the Union to the Confederate privateers. "Retaliation," Davis warned, would be extended as far as necessary to force the United States to abandon its treatment of privateers as pirates, a treatment that Davis insisted was "unknown to the warfare of civilized man, and so barbarous as to disgrace the nation which shall be guilty of inaugurating it."

The problem of southern privateers caused Secretary of State Seward to revisit the country's embarrassing Declaration of Paris episode. In 1856, Great Britain had deftly outmaneuvered the United States when it arranged a multilateral treaty that adopted American neutral rights principles while prohibiting the use of privateers. Unwilling to abandon its longstanding reliance on privateers, the U.S. had rejected the treaty as a ruse by more powerful European states. Five years later, now occupying Britain's customary place as the stronger sea power in an armed conflict, the United States switched its position. Seward saw an opportunity to strike at the Confederate privateers by signing on to the Declaration's prohibition on privateering. The secretary of state authorized Charles Francis Adams in London to accept belatedly the British invitation of 1856 to join the Declaration. If Britain were to refuse, Seward added, it could "only be because she is willing to become the patron of privateering when aimed at our devastation."

Seward's gambit failed, however, and it failed because invoking the laws of war had consequences. The United States' attempt to characterize the South's privateers as criminals and pirates followed fast on its description of the South as a legitimate belligerent for purposes of the blockade. The contradiction was too much for many to swallow. William Howard Russell, correspondent for *The Times* in London, scoffed that "[t]he inconsistencies of the Northern people multiply ad infinitum." It seemed to Russell a "farce" to try the privateers as pirates for acting on "the authority of a pretended letter of marque from one Jefferson Davis." "One Jeff Davis," Russell quipped, "is certainly quite enough for them at present."

British statesmen saw the situation in much the same way. When Seward and Adams asked for admission to the Declaration of Paris, Lord Lyons agreed to allow it but only as applied to future conflicts, not in the war that had already broken out with the South. Seward answered with the administration's standard line on the privateers. The conflict with the South, he replied, was not a war but an insurrection, and as such the Declaration would apply to bar southern privateers even though the insurrection was already underway. To this, Lord Lyons had a devastating reply. "Very well," he told Seward. "If they are not independent then the President's proclamation of blockade is not binding. A blockade, according to the definition of the convention, applies only to two nations at war." Invoking international law's powers in April to erect a blockade had made denying its protections in May far more difficult. Did the United States plan to treat Confederate soldiers as criminals, too? For it was hard to see why there ought to be a difference in the treatment of the South's privateers and its soldiers on land. Britain, explained the British foreign secretary Lord Russell, would try to keep the conflict at sea and on land "within the rules of modern civilized warfare."

S EWARD'S DECLARATION OF PARIS ploy may have failed, but the piracy prosecutions proceeded nonetheless. In light of the British pressure and Jefferson Davis's retaliation threats, a stark question arose. Did Lincoln have the courage to hang Calvo and the other alleged pirates?

At first it seemed he did. On July 16, a federal grand jury in New York indicted as pirates twelve crew members from the Charleston privateer *Savannah*. In August, a grand jury in Philadelphia did the same for five men from the privateer *Jefferson Davis*.

The trials that ensued in October were national spectacles. The nation's most prominent lawyers argued before packed courtrooms. National political figures sat in the galleries. Supreme Court Justice Benjamin Grier presided in Philadelphia, where the first piracy trial started on October 22. After just three days of argument in the courtroom, the jury took a half hour to return a verdict of guilty against William Smith, the captain of the prize crew from the *Jefferson Davis*. The court sentenced him to death by hanging. In the subsequent days another Philadelphia jury returned guilty verdicts against three more men from the same crew.

The New York trial of the officers and crew of the *Savannah* began a day after the commencement of the Philadelphia trial. It had all the same pomp and circumstance. Supreme Court Justice Samuel Nelson presided. But the New York trial produced a very different outcome.

For the defense, the renowned criminal defense lawyer John Brady teamed up with the dean of the New York bar, Daniel Lord, and a rising young lawyer named Algernon Sullivan. They squared off against the government's favorite hired gun, William Evarts, whose mentor Lord was now his adversary in one of the biggest cases of their careers.

From the start, the case proved to be a bitter fight. Even before the trial began, Secretary of State Seward threw the defense lawyer Algernon Sullivan into prison for seditious contact with the enemy. (Sullivan had corresponded with Confederate officials in Virginia on behalf of his clients.)

Daniel Lord represented John Harleston (the first mate of the *Savannah* and the son of one of Lord's Yale College classmates) and insisted that the government's position was hypocrisy through and through. Right down the hall in the very same courthouse, Lord spluttered, federal judge Samuel Betts was condemning Confederate vessels captured by a Union blockade force that presupposed a state of war between North and South. But if the Confederacy was capable of carrying on a war, then it ought to be able to commission privateers, too. Almost beside himself, Lord fumed about a government that claimed to treat southerners "as enemies, for the purpose of confiscation" but "as traitors and pirates, for the purpose of execution." It was "a glaring inconsistency," Lord exclaimed. Sullivan, released on an oath of loyalty from the dungeons of Fort Lafayette in New York Harbor only days before, pushed his luck by exhorting the jury to remember that their fathers had been revolutionaries, too, and that they had "judged for themselves what Government they would have."

For all the controversy in the *Savannah* case, there was little disagreement about the essential facts. The dispute was over how to characterize them. Was the Civil War a conflict in which commissioned private vessels were legitimate privateers like the American privateers of the War of 1812? Or was it a criminal conspiracy in which the so-called privateers were really mere pirates like the members of so many antebellum filibustering expeditions in South America? For six days, the lawyers debated the case. And in the end, the defense arguments won out. When the jury came back deadlocked, Justice Nelson sent them back to the jury room to try again. But when the jury again failed to reach a decision, the government's case collapsed. For all his persuasive capacity, William Evarts had simply been unable to persuade the jury that the armed conflict with the South—then finishing its sixth month—was anything other than a war.

Prosecutors planned to retry the *Savannah* crew on the same piracy charges, but the hung jury took the wind out of the prosecution's sails. For men like Calvo waiting in the Tombs, the government's inability to get a conviction in the *Savannah* case meant that their day in court would never come. In Philadelphia, plans to execute Smith and his crew were quietly put on hold. And late in the fall, Lincoln and Seward abandoned the piracy prosecutions altogether. By February 1862, the privateers imprisoned in New York were transferred from the Tombs to Fort Lafayette and redesignated as prisoners of war. At the end of May, Calvo and the privateers from the *Savannah* and two other Confederate privateering vessels were discharged as part of a prisoner exchange between North and South.

*   *   *

O NE THING THAT had happened between the captures of the privateers in June and their trials in the fall was the first great land battle of the war. At Bull Run, on July 21, 1861, almost 500 Union soldiers lost their lives, as did almost 400 from the Confederate Army. Altogether, another 2,700 were wounded.

More important for the course of the conflict were the 1,300 Union soldiers captured by the Confederacy. Two weeks after Jefferson Davis sent his ominous retaliation letter to Lincoln in early July, Bull Run had made retaliation a credible threat. The South could now impose the laws of war on the North by sheer force. From the end of July onward, reciprocity between the two sides became a tacit basis for abandoning the piracy prosecutions and steadily expanding the role of the laws of war in the Union war effort. Indeed, Lincoln and Seward decided to change the privateers' legal status from pirates to prisoners of war after an interview with Congressman Alfred Ely of New York, who himself had been captured at Bull Run. Ely had been one of the numerous northern spectators captured in the chaos of the end of the battle. In November 1861, after the Philadelphia convictions and while retrial of the *Savannah* officers was still a live possibility, Ely had been forced by his Confederate captors to draw from a tin the names of the Union officers who would stand as hostages for the humane treatment of the Confederate privateers in Union hands.

Yet if Lincoln's piracy prosecutions came to naught, so did the Confederacy's privateering plans. Despite predictions of hundreds of vessels disrupting Union commerce, the Confederacy ultimately commissioned only fifty-two privateers, many of them barely fit for service and some of them so small and poorly armed as to be no threat to northern merchant vessels at all. When it turned out that the Union blockade had made it too difficult for Confederate privateers to reach the high seas, let alone get their prizes back into southern ports, southern ship owners lost interest in privateering as quickly as they had taken it up.

In the end, the problem of privateering took care of itself. But the piracy trials had revealed something important to the Lincoln administration. Invoking the laws of war to mobilize the power of the blockade was not free. It had come with consequences. It had bound and constrained the Lincoln administration in the federal court in New York City in October 1861 when the jury refused to convict the southern privateers. In the months and years to come it would do the same in the court of public opinion and in the diplomatic courts of Europe. As 1861 came to a close, however, Lincoln and Seward were about to learn that sometimes being constrained by the laws of war could be useful.

Hero of the Hour

C APTAIN CHARLES WILKES was a national celebrity. In July 1842, he had returned with fantastic discoveries after four years in command of the United States Exploring Expedition in the South Pacific. In the hulls of the expedition's two surviving vessels (the expedition had started out with six), Wilkes carried 2,000 previously unidentified species of plants and animals. Wilkes and his crew had logged 87,000 miles and mapped 280 Pacific islands. His flagship, the *Vincennes*, carried a dying Fijian man whose skull (along with 40 tons of specimens and artifacts) would soon become part of the founding collection of the Smithsonian Museum in Washington. Wilkes had discovered a continent—Antarctica—a massive part of which (1500 miles of coastline) would be named after him: Wilkes Land. He was a modern-day Columbus. As Mark Twain later remembered, "the name of Wilkes, the explorer, was in everybody's mouth."

Yet as a commander, Wilkes had been erratic, abusive, and self-promoting. In the midst of his triumphant return, Wilkes's subordinate officers dragged him before a court-martial, which convicted him of illegally flogging the seamen on board the expedition's vessels. The commander quickly became as renowned for his pugnacious temperament as for his discoveries. And in late 1861, almost twenty years later, the irascible Wilkes nearly touched off a war with Great Britain—a war that the beleaguered United States could ill afford.

W HEN THE CIVIL WAR began in April 1861, Navy Secretary Gideon Welles appointed Wilkes to the command of the *San Jacinto*, a 12-gun sloop of war stationed off the western coast of Africa to suppress the slave trade. Wilkes was to report to Philadelphia to serve under Captain Samuel F. Du Pont in the Union Navy's impending assault on Confederate-held Port Royal in the South Carolina Sea Islands. But Du Pont had served on the court that convicted Wilkes in 1842, and the embittered Wilkes had no intention of subordinating himself to his former judge. Violating his orders, Wilkes combed the waters of the eastern Atlantic, hoping to capture Confederate privateers and bring renewed fame (not to mention fortune) to his name. Failing to find any, he sailed to the Caribbean to do more of the same. Then fate intervened. In early November, Wilkes heard rumors that two senior Confederate statesmen—James Mason of Virginia and John Slidell of New Orleans—had run past the Union blockade and booked travel on a British mail steamer called the *Trent*, sailing out of Havana.

Mason and Slidell had been appointed commissioners to represent the Confederacy in Great Britain and France. But Wilkes had other plans for them. On November 9, he spied the British vessel and fired shots across its bow, forcing it to heave to. Sending a boarding party to the *Trent*, Wilkes ordered Mason and Slidell and their secretaries forcibly taken from the British vessel while an angry British captain and passengers looked on. Slidell's seventeen-year-old daughter tried to stop the boarding party single-handedly by slapping Wilkes's second-in-command in the face.

Wilkes had scoured the law books that he (like many naval captains) carried on board the *San Jacinto*—books by the Americans Kent and Wheaton and the ubiquitous Vattel. He concluded that although he could find no authority exactly in his favor, it was nonetheless his right and indeed his duty to seize the two men. Wilkes believed he also had the right to seize the *Trent* itself. But partly because he could ill afford to spare any members of his already overstretched crew, and partly out of consideration for the passengers and crew of the British mail steamer, Wilkes and his officers decided to release the *Trent* to continue on its way.

W HEN WORD REACHED the United States of Wilkes's coup, supporters of the Union reacted in wild euphoria. Since late July and the disaster at Bull Run, the North had longed for good news. The capture of Mason and Slidell provided a desperately needed morale boost. William Howard Russell from *The Times* of London reported "a storm of exultation sweeping over the land." Wilkes, he wrote in his diary, was "the hero of the hour." When Wilkes sailed into Boston with the two Confederate statesmen, patriots greeted him in celebration. Governor John A. Andrew spoke at a banquet held in Wilkes's honor at the Revere House. Secretary Welles told Wilkes that his "conduct in seizing these public enemies" had "the emphatic approval of this Department."

The difficulty was that public indignation in Great Britain was soon aroused as well. When word of Wilkes's seizure of the British mail steamer reached England on November 27, the case became a cause célèbre. From London, a friend of Seward wrote that he had never before seen "such a burst of feeling" among the British people; "were the country polled," he added, "I fear that 999 men out of 1,000 would declare for immediate war." Charles Wilson, the secretary of the American legation in London, wrote "in very great haste" to Washington that news of the *Trent* affair had "raised excitement to the highest pitch." Thurlow Weed, whom Lincoln had sent to Europe to discourage British support for the South, reported that "England is exasperated" and warned Seward that talk of war raced through Britain. By December 11, Weed wrote urgently that war had been "deliberately settled upon" by the British unless Seward could avert the crisis. But averting the crisis meant releasing Mason and Slidell, and releasing Mason and Slidell would doubtless set off a firestorm of opposition in the United States.

The heart of the problem was that American and British observers came to radically divergent answers to the questions that Wilkes had first tried to parse on board the *San Jacinto* on November 7. Could a belligerent stop a neutral vessel traveling between neutral ports to seize enemy ministers? Lincoln's attorney general, Edward Bates, was certain that Wilkes's act was legal. ("The law of nations," he said, "is clear upon the point.") As Wilkes himself had reasoned, the law treated enemy dispatches as contraband, and even though Wilkes had been unable to find dispatches, the commissioners themselves were (as Wilkes put it) the "embodiment of dispatches" and thus contraband subject to confiscation. Former U.S. attorneys general and secretaries of state, law professors at Harvard, and leading prize court lawyers all stepped forward and agreed with Wilkes's conclusions in the strongest terms.

The British, however, were just as certain the opposite was true. Lord Russell, the British foreign minister, insisted that Wilkes had "superseded the authority of the Courts instituted and recognized by the Law of Nations." "The ingenuity of American lawyers," he warned Lyons, would doubtless "entangle you in endless arguments on Vattel, Wheaton, and Scott." But British lawyers and statesmen contended that Wilkes had engaged in a clear violation of neutral rights by intercepting a neutral vessel traveling between neutral ports. The contraband rule, they pointed out, had no application to goods traveling between neutral ports, and in any event they denied that ministers could be contraband of war. Accordingly, Lord Russell instructed Lyons to demand the release of Mason and Slidell and "a suitable apology for the aggression which has been committed." If release of the men and an appropriate apology were not forthcoming within seven days, Lyons was to request his passports and leave the country.

* * *

FOR NINE MONTHS Lincoln had been trying to make sure the United States fought one war at a time. But now many thought war with Britain was inevitable.

On the one hand, Lincoln faced the fervent pro-Wilkes sentiment of northern supporters of the war effort: any effort to turn over Mason and Slidell to the British would seem to the American public, as Bates put it, no more than "timidly truckling to the power of England." On the other hand, he faced the angry demands of the British government for the two men's immediate release. As Britain's deadline approached, Lincoln found himself in what naval historian Craig Symonds has called his "Cuban Missile Crisis moment."

On Christmas Day, 1861, Seward delivered a brilliant solution, one rooted in the very same laws of war whose confusions had so far only exacerbated the problem. In the British view, Wilkes had actually made two mistakes. Not only had he lacked the right to seize Mason and Slidell, he had also failed to bring the *Trent* to the federal courts in the United States to have the legality of his capture determined by law. There were mitigating considerations, to be sure. Wilkes had cited the inconvenience to the *Trent* and its passengers in deciding to let the vessel continue on its way. Moreover, in releasing the vessel, he had abandoned any personal claim on it or its cargo, valued at over $1 million in 1861 dollars. Nonetheless, bringing captured vessels before a prize court was absolutely required by the laws of war. By not doing so, Wilkes had (as Lord Russell observed in the midst of the crisis) "taken into his own hands, by virtue of his cannons and cutlasses," the question of whether he had been in the right in stopping the *Trent* and intercepting the commissioners.

Lord Russell had made this point to Lyons in early December, and Lyons in turn passed the objection along to Seward. Once Seward realized the gravity of the situation, he also grasped the opportunity this second British objection offered. When the cabinet assembled on Christmas Day to consider the British ultimatum, Seward read them a draft memorandum that held strong to the ground Wilkes had claimed in November. The Confederate commissioners Mason and Slidell, Seward insisted, were contraband of war, as were any dispatches they were carrying. Wilkes had merely exercised the lawful right of a nation at war to stop and search neutral vessels, and he had done so in a lawful manner. So far, Seward had sustained even the strongest claims of American public opinion. But when Seward reached the question of whether Wilkes had followed the procedural requirements of the laws of maritime warfare, he did an abrupt about-face.

It was true, Seward observed, that Wilkes had declined to follow the procedural requirements of the laws of war at sea. Out of an excess of consideration for the passengers and crew of the *Trent*, whose voyages would have been badly waylaid by a detour to the United States for adjudication, Wilkes had let the vessel go on its way. (Seward left out the fact that Wilkes had also been motivated to avoid losing a portion of his crew.) But good motives were irrelevant, Seward said. Wilkes had erred in failing to have the capture evaluated by a prize court, and as a result Mason and Slidell and their secretaries were entitled to be released.

Seward's final move was inspired. If anyone thought for even a minute that Seward had stooped to making pro-British and anti-American arguments, Seward reminded them that he "was really defending and maintaining . . . an old, honoured, and cherished American cause" based on the "distinctive policy" of the United States with respect to neutral rights in wartime. James Madison himself, while secretary of state in 1804, had insisted that every capture be "carried before a legal tribunal" for regular trial and adjudication. "If I decide this case in favour of my own Government," Seward wrote, "I must disallow its most cherished principles."

Lincoln himself (at Sumner's urging) had hoped to arrange an arbitration of the dispute by France or Prussia. But by Christmas he was persuaded that arbitration would be futile (European views of the affair sided with Great Britain) and that the British deadline was not to be trifled with. Lincoln and a unanimous cabinet approved Seward's memorandum the day after Christmas. Mason and Slidell were released shortly thereafter, and the crisis was averted. Lyons even forgave the absence of an apology in the American response, which Lord Russell grudgingly accepted.

The curiosity of the *Trent* affair's culmination was that it turned on what Treasury Secretary Salmon Chase irritably called "a technical wrong"—a legal technicality. And so for a century and a half, historians have viewed the end of the affair as absurd, as evidence that the entire episode was the result of a kind of national madness. Charles Francis Adams, Jr., whose father had been the minister to Great Britain during the controversy, later wrote that it was precisely these sorts of moments that "bring law into contempt" and reveal the "quite unintelligible and somewhat ludicrous state of what is termed Law, of the international variety." Indeed, according to Adams, the futility of international law was "the one real world lesson the world derived from the *Trent* affair."

Historians ever since have followed Adams's interpretation. But Adams was wrong. Badly wrong. It was the law (technicality or otherwise) that had helped Lincoln and Seward solve their seemingly intractable problem. It offered a principled reason for departing from the wild enthusiasms of American public opinion without abandoning the American view of the merits of the case. And it was the law that had allowed Seward to save face by rooting Lincoln's position in the proudest traditions of the founding fathers. The law had given Lincoln and Seward room to maneuver in what was otherwise a very tight spot. By the end of 1861, it was fair to say that Lincoln had learned a thing or two about practicing the laws of war, even if the law of nations had not made its way into the frontier law courts of Illinois. Under the stewardship of Lincoln and Seward, it was the law of war (not Wilkes) that had proven to be the unsung hero of the hour.

M UCH OF THE administration's work on the blockade, the privateers, and the *Trent* affair had consisted of updating the United States' embarrassingly outdated positions in the laws of war at sea.

On land, the situation was just as bad and maybe worse. Since the founding, American statesmen had adopted positions that were at the leading edge of the Enlightenment tradition of restraints on war's violence. They had proposed rules to limit the destruction of private property in wartime. They had castigated the British for the destruction of Washington, D.C., in the War of 1812. Most of all, the United States had argued that emancipating an enemy's slaves was a gross violation of the laws of civilized warfare.

The *Trent* crisis had led impassioned Lincoln supporters (even some with little sympathy for slaves) to call for an expanded war effort, one that ever more northerners now urged should emancipate the slaves and arm "every negro of every rebel" so as to "crush out the last vestige of the Slave Aristocracy." But ever since the royal governor Lord Dunmore had tried to free the slaves of Virginia's founding fathers, American statesmen had denounced such efforts as the very definition of savagery in wartime. If Lincoln was to take on the problem of slavery, the United States would need to utterly transform its traditional view of the customs and usages of war.

As it happened, in February 1862 the man who was best qualified to accomplish that transformation was making his way across the country from New York to the Ohio Valley. Chased by personal demons, and without so much as a plan, the man hoped to find a gravely wounded son who had been injured in bitter fighting along the Cumberland River.

Chapter 6

Blood Is the Rich Dew of History

————◦————

The shorter war is, the better; and the more
intensely it is carried on, the shorter it will be.

—Francis Lieber, 1861

A T 6 A.M. on Saturday, February 15, 1862, on the Cumberland River
in Tennessee, First Lieutenant Hamilton Lieber and the 1,000 men
of the 9th Illinois awoke from a restless night of snow and sleet to the sound
of the antiquated British Tower Pattern muskets carried by the Western
Department of the Confederate Army. For two days, a Union army of
15,000 men under Brigadier General Ulysses S. Grant and a fleet of four
ironclad steamboats led by Union flag officer Andrew H. Foote had pounded
21,000 Confederate soldiers penned up in and around Fort Donelson. Now
even more Union troops were arriving. Brigadier Generals John B. Floyd
and Gideon Pillow of the Confederate Army had decided to launch a last-
ditch offensive to break out of the Union cordon and escape down the road
to Nashville.

The 9th Illinois occupied the extreme right of the Union line. Its mission
was to extend the Union position and anchor it along a creek to the south
and east of the fort, thus blocking the road that ran along the creek toward
Nashville and safety for the Confederate Army. At daybreak, when three
Confederate regiments led an assault on Union positions, the 9th Illinois
stood directly in their path.

The 101 men of Hamilton Lieber's Company B had seen action briefly
in October 1861 when they participated in a rout of 300 Confederate cavalry at Eddyville, Kentucky. But the early hours of February 15 marked the

first time in combat for most of the Illinois volunteers. Inexperience had led them to position themselves poorly on the rolling terrain, and try as they might, the Union regiments had been unable to stretch their lines all the way to the creek. A thick wet snow hung heavily in the underbrush, rendering visibility poor. To make matters worse, at this early stage of the war the two armies' uniforms were still unstandardized. Some Union soldiers wore militia gray. Some Confederate companies still dressed in standard-issue United States blue. In the confusion and the disorder, nervous Union troops fired on their comrades. Underfoot, the slippery cold mud from the snow and rain and the swollen Cumberland made movement of any kind difficult at best.

Taking advantage of the gap between the Illinois volunteers and the creek, Nathan Bedford Forrest's cavalry and Colonel Joseph Drake's Third Brigade of Mississippi, Arkansas, and Alabama troops quickly turned the right flank of the Union line. The green Union soldiers were suddenly exposed on two sides. The Confederates pressed their advantage. Moving forward in large masses six to eight files deep, each rank of Confederate infantrymen fired and stepped aside to allow the next rank to do the same. Under what one Illinois volunteer remembered as incessant fire, the Union troops soon fell into disarray. As the Confederate advance continued and the Union lines broke,

The harrowing rebel assault on the Union right at Fort Donelson
nearly reversed what became the Union's first great victory of the war.

the fight became a bitter and chaotic struggle at close range. Men dropped all around. Supply wagons had been late in arriving, and those still standing on the Union side ran low on ammunition. The men of the 9th Illinois must surely have been afraid. It was the first time in the western theater that Union soldiers had heard the high-low call of the rebel yell. But like soldiers in wars before and since, they were stunningly brave. One wounded volunteer officer from Illinois recalled that every single volunteer in his regiment stood and fought, though many must have felt an urge to run. When told to retreat and regroup, men whose ammunition had run out protested that they could fight with bayonets alone.

Lieutenant Lieber and Company B of the 9th Illinois held out as long as any of the first defenders of the Union right. It helped that Company B was held together by tight bonds. Virtually every man of the company was of German-American birth, and most hailed from the close-knit communities of southern Illinois. They were farmers, tradesmen, and artisans with names like Geist, Schwarzkopf, Cropp, and Lugenbuehler. Hamilton Lieber himself was a twenty-seven-year-old farmer whose father had been born in Berlin. He was an officer in part because he had formal military training. Before the war, he had enrolled in the Naval Academy at Annapolis. He quit when he proved unable to master the mathematics curriculum. In Illinois, however, Hamilton had quickly gained a reputation for prodigious strength and bravery. Both were on full display in the Union defense outside Fort Donelson. Again and again he rallied the men of Company B. When a shot struck him in the left arm, he tied a kerchief around it and soldiered on in the snow and the cold trying desperately to hold the right end of the Union line. Around 9 or 10 a.m., a minié ball from a Confederate rifle smashed the elbow of the same left arm that had already been struck. The ball pulverized the bones on both sides of the elbow. Most of the brigade had already retired from the field. Now a badly wounded Hamilton Lieber would too.

Union casualties on that morning were staggering. A surgeon arriving late in the afternoon said it was like the aftermath of a "death storm." Almost 2,000 Union soldiers were wounded, many (including Hamilton Lieber) seriously. Four hundred Union men lay dead. Only the 8th Illinois and 18th Illinois suffered worse casualties than Hamilton's 9th that morning. Before the day was out, 201 of the regiment's 1,000 men had been killed, wounded, or captured. Company B's casualties were especially gruesome. Nine had been killed and twenty-eight wounded, higher figures than in all but one of the 9th Illinois's nine other companies. Hamilton was carried to a makeshift field hospital, where he sat untreated and bleeding among the dead and the dying and the amputated limbs, which lay strewn around like terrible surgeons' trophies. Only that night, after a team of doctors from the U.S. Sanitary Commission arrived and after he was able to catch the attention of a navy surgeon, did Hamilton receive medical attention. The only course of action was to amputate the limb as mortification set in.

Back on the Union right, the heroics of men like Hamilton paid off. The massed lines of Confederate soldiers under Gideon Pillow had been unable to break through cleanly in the opening hours of the battle. When Pillow hesitated, unsure what to do next, Grant rushed reinforcements to the Union right and stopped the Confederate advance. Unable to escape, the Confederate forces at Fort Donelson (now reduced to 15,000 men in all) had no choice but to surrender. They did so the next morning, on Grant's stern terms: "unconditional and immediate surrender."

The battle at Fort Donelson provided the Union its first great strategic victory of the war. Along with Grant's victory the week before at Fort Henry, the capture of Fort Donelson opened up to Union forces the river routes into Tennessee, Alabama, and Mississippi. The fall of Fort Donelson left important Confederate ironworks defenseless and cut off Richmond from one of its principal sources of grain and pork. General Albert Sidney Johnston, the brilliant commander of the Confederacy's Western Department, called the loss of Donelson "most disastrous and almost without remedy." Historians have called it a campaign that helped decide the Civil War. Hamilton would etch the date of the battle into the hilt of his officer's sword. He had missed its conclusion. But his experience that morning set in motion events that would shape the course of the war and remake the laws of warfare in ways no one could have anticipated in the snow and sleet and mud of the Cumberland.

Would to God, I, Too, Could Act!

ONE THOUSAND MILES AWAY, on East 34th Street in New York, Francis and Matilda Lieber waited anxiously for news of their son as the battle of Fort Donelson raged.

Sixty-four-year-old Francis, or Frank as he was known to intimates, was born in Berlin in 1798. His first memory was watching Napoleon's soldiers march through Berlin past his family home in 1806 after epic battles at Jena and Auerstadt in which Napoleon had swept the Prussians from the field. The Berlin of his youth was full of men committed to casting off the yoke of the French. His older brothers joined Prussia's secret military. His father, Frederick, served as district inspector for the *Landsturm*, an organization for Prussian home defense.

Francis was too young for military service in 1806, but he too dreamed of evicting the hated French. At the age of fifteen he decided he would learn French and disguise himself for the purpose of assassinating Napoleon. The plan seems never to have gone very far. But shortly thereafter he took up a leading role in Friedrich Ludwig Jahn's gymnasium movement, the motivation for which was much the same. Jahn aimed to improve the fitness of a new generation and create a body of men that would be "able to expel the French from Germany." Jahn's system of youth athletics established modern gymnastics.

When Napoleon returned from exile in Elba in 1815, a seventeen-year-old Lieber at last got his chance to fight the hated French. Lieber and three brothers enlisted in the legendary Colberg Regiment, which had been the last to hold out against the French in 1806 and 1807. In June, the Lieber brothers took part in the fighting at the Belgian village of Ligny. The next day, they waited in reserve as the Prussian and British armies defeated the French at Waterloo.

For a day and a half, Lieber's regiment chased Napoleon and the French back toward Paris. As his company charged down a hill into the town of Namur, Francis Lieber was shot by a French grenadier. Years later he remembered the event as if it had just happened:

> I suddenly experienced a sensation as if my whole body were compressed in my head, and this, like a ball, were quivering in the air. I could feel the existence of nothing else; it was a most painful sensation.

A PASSING PRUSSIAN told Lieber he had been shot through the neck. As he lay on the field outside Namur, he was struck by another French volley, this time in the chest. He was certain he would die. And when late that evening he was pulled off the field, his comrades thought so too.

Miraculously, the young man lived. Even more miraculously, his wounds left him no less enamored of the life of the soldier. To the contrary, he felt that on the battlefield he had experienced life in its fullest. Five years later, he joined an international brigade of Danes, Poles, Frenchmen, Italians, and Germans to fight for Greek independence against the Turks. Like Lord

Byron, he imagined himself to be rescuing the glories of Greece from the clutches of the Ottoman Empire, but he quickly concluded that modern-day Greeks bore little resemblance to the heroes of antiquity. They seemed disorganized, drunken, unreliable, and thieving. On closer examination, he came to think that Turk atrocities were matched by Greek disgraces. The conflict could barely be described as a respectable war. Within weeks of his arrival in Greece, Lieber concluded that "if there should not be any opportunity to engage in warfare," he would see the sights of ancient Athens.

In his childhood, then at Waterloo, and then again in Greece, Lieber showed a deep attraction to war. He tingled at the "indelible horror" of death and destruction around him. He remembered a bewildered boy who had stumbled into the thick of the action at Ligny and seemed certain to die. He remembered birds trying to protect their young from the "tremendous uproar and carnage" and he remembered pulling cannon "over the mangled bodies of comrades" who writhed "in agony when the heavy wheels crossed over them." Outside Waterloo, he had threatened to shoot a Belgian peasant for bread after the long day of fighting. ("I told my comrade to hold him while I would seem to prepare to shoot him," he later wrote.) Days afterward, while he lay on the field at Namur, the local peasants had their revenge, stealing his watch, his money, and his clothes, and aggravating his wounds. War was full of terrors. But terror did not mean repulsion, or at least not repulsion alone. For it was war's glory that had delivered Prussia from the grip of the hated French.

T HE YEARS AFTER Waterloo ought to have been a time of celebration for Lieber. But the political enthusiasms of men like Lieber and Jahn made them suspect in the reactionary politics that descended on Europe after Napoleon's defeat. In 1819, Lieber was arrested and imprisoned for four months on suspicion of political subversion. He managed thereafter to earn a doctorate in mathematics at the university at Jena. But most universities in Prussia were placed off limits to him.

In 1826, Lieber left the political repression of Prussia behind and traveled to England. In London, he sought out and befriended some of the leading intellectuals of the country, including the aging utilitarian philosopher Jeremy Bentham and a young John Stuart Mill. He also met Matilda ("Matty") Oppenheim, whom he would marry three years later. Though there was talk of a teaching post for Francis in London, none of his connections produced gainful employment. And so in 1827 he traveled to Boston, where he took up a position as the first permanent director of a new gymnasium that a group of wealthy Boston men had established in the Prussian fashion of Lieber's old mentor Jahn.

The gymnasium failed after a year. But its connections to the latest European ideas about education launched Lieber into a career as one of the most garrulous and peripatetic public intellectuals of his day. As in London, he eagerly pursued the leading men of the country. In the young United States, Lieber's cosmopolitan background opened doors more readily than it had in England. President John Quincy Adams swam at his gymnasium. A generation of Europhile intellectuals took him into their social circles: men like the Supreme Court justice and Harvard law professor Joseph Story, the young lawyers Charles Sumner and Francis Hilliard, and the poet and Harvard literature professor Henry Wadsworth Longfellow. Within a few years he was dining with President Andrew Jackson and befriending the U.S. senator from New York and future cabinet member William Marcy.

Casting about for a way to turn his intellectual background into cash, Lieber entered the publishing business with a prominent Philadelphia printer, Matthew Carey. Between 1829 and 1833, Lieber published the *Encyclopaedia Americana,* a fabulously successful venture whose thirteen volumes and 7 million words quickly found their way into virtually every well-to-do home in the country. President Jackson had a set in the White House. A young frontier lawyer named Abraham Lincoln owned a set in his offices. Later editions would become the second-best-selling encyclopedia in the world, behind only the *Encyclopaedia Britannica.*

With the success of the *Encyclopaedia* under his belt, Lieber pursued the possibility of a history chair at Harvard College. But despite his publishing success and his many friends, Lieber would always be an outsider among the Boston elite, and no teaching post at Harvard was forthcoming. With two young boys (Oscar, age five, and an infant named Hamilton), Lieber needed to find a steady source of income. In 1835, the family moved to Columbia, South Carolina, where he took a professorship in history and political economy at South Carolina College.

At South Carolina, Lieber proved to be a desultory teacher, but mostly because he lacked the patience to give his students a chance to get a word in edgewise. He loved to talk, and when he could find no one to listen, his torrent of words spilled out through his pen. So prolific was his correspondence and his never-ending stream of pamphlets, books, and articles that he seemed almost never to sleep. He was intellectually eccentric. Even his friends noted that he spoke in strange and idiosyncratic formulations. He had a certain charisma. But he could be egomaniacal and off-putting as well. Joseph Story quipped that Lieber needed conversation and correspondence like he needed food and oxygen. Lieber would die, Story wrote, "for want of a rapid, voluminous, and never-ending correspondence." The Boston lawyer Rufus Choate wrote that Lieber was the "most fertile, indomitable, unsleeping, combative and propagandising person of his race."

WHAT LIEBER LOVED to talk about most was war. As a student in 1821, he had studied military mathematics and geometry of the kind taught at the U.S. Military Academy at West Point. But Lieber thought that the study of war and strategy was irreducibly historical, not mathematical. He was an intuitive student of great battles in history. He dated his correspondence by reference to the Napoleonic battles at Ligny, Leipzig, Jena-Auerstadt, and Waterloo.

As Lieber saw it, modern warfare had undergone a dramatic transformation. The age of gunpowder had transformed war into a mass phenomenon. The "individual," he wrote, was "lost more and more in the mass."

But even in an age of mass violence—especially in an age of mass violence, an age in which armies hurled as many as 100,000 men toward one another—Lieber believed that war had a deep and profound moral significance. In his two-volume *Manual of Political Ethics*, published in 1838 and 1839, Lieber contended that pacifism was a view held "by persons who have an inadequate idea of what war actually is." Lieber knew war, and in his view war was not only morally permissible, it was morally imperative. War's moral virtues were the qualities of "energy and independence of thought, elevation and firmness of character, intensity of action." War brought out in men a "peculiar attribute of greatness of intellect." It communicated "the spark of moral electricity."

Indeed, Lieber wrote, the "choicest pages of history" were written of war. "Every single thread of that great web we call our civilization," he told his students, "has at one time or another been saved by battle or protracted war." At Marathon, Athens held off the Persians and saved Greek civilization. At Tours in the year 732, Christianity turned back Islam. At Leipzig ("the greatest battle ever fought"), Europe had crushed Napoleon. Battles such as these had been the engines of history, and Lieber said as much time and time again throughout his adult life. ("Blood," he wrote in 1844, was the "vital juice" of history.) This was the lesson of Prussia in 1806, when Napoleon humiliated Berlin but created the patriotic energy that fueled Prussia's rebirth. It was the lesson of Prussia's resurgence in 1813 and 1815. And it was the lesson of American history as well. When, after all, had the United States exhibited the "best and purest examples" of patriotism and public spirit? In the Revolution, of course, for wars such as the War of Independence restored the moral vitality of a people. The "protracted peace" of the years after 1815, by contrast, had produced the culture of "sordid selfishness and degrading submissiveness" that Lieber believed the residents of his adopted country could see firsthand all around them. What, Lieber asked rhetorically, could better exemplify "the nobleness of human nature" than "a devoted, humble citizen bleeding and dying for his beloved country, her laws and liberty, the freedom of his children"? To the pacifist, such glorious virtue counted as nothing. But to Lieber, it was the most honorable calling of mankind.

Lieber held justice, not peace, as the highest ideal. He denied that human life was "the greatest good." Nor, he insisted, was death "the greatest evil." By mistakenly making human pleasure their highest aspiration, their *summum bonum*, philosophers in what Lieber disparaged as the age of happiness had extinguished "that lively feeling of justice, without which no free state can flourish," producing a "habitual submission to injustice, plunder and insult." Just wars, by contrast, were "not demoralizing." To the contrary, when carried on by civilized peoples, just wars were the way civilization spread.

LIEBER'S INTENSE and heartfelt engagement with war led him to take unorthodox positions on some of the most controversial episodes of the day. In 1840 and 1841, for example, he defended New York's right to prosecute Alexander McLeod for murder in the *Caroline* episode. Where Secretary of State Webster insisted that the British had used force illegally, but that McLeod had a soldier's immunity from prosecution, Lieber adopted exactly the reverse view. Lieber's position—which he personally urged on Webster, President John Tyler, and others—was that soldiers were morally responsible for their actions in war or otherwise. In this he agreed with Governor Seward and the New York prosecutors. He saw no sharp moral or legal divide separating war from peace; moral imperatives governed both. But unlike the New York officials, Lieber insisted that McLeod had committed no crime because Britain had been fully within its rights in crossing the U.S. border and using force against MacKenzie's expeditionary unit. If he had been on the jury, Lieber wrote his friend Charles Sumner, he would have acquitted McLeod even if he concluded that McLeod had killed the American passenger.

For a time, Lieber's passionate views on war cost him his close friendship with Sumner. Beginning in 1834, the two had been fast friends. For more than a decade, they wrote hundreds of letters to one another. But on July 4, 1845, Lieber sat in Tremont Temple in Boston and listened to his friend's electrifying and controversial speech denouncing war as the moral equivalent of crime. Sumner's address, Lieber thought, was "the worst advised, and one of the worst reasoned speeches I have ever heard," and he told Sumner so. After several more years of increasingly acrimonious relations, the two men broke off their correspondence completely.

Lieber took Sumner's apostasy on war as seriously as he did because for Lieber war was a high moral calling. Sumner's view, he thought, displayed "elevated intention, but a lack of philosophical grasp and unraveling penetration." Lieber was no warmonger; he opposed the Mexican War, for example, even though he felt a powerful urge to enlist. But Lieber saw war as a vital part of the moral progress of vigorous nations. On his mantelpiece he kept a treasured leaf from the field at Waterloo. As a visitor to West Point, he thrilled at the march of the cadets. Indeed, for much of his adult life Lieber experienced a kind of self-loathing for living a life of ease so far removed from war. He always considered his own career of writing and teaching distinctly inferior to a life of action. The "spheres of action" of the statesman and the commanding general, he wrote, were "infinitely superior" to that of a mere professor. Lieber wanted a role "shaping history in the field, instead of teaching it in the lecture-room." In his grandiose moments (which some thought he experienced too often), he convinced himself that he had missed his true calling. "I was born for action, and for action in troubled times," he insisted to a friend in 1854. And when the Civil War broke out in 1861, his old instincts came flooding back. "Would to God, I, too, could act!" he cried.

Lieber would act. So, too, as it happened, would Sumner, who in 1861 abandoned his pacifism to fight against slavery, resuming his friendship with Lieber in the process. But in the Civil War, Lieber's contribution would be radically different from the one he had made at Waterloo.

Clausewitz in New York

I N 1856, Lieber resigned from his post at South Carolina College. He had always experienced life in the small town of Columbia as a kind of exile. ("Oh! my poor life!" he exclaimed more than once.) In 1851, he was passed over for the college presidency. At the same time, South Carolinians rightly began to suspect that Lieber held heterodox views on states' rights and slavery. Francis and Matty moved to New York City with their youngest son, Norman, who was now nineteen. Twenty-one-year-old Hamilton had gone off three years before to Illinois to try his hand at farming after his failed venture at the Naval Academy. Their oldest boy, the twenty-seven-year-old Oscar, stayed behind in South Carolina.

Francis had never felt at home in the South ("a Slave State!" he exclaimed), and was eager to try one last time to make a life in the North. To his good fortune, Columbia College in New York was establishing a law school and increasing the size of its faculty at just the time of his arrival in the city. In 1857, Columbia appointed him Professor of History and Political Science.

The move to New York made the growing split between North and South intensely personal for the Lieber family. Oscar had lived virtually his whole life in South Carolina, and as tensions increased, he took the side of his home state. When Francis wrote to Oscar in 1860 to say that he expected to vote for Abraham Lincoln, the split in the family became irreconcilable. In March 1861, Francis learned that Oscar had enlisted in Hampton's Legion, an elite unit of the Confederate armed forces led by Francis's former student, the wealthy young South Carolina planter Wade Hampton. Hamilton and Norman would soon join the armed forces of the Union. "Behold in me," Francis wrote a friend, "a symbol of civil war."

Francis was no less vigorous in his support of the Union war effort for his family's split. Indeed, the sharpness of his break with Oscar may have had the opposite effect. As the spring of 1861 unfolded, Lieber concluded that the American Civil War would be one of the great conflicts in the history of civilization. To his wide circle of well-placed friends and correspondents, Lieber issued repeated calls to arms. He struck up new correspondence with members of Lincoln's cabinet such as Attorney General Edward Bates. In 1862, he began corresponding regularly with Secretary of War Edwin Stanton. His message to all was the same. "Strike, strike and strike again," he urged. He called on the Union "sledgehammer" to deliver "a death blow" to the rebels. "Blow upon Blow ought to be our motto," he wrote. "Hard, Harder, Hardest." To Attorney General Bates, Lieber urged that the Union "drive back the enemy." He took to adorning his letters with an arm-and-hammer sketch representing the appropriate posture of the Union toward its enemy.

Lieber delivered the same message to Lincoln himself in July when he traveled to the White House to give the president an honorary degree from Columbia College. The two men talked for a half hour, at the end of which Secretary of State Seward scolded the president for having failed to wear his afternoon coat. ("I intended to do so," Lincoln replied, "but the Dr. will excuse me, I was not aware it was so late.") Lieber and Lincoln ran into one another again several times that summer. "Mr. President," Lieber said on one occasion, "won't you give us at least a little fight?" The president's reaction was not encouraging. (He was "evidently pained at the idea," Lieber reported). Each time they met, Lieber worried that the president would not muster the courage to strike the South with sufficient force. Lincoln seemed to Lieber a gentle soul, "a peculiarly truthful simple hearted man."

LIEBER'S ENTHUSIASM FOR fierce measures (perhaps combined with Oscar's enlistment in the Confederate Army) focused his attention more closely than ever before on the moral limits of war. The subject was not entirely new to him. In his earlier writing on war, he had insisted that "war does not absolve us from all obligations to the enemy." Those obligations, he believed, were contained in the laws of civilized war. And in the summer of 1861, he began to study the subject with greater urgency. In the weeks after Bull Run, for example, Lieber wrote influential public letters in the *New York Times* urging prisoner exchanges with the Confederacy and arguing that they did not entail any recognition of the South as an independent country. In this, he assured his readers, he was "guided by no false sentimentality," nor by any sympathy for "the whining peace party," but only by the fierce conviction that "the enemy must be beaten."

But as Lieber focused on the customs and usages of war, his distinctive views about war led him to striking departures from the orthodoxy in the field. Lieber unveiled his thinking on the laws of war in a lecture course he initiated at Columbia College's new law school in the fall of 1861. Titled "The Laws and Usages of War," the lectures drew virtually every student in the school, as well as assorted observers and members of the press. Lieber estimated his audiences at around 100 people. He took them on an epic tour of international law. He reviewed customs for the treatment of prisoners, the distinction between soldiers and noncombatants, and the use of tactics such as poison and assassination. The lectures were long and rambling, but they held the attention of his listeners. For an entire term, from October 1861 into March 1862, Lieber's lectures were carried in the *New York Times* and reprinted in newspapers across the country.

According to their author, the lectures promised simply to restate the customs of civilized war as they had developed since the middle of the eighteenth century. But his uncharacteristic modesty masked a deeper ambition. Lieber aimed not so much to restate the law of war as to seize it back from the peace societies and their mawkish fellow travelers. As Lieber saw it, Enlightenment jurists such as the Swiss Vattel—"Father Namby Pamby," Lieber called him disdainfully—had led thinking about the laws of war badly astray. Their mistake, Lieber thought, was separating the regulation of conduct in war from the justice of war's aims. Vattel and his followers had developed an array of hard-and-fast rules to allow for a law of war that could regulate conduct in armed conflict without reference to the legitimacy of the war aims of either side.

Lieber jettisoned Vattelian orthodoxy in favor of an updated version of the very approach Vattel and his followers rejected. He would measure an act's permissibility by reference to its intended object. He would, in other words, relate means to ends in a way that took ends seriously.

Lieber began his lecture series with an arresting idea: the extended European world had suddenly entered a period of war, "a period of peculiar martial character," after a long era of peace. For decades, since 1815, observers had hoped that war might not visit Europe and its former colonies again. Peace societies had flourished. Men had dreamed of an International High Court that would deliver peaceful resolutions to the kinds of disputes that had once led to war. Following the philosopher Immanuel Kant, men had written of "perpetual peace," and though Lieber told his audience that Kant's essay on the topic was one of the philosopher's "least profound works," it was representative of what Lieber called "the Happiness Period" of human history, an age that aimed to minimize suffering and maximize human happiness. But Lieber insisted that "utilitarian happiness" was not the greatest good. "Freedom, right, truth, justice, real culture, purity, and humanity"—all these values "stand far higher" than happiness or wealth, he insisted, and sometimes they demanded the use of force in their defense. "Freedom," Lieber announced, "is a goddess who cannot afford to sheathe her sword forever."

The goddess of war seemed to have returned to the field with a vengeance. War had visited North America in the Mexican conflict of 1846. It split Europe into warring factions in the Crimea in 1854. It pitted Austria against France in northern Italy in 1859. Now it had occasioned civil war in the United States, and Lieber heard the rumble of war drums in Europe, too, as his native Prussia surged toward German unification. But by Lieber's lights, the grave new era of war held within it a new promise of redemption for Europe and America alike. The period of prolonged peace had "thrown us into a trifling pursuit of life." It had undermined the moral character of the European world and had "loosened many a moral bond." War would be "a grave school-master." It would teach Americans to be morally vigorous just as it had fostered the virtue of the founders.

War could accomplish these rigorous ends, Lieber believed, because properly understood it did not consist of lawless and undisciplined violence. War existed within a system of constraints that had developed over centuries in the European world, much as the common law had developed incrementally in England and the United States. The laws and usages of war thus comprised practices that had recommended themselves over time to the common sense of mankind. To be sure, these laws often functioned quite differently than the ordinary law of a particular nation. The laws of war, Lieber explained, were not "a rule of action, unconditionally prescribed by higher authority." After all, "there was no higher authority"—that was the very nature of relations between nations. It was what distinguished a dispute between countries from a dispute between individuals. But the absence of higher authority—the absence of a common judge—hardly meant that war was governed by "the law of mere force." That would be no law at all. To the contrary, what made the laws and usages of war significant was that they could not be violated without incurring "the general hostile opinion of mankind"—and without giving an enemy the right to retaliate in return.

B UT WHAT WERE the laws and usages of war? In his lectures at Columbia in the fall and winter of 1861–62, Lieber proposed a stark rule. The only question of law, he announced, was a simple one: Was the destruction "greater than necessary"?

Cruelty—inflicting pain for its own sake—was not permitted, because cruelty was the opposite of necessity. Cruelty consisted of the "unnecessary infliction of pain, pain for its own sake to satisfy the lust of revenge or a fiendish hatred." But the rule against cruelty left vast room for destruction and violence. The use of poisons, for example, was clearly forbidden, according to Vattel and his followers. Lieber conceded that there was "something fiendish" in their use. But it did not follow from this that the laws and customs of civilized war set poisons outside the pale. It might well be, Lieber observed, that there were very few situations in which poisons were necessary. But who was he to say that there were none? Where a weak nation was put to the task of preserving its very existence against a ruthless enemy, for example, and where that object could only be obtained "by poisoning wells and by no other means," Lieber could not see "why it would not be lawful to resort" to such a course of conduct, terrible though it would be.

In his lectures, Lieber allowed one important but narrow exception to the necessity principle: torture. Some kinds of pain counted as cruel even where the pain was inflicted for the sake of the war effort. "No doubt," Lieber said, "the whole world would condemn it as cruel, if pain were inflicted upon an enemy to extract an important secret—e.g., by application of torture." Torture was not allowed in civilized war, not even against savages. "Can we roast Indians," Lieber asked rhetorically, "though they may have roasted one of our own?"

Here then was a compelling but potentially ferocious framework for the laws of war. Outside of torture, virtually all destruction seemed permissible so long as it was necessary to advance a legitimate war effort. The law thus permitted the use of any weapon, including "those arms that do the quickest mischief in the widest range and in the surest manner." And it did so for a simple reason. As Lieber said more than once in the course of his lectures, short wars were more humane wars, and the way to ensure short wars was to fight them as fiercely as possible. The prospect of fierce wars might even prevent war from breaking out in the first place. It was thus critical that statesmen "not allow sentimentality to sway us in war," he warned. "The more earnestly and keenly wars are carried on, the better for humanity, for peace and civilization."

The idea seemed innocuous enough. But the notion that short and sharp wars were more humane represented a deeply subversive critique of the system of humanitarian limits in wartime. It meant that humanitarian limits might be not merely ineffective but pernicious, increasing war's horrors, not diminishing them. For centuries, unsentimental statesmen had articulated this very critique of the laws of war. Machiavelli had called for wars that were "short and strong" ("*corte e grosse*," he said). Frederick the Great advocated wars that were "short and lively" ("*kurz und vives*"). In the nineteenth century, international jurists sometimes despaired that nothing could be done to lessen war's calamities "but to make the calamity shorter at the cost of making it fiercer and more terrible." But if the sharp war thesis was correct, it called into question the very idea of humanitarian constraints in war.

T HE LAW OF WAR'S fiercest nineteenth-century critic was the Prussian military genius Carl von Clausewitz. Clausewitz served in the Prussian army in the wars of 1793 and 1794 and then again in the wars of Napoleon. After Prussia's defeat in 1806, he briefly joined the Russian army to continue the fight against the French. In the years after 1815 he served as director of the military school at Berlin.

Clausewitz argued that rules existed to govern the details of a campaign: for the "minutiae of service," things like "telling us how to set up a camp or leave it, how to construct entrenchments, etc." But rules could not tell men how to act in moments of extremity. Criticizing Baron de Jomini's system of arithmetic propositions for military strategy, Clausewitz insisted that there were "no rules for conducting a campaign or fighting a battle." The lawless condition of battle vitiated legal rules, too. In his book *Vom Kriege (On War)*, published posthumously in 1832, Clausewitz insisted that the "international law and custom" of warfare was barely perceptible; indeed, he dismissed it as "hardly worth mentioning." In the harsh world of war, Clausewitz warned his countrymen, it was simply foolish to dull one's sword "in the name of humanity." If we did such a thing, he stated bluntly, "sooner or later" an enemy would "come along with a sharp sword and hack off our arms."*

Historians have usually thought that Clausewitz's fierce views became influential in the United States 100 years after the Civil War, following publication of a new American translation of *On War* in 1943. Clausewitz's writings were not available in English at all until ten years after the Civil War, when an English edition was published in London. But Lieber knew the work of his fellow Prussian even before the publication of the German-language first edition of *Vom Kriege*, and Clausewitz's views had a powerful influence on his thinking as early as the late 1820s. Clausewitz famously said time and again in his writings that war was "the continuation of politics by different means." Lieber thus thought of war as continuous with peacetime politics, not (as Vattel and his followers had argued) a separate domain of social life (the "state of war") with a moral and legal logic of its own. Lieber understood war as a way of achieving political ends. The force brought by warring armies, he argued, was a species of the same coercion exercised all

---

*Clausewitz did feel that he needed to explain the relatively limited structure of eighteenth-century warfare in Europe before Napoleon. Wars "between civilized nations" in the eighteenth century, he conceded, seemed "far less cruel and destructive than wars between savages." But the reason was not the existence of so-called rules for legitimate warfare. Rather, as Clausewitz said with the cultural chauvinism characteristic to his age, it was because European nations used their intelligence more effectively than the savage and barbarian peoples in the rest of the world. Civilized states simply adopted "more effective ways of using force than the crude expression of instinct." In the same passage, Clausewitz also suggested that the explanation for limited wars in the eighteenth century lay in "the social conditions of the states themselves and in their relationships to one another." The laws and customs of war of which he was so dismissive were doubtless a part of those social conditions and those relationships, but Clausewitz seems not to have understood the point.

the time within countries by courts and the police. Clausewitz wrote that war was "an act of force to compel our enemy to do our will." Lieber recited Clausewitz's definition and agreed, writing that war was fought against an enemy "to compel him to peace at my will," and argued that so long as this was the goal, armies had "a right to use all means" suited to that end.

Yet as Lieber read him, Clausewitz did not endorse an abandonment of moral standards in wartime altogether. In war, Lieber told his students, "morality floats above the whole." Where Vattel and his followers had crafted a specialized body of moral norms peculiar to the condition of war, Lieber took Clausewitz to mean that the moral obligations of ordinary life extended to armed conflict. Killing was permitted in wartime, for example, but only when killing in war was justified according to ordinary morality, not because war permitted things that would otherwise have been unlawful. The key idea Lieber drew from Clausewitz was that to know whether a killing was justified, one had to know why it had occurred. Clausewitz thus offered an approach to thinking about the moral obligations of men in war that eschewed the quintessential strategy of the Enlightenment jurists. In Vattel's separate legal domain of war, legal constraints were indifferent to the moral significance of a soldier's cause. Clausewitz's theory, by contrast, asked the statesman, the general, and the soldier to take the objectives of their conduct into account at all times. Ends, in Lieber's view, could not be separated from means; to the contrary, they helped determine the scope and character of the conduct appropriate to the situation. For something so destructive as conduct in war, only weighty objectives would suffice as a justification. Even the weightiest ends, Lieber declared emphatically, did not justify means such as torture.

O F COURSE, means and ends were not mere abstractions for Lieber and his family. As Francis's law lectures wound down in February 1862, he and Matty followed every movement of their son Hamilton's 9th Illinois. With a mixture of pride and worry, they read the newspaper coverage of Ulysses S. Grant's move down the Tennessee and Cumberland rivers into the heartland of the South. They rejoiced at the Union victory at Fort Henry on February 6. They celebrated word of Fort Donelson's capture. But the news from the West soon brought bad tidings. Hamilton was among the wounded.

Guerrillas in Missouri

COUNTLESS FATHERS SEARCHED for wounded sons in the aftermath of Civil War battles. The Boston poet and physician Oliver Wendell Holmes sought out his wounded son, the future Supreme Court justice of the same name, not once but twice. In the elder Holmes's account, published in the *Atlantic Monthly* in late 1862 after the battle at Antietam, the train to Maryland was packed with fathers seeking sons. In a war in which medical care was not far advanced beyond what it had been 100 or 200 years before, parents wanted desperately to rescue their young men from Civil War hospitals full of the wounded and the dying.

Most parents would barely have known where to begin their search, and Francis Lieber was no exception. Administrative chaos reigned in the new mass armies of the Union. On the eve of the war, some 16,367 officers and enlisted men served in the U.S. Army. Such numbers could not even begin to match the scale of the Civil War. In July 1861, the Congress authorized an army of half a million volunteers. By the end of the war, more than 2 million men would serve in a Union uniform and 1 million more would fight in the Confederate States Army. The infrastructure for these modern armies had barely been imagined, let alone put into place. Union wounded at Fort Donelson, for example, went to at least half a dozen different places, with no centralized information source or tracking mechanism for keeping records on who went where. And so when Francis Lieber went on his frantic search for Hamilton, he could not find him. (Later that year, Holmes the father would travel in circles for days before finding his son.) Hamilton was not at Cincinnati, where Francis went first. He went next to St. Louis, where he was directed on to Mound City. After ten days of walking through Union hospitals and peering into ambulances, Francis at last found Hamilton recuperating in a makeshift Union hospital. "I knew war as [a] soldier, as a wounded man in the hospital, as an observing citizen," he told Sumner; but he had only now learned it as "a father searching for his wounded son."

FRANCIS LIEBER'S ANXIOUS search produced a fortuitous reunion. Francis had almost forgotten, but on one of his usual summer trips to the North in July and August of 1845, he had dined regularly at the U.S. Army installation on Governors Island in New York Harbor. The main topic of conversation had been Charles Sumner's controversial antiwar speech, which had been delivered only a few weeks before. Lieber's dinner-table denunciations of Sumner and the peace societies had powerfully impressed a lieutenant of engineers named Henry Halleck. Now, seventeen years later, Halleck was stationed in St. Louis commanding the Union Army's Department of the Missouri. It was Halleck who directed Lieber to Mound City and to his son Hamilton.

The old acquaintances quickly struck up a renewed correspondence, for Halleck found himself in need of Lieber's expertise. Halleck was an engineer trained in the orthodox West Point style. His views of war rested on the rational geometry and engineering axioms that dominated the Academy's antebellum curriculum, not on the rule-defying art of the Prussian Clausewitz. Clausewitz had emphasized the irreducibly contingent and probabilistic character of war. But Halleck had entered the war believing with Jomini and against Clausewitz that "war is not, as some seem to suppose, a mere game of chance." War, he had written, constituted "one of the most intricate of modern sciences." The general who understood how to apply its rules and principles, Halleck thought confidently, could "be morally certain of success."

On the very eve of the war, Halleck wrote a long book that adopted a similarly tidy view of the legal rules governing warfare. The book, titled *International Law; Or, Rules Regulating the Intercourse of States in Peace and War*, described a law of war that had proved capable of channeling war into fixed and durable configurations. In the laws of war at sea, he insisted, the law had "been rendered clear, definite, and stable." The laws of war on land, he thought, had also witnessed crisp moral triumphs. Statesmen and generals alike, Halleck affirmed confidently, were "bound by rules" that governed "the conduct of hostile forces."

Yet by early 1862, when Halleck was reunited with Lieber in St. Louis, the aging engineer's confidence in the laws of war had begun to waver. In Halleck's Missouri, the Civil War was veering rapidly away from the orderly warfare described in Jomini's theories and in Halleck's treatises. Indeed, after October 1861, when Major General Sterling Price and the pro-Confederate Missouri State Guard withdrew from the state, there hardly seemed to be an army to fight. Instead, bands of irregular soldiers and armed Confederate sympathizers vied with Union-allied Kansas jayhawkers and antislavery Missouri men in a bitter partisan conflict inside Union-controlled Missouri. Confederate fighters ambushed Union detachments. They struck in Sedalia and Warrensburg in the west of the state, where terrorist violence between proslavery bushwackers and free state jayhawkers had been going on ever since the savage violence of 1854 and 1855, when proslavery forces had battled abolitionists such as John Brown to decide whether neighboring Kansas would be a slave state or free. They struck in Springfield in the south of the state. They struck in Palmyra in the northeast. Union supply lines were often vulnerable to attack. But guerrilla violence aimed at defenseless civilian targets as well. Guerrillas engaged in indiscriminate violence against Union soldiers, prisoners, and civilians alike. In attacks by increasingly notorious guerrillas like Bloody Bill Anderson and William Quantrill, Union soldiers reported encountering grim evidence of mass executions and the mutilation of bodies.

As Union forces began to occupy substantial parts of the South, irregular warfare became more widespread. The influential southern magazine *De Bow's Review* had supported partisan-style warfare from the outset of the conflict, and now its editors urged that the South abandon "all fastidious notions of military etiquette" and expel the Union "by every means." Irregular bands sprang up in western Virginia and eastern Tennessee in the fall of 1861 and in the rest of Tennessee by February 1862. By April, they were appearing in and around Union-occupied New Orleans and in northern Louisiana and Arkansas. By the early summer, Union incursions into

Guerrillas such as the infamous William Quantrill harassed Union sympathizers in and around Missouri from 1861 onward. Here Harper's Weekly *depicts Quantrill's raid on Lawrence, Kansas, in 1863.*

northern Alabama and Mississippi occasioned the formation of irregular self-defense companies there too. Later in the summer, guerrilla units rose in eastern North Carolina in and around New Bern. Everywhere Union soldiers went, citizens who seemed loyal Unionists by day turned into Confederate irregulars by night.

In the spring of 1862, the leadership of the Confederacy decided to authorize and expand the irregular effort. In April, the Confederate Congress enacted the Partisan Ranger Act, which authorized Jefferson Davis to commission officers to form "bands of partisan rangers" who were to be in the service of the Confederacy, paid by the Confederacy, and subject to "the same regulations as other soldiers" in the Confederate armies. Similar calls for guerrilla units followed quickly in places like Arkansas and Missouri. Statesmen like Davis and General Robert E. Lee had been reluctant to adopt partisan warfare. Such men had been critical of guerrilla warfare in Mexico a little more than a decade before. But Union occupation of substantial parts of the South left them with little choice. Davis in particular hoped that putting the irregular bands of local defenders on an official footing would make such groups more effectively controllable from Richmond. But very soon such hopes proved unwarranted.

Southern expansion of the irregular war efforts produced new cycles of violence. Prominent southerners talked wildly of mounting irregular invasions of the North that would devastate civilian resources; Edmund Ruffin of Virginia urged that guerrillas "might lay waste to Philadelphia with fire and sword, or lay Cincinnati & even Chicago in ashes." And for a while, it looked as if Ruffin's terrible dream might come true. For virtually the entire month of July 1862, John Morgan's brigade raided north past Union lines into Kentucky, nearly reaching Cincinnati, and disrupting Union operations the whole way. The expansion of irregular forces also occasioned a sharp rise in indiscriminate violence. More cautious observers than Ruffin worried that Confederate guerrillas were turning out to be "robbers and jayhawkers" who competed with Union troops in "plundering, devouring and wasting the subsistence of loyal Southerners." Confederate brigadier general J. O. Shelby in Arkansas condemned the irregulars who served in his district as having "no organization, no concentration, no discipline, no law, no anything."

On the other side, Union soldiers in southern territory began to act as U.S. troops had in Mexico in 1847. Already in 1861, the proslavery *Missouri Republican* decried the "hurricane violence" of Union reprisals that had shed "the blood of friends and kindred" throughout the state. Halleck complained to Secretary of War Edwin Stanton about Kansas jayhawkers ("robbers,"

Halleck called them) who wore Union uniforms and received Union pay, but whose "principal occupation for the last six months seems to have been the stealing of negroes, the robbing of houses, and the burning of barns, grain, and forage." In northern Alabama, Union forces under Major General Ormsby M. Mitchel burned the town of Paint Rock in retaliation for guerrilla attacks on Union transport trains. That same month, May 1862, Colonel John Basil Turchin—a former Russian army officer who had served the czar in the Crimean War—allowed his troops to sack the town of Athens, Alabama, in retaliation for civilian participation in a Confederate cavalry attack. In September, William Tecumseh Sherman ordered the burning of Randolph, Tennessee, after guerrillas fired on an unarmed Union mail steamer there. When his regiment returned from torching the town, Sherman simply reported to his commander that Randolph was gone.

C AUGHT IN THE maelstrom of irregular warfare, Union commanders cast about desperately for solutions. As early as August 1861, Major General John C. Frémont (Halleck's predecessor in Missouri) declared martial law and announced that he would execute "all persons who shall be taken with arms in their hands" within Union lines. In December, Halleck ordered the same treatment for persons "not commissioned or enlisted" in the Confederate service; they would be tried as criminals, for it was a "well-established principle" that only those men "duly enrolled in the service of an acknowledged enemy" were entitled to prisoner of war status. "Insurgents and marauding, predatory, and guerrilla bands" were "not entitled to this exemption" from the criminal laws. Such men, by the laws of war, were "regarded as no more or less than murderers, robbers, and thieves," and nothing in their "military garb" or their assumed company name could "change the character of their offenses" or "exempt them from punishment."

Halleck's position in late 1861 and January 1862 drew on the orthodox view of who counted as a soldier. For more than a century, the law of who was entitled to fight in war had been simple: the duly authorized soldiers of sovereign states were entitled to go to war. The English jurist William Oke Manning stated the basic rule in 1839 when he wrote that legal violence in war was "only allowed" by those who were "expressly authorized" to act "by the sovereign power." The German Georg Friedrich von Martens had said the same thing a few decades earlier. The Swiss Vattel wrote that only "a commission from their sovereign" afforded men "such treatment as is given to prisoners taken in regular warfare." And on the eve of the Civil War,

Theodore Dwight Woolsey, the president of Yale College, said that the laws of war offered no protection to those who fought "without a sanction from their governments." Halleck's own book, *International Law*, adopted the same rule: "partizan and guerrilla troops" who fought without "commissions or enlistments," he wrote, were not entitled to the privileges of the laws of war; when they were "authorized and employed by the state," however, "they become a portion of its troops."

It was no wonder, then, that in the winter 1861–62, Halleck distinguished between those men who were "commissioned or enlisted" in the Confederate Army, on one hand, and self-organized guerrilla bands, on the other. But the official Confederate embrace of partisan rangers in the spring of 1862 revealed a potential flaw in the orthodox Enlightenment approach. For what the Confederacy had shown in the Partisan Ranger Act was that a belligerent could very easily extend commissions to irregulars and thus give them the status of soldiers deserving prisoner of war treatment. Moreover, a belligerent could do so without changing the behavior of the irregulars at all. Halleck's own book had suggested—indeed, it had stated clearly—that commission or enlistment was the key criterion. But now this view seemed impossibly naive. Merely issuing "commissions or licenses" to the bandits who terrorized the state, he now reasoned, ought not change their legal status. "You must be aware, general," he wrote reprovingly to his Confederate counterpart Sterling Price, "that no orders of yours can save from punishment spies, marauders, robbers, incendiaries, guerrilla bands, etc., who violate the laws of war." Halleck's conclusion was firm: "You cannot give immunity to crime."

Price replied that his men were "specially appointed" and instructed to act in accordance with "the laws of warfare." In Arkansas, Confederate general Thomas C. Hindman likewise insisted that official recognition transformed criminal guerrillas into legal soldiers. His irregulars, he told Union colonel Graham N. Fitch, were "recognized by me . . . as Confederate troops," and Hindman asserted "as indisputable" his right "to dispose and use those troops" as he saw fit. "We cannot be expected to allow our enemies to decide for us," complained another Confederate general later in the year, "whether we shall fight them in masses or individually, in uniform, without uniform, openly or from ambush."

The problem of the partisan rangers sprang up in western Virginia, too, where Governor John Letcher argued that all those "acting under the authority" of Virginia, "with commissions issued in pursuance of law and under the seal of the State," were entitled to protection as soldiers and prisoners of war. Confederate secretary of war George Randolph agreed and fiercely defended the partisan rangers against the accusation that they were not soldiers entitled to the protections afforded to soldiers. The stakes were very real. For if the Union were to execute men carrying Confederate commissions, the Confederacy would retaliate in kind against Union soldiers in Confederate custody.

E VEN AS THE controversy over guerrilla warfare was heating up, Matty and Francis Lieber received heartrending news from Virginia. In late June they learned that their oldest son, Oscar, had been killed while fighting for the South in the Battle of Williamsburg. "Civil war," Lieber wrote to his rediscovered friend Halleck, "has thus knocked *very* loudly at our door."

Personal tragedy notwithstanding, Lieber's importance in the Lincoln administration was growing. Behind the scenes in 1861 he had helped to organize the administration's defense of its suspensions of the writ of habeas corpus. Now, in the summer of 1862, President Lincoln and Secretary of War Stanton promoted Lieber's friend Halleck to general-in-chief of the Union armies. Halleck and Stanton began to call on Lieber to solicit his advice on some of the most difficult questions of the war effort.

As one of his very first acts as general-in-chief, Halleck asked Lieber to prepare a formal memorandum of the international laws of war governing the guerrilla controversy. Lieber threw himself into the task, and in a week's time, he sent Halleck a long essay entitled *Guerrilla Parties Considered with Reference to the Laws and Usages of War.* Halleck liked it. ("I highly approve," he told Lieber.) Before the month was over, the general-in-chief had ordered 5,000 copies for distribution in the Union armies. The document would help guide Union policy toward irregular fighters until the end of the war.

Halleck could be enthusiastic about *Guerrilla Parties* because Lieber's treatment neatly solved the problem of the commissioned irregular by reorganizing the law of combatants. In Mexico, Winfield Scott's councils of war had treated the soldier in a guerrilla unit as a special kind of criminal. Halleck and Lieber were now asking who was a soldier in the first place. And Lieber's answer went beyond the formal question of whether a band of fighters was commissioned by a legitimate belligerent. Instead, Lieber asked himself what were the working characteristics that made men soldiers. The regular soldier, Lieber decided, was defined by a number of different features. The soldier typically served in a regular army. He was usually paid and provisioned by that army, which eliminated the imperative to engage in pillage. His band was permanent (or at least durable) in its formation. His movements were dictated by a central command structure that enforced discipline over him and his comrades. He wore the garb of a soldier, or at least some badge of his status, in a way that distinguished him from the peaceful citizen. He followed the laws of war and took prisoners when his enemy surrendered.

For Lieber, the formal existence or absence of a commission from a state (or as he put it, whether a band of fighting men was "self-constituted") was relevant to, but not determinative of, soldier status. Echoing Halleck's letters to Price, Lieber wrote that it could not be "maintained in good faith" that an armed prowler or bushwacker would "be entitled to the protection of the law of war" simply because "his government or his chief has issued a proclamation" authorizing such violence. Instead, determining whether a fighter qualified as a soldier required careful consideration of the relevant criteria in light of the underlying goals of the laws of war: uniforms or badges that separated fighters from civilians; an organized command structure that could enforce discipline and the rules of combat; and the institutional capacity to take and keep prisoners.

Commentators would later criticize Lieber's guerrillas paper as verbose and rambling. There is something to the criticism, to be sure. Lieber was prone to long-windedness, and the paper (whose readership was made up of hard-pressed officers in the field) ran to 6,000 words. It provided lavish historical examples that ranged from the Greek Civil War to Napoleon's Peninsular Campaign, from the ancient world to the sixteenth-century Dutch revolt against the Spanish. It lingered on Lieber's beloved Prussian resistance to Napoleon and it reviewed at great length obscure European treatments of the laws of war. The paper, in short, engaged its topic as a philosophical problem as much as a military imperative.

But if Lieber's *Guerrilla Parties* paper was wordy, that was so in substantial part because it forged new ground. Lieber's new criteria were linked together by a common thread. Each of them substituted functional considerations for the formal question of whether a fighter had been commissioned by one of the warring sides. Clausewitz had described the formal customs of eighteenth-century war as an artifact of relations among the states of Europe. Now, in a new political context in which war was being fought outside the confines of nation-states, the simple structure of those customs no longer seemed adequate to commanders like Halleck. Lieber grasped that war had overflowed its eighteenth-century political constraints, and that in the sprawling and disorganized wars of the modern age, the laws of war would need reorganization.

The innovation Clausewitz inspired and Lieber made in August 1862 is still in our law today. We can see it in the Third Geneva Convention of 1949, which defines the soldier by reference to the considerations Lieber's essay first raised.* And it influenced the practice of Civil War commanders as well. Within weeks of its drafting, the approach Lieber adopted for Halleck made its way back to the western theater. In September 1862, when William Tecumseh Sherman denied that Confederate guerrillas were entitled to prisoner of war treatment, he cited the arguments that Lieber and Halleck had articulated a month earlier. "Whether the guerrillas or partisan rangers, without uniform, without organization except on paper, wandering about the country plundering friend and foe, firing on unarmed boats filled with women and children" were "entitled to the protection and amenities of civilized warfare," Sherman wrote drily to his Confederate counterpart Thomas Hindman, "is a question which I think you would settle very quickly in the abstract."

Even if Lieber's analysis of the irregular warfare problem was influential, it was hardly definitive. It left wide discretion in the hands of officers in the field. One of the most striking features of Union treatment of guerrilla fighters for the rest of the war was its variability from region to region and command to command. Some Union soldiers and statesmen, from line infantrymen to officials in the War Department and right up to the attorney general of the United States, favored summary field executions for guerrillas—executions that left precious little time for close inquiry into who qualified as a soldier and who did not. Lieber did not reject such executions out of hand. ("The most disciplined soldiers," he wrote, "will execute on the spot an armed and murderous prowler found where he could have no business as a peaceful citizen.") But he was cautious in endorsing a harsh policy of field executions for fear that doing so risked a vicious spiral of retaliation. Other Union officers adopted military commissions on the model of General Winfield Scott's in Mexico. And some officers even worked to find ways to treat guerrillas as prisoners of war when the situation so warranted.

Lieber's great success was to establish a new functional basis for Union treatment of Confederate irregulars, one that the Confederacy came to accept, if only grudgingly. Lieber's approach treated many of the partisan

---

*Article 4 of the Third Geneva Convention of 1949 extends prisoner of war status to "members of the armed forces of a Party to the conflict," as well as to members of militias or other volunteer groups so long as they can show that they operate under a responsible command; they have a "fixed distinctive sign recognizable at a distance"; they "carry[] arms openly"; and they "conduct[] their operations in accordance with the laws and customs of war.

rangers commissioned under the April 1862 Confederate legislation as legitimate soldiers, but distinguished those who fought without outward badges of identification, without organized command structures, or without adherence to the basic laws of war.

Abraham Lincoln shared Lieber's tough humanitarianism. He tacitly approved the policy of death sentences for guerrillas, a policy that was discussed in the cabinet. Yet time and again he commuted such sentences to imprisonment at hard labor for the duration of the war. Aggressive soldiers sometimes arranged for summary executions precisely to avoid the lengthy delays that inevitably accompanied Lincoln's formal military commissions process.

I N FRANCIS LIEBER'S study on 34th Street in New York (just steps from where the Empire State Building now stands), a tablet on the mantelpiece displayed the names of every soldier who had fought at Fort Donelson in his son Hamilton's 9th Illinois. With the 9th Illinois looking down on him, Lieber's message to Halleck and Sumner and Lincoln—indeed, to virtually anyone who would listen—never varied. Lieber encouraged Lincoln and his administration to wage what Clausewitz had described as "war in earnest." Such a war eschewed many of the constraints of limited eighteenth-century warfare, for too often those constraints seemed to Lieber to have little application to the great struggle of North and South for the future of civilization in North America. War, as Lieber saw it, was no trifling matter to be constrained by mawkish social conventions. It was the forward motion of civilization. "Blood," he wrote Halleck, "is occasionally the rich dew of history."

What made the Civil War an epochal event in Western history, according to Lieber, was what he saw as its underlying cause. The war pitted a free people against slavery. As summer turned into fall in 1862, slavery took center stage in the war. Lincoln and Stanton and Halleck would soon require answers to the new set of problems that Emancipation raised.

Chapter 7

Act of Justice

❧

The extraordinary spectacle is presented to the contemplation of civilized man in this boasted nineteenth century of the Christian world, of a nation claiming to be civilized . . . inaugurating deliberately servile war by stimulating the half-civilized African to raise his hand against his master and benefactor. . . .

> —Brigadier General Daniel Ruggles, Confederate States Army, 1862

ABRAHAM LINCOLN TRIED his best to avoid the question of whether he could free the South's slaves. But when the war forced his hand, the first answer Lincoln gave was that he could not.

It was Major General John C. Frémont, the handsome but politically clumsy commander of the Western Department, who pushed the slave question onto Lincoln's agenda. Born in 1813 as the illegitimate son of a planter's wife and her French émigré dance teacher and lover, Frémont had risen by some combination of good luck, good looks, and personal charm to become an officer in the U.S. Army Corps of Topographic Engineers, surveying the trans-Mississippi West. In 1841, he had eloped with Jessie Benton, the seventeen-year-old daughter of powerful Missouri senator Thomas Hart Benton. When he won over her father as well, he made himself part of one of the country's most influential political families. For the next decade, Frémont led widely publicized exploring expeditions into the Oregon country and California. When gold was discovered on lands he had acquired near what is now Yosemite National Park, Frémont became a wealthy man. Several years later, his burgeoning fame won him the fledgling Republican Party's 1856 nomination for president. And in July 1861, his political clout—and especially his influence in the critical border states—led Lincoln to appoint him commander of the Western Department, headquartered in Missouri.

The problem was that Frémont's fame and political connections far outstripped his competence. He arrived in St. Louis at the beginning of Missouri's bitter guerrilla war. Frustrated by anonymous attacks on trains and Union soldiers, and badly out of his depth, Frémont issued a hastily drafted, ill-considered, and unauthorized declaration of martial law. The declaration, dated August 30, 1861, ordered the execution of armed Confederates found behind Union lines. It also confiscated the property of all persons in the state of Missouri who were in arms against the United States. To this Frémont added the most controversial provision of all: "Their slaves, if any they have, are hereby declared free."

Frémont's emancipation declaration thrilled abolitionists, but it left moderate Lincoln supporters aghast and southerners spluttering. Lincoln had chosen Frémont in order to shore up Union loyalties in the border states. The general's rash declaration risked alienating the very constituency he had been appointed to reassure. Joseph Holt, the former secretary of war during President James Buchanan's crisis-filled final weeks in office, warned Lincoln that Frémont's order was inspiring outright terror in the loyal slaveholding states. As protests from Kentucky and Missouri poured in, Lincoln concluded that he had no choice but to countermand the order. Writing to Frémont, the president warned that "liberating [the] slaves of traitorous owners" threatened to "alarm our Southern Union friends, and turn them against us." Such a policy might cause Kentucky to leave the Union. To lose Kentucky, Lincoln believed, would be "nearly the same as to lose the whole game."

Even if Lincoln had thought it prudent to emancipate slaves in Missouri, he concluded that the customs and usages of warfare prevented him from doing so. It would be one thing, he reasoned, for a military commander to seize property and hold it "as long as the necessity lasts." Such a seizure would be "within military law, because within military necessity." But to appropriate property permanently was another thing altogether. To say, for example, that a farm "shall no longer belong to the owner, or his heirs forever," even after the farm was "no longer needed for military purposes," was to make a political pronouncement, not a military one. The same held true for slaves. "If the General needs them," Lincoln explained to his Illinois friend Orville Browning (now serving as a U.S. senator), "he can seize them, and use them; but when the need is past, it is not for him to fix their permanent future condition."

In overruling Frémont, Lincoln carried on a tradition that ran back to the founders, back all the way to Lord Dunmore's slave emancipation decree in 1775. American statesmen had proclaimed time and again that the laws of war protected slavery from war's ravages. Civilized warfare, the United States had insisted, prohibited acts that might incite slaves into a war of servile insurrection and indiscriminate violence.

That Lincoln walked in the footsteps of his predecessors in September 1861 was unsurprising. What was remarkable was that in less than a year he would change his mind.

Worse Than Savages

EVER SINCE Thomas Jefferson's Virginia Constitution of 1776 indicted the king for causing "negroes to rise in arms" against the colonists, emancipations had been closely linked in the minds of white Americans to violence that defied the civilized constraints of modern war.

For one thing, slaves were private property, and as General-in-Chief Henry Halleck's 1861 book on international law explained, "private property on land is now, as a general rule of war, exempt from seizure or confiscation." Chief Justice Roger Taney had endorsed the same idea when he was attorney general of the United States in 1833, as did the late Henry Wheaton, whose *Elements of International Law* was still a leading authority on the laws of war. According to the editors of the widely respected Massachusetts-based *Monthly Law Reporter*, the rule had been asserted so often by the State Department that it could not be abandoned now without great embarrassment. "The just fame which the United States have acquired in their efforts to soften and ameliorate the code of war," the editors wrote, "forbids that they should seek to exercise those rights, the legality of which they have steadily denied."

Slaves, moreover, were a peculiar kind of private property. As the Georgia lawyer Thomas Cobb had put it before the war, slaves had "a double character," at once property and person, and in wartime their personhood seemed to many to create a grave humanitarian danger. Wartime emancipations might let loose unimaginable waves of violence. Slave uprisings in the midst of civil war threatened to produce atrocities and destruction enough to set the South back decades, perhaps centuries. The region might be left a dismaying ruin, with rapes and murders from the Atlantic to the Mississippi.

History provided terrifying examples. The editors of the *North American Review* offered their readers lurid descriptions of the servile wars of antiquity ("the constant terrors" of ancient Rome). More recent episodes lay close at hand, too. In 1791 in the French colony of Saint-Domingue in the Caribbean, slaves had massacred their masters and burned plantations at the beginning of what became the Haitian Revolution. A decade later, as Napoleon tried to wrest control of the island away from the revolutionary leaders Toussaint L'Ouverture and Jean-Jacques Dessalines, both sides fought wars of racial extermination, executing prisoners and moving across the countryside in waves of terrifying destruction that left much of the once wealthy island a smoking hulk. Even nearer to home, domestic slave revolts such as Nat Turner's rebellion in Virginia in 1831 provided fresh reminders that under the right conditions, slavery's suppressed war could quickly erupt into a violence that no laws of warfare could hope to contain.

The South's military vulnerability to slave rebellion had become conventional wisdom in the years leading up to the war. In 1856, while trying to block the Treaty of Paris's prohibition on privateering, the American diplomat Alexander Dallas had warned that without privateers, European navies would be able to land at any "point of our immense coast" and from there touch off a "servile insurrection." British military men had long boasted that, with or without privateers, attacking the American South would be like striking a spark into a tinderbox. Indeed, as tensions mounted between North and South, many in the North argued that a slave society such as the South could never fight a war in earnest. As one northerner put it in casual conversation with a southern tourist on a Hudson River steamboat, "You cannot fight! Your worst enemy is in your midst. Let us but sound the tocsin of war and your slaves will rise! Why, you will have murder and cutting of throats in every house."

The most radical abolitionists in the North advocated precisely such an uprising. Before war broke out, an abolitionist pamphleteer from Massachusetts named Lysander Spooner called for citizen associations to raise money and arms for a "private war" of abolitionists and slaves against the master class of the South. Spooner stopped circulating his pamphlet at the request of John Brown, a veteran of antislavery violence in Kansas who worried that Spooner's efforts would hinder the raid he himself was planning. In 1859, Brown led precisely the kind of raid Spooner had proposed when Brown tried unsuccessfully to start a slave uprising at Harper's Ferry, Virginia. Even moderates in the North thought they might have to choose between disunion and a slave uprising as the war approached. Harvard law professor Joel Parker said that he, for one, would rather risk the "consequences attendant on a servile insurrection" than allow the United States to fall apart.

On the eve of the war, talk of slave uprisings reached a fever pitch. Outgoing president James Buchanan blamed abolitionists for encouraging "servile insurrections." South Carolina listed northern incitement of slave rebellion as a ground for secession. Thomas J. Jackson of Virginia (known to history as "Stonewall" Jackson for his courage at the First Battle of Bull Run) accused the North of conspiring to excite slaves to a "servile insurrection in which our families will be murdered without quarter or mercy." In Charleston, women of the planter elite such as Mary Boykin Chesnut whispered to one another about the slave uprising that would surely come once war began.

As state after state seceded, rumors of abolitionist and slave conspiracies raced across the South. Stories of secret caches of gunpowder circulated in Virginia. Suspicious arson in Texas produced near hysteria and led to the execution of fifty men, most of them black slaves, at the hand of vigilante mobs and the state's home guard. Louisiana planters got wind of a slave conspiracy planned for March 4, the day of Lincoln's inauguration. Slaveowners in Tippah County, Mississippi, talked of "an insurrection of the black population" and cited attempts to poison masters and burn their homes in the night. In May, fear of uprisings washed across the countryside near Huntsville, Alabama. By July, rumors flew around upcountry North Carolina that slaves were rising against their masters and that "whole families" had been "brutally butchered at midnight." Indeed, for the first half of the year letters poured into the offices of state governors around the South warning of supposed insurrections.

Virtually nothing appeared in the newspapers, lest the slaves themselves learn about the suddenly improved prospects for uprisings. In the War of 1812, newspapers in the South had manufactured stories of British officers selling Virginia slaves into the West Indies in order to discourage slaves from running off to British lines. Now papers like the *Mobile Register* made up outlandish stories about horrific northern plans to abolish slavery by mass murder of the South's 4 million slaves. The story was so implausible the author could barely muster the energy to see it through. The master class, he concluded weakly, would "in this, as in all other instances" be the slaves' "protectors and saviours."

*　*　*

Fear of a slave uprising shaped the conduct of both southern and northern armies in the early months of the war. Southern state governors declined to hand over confiscated federal weapons to Confederate authorities out of fear that the arms would be needed for local defense against slave rebellions. Local reluctance to turn over weapons to Richmond officials kept as many as 200,000 Confederate troops out of the field in the first year of the war.

Union commanders made suppressing slave insurrections one of their first priorities as well. Along the Mason-Dixon line, the aged and doddering Major General Robert Patterson, a veteran of the War of 1812, instructed soldiers in the Department of Pennsylvania that it was their duty to "suppress servile insurrection." Brevet Major General George Cadwalader of Philadelphia issued the same orders. So did the commander of Union forces in western Virginia. And when Brigadier General Benjamin Butler of the Massachusetts militia heard rumors of slave insurrection in Maryland in April, he offered the assistance of his Massachusetts forces to Maryland governor Thomas Holliday Hicks.

Historians usually describe Butler as the man who put the Union on the path to emancipation. In late May, when three fugitive slaves named Frank Baker, Shepard Mallory, and James Townsend rowed four miles across the mouth of the James River to Butler's command at Fort Monroe, Butler refused to hand them over to the Virginia officer who came under a flag of truce to collect them. The three slaves had been working to build a battery opposite the Union position, and Butler decided that their usefulness in the southern war effort made them "contraband of war." The term was an ill-fitting one. Its technical use was to describe weapons and other kinds of property that could be seized in warfare at sea, even though belonging to a neutral owner or shipped on a neutral vessel. The black abolitionist Frederick Douglass said the term was better suited to pistols than to people. Nonetheless, Butler had hit on a way to finesse the Union treatment of fugitive slaves, and during the first year of the war the term "contraband" quickly took on vast significance as slaves gathered at Union encampments all around the edges of the South.

Yet focusing only on the contraband episode mischaracterizes Butler and ignores a problem that loomed as large as fugitive slaves in the opening weeks of the war. Butler was no abolitionist, at least not at the beginning of the war. In the election of 1860, he had been a lonely northern supporter of Jefferson Davis for the presidency. In 1862, at New Orleans, he would turn slaves away from Union lines, a decision that prompted the Congress to enact legislation barring Union forces from doing so. When Butler offered to suppress slave insurrections for Governor Hicks in April 1861 (a full month before he received the first contrabands at Fort Monroe), he expressed a keenly felt fear that the Union Army's appearance in the South would trigger a slave rebellion.

Butler's position on slave uprisings produced instant controversy. Angry abolitionists across the North argued that to relieve slaveowners of this risk was to do their dirty work for them. Governor John Andrew of Massachusetts protested to Butler that the South's vulnerability to slave insurrection was not the Union's problem, but "one of the inherent weaknesses of the enemy." Butler's reply put in sharp focus what was fast becoming a central humanitarian question in the first months of the war. "In what manner," he asked rhetorically, "shall we take advantage" of the South's weakness as a slave society? Should the Union, Butler demanded, allow the slave population "to rise upon the defenseless women and children of the country, carrying rapine, arson and murder?" In Butler's view, a servile insurrection in the United States would have "all the horrors" of Haiti, only "a million times magnified." Once the slaves had "tasted blood," Butler warned, they might "turn the very arms we put in their hands against ourselves, as a part of the oppressing white race." The founding fathers, Butler reminded Governor Andrew, had complained bitterly when the British armed "the red man with the tomahawk and the scalping knife against the women and children of the colonies." Surely the Union could not now justify itself "in letting loose four millions of worse than savages upon the homes and hearths of the South." In the Revolution, the British had been willing to use "all the means which God and nature" gave them "to subjugate the colonies." But the United States could do no such thing, at least not if the conflict was to consist of "honorable warfare."

L ONG-STANDING IDEAS ABOUT honorable warfare exerted powerful influence on Union policy toward slavery in the first year of the war. But already some urged Lincoln to move toward emancipation. And when they did, they ran headlong into the well-established American position protecting slavery in wartime.

A current of dissent on the slavery question ran through American history from the founding of the republic right up to the Civil War, but it was plagued by an embarrassing ancestry. For the clearest statement of the abolitionist view of slavery in wartime had come not from an American but from the commander of British forces in North America at the close of the Revolution. In 1783, Sir Guy Carleton had issued a "Précis Relative to Negroes in America," contending that slaves crossing into British lines during the Revolution were thereby made free.

In the decades since Carleton, John Quincy Adams had offered extensive and compelling arguments on the same point. But Adams's arguments were almost as compromised as Carleton's were awkward. For a decade and a half after the War of 1812, Adams had championed the proslaveholder argument on the status of slaves in wartime in his capacity as diplomat, as secretary of state, and finally as president. Indeed, no one had done more to associate the United States with the view that civilized nations sheltered slavery from war's destruction.

In the second half of his career, as a senior statesman in the House of Representatives, Adams rediscovered his antislavery commitments and reversed course. Contesting the so-called gag rule barring antislavery petitions on the floor of Congress, Adams argued that the federal government *did* have a power over slavery—the war power. By the laws of war, Adams said in Congress in 1842, the "laws and municipal institutions" of the territory being fought over were "swept by the board." In their place stood the laws of war, which Adams said gave armies awesome powers, including the power to emancipate slaves. How else could the emancipations in revolutionary South America be explained? Indeed, could it possibly be the case, Adams asked his colleagues in the House of Representatives, that the federal government possessed no authority to intervene if "servile war" broke out in the South? With astonishing foresight, Adams told his colleagues that it was "in the very nature of things" that the "Southern and Southwestern States" would one day "be the Flanders of these complicated wars, the battle field upon which the last great conflict must be fought between slavery and emancipation."

Building on Adams's unorthodox late-career account, antislavery men in 1861 and 1862 argued that, properly understood, the laws of war permitted the emancipation of enemy slaves. Writing to Lincoln shortly after the Frémont debacle, Senator Orville Browning of Illinois insisted that Frémont's proclamation "was fully warranted by the laws of war." In Browning's view, contrary to the spirit of the American authorities on the question, private property was "subject, by the law of nations, to be taken, and confiscated, and disposed of absolutely and forever" in wartime. If a belligerent could "turn loose horses," Browning asked Lincoln, "why may he not negroes?"

Charles Sumner pressed the case most strongly. As the powerful chair of the Senate Foreign Relations Committee, and as a confidant of Lincoln in the early months of the war, Sumner encouraged the president from the day Fort Sumter was shelled in April 1861 to make use of the war power to emancipate slaves. After the military debacle at Bull Run in July, Sumner became convinced that emancipation was imperative. In a long and intense conversation that went late into the night, he tried unsuccessfully to persuade Lincoln to exercise the war power authority to free the South's slaves. In September, after Lincoln had reversed Frémont's emancipation order, Sumner wrote his rediscovered friend Francis Lieber to complain that Lincoln had abandoned what Sumner thought to be the most viable path to emancipation. And once Lincoln seemed to have rejected the war power case for emancipation, Sumner took his argument to the public. The laws of war, he declared in an October 1861 speech before the annual convention of the Massachusetts Republican Party, knew no master but necessity. If necessity so warranted (and Sumner contended it did), armies could emancipate an enemy's slaves.

Sumner's speech called forth fierce opposition. A Pennsylvania newspaper wrote scathingly that Sumner had endorsed a "horrid policy of unloosing the bonds of four million slaves, and setting them against the Caucasian race,—to murder, pillage, and destroy, without stint, until their barbarous appetites may be appeased."

But if Sumner's controversial October address sparked a firestorm of criticism, it generated a groundswell of support as well. The editors of the *New York Journal of Commerce* opined that "the slave property of rebels is unquestionably the subject of confiscation as much as their horses or their cotton." *Harper's Weekly* reached a conclusion that would have been startling a few months before: "nothing is truer than that emancipation may become an incident of the war." Even the moderate *Christian Intelligencer*, the official journal of the American Reformed Church, decided that it was time to "let slavery feel the war." By the spring of 1862, a Harvard Law School graduate named William Whiting (soon to be appointed as the lawyer for the War Department) prepared a long pamphlet defending a broad war power of the president to emancipate enemy slaves in wartime. Whiting later exaggerated his own importance when he claimed that his essay ran through forty-three separate printings. But the pamphlet was distributed widely nonetheless, coming out in ten editions by 1864.

Some in the North also began to push back against the idea that emancipation would inevitably lead to the horrors of servile insurrection. Nathaniel Eggleston, a congregational pastor in Connecticut, complained that every mention of emancipation was met with the frantic claim that abolition would be "like the letting loose of so many wild beasts to devastate and devour." Sumner argued that only emancipation could save the South from the fate it feared most. Without the salutary influence of the armies of the North, Sumner predicted "wild and lawless" slave insurrections. "If Liberty does not descend from the tranquil heights of power," he warned, "it will rise in blood." Others such as Henry Ward Beecher of Brooklyn, the North's most influential pastor, argued that if a slave uprising occurred it would be the result of the slave system itself, not the product of Union policy. "Servile insurrections and war," he said, "are just as certain, as it seems to me, as explosions are, where fire comes to gunpowder." His sister Harriet Beecher Stowe, the author of *Uncle Tom's Cabin*, agreed: "What are these madmen now doing," she asked of the South's secessionists, "as they sit on their powder magazine and fire hot shot to right and left?"

And yet for all this, the memory of Haiti and the threat of indiscriminate bloodshed prompted continued caution. "Experiments of emancipation by martial law," warned Charles Francis Adams, Jr., would produce "terror and confusion" across the South. "Can a torch be thrust into a magazine," he asked, "without an explosion?—if it can, the powder is worthless. Will two centuries of grinding oppression produce no spirit of revenge? If it does not, then indeed is the African unfit to be a freeman." Emancipation would "force millions of irresponsible barbarians into society" where they would wreak a "just vengeance for their own wrongs." It would, Adams thought, create "convulsions before which humanity must stand aghast!"

L INCOLN WAS NO STRANGER to controversies over slaves in wartime. He had been almost twenty years old in 1828 when John Quincy Adams distributed the last compensation funds to American slaveholders whose slaves had been carried off by the British in the War of 1812. Two decades later, in 1849, as a member of the Thirtieth Congress, Lincoln debated whether the United States was obliged to compensate the descendants of a slaveowner whose slave had been hired by the U.S. Army as a guide and then escaped to freedom with the Seminoles during the Second Seminole War. Lincoln cast a losing vote to deny compensation; along with most northern congressmen, he seems to have objected to giving slavery protected status under the federal Constitution. The southern legislators who won the vote had turned the debate into a referendum on the basic standards of civilized conduct in wartime. "Every civilized nation on earth," they insisted, compensated property owners for property destroyed in wartime, including slave property.

Once the Civil War began, Lincoln heard almost constantly about the risk of slave insurrection. Letters warning of the risk of uprisings poured in from the day of his election forward. In the critical days of April, Attorney General Bates warned Lincoln repeatedly that armed conflict between North and South would "bring on a servile war, the horrors of which need not be dwelt upon." (Bates advised the president to abandon Fort Sumter in order to avert the danger.) And as word spread of Frémont's emancipation decree in September, loyal Unionists in the border states turned once again to the familiar theme. "All of us who live in the slave states," Lincoln's friend the Kentucky slaveowner Joshua Speed wrote to the president, "have great fear of insurrection." If "such a proclamation" were read by the slaves, Speed complained, would it not "incline them to assert their freedom"?

Lincoln tried to dampen emancipation enthusiasm as best he could. He quietly approved Butler's narrow "contraband" policy at Fort Monroe in May 1861. But he publicly rebuked Frémont in September. And when his beleaguered first secretary of war, Simon Cameron, endorsed arming slaves in an early draft of his annual report in December 1861 (a draft that was quickly leaked to the press), Lincoln removed him and unceremoniously shipped him to Russia as America's minister to the czar.

Lincoln knew well that emancipation and indiscriminate violence were closely connected to one another in the minds of white Americans. Indeed, the risk that fighting might lead to race war in the South seems to have worried him a great deal. For one thing, predictions of atrocity-filled slave uprisings turned on estimations of what kind of people the slaves were, and as the historian Eric Foner has recently emphasized, Lincoln had very little contact with blacks before becoming president. One of his few interactions had come when a group of black men assaulted him while he was shipping farm goods down the Mississippi. "Seven negroes," he later remembered, had tried to "kill and rob" him, but he and his partner managed to drive them from the vessel. That was 1831. Now, thirty years later, Lincoln found himself wondering whether unloosing the bonds of slavery would reproduce the kind of violence he had experienced then, only on a massive scale and in all likelihood with much less happy results.

Yet as the months wore on, Lincoln quietly shifted his ground on emancipation. In May 1862, Major General David Hunter repeated Frémont's premature emancipation decree, this time in the Department of the South, which consisted of South Carolina, Georgia, and Florida. Declaring martial law as a matter of "military necessity," Hunter followed Guy Carleton's 1783 reasoning and announced that "slavery and martial law in a free country" were "entirely incompatible." All persons "heretofore held as slaves" in the three states under his command, he declared, were "forever free." Hunter's order was even more ambitious than Frémont's. Frémont's order had applied only to the slaves of those who took up arms against the United States. Hunter's emancipation order contained no such limit. It purported to free the slaves in three southern states with a single blow. But where Lincoln had reversed Frémont's order on the ground that neither he nor Frémont could free slaves under the laws of war, now he countermanded Hunter's order because it claimed to make decisions that were the president's alone to make. "Whether at any time, in any case, it shall have become a necessity indispensable to the maintenance of the government, to exercise such supposed power," Lincoln explained, "are questions which, under my responsibility, I reserve to myself."

The implication was clear: emancipation was permissible if necessary, and Lincoln himself would decide when the necessity had arrived. But that was not all. For if emancipation came, the president added, it mattered how it came. "Rending or wrecking" the social life of the South would not do. If done right, Lincoln said, emancipation would arrive as "gently as the dews of heaven."

The Highest Principles Known to Christian Civilization

HEAVEN WAS FAR from Lincoln's mind as he reviewed the military situation in the early summer of 1862. The Union war effort in the East was badly stalled.

In March, Major General George B. McClellan had taken the Army of the Potomac—some 100,000 strong—down the Chesapeake aboard a flotilla of 500 vessels and landed sixty-five miles southeast of Richmond on the peninsula between the Rappahannock and the James rivers. McClellan's plan was to skirt the defenses of General Joseph E. Johnston's Confederate Army of Northern Virginia by entering the Confederate capital through the back gate. But the campaign had gone badly from the start. At Yorktown, where Washington had trapped Cornwallis and sealed an American victory in the War of Independence eighty years before, McClellan was fooled by the theatrical parading of Confederate brigadier general John B. Magruder into badly overestimating the strength of the Confederate forces. A mere

13,000 Confederate soldiers held off McClellan's army for a month while Johnston repositioned his forces to block McClellan's advance.

Without the element of surprise, McClellan inched toward Richmond for the next two months, wasting precious political support with each passing day. "I have never written you, or spoken to you, in greater kindness of feeling than now," Lincoln wrote him in early April. *"But you must act."* On the last day of May, McClellan won an ugly victory at Seven Pines that left his army on the verge of the Southern capital. "Our left is now within four miles of Richmond," he wrote Secretary of War Stanton, "I only wait for the river to fall to cross . . . & make a general attack." But the Union commander lost his nerve. June was nearly over when the fight for Richmond began again in earnest. And when it did, in a series of engagements known as the Seven Days' Battles, McClellan failed utterly to seize the advantages his superior forces afforded. After an artillery barrage that left the Army of Northern Virginia in disarray, McClellan unaccountably retreated to Harrison's Landing on the James River to regroup. His officers were stunned. Brigadier General Philip Kearny fumed that McClellan was either a coward or a traitor. "We ought instead of retreating to follow up the enemy and take Richmond," he argued. As to tactics, Kearny was probably right. But he was overruled. The Peninsula Campaign ground to a halt.

McClellan's problem was that he loved the aesthetics of battle, but could not abide its harrowing reality. This had profound effects on the way he fought. At West Point, where he had graduated second in his class, McClellan learned to think of warfare as a kind of chess match, to be played by professionals in bloodless and honorable competition. His proudest moments were those when "by pure military skill," as he put it, he won apparent victory with a "trifling" loss of life.

But bloodless triumphs such as the month-long siege at Yorktown (one of his two "brightest chapters," McClellan called it, alongside his role at Bull Run) were Pyrrhic victories if they produced weeks of delay and allowed the escape of enemy armies in the process. After his first major engagement on the peninsula, McClellan wrote to his wife that he was already "tired of the sickening sight of the battlefield, with its mangled corpses and poor suffering wounded." Every casualty haunted him, he told her. Such affections endeared him to his soldiers. But they made him a poor general.

Talk of ending slavery was especially aggravating to McClellan. The commander of the Army of the Potomac shared the engrained racism of most of his colleagues in the Union officer corps, though he expressed it with distinctively ugly force. "I confess," he wrote shortly after the war, "to a preju-

Alfred Waud's sketch of George McClellan's headquarters during religious services on a Sunday in July 1862. The Union commander espoused a civilized and Christian model of warfare.

dice in favor of my own race, & can't learn to like the odor of either Billy goats or niggers."

Emancipation, McClellan believed, would produce a bloody wave of indiscriminate racial violence. In his first command, McClellan had gone out of his way to assure the whites of western Virginia that he would use "an iron hand" to "crush any attempt" at slave insurrection. In the summer of 1861 he warned Charles Sumner that "sudden and general emancipation" would require precautions "to guard against" the "four and a half millions of uneducated slaves" that such a policy would set loose upon the nation. When McClellan ran for president against Lincoln in 1864, the Ohio abolitionist congressman Gerrit Smith reminded voters that it was McClellan "who assured the slaveholders that he would guard their homes, their wives and children from servile insurrection." In doing so, Smith observed pointedly, McClellan had left the white men of the South free to swell the armies of the rebellion.

ON JULY 8, 1862, Lincoln traveled to Harrison's Landing to confer with his cautious general. McClellan greeted the president with a carefully prepared statement on the basic standards of civilized warfare. At the letter's heart lay the problem of slavery. The conflict, McClellan wrote, "should

be conducted upon the highest principles known to Christian Civilization." The war "should not be a war looking to the subjugation" of a people,
not "at all a war upon population," but exclusively a war "against armed
forces and political organizations." Most important, "neither confiscation
of property" nor the "forcible abolition of slavery should be contemplated
for a moment."

McClellan had evidently paid attention to his law of war training at
West Point (meager though it was). His letter was a near-perfect restatement of the American establishment orthodoxy on the laws of war. He presented a vision of war without passions, war that left private citizens almost
completely untouched. "All private property and unarmed persons should
be strictly protected," he told the president, "subject only to the necessities
of military operations." In the event private property had to be taken for
military use, compensation was required. "Pillage and waste" by Union soldiers "should be treated as high crimes"; unnecessary trespasses were to be
"sternly prohibited," and any "offensive demeanor by the military towards
citizens" was to be "promptly rebuked." McClellan was even willing to concede that limited and targeted emancipations might be warranted "upon
grounds of military necessity," though only with compensation to the owners. But any "declaration of radical views" on slavery would "rapidly disintegrate our present armies" and undo the nation's long-standing attachment
to civilized war.

McClellan's letter had a powerful effect on Lincoln, but it was not the one
McClellan had intended. Coming at the low point of a mostly dismal year of
war, McClellan's letter resolved Lincoln on a new departure in Union policy
toward slavery. For three agonizing months, McClellan's version of civilized
war had been unable to take Richmond. Now the clarity of his letter forged
an unmistakable connection between limited Enlightenment-style war and
the failure of Union forces to bring the war nearer to a close.

As Lincoln returned from Virginia to Washington, he decided to throw
off the constraint on which McClellan had insisted most strongly. On Sunday, July 13, in a carriage on the way to the funeral of Secretary Stanton's
infant son, Lincoln confided to Welles and Seward that he had "come to the
conclusion" that emancipating the slaves "was a military necessity absolutely
essential for the salvation of the Union." It was, the president revealed, "the
first occasion" on which "he had mentioned the subject to any one." A little
more than a week later, Lincoln quietly dropped his bombshell in a cabinet meeting. In the final sentence of a proposed order executing Congress's
Second Confiscation Act, Lincoln proposed "as a fit and necessary military

measure" for restoring the Union, that "all persons held as slaves" within the Confederacy on January 1, 1863, "shall then, thenceforward, and forever, be free." Lincoln had resolved on emancipation.*

WITHOUT EVER PUTTING it in so many words, Lincoln had come to his decision by rehearsing the basic moral structure of Enlightenment just war thought. As he often did, he sat down with a pen and worked through the problem. His initial proposition was, he thought, self-evident: "The will of God prevails." But the difficulty of thinking about God's will in war was immediately apparent as well: "In great contests," Lincoln continued, "each party claims to act in accordance with the will of God." But of course the contending sides could not both be right. "Both *may* be, and one *must* be wrong," Lincoln wrote to himself, because "God cannot be *for*, and *against* the same thing at the same time." The great problem, he concluded, was that people could never know for sure whether God had chosen them to be his "human instrumentalities."

In a few short strokes, Lincoln had come to the idea underlying the entire array of Enlightenment rules for civilized warfare. Human beings could never know for sure that they comprehended God's justice. Legal limits on war reflected the fact that both sides inevitably believed they were in the right. But now Lincoln grasped a conceptual puzzle at the root of the idea. Didn't war itself require certainty about the justice of one's cause? Why go to war at all—why set in motion war's terrible violence—if you were not sure you were right? The Union armies had already suffered almost 200,000 casualties in little over a year of fighting. At least 150,000 southerners had been killed, wounded, or captured as well. If the war were justified, there had to be something more than moral uncertainty to sustain it. And so Lincoln took a tentative next step, one that cut against the grain of the Enlighten-

---

*There is considerable debate over the precise timing of Lincoln's decision. David Donald, one of the giants of Lincoln scholarship and the history of the Civil War, believed that Lincoln made his decision in June, or even May, well before the Harrison's Landing episode—Donald, *Lincoln*, 363–64. In my view, the more likely timing is that proposed by Eric Foner, Allen Guelzo, and others, who date the decision to shortly after the July 8 Harrison's Landing meeting with McClellan—Eric Foner, *The Fiery Trial*, 217, and Allen Guelzo, *Lincoln's Emancipation Proclamation*, 141–46. There is evidence on all sides, but the earlier dating rests in significant part on stories told by interested witnesses long after the fact. Most persuasive to me is the fact that on July 1, 1862, Lincoln showed his friend Orville Browning a memorandum on his thinking about the slavery question that contained no hint of the dramatic policy Lincoln would unveil later that same month—Pease & Randall, eds., *Diary of Orville Hickman Browning*, vol. 1, p. 555.

ment's approach to limiting just wars. In uncharacteristically hesitant language, Lincoln continued his notes: "I am almost ready to say this is probably true—that God wills this contest."

Lincoln gave voice to his thinking on the subject in September when a church delegation from Chicago came to the White House to present a memorial endorsing emancipation. By now Lincoln had privately resolved on emancipation. But he was still considering the reasoning behind his momentous decision. He told the delegation that religious men regularly approached him with advice. They were invariably "certain that they represent the Divine will." But they came with radically opposing views ("the most opposite opinions and advice"), and not all of them could be right. It might even be that all of them were wrong. And there was the nub of the problem. How could one learn God's will, and if one could not, how could one make the grave decision to increase the destructiveness of the war? "If I can learn what it is I will do it!" Lincoln said. But God's justice was inscrutable. "These are not," he reminded his memorialists, "the days of miracles." There would be no "direct revelation." In a moment of playfulness, Lincoln suggested facetiously that rebel soldiers might well be "praying with a great deal more earnestness . . . than our own troops." The more serious point was that Confederate soldiers were no doubt "expecting God to favor their side" just as Union men thought that God would favor theirs.

Lincoln had stated the case for restraint in wartime. Moral uncertainty demanded moderation. But the Chicago Christians replied with a much older idea, one that tracked the just war framework not of the Enlightenment but of the Middle Ages. Unbeknownst to them, their reply followed the course Lincoln's own thinking had been taking over the previous weeks. Moral uncertainty, they observed, could not excuse paralysis. "Good men," they conceded, "differed in their opinions." But "*the truth was somewhere*," and men could not merely set one opinion against another and throw up their hands. The moral leader had to act, had to bring "facts, principles, and arguments" to bear and come to a conclusion as to what justice required. Lincoln had already made his decision, though he had not told them so. And when the interview closed, it was clear that Lincoln and his Chicago petitioners were not so far apart after all. "Do not misunderstand me, because I have mentioned these objections," Lincoln told them. "Whatever shall appear to be God's will I will do."

* * *

G OD'S WILL OR otherwise, Lincoln's advisers urged caution. When the
president shared his plan with the cabinet, Secretary of the Treasury
Salmon Chase (the most antislavery member of the cabinet) immediately
urged that any emancipation policy aim to avoid the "depredation and massacre" so many feared would follow freedom for the slaves. Chase proposed
instead that Lincoln allow local commanders "to organize and arm the
slaves," since officers who were close to the ground would be in a better
position to manage and police slave populations. Attorney General Bates
had long worried about the risk of a slave uprising, and he insisted that the
proclamation be coupled with a deportation measure to remove the dangerous population of former slaves from the country.

William Seward, another strong antislavery man, spoke up as well. Given
the condition of the Union war effort, he noted, emancipation might be
viewed as a sign of weakness, or (worse yet) a sign that the Union had decided
to ask the slaves for help in winning the war. It would look, Seward said, as if
the government was "stretching forth its hands to Ethiopia, instead of Ethiopia stretching forth her hands to the government." Given the widespread
controversy going back before the war over the propriety of a civilized nation
setting slaves in arms against their masters, no one could doubt Seward's
meaning here. It was not merely that issuing a call for emancipation from
a position of weakness would look desperate. The problem Seward saw was
that an emancipation announcement would appear as the last throes of a
government that had cast away the limits of civilized warfare. Seward's idea,
Lincoln later recalled, was that emancipation "would be considered our last
shriek." The observation struck the president with "great force." At Seward's
urging, Lincoln put off announcing emancipation to await a Union victory
on the battlefield.

It took two months for such a victory to come about. The Union war
effort got worse before it got better. At Bull Run, where the Union had
suffered its embarrassing first major defeat of the war, Union forces, now
fighting under Major General John Pope, were badly defeated for a humiliating second time. Many, including Lincoln himself, believed that McClellan and his trusted ally, Major General Fitz John Porter, had secretly hoped
for Pope's defeat.

Only after the Union's grim victory at Antietam on September 17 did
Lincoln resolve to announce the emancipation plan to the nation. Calling
together his cabinet on Monday, September 22, Lincoln told them that he
had promised himself he would issue an emancipation proclamation if the

Union turned back Robert E. Lee and the Army of Northern Virginia at Antietam. Hesitating just a little, Lincoln added that he had made a promise with his Maker, a covenant with God, that if God "gave us the victory" at Antietam, he would "consider it an indication of Divine will" on the emancipation question. It was hard to imagine that the age of miracles had really returned on the bloody battlefield in Maryland. September 17 was the deadliest single day of the entire war. McClellan, restored just weeks before to command of the Army of the Potomac, had characteristically failed to follow up his terrible victory and deliver a decisive blow. Yet Lincoln viewed the day's events as a sign from heaven. "God had decided this question," Lincoln said, "in favor of the slaves."

In language that was Lincoln's own, his proclamation announced that on January 1, 1863, all people held as slaves within a state in rebellion against the United States would be "forever free." The armed forces of the United States, the president resolved, would thenceforward "recognize and maintain the freedom" of the former slaves and would "do no act or acts to repress" the freedpeople "in any efforts they may make for their actual freedom."

In deciding on emancipation, Lincoln had not so much solved the problem of moral uncertainty as he had chosen one side of the dilemma and decided to stick with it. His annual message to the Congress in December 1862 offered a kind of coda to the agonizing deliberations of the summer and fall. "We *say* we are for the Union," Lincoln wrote. "The world will not forget that we say this. We know how to save the Union. The world knows we do know how to save it. We—even *we here*—hold the power, and bear the responsibility." This, of course, had been the message of the Chicago petitioners. Lincoln had not chosen war lightly. Rescuing the Union was his sacred cause, and if there were means available, it was imperative that he exercise them. His stirring conclusion defended Emancipation in the same terms:

> We shall nobly save, or meanly lose, the last best, hope of earth. Other means may succeed; this could not fail. The way is plain, peaceful, generous, just—a way which, if followed, the world will forever applaud, and God must forever bless.

Here, then, was a Christian answer to McClellan's "highest principles known to Christian Civilization," an answer that was rooted in the justice of the path selected. "The dogmas of the quiet past," Lincoln told the Congress, "are inadequate to the stormy present." It was apparent that there were means that might advance the desperate end of saving the republic. If we could "disenthrall our selves" from the orthodox nostrums of constraint, the president now argued, "then we shall save our country."

Abstain from All Violence

As Chase and Seward had guessed, critics saw Emancipation as a plan not to save the Union but to destroy the South in a wave of indiscriminate violence. The United States, fumed Jefferson Davis, hoped to "inflict on the non-combatant population of the Confederate States all the horrors of a servile war." As Davis saw it, Lincoln had made clear "not only his approval of the effort to excite servile war within the Confederacy, but his intention to give aid and encouragement thereto." Southern state legislatures condemned Lincoln for "seeking to bring upon us a servile war by arming our slaves." In New Orleans, a young society woman named Julia Ellen LeGrand excoriated northern abolitionists for urging "that our homes should be burned and that Southern women and children should be startled at midnight by the wild beasts which Africans become after having scented blood." Thomas Jenkins Semmes, a member of the Confederate Senate, called Emancipation "an invitation to servile war." The *Richmond Enquirer* opined that Lincoln had issued a proclamation "ordaining servile insurrection" and employing means that "the most callous highwayman should shudder to employ."

The Confederate Congress took up a blizzard of retaliatory resolutions. One bill resolved that "all rules of civilized warfare should be discarded in the future defense of our country." Another proposed that "every person pretending to be a soldier or officer of the United States" captured after January 1 should be presumed to intend "to incite insurrection and abet murder" and therefore "suffer death" as a criminal. The Confederate Congress's final joint resolutions described the Emancipation Proclamation as an effort to encourage slaves to take up a servile war that would be "inconsistent with the spirit of those usages which in modern warfare prevail among civilized nations."

Many observers in the North and in the border states were almost as critical as the rebels. Two days after the Proclamation was made public, McClellan wrote privately to his wife, Ellen, that he would not "fight for such an accursed doctrine as that of a servile insurrection—it is too infamous." The *Louisville Journal* observed angrily that Emancipation freed enemy slaves and incited "servile insurrection," both of which were "condemned by the laws of civilized warfare." Further west, in Dubuque, Iowa, critics of Emancipation saw it as tending toward "a servile war, instigated by the President's proclamation." In Lincoln's old haunts of Springfield, Democrats accused him of unloosing "the lusts of freed negroes who will overrun our country." Former Supreme Court Justice Benjamin Curtis conjured up "scenes of bloodshed, and worse than bloodshed." The governor of New Jersey, Joel Parker (no relation to the Harvard professor of the same name), predicted a slave uprising that would lead to the genocidal massacre of all the South's blacks. Similar nightmarish stories raced through the salons of Britain and France in the winter 1862–63, creating speculation that the threatened terrors of Emancipation might lead the two European states to recognize the South and impose a mediated peace.

Detractors focused in particular on one aspect of the September 22 preliminary Emancipation Proclamation: Lincoln's promise that the armed forces would "recognize and maintain" freedom and not "repress" the efforts of former slaves to turn the Proclamation into "actual freedom." Outraged newspaper editors spluttered that Lincoln was practically "inviting the negroes to the commission of any atrocity which their brutal passions may suggest." With Lincoln's active assistance, Emancipation would lead "a barbarous and servile race" to wreak violence on the white women and children of the South.

F OR EMANCIPATION'S CRITICS, the Proclamation seemed to signal the end of restraint. But in this they were badly mistaken.

Like Butler at the outset of the war, Lincoln and his cabinet remained gravely concerned about the risk that slave uprisings would give rise to an indiscriminate bloodbath. Secretary of War Stanton thought enough of the concern to assure the Congress in his December 1862 annual report that "under no circumstances has any disposition to servile insurrection been exhibited by the colored population in any Southern State." And when Lincoln issued the final Emancipation Proclamation on January 1, 1863, he aimed to allay precisely these worries. All persons held as slaves in the rebellious states, the Proclamation reaffirmed, "are, and henceforward shall be free." But where the preliminary Proclamation in September had promised Union aid to slaves' own efforts to achieve "actual freedom," now Lincoln substituted a stern warning against self-help: "I hereby enjoin upon the people so declared to be free," he wrote, "to abstain from all violence, unless in necessary self-defence." Indeed, Lincoln went further, urging the newly freed blacks of the South to refrain from any attempt to challenge the allocation of power and wealth in the southern states. "I recommend to them," he continued, "that, in all cases when allowed, they labor faithfully for reasonable wages." A year later, in his 1863 message to Congress, Lincoln proudly reported on the status of the Emancipation Proclamation and on the Union's military successes since its implementation: "No servile insurrection, or tendency to violence or cruelty," the president said, "has marked the measures of emancipation and arming the blacks."

Emancipation did not entail the elimination of restraints. But it did mean a different way of talking about them. As Francis Lieber told his students a year before, jurists in Europe and America had sought for a century and more to maintain a sharp separation between rules for combat, on the one hand, and the justice of the cause, on the other. Jurists like Vattel had done this by articulating hard-and-fast prohibitions that could be followed without reference to the cause of the underlying conflict. Lieber's lectures aimed to dismantle the partition between means and ends, and most of Vattel's rules had come tumbling down in the process. Now Lincoln experimented with the same move. Like Lieber's lectures, Emancipation pressed humanitarian limits and justice back together by measuring the limits on conduct by reference to the justice of its ends. Lincoln had announced the Emancipation Proclamation "as a fit and necessary war measure," one that was "warranted by the Constitution, upon military necessity." The military necessity test tethered the means allowed to the justice of the end in view. Justice—God's justice—was precisely what Lincoln had in mind. "Upon this act, sincerely believed to be an act of justice," the president wrote in the final Emancipation Proclamation, "I invoke the considerate judgment of mankind, and the gracious favor of Almighty God."

O DDLY, the grave reasoning of the Emancipation Proclamation has been missed by most of its readers. For a century and a half, even sympathetic observers have criticized the Proclamation's text as morally impoverished. The abolitionist Lydia Maria Child—who had sympathized openly with John Brown's raid on Harper's Ferry just four years before—complained that the Emancipation Proclamation was "merely a war measure." Child said it made "no recognition" of the "principles of justice or humanity" that had prompted it. The influential twentieth-century historian Richard Hofstadter dismissed the document as having "all the moral grandeur of a bill of lading." It was, Hofstadter protested, based on nothing more than "military necessity."

What Child and Hofstadter missed is that military necessity *was* morally momentous. As a war measure based in military necessity, the Emancipation Proclamation condensed a millennium of moral and legal reasoning into its short text. It contained an entire world of moral considerations about the relationship between means and ends. In cutting against the grain of the hard-and-fast rules that had populated the laws of war since the Enlightenment, Lincoln moved the war to a dangerous new footing—one that not only undid one of war's limits but also threatened to undermine the very moral structure of just wars in the modern tradition. Yet it was hardly a lawless vision of war that Lincoln offered. Even the flat affect of the Proclamation itself was exquisitely attuned to moral restraint in warfare and to what men like Seward were telling the president might be the "vast and momentous" consequences of his act. Lincoln knew precisely the risks posed by bringing justice back into the conduct of war. He thus did so quietly, omitting rhetoric calculated to stir the passions of the conflict. Lincoln announced Emancipation with the modesty of a man who knew that he could never understand for certain how God willed him to act, but who knew that he had to act nonetheless.

If uncertainty was man's fate, if there were to be no miracles, then the Lincoln administration would have to attend very carefully to the risks that Emancipation occasioned. Recruiting the newly free men into the Union Army would turn those risks into one of the most pressing problems of the entire war.

Chapter 8

To Save the Country

> _To save the country is paramount to all other considerations._
>
> —Instructions for the Government of Armies
> of the United States in the Field, 1863

A s the moon sank low in the night sky over eastern Florida on March 8, 1863, 900 soldiers of the Union Army made their way up the St. John's River from the Atlantic coast aboard the steamer *John Adams* with an escort of Navy gunboats. Even under ordinary circumstances, the raid would have been a daring and complex one. The mission was to travel twenty miles upriver under cover of night and make a dawn landing at the sharp bend in the St. John's that sheltered the isolated village of Jacksonville, population 2,000. If all went as planned, the village would be occupied before local Confederate forces even knew what was happening.

But these were not ordinary circumstances. This operation was different from any the Union had carried out in two years of war. Months earlier, all 900 of the enlisted men aboard the *John Adams* had been slaves on the sea island plantations of South Carolina. Now, in March 1863, they were black soldiers of the South Carolina Volunteers on a mission to spread word of the Emancipation Proclamation among the blacks of Florida.

The South Carolina Volunteers, as one newspaper observed, were "not the phantom" of servile insurrection. They were its reality. The Union had occupied Jacksonville once before in an effort to interrupt the shipment of cattle and hogs to the Confederate armies. This time the Union mission in Jacksonville was different. The regiment's white officers, Colonel Thomas

Wentworth Higginson and Colonel James Montgomery, had been radical abolitionists before the war. Higginson was an admirer of John Brown. Montgomery was an antislavery Kansas jayhawker, raiding slave plantations across the Missouri border in the lawless violence of the 1850s. With Higginson and Montgomery in command, the Volunteers aimed to use Jacksonville as a base for arming Florida's freedmen against their former masters.

Obstructions along the St. John's delayed the Union vessels by several hours. At eight in the morning stunned residents of Jacksonville watched the *John Adams* steam around the bend. As they realized the race of the men in the Union uniforms, the surprise of the white onlookers gave way to terror. For months, Confederate authorities had been warning that Emancipation would mark the beginning of a Union effort to foment slave uprisings across the South. Now the white inhabitants of Jacksonville—"in mortal dread of the sable soldiers," as one correspondent reported—expected an indiscriminate massacre. Around the country, observers expected that raids such as the one led by the South Carolina Volunteers would be like "a great volcano ... bursting" upon the South. Critics of the Lincoln administration in the North condemned the expedition (the "wretched business of negro soldiering") as war "against the women and children on the plantations, and not against the armed force in the field."

Thomas Wentworth Higginson, commander of the 1st South Carolina Volunteers, and his first sergeant Henry Williams led raids to bring away slaves from the backcountry of the Deep South.

Union officials were painfully aware of the passions raised by the mission. Secretary of War Stanton, who had authorized the recruitment of the black regiment in August, warned the commander of the South Carolina Sea Islands, Brigadier General Rufus Saxton, to use only those means "consistent with civilized warfare." Saxton, in turn, had expressly limited Thomas Higginson to those measures "consistent with the usages of civilized warfare." Indeed, Higginson himself believed that his men could easily be turned into savage warriors like the Seminole Indians who had fought U.S. troops in Florida for decades. They were, he wrote, especially suited to "partisan warfare" and "could easily be made fanatics" if their commander chose to train them as such. But Higginson insisted that he would "have none but civilized warfare" in his regiment. The eyes of the nation, he told his men, were upon them.

No one knew better than the black soldiers themselves just how fraught their raid into the Florida interior was. It had not escaped them that in the event of their capture, Confederate forces would treat them not as enemy soldiers but as armed slaves encouraging a general uprising. The penalty for stirring up slave rebellion was death. Even before the announcement of Emancipation in September 1862, southern whites had demanded that southern blacks captured in arms be executed. Since Lincoln had made Emancipation public in September, the Confederacy had made execution or re-enslavement its official policy. "Dere's no flags ob truce for us," Higginson's men observed. None of the Enlightenment's constraints protected them. "When the Secesh fight de Fus' South," one of the Volunteers remarked, "he fight in earnest."

And yet despite the fears that raced through the town at the arrival of the black South Carolina Volunteers, no massacre ensued. To the contrary, Higginson and his men took the town with such speed and skill that it was completely surrounded before the people of Jacksonville had become fully aware of their presence. When reports of the Volunteers' success reached the North, newspaper editors reacted with joy. The *Boston Daily Advertiser* gushed that the use of black troops had been shown to be "something far different from an attempt to arouse servile insurrection, with the horror anticipated from it." The "conduct of the freedmen" had been "free from excess or disorder," far more so (the editors were "very sorry to say") than the conduct of most white regiments. The raid on Jacksonville had been "an act of regular warfare under the established rules of nations."

* * *

THE FREEDMEN OF the South Carolina Volunteers are little remembered today. Unlike the black soldiers of the better known 54th Massachusetts, who under their commander Colonel Robert Gould Shaw led a heroic but ill-fated assault on Fort Wagner near Charleston in July 1863, the Volunteers fought no famous pitched battles. In Jacksonville, it was precisely the absence of violence that marked the Volunteers' success. What observers North and South understood very well at the time was that Lincoln and Stanton's decision to expand Union reliance on black soldiers depended crucially on their performance. There might never have been a 54th Massachusetts if it were not for the successes of the South Carolina Volunteers.

The legacy of the black soldiers from South Carolina has remained with us in another, less salient way as well. Even as the South Carolina Volunteers occupied Jacksonville, the Union was putting the finishing touches on an effort to establish that Emancipation and the arming of black soldiers were aligned with the highest humanitarian ideals of the age. The very project that threatened to cause a conflagration across the South helped spark the modern laws of war.

Simply as Men

THE CONFEDERACY HAD no need to produce a new chapter in the laws of war. Their aim was not to transform those laws but to embrace them in the form they had taken since the earliest days of the republic.

Within days of the firing on Fort Sumter, Confederate president Jefferson Davis proclaimed his commitment to "the usages of civilized warfare" as they had been understood since the War of Independence. Davis and the Confederate Congress championed broad rights for neutral shipping and affirmed the old American principle that free ships made free goods. They attacked the Union's blockade as an unlawful paper blockade and adopted the general principles of the 1856 Declaration of Paris, except for its ban on privateering. After southern privateers began to seize Union vessels on the seas, Davis and his administration gleefully mocked the Union's sudden and transparently self-interested about-face on the Declaration's privateering provisions.

With more bitterness than glee, Confederate statesmen also excoriated the Union for its treatment of private property on land. After Lincoln signed the first Confiscation Act into law in August 1861, the Confederate Congress announced that the Union had "departed from the usages of civilized warfare" by "confiscating and destroying" Confederate property whether "used for military purposes or not." The South's retaliatory Sequestration Act ultimately scooped up more property than the Union's confiscation legislation ever did. But the South only seized and held Union property in reprisal for Union confiscations and as security to ensure that Confederate citizens were indemnified for their unlawful losses.

All of this aligned the South with a long American tradition of limits on war's destruction. When Lincoln decided to prosecute southern privateers as pirates, Jefferson Davis had virtually stood in the shoes of George Washington outside Boston demanding that the British treat his men as soldiers instead of as criminals. Davis wrote to Lincoln that it was "the desire of this Government so to conduct the war now existing as to mitigate the horrors as far as may be possible."

The Confederate position on emancipation and the arming of slaves followed easily from its embrace of long-standing American views on the laws of war. As early as June 1862, southern whites wrote to Davis to demand that the Confederate Army deny prisoner of war status to black Union soldiers and treat them instead as slaves engaged in a criminal uprising. In August, in response to early efforts to recruit black regiments in the Department of the South and the Department of the Gulf, authorities in Richmond ordered that Major General David Hunter and Brigadier General John W. Phelps "be no longer held and treated as public enemies of the Confederate States, but as outlaws." In the weeks after Lincoln announced Emancipation in September 1862, members of the Confederate Congress introduced bills that would have treated Union officers as agitators inciting slaves to rebellion and thus as criminals, not soldiers. By the end of the year, Jefferson Davis announced that armed "negro slaves" and the commissioned officers found serving with them would be delivered to state authorities for prosecution.

T HE CONFEDERACY HAD simply reproduced the views of American statesmen from Jefferson and John Quincy Adams to Franklin Pierce and William Marcy. But as Emancipation approached, and as the Union moved rapidly toward arming black soldiers, Lincoln enjoyed no such luxury.

One alternative that crossed Lincoln's mind was to revisit the decision to apply the laws of war to the conflict with the South. In setting up the blockade and in abandoning the privateering trials, Lincoln had backed his way into treating the South as entitled to the basic rights of the laws of war. But as the Confederacy threatened to abandon the rules of civilized warfare in retaliation for Emancipation, some thought the only sensible response was to insist that it was the slaveholders who were savage violators of the basic standards of civilization.

The best developed argument on this score came from an unlikely source on the other side of the Atlantic. John Elliot Cairnes was a distinguished professor of jurisprudence and political economy at Queen's College, Galway, in Ireland. Just two years before the war, Cairnes's friend the British philosopher John Stuart Mill had forcefully observed that the laws of civilized war did not apply in war with savage peoples. Mill made the observation in the course of defending the use of force in the far reaches of the British Empire. As a description of the limits of the European tradition, he was right. If one thing was clear, it was that the rules of civilized conflicts were inapplicable in fighting against savages and barbarians. This was the basis for Jefferson Davis's argument that enlisting black soldiers against the Confederacy was an act of barbaric warfare.

Cairnes's insight was to see that the same idea Mill invoked for the wars of empire and that Davis used to demonize the North could be turned against the South. As the war of words over Emancipation heated up, Cairnes contended that the barbaric people were not the slaves but the slaveholders. Slaveholding was a backward institution, he insisted, at odds with the moral progress of the modern world. It sapped the moral fiber of peoples who practiced it. And if the slaveholders were barbarians, Cairnes asked, then why should the laws of war bind those who fought against them any more than it did those who fought against the savages and barbarians of faraway lands?

Cairnes's book was instantly reprinted in the United States, and it garnered widespread interest and much favorable attention. Lincoln himself referred to Cairnes's idea when he wrote a draft resolution to be issued by English supporters of the Union cause. No state founded on "human slavery," Lincoln proposed in early 1863, should "ever be recognized by . . . the family of Christian and civilized nations." Lincoln's main interest here was to hold off the continuing threat of English recognition of the Confederacy as an independent nation. His careful choice of words suggested a further step: refusing recognition not just as a state, but as a *civilized* state, a member of the "family of . . . civilized nations." Lincoln may not have started out as an expert in the international laws of war. But he was learning fast, and he knew very well that only "civilized nations" were entitled to the rules that attached in violent squabbles within the family of European states.

By the time Lincoln proposed his 1863 resolution, however, he also knew that implementing Cairnes's approach was impossible as a practical matter. From the collapse of the privateering prosecutions in late 1861 onward, the president had come to understand that he could not treat the South as categorically outside the laws of war except at terrible cost. Davis would no doubt retaliate in kind against captured Union soldiers for any punishment of Confederate soldiers. In a world in which tens of thousands of Union prisoners were in Confederate hands, Lincoln would have to work inside the laws of war. His administration would need a different response to Jefferson Davis's position on Emancipation and black soldiers.

B Y THE SUMMER of 1862, Francis Lieber had emerged as the Lincoln administration's closest adviser on matters relating to the laws of war. Lieber shared Cairnes's view of slavery as a deeply backward institution. He shuddered when he saw slaves punished by their masters and families separated by sale. Slavery, he thought, was antithetical to the moral progress of the age. "It is not the North that is against you," he wrote in an unsent letter to the aging defender of slavery John Calhoun in 1850; "it is mankind, it is the world, it is civilization, it is history, it is reason, it is God, that is against slavery." The South's peculiar institution was akin to barbaric practices the world over such as polygamy and concubinage, all of which Lieber thought were dying out across the civilized world. Slavery would soon follow. "The whole movement of history," he said, was against it.

Such ideas were commonplace in the North in 1862. Yet Lieber was differently positioned from most who held this view. For Lieber had been a slaveowner himself only a few years before. Shortly after arriving in South Carolina in 1835, he had spent $1,150 on two slaves: a woman named Betsy and her daughter Elsa, whom he bought from a slave dealer at the state courthouse in Columbia. In his diary he noted their "good looks" and "healthy, cheerful, and bright appearance." Over the next twenty years he bought more slaves, carefully checking their teeth to gauge their health and examining their backs for signs of whipping to judge their behavior. When Elsa and her baby died in childbirth, Lieber observed privately that the deaths cost him "fully one thousand dollars—the hard labor of a year." Lieber failed to note that a successful birth of the child, who under the slave law of South Carolina would have belonged to him, would have yielded a fabulous return on his initial investment.

Lieber excused his ownership of slaves by reasoning that in a place where slavery existed, it was better to own slaves and treat them well than to leave them to other, less benign owners. During his South Carolina years he had defended southern slaveowners' treatment of their slaves and condemned radical abolitionism. His erstwhile friend Sumner had accused him of becoming "a proslavery man."

Perhaps because of his own experience with slavery and with living in the South, or maybe because his late son had fought on the side of the rebels, Lieber was unwilling to conclude that the slaveholding South was ineligible for the laws of civilized warfare. To the contrary, Lieber saw the war as an opportunity to increase the prestige and significance of the laws of war. Early in the conflict, he proposed an international congress of jurists to resolve open questions in the laws of civilized warfare. If not an international congress, then Lieber suggested to Sumner "a little book on the Law and Usages of War." ("A catechism for belligerents and neutrals," Lieber called it, though he assured Sumner that his idea arose from "no sickly philanthropy" or "morbid feeling about war.") Lieber took up the subject of prisoner exchanges and the law in the pages of the *New York Times*. The lectures Lieber delivered in New York in the fall and winter of 1861–62 put the laws of war at the center of the conflict. He hoped to make the Civil War an epochal war for civilization, the capstone of centuries of moral development.

If civilization abhorred slavery, it followed for Lieber that slavery could not possibly be protected by the law of war among civilized nations. Slavery, he thought, was a creature of the laws of particular nations, and backward-looking ones at that. War, however, took place in what Lieber (following many before him) called the state of nature, where no one nation's laws could claim authority. Slavery was therefore at great risk in wartime. After the Mexican War, for example, Lieber had written that slavery did "not exist in conquered Territories" unless authorized in new affirmative legislation by the conquering state.

Lieber's view had powerful implications for the status of slaves arriving in Union lines. Along with Thurlow Weed and Senator Henry Wilson of Massachusetts, Lieber visited Fort Monroe and discussed the problem of fugitive slaves with General Benjamin Butler. Lieber thought the term "contraband" was ill adapted to the problem, though he agreed that it had been taken up into the culture "amazingly." The true principle, Lieber contended, was that when fugitive slaves came into Union lines, they instantly "must be, and are by that fact, free men," whether or not they were useful for the Confederate or Union war efforts. The race of the slaves made no difference. Since "war is carried on by the law of nature," no nation was bound to recognize the racial status laws of any other, let alone of an enemy. The "law of nature," he insisted, "does not acknowledge difference of skin."

Lieber's law lectures concluded with a long treatment of the status of slaves in wartime. Following Montesquieu and Blackstone, he condemned the traditional justification for slavery as arising from the capture of prisoners of war. When a fugitive slave presented himself for protection to a military commander, Lieber explained to his students, the commander had no capacity and indeed no authority to apply the enemy's "peculiar" laws authorizing slavery. Any such fugitive was therefore necessarily free. Soon Lieber was collecting notes for his friend Sumner to show that John Quincy Adams had erred as secretary of state in the 1810s and 1820s when he said that the usages of civilized war prohibited the emancipation of fugitive slaves.

Lieber's outspoken position on the implications of the laws of war for slavery soon attracted the attention of the Lincoln administration. Lieber had been scandalized in 1861 when McClellan promised to put down servile insurrections with the Army. Did McClellan propose, Lieber wondered, to "step back and fight the masters again" once any such slave insurrection had been suppressed? A year later, when Edward Stanly, Lincoln's military governor for eastern North Carolina, began returning fugitive slaves to their putative owners, Attorney General Bates asked Lieber for a formal opinion on the status of slaves in wartime. Lieber's opinion, which ran in newspapers in New York and Chicago, drew on his lectures to argue that fugitives who reached Union lines were free. In the laws of war, Lieber argued, "men stand opposed to one another in war simply as men." Their legal status as husbands, employees, servants, or slaves, fell away "like scales." When "a negro presents himself to our troops as coming from the enemy and claiming our protection," he was therefore a free man. A month and a half later, at the beginning of August 1862, Secretary Stanton asked Lieber to prepare a formal opinion on the "military use of colored persons." Lieber quickly produced another memorandum arguing that the use of slaves in armies was admitted by the "acknowledged law of war," and urging that the Union Army make more organized use of them in the war effort. By 1863, he was arguing that the enlistment of blacks was "one of the historic facts" of the war. "If only we can prevent regular servile war," Lieber wrote, "it would be very desirable."

As 1862 CAME to a close, Lieber's views on the slavery question became more salient than ever. Even as the Union began to arm black soldiers in earnest, and even as Thomas Higginson drilled his South Carolina

Volunteers, Jefferson Davis issued proclamations excoriating the impending emancipation and ordering that armed "negro slaves" (and the commissioned officers found serving with them) be treated as criminals and delivered to state authorities for prosecution. Rumors began to circulate in Washington that the Confederacy was selling into slavery black freemen captured alongside Union forces. News reports suggested that Confederate soldiers had even begun to execute black teamsters accompanying surrendering Union troops. (The reports, it turned out, were true.)

All of this put enormous pressure on the Lincoln administration as January 1—the appointed day of Emancipation—drew near. Radicals in the Senate demanded to know what Stanton and the War Department planned to do in response to the South's provocations. And once the administration turned from the work of preparing its annual message to Congress in early December, Lincoln's secretary of war and his general-in-chief Henry Halleck wired Francis Lieber in New York with an urgent message to come to Washington.

Responsible to God

T HE TELEGRAPH FROM Halleck spelled Lieber's name wrong. It was addressed to the wrong house as well. But it made its way to Lieber nonetheless, and when he arrived in Washington on December 12, Halleck and Stanton appointed him to a small board of advisers charged with revising the Articles of War. More ambitiously, they asked Lieber to draft "a code of regulations" drawn from "the laws and usages of war."

Lieber had been lobbying men like Halleck and Sumner for more than a year to commission precisely such a code to address what he called "the most urgent issues" in the law of war. As he told a historian soon after the war, it was confusion over the status of slaves in the war that had first prompted him to call for a restatement of the laws of war. But there was no shortage of questions that needed addressing. There were still grave disagreements over the status of guerrilla fighters in places like Missouri. In the Shenandoah, Major General John Pope issued a set of harsh orders for property destruction and seizure in August 1862, orders that critics decried as beyond the pale of civilized combat. A second Confiscation Act, passed by Congress in July, had produced similarly widespread controversy over questions of enemy property in wartime. Meanwhile, Union commanders had been holding hundreds of military commissions, trying Union soldiers,

Confederate soldiers, and civilians alike with virtually no formal guidance from the War Department. Joseph Holt, the judge advocate general beginning in September 1862, reached out to Lieber for guidance on problems arising in the prosecution of spies and violators of the laws of war. Prisoner of war populations were reaching new heights on both sides, raising myriad questions about their treatment. The Union had assembled a set of instructions for the treatment of prisoners early in 1862. In early December, it issued new instructions on who counted as a prisoner of war. But further questions abounded. The Confederacy, meanwhile, had adopted a policy of paroling thousands of U.S. troops on the battlefield—releasing them in return for a promise not to serve until the end of the war or until exchanged for a captured Confederate soldier. At Harper's Ferry and at Richmond, Confederate officials had paroled 13,000 Union officers and enlisted men in September 1862 alone. The Union protested that such paroles asked soldiers to give up something they had no right to trade away, namely, their obligation to serve their nation. The paroles, Union officials suspected, were transparent attempts to transfer the costs of feeding, clothing, and housing captured soldiers over to the Union.

The men Halleck and Stanton appointed to help Lieber prepare the new code were well chosen to deal with these questions. Major General Ethan Allen Hitchcock, the grandson of Revolutionary War hero Ethan Allen and a sometime confidant of Lincoln on matters of military policy, was the Union's commissioner for the exchange of prisoners and the drafter of the new regulations for the Union treatment of Confederate soldiers in captivity. He was also a former instructor at West Point with decades of experience in courts-martial. Major General George Cadwalader of Pennsylvania, a veteran of Winfield Scott's army in Mexico and a lawyer by training, had been among the first Union military men to raise the question of what to do in the event of slave uprisings across the South. Major General George L. Hartstuff was a West Point graduate and combat veteran who had been shot three times, once in the chest, fighting Seminoles in Florida before the war; now he was recuperating from severe injuries he had received while leading a regiment at Antietam. Brigadier General John Henry Martindale—a lawyer from Rochester and another West Point graduate—was the military governor of Washington, D.C., and a veteran of McClellan's failed Peninsula Campaign whose opposition to McClellan's cautious tactics had been publicly vindicated at a court of inquiry weeks before his appointment.

Of all the men on the board, however, Lieber had far and away the most expertise on questions of the laws of war. The board gave him wide discretion to draft a set of instructions for the Union Army on the topic, and Lieber set to work almost immediately. Working closely from his lectures and his memoranda for the administration over the previous year and a half, Lieber spent Christmas in the capital working furiously on his draft. For another month he worked on it back at his home in New York among his books. It was, he thought, like nothing that had ever been written before.

I HAD NO GUIDE, no groundwork, no text-book," Lieber later remembered. "No country," he wrote, "has anything of the kind."

In one sense, Lieber's descriptions of the novelty of his project were misleading. The Prussian military's decade-long effort to overcome the legacy of its ignominious defeat by Napoleon in 1806 had occasioned a proliferation of military manuals, many of which included shorthand information on the laws of war. Indeed, the Prussian tradition of field manuals, with which Lieber had at least passing familiarity, went back into the eighteenth century to the time of Frederick the Great. One such handbook, *Das Krieges oder Soldatenrecht (The Laws of War or of Soldiers)*, was in Lieber's private library.

But in a more important sense, Lieber was correct. In the modern era of the laws of war, there was nothing like the code he sat down to write. The Prussian manuals had been concerned principally with tactics calculated to counter the military genius of Napoleon. Manuals such as the Prussian handbook Lieber owned focused on the rights war conferred on the princes of Europe, where battle served as a substitute for lawsuits in disputes between sovereigns.* Lieber, by contrast, aimed to write a distillation of the laws of war for the age of democratic nations and mass armies.

When he was done, the code's 157 articles covered a dazzling array of questions. The code set out procedures for flags of truce and safe-conducts. It prohibited further injury to men "already wholly disabled." It regulated the exchange of mails and the interaction of ambassadors. It authorized the execution of spies and it detailed the offense of trading with the enemy. It permitted the conscription of local guides and set out rules for prisoner exchanges. It established special yellow markings for war hospitals. And it prescribed the procedures for armistices and surrenders. It banned assassination, which it defined as proclaiming an individual enemy to be "an outlaw,

---

*On the law of battles, see James Q. Whitman's brilliant new book, *The Verdict of Battle: The Law of Victory and the Making of Modern War* (Cambridge, MA: Harvard University Press, 2012).

who may be slain without trial by any captor." Drawing on his guerrilla war paper for Halleck in August, Lieber wrote that guerrillas or others who divested themselves of the appearance of soldiers from time to time, and moved back and forth between armed conflict and "peaceful pursuits," were "not public enemies." If captured, they were "not entitled to the privileges of prisoners of war, but shall be treated summarily as highway robbers or pirates." And responding to the mass paroles by Confederate armies of captured Union troops in the fall at Harper's Ferry and Richmond, the code provided that paroles were only valid if approved by a captured soldier's government. Battlefield paroles were invalid because no soldier could trade away his nation's interest in his own service. Prisoner paroles, the code explained, were not private agreements.

Many of the code's terms drew on the orthodox law of war as it had developed since the eighteenth century. But like Lieber's lectures in New York the previous winter, the code also reflected Lieber's own fierce personal views. The treatment of prisoners, for example, elaborately reproduced the most civilized terms with respect to captured enemy soldiers. The previous summer, Lieber had worried that his son Norman might have been captured in the Seven Days' Battles. It was a source of grave concern for him, because Lieber believed that nothing "so plainly characterizes the barbarity and demoralization of the South . . . as the continued . . . treatment of the American prisoners." Not surprisingly, his code provided that "all soldiers, of whatever species of arms," including those "who belong to the rising en masse of the hostile country," were "prisoners of war" and "subject to no punishment" for their fighting. No revenge was to be wreaked upon the prisoner by the intentional infliction of suffering, nor by "disgrace, by cruel imprisonment, want of food, by mutilation, death, or any other barbarity." Prisoners were to be fed "plain and wholesome food" and "treated with humanity." Their private property was protected against appropriation. No violence could be used upon them to extract information, and no torture was permissible to "extort confessions." The principle behind the code's treatment of prisoners was the principle that lay at the foundation of the entire modern laws of war. When "a man is armed by a sovereign government," Lieber wrote, "his killing, wounding, or other warlike acts, are no individual crimes or offences."

Yet the rules for prisoners also signaled the hawkish spirit that animated Lieber's thinking about war more generally. Any prisoner, the code provided, was subject to retaliation for violations of the laws of war by his nation, regardless of his personal responsibility for the violation. Lieber made clear furthermore that although the prohibition on injuring and killing prisoners was a central feature of civilized modern war, it was not absolute. In his initial draft, Lieber wrote that a "chief commander" could "permit a regiment or division to declare, for the duration of the war, that it will not give, and therefore does not expect, quarter." Halleck edited the passage out, but the final order nonetheless allowed the execution of prisoners in extreme situations. A commander, Lieber wrote, was "permitted to direct his troops to give no quarter" when he found himself "in great straits" such that "his own salvation" made it impossible to encumber himself with prisoners. Nor could those soldiers who violated the rules of war expect to enjoy their benefits. Soldiers "known or discovered to give no quarter" received none themselves. Nor did soldiers who fought in enemy uniforms, or disguised themselves under an enemy standard, or went into combat "without any plain, striking, and uniform mark" to distinguish themselves. All such combatants could be executed summarily upon capture.

The code's treatment of civilians showed the same mix of moral limits and unforgiving war. It was a mark of civilization's advance, Lieber announced, that "the unarmed citizen is to be spared in person, property, and honor as much as the exigencies of war will admit." And yet even as the code set out humanitarian limits, it tore down the wall between soldiers and noncombatants that Enlightenment jurists had tried to build. Jean-Jacques Rousseau had written that war was "a relationship between one state and another, not between their citizens." But the code instructed that "each citizen or native of a hostile country" was an enemy and as such "subjected to the hardships of the war." It authorized the starving of noncombatants "to hasten on the surrender" of the enemy. It permitted commanders to bombard cities without notice (though it discouraged doing so where unnecessary). And in a civil war, it authorized a commander to "throw the burden of the war, as much as lies within his power, on the disloyal citizens."

The code dealt out its double-edged treatment to property as well. It announced that the United States would "acknowledge and protect . . . strictly private property." It gave special protections to cultural property such as museums, universities, and libraries. But nowhere did it rule out confiscating the private property of enemy noncombatants or the cultural monuments of an enemy nation. Cultural property that could be removed without injury or destruction might be "seized and removed for the benefit" of a conqueror, with the "ultimate ownership" to be settled by the peace treaty at the end of the war. (Napoleon had famously appropriated works of art and cultural monuments everywhere his armies went.) Most of all, the limits of modern warfare did nothing to interfere with the right of the victorious invader to tax the population or billet soldiers in their homes, or to appropriate property "for temporary and military uses." Lieber had little but disdain for the "over-trained idea that soldiers must take nothing." Seizure of enemy private property, he wrote, "cannot be prevented, nor ought it to be."

What Lieber did insist on was that "useless destruction" be prohibited, and that all destruction and appropriation be in the service of the nation and its war effort. "All captures and booty," the code provided, "belong . . . to the government of the captor." Neither "officers nor soldiers" were permitted to use their position "for private gain."

T HE MASTER PRINCIPLE that animated the code was the same one that had appeared in Lieber's lectures and had provided the justification for Lincoln's Emancipation Proclamation. Virtually any use of force was permissible if required by military necessity. As Lieber put it in notes for an unfinished book on the laws of war, destruction in wartime was "lawful only as a means to obtain the great end for which a war is undertaken, and not for its own sake." As he saw it, this was "the chief difference between the wars of barbarous ages and the armed contests of civilized people." The code said the same thing: "Unnecessary or revengeful destruction of life is not lawful." Virtually every limit in the code was shadowed by a necessity exception. This was why prisoners could be executed "in great straits." It was why private property and cultural monuments (though "acknowledged and protected") were subject to appropriation. It was why even war hospitals were protected only "as much as the contingencies and the necessities of the fight will permit."

In Lieber's hands, military necessity was both a broad limit on war's violence and a robust license to destroy. He carefully explained that necessity authorized only acts in the service of the nation's public war effort; his code disclaimed "all cruelty and bad faith . . . all extortions and other transactions for individual gain; all acts of private revenge." But its warrant for violence was daunting nonetheless. Military necessity, Article 15 provided,

admits of all direct destruction of life or limb of *armed* enemies, and of other persons whose destruction is incidentally *unavoidable* in the armed contests of the war; it allows of the capturing of every armed enemy, and every enemy of importance to the hostile government, or of peculiar danger to the captor; it allows of all destruction of property, and obstruction of the ways and channels of traffic, travel, or communication, and of all withholding of sustenance or means of life from the enemy; of the appropriation of whatever an enemy's country affords necessary for the subsistence and safety of the army, and of such deception as does not involve the breaking of good faith. . . .

Lieber summarized the principle in a sentence: "Military necessity, as understood by modern civilized nations, consists in the necessity of those measures which are indispensable for securing the ends of the war, and which are lawful according to the modern law and usages of war."

These were the key words: *indispensable for securing the ends of the war.* Lieber had borrowed the term "indispensable" from Lincoln's rebuke to Hunter's emancipation order in 1862. Whether Emancipation was an "indispensable" necessity, Lincoln had said, was a question he would reserve to himself. But what did the word mean? One thing was certain. It did not mean that armies were permitted to take only those actions that were necessary in the sense of leaving no other choice. Read this way, the necessity principle would have prohibited virtually every act of war, for it was rarely the case that any course of conduct (in war or otherwise) offered the only available path forward. McClellan's Peninsula Campaign was not necessary in this sense, because he could have approached Richmond more directly. Nor was the South Carolina Volunteers' occupation of Jacksonville, since there were other ways for the Union to bring word of Emancipation to the Deep South. The narrow meaning of necessity would have made war impossible to fight. If there were good reasons to fight wars, then the most rigid interpretation of the necessity standard was not plausible.

Lieber certainly did not see military necessity in this narrow way. Nor did he mean to invoke a less restrictive but still demanding approach that would have prohibited acts of force for which there were less destructive substitutes. This has been an appealing notion for humanitarian lawyers ever since, some of whom have sought to adopt a least-destructive-means requirement to lessen the human suffering of war. But Lieber thought that the attempt to reduce the human suffering arising out of any one decision in wartime might well increase suffering in warfare more generally. "When war is begun," Lieber told his students, "the best and most humane thing is to carry it on as intensely as possible so as to be through with it as soon as possible." He repeated the same idea in the code. "The more vigorously wars are pursued, the better it is for humanity. Sharp wars are brief." If this was so, then the least destructive means were not necessarily the most humane. The opposite might be true. Indeed, if war was sufficiently terrible, there might be fewer wars. Human suffering from warfare might be reduced most by a rule that not only permitted but required the greatest possible destruction.

Lieber had written into the code the essentially Clausewitzian perspective that underlay his views of war. "War," he wrote in Article 30, echoing Clausewitz, "has come to be acknowledged not to be its own end, but the means to obtain great ends of state." He said the same thing in Article 68, sounding more Clausewitzian still: "The destruction of the enemy in modern war, and, indeed, modern war itself, are means to obtain that object of the belligerent which lies beyond the war." For Lieber, like Clausewitz, the idea that modern wars were a means to advance the political ends of states meant that the old "conventional restrictions of the modes adopted to injure the enemy" were no "longer admitted." Indeed, this was pure Clausewitz. Lieber's "conventional restrictions" were the "self-imposed, imperceptible limitations" Clausewitz had derided as "hardly worth mentioning." Modern war, in this view, was less savage than its predecessors not because of its humanitarian ideals but because it had been shorn of irrational excesses. Force had been channeled and directed into those forms of destruction and violence that most rationally advanced a nation's war ends. Private violence for vengeance or sadism was no longer tolerated. But violence in pursuit of a nation's goals was virtually unmoderated. "To save the country," Lieber wrote in the code's most startling passage, "is paramount to all other considerations."

To be sure, the necessity principle did not sweep the field, displacing all constraint. For as soon as he had done away with the "conventional restrictions" of the laws of war, Lieber introduced a new set of limits. "The law of war," he wrote, "imposes many limitations and restrictions on principles of justice, faith, and honor." And while many of the limits in the code contained overrides for necessity, others did not. Lieber said that necessity did not permit "torture to extort confessions" or "the use of any violence against prisoners" to extract information. To Halleck, Lieber cited an example that he had used in his lectures the year before: "If Indians slowly roast our men, we cannot and must not roast them in turn." To do so was to "sink to the level of fiends." The basic standards of humanity imposed further obligations as well. Reversing a position he took with his students at Columbia, he now insisted that the laws of war did "not admit of the use of poison in any way"; to use poisons "in any manner" was to put oneself "out of the pale of the law and usages of war." Nor did the law of war permit the breaking of faith or the violation of truces. Echoing writers on the laws of war from Augustine in the fifth century to Kant in the eighteenth, Lieber added that "military necessity does not include any act of hostility which makes the return to peace unnecessarily difficult."

Yet if it contained limits, the code's necessity principle also licensed frightful new forms of destruction. As the war progressed, Union authorities approached Lieber with questions about any number of new killing devices. At Yorktown, the Confederates buried explosive shells in abandoned entrenchments—primitive land mines that killed the Union soldiers who tripped them off. Lieber heard of booby-trapped bodies and new submarine torpedoes. He learned about "incendiary balls" or "rifle bombs," akin to the explosive projectiles multilateral treaties would later prohibit. Time and again, his reaction was the same. As he told Halleck in 1863, "the soldier within me revolts at the thing. It seems so cowardly." But "the jurist within me cannot find arguments to declare it unlawful." Wars, he said, "are no Quixotic tournaments." Lieber may have abandoned the position he took in his lectures as to poisons. But the same logic he had applied to poisons in the lectures animated his approach to novel weapons. The real question was whether the use of such weapons would advance the war effort, and do so not at the least cost in lives and property, but at an acceptable cost, one that did not unduly impede the restoration of the peace. Lieber made clear that there were moral limits on the conduct of men at war. But he was unwilling to say, as jurists like Vattel had said before him, that those limits could be readily translated into hard-and-fast rules of general application. Lieber summed up the moral theory of the code in one of its first articles: "Men who take up arms against one another in public war, do not cease on this account to be moral beings, responsible to one another and to God."

A BRAHAM LINCOLN TOOK no role in commissioning the code, at least not one that we know of. Halleck and Stanton handled that themselves. Nor did Lincoln participate in editing or revising the code. Halleck did most of that. Indeed, there is little reason to think that Lincoln ever saw the text until it was near completion and ready to go out as an order under his name. But when it was issued in May 1863, the code was issued as General Orders No. 100 of the United States War Department, "approved by the President of the United States."

Lincoln approved the code because (as Halleck and Stanton well knew) it expressed a view of military necessity very close to that which Lincoln had been developing since his July 1862 encounter with McClellan at Harrison's Landing. In September 1861, Senator Orville Browning told Lincoln that the law of war gave a nation the "liberty to use violence against" its enemy "in infinitum" and permitted the destruction of "all things belonging to the enemy," so long as their destruction bore "some relation to the design of the war" and would "in some measure weaken the enemy." In response, Lincoln had adopted something akin to the narrow view that military necessity licensed only those acts of force that lacked less destructive alternatives.

By the late summer and fall of 1862, Lincoln had come around to the view Browning had urged on him and that Lieber and the board of military officers would soon write into the code on the law and usages of war. To the Union loyalist Cuthbert Bullitt of New Orleans, who had passed along complaints about interference with slavery in Union-occupied New Orleans, Lincoln said he would not leave "any available means unapplied. . . . I shall not do *more* than I can, and I shall do *all* I can to save the government." ("What would you do in my position," Lincoln asked impatiently, "would you prosecute it [the war] . . . with elder-stalk squirts, charged with rose-water?") In early August, he assured Secretary Chase that "he was pretty well cured of objections to any measure except want of adaptedness to put down the rebellion." And at the end of the month, when Horace Greeley sent him a public letter urging him to abandon his "mistaken deference to Rebel Slavery," he replied by invoking the same moral logic. In words that have been quoted countless times since, Lincoln explained his thinking without disclosing that he had already resolved on emancipation:

> If I could save the Union without freeing *any* slave I would do it, and if I could save it by freeing *all* the slaves I would do it; and if I could save it by freeing some and leaving others alone I would also do that. What I do about slavery, and the colored race, I do because I believe it helps to save the Union; and what I forbear, I forbear because I do *not* believe it would help to save the Union. I shall do *less* whenever I shall believe what I am doing hurts the cause, and I shall do *more* whenever I shall believe doing more will help the cause.

In September, Gideon Welles observed that Lincoln had "come to the conclusion that it was a military necessity absolutely essential for the salvation of the Union, that we must free the slaves." And the following year, Lincoln defended the Emancipation Proclamation on grounds that almost perfectly reproduced the logic of Browning and Lieber. "Civilized belligerents," the president insisted in 1863, "do all in their power to help themselves, or hurt the enemy, except a few things regarded as barbarous or cruel." No longer did military necessity, in his view, require a nation to exhaust less destructive means. Acts of force in war, Lincoln continued, were warranted by military necessity not because they were indispensable in the sense of being the only means available, but because they were helpful in the war effort. "To whatever extent the negroes should cease helping the enemy," he argued, "to that extent it weakened the enemy in his resistance"; "whatever negroes can be got to do as soldiers, leaves just so much less for white soldiers to do, in saving the Union." Emancipation was rationally connected to the advancement of the war effort, and that was enough for it to fall within the wide warrant of military necessity.

Indeed, by the time Stanton and Halleck had called on Lieber and his board to craft a new law of war code, Lincoln had determined to abandon the "rose-water" tactics of the war's first year and to take full advantage of his newly expanded conception of military necessity.

But for Lincoln, as for Lieber, stepping up the war effort did not mean abandoning limits. The president's notion of warfare made the vital moral distinction between violence in pursuit of the war effort, on the one hand, and private violence in the name of vengeance or individual profit, on the other. In November and December 1862, when Lincoln reviewed the sentences of more than 300 Sioux Indians from Minnesota who had been sentenced to death for their roles in a massacre of white settlers in the territory, he carefully separated those who engaged in battles from the much smaller group that seemed most likely to have engaged in indiscriminate killings and crime. (When Minnesota's governor quipped that Lincoln would have received more votes in Minnesota if he had hanged them all, Lincoln replied drily that he "could not afford to hang men for votes.") In orders he drafted in his own hand, Lincoln authorized the confiscation of property "where necessary for military purposes," and enjoined that "none shall be destroyed in wantonness or malice." Later, when he defended a Union officer in Missouri against charges of unwarranted actions against the civilian population, Lincoln warned against the wanton private violence that too often followed on war's coattails. "Murders for old grudges, and murders for self," he observed, smuggled themselves in under the cloak of war's violence. Men's ideas, he said, were "forced from old channels into confusion. Deception breeds and thrives. Confidence dies, and universal suspicion reigns." Soon "each man feels an impulse to kill his neighbor, lest he be first killed by him." The result was "revenge and retaliation."

* * *

CONTAINING THE VIOLENCE of the war took on new importance for the president in the winter of 1862–63 because of his new commitment to arming black soldiers. "The colored population," Lincoln told Andrew Johnson, his future vice president and the war governor of Tennessee, was "the great available and yet unavailed of force for restoring the Union." Just imagine, he urged Johnson, "the bare sight of 50,000 armed and drilled black soldiers upon the banks of the Mississippi." Such a force "would end the rebellion at once." To Major General David Hunter in the Department of the South, whose premature proclamation on slavery he had recalled just a year before, Lincoln now wrote telling him that it was just as "important to the enemy" that a black Union Army not "grow, and thrive, in the South" as it was "important to us that it shall."

If blacks were to be enlisted in the Union armies by the tens of thousands, however, the Confederacy's uncompromising stance on the impermissibility of black soldiers in civilized war would have to be addressed head-on. And that is precisely what the code Halleck and Stanton commissioned Lieber to draft aimed to do. It took up the moral theory of the war Lincoln had embraced and remade the American law of war tradition for the age of Emancipation and the era of black soldiers.

No Distinction of Color

NO FEWER THAN a dozen articles of the code, and arguably more, dealt with some aspect of the question of Emancipation or with the arming of blacks: more than the number dealing with torture, civilian targets, wounded soldiers, war hospitals, and spies combined. Moreover, in a code that mostly borrowed its substantive provisions from the existing literature on the laws of war, the slavery sections were the most original parts of the document.

The slavery passages received much of the attention in the drafting stages. With the exception of a section on the laws of war in civil wars that Halleck asked Lieber to add, most of the code was approved almost exactly as Lieber drafted it, though some of its sections were reordered. Not so with the articles dealing with slavery. In February, Lieber sent out a printed first draft of the code to the members of the board and to a select group of well-placed friends. The passages he asked about were the slavery sections. Lieber readily confessed that these were the passages of which he was most proud. Even so, Halleck edited the slavery sections carefully, making important additions and omitting clauses he thought too embarrassing in view of the long history of American support for views diametrically opposed to those set out in the code. Lieber's other correspondents wrote him about the slavery sections as well. Hamilton Fish, a trustee of Columbia College and future secretary of state under President Ulysses S. Grant, told Lieber that although most of the code merely restated "admitted principles recognized by modern nations," the draft's slavery provisions were "better than the Emancipation Proclamation." Unlike Lincoln's Proclamation, Fish thought that Lieber's draft articles did not afford the "Southerners of the North" an opportunity to attack Lincoln for stirring up internal rebellions. Brigadier General Napoleon Bonaparte Buford's response to the slavery sections was so enthusiastic that when he received a copy of the committee print at the headquarters of the Division of Cairo in the western theater, he declared the draft slavery articles to be of "vast importance" and impulsively sent them to be published in the *Chicago Tribune*, where (he assured a startled Lieber) they would be "much read by the army of the west."

In the final version, the slavery passages themselves ranged from Article 32, which provided that a victorious army had the authority to abolish "the relations which arise from the services due, according to the existing laws of the invaded country, from one citizen, subject, or native of the same to another," to Articles 40 and 41, which announced that the law of any one nation at war with another had no effect "between armies in the field" and that only "that branch of the law of nature and nations which is called the law and usages of war on land" applied. Article 42 explained why that mattered. Drawing on his memorandum for Attorney General Bates the previous summer, Lieber wrote that the "law of nature and nations has never acknowledged" slavery, which "exists according to municipal law only." But if municipal law—by which Lieber meant the domestic law of any given nation—did not apply as between contending armies, and if only the law of nations applied, then slavery could not exist in wartime. "Fugitives escaping from a country in which they were slaves" were thus free. Article 43 restated the principle:

Therefore, in a war between the United States and a belligerent which admits of slavery, if a person held in bondage by that belligerent be captured by or come as a fugitive under the protection of the military forces of the United States, such person is immediately entitled to the rights and privileges of a freeman. To return such person into slavery would amount to enslaving a free person, and neither the United States nor any officer under their authority can enslave any human being.

In a passage that Halleck added in the editing process, Article 43 provided further that after a war's conclusion, "a person so made free by the law of war" could not be reclaimed by a former owner; such a freedperson was "under the shield of the law of nations," and a former owner could make no claim for services owed.

As statements of existing law, articles 42 and 43 were misleading. It was simply wrong to say, as Lieber did, that the law of nations had never acknowledged slavery. For centuries, capture in war had been a principal justification of slavery, which seemed preferable to execution. Only in the eighteenth century had writers like Montesquieu and Blackstone observed that the end of prisoner executions fatally undermined the capture justification for slavery. What Lieber was drawing on in Article 42 was not so much the laws of war as the more general idea in the law of nations that slavery could exist only where there was some affirmative act of legal authority recognizing its validity. This was the idea articulated most prominently by the leading British judge Lord Mansfield in 1772 when he determined in his famous decision in *Somerset's Case* that a slaveowner could not forcibly seize a man who had been his slave in Virginia and return him to the Americas when the alleged slave lived in England as a freeman. Now ninety years later, the same idea reappeared in Lincoln's General Orders No. 100 as the justification for freeing slaves upon their arrival in Union lines.

Article 82 referred to slavery more obliquely, but it was as important a passage as any in the code. If "men, or squads of men" committed hostilities "without being part and portion" of an organized army, "without sharing continuously in the war," and without retaining "the character or appearance of soldiers," the Article instructed, such men were "not public enemies" and therefore "not entitled to the privileges of prisoners of war." Lieber drew on the experience of Napoleon in Spain and northern Italy to formulate the provision. Its terms bore the hallmarks of his work on guerrillas in Missouri for Halleck in the summer of 1862. But in the context of the Civil War, one of its most natural applications was to uprisings of freedpeople behind Confederate lines. Article 82 announced that the Lincoln administration would not insist that the South treat freedpeople rising up against the Confederate government as soldiers and prisoners of war.

Whether slaves in an uprising would be considered as legitimate soldiers was a live question, for the French Revolution's *levée en masse* had licensed the people of a nation under attack to rise up against an invader. Since the relationship between slave and master had long been associated with a kind of suppressed warfare, it was only natural to think that the *levée en masse* idea might be extended to slave insurrections. That, after all, was the great fear southern whites had experienced in reading Lincoln's preliminary Emancipation Proclamation in September 1862, with its promise of Union Army support for "any efforts" by blacks themselves to achieve "their actual freedom." The final Emancipation Proclamation had pulled back on that promise subtly but significantly, replacing it with an injunction to the freedpeople "to abstain from all violence" except in "necessary self-defense." Now, five months later, Lieber's instructions repeated the message of the January 1863 Proclamation and disavowed one possible form of Union support for a black uprising. Together, the January Proclamation and the May instructions left the freedpeople with self-defense rights under the criminal law while limiting the claims they could make on the laws of war if they rose up collectively against their former masters.

Article 57 firmly took the opposite position for black soldiers enlisted in the Union armed forces. "No belligerent," announced Article 57, "has a right to declare that enemies of a certain class, color, or condition, when properly organized as soldiers, will not be treated by him as public enemies." Article 58 further elaborated the same idea: "The law of nations knows no distinction of color," it proclaimed, providing that "if an enemy of the United States should enslave and sell any captured persons of their army, it would be a case for the severest retaliation." And because the United States could not and would not retaliate by enslaving captured Confederate soldiers, the code authorized the execution of an equivalent number of Confederates in retaliation for black soldiers enslaved.

The Confederate policy toward black soldiers was at the heart of Article 62 as well. Rumors suggested that many Confederate officers planned to give such men no opportunity to surrender. They would, in the language of warfare, give black soldiers "no quarter." Article 62, in turn, provided that "All troops of the enemy known or discovered to give no quarter in general," or (crucially) to give no quarter "to any portion of the army," would themselves "receive none" in return. The Confederate position, of course, was that black soldiers were impermissible combatants in civilized warfare because they were savages. Article 67 squarely took on that claim: "The law of nations . . . admits of no rules or laws different from those of regular warfare, regarding the treatment of prisoners of war, although they may belong to the army of a government which the captor may consider as a wanton and unjust assailant."

Even passages that seemed to have little to do with the slavery question were powerfully influenced by it. Toward the end of the code, Lieber included an enigmatic passage prohibiting assassination as beyond the pale of civilized combat. "The law of war," provided Article 148, "does not allow proclaiming either an individual belonging to the hostile army, or a citizen, or a subject of the hostile government, an outlaw." Readers have puzzled over the meaning of Lieber's assassination provision ever since, in no small part because it would be invoked after Lincoln's assassination in 1865. But slavery and the black soldier controversy provided the context. When Union forces in the Department of the South and the Department of the Gulf began to raise black regiments from the swelling ranks of contraband slaves, the Confederate government in Richmond had issued outlawry orders against the principal Union organizers, Major General David Hunter and Brigadier General John W. Phelps. Two days before Christmas 1862, while Lieber was hard at work on the code, Jefferson Davis issued another outlawry proclamation, this time aimed at Major General Benjamin Butler, now commanding Union forces in New Orleans. Davis excoriated Butler not only for exciting "African slaves . . . to insurrection by every license and encouragement," but for arming "numbers of them . . . for a servile war," a war that would far exceed "in horrors the most merciless atrocities of the savages." Davis ordered that Butler no longer be treated as a "public enemy" but "as an outlaw and common enemy of mankind," liable to immediate execution by any officer capturing him. When Lieber wrote into the code that "civilized nations" looked "with horror" upon outlawry and assassination "as relapses into barbarism," he had the outlawry orders against Hunter, Phelps, and Butler close at hand.

P ARTS OF THE code dealing with less politically sensitive questions such as prisoner paroles were issued early in the spring of 1863 without awaiting the approval of Stanton and Lincoln. But the rest of the code, including its principal slavery sections, required the authorization of the secretary of war and the president. In May, Lincoln issued it as General Orders No. 100 of the Union Army.*

On May 23, William Ludlow, the Union officer for prisoner exchanges at Fort Monroe in Virginia, met his Confederate counterpart for their regular appointment along the James River near Richmond and handed him a copy of the code. Its terms, Ludlow announced, would govern the two armies and would be the basis for prisoner paroles and exchanges for the rest of the war. The Confederate reaction was instantaneous and unsparing. Secretary of War James Seddon, who as a congressman during the Mexican War had praised the laws of war as "the boast of modern times" and "the blessing . . . of Christianity and civilization," lambasted the code as a "confused" and "undiscriminating compilation" of obsolete and repudiated notions. The code's military necessity principle, Seddon argued, meant that an army could either fight with "faith" and "honor," or behave like the "barbarous hordes" of the Middle Ages, committing "acts of atrocity and violence" that would "shock the moral sense of civilized nations." The Confederate agent of exchange in Virginia told his Union counterpart that the code was "a license for a man to be either a fiend or a gentleman." In his annual message to the Confederate Congress at the end of the year, Jefferson Davis quoted at length from the code's military necessity passages to contrast its "inhuman" terms with the "moral character" of the South's "Christian warriors."

The parts of the code that most provoked Confederate authorities ("the most prominent of the matters treated in Order No. 100," Seddon said) were those that took up the slavery question. Within a few weeks of delivering the code to the Confederacy, the Union's agent for the exchange of prisoners was embroiled in a hot dispute with the Confederate agent of exchange over black prisoners. "Discrimination among our captured officers and men," protested Lieutenant Colonel William Ludlow for the Union, was a violation of "the laws and usages of war." Drawing on the code, Ludlow told the Confederate agent of exchange that the Union would "throw its protection around all its officers and men without regard to color."

The Confederacy's official response went straight to the core of the matter. "The employment of a servile insurrection as an instrument of war," Secretary Seddon argued, "is contrary to the usages of civilized nations." In "the

---

*General Orders No. 100 bore the date April 24, but that seems to be the date on which Stanton and Lincoln approved it; few people inside or outside the Union Army seem to have seen the final version until the second and third week of May.

better days of the Republic," he maintained, the United States "would have regarded an attempt of the kind as dishonoring to the State or people who might be guilty of adopting it." The nation's diplomatic history and its treaties showed that it had once insisted on "reclamations for the value of escaping slaves and of slaves abducted by a military force in time of war." And so, Seddon concluded:

> The enlistment of negro slaves as a part of the Army of the United States cannot be regarded as having any object but one. It is a part of the system of the United States Government to subvert by violence the social system and domestic relations of the negro slaves in the Confederacy and to add to the calamities of the war a servile insurrection. The savage passions and brutal appetites of a barbarous race are to be stimulated into fierce activity.

In Seddon's view, the code was thus not a restatement of the law of war at all, but a reversal of that law's most cherished principles. A war carried on under its terms would entail "the abandonment of all rules, conventions, mitigating influences, and humanizing usages" developed over two centuries of moral progress. An enemy that adopted "such auxiliaries" as black soldiers was one that proclaimed its "desire as well as design that the war shall be one for mutual extermination."

Newspapers quickly picked up the new order, and they too concentrated on the slavery sections. In the North, long excerpts appeared in the *Boston Herald*, in Washington's *Daily National Intelligencer*, and in the *New York Times* and the *New York Herald*. In the South, the *Charleston Mercury* and *New Orleans Daily Picayune* published detailed reports. The black newspaper *L'Union* in New Orleans translated large sections of the code into French. The *Louisville Daily Journal* published the entire text over several issues. Extensive treatments soon came out in the *Baltimore Sun*, the *New Haven Daily Palladium*, the *Boston Daily Advertiser*, the *Daily Cleveland Herald*, the *Milwaukee Daily Sentinel*, and the *Daily Evening Bulletin* of San Francisco.

Newspapers acknowledged Lieber's draftsmanship, but laid the code at Lincoln's feet, and not just because it was issued under his authority or because the buck stopped with the president. They talked about the code as Lincoln's because they understood it to be bound up in Emancipation, the most important policy of his presidency. The *Daily Intelligencer* praised the code as Lincoln's response to the Confederacy's policy of criminal prosecutions against black soldiers and their white officers. "The President, by

1

George Washington strove to be the embodiment of civilized conduct in the War of Independence after being accused of atrocities twenty years before. He is depicted here by John Trumbull as the calm before the storm.

2

An artist's rendering of the Capitol building after it was burned by the British in 1814; President James Madison accused the British of violating the "rules of civilized warfare."

3

4

From 1815 to 1828, as the U.S. minister in London, as secretary of state, and then as president, John Quincy Adams insisted that it was unlawful to carry off enemy slaves in wartime.

Serving in the Congress in the 1830s and 1840s, Adams reversed his position and predicted that slavery would end in a terrible war laying waste to the South.

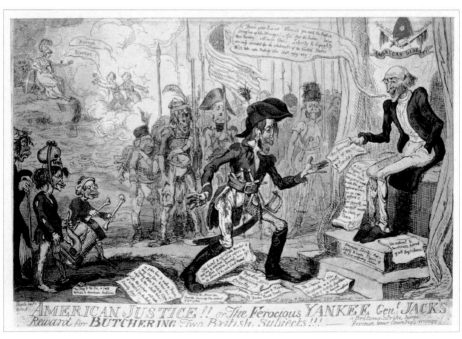

5

The London press lampooned Andrew Jackson as a bloodthirsty butcher leading a Tennessee militia of desperate savages. President James Monroe is seated at right.

6

7

A young Charles Sumner condemned the laws of war as legitimating lawless violence. By 1861, he defended a war against slavery and helped introduce Lincoln to John Quincy Adams's late-career arguments about the fate of slavery in wartime.

The first week of the war presented President Abraham Lincoln with a crisis in the laws of war at sea; controversy dogged his decision to blockade the South and treat Confederate privateers as pirates.

8

Secretary of State William Henry Seward (seated with hat on knee) used social occasions with the European diplomatic corps to craft the Lincoln administration's distinctively pragmatic approach to the laws of war.

9

The Union blockade of southern ports was notoriously porous, but its basis in the laws of war helped accomplish the crucial goal of holding off European intervention in the war. Alfred Waud's Civil War sketch for *Harper's Weekly* captured the life of the blockade that Lincoln, Seward, and Secretary of War Gideon Welles constructed.

POLICEMAN WILKES, noticing by the last Number of *Harper's Weekly*, that the well-known Rogues, MASON and SLIDELL, were about to Pawn some of their late Employer's Property at Messrs. *Bull, Cropout & Co.'s* Shop, kept a bright look-out for'ard, and nabbed them in the nick of time."

10

Captain Charles Wilkes seized Confederate diplomats Mason and Slidell from a British vessel in November 1861. This early controversy over neutral and belligerent rights at sea nearly brought Britain (depicted as the angry John Bull in the rear) to war against the Union.

At the outset of the war, Francis Lieber was teaching the laws of war at Columbia College in New York City after living in South Carolina for two decades.

When Lincoln elevated the bookish Henry Halleck to general-in-chief in 1862, he brought an expert on the laws of war into the Union high command.

Fugitive slaves streaming into Union lines forced the issue of slavery onto the Union agenda.

14

15

The long history of slave rebellions in war-time led to widespread beliefs in the North and South alike that freeing the slaves would produce indiscriminate bloodshed and terrible atrocities, like those in Haiti shown here.

By the fall of 1862, when Lincoln traveled to the battlefield at Antietam in Maryland, he had announced Emancipation. He is pictured here with Major General George B. McClellan, who bitterly opposed freeing slaves as a dangerous and uncivilized step in warfare.

16

Southern sympathizer Adalbert Johann Volck's cartoon depicted lead-ing Union men as infidels justifying Emancipation by the terrible motto inscribed on the altar of Negro Worship: "The End Sanctifies the Means."
Photograph © Museum of Fine Arts, Boston.

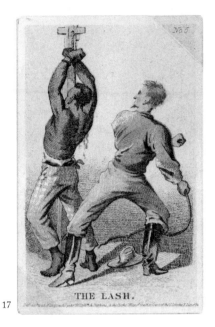

17   THE LASH.

BLOW FOR BLOW.   18

With the decision not only to emancipate the slaves behind Confederate lines but to enlist them and other blacks into the Union Army, it seemed that the Civil War had turned the violence of slavery upside down.

19

By late 1862, when he began work on a code for the laws of war, Francis Lieber had lost one son killed fighting for the Confederacy and seen a second gravely injured while fighting for the Union. The costs of the war are etched on his face in this grave portrait for the Columbia College 1862 class book.

36

37

A nasty conflict with Modoc Indians in Oregon in 1873 reprised the scalping scenes of the pre–Civil War era.

"Captain Jack," standing at right, led the Modoc band before being executed for killing a U.S. officer under a flag of truce. Men like Andrew Jackson had executed the Indians they captured without any formality; now captured Indian warriors like Jack were tried by military commission.

38

President Grover Cleveland proposed to execute Geronimo, but he and his band of Chiricahua Apache—men, women, and children alike—were taken by train to Florida from their native Southwest and spent more than two decades as prisoners of war.

39

After the Civil War, the Union's law of war instructions of 1863 began to spread around the world. The Franco-Prussian War of 1870–71 saw the code's principles applied to the irregular French fighters who resisted Prussian occupation.

40

41

A Swiss-born jurist named Johann Caspar Bluntschli translated the American code into German and spread its influence in Europe.

The formidable Alfred Thayer Mahan dominated the U.S. delegation at a conference in The Hague in 1899 that set the terms for the laws of war the world over.

42

U.S. armed forces in the Philippines engaged in the widespread use of torture tactics such as the water cure, demonstrated here by a team of American soldiers.

43

Colonel Edwin F. Glenn led a team of water cure experts in the Philippines and was court-martialed for violating the 1863 code's prohibition on torture. Twelve years later, he drafted the field manual on the laws of war that American officers would carry into two world wars.

approving these declarations," wrote the editors, had squarely answered the threats of "the insurgent authorities." Critics of Emancipation agreed that the code's central passages were the slavery sections. The anti-Lincoln editors of the *New York Herald*, for example, said that parts of the code were "very good," but condemned the sections relating "to the escape of fugitive slaves from the South into the lines of our armies" as "a complete fallacy." The *Herald* editors could hardly believe that the president meant to abandon so decisively the position the United States had taken at the close of the last major war fought on American soil. At the end of the War of 1812, they pointed out, more than a decade of diplomatic controversy had been dedicated to showing that "the slaves taken by the belligerents" needed either to be "returned or their price paid."

For the Lincoln administration, however, transforming the United States' position on the question of slavery in wartime was precisely what the code aimed to do. Major General Hunter in the Department of the South put the code to work immediately upon its publication by sending a copy to the regiment whose work had helped inspire it: the South Carolina Volunteers. Hunter told Colonel James Montgomery that the code was especially important for the "employment of colored troops" so as to avoid grounds for recriminations by the South or by European observers. Hunter continued:

> If, as is threatened by the rebel Congress, this war has eventually to degenerate into a barbarous and savage conflict, softened by none of the amenities and rights established by the wisdom and civilization of the world through successive centuries of struggle, it is of the first moment that the infamy of this deterioration should rest exclusively and without excuse upon the rebel Government.

Hunter called on Montgomery to enroll and arm as soldiers any fugitives reaching his lines, but always to follow with "utmost strictness" the code's instructions on the limits of civilized warfare.

L INCOLN HIMSELF SOON put the code to use in the project of arming black soldiers. That same spring, a joint resolution of the Confederate Congress recommitted the Confederacy to its policy on black Union soldiers. Some in the North thought the code was response enough. But others insisted that a more specific statement was needed. The code announced only what the laws of war *allowed* a nation to do, not what it *would* do. The editors of the *Boston Daily Advertiser* worried moreover that "not one person in a hundred" knew of the code. Even if it were widely known, some thought that the code was "not of a character to strike the mind very forcibly." What was needed was a "formal announcement from the highest authority," something that would "impress the rebels" of the Union's seriousness of purpose.

And so on July 31, after what Halleck later described to Lieber as a "full conversation" with his advisers, Lincoln issued a retaliation order that tracked almost word for word the language of the code he had approved two months earlier. Drafted for Lincoln in Stanton's War Department by someone who almost certainly had the text of the code before him, the order denied enemies the right to declare unlawful any soldier on the basis of "class, color, or condition" and insisted that the "law of nations" permitted no "distinction" of "color." To "sell" or "enslave" a "captured person" was what the code and Lincoln's retaliation order each called a "relapse into barbarism." Lincoln did not exercise all the authority Lieber's account of the laws of war afforded him. He stopped short of ordering executions in retaliation for enslavement, providing simply that for every soldier enslaved, one rebel soldier would be put to hard labor.

The code's retaliation provisions and Lincoln's retaliation order had at least some of their intended effect. After July 1863, the Confederate government retreated from its strong initial position and discouraged public proceedings against black soldiers as criminals in order to minimize the risk of northern retaliation. Secretary of War Seddon decided to make a distinction between black Union soldiers who had been free blacks in the North before the war, who would be "held like other captives," and black Union soldiers who had been slaves in the South before enlistment. Only the latter would be treated as criminals. Ethan Allen Hitchcock, the commissioner for prisoner exchanges and the lead member of Lieber's board of advisers, cited the code as a vital step toward addressing the Confederacy's harsh stance on black soldiers and their officers. Lieber's work "in suggesting and building up the Code," he wrote in October, had "already done great good."

Of course, the code could not have been expected to change the Confederate position single-handedly. But it became an instrument for denouncing the South's stance as a grievous violation of the norms of modern warfare. When Confederates under Nathan Bedford Forrest engaged in a horrific massacre of black soldiers at Fort Pillow in April 1864, Union officers directed attention to the code once again. Protesting Forrest's conduct, Major General Cadwallader Washburn of the Union's western district of Tennessee sent the Confederate general a copy of General Orders No. 100.

As Washburn wrote sternly, he sent the order "that you may know what the laws of war are." A "candid world," Washburn concluded, would judge Forrest's conduct.

I N ONE SENSE, men like Jefferson Davis and James Seddon were deeply wrong about the absence of limits in the document that Lieber eventually came to call "Old Hundred." The code contained hard limits on the use of poisons, on the use of certain kinds of torture and violence against prisoners, and on perfidy or bad faith. It also featured the more elastic limit of military necessity.

The code also adopted a constraint for which the statesmen of the South had a special blind spot. For it not only licensed Emancipation, it shared in the Lincoln administration's effort to lessen the risk of slave uprisings in its wake. When Lincoln ordered that men fighting outside organized armies and without retaining the character and appearance of soldiers were "not entitled" to the protection of the laws of war, and that the Union would not insist that the South treat such people as prisoners of war, he was trying to shape the way Emancipation would unfold, and he was announcing limits on what the Union would be willing to do to see its new policy through.

Yet even as the code contained limits on the freedom it authorized, it also continued Emancipation's startling departure from the spirit of the eighteenth-century laws of war. By relying so heavily on the doctrine of military necessity, by insisting on the lawfulness of Emancipation, and by demanding the equal treatment of black soldiers, the code (like Emancipation itself) integrated the concept of justice into a body of law that had been designed to set justice aside for the sake of humanity.

Asserting the priority of justice over humanitarianism had almost immediate practical consequences. International lawyers have long touted Lincoln's code for lessening the suffering of the Civil War. But this gets the president's order exactly backward. Embracing Emancipation and demanding equal treatment for black soldiers were the right things to do. But they did not reduce the suffering in the conflict. To the contrary, Lincoln's code helped produce some of the war's most enduring humanitarian crises.

Chapter 9

Smashing Things to the Sea

———◆◆◆———

The law of war imposes many limitations and
restrictions on principles of justice, faith and honor.

—Instructions for the Government of Armies of
the United States in the Field, 1863

War is simply power unrestrained. . . .

—William Tecumseh Sherman, 1864

I N A WAR FILLED with controversies, none is remembered more bitterly
than William Tecumseh Sherman's assault on Atlanta in the summer of
1864.

Since early May, Sherman and his army of 100,000 men had been
engaged in an elaborate series of feints and parries with Confederate general Joseph E. Johnston's 65,000 soldiers. Moving south from Chattanooga
across the Georgia border and into the heartland of the South, Sherman
aimed to take Atlanta and its railroads and thereby destroy the economic
foundations of the Confederacy. Johnston tried to block the Union force
at every turn. But time and again, the southerners dug in only to fall back
once more. Desperate to stop the Union advance, Jefferson Davis replaced
Johnston with the more aggressive John Bell Hood. Yet Hood's attacks did
little to stop Sherman's progress. Now, on July 20, as Hood fell back to positions on the outskirts of the city, Sherman ordered his commanders to cut
off Atlanta's railroads and shell the city into submission.

For the next five weeks, Union guns pounded the city blocks that lay just beyond Hood's entrenchments. On August 9 alone, 5,000 rounds fell in Atlanta. Sherman called in heavier siege guns the very next day. Sherman marveled at the capacity of his fantastic modern guns to single out particular homes from a mile away, but the Union fire was often indiscriminate anyway. He urged his commanders to concentrate their fire at night (one Union shell killed a father and his daughter while they slept). His aim, he told Major General Oliver Otis Howard, was to "destroy Atlanta and make it a desolation." Writing to Henry Halleck in Washington, Sherman said he would "make the inside of Atlanta too hot to be endured." Whether he took Atlanta or not, Sherman aimed to leave the city all "used-up" by the time he was done.

The Union onslaught damaged virtually every structure in the city's most densely built district. Casualties were relatively low thanks to the evacuation of three quarters of the city's population; by the best count, the Union barrage killed around 20 noncombatants and wounded between 100 and 200 more. But Sherman could claim no credit for the low number of injuries. He announced that he would go forward with his assault "even if it result in sinking a million of lives and desolating the whole land," and ordered his artillery officers to give "no consideration" to whether their targets were "occupied by families." His guns, he told an Alabama man at the time, were "seeking the lives" of Atlanta's people.

Sherman later accused Hood of digging in so close to the city that Union guns aimed at the Confederate lines occasionally overshot their mark. But the sheer volume of rounds that fell on Atlanta belied his claim. And when Atlanta finally fell into Union hands in the first days of September, Sherman moved to complete his assault by ordering the remaining 4,000 residents removed from the town by force. The Union sympathizers he sent north. Rebel families he expelled south to the protection of Hood's forces. He would not saddle himself with a city full of rebels. "If the people raise a howl against my barbarity & cruelty," he wrote to Halleck, "I will answer that War is War & not popularity seeking. If they want Peace, they & their relations must stop War."

Sherman's opponents did indeed howl. General Hood protested "in the name of God and humanity" that forced removal of the city's population was an "unprecedented measure," transcending "all acts ever before brought to my attention in the dark history of the war." The mayor of Atlanta, James M. Calhoun, begged Sherman to think of "the woe, the horrors, and the suffering" his evacuation order would cause to the pregnant women, the mothers, and the small children of the city.

But Sherman would have none of it. It was an act of "kindness" to remove the families of Atlanta, he insisted. "You cannot qualify war in harsher terms than I will," he warned Mayor Calhoun. But once begun, war's logic was inexorable. "War is cruelty and you cannot refine it, and those who brought war into our country deserve all the curses and maledictions a people can pour out." "If we must be enemies," he told Hood, "let us be men, and fight it out as we propose to do, and not deal in such hypocritical appeals to God and humanity." God, Sherman concluded, would "judge us in due time," and God would decide "whether it be more humane to fight with a town full of women and the families of a brave people at our back, or to remove them" to safety. To Hood's condemnation of his bombardment of Atlanta, Sherman replied furiously: "I was not bound by the laws of war to give notice of the shelling of Atlanta, a 'fortified town with magazines, arsenals, foundries, and public stores.' You were bound to take notice. See the books."

IN THE TWENTIETH and twenty-first centuries, Sherman's conduct at Atlanta and in the March to the Sea that followed have come to represent the beginnings of modern total warfare and proof that the laws of war cannot constrain the machinery of industrialized warfare. Surely, the critics say, Sherman's conduct shows that the code Lincoln issued in 1863 made no difference to how the Union waged the war. General Orders No. 100 contained terms bearing directly on Sherman's conduct, but there is no evidence that he consulted them. To leading historians, the law of war has seemed little more than a "moral cloak" for the Union's conduct in the last two years of the conflict.

But the skeptics miss the real story. The laws of war and the order that codified them powerfully shaped the war experience of tens of thousands of people on both sides of the conflict. Sherman's assault on Atlanta, in turn, was not a betrayal of the law of war. It was the practical embodiment of the code's unsettling critique of the orthodox laws of war.

A Most Solemn Obligation

THE FIRST PRACTICAL thing the newly codified laws of war accomplished was to make Major General Ethan Allen Hitchcock's life much harder.

Hitchcock, who oversaw the writing of the 1863 code as president of the board of advisers appointed to assist Lieber, was one of the great crusty characters of the war. Born into the family of Vermont War hero Ethan Allen, Hitchcock graduated from West Point in 1817, and returned to the Military Academy as an instructor in infantry tactics. For a decade, he taught the men who would one day become the Civil War's leading generals. On the Union side, his students included Sherman, Joseph Hooker, George Gordon Meade, Samuel Curtis, Samuel Heintzelman, and John Sedgwick. On the Confederate side, he taught Joseph Johnston, Robert E. Lee, John Magruder, Jubal Early, and Leonidas Polk, not to mention Jefferson Davis himself. Hitchcock was on his way to becoming one of the academy's legendary instructors. But when President Andrew Jackson began to meddle in the academy's affairs, the uncompromising Hitchcock soon got into political trouble. Jackson exiled him to the Indian-fighting posts of the frontier.

In the West, Hitchcock came to regard American military policy toward the Indians as a moral abomination. The U.S. policy, he wrote, was "a picture of cruelty, injustice, and horror." Serving in the interminable Seminole Wars in Florida in the 1840s, he concluded that bad faith on the part of the United States was responsible for the conflict. Americans typically treated the Indians, he said, "as white men on this continent have always treated them": as "barbarians and 'insurgents,'" especially when the Indians "presumed to set up a claim to anything" the white men wanted. The "Puritans and their descendants," Hitchcock decided, were as savage as the Pequots and theirs.

Hitchcock was not only a man of unusual principle, he was also an intellectual eccentric of the first order. In the early 1840s, while stationed on the Gulf Coast in Tampa, he read the political tracts of Thomas Hobbes and John Locke and pored over the metaphysics of Kant and Hegel. On the western frontier he turned to histories: Napier's history of Napoleon's Peninsular Campaign, the Roman history written by the great Prussian historian Barthold Georg Niebuhr (an old mentor of Francis Lieber), and Thomas Babington Macaulay's *History of England*. While fighting Indians he found spare moments to delve into Jeremy Bentham's works on utilitarianism. In Texas and Mexico, he read the seventeenth-century Dutch-Jewish philosopher Baruch Spinoza. Indeed, in the 1840s, Hitchcock published a philosophical tract of his own, one that purported to unify the doctrines of Spinoza with those of the Christian mystic Emanuel Swedenborg. After resigning from the Army in 1855, Hitchcock published a stream of additional works, each one more esoteric than the last. *Remarks Upon Alchemy and Alchemists* (1857) featured his account of the religious mysticism that lay behind alchemy's dream of transfiguring lead into gold. In 1861, just as the guns were firing on Fort Sumter, Hitchcock's abstruse *Christ the Spirit* argued controversially that Jesus had not existed at all except in the imagination of ancient Jewish mystics.

At the age of sixty-four, in the second year of the Civil War, Hitchcock rejoined the Army as a major general serving on Secretary Stanton's staff. In the summer, he inspected Union prisoner of war camps. In November, Stanton appointed him commissioner for the exchange of prisoners. A month later, he was added to the board of advisers tasked with helping Francis Lieber prepare a code of regulations for the laws of war.

H ITCHCOCK WAS AMONG the first to realize there was a serious flaw in the code he had helped produce. Since July 1862, an agreement negotiated by John Dix for the Union and Daniel Harvey Hill for the Confederacy had produced a regular system of prisoner exchanges. But by early 1863, the exchange cartel had begun to break down. The South was increasingly desperate to restore men to its depleted lines. After the major engagements in 1862 at Bull Run, Antietam, and Fredericksburg, the Union held 10,000 more prisoners than the Confederacy. In the Union, meanwhile, acute problems were arising out of the South's practice of paroling captured Union soldiers pending their exchange. Northern camps established to house idled Union soldiers on parole turned into breeding grounds for disease, discontent, and crime. Some paroled prisoners never bothered to report to the camps but went home instead; they were scattered around the country and often unavailable for a return to service after they had officially been exchanged. The parole of thousands of captured Union soldiers at Harper's Ferry and Richmond in the fall of 1862 exacerbated an already deteriorating situation.

Hitchcock responded by trying to end the Confederate practice of mass battlefield paroles. As commissioner for exchanges, he took the position that battlefield paroles were of no legal effect because the terms of the Dix-Hill exchange cartel required that paroled Union soldiers be sent through officers of exchange at Dutch Gap in Virginia or at Vicksburg in the West. Only then could a parole be binding. Noncompliant paroles, Hitchcock contended, were like escapes: they simply released a prisoner to serve in the lines again.

Francis Lieber's project aimed to bolster the Union position on paroles by adding a second objection to battlefield paroles. The code asserted that as a matter of international law no soldier could trade away his obligation to serve his country. Release on parole was "not a private act." Paroles were only valid if consented to by the commanding officer in the field and the parolee's government. Article 131 provided that "if the government does not approve of the parole, the paroled officer must return into captivity."

There was the mistake: "must return into captivity." The intended Union position was the one that Hitchcock had announced the previous winter: that invalid paroles were the functional equivalent of escapes and that prisoners discharged on an invalid parole were eligible to return to Union lines immediately. But that's not what Article 131 said. The Union's own statement of the laws of war now required its illegally paroled men to report to the South to be duly imprisoned as prisoners of war.

Lieber's code was a blank check for Confederate forces to issue wholesale paroles to captured Union soldiers at no cost to themselves. Confederate secretary of war James Seddon initially protested the code's limits on paroles. (The Confederacy's battlefield paroles had spared Seddon the considerable cost of prisoner upkeep and transportation.) But as the significance of Article 131's error became clear, the Confederacy quickly shifted its position. Moving into the North in June 1863, Robert E. Lee's Army of Northern Virginia captured Union soldiers by the thousands and simply turned them loose on an oath not to serve again until exchanged, keeping long lists of the men who had so sworn. Southern commanders like Jubal Early freely disregarded the rules for proper paroling practice set out in the 1862 cartel and the 1863 code, confident that doing so would free southern armies of the onerous work of escorting prisoners back into the South.

Stanton and Halleck scrambled to rectify the error. On July 3, while the year's two most important battles raged at Gettysburg in the east and Vicksburg in the west, Stanton rushed out an order announcing that henceforth paroles not complying with the code and the Dix-Hill cartel were to be regarded as "null and void." Halleck instructed Hitchcock to take the position that General Orders No. 100 had not superseded the 1862 cartel. But the Confederate agent of exchange Robert Ould would have no part of Halleck's dodge. Ould gleefully proposed that paroles be respected according to the position of the Union's own orders—orders that required the Union either to recognize the paroles of the Gettysburg campaign or to deliver the discharged Union soldiers back to their Confederate captors.

B Y AUGUST 1863, prisoner exchanges had broken down irretrievably for reasons much more grave than Lieber's careless mistake.

The long-term threat to prisoner exchange was the South's refusal to treat black soldiers and their white officers as eligible for exchange under the 1862 cartel. Jefferson Davis and the Confederate Congress continued to treat them as fugitive slaves, insurrectionists, and criminals, not as soldiers. In the spring, two free black boys captured while accompanying a Union regiment from Massachusetts were sold into slavery by Texas officials. In August, Secretary of War Seddon ordered General Kirby Smith to execute white officers of colored regiments "red handed on the field or immediately thereafter"; blacks in arms, he told Smith, were to be viewed as "deluded victims" of Union hypocrisy and handed over to state officials. State governors across the South put in place procedures for re-enslaving blacks taken in arms. Newspapers listed the names of blacks captured in battle and called on owners to reclaim those whom they believed belonged to them. Unclaimed prisoners were sold into slavery for the benefit of state coffers.

Some Confederate officers simply executed black soldiers on the spot. When the first black soldiers were captured in November 1862, Seddon had recommended summary execution to Jefferson Davis, and the idea never entirely went away. Kirby Smith instructed Confederate officers west of the Mississippi to give "no quarter" to both "negroes and their officers captured in arms." Entire detachments of captured black soldiers were killed on the pretext that they had attempted to escape. Officially, the Confederate War Department discouraged such practices, at least with regard to black soldiers themselves, whom they viewed as the dupes of a wicked northern scheme. But officials such as Robert Ould, the agent of exchange in Richmond, also knew that if done quietly enough, summary executions would reduce the tensions that Confederate policy had produced in the exchange system by keeping the number of black prisoners to a minimum. When one cavalry officer reported to his superiors that he had assisted in executions with his own revolver, the Confederate command decided simply that it was not in "the interest of the service" to investigate the matter further.

Harper's Weekly *depicted Confederate soldiers shooting captured*
black Union teamsters in May 1864.

It was hard to keep such executions quiet. Summary executions culminated in bloody massacres at places like Saltville, Virginia, where Confederate guerrilla Champ Ferguson and his men executed dozens of blacks in October 1864. At Mark's Mill, Arkansas, one Confederate veteran later remembered that "no orders, threats, or commands could restrain the men from vengeance on the negroes" they had captured. At nearby Poison Springs, Union colonel James Williams reported that the wounded men of the 1st Kansas Volunteers were "murdered on the spot" when they fell into Confederate hands.

The most notorious race massacre took place when Major General Nathan Bedford Forrest's cavalry assaulted the Union garrison at Fort Pillow in Tennessee in April 1864. Of the 600 Union men guarding the fort, about half were black soldiers. Most had been slaves until very recently, and many of them had lived in the vicinity of Fort Pillow. Some were even well known to members of Forrest's forces. When Forrest overran the Union positions, his men allowed white Union soldiers to surrender. But as a Confederate newspaper correspondent reported, "the negroes were shown no mercy." A sergeant in Forrest's cavalry told his wife that words could not "describe the scene" that followed. The "poor deluded negroes," he wrote shortly after the event, "would run up to our men fall upon their knees and with uplifted arms scream for mercy," only to be "ordered to their feet and then shot down." Two-thirds of the 300 black soldiers who were in the fort that morning were dead by nightfall. Forrest would later deny accusations that he or his men had executed blacks. But the evidence shows (and most historians now agree) that they did. Indeed, the Fort Pillow executions were not so much surprising as they were inevitable. They were simply the logical outcome of the South's official denial that blacks could be lawful soldiers. Forrest, who founded the Ku Klux Klan shortly after the war's end, treated black Union soldiers at Fort Pillow as he would have treated slaves in an armed insurrection before the war. They were criminals for whom the laws of war had nothing to say.

I N THE SUMMER of 1863, Lincoln, Stanton, Halleck, and Hitchcock decided the Union would not take part in any system of exchange so long as the South persisted in its treatment of black soldiers as criminals.

It was an extraordinarily unpopular policy. Many northern whites could hardly believe that the Lincoln administration would put black soldiers ahead of white ones. White soldiers in the southern camps petitioned angrily for a change in policy, observing caustically that the southern policy on black soldiers sometimes worked out to the benefit of captured blacks, who were "seldom imprisoned" but put to work and fed and clothed in order to maintain their strength. White soldiers complained that they were "starved and treated with a barbarism unknown to civilized nations," while black soldiers

Two hundred black soldiers died in the grisly massacre at Fort Pillow.

were "neither starved, nor killed off by the pestilence in the dungeons of Richmond and Charleston." The editors of the *New York Times* demanded resumption of prisoner exchanges lest "ten or twelve thousand of our soldiers be starved to death." Walt Whitman took to the newspapers to decry Secretary Stanton for turning thousands of white soldiers into hostages for the benefit of a few black men. Responsibility for their deaths, Whitman angrily asserted, would "rest mainly upon the heads of members of our own Government."

The Union's newly codified account of the laws of war played a vital role in the controversy. With a clarity that appeared nowhere else in the law of nations, the code's terms denied that a nation at war could discriminate among enemy soldiers on the basis of their race. The crisp terms provided a script for Union officials for the rest of the war. Within weeks of the code's publication, Union exchange agent William Ludlow drew on it to protest to his counterpart Robert Ould that under "the laws and usages of war" a capturing army was forbidden to withhold prisoner of war treatment on the basis of race. Halleck committed the United States to offering "protection to all persons duly received into the military service" and demanded that the Confederacy comply with this basic feature of the "rules of civilized war." In the Department of the South, David Hunter insisted that exchanges stop until the South treated Union soldiers equally "irrespective of their color." Near Vicksburg, Mississippi, Ulysses S. Grant announced that the U.S. government was "bound to give the same protection" to black troops "that they do any other troops." Benjamin Butler, who became a special agent for the exchange of prisoners in December 1863, told Ould (at Hitchcock's instruction) that it would be consistent with neither "the policy, dignity, nor honor of the United States" to allow those who had "borne arms in behalf of this country" to "remain unexchanged and in the service of those who claim them as masters."

Hitchcock also relied on the code's race discrimination provisions when he took the Union's case to the unsympathetic northern public. Hitchcock had taken positions of principle many times in the course of his long and curious career, often to his own detriment. Now, in an open letter to the editor of the *New York Times*, he made one more stand. Union soldiers in the prison camps of the South, he conceded, were undergoing "extreme sufferings" that had "naturally aroused the sympathies of our people." Why then had they not been exchanged? The answer, Hitchcock explained, was that in employing black troops, the United States had incurred a "most solemn obligation" to protect all of its soldiers and ensure that they were "treated with that humanity which is due to all other troops in like circumstances according to the laws of civilized warfare."

S KEPTICS DOUBTED HITCHCOCK's sincerity in 1863 and have continued to doubt it ever since. The skeptics argue that protecting black soldiers was merely a pretext for the real reason the Union discontinued exchange: promoting its strategic interests. As the critics observe, Union leaders such as Stanton had come to think that exchanging all the Union's southern prisoners would hand the Confederacy "a new army 40,000 strong" while getting little in return for the North. The arithmetic of prisoner exchange had often worked against the Continental Army in the War of Independence. Now exchanges seemed likely to work against the Union. Prisoners held by the Confederacy were often too weak to be returned to the front lines. Many Union soldiers' three-year enlistments would expire in the summer campaign season anyway.

Yet the treatment of black soldiers was no mere excuse for self-interested Union tactics. As far back as December 1862—long before conditions in southern prisons raised political pressure on the exchange question—Lieber, Hitchcock, and Halleck had made the equal treatment of black soldiers a central feature of their project to codify laws of war. While the code was still in the drafting stage in January 1863, Stanton told the governor of Massachusetts that "the United States was prepared to guarantee and defend, to the last dollar and the last man . . . all the rights, privileges and immunities that are given, by the laws of civilized warfare." And in their private correspondence, Union officials expressed the same position. Early in the fall of 1863, weeks before he wrote his public letter to the *Times*, Hitchcock told Lieber that "if the government employs colored soldiers, their officers (& themselves also) must be protected according to the laws of war."

Justifying an otherwise unpopular policy by appealing to the equality of black and white soldiers would have been a singularly poor political tactic. Popular reaction to the Union policy was so hostile that Hitchcock offered his resignation within days of the publication of his open letter. (Stanton declined to accept it, and Hitchcock served to the end of the war.) The policy of refusing discriminatory rebel exchange offers became more controversial with every passing month. Even Secretary of the Navy Gideon Welles believed that stopping the exchanges because southern slaveowners "held on to their slaves" when they were captured "was an atrocious wrong." Prisoners moldering at the prison camp at Andersonville, Georgia, were positively venomous toward a policy that resulted in the deaths of hundreds of their white comrades, sometimes at a rate of more than 100 each day. "The Everlasting Nigger must be protected," seethed a Massachusetts prisoner, "and the soldier may take care of himself." A Vermont sergeant complained that "we must stay here because they can't agree on some nigger question." A New Yorker wrote that he had "no desire to be immolated upon the altar of the 'irrepressible nigger.'" William Farrand Keys, a schoolteacher from Pennsylvania, bitterly expressed what many in the camps thought: "it appears that the federal government thinks more of a few hundred niggers than of the thirty thousand whites here in bondage." If refusal to resume the exchange cartel was not actually based on the South's refusal to treat black Union men as soldiers, the administration had chosen a singularly bad public justification for its policy.

The Union position on prisoner exchanges was not based solely on principle, of course. It had strategic implications as well, though not only the ones the critics typically cite. White men available for army service had grown scarcer in 1863. As the Union turned to unpopular measures such as the draft, the availability of black soldiers became an increasingly critical part of the Union war strategy. Almost 200,000 would serve in arms by the war's end. By the summer of 1863, however, free blacks such as Frederick Douglass had made clear that if the Lincoln administration wanted to recruit black soldiers into its armed forces, it would have to insist on prisoner of war treatment for black soldiers. A black man from New York named Theodore Hodgkins put it bluntly: If the government did not protect its black soldiers, he wrote to the president, "it may as well disband all its colored troops, for no soldiers whom the government will not protect can be depended upon." In the war's waning weeks, when black recruitment was no longer as urgent a concern, Grant agreed to resume exchanges without insisting on a policy of nondiscrimination.

The greatest problem of all for the skeptics is that, as Hitchcock reminded Stanton after the war was over, all the Confederacy had to do to resume prisoner exchanges was agree to exchange black soldiers man for man alongside whites. The Union offered precisely these terms repeatedly in 1863 and 1864. Grant himself offered to enter into such an exchange with Lee in October 1864. But each time, the South refused to take up the Union's offer. Ould told a Union exchange officer that southerners would "die in the last ditch" before they agreed to treat blacks as soldiers. Even many captured Confederate soldiers opposed any agreement to exchange black soldiers, despite the fact that such an arrangement would have sped their release. One Alabama

*Exchanges resumed in the last weeks of the war; artist Alfred Waud
sketched recently exchanged Union soldiers receiving new clothes in
December 1864.*

man, captured at Chattanooga in November, speculated in his diary that
the Union had enlisted blacks for the very purpose of stopping prisoner
exchanges. "They well know," he observed, "we can never treat our slaves
as prisoners of war." No wonder, then, that in their private correspondence,
Ould and Seddon characterized the Union's insistence that former slaves
in Union uniforms be treated as prisoners of war as "the chief" and "insurmountable" obstacle to the restoration of the exchange system.

IN THE CONTROVERSY over prisoner exchanges and black soldiers, the
laws of war did not oblige the United States to take the stand it did. The
code Lieber drafted in 1863 asserted only that the South could not discriminate among regular Union soldiers without facing the risk of Union
reprisals. It was up to the Union to decide whether to insist on prisoner of
war treatment for its soldiers. What the laws of war did was to offer support
for the unpopular policy of refusing to enter into discriminatory prisoner
exchanges. The code, in short, helped the Lincoln administration stand its
ground.

Therein lies a startling paradox for the beginnings of the modern laws of war. For by insisting on nondiscrimination, Lincoln's code had a hand in the greatest humanitarian disaster of the last two years of the war. Some 55,000 men died in Civil War prison camps. Had exchanges been allowed to go forward on the South's terms, countless of those men would have lived. If the law of war's only goal were reducing human suffering, this would have been a searing indictment of its legacy. But the Union's code embodied a mix of purposes. Lessening humanitarian suffering was one. But so was justice for black soldiers and victory for the Union.

Holt's Bright Young Men

NO ONE HAD a fiercer vision of justice in wartime than the intense man in charge of military justice in the Union War Department. Joseph Holt was born in Kentucky in 1807. After a brief but lucrative career as a lawyer in the cotton boomtown of Vicksburg, Mississippi, he had retired back to his home state, a wealthy man at the age of thirty-five.

Holt soon became involved in Democratic Party politics. In 1857, President James Buchanan appointed him commissioner of patents. Two years later, Buchanan named Holt to his cabinet as postmaster general of the United States. And when Secretary of War John Floyd of Virginia resigned in the weeks after Lincoln's election, Buchanan appointed Holt to replace him. From December 1860 until March 1861, Holt worked feverishly to bolster federal defenses around Washington and to defend military outposts in the fast-seceding states of the South, including Fort Sumter in Charleston Harbor. In March, following Lincoln's inauguration, it was Holt who delivered to the new president the grim news that Fort Sumter could not hold out more than a few weeks without new supplies.

Secession radicalized Holt. He had always been prone to fierce obsessions. Before the war, President Buchanan thought that the Kentucky-born Holt "went further in his hatred of the abolitionists than Christian charity would have warranted." Now Holt turned his zeal to preserving the Union against the secessionists. For much of 1861, he delivered fiery speeches decrying secession and condemning what he called "the fallacy of neutrality"—the idea that his home state of Kentucky could carve out a noncommittal posture in the conflict. When Lincoln fired his first secretary of war, Simon Cameron, in January 1862, he nearly chose Holt as Cameron's replacement. Lincoln ultimately settled on Holt's friend and ally from the

Buchanan administration, Edwin Stanton of Pennsylvania. In September, at Stanton's urging, Lincoln appointed Holt to the new position of Judge Advocate General, making him the Army's top lawyer.

JOSEPH HOLT'S APPOINTMENT marked a turning point in the Union's use of the laws of war. When the war began, the law governing soldiers in the armies of the United States was badly out of date. The Articles of War had not been updated for half a century. The office of the Judge Advocate of the Army dated back to the Revolution, but it had been ignored and sometimes even allowed to lapse into nonexistence in the years since. From 1821 to 1849, there had been no judge advocate at all.

At the war's beginning, the Army's judge advocate was John Fitzgerald Lee. Lee, who had held the office since its renewal in 1849, was a Virginian by birth and a cousin of Confederate general Robert E. Lee. Like George McClellan, John Lee opposed the disruption of slavery by Union soldiers. He also believed that military commissions—the tribunals crafted by Winfield Scott in 1847 to try offenses for which Congress had not given authority to the traditional courts-martial—had no place in the conflict between North and South. He doubted military commissions' authority to try captured Confederate soldiers for offenses against the laws of war. But he denied in particular that they had any jurisdiction over civilians, who under the Constitution enjoyed rights of due process and trial by jury in a federal court. When Henry Halleck, as commander of Union forces in the West, prosecuted a Missouri man named Ebenezer Magoffin before a military commission for killing a Union sergeant "when not a legitimate belligerent," Lee objected that a man who was not a "public enemy in arms" had the right to a trial by jury in open court. "Military commissions," Lee wrote Stanton in April 1862, "are not a tribunal known to our laws." Stanton believed that the power to use military commissions was vitally important to the Union war effort. He fired Lee before the summer was over.

Holt determined to adopt a much more expansive approach to military justice. He gathered around him a team of ambitious and well-connected lawyers. Over the next two and a half years, Holt recruited thirty-three men from among the best and the brightest of the northern antislavery elite; Lincoln personally appointed each of them as judge advocates to work under Holt's direction. Most had roots in the prewar Republican Party. Levi C. Turner, who acted as judge advocate between the discharge of John Lee and the appointment of Holt and stayed on as Holt's assistant, was a Columbia

College–educated lawyer and a founder of the New York Republican Party. John A. Bingham and William McKee Dunn were Republican members of Congress until being turned out in the 1862 midterm elections. Dunn, who had graduated from Yale College, lost because his early support for enlisting black soldiers was highly unpopular in his home state of Indiana. Bingham would later draft the first section of the Fourteenth Amendment to the U.S. Constitution, guaranteeing constitutional privileges and immunities, due process, and the "equal protection of the laws" for the freedpeople. John Bolles, the former Massachusetts secretary of state, grew up in an abolitionist family before graduating from Brown University and writing a prize-winning essay for the American Peace Society. John Knox was the scion of one of Pennsylvania's most prominent families, a descendant of the republic's first secretary of war, Henry Knox, and himself a former state attorney general. DeWitt Clinton was the grandson of the great New York governor of the same name. Lucien Eaton was the son of Andrew Jackson's first secretary of war and a graduate of Harvard Law School.

The law school at Harvard produced five judge advocates in all, including John Chipman Gray (later a professor at the school and founder of one of the country's leading law firms) and William Winthrop, a descendant of the first governor of the Massachusetts Bay Colony and a graduate of Yale College. Fifteen of the thirty-three judge advocates appointed by Lincoln were educated at one or more of the schools that would later come to be known as the Ivy League universities of the Northeast. Others attended prominent liberal arts schools like Union College in New York or Wheaton College in Illinois.

The judge advocates adopted an aggressive stance that perfectly matched the stepped-up intensity of Lincoln's approach to the war in the fall of 1862. The very first opinion out of the new Judge Advocate General's office affirmed the president's power under the laws of war to seize slaves working on Confederate fortifications. In subsequent weeks, Holt vigorously defended Emancipation and the enlistment of blacks into the Union armies ("a most powerful and reliable arm of the public defense," he told Stanton). He championed the self-defense rights of newly free black men prosecuted for acts of violence against their former owners. (When one black man in Arkansas nearly severed the head of his former master in self-defense in December 1863, Holt told Lincoln that only an acquittal would properly recognize the former slaves "as occupying the status of freedmen.") In the field, the judge advocates worked to track down rumors that Confederate captors were quietly executing colored soldiers. And back in Washington,

Holt encouraged harsh punishments for whites who continued to buy and sell slaves after January 1, 1863. Failure to punish such men for their "barbarous avarice," Holt told Lincoln, would "set at naught the proclamation of emancipation" and dishonor the black men who now risked "the perils of battle" and "the horrors of massacre" in the service of the Union armies.

Where Judge Advocate General John Lee had denied that the Union possessed the legal authority to use military commissions as a tool for punishing its enemies, Holt and his team believed that the laws of war vested the president with a wide-ranging power to try civilians and Confederate soldiers alike in military commissions. Lincoln agreed. Three weeks after Holt's appointment, on September 24, 1862, Lincoln suspended the writ of habeas corpus around the country—effectively precluding judicial inquiry into the legality of arrests—and authorized the trial by military commission of anyone "affording aid and comfort" to the enemy.

Holt's most significant contribution during his first year in office was a creative act of lawyering that turned the laws of war into a broad warrant for Lincoln's military commissions. On March 3, 1863, the lame duck Thirty-seventh Congress authorized Lincoln to do what he had already done on his own on September 24, and indeed had been doing in an *ad hoc* fashion since April 1861: suspend the writ of habeas corpus. Future judge advocate John Bingham was the House floor manager for the crucial legislation. But the legislation also created a new constraint on the president. The second section of the act, sponsored by Senator Lyman Trumbull of Illinois, required the president to submit reports to the federal courts listing all persons held as "state or political prisoners, or otherwise than as prisoners of war." Any person so listed was to be discharged from imprisonment if the next grand jury session of the court came and went without producing an indictment charging him with a crime. Violating the reporting and discharge obligations was a crime punishable by fine and six months imprisonment.

The statute was clear enough. It artfully removed the legal cloud that had hung over Lincoln's unilateral suspension of habeas corpus since the first month of the war, while also limiting the administration's ability to seize people and hold them indefinitely. But Holt ingeniously reasoned away the act's constraint on executive power. Contending that its terms were "extremely difficult of construction" and potentially at odds with what he delicately called "the exigencies" of the Union war effort, Holt read the statute in such a way as to restore Lincoln's freedom to arrest noncombatants who aided the enemy. With Stanton's blessing, Holt decided that the act distinguished between military and political prisoners and applied its requirements only to the latter, excluding not only soldiers held as prisoners of war but also anyone convicted by a military commission for offenses against the laws of war.

As Holt saw it, the act's constraints on the president's power had no bearing on prisoners held pursuant to the president's law of war authority. In so construing the act, Holt set the stage for a radical expansion in the scope of the laws of war.

H ISTORIANS OF THE Civil War often cite the postwar prosecution of Captain Henry Wirz, the Confederate commander at Andersonville prison camp in Georgia, as the war's only trial for war crimes. But this is badly mistaken. Nearly 1,000 individuals were charged with violating the laws of war during the course of the conflict. Of the approximately 4,000 military commissions held by the North during the war, one in four dealt with a law of war violation.* Indeed, violating the laws of war (as Judge Advocate William Winthrop later remembered) was "the most common form of charge before military commissions."

The charges were strikingly different from the kinds of prosecutions for law of war violations that would become typical in the twentieth and twenty-first centuries. Since World War II, violations of the laws of war have usually involved crimes such as abusing prisoners of war, killing civilians, or shooting soldiers who are attempting to surrender. Military commissions in

---

*The numbers are very difficult to arrive at, which is part of why no one to my knowledge has heretofore compiled an estimate of the number of persons accused of violations of the laws of war in military commissions. I arrived at this estimate in two different ways. First, a research assistant named Gideon Hart and I counted military commissions charging law of war violations in the printed General Orders volumes that are scattered in libraries and archives around the country. We were unable to locate General Orders volumes for every Union military department, but we counted 712 military commissions charging law of war violations. (The full results from Hart's massive efforts, along with full documentation, can be found in his article in vol. 203 of the *Military Law Review*, published in the spring of 2010.) I did an independent count using the database of court-martial and military commission records compiled by Tom Lowry and the Index Project from the files contained in the National Archives in Washington. Lowry's files indicate 875 military commissions charging law of war violations. I subsequently double-checked the Lowry data by examining a subset of the files he indexed. My estimate of the total number of military commissions slightly reduces Mark Neely's standard estimate of 4,271 because Hart and I found that Neely's count included some number of trials that were properly categorized as courts-martial. Lowry counts 5,562 military commissions, including commissions that took place after April 1865. See Mark E. Neely, Jr., *The Fate of Liberty: Abraham Lincoln and Civil Liberties* (New York: Oxford University Press, 1989), 168; Thomas P. Lowry, *Merciful Lincoln: The President and Military Justice* (Charleston, SC: Thomas P. Lowry, 2009), xi.

the Civil War occasionally charged men with violating the laws of war for committing such acts. But the overwhelming majority of prosecutions arose out of very different kinds of conduct. Against members of the regular armed forces of the Confederacy, for example, the most common violation of the laws of war charged in the military commissions was lurking behind Union lines as a spy. Breaking oaths of allegiance to the Union, parole violation, and recruiting for the Confederacy behind Union lines often led to charges against Confederate soldiers as well.

Far and away the most common defendants were not Confederate soldiers but noncombatants and guerrillas, who constituted nearly 85 percent of the people charged with law of war violations before Union military commissions. Judge advocates charged such defendants with violating the laws of war for a stunningly wide array of conduct. Some charges were for acts closely tied to the war. Judge advocates in Missouri prosecuted suspected members of the notorious William Quantrill's band of guerrillas for law of war violations when they robbed and killed Union sympathizers. Other charges, however, accused defendants of violating the laws of war for conduct that was a good deal less closely tied to the conflict. In Kentucky, where the courts remained open for much of the war, judge advocates charged noncombatants with violating the laws of war by "using disloyal language" and kidnapping "a contraband negro." The judge advocates charged forgery artists with violating the laws of war by forging false discharge papers. Assisting desertion was a war crime. So was making a false claim for damages against the U.S. armed forces and corruptly facilitating the release of convicts to serve as substitutes for conscripted men. Neglect of duty by military contractors and service providers could be a violation. So could forging medical certificates or furlough extensions, evading militia service, harboring rebel guerrillas, refusing to take an oath of allegiance to the United States, running the blockade (though not when committed by the nationals of neutral states like Great Britain), obstructing the recruitment of black soldiers, killing a freedman, sending blacks deeper into Confederate territory after Emancipation, attacking black soldiers' families, conspiring to deprive soldiers of the vote, and desecrating the bodies of dead Union soldiers.

In the border states of Missouri, Kentucky, and Maryland, trading with the enemy was a common way for northern civilians to violate the laws of war. Going into the South without a pass was a law of war crime. (In the border states, citizens with obligations of allegiance to the North were prosecuted for violating the laws of war when they joined the rebel army or evaded service in the Union armed forces, something which Union lawyers did not treat as criminal at all when done by residents of the states that voted to secede.) One St. Louis woman was charged and convicted of violating the laws of war for writing encouraging letters to acquaintances in the South. (A Baltimore woman was similarly prosecuted for sending a sword to a rebel officer, as was the person who purchased the sword in New York City and the two people in Baltimore who took possession of the sword on her behalf.) Horse-stealing could be a war crime. Expressing anti-Union views was chargeable as a war crime in some parts of Missouri in 1862. Even private violence by one noncombatant against another could become a violation of the laws of war so long as it had sufficient connection to the war effort.

Judge advocates sometimes charged Union soldiers with violations of the laws of war, too, for ransacking civilian property or threatening civilians or for attempting to rape noncombatants. But such charges were rare: there were only about thirteen such trials between 1861 and the end of the war. Partly this was because Union commanders could use courts-martial to try their own soldiers for conduct that might otherwise have been charged as war crimes. No doubt the small number of Union soldiers so charged also reflected bias in favor of the Union's own men.

More fundamentally, the rarity of prosecutions against Union soldiers accused of violating the laws of war reflected the basic function of the military commission and the laws of war in the work of the judge advocates. Since the days of Alexander Hamilton, American statesmen had used the laws of war as a vehicle for expanding the authority of the federal government and of the executive branch in particular. This was Holt's aim as well. Union judge advocates charged noncombatants with violating the laws of war to establish that they were military prisoners, not political prisoners, and thus (under Holt's aggressive interpretation) outside the reporting and discharge requirements of the March 1863 habeas legislation. Those who violated the laws of war could also be tried before a military commission even where the regular courts were open for business. By charging violations of the laws of war, Holt's team of judge advocates was able to circumvent both Congress and the courts and either try or detain military prisoners— whether they were civilians or regular soldiers—as they saw fit.

The judge advocates created an institutional footprint for the laws of war such as had rarely been seen before in American history, if not the history of warfare more generally. Not since the days of the Philadelphia prize lawyers of the early republic, when men like Peter Stephen Du Ponceau, Jared Ingersoll, and William Rawle argued fine points of the laws of maritime warfare in the federal courts, had there been such a concentrated pool of law of war knowledge in the United States. In June 1864, Congress belatedly recognized this by organizing Holt's judge advocates into the Bureau of Military Justice and promoting the Judge Advocate General to the rank of brigadier general. The law of war now had boots on the ground.

W HEN JUDGE ADVOCATES marched into the field, they carried with them the pocket-sized pamphlet code of rules issued by Lincoln and written by Francis Lieber.

At the start of the war, military tribunals were badly disorganized. Commanders like John Frémont in Missouri tripped over the knotty details of military law. (So did Ulysses S. Grant.) Even into 1862, for example, military tribunals purported to try civilians for treason, a crime the Constitution makes prosecutable only in the courts.

The 1863 *Instructions for the Government of Armies of the United States in the Field* offered a blueprint for organizing the Union's military commissions. Article 13 of the code, which Halleck edited so heavily he had virtually drafted it himself, resolved Frémont's early confusion by carefully distinguishing the two kinds of military tribunals: courts-martial, whose power was "conferred and defined" by the 1806 Articles of War; and military commissions, whose authority was "derived from the common law of war." Judge advocates cited particular code provisions by number and relied on Lieber for advice in hard cases. (On the rare occasions where the accused was represented by counsel, both the prosecution and the defense often referenced Lieber's writings.) Connections between the code and the judge advocate corps were cemented in 1863, when Lincoln appointed Lieber's son Norman (an 1858 graduate of Harvard Law School) as the judge advocate in Union-occupied Louisiana.

The code's broad view of military authority helped spur a dramatic expansion in the number of military commissions in Union military departments around the country. Before the end of 1862, only Missouri had seen a significant number of military commissions. Once Lincoln issued the code and Stanton distributed it to thousands of officers, however, military commissions spread to military departments around the country. The second half of 1863 witnessed as many military commissions outside Missouri (150) as had been held outside the state in the entire first two years of the war. In 1864, 750 military commissions were held outside the state.

Lieber's pamphlet code also bolstered the commissions' conceptual basis. What business, after all, did Lincoln and Holt have trying thousands of

U.S. citizens in military courts? Judge Advocate John Lee had objected to military tribunals in 1862. As late as 1864, John A. Dix, commanding the Union's Department of the East, asked Lieber to explain how military commissions could "take cognizance of . . . any violation of the law of war" by a U.S. citizen when the citizen was not "connected in any wise with the military service of the United States." Lieber's stern answer was that war implicated entire populations, not merely (as Rousseau had posited a century before) their armies in the field. "War is not carried on by arms alone," Lieber's code stated. The "native of a hostile country" was as much an enemy as the armed soldier, and martial law under "the laws and usages of war" extended "to property, and to persons," regardless whether they were soldiers or civilians. Lieber told Dix that under the conditions of the Civil War, citizens could ("or rather must," he corrected himself) "be tried by military courts, because there is no other way to try him and repress the crime which may endanger the whole country." Indeed, Lieber was not only satisfied with the legality of the military tribunals that Holt's judge advocates oversaw, he was proud of the United States' role (and his own part in it) in expanding the reach of the law into domains once dominated by sheer violence. The "careful trials of spies [and] brigands," he wrote to Halleck, were "a novel feature in the history of the Law of War." After one spying case, Lieber boasted to Holt that "no person accused of being a spy, in the whole history of war, had ever so dignified and elaborate a trial."

HOLT'S EFFORTS AND Lieber's code went to the U.S. Supreme Court after the elaborate (but hardly dignified) arrest and military commission trial of the Lincoln administration's most implacable northern critic.

In the early morning hours of May 5, 1863, an entire company of Union soldiers—as many as 100 men by some accounts—made its way by unmarked train to Clement Laird Vallandigham's home in Dayton, Ohio, stormed it with fixed bayonets, and arrested Vallandigham in his bedroom as his wife and sister-in-law cowered behind him. Vallandigham was Ohio's (and perhaps the North's) most vocal opponent of the war. A former Democratic Party congressman, he had been giving incendiary antiwar stump speeches throughout the state, excoriating "Lincoln and his minions" and denouncing the conflict as "a war for the freedom of the blacks and the enslavement of the whites." The new Union commander of the Department of the Ohio, General Ambrose Burnside, worried that Vallandigham's speeches would undermine the Union's ability to attract new recruits. Drawing on Lieber's unpublished early draft of the rules of war, Burnside declared that "all persons found within our lines who commit acts for the benefit of the enemies of our country will be tried as spies or traitors, and, if convicted, will suffer death."* After another incendiary speech (delivered while Burnside's undercover agents took notes in the crowd), Burnside ordered Vallandigham's arrest.

The next day, May 6, Burnside hauled Vallandigham before a military commission in Cincinnati and charged him with publicly expressing sympathy for the rebellion with the purpose of hindering the U.S. government's efforts to suppress it. Vallandigham refused even to enter a plea of not guilty: he was not, he insisted, triable by a military tribunal, for he was a U.S. citizen, and as such entitled under the Constitution to due process and a public jury trial in a court of law. But the commission, made up of seven officers from Burnside's Department of the Ohio, refused to entertain the objection. After two days of trial, the officers adjourned to deliberate.

Not content to await the verdict, Vallandigham sought a writ of habeas corpus from Judge Humphrey Leavitt in the federal circuit court. The government's response unveiled the legal strategy that had been forged by Holt and that was advanced in the code the Union would release in its final form just days later. To deliver it, Burnside sent two men with close ties to the Lincoln administration: Aaron Fyfe Perry, a leading Ohio Republican who had turned down a seat on the Supreme Court in 1861, and the federal district attorney, Flamen Ball, a former law partner of Treasury Secretary Salmon Chase. Perry argued that Burnside had arrested and tried Vallandigham under the international "laws of war, or martial law," or what Perry (adapting language Halleck had inserted into Lieber's draft code) called the "common law of nations." Lieber's draft, which was in its final stages of review by Stanton, expressed exactly the same idea, defining martial law as "military authority . . . in accordance with the laws and usages of war." A nation at war, Perry recited, could "lawfully secure and make prisoners" of any "persons belonging to the opposite party (even the women and children)." Chase's longtime law partner Flamen Ball summed up the broad implications of the U.S. position. "Ohio," he said, "is at war because the United States are at war."

---

*Lieber's draft had instructed that anyone in a place under martial law who "gives information to the enemy," or otherwise assisted the enemy, was punishable by execution; so, too, were "armed prowlers" or "persons of the enemy territory who steal within the lines of the hostile army." Burnside's order simplified and combined Lieber's terms. See [Francis Lieber], *A Code for the Government of Armies in the Field as Authorized by the Laws and Usages of War on Land*, unpublished ms., Huntington Library, San Marino, California.

And in wartime, "the citizens of the state of Ohio are liable to the operation of the laws of war as administered *ex necessitate rei* [out of the necessity of things], by courts-martial or military commissions." Sensing that he was in over his head, an overmatched Judge Leavitt ruled in the government's favor.

After a week of deliberations, the commission pronounced Vallandigham guilty and sentenced him to prison for the remainder of the war. Lincoln promptly reduced the sentence to banishment from Union lines. But Vallandigham could not be bought off so easily. He petitioned the U.S. Supreme Court to reverse the conviction and sentence of the military commission. When the Court took up the case in February 1864, it let stand the Lincoln administration's broad assertion of a law of war authority. The opinion by Justice James Moore Wayne noted that Burnside had acted "in conformity with the instructions approved by the President of the United States," the instructions that (as the Court noted) had been prepared by Francis Lieber and Major General Ethan Allen Hitchcock. Quoting from the code's Article 13, Justice Wayne observed approvingly that military commissions tried and punished offenses "under the common law of war."

T HE WORK OF Holt and his judge advocates had no analogue in the Confederate States of America. A small rebel office headed by assistant secretaries of war Albert Taylor Bledsoe, a former lawyer turned mathematics professor at the University of Virginia, and then John A. Campbell, a former justice of the United States Supreme Court, presided over a few military tribunals. When Confederate forces caught twenty-two Union raiders trying to destroy the railroad connecting Atlanta to Tennessee in the spring of 1862, for example, military tribunals convicted eight of the raiders as spies and executed them by hanging. But the Confederate Congress refused to appoint a judge advocate general or a judge advocate corps. In the very months of 1863 in which Holt, Lieber, and Halleck were crafting the Union's expansive conception of the laws of war as a source of authority, the Confederate assistant adjutant general responsible for military justice denounced the idea of martial law as anathema to the Confederate Constitution. Officials in the rebel War Department ruled that there could be no military tribunal jurisdiction over persons residing in the Confederate States of America other than soldiers.

The shrinking Confederate lines of 1863 and 1864 meant that the Confederacy never had the need to develop anything like the Union's judge advocate staff to dispense justice in occupied enemy territory. Campbell, the former justice, deprecated the significance of his work for the Confederacy as "irksome, uncongenial, and in most cases, trivial labor." Captured black soldiers might have produced an expansion of the authority of Confederate military tribunals, but instead of treating their actions as war crimes, Jefferson Davis and the Confederate Congress sent black prisoners to the states to be dealt with under the state criminal laws.

It was the North, then, that made the law of war part of its strategy for winning the war. But in so doing, the Union raised a tension that has haunted the law throughout its history. Holt and the judge advocate corps treated the law of war not only as a restraint but as an instrument for increasing the power of a nation at war. In this sense, the law of war was not at odds with campaigns such as Sherman's March to the Sea. Both were efforts to bring to the South what Sherman called the "hard hand of war."

Which Party Can Whip

S HERMAN'S MARCH THROUGH Georgia and South Carolina comes down to us differently than most of the moral controversies of the Civil War.

Consider the destruction of Athens, Georgia, in 1862. When Colonel John Basil Turchin allowed Union troops to sack the city, rebels cried foul. Surely this was a clear-cut violation of the standards of civilized conduct. But making sense of the episode quickly became difficult. Turchin claimed that he had been engaged in lawful reprisals against noncombatants who had fired on Union troops from their homes and participated in the execution of Union prisoners. Or consider the events at Chambersburg, Pennsylvania, in July 1864, when Confederate forces burned the town after it refused to hand over $100,000 in gold. Confederate generals John McCausland and Bradley T. Johnson defended their actions as retaliation for Union general David Hunter's destruction of the Virginia Military Institute (McCausland's alma mater) and the Virginia governor's mansion. The same pattern emerged in Missouri. When Colonel John McNeil ordered ten captive Confederate soldiers taken out and shot by firing squad in Palmyra, Missouri, he defended his actions as justified retaliation for the execution of a local Union sympathizer by Confederate forces. When Confederate sympathizers protested Union general Thomas Ewing's order that four counties be completely depopulated, Ewing (who had grown up in the same home as William Tecumseh Sherman) countered that the population had provided crucial support for the rebel guerrilla William Quantrill, whose bloody raid on Lawrence, Kansas, just days before had killed 150 Unionist men and boys. Quantrill in turn cited a history of internecine violence between anti- and pro-slavery guerrilla forces that stretched back before the war to the days of John Brown in the 1850s.

Again and again, moral controversies over conduct in the war lay obscured by a thick fog of charge and countercharge, with no discernable stopping point. The same troubles plagued bitter guerrilla actions across the Upper South; each side accused the other of the first atrocity. The first wrongdoer usually proved elusive. Rumors of exploding bullets used by one side were matched by claims of barbaric incendiary devices said to be used by the other. When the Union blockaded Charleston by sinking old vessels in the mouth of the harbor, the South booby-trapped bodies along South Carolina's coast. Even at Fort Pillow, where historians are confident that most of the postwar denials were false, students of the war have had to wade through thick layers of obfuscation to find the truth.

But if most of the war's contested episodes lay hidden in the fog of war, Sherman's march comes to us as if in the bright sunshine of a cloudless day. For Sherman did not claim that his actions were aberrations justified by his enemy's atrocities. He aimed to fight a war that would be as candid as it was uncompromising.

L ITTLE IN SHERMAN's background suggested the unforgiving mode of warfare for which he would become known. A West Point graduate of the class of 1840, where he graduated sixth out of forty-two, Sherman had been brought up in the orthodox world of antebellum military thought. He happily spent much of his early military career stationed in the South and disapproved when his stepbrother Thomas Ewing took up antislavery politics. After a series of failed business enterprises in California and Missouri, he took a job as the superintendent of the Louisiana Military Seminary and settled down comfortably in slaveholding Baton Rouge in 1859 on the very eve of the secession.

Sherman's initial approach to the conflict closely resembled McClellan's idea of enlightened warfare. In the Department of the Cumberland in 1861, he punished soldiers for property offenses against noncombatants and provided compensation for property taken by his men. As the historian Charles Royster rightly put it, Sherman's "standard of conduct was the West Point ideal of a regular army, keeping warfare away from noncombatants for the sake of both humanity and strict discipline." After the First Battle of Bull Run, Sherman cursed the volunteers: "Goths or Vandals," he called them, who had no "respect for the lives and property of friends and foes." He complained that "petty thieving and pillaging" by Union soldiers did the Union cause "infinite harm." Sherman shared McClellan's views on slavery as well, instructing his officers that "fugitive slaves must be delivered up on application of their masters." His thinking reflected Rousseau's idea that the enemy was an army, not a people.

As the war ground forward, however, Rousseau's notion no longer appeared to Sherman as a tenable description of the conflict. Serving as the military governor of Memphis in the summer of 1862, Sherman found himself fighting an unending battle not against southern armies but against shadowy guerrillas. The South, he came to see, was sustained not only by its armies but by the farmers who at night turned into fighters, by the newspapers that kept up Confederate morale, and by the women who made sure production on the plantations continued apace in the absence of their husbands. By August, Sherman was becoming convinced that "all in the South are enemies of all in the North," that the "entire South, man, woman, and child, is against us, armed and determined." In the war between North and South, he wrote, "all the People of the one" side were "enemies of the other." Perhaps European wars of the eighteenth century had lived up to Rousseau's model. But Sherman told Henry Halleck that the Civil War was unlike those conflicts because the United States was "not only fighting hostile armies, but a hostile people." Sherman laid out the implications: We must, he told Halleck, make not only the "organized armies" of the South but also the "old and young, rich and poor, feel the hard hand of war."

Once Sherman had come to see the population of the South as his enemy, it was an easy step to adopt a strategy of attacks on civilian infrastructure. Newly promoted to general-in-chief, Ulysses S. Grant had already ordered Sherman to inflict "all the damage you can" against the "war resources" of the South. Now, as Sherman prepared to set out from Atlanta on what would become the most celebrated (and reviled) military campaign in American history, Halleck advised him to "destroy every mill and factory within reach." Sherman took to the plan with a stern enthusiasm. He would, he said, "make a wreck of the road and of the country" behind him, destroy Atlanta, and then move with his most battle-hardened 60,000 men, "smashing things to the sea" and ensuring "the utter destruction" of Georgia's "roads, houses, and people" so as to "cripple their military resources." After Sherman took Savannah in December, Halleck urged him to proceed to Charleston and destroy it for generations to come: "If a little salt should be sown upon its site," Halleck encouraged, "it may prevent growth of future crops of nullification and secession."

But Sherman did not stop at attacks on infrastructure. He attacked the morale of the southern people, taking the war directly to southern noncombatants to destroy the population's willingness to fight. "I propose," he wrote in mid-October, "to demonstrate the vulnerability of the South, and make its inhabitants feel that war and individual ruin are synonymous terms." To Grant, he said: "I can make the march, and make Georgia howl!" To Lincoln, he wrote that he and his army would commit themselves to "desolating the land as we progress" until Georgia withdrew its quota from the armies of the South. To win the war, he told Halleck in September 1863, required a conquest of the South so unrelenting that it would cause "all idea of the establishment of a Southern Confederacy" to be abandoned. "I would not coax them, or even meet them half-way," Sherman said, "but make them so sick of war that generations would pass away before they would again appeal to it."

Sherman's idea of war against the South contained limits. It did not extend to personal violence directed at noncombatants. He aimed to limit the violence against white southern noncombatants almost entirely to property destruction.

The destruction Sherman wrought was vast nonetheless. On November 12, he set out from a ruined Atlanta. For the next month, the two wings of his massive army carved a path of destruction 30 to 60 miles wide and almost 300 miles long, annihilating or confiscating "anything of any military value" between Atlanta and the sea: "railroad tracks, machinery, cotton mills, horses, mules, and foodstuffs—and much more." In Georgia, his men confiscated or destroyed 90,000 bales of cotton worth some $36 million, along with almost 7,000 mules and horses, more than 13,000 head of cattle, 10 million pounds of grain and another 10 million pounds of fodder, as well as 6 million rations of beef, bread, coffee, and sugar. Sherman later estimated the total value of goods confiscated and destroyed at $100 million, though he thought that only $20 million of that had been used by his men. ("The remainder," he stated, "is simple waste and destruction.") When Sherman's army encountered the homes of prominent secessionists, the destruction became purposefully more punishing still. At the residence of former U.S. senator Howell Cobb, Sherman instructed his men to "spare nothing," and that night, he later remembered, "huge bonfires consumed the fence-rails" and virtually everything else that would burn on Cobb's plantation.

Once Sherman's men moved north from Georgia into South Carolina, the destruction became even greater. The "whole army," Sherman told Halleck, "is burning with an insatiable desire to wreak vengeance upon South Carolina." And wreak vengeance they did. Sherman's troops burned entire towns along their march to the state capital, Columbia. The capital itself was almost completely destroyed. Who started the fires in Columbia has long been contested. On a windy day, Wade Hampton's Confederate cavalry had tried to burn the city's cotton in order to deny it to Sherman's approaching army. Those fires almost certainly spread to nearby structures. But there is little doubt that many of Sherman's men aided in the destruction of Columbia by setting new buildings ablaze.

WHAT MAKES SHERMAN'S campaigns of 1864 and 1865 so memorable is that he put a torch not only to southern property but to the conventional moral language of warfare. His disdain for "hypocritical appeals to God and humanity" represented a decisive rejection of the notion of war for which he had been trained at West Point. For Sherman, "outrages, cruelty, [and] barbarity" were mere "side issues" in war. Like Clausewitz, Sherman believed that focusing on such considerations was thus "idle and nonsensical." The "only principle," he insisted, was "which party can whip." Sherman dismissed the war's humanitarian missionaries with contempt. He snubbed the agents of the U.S. Sanitary Commission and the delegate-missionaries of the U.S. Christian Commission as "crowds of idlers" and "curiosity hunters." (In Atlanta, Sherman summarily put one Indiana sanitary commission agent out of business.) Even the torment of Union prisoners was not enough to distract him from his single-minded focus on bringing the war to a speedy and hard end. When given the opportunity, Sherman declined to exchange the Confederate soldiers he held for all the Union soldiers at the Andersonville prison camp; exchanges, he feared, would "slow the progress of his army and prolong the conflict." After he authorized a failed cavalry raid to free the prisoners at Andersonville in the summer of 1864, Sherman reproached himself for making a bad tactical mistake. He even wondered whether the modern practice of taking prisoners was a wise policy. "At times," he mused, "I am almost satisfied it would be just as well to kill all prisoners.... They would be spared these atrocities."

Nothing could have been further removed from the Enlightenment model of the laws of war. Sherman often spoke in dangerously loose terms. "To secure the navigation of the Mississippi," he declared in 1863, "I would slay millions." He repeatedly urged the mass relocation of the southern population and the resettlement of their land by loyal Unionists from the North, though he pursued this policy in only two isolated instances, once at the Confederate cotton works at Roswell, Georgia, and then again at Atlanta. These were ways of talking about armed conflict that diverged sharply from the Enlightenment's moral logic of war. But Sherman found himself thinking that the orthodox approach to constraints on warfare took a crabbed and distorted moral perspective.

Sherman coined a phrase for the peculiar moral vision adopted by the conventional international laws of war: "the humanities of the case," he called it. What he meant was that his humanitarian critics evaluated each situation—each case—in isolation, as if unconnected to the broader war effort, its aims, or its future ramifications. They condemned no-quarter warfare or violence against civilians without regard to the ends in view. What Sherman had keenly grasped was that the laws of war in the modern age had set aside the just war tradition's concerns with right and wrong and replaced them with a new ethic of humanitarian constraint, an ethic that dismissed questions of justice as ultimately unresolvable.

In place of the narrow focus of the case-specific approach, Sherman adopted a wider lens that aimed to bring war to a just end with a minimum of unnecessary suffering overall. In this approach, reducing long-term suffering sometimes meant increasing war's short-term destruction. That was what Sherman had in mind when he told Mayor James Calhoun of Atlanta that the way to end the suffering of his people was to end the war quickly. In early 1865, Sherman expressed the idea more bluntly: "the more awful you can make war the sooner it will be over." Francis Lieber had proposed the very same notion in his code. Sharp wars were short wars, and all things considered, short wars were often more humane, even when they involved destructive tactics.

No one can be entirely sure when Sherman first said, "War is hell." No one can even be sure whether he said it at all. One officer under his command later remembered Sherman saying the words over dinner in South Carolina in early 1865. But Sherman himself could not recall the occasion on which he had uttered the words for the first time. And for good reason. In one way or another, he said the same thing in so many words time and time again. "War is barbarism," he said at Jackson in 1863. At Vicksburg in 1864, he wrote that "war is simply power unrestrained by constitution or compact." In Atlanta, he told the Confederates that "war is cruelty." Fifteen years after the end of the Civil War, he told a gathering of veterans what they knew only too well: "Boys, it is all hell."

Most historians have seen Sherman's disillusioned realism as antithetical to the very idea of legal constraints on warfare. They have aligned themselves with Jefferson Davis's account of Sherman's conduct in Atlanta, which Davis labeled a "barbarous cruelty" like none since "the sixteenth century," or with Davis's evaluation of Sherman's actions at Columbia, South Carolina, which Davis called "an act of cruelty" as barbarous as the excesses of "the Thirty Years' War." But this is far too complacent a conclusion. It rescues the easy nostrums of restraints in wartime without subjecting them to the scrutiny that men like Sherman and Lieber believed they deserved. Sherman's conduct departed from the Enlightenment model of war. But so did the most exhaustive statement of the laws of war in American history to date. The Union's code of May 1863 and Sherman's march shared the same grim engagement with the moral limits of war.

L IEBER FOLLOWED SHERMAN'S campaign via private reports he received from Henry Hitchcock, an officer on Sherman's staff and the nephew of Lieber's colleague Ethan Allen Hitchcock. In 1862, after the battle at Fort Donelson, the younger Hitchcock's mother-in-law had taken care of the injured Hamilton Lieber in St. Louis. Now his letters kept the professor well informed on the progress of Sherman's army through the Deep South.

The reports left Lieber deeply impressed with some features of Sherman's campaign. "Sherman moves his army better than Uncle Sam [delivers] our letters," Lieber gushed. Here at last was a Union commander who seemed to grasp the nature of Lieber's fierce thinking about war.

Yet the more Lieber learned about the events unfolding in Georgia and the Carolinas, the more he worried that Sherman's destruction threatened to get out of control. Lieber approved of the general's basic strategy, but the unorganized destruction his men wrought filled him with dread. "Assuredly my name is not namby-pamby," he wrote to Halleck. He approved of "a manly, unflinching yet un-impassioned sternness" in war. Nonetheless, Lieber pleaded that it was vital to "stay the hand of mere ruthless revenge" by Sherman's army in South Carolina. Mere "ruthless burning, killing," and rape, he warned, "demoralizes an army." Napoleon's rise from popular general to dictator loomed large for the Prussian émigré Lieber. An undisciplined democratic army, he worried, was only a few steps away from becoming a politically destabilizing mob.

The difficulty was that even Sherman did not fully grasp the ethical implications of his march. Cutting free from his supply lines, Sherman had embarked on a kind of warfare that delegated radical discretion to individual soldiers. When the general ordered his army to "forage liberally on the country during the march," he inadvertently touched off a revolution in modern military strategy. He had aimed to manage the foraging process from the top down by organizing formal foraging parties of fifty men "under the command of one or more discreet officers" who were to do the work of collecting provisions for each brigade. (It was, he told his men, "most important" that they "keep their places and do not scatter about as stragglers or foragers.") Yet almost immediately the decentralizing imperatives of the campaign undid the fragile limits Sherman had sought to impose. Only one day out of Atlanta, Sherman described how a "soldier passed me with a ham on his musket, a jug of sorghum-molasses under his arm, and a big piece of honey in his hand." "Forage liberally on the country," the soldier joked in a stage whisper, quoting Sherman's order back to him. Within days, the brigades' official foraging parties were being supplemented by foragers from virtually every company in the army.

The logic of decentralized foraging quickly led to a dynamic that would embitter generations of white southerners. Competing with one another for the best provisions they could find, "Sherman's bummers" (as the foragers came to be called) evolved into a system of individual initiative perfectly (if accidentally) designed to vacuum all the usable goods from a path fifty miles wide along the road from Atlanta to the sea. Some foragers tried to restrain themselves and leave the Georgia families they encountered with enough food to make it through the winter. But whatever one party of bummers left behind was likely to be taken by the next. To leave provisions on a plantation was thus no humanity at all, but merely to deprive one's own closest comrades of provisions that would doubtless be scooped up by the next foragers to come along. What the 16th Iowa left, the 53rd Illinois would take. The very structure of the competitive foraging system undercut restraint. It produced instead a race to the bottom in which foragers swept up more provisions than centrally directed foraging parties possibly could have managed.

All too often the race led to downright lawlessness. Bummers hanged Georgia farmers by the neck from tree limbs until almost dead in order to make them reveal the location of hidden supplies. Where the farmers had already fled, foragers held loaded pistols to the heads of blacks on the plantation to force them to disclose the whereabouts of their former masters' goods. Torture and threats quickly moved from provisions to booty like jewels, silver, and cash. Executions sometimes followed for those who refused to cooperate. The five or six miles on either side of Sherman's army became a kind of lawless zone of unconstrained violence. Confederate home guards and guerrillas roamed the byways of the country and executed foragers whenever they could, hanging them along the roadsides as grim warnings. By the time the march was complete, the Union command counted 173 of its men hanged or shot at close range. Plantation owners booby-trapped false caches of treasure and provisions before fleeing from Sherman's onslaught. Sherman, in turn, ordered the execution of Confederate prisoners in retaliation.

The decentralized structure of the campaign produced similar effects when it came to property destruction. At the outset of the campaign, Sherman ordered that only "corps commanders" were authorized "to destroy mills, houses, cotton-gins, etc." Even commanders were to forbear from destruction in neighborhoods whose residents allowed the army to pass unmolested. But Sherman's men were vested with too much discretion to ever ensure that such orders were carried out. As they departed Atlanta, "firebugs" among his soldiers burned some 5,000 homes, despite his instructions against doing so. One New Jersey officer remarked in South Carolina in early 1865 that it seemed "almost as though there was a Secret organization among the men to burn Every thing in the State for thus far, in spite of orders, & the utmost efforts of officers, houses, in Some way, get on fire & Nearly all we have passed thus far are I think in ashes." But the destructiveness of Sherman's army was less the result of a secret organization than it was the effect of the purposeful organization of the campaign: its devolution of initiative down the chain of command.

Some of Sherman's officers tried harder than others to interrupt the dynamic of destruction. (General Oliver Otis Howard was one who detested what he called the "inexcusable and wanton" looting of trunks and silver plate.) But Sherman himself quickly became resigned to the actions of his bummers. "I never ordered the burning of any dwelling," he told one of his officers, "but it can't be helped." Sherman's claim of innocence was not strictly true, and he knew it. "I say Jeff Davis burnt them," he said slyly. When Sherman turned away one white woman who requested that he post a guard at her home, he turned to an officer and acknowledged that "the soldiers will take all she has." After the war, Sherman would confess that "many acts of pillage, robbery, and violence, were committed" by his bummers. Belief that Sherman tacitly authorized such acts was sufficiently widespread that one man arrested for unauthorized destruction cited Sherman's approval in his defense.

Halleck and Stanton had commissioned Lieber's 1863 code in part to respond to the decentralization of authority that the war had already called into being in the second half of 1862. That was why it was issued as a General Order and printed as a pamphlet that was distributed to officers around the Army. That was why it was styled as instructions to the U.S. armies "in the field." When Halleck passed the code along to his commanders in the field in May and June of 1863, he stressed the imperatives of decentralization and initiative, explaining that the application of the rules "in particular places" would "be left mainly to the good judgment and discretion of the commanders." Lieber, too, had helped usher the laws of war into the age of entrepreneurial initiative. In the weeks after Lincoln issued the code as General Orders No. 100, a commercial publishing company in New York printed still more copies, packaging Lieber's text together with advertisements for the publisher's popular science texts and its volumes on ordnance, gunnery, and infantry tactics.

In Sherman's march, however, the centrifugal forces of military decentralization outraced the technological advance the code represented for the laws of war. The difficulty was that Sherman's men had begun sounding like the commander himself. "War is an uncivil game," pronounced a soldier in Sherman's ranks, "and cant be civilized." "Truly," said another, "war is cruelty." Crossing into South Carolina, one of Sherman's men crowed, "Boys, this is old South Carolina, let's give her h-ll!"

It was one thing for Sherman to step outside the sometimes artificially constraining moral limits of the laws of war and to set aside case-by-case humanitarianism for an ethic of the long run. But it was entirely another to vest discretion to do so in tens of thousands of individual soldiers. What if 60,000 men took it upon themselves to decide when the orthodox rules ought to apply and when they were best set aside in the name of a higher morality or an all-things-considered humanity? One Ohio officer gave a grim answer. The "country behind us," he said, "is left a howling wilderness, an utter desolation."

I RONICALLY, the chief prophet of the new way of war was also among the least enthusiastic Union commanders when it came to using the war to reorganize the social life of the Confederacy. Only a massive transformation of the social structure of the South would bring a measure of equality to the 4 million people freed by the war. But as his march through the Carolinas neared its end, and as the armies of the South collapsed, Sherman hoped peace would restore the Union to its prewar condition—without slavery, to be sure, but otherwise unaltered. So did millions of other northerners. And that helps to explain the startling development at the war's end. While Sherman was living out the radical new conception of the laws of war that Lieber had drafted and Lincoln had issued, a far more traditional idea of the laws of war surged back into view.

Chapter 10

Soldiers and Gentlemen

With malice toward none; with charity for all;
with firmness in the right, as God gives us to see the right,
let us strive on to finish the work we are in. . . .

—Abraham Lincoln, Second Inaugural Address, March 1865

W HEN Ulysses S. Grant and Robert E. Lee met on April 9, 1865, at Wilmer McLean's farm in Appomattox Courthouse, Virginia, their armies were no longer comparable. Lee's Army of Northern Virginia was on its last legs. Hunger and desertions had decimated its ranks. Neither, in Grant's view, were the two armies morally alike. Sitting with Lee at the McLean farm, Grant reflected to himself that his counterpart's cause was "one of the worst for which a people ever fought."

Yet the Union commander had no doubt about the Confederate general's sincerity. Grant thought "the great mass" of Confederate soldiers had fought with the same earnestness, and this made all the difference. The human tendency to persuade oneself of one's cause was the starting point for the rules of Enlightenment warfare that Grant and Lee had learned at West Point. It was why civilized armies did not hold their enemies' causes against them, even when they seemed heinous. And it was why, despite all their differences, the two men met that day as equals in the eyes of the law.

In keeping with the customs and usages of enlightened soldiers, Grant accepted Lee's surrender on remarkably magnanimous terms. Some 25,000 Confederate soldiers went home on the promise not to take up arms again. Grant promised that so long as they kept their oaths, they would not be punished by the United States for their role in the conflict.

What Grant and Lee and every other West Point graduate knew was that civilized wars ended in agreements to forget the perceived wrongs of the contending sides, not in the punishment of a vanquished enemy. Once war was over, the need to retaliate for past violations of war's rules in order to ensure future compliance virtually disappeared. Moreover, the prospect of punishment threatened to make war a ghastly fight to the bitter end. Men facing punishment and death might never surrender.

The favored practice in the age of enlightened warfare was to grant amnesty to the subjects of the warring states for their actions in the conflict, consigning violations of the laws of war to what eighteenth-century peace treaties called "a general oblivion." As Francis Lieber's old Prussian handbook put it, peace offered "forgetting and amnesty" (*Vergessenheit* in the German) for "all discord, enmity, hostilities and of whatever deeds had been committed during the war." Nine days after Appomattox, William Tecumseh Sherman and General Joseph Johnston (two more West Point graduates) agreed to magnanimous terms recognizing the rebel state governments, restoring the citizenship and rights of rebels, and offering a broad amnesty. Newly sworn-in President Andrew Johnson refused to accept the Sherman-Johnston agreement on the grounds that Sherman had badly exceeded his authority, but barely a month later the president issued an amnesty for all rebel soldiers, excepting high-ranking officers and those who had treated captured Union soldiers unlawfully. Peace treaties the following year between the United States and five Indian tribes that had allied themselves with the South took the same approach, adopting a "general amnesty of all past offences."

Yet there was an alternative approach to the end of war, one that had long been adopted in civil wars. In the seventeenth century, the English Civil War had closed with the execution of prominent royalists. Widespread executions and purposeful starvation marked the grim finale of the uprising in Scotland in 1745. A half century later, Lord Charles Cornwallis (seventeen years removed from his defeat at Yorktown, Virginia) executed thousands of defeated Irish rebels. In the first decade of the nineteenth century, Napoleon imposed terrible punishments on men caught up in guerrilla insurgencies against his puppet governments, first in Calabria and then in Spain.

The code Lincoln issued in 1863 balanced precariously between the honorable soldier's amnesty and the much harsher approach characteristic of civil wars. The fierce vision embodied in the code had already underwritten nearly 1,000 war crimes trials during the war. By its terms, it authorized treason prosecutions of rebels in the war's wake, too. After John Wilkes Booth assassinated Lincoln on April 14, a mere five days after the courtly meeting of military commanders at Appomattox, northern sentiment tipped toward a fierce justice for the postwar world. Arrests of high-ranking Confederate officers and civilian officials followed hard on the heels of the April surrenders. The Union Army cast Jefferson Davis into solitary confinement at Fort Monroe in Virginia and held his vice president, the diminutive Alexander Stephens of Georgia, at Fort Warren in Boston Harbor. In quick succession, Union forces arrested the former justice of the U.S. Supreme Court John Campbell and Confederate cabinet officials George Trenholm, James Seddon, John Reagan, Robert Hunter, and Stephen Mallory. Governors Zebulon Vance of North Carolina, Abraham Allison of Florida, and Joseph Brown of Georgia soon found themselves in prison, as did the Confederacy's Canadian agent Clement Clay, Senator Benjamin Harvey Hill of Georgia, the Confederate agent for exchange Robert Ould, and a number of others. In May, the Lincoln assassination conspirators went on trial. Captain Henry Wirz, the commandant of the Andersonville prison camp, sat in the Old Capitol Prison in Washington, D.C., awaiting his own trial for abusing Union soldiers. And in midsummer, Secretary of War Stanton sent Francis Lieber into the Confederate archives on a mission to uncover evidence of complicity by Jefferson Davis and other high officials of the Confederacy in the crimes of the war.

Lieber's foray into the rebel archives promised to undo the magnanimous spirit of Grant and Lee at Appomattox. His project aimed to support a vast system of war crimes trials and to carry the uncompromising approach to the laws of warfare into the postwar world. But it was not to be. Within two years, Jefferson Davis would walk out of Fort Monroe arm-in-arm with his wife. Eighteen months thereafter, Johnson would issue an amnesty for Davis and the last few Confederate officials yet to be pardoned. The project of turning the laws of war into a vehicle for prosecuting Confederate leaders had come to naught. But why?

To Assassinate Everybody

JOHN WILKES BOOTH's bullet denied Lincoln the chance to elaborate a full-blown plan for dealing with the rebels in the postwar world. But the martyred president left clues.

In his Second Inaugural Address, delivered on March 4, 1865, Lincoln voiced the thoughts that had preoccupied him in the fall of 1862 as he considered Emancipation and a more aggressive Union war effort. The problem, he told the inaugural crowd, was that each side to the conflict imagined it was in the right. Men in the North and the South "read the same Bible, and pray to the same God; and each invokes His aid against the other." It seemed impossible that those who fought to defend the evils of slavery could lay claim to God's authority. But Lincoln cautioned against overconfidence. "Let us judge not that we be not judged," Lincoln said, echoing the New Testament's Matthew 7:1 God would judge, for there was sin enough for both sides. ("He gives to both North and South, this terrible war, as woe due to those by whom the offence came. . . .") Our role on earth was to leave revenge behind and to move forward to "bind up the nation's wounds." Exquisitely attuned to the limits on man's capacity to know for certain whether his way is the way of God, Lincoln finished the address with words that balanced humility with righteousness: "With malice toward none; with charity for all; with firmness in the right, as God gives us to see the right, let us strive on to finish the work we are in . . . to do all which may achieve and cherish a just, and a lasting peace, among ourselves, and with all nations."

Lincoln's thinking in the final weeks of the conflict was singularly forward-looking. Charles Sumner remembered that the president "had been gentle & forgiving" down to the last. The president, Sumner recalled, "said nothing harsh even of Jefferson Davis," and urged fellow Union men to "repeat the words quoted in his late address, 'Judge not that ye be not judged.'" Lincoln's actions matched his words. In December 1863, he offered full pardons to rebels willing to swear an oath of loyalty to the Constitution of the United States and respect all laws and presidential proclamations regarding Emancipation. (Lincoln excluded several classes of rebels, including high-ranking military officers, civil or diplomatic agents, and anyone who had treated black Union soldiers or their officers "otherwise than lawfully as prisoners of war.") A year later, in his December 1864 message to the Congress, the president assured the nation that the offer remained open, though he warned that it would not remain open forever. All but Jefferson Davis, he said, would be allowed to "reaccept the Union." (Privately he hoped Davis would escape abroad.) In February 1865, Lincoln even presented a plan to his cabinet that would have paid the South $400 million in compensation for Emancipation (equal to the cost of 200 days of war) and offered amnesty for treason if the rebels would agree to put down their arms.

When prominent American actor and Confederate sympathizer John Wilkes Booth assassinated Lincoln at Ford's Theatre in Washington, he eliminated the Union leader most committed to the amnesty tradition in postwar justice. For there was a powerful backward-looking and sometimes vengeful streak in Union sentiment as well. In the Congress, Senator Benjamin Wade and the powerful Joint Committee on the Conduct of the War had been pressing since January for retaliation against the South for its treatment of Union soldiers and other atrocities. "If you go to war," Wade thundered, "you have departed from the great principles laid down by Christ and His followers." The forgiveness principle of the Sermon on the Mount, Wade insisted, thus had no application to conduct in war. Sumner disagreed, and cited his friend Lieber as an authority on the dangers of retaliation. But others, such as Senator Timothy Howe of Wisconsin, sided with the Joint Committee. The better biblical frame of reference, he said on the Senate floor, was not New Testament forgiveness but Old Testament retaliation: the law of an eye for an eye. "If they take a tooth," Howe announced, the Union ought "to take another" in reprisal.

JOSEPH HOLT IN the War Department's Bureau of Military Justice believed the assassination of Lincoln demanded severe postwar measures. But where Wade and Howe had pressed for retaliation, Holt sought the criminal punishment of Confederate leaders. In the spirit of his departed president's code, he aimed to adapt the fierce law of war of the wartime military commissions for the postwar world.

In the days after Booth shot Lincoln, the assassination of the president was Holt's overwhelming preoccupation. Booth had leapt to the stage and escaped (hobbled by his fall) through a back door. In the hours that followed, even before the president was dead, Edwin Stanton personally launched a fevered investigation, which he soon handed off to Holt and the Bureau of Military Justice. Within ten days, the government had arrested seven people Holt believed had conspired in the assassination. On April 26, Union troops tracked down and killed Booth in a Virginia barn seventy-eight miles from the capital and arrested his companion, the impressionable David Herold.

Stanton and Holt thought that the authority of their wartime military tribunals extended to the eight alleged conspirators in custody. Less than twenty years after Winfield Scott had pioneered the idea of the military commission in Mexico, the criminal punishment of those who violated the laws of war had become standard operating procedure in the Union war effort. The code of 1863, which set out much of the law that the military commissions applied, listed assassination as a violation of the laws of war. Though the provision had been drafted with the Confederate outlawry of Benjamin Butler and David Hunter in mind, it would apply just as well to the killing of Lincoln. The trial of the assassination conspirators would proceed in a military tribunal, as had hundreds of trials for violations of the laws of war in the preceding four years.

The new attorney general of the United States, James Speed, agreed. Lincoln had appointed Speed in December 1864 to replace the aging and ill Edward Bates. As a longtime antislavery lawyer from Kentucky, his instincts now ran to the protection of the freedpeople, something that became more apparent with time and that ultimately led to his resignation in 1866. But he was not the sharpest lawyer. Lincoln had chosen him for his border state political connections, not his legal acumen. An unsympathetic Justice Samuel Miller wrote that Speed was "one of the feeblest men" he had seen argue before the Court. And when President Johnson asked him whether the Lincoln conspirators could be tried in a military commission, Speed made what would prove to be a fateful error. In a long opinion, Speed contended not only that the assassination could and should be tried by military commission but that it could not be tried in any other forum. "If the persons charged have offended against the laws of war," Speed opined, "it would be as palpably wrong for the military to hand them over to the civil courts, as it would be wrong in a civil court to convict a man of murder who had, in time of war, killed another in battle."

Perhaps Speed was not to be blamed for erring. The law governing punishment for violations of the laws of war was startlingly new; the term "war crime" had not yet even come into use. But his mistake was an important one. There was no reason to see resort to the courts as legally unavailable. The theory of the prosecution was that Booth and his accomplices were not acting as lawful soldiers and therefore could not claim the privilege to kill that the law of war afforded. There was thus no need to charge Booth's accomplices with war crimes at all. They might just as well have been charged with conspiracy to commit murder. But given the standard operating procedures of Holt's Bureau of Military Justice, and given that the White House was in post-assassination disarray, little or no thought was put into whether the trial might better have taken place in the federal courts in Washington, D.C. Speed had reached his conclusion by May 1. And once the case was set for trial in a military commission, a series of tactical mistakes ensued, mistakes that almost certainly would not have been made in a civilian courtroom and that would soon come back to haunt Holt's postwar effort to bring rebel leaders to trial.

* * *

WHEN THE LINCOLN assassination commission opened on May 9, 1865, six male defendants shuffled into a low-ceilinged room in the Old Arsenal Penitentiary in Washington. They were dressed in black and hooded so that they could not see. The two defendants who followed close behind—a woman named Mary Surratt and a seventh man named Dr. Samuel Mudd—were spared the indignity of the hood, but all the defendants wore shackles of one kind or another. Some were chained to heavy iron balls. At Holt's order, the room had been closed to the public.

Having persuaded themselves that a military commission was necessary, Holt and his judge advocates had pressed the commission to its limits. Brevet Major General August Kautz, who sat as one of the members of the commission, thought the scene looked like something out of the Spanish Inquisition. "I was quite impressed with its impropriety in this age," Kautz later recalled. Holt soon pulled back. On subsequent days, the hoods disappeared. The secrecy rule was lifted when the newspapers protested and Holt realized that he would not be able to prevent selective leaks. But the damage was done. The shackles remained, and so did the lasting image of the hooded defendants before a secret tribunal.

Two of the most trusted members of Holt's wartime judge advocate team, John Bingham and Henry Burnett, assisted the judge advocate general in the trial. The three men presented a stream of witnesses whose testimony connected the defendants to Booth. Against six of them, the evidence (while not bulletproof) was relatively clear. George Atzerodt, who was supposed to have attacked Vice President Johnson but had failed to do so, had taken a room at the Kirkwood House hotel where the vice president was staying; weapons and a bankbook in Booth's name were found in the room. Lewis Powell, who had been assigned to kill Secretary of State Seward and had nearly accomplished his goal, was identified by multiple eyewitnesses to his brutal knife attack on Seward in the secretary's Washington home. David Herold had been captured with the assassin. Statements by one of the defendants, Samuel Arnold, convincingly connected Arnold and his co-defendant Michael O'Laughlin to an earlier plot by Booth to kidnap Lincoln, though there was little to suggest that either man had been involved in the events immediately surrounding the April 14 assassination. Edman Spangler, a stagehand and carpenter, was implicated by testimony showing that he had helped Booth get away down the back alley behind the theater.

The cases against Mary Surratt and the Virginia doctor named Samuel Mudd, the remaining two defendants, were considerably more controversial. Fleeing Washington, Booth and Herold had sought medical assistance at

Mudd's home within hours of the assassination; Mudd set Booth's broken leg and failed to alert authorities to the possibility that his patient might have been the fugitive assassin. A boarder at Mary Surratt's boardinghouse named Louis J. Weichman further testified that he had spent time together with Mudd and Booth in the capital weeks before Booth sought medical assistance from Mudd in Virginia.

Weichman also implicated Mary Surratt, testifying that Atzerodt, Powell, Herold, and Booth had all frequented the Surratt boardinghouse in the weeks leading up to the assassination and that Booth had spoken secretively with Mary and her son John, who later fled the country to evade arrest. Another witness, John Lloyd, also testified against Surratt. Lloyd, who had leased a farm and tavern from Surratt at the tiny Virginia crossroads known as Surrattsville, swore that John Surratt along with Herold and Atzerodt had left guns and ammunition at the tavern several weeks before the assassination, and that Mary Surratt had checked to make sure the guns were at the ready in the days before the assassination and had done so again on the fateful day itself. Also weighing against Surratt was the inconvenient fact that Powell had implicated her by his actions. He had been arrested three days after the assassination when he arrived poorly disguised at her boardinghouse while investigators were searching the premises.

The testimony of Weichman and Lloyd laid powerful, if circumstantial, cases against Surratt and Mudd. Had Holt stopped there, and especially if Surratt had been imprisoned with Mudd rather than executed, the Lincoln assassination trial might not have generated the controversy it has for the past 150 years. But Holt was not satisfied with pursuing the eight defendants before the commission. The charges named Jefferson Davis and seven Confederate agents in Canada as unindicted co-conspirators in the assassination plot. And when the case delved into this broader conspiracy theory, it began to come apart at the seams.

T HE PRINCIPAL STRATEGY of the defense was to contest the authority of the military commission to try the defendants for violating the laws of war. Senator Reverdy Johnson of Maryland represented Mary Surratt and took the same position that John Lee had adopted when he was the Union judge advocate in 1862 and that Clement Vallandigham had advanced in 1864. Military tribunals, Johnson told the commission, had jurisdiction only over soldiers and moreover could try only those crimes that were specified in Congress's Articles of War from 1806. Johnson willingly conceded that there might be an exception when the U.S. military operated outside its own borders, as it had in Mexico when Winfield Scott instituted military commissions in 1847. But to do so in the United States was an entirely different matter. The defendants here were not enemy aliens, they were U.S. citizens, living in the nation's capital and in Maryland. Under such circumstances, Johnson contended, military tribunals were illegitimate substitutes for the kinds of treason prosecutions that the Constitution expressly committed to the federal courts. Indeed, Thomas Ewing, Jr. (the foster brother and brother-in-law of William Tecumseh Sherman and veteran of the bitter Missouri guerrilla war), argued on behalf of Dr. Mudd that the tribunals operated without law at all.

Holt's team had powerful responses at the ready. Could it be the case, Bingham replied, that the military was empowered to shoot down Booth in cold blood but not to put assassins on trial under the laws of war? "By what law" was a president justified in killing one of the conspirators, but condemned for "subjecting to trial" others "according to the laws of war"? Attorney General Speed made the same argument in his opinion supporting the authority of the military tribunal. Military tribunals were the self-imposed restraint that soldiers adopted to be sure the particular person before them deserved death. War usually brought death to its victims with far less individualized attention to justice. No one other than pacifists (of whom there were precious few in 1865) doubted the legality of legitimate military killings in wartime. How, then, could trying and executing the same people for violations of the laws of war be unlawful?

As Speed saw it, "the civil courts have no more right to prevent the military, in time of war, from trying an offender against the laws of war than they have a right to interfere with and prevent a battle." Was it really the defendants' position that the military should give way to the civilian authorities in precisely the domain in which it was already seeking to exercise restraint? "It is curious," Speed concluded, "to see one and the same mind justify the killing of thousands in battle because it is done according to the laws of war, and yet condemning that same law when, out of regard for justice and with the hope of saving life, it orders a military trial before the enemy are killed." The implication of Speed's and Bingham's words was only too clear: If the defendants were right, the military would in the future resort to more traditional modes of military force, ones that would not be nearly as discriminating or restrained as those exercised by the commission.

Ultimately, Bingham and Holt could barely even understand the nature of the defendants' objection. Had the defendants' lawyers not noticed the hundreds of military tribunal prosecutions in which the United States had prosecuted rebels for violations of the laws of war over the previous four years? The work of the judge advocates had been to mobilize what the Union's 1863 code and Justice Wayne's opinion in the *Vallandigham* case had called "the common law of war." By "what code or system of laws is the crime of 'traitorously' murdering" defined, Ewing demanded to know on behalf of the defendants. Holt's reply was straight from the vigorous version of the customs and usages of war crafted by Lieber and issued by Lincoln at the nadir of the Union war effort: "the common law of war," he answered. If there was any doubt whence Holt derived the authority for the charges, he dispelled it on June 8 when he offered into evidence for the prosecution a copy of General Orders No. 100, Lieber's *Instructions for the Government of Armies of the United States in the Field*.

Holt's arguments carried the day before the military commission. After deliberating for several days, the commission returned guilty verdicts for all eight defendants on June 30. President Johnson approved the commission's findings on July 5. Arnold, O'Laughlin, and Mudd received terms of life imprisonment. The commission sentenced Spangler to six years at hard labor. But as for Atzerodt, Herold, Powell, and Surratt, the commission sentenced them to be hanged by the neck until dead. Two days later, Judge Andrew Wylie of the District of Columbia courts reluctantly acquiesced in the president's refusal to recognize Mary Surratt's emergency habeas petition. (Johnson insisted that the writ of habeas corpus was still suspended, but just in case it was not, he issued a special order suspending it for Surratt's case in particular.) Within hours, Union military officials hanged Atzerodt, Herold, Powell, and Surratt from a newly built scaffold in the south yard of the Old Arsenal Penitentiary.

T HE LINCOLN CONSPIRATOR trial raised serious questions about flaws in the military commission system and accordingly about the utility in the postwar world of the fierce version of the laws of war that Lincoln and Lieber had advanced in early 1863.

The military commission placed virtually no constraints on the scope of the conspiracy theory that Holt's team proposed. A court would almost certainly have required that the judge advocates stick closer to the defendants in the dock. But lacking any such limit, Holt and his team exhausted themselves trying to connect Booth's accomplices to the highest reaches of the Confederate government. Calling a shadowy network of informants as witnesses, they aimed to prove the existence of a nefarious plot reaching from the Confederate capital at Richmond to agents in Canada and back to Booth in Washington. The commission heard about surreptitious Confederate plots to burn the North's major cities and destroy its ports. The prosecution presented evidence of efforts to destroy civilian steamboats and blow up the Union supply lines at City Point in Virginia by means of a new torpedo device. Witnesses testified to plots to burn New York City, to introduce infectious diseases in the North, and to starve captured Union soldiers at prison camps in the South. Holt's team submitted testimony describing Confederate agents' involvement in a raid on civilian property at St. Albans, Vermont, launched from across the Canadian border.

Most important, Holt relied on a man he introduced to the commission as Sanford Conover. Conover testified that he had worked as a Confederate agent in Canada under the alias James Watson Wallace and that he had there met with numerous Confederate agents (including some named as co-conspirators in the charges against Booth's accomplices) to arrange "the plot to assassinate Mr. Lincoln and his cabinet." Conover helped expand Holt's case against the alleged accomplices into a wholesale attack on the war methods of the South. He testified to schemes to attack Union prison camps and release entire regiments of captive Confederate soldiers to plunder the interior of the Union. He described a plan to destroy the Croton Dam, which supplied New York City with its water. He detailed plans to set off a yellow fever epidemic by sending infected goods to the North's most populous cities. Most of all, he connected the schemes to the highest levels of the Confederate government.

Holt's reliance on Conover backfired even before the trial had come to a close. Conover, whose real name was Charles Dunham, was actually a con man. By mid-June, reports were circulating in the press to indicate that Conover had concocted a fantastic series of lies. A Canadian came forward to say that he was the real James Watson Wallace and that he had no knowledge of the conversations Conover claimed to describe. The *Toronto Globe* published evidence that Conover had simply made up his stories from whole cloth. The *New York Times* reported that the testimony that had "caused such a sensation" now "seem[ed] to be in a muddle." In late June, John A. Dix, commander of the Union's Department of the East, privately warned Holt that Conover was a notorious character. But blinded by his zeal to connect the Confederate hierarchy to the assassination and to an entire scheme of unlawful warfare, Holt plunged forward in reliance on his dubious witness nonetheless.

Holt's team reached too far in its arguments about the law as well. Law of war commissions had become a basic part of the Union war effort. Yet Bingham in particular sought to use the trial to establish a breathtaking expansion in the scope of the military commissions. Arguing before the commission, he insisted that every single rebel soldier was implicated in the assassination, or at the very least in unlawful killings. "Everybody" who "entered into the rebellion," he thundered, "entered into it to assassinate everybody that represented this Government." Assassination and unlawful killing were the natural consequences of the rebellion; they were the very purpose for which men had joined the southern armies. Thomas Ewing grasped the implications. Why, he asked the commission, had the prosecution adopted such a novel position? It was for the same reason that Achilles immolated a dozen Trojans at the funeral pyre of Patroclus: "simply because they were Trojans, and because Patroclus had fallen by a Trojan hand." Now Holt and Bingham were threatening to burn every rebel at the pyre. Indeed, Ewing warned, it could even prove to be worse. In his view, the eight people accused of being the accomplices of Booth were no more subject to military jurisdiction than any other American—unless, that is, military law extended over and embraced "all the people of the United States."

E WING'S CLAIM WAS an exaggeration, but it was not as much of one as it has seemed in the years since. Though it has long been forgotten by historians, the men participating in the Lincoln conspiracy tribunal knew full well that dozens of war crimes trials were taking place all around the country in the waning days of the conflict and in its immediate aftermath. Many such trials took place far from the spotlight. Others, though a good deal less prominent than the prosecution of the Lincoln assassination conspirators, were nonetheless high-profile affairs.

In January 1865, a military commission in Cincinnati had attracted nationwide press attention when it tried and convicted a group of seven men, including a swashbuckling British mercenary named George St. Leger Grenfell, for conspiring in violation of the laws of war to set fire to Chicago and free the captured rebel soldiers held there at the Union's Camp Douglas. The next month, one of Holt's close associates, Judge Advocate John Bolles, led the closely watched prosecution of a well-connected young Virginian named John Yates Beall at Fort Lafayette in New York Harbor. A military commission convicted the handsome but impetuous Beall of unlawful attacks on vessels in the Great Lakes, attempted sabotage of civilian railroads in upstate New York, and being a spy. "It is a murder," declared Beall as he mounted the scaffold and turned to face his beloved South. (Orville Browning would later wonder whether John Wilkes Booth had hoped to avenge Beall's death when he entered Lincoln's box at Ford's Theatre a month and a half later.) At around the same time, Union officials in New York also tried, convicted, and executed a Confederate agent named Robert Kennedy on charges of violating the laws of war and spying in connection with a failed attempt to set a great fire in Manhattan. Little damage had been done, in part because Kennedy had been drunk the whole time. P. T. Barnum's museum, which was one of Kennedy's targets, had a wax figure of the dead Confederate saboteur on display less than a month after his execution.

The end of open hostilities did little to slow the pace of the commissions, at least not at first. Even as Holt was overseeing the trial of Booth's accomplices, his office presided over dozens of military commissions for violations of the laws of war. Commissions trying such violations moved forward in the Department of the Cumberland under Major General George H. Thomas; in the Department of the East under John Dix; in Virginia

Champ Ferguson in custody: pictured in front at center with an armed Union guard, Ferguson was one of the most feared southern guerrilla leaders. After the war he was tried and executed for war crimes, including the execution of captured black soldiers.

and North Carolina under Benjamin Butler; in the Department of the Gulf under Major General Stephen A. Hurlbut; and in Missouri under Major General Grenville Dodge. All through the summer in Nashville a military tribunal tried and convicted Champ Ferguson for unlawful guerrilla warfare and the systematic execution of black soldiers at Saltville, Virginia. Ferguson was executed in October. That same month, another commission in Wilmington, North Carolina, tried and convicted two men for the murder of a Union guide in violation of the laws and customs of war.

F AR AND AWAY the most prominent case tried in the wake of the Lincoln conspiracy trial was the prosecution of Captain Henry Wirz, the commander responsible for overseeing captured Union soldiers held at Andersonville, Georgia. It did almost as much damage to the reputation of military commissions as the worst excesses of the Lincoln assassination trial had done just weeks before.

When the first Union prisoners had arrived at the tiny hardscrabble town of Andersonville in southwestern Georgia in February 1864, they found a bleak seventeen-acre camp with no structures surrounded by an eighteen-foot stockade fence. A creek ran down the middle of the camp. Around the compound's edges ran a "dead line" about twelve feet inside the stockade wall. Andersonville had been designed to hold 10,000 Union men, though given the absence of buildings it would not have held even that number comfortably. But over the course of the next year, the camp at Andersonville took in between 41,000 and 45,000 Union soldiers. As many as 32,899 prisoners resided inside the stockade at any one time. For six months in 1864 and early 1865, the press of prisoners turned the little town into the fifth most populous city in the South. Conditions were deplorable. The camp's principal water source quickly became foul and polluted. Gangrene and disease ran rampant among the prisoners. Three quarters of the patients admitted to the camp hospital died. All told, more than a quarter of those who entered the stockade—some 12,912 men—never left.

In May 1865, Union officials arrested Wirz for his conduct as commander of the prison interior. Wirz seemed to be a comic book villain. With a thick accent and a temper made worse by a festering wound received in the Peninsula Campaign in May 1862 that had rendered his right arm almost completely useless, the Swiss-born Wirz was reviled by former prisoners and disliked by many of his own men as well. Lew Wallace, who served as president of the military commission that tried Wirz, described him as having the eyes of a cat "when the animal is excited by a scent of prey." Wirz, Wallace decided, was "altogether well-chosen for his awful service in the Confederacy."

Yet the trial got off to a bumpy start on August 21. When the judge advocate handling the case, Norton Parker Chipman, filed charges against Wirz that named Jefferson Davis, Robert E. Lee, and Confederate secretary of war James Seddon, an angry Stanton called a halt to the proceedings and demanded that Chipman redraft the charges to leave out the Confederate leadership. With Lieber's help, Stanton was trying desperately to find evidence that would support Holt's accusations at the trial of the Lincoln assassination conspirators by definitively linking Davis to the worst atrocities of the war. The last thing Stanton needed was for the Wirz prosecution to force his hand before he had found the evidence he needed. Nor did he want to create an occasion for bringing Davis to the capital.

The trial resumed three days later with new charges that left out Davis and the Confederate high command. But Wirz's two lawyers both dropped out immediately. The lawyers who replaced them, Orrin Baker and Louis Schade, threatened to walk off the case themselves when the tribunal frustrated their attempts to call certain witnesses on Wirz's behalf. The judge advocate arrested James Duncan (Wirz's subordinate at Andersonville) while Duncan waited to testify for the defense. And when Schade sought to call Robert Ould to testify to the Union's responsibility for the collapse of the 1862 prisoner exchange cartel, Chipman chased him back to Virginia on the threat of arresting him for breaking the terms of his parole if he left his home state. A court reporter delivered Wirz's closing statement when the tribunal refused to give Baker the two weeks he requested to prepare his final arguments.

Such procedural irregularities were bad enough, but the case prepared by Chipman and Holt was plagued by a deeper problem too, one that Chipman's ill-advised initial charges had inadvertently betrayed. Chipman made heroic efforts to bring out testimony that would tie prison conditions at Andersonville to Confederate officials in Richmond. Doing so suggested a wide and nefarious conspiracy. But such efforts also cast doubt on Wirz's personal responsibility for the prison conditions that had killed so many Union men. Multiple witnesses (some unreliable, others more credible) testified to instances of abuse by Wirz, including the shooting and beating of individual prisoners. But the real burden of the case was to charge Wirz with responsibility not for isolated incidents of brutality, but for the deaths of thousands. And here the evidence was far less clear. Wirz, it came out, had sought on more than one occasion to bring the miserable conditions at his camp to the attention of Richmond officials. He made plans to improve the camp bakery and petitioned Richmond for improved rations. He enlarged the space enclosed in the stockade. And he looked into relocating the hospital to cleaner, less crowded space outside the stockade altogether. Wirz also put together a plan to create an elaborate series of dams and floodgates to improve the water quality at the camp and began work on the project, though it was never completed.

Wirz doubtless could have done more. He failed to carry out most of his plans to improve conditions, and his notoriously erratic temper made life worse for many of the men under his care. But the evidence brought out in the tribunal also made clear that he had possessed little control over the resources his superiors provided to the prisoners. Wirz's lawyers argued that he was merely "a servant and instrument in the hands of the Southern authorities." The Swiss consul-general remonstrated on Wirz's behalf with President Johnson, conceding that Wirz was "detestable," but arguing that he had been the "tool of monsters in human form." "Shall the hand suffer," he asked, "for the arm that wielded it, for the soul and mind that controlled its ultimatum of crime?" As the proceedings unfolded, it came to seem that Confederate brigadier general John Winder—who had established the prison, presided over the selection of its site, and overseen all Confederate prisons from November 1864 onward—would have been a far better target for the Union's ire. One witness testified that Winder had planned to improve conditions by a horrible attrition; he would leave the prisoners "in their present condition until their number has been sufficiently reduced by death to make the present arrangements suffice for their accommodation." Even Winder objected to the quality and size of the prisoners' rations and wrote Richmond seeking improvements. But his responsibility for prison conditions seemed far clearer than Wirz's. If he had not died of a heart attack while inspecting a South Carolina prison in February 1865, he surely would have been on trial alongside his German-speaking subordinate.

The Wirz prosecution also threatened to raise embarrassing questions for the Union. Conditions at some prisons in the North, and especially the notorious prison at Elmira, New York, had been almost as bad as those at Andersonville. Death rates in northern camps rivaled those in the South, and northern officials bore their share of the responsibility for conditions that led to the unnecessary deaths of Confederate soldiers.* Prisoner of war camps on both sides had simply never caught up to the massive organizational task of maintaining populations of thousands and even tens of thousands of men.

In particular, Wirz and his defense lawyers worked to turn attention back on Union authorities' unpopular refusal to engage in prisoner exchanges after the summer of 1863. That was why they had called Robert Ould (the Confederate agent for exchange) to testify, and it is almost certainly why the judge advocates chased Ould back to Virginia on the threat of arresting him for breaking his parole. Even so, the defense's cross-examination of government witnesses directed attention to the question of prisoner exchanges and the collapse of the exchange cartel. And in his closing statement, Wirz did so again, urging on the commission his view of "where the responsibility rested for non-exchange of prisoners of war."

None of these difficulties affected the outcome of the case. Enough witnesses, including Confederate and Union veterans alike, testified to brutal acts by Wirz that his responsibility for atrocities at Andersonville was well established. With characteristic fury, Holt described the trial as giving the picture of Wirz "rather as a demon than a man." In late October, the commission returned verdicts of guilty on the charges of murder and conspiring against Union prisoners in violation of the laws of war. It sentenced Wirz to death. On November 10, Wirz was hanged at the Old Capitol Prison, the site where John Marshall's fellow justices had stayed while deliberating over prize cases a half century before and where in 1819 Congress had debated Andrew Jackson's conduct in Florida. Wirz's body was interred next to the Lincoln conspirator Atzerodt in the Old Arsenal Penitentiary.

C ONVICTIONS IN THE Lincoln assassination case and the Wirz prosecution distracted the single-minded Joseph Holt from difficulties that his military commissions were fast running into. Rather than being chastened,

---

*Death rates overall were significantly higher in southern camps (15.5%) than in northern ones (12.1%). One problem with comparative death rates is that they reflect in part the condition of the men who entered the prison. James McPherson has usefully pointed out that whereas Union soldiers were 68 percent *more* likely to die in Confederate camps than they were to die of disease while with their own army in the field, soldiers from the South were 29 percent *less* likely to die in Union prisons than of disease while serving in their own army—James M. McPherson, *Ordeal by Fire: The Civil War and Reconstruction* (New York: McGraw-Hill, 1982), 451 & 451n.

Holt began to plan on expanding the use of military commissions to try the Confederate officers whose names came up during the Wirz proceedings.

Yet the difficulties that arose in the two most prominent trials of the summer and fall of 1865 showed up in less closely watched prosecutions as well. At Beall's trial in February, James T. Brady, the prominent trial lawyer, had accused the Union of hypocrisy. "Where do you make the distinction," he wondered

> between the march of Major-General Sherman through the enemy's country, carrying ravage and desolation everywhere, destroying the most peaceable and lawful industry, mills and machinery, and every-thing of that nature; where do you draw the line between his march through Georgia and an expedition of twenty men acting under com-mission who get into any of the States we claim to be in the Union, and commit depredations there?

In retrospect, even the Lincoln assassination case seemed troubled. What, after all, was assassination? Why was killing the commander in chief of the Union armies unlawful while killing a conscripted private on the battlefield was not? It was not that there were no answers to these questions. Booth had acted without a uniform or any other distinguishing mark to set himself off as a combatant. So, too, with John Yates Beall on the Great Lakes, Robert Kennedy in New York City, and George St. Leger Grenfell in Chicago—all had engaged in a kind of violence that threatened to undo the distinction between soldiers and noncombatants. But the differences were subtle ones, the categories new and unfamiliar to combatants and lawyers alike.

Sure enough, as Wirz's trial was getting underway, a military commission trial of guerrillas in Texas resulted in the acquittal of all the defendants. In December 1865, a commission in the Department of North Carolina con-cluded that it lacked jurisdiction to prosecute Confederate general George Pickett (of Pickett's Charge fame at Gettysburg) for executing twenty-two North Carolinians captured while serving in the Union Army after desert-ing from Confederate service. Holt was infuriated (Lieber was too), but he dropped the case after a second tribunal could not find enough evidence to show that the executed men had been entitled to prisoner of war treatment. (It did not harm Pickett's prospects that Ulysses S. Grant intervened on his old friend's behalf.) A January 1866 commission acquitted Confeder-ate general Hugh W. Mercer of charges that he murdered seven captured Union soldiers near Savannah in 1864. In June, a military commission trial in Raleigh of Major John H. Gee, the prison commandant at the smaller Salisbury camp in North Carolina, resulted in yet another acquittal. By some measures, conditions at Salisbury had been worse even than those at Andersonville; Union prisoners died faster there than at any other southern prison. Yet the commission vindicated Gee against charges of abusing and murdering prisoners in violation of the laws of war. After James Duncan was arrested in the Wirz commission courtroom, a commission in Savannah managed to convict him of manslaughter and violation of the laws of war for his gross abuse of Union prisoners while serving as the quartermaster at Andersonville. But the commission split on the sentence and could not agree on more than fifteen years' imprisonment at hard labor. When Duncan escaped a year later, no one seems to have looked very hard for him. For the next thirty years he lived more or less openly with his wife in Pennsylvania.

As actual hostilities receded into the past, problems for the military commissions grew still more acute. The simple fact of the war having come to a close created difficulties. Grant insisted that Confederate soldiers covered by the surrender agreements of April 1865—including controversial partisans such as John Singleton Mosby—were immune from prosecution under the terms of their paroles. Holt maintained otherwise. His commissions had proceeded in the face of such objections in the past; Wirz's lawyers had made the same argument. But now Grant successfully prevented the trial of Harvard Law School graduate Bradley T. Johnson, one of two Confederate brigadier generals in command at the burning of Chambersburg, Pennsylvania, in 1864. Johnson had also served as the commander of the grim prison camp at Salisbury, North Carolina, in the final months of the war. Nonetheless, Grant insisted that "the terms of the parole given by officers and soldiers . . . exempt them from trial for acts of legal warfare." Moreover, when President Johnson announced the formal end of the insurrection in all states other than Texas on April 2, 1866 (Texas followed on August 20), many doubted that the authority of the military commissions would continue at all.

Most of all, the commissions seemed not to be targeting the leaders of the Confederacy, but to be scapegoating its minor players. Republican congressman James G. Blaine (later secretary of state under Presidents James Garfield and Chester Arthur) said at the time that prosecuting Wirz "seemed like skipping over the president, superintendant, and board of directors in a great railroad accident and hanging the brakeman on the rear car." John Gee's lawyers made the same objection, and the commission that tried him agreed; its report concluded that it could attach "no responsibility" to Gee "other than his weakness in retaining a position when unable to carry out the dictates of humanity."

Yet for all the difficulties the commissions faced, Holt's severe temperament and stubborn personality prevented him from understanding that public opinion was shifting the ground beneath his feet. Nowhere was the seismic shift clearer than in the debates that raged in the Congress over Reconstruction and the condition of the former slaves.

A Citizen of Indiana

FOR ALMOST A CENTURY, the laws of war had played a role in heated controversies around the question of slavery. In the months after Appomattox, those same laws occupied center stage in a new debate over how to incorporate 4 million freedpeople into the Union.

Since late May 1865, President Johnson had been appointing provisional governors for the rebel states and authorizing those who had been qualified to vote under prewar law to reorganize their states. Johnson urged that they ratify the Thirteenth Amendment abolishing slavery, but otherwise he allowed them to regulate the conditions of the freedpeople as they saw fit. White southern governments, presided over by the same men who had led their states into open rebellion, ratified the amendment while enacting new laws called Black Codes designed to reinstitute slavery in all but name.

When the Thirty-ninth Congress met for its first session in December 1865, the Republican majorities in the House and the Senate rejected Johnson's plan, shut out the would-be representatives of the rebel states, and turned immediately to the business of preventing the white South from denying blacks their basic civil rights. Two bills introduced by Senator Lyman Trumbull of Illinois—what Senator Garret Davis of Kentucky called the "Siamese twins" of the Thirty-ninth Congress—quickly came to the fore. The first was an extension and enlargement of the wartime Freedmen's Bureau Act, which had created a federal agency in the War Department for control of all subjects relating to refugees and freedpeople in the rebel states. The second was a bill to protect the civil rights of the freedpeople, including their right to make contracts, their right to sue, and their right to give evidence.

For all their centrality to the Republican agenda for 1866, the two bills at first shared a fundamental difficulty. The question confronting both bills was whether the federal government had the authority to enact them. The Constitution of 1787 had protected the states against federal power in all but a set of carefully enumerated federal domains. Once the states had ratified the Thirteenth Amendment to the Constitution prohibiting slavery and authorizing Congress to enact appropriate legislation to enforce its terms, the problem of federal authority to enact the civil rights bill seemed less acute. But the Freedman's Bureau bill still seemed beyond any of the conventional powers of Congress. What license did the government have to try to govern day-to-day life in the states?

A T THE OUTSET of the Thirty-ninth Congress, radical firebrand Thaddeus Stevens of Pennsylvania and Jacob Howard of Michigan offered an answer that drew on the lessons of the past four years and harkened back to the arguments of Alexander Hamilton in the 1790s. The laws of war, they argued, represented a powerful source of authority in a constitutional system that had otherwise hedged and constrained the power of the federal government.

As Senator Howard put it in urging the establishment of a joint committee on Reconstruction in the opening days of the Thirty-ninth Congress, the "status of the rebel States" was simply that of "conquered communities, subjugated by the arms of the United States." If that were so, the Congress had all the rights of a conquering nation as set out in the international laws of war. In the House, Stevens—who just four years before had berated Lincoln for acceding to the idea that the laws of war had any bearing at all on the conflict between the states—agreed and elaborated on the implications. "Unless the law of nations is a dead letter," he announced on the floor of the House, the southern states were "in the condition of a foreign nation with whom we were at war." Indeed, precisely because the Union had extended to the rebel armies the protections of the laws of war in battle, the southern states were now "subject to the absolute disposal of Congress."

Moderate Republicans in Congress disliked the conquered province theory. It seemed to concede the rebels' own wartime argument that the seceding states had left the Union and become an independent nation. Representative William Finck of Ohio complained that Stevens's "views on this point coincide with those of the most rabid secessionists." Congressman Henry Raymond of New York, the founder of the *New York Times* and a close ally of the new president, added that Stevens's theory would preclude prosecuting any rebel, including Jefferson Davis, for treason. Indeed, as Representative William Niblack of Indiana jumped in to observe, the conquered territory theory would characterize the loyal Union men of the

South as having been traitors when they sided with the Union against their home states.

Yet the most commonly cited alternative to the conquered territories theory was barely more appealing. A number of Republicans cited a clause in Article IV of the Constitution guaranteeing each state a republican form of government. The difficulty was explaining how the southern states as they existed in the winter of 1865–66 were somehow not republican governments under the Constitution. For more than seventy years, since at least the ratification of the Constitution in 1788, the federal government had proceeded as if slavery was perfectly compatible with republican government. Could it really be that in order to have a republican form of government a state now not only had to abolish slavery, but also had to adopt legal protections for the civil rights of those who had once been slaves? Many doubted the republican government guarantee could be read so liberally. (President Johnson had relied on the clause in endorsing his own far less ambitious restoration of white state governments.) Moreover, if the republican government clause could be construed so broadly, it threatened to make Article IV an ongoing warrant for open-ended federal government intervention into the affairs of the states. At least the conquered territory theory was limited to the South and to the context of the war. The republican guarantee approach threatened to undo entirely the allocation of powers between states and the federal government.

What a theoretical basis for Reconstruction needed to accomplish was to adopt the limitations of the conquered territories idea without seeming to concede that theory's capitulation to the rebel idea that the states had indeed possessed a right to secede and had been independent nations of their own during the war.

The solution the Republican Congress soon hit upon was the very same idea that Lincoln had pursued in 1861 when he set up a blockade while refusing to concede that the South was an independent nation. The idea was that Congress could have it both ways. Sumner had developed the notion in the Congress as the "double" theory of the war. Lieber had followed it, too, by expressly reserving in General Orders No. 100 the right to prosecute rebels for treason. The Supreme Court had embraced it in *The Prize Cases* in 1863.

Richard Henry Dana, who had argued *The Prize Cases* for Lincoln, was among the first to apply the idea to the Reconstruction conundrum when he told a black suffrage meeting at Faneuil Hall in Boston in June 1865 that Congress could insist on black voting rights in the rebel states as a condition of representation in the Congress. Under the laws of war, Dana explained, the U.S. was a "conquering party" and could thus "hold the other in the grasp of war until it has secured whatever it has a right to acquire." As in *The Prize Cases*, Dana contended that the law of war argument for congressional power did not require the Congress to see the rebel states as having been a foreign enemy. In civil wars, as Dana had put it in 1863, "the sovereign may exercise belligerent powers, as well as the powers of municipal sovereignty," without contradiction.

Congress soon took up Dana's "grasp of war" idea to sustain its postwar Reconstruction program. Charles Sumner, who had proposed a grab bag of theories for Congress's authority to reconstruct the South, eulogized Abraham Lincoln in June 1865 by insisting that "the same national authority that destroyed Slavery must see that this other pretension is not permitted to survive." There was, he thought, no doubt that "the authority which destroyed Slavery" was now "competent to the kindred duty" of guaranteeing the rights of the freedmen. In December, his fellow senator from Massachusetts, Henry Wilson, cited the same theory in proposing a civil rights bill that would make "null and void" any law of the rebel states establishing "any inequality of civil rights and immunities among the inhabitants" thereof. "The men who went into rebellion have been defeated in battle," Wilson explained; "they have been conquered and subjugated; they are at the mercy of the Government of the United States to-day." In late April 1866, when the Joint Committee on Reconstruction issued a plan for restoring the rebel states and ratifying the Fourteenth Amendment to the Constitution, the committee based its authority on principles crafted by Dana and carried forward by Sumner, Wilson, and others. "Conquered rebels," stated the committee report, were "at the mercy of the conquerors."

A NDREW JOHNSON HAD exercised war powers as the Union's military governor in wartime Tennessee. In 1860, as a member of the Senate, he had been an early champion of the argument that would later be known as Thaddeus Stevens's conquered territories theory of Reconstruction. Yet as president in 1865 and 1866, he turned into a sharp critic of bringing the law of war to the postwar South.

President Johnson's program of speedy amnesty and state restoration was deeply at odds with the continuing military commissions of Joseph Holt and James Speed. Like the president, Holt and Speed were southerners by birth, with prewar connections to the Democratic Party. The war had changed the two men. Holt and Speed found themselves advocating for the freedpeople and for using the authority of military commissions to uphold their rights. But the war had not changed Andrew Johnson, at least not in the same way. Johnson chafed at the continuing war powers of the federal government. In February 1866, he ordered that no steps be taken toward the prosecution of Confederate naval officer Raphael Semmes for violations of a truce flag that occurred when the Union vessel *Kearsarge* sank his ship, the *Alabama*, off the coast of France in 1864. Holt had arrested Semmes for escaping from the sinking *Alabama* after flying a white flag of surrender. Semmes's conduct undoubtedly violated the customs of truce flags, which forbade the use of white flags to enable escape. But Johnson thought that in arresting Semmes, Holt had taken his vindictiveness a step too far. Johnson told Secretary of the Navy Welles that he "wished to put no more in Holt's control than was absolutely necessary," and called Holt a "cruel and remorseless" man whose "tendencies and conclusions were very bloody." Welles, for his part, thought Holt a "dupe of his own imaginings."

Later in the same month, Johnson's veto of the Freedmen's Bureau bill set forth publicly the president's fierce hostility to the persistence of military commissions. They were, he insisted, "arbitrary tribunals" inconsistent with the Constitution. On April 2, 1866, when the president declared the war over, he elaborated further. Martial law and military tribunals, he maintained, "are in time of peace dangerous to public liberty, incompatible with the individual rights of the citizens, contrary to the genius and spirit of our free institutions, and exhaustive of the national resources."

Holt continued to press forward, but his efforts were increasingly clumsy. The prosecution of rebel captain Richard B. Winder (John Winder's cousin) for crimes at Andersonville collapsed when Holt's best witnesses failed to appear. In late March 1866, Holt confidently insisted that he was prepared to move forward with a prosecution by military commission of Jefferson Davis and Clement Clay for their complicity in the Lincoln assassination. But the hurdles to Holt's military commission program were about to get much higher.

THE SUPREME COURT had lent its support to wartime military commissions in 1864 in the case of Clement Vallandigham; Justice Wayne had intimated the Court's approval for the military trial of offenses "under the common law of war." A year later, however, when a citizen of Indiana named Lambdin Milligan challenged his conviction by a military commission, circumstances had changed.

Milligan belonged to a quasi-military organization known as the Sons of Liberty, in which he held the position of supreme commander. In July and August 1864, the Sons of Liberty worked with Confederate agents to organize an uprising in the northwestern states of Indiana, Illinois, Ohio, Missouri, and Kentucky. They aimed to detach the Northwest from the Union and to free the tens of thousands of Confederate soldiers held in the Union prison camps at Chicago and on Johnson's Island in Lake Erie. With suitcases of cash supplied by the Confederate agents, the plotters purchased shipments of firearms to make good on their plans. But Union men had infiltrated the Sons of Liberty for months. And when Indiana officials discovered the arms, the plot unraveled quickly. Along with six other men, Milligan was arrested in October by forces under Alvin P. Hovey, commander of the military district of Indiana. When one of the plotters agreed to testify for the government, Judge Advocate Henry Burnett (who would soon assist Holt in the Lincoln assassination trial) tried and convicted Milligan in a military tribunal for conspiring against the United States, aiding and comforting the rebels, inciting insurrection, and violating the laws of war by introducing Confederate agents behind Union lines and running an organization of unlawful combatants. The tribunal sentenced Milligan to death.

Milligan petitioned for a writ of habeas corpus in May 1865. When his case got to the Supreme Court in February of the following year, his lawyers rehearsed all the arguments that had been made by the critics of military commissions since 1862. Milligan's position was that, as "an inhabitant, resident, and citizen of Indiana," he could not be accused of violating the laws of war. Only a soldier could violate the laws of war, he insisted, though Union practice on this point had been otherwise for most of the war. The Civil War hero and future president James Garfield argued for Milligan in the Supreme Court alongside Jeremiah Black, former attorney general of the United States under James Buchanan, and the prominent New York lawyer David Dudley Field, brother of Supreme Court Justice Stephen Field.

Garfield led off, and Field spoke longest, but Black's argument won the day. As attorney general, Black had maintained that the federal government lacked the authority to use force against the seceding states. Now he contended that U.S. military commissions could not exercise a law of war authority to try citizens accused of offenses committed outside a war zone when the civil courts were open for business and the civil authorities were "in full exercise of their functions." The Constitution, he said, forbade such military commissions. Arguing for the government, his opponents contended that "the laws of war must be treated as paramount." But in Black's view the Constitution was supreme. It was the sovereign prerogative of the people of the United States to deny their government powers regardless of whether the laws of war allowed those powers to other nations. As to Attorney General Speed's defense of the military commission in the Lincoln assassination case, Black could hardly contain his contempt. Could the armed forces really "take and kill" or "try and execute . . . persons who had no sort of connection with the Army or Navy"? Black condemned the entire apparatus of Holt's Bureau of Military Justice as a "dark and bloody machinery" of death.

Arguing for the United States, Ohio lawyer Henry Stanberry (a close confidant of the president) entered a brief objection to the Court's jurisdiction. But Stanberry, whom Johnson would soon make attorney general after pushing Speed out of office, quickly made way for the sitting attorney general and Benjamin Butler, who took breathtakingly broad positions in defense of military commissions. Once war was declared, they contended, "all peace provisions of the Constitution" and "all other conventional and legislative laws and enactments" fell "silent amidst arms." The president in wartime had at his disposal "all the means and appliances by which war is carried on by civilized nations." In short, they argued, the only limit on the president's power in wartime was set out by the laws of war.

Speed left it to Butler, who had received the first contraband slaves at Fort Monroe in May 1861, to defend the argument. Butler urged the Court to heed the lessons of the war's great turning point. What, after all, had been the basis for Emancipation other than the president's awesome law of war authority? Had not John Quincy Adams argued that the federal government could seize slaves in wartime on the ground that the law of nations replaced "all municipal institutions" in time of war? Contesting the gag rule against antislavery petitions in the Congress, Adams had argued that "all the powers incident to war are by necessary implication conferred upon the government of the United States" in wartime, not from "any internal, municipal source, but from the laws and usages of nations." The law of war, Adams had contended in the 1830s and 1840s, "breaks down every barrier so anxiously erected for the protection of liberty, property, and life." As Butler could not resist observing, Adams was the son of a founding father, the son of the second president of the United States, and himself the sixth president. And it was his arguments on slavery and the laws of war that Lincoln, the sixteenth president, had taken up to emancipate the slaves on January 1, 1863. If Adams's arguments would sustain Emancipation, Butler contended, surely they would support military commissions as well.

Observers of the *Milligan* case have been mystified ever since by Speed's and Butler's arguments. The case had made available to them a much more modest position. During the course of the conflict there had been nearly 1,000 military commission prosecutions for violating the laws of war. Justice Wayne had approved such a commission in the *Vallandigham* case just two years before. Lambdin Milligan had been tried and convicted of (among other things) violating the laws of war. Nonetheless, Butler and Speed defended the Milligan commission not as a device for punishing violations of the laws of war, but as a legitimate exercise of martial law generally. They contended that the laws of war afforded the president and the Army the power to declare martial law even outside active war zones and to prosecute U.S. citizens and others before military tribunals so long as the "quality of the acts" charged made them the "proper subject of restraint by martial law." They had made a broad argument where a narrow one would have sufficed to sustain Milligan's conviction.

The reason was that Speed and Butler were not really arguing about Lambdin Milligan at all. Their arguments were calculated not to sustain his conviction but to defend the authority of military commissions and martial law during postwar Reconstruction. That was why Butler made Emancipation so central to his argument. The *Milligan* case would be a referendum on the future of the project that Lincoln had begun in the fall of 1862, the project that had produced Lieber's General Orders No. 100 and that underlay the Union's uncompromising approach to the laws of war. It would have been no great victory to win a slender ruling upholding Milligan's confinement. The federal courts sustained precisely such a narrow defense of military commissions two years later when a judge in Florida ruled that Dr. Samuel Mudd's conviction in the trial of the Lincoln conspirators had been a lawful one. (One hundred and fifty years later, a federal judge in Washington, D.C., would rule the same way when he rejected Dr. Mudd's grandson's challenge to the accuracy of the military records in his grandfather's case.) What was unclear in early 1866, and what Speed and Butler hoped to vindicate, was the availability of the laws of war as a basis for federal authority moving forward into Reconstruction.*

---

*In 1871, Milligan won a civil case for damages against Major General Alvin P. Hovey for arresting and holding him unlawfully. An unsympathetic jury awarded Milligan only nominal damages, but the fact that he won even a nominal victory suggested that Speed and Butler might not have been able to sustain Milligan's conviction even on the narrow argument. Future president Benjamin Harrison represented Milligan in his civil case. See *Milligan v. Hovey*, 17 F. Cas. 380 (C.C. D. Ind. 1871).

The justices of the Supreme Court understood exactly what was at stake. One day after the president's April 2, 1866, peace proclamation, the Court signaled its rejection of Speed's arguments, ruling without explanation that the military tribunal lacked authority to try Milligan and that he ought therefore to be discharged from custody. In December, when the Court resumed session, Justice David Davis issued an opinion explaining the Court's April ruling. Davis had once claimed (wrongly) that Lincoln never supported the use of military tribunals against anyone other than soldiers. But Davis must have confused his own resistance to the tribunals for his friend's, for he now soundly rejected the tribunals that Lincoln had helped to set in motion in September 1862 and whose decisions Lincoln had reviewed for the rest of the war. The Constitution, Davis wrote, was the law "equally in war and in peace ... at all times, and under all circumstances." To the contention that the laws and usages of war allowed military courts, Davis replied that such laws could have no application to citizens in loyal states where the courts were open. And to the argument that the writ of habeas corpus had been suspended by Congress for prisoners like Milligan in March 1863, Davis replied that the interpretation Holt and Stanton had given to the 1863 habeas legislation for more than three years was wrong. The War Department had contended that the habeas legislation had no application to men charged with violations of the laws of war. That was why the wartime military commissions had relied so heavily on the laws of war to circumvent the Congress and the courts. But Davis countered that Milligan—a citizen of Indiana never in the Confederate service—could not possibly be counted as a prisoner of war. Adopting Milligan's argument that he could not be charged with violating the laws of war unless he was a lawful combatant, Davis charged the government with wanting to have its cake and eat it too: "If he cannot enjoy the immunities attaching to the character of war, how can he be subject to their pains and penalties?"

Indeed, Davis went further. Just weeks before he issued the opinion of the Court, the elections of 1866 had produced a landslide in favor of the Republicans in Congress, a victory that was certain to strengthen the hand of the Republican program of Reconstruction. Knowing this, and knowing full well that the Congress would very likely rely on its war powers to extend military tribunals, Davis held not only that the president could not employ a military tribunal in Milligan's case, but that the Congress could not do so either. Chief Justice Chase, who had been one of the strongest antislavery voices in the Lincoln cabinet, dissented from this last point along with three other justices. Looking forward to the Reconstruction efforts on the horizon, Chase insisted that Congress might do what the president alone could not. But Chase's opinion captured only a minority of the Court's votes.

Justice Davis left open a slim chance that military commissions in the former rebel states might be treated differently. He would have allowed commissions in states that were "the locality of actual war." But few at the time doubted that the *Milligan* decision signaled the Court's intent to put tight limits on the law of war powers of the Congress in the era of Reconstruction. Many Republicans likened the ruling to the *Dred Scott* decision of 1857. (Thaddeus Stevens insisted that *Milligan* was worse.) Other critics, including the usually restrained *New York Times,* accused the Court of taking the side of those who had so recently "assailed the Union." White southerners rejoiced when President Johnson cited the decision as grounds for releasing whites convicted by military commissions of crimes against freedpeople. At last, the editors of the *Richmond Enquirer* wrote, "the revolutionary proceedings of the Congress are promised a check."

A month after he issued his opinion, Davis commissioned former justice Benjamin Curtis to write a defense of the Court's *Milligan* decision. It was Curtis who in 1862 had written a stinging critique of Lincoln's Emancipation decision. It was Curtis who had lent his voice to warn of the "scenes of bloodshed, and worse than bloodshed" in the servile insurrections he was sure would follow on Emancipation's heels. It was Curtis who had denied that civilized peoples could free their slaves in wartime. Now it was Curtis to whom Justice Davis turned to help bring an end to the awesome powers that the laws of war and Emancipation had created.

As the Supreme Court checked and constrained the law of war powers of the legislative branch, members of the Thirty-ninth Congress had been working hard to establish a new source of federal authority in the formerly rebel states, one that would no longer rest on the authority offered by the international laws of war. At the end of April 1866, the Joint Committee on Reconstruction reported a draft of what would become the Fourteenth Amendment to the Constitution. After weeks of debate and compromise, the House and the Senate proposed a final version on June 16, 1866. If ratified by three quarters of the states, Section 1 of the amendment promised to prohibit states from abridging the privileges or immunities of citizens of the United States, depriving "any person of life, liberty, or property, without due process of law," or denying any person "the equal protection of the laws." Section 5 would provide the Congress the "power to enforce, by appropriate legislation," the amendment's substantive provisions. Here at last was a durable basis for the federal government's authority in the South.

But Congress's effort to move away from the "grasp of war" theory quickly ran into obstacles of its own. Encouraged by the president, all but one of the white southern state governments refused to ratify the Fourteenth Amendment proposed by Congress. Race riots in which whites assaulted blacks in Memphis and New Orleans, as well as a spate of violence against freedpeople and Union men across the South, recalled the bitter skirmishes of the war itself. Emboldened by the election results of the fall of 1866, a frustrated Thirty-ninth Congress temporarily returned to the laws of war for one last time in the Reconstruction saga.

O N MARCH 2, 1867, Congress passed the Military Reconstruction Act over Johnson's veto. The act, which became law on the very last day of the Thirty-ninth Congress, divided the ten rebel states (all but Tennessee, which had already been restored to the Congress) into five military districts and set out the conditions under which their representatives would be readmitted to the Congress, conditions that included ratification of the Fourteenth Amendment and adoption of new state constitutions with universal male suffrage. The legislation ran directly contrary not only to Johnson's efforts to restore the southern states but also (as its opponents noted) to the Supreme Court's *Milligan* decision. For it aimed to put the relations between the federal government and the rebel states back on a war footing, where the laws of war would supply Congress with wide-ranging authority. Indeed, the legislation's central justification was precisely the "grasp of war" theory that had sustained the Freedmen's Bureau Extension Act the year before.

Thaddeus Stevens introduced the military reconstruction bill in the House by rehearsing his theory of the power of conquerors under the law of nations. Most Republicans, however, followed Congressman John Bingham of Ohio, Holt's old colleague in the Judge Advocate General's office and veteran of the Lincoln assassination trial, by citing the "unlimited power for the common defense" that the "law of nations" conferred on all countries. Zachariah Chandler, a Republican senator from Michigan, argued that the "laws of war" had given Lincoln the power to appoint military governors and concluded that the same laws of war authorized the Congress to order the reorganization of the former rebel states. William D. Kelley, the founder of a family dynasty in Philadelphia politics and a stalwart Republican, argued that the bill did only what the "law of nations and his oath of office justified Abraham Lincoln in doing."

Notwithstanding that the Supreme Court majority in the *Milligan* case had seemed to put military commissions beyond Congress's control, the act expressly authorized military commissions whenever military district commanders believed they were necessary. The act's critics thus contended—with good reason—that it could not possibly survive constitutional scrutiny in the courts. Writing for the president, Attorney General Henry Stanberry revealed why he had left the argument on the merits of the *Milligan* case at the Supreme Court to Speed and Butler. In a blistering opinion, he condemned the use of military commissions.

Yet if the Reconstruction Act had returned once more to the law of war power that Lincoln developed, it also set in motion the return of constitutional normalcy and the end of the era in which the federal government could invoke the laws of war to exercise extraordinary powers. John Bingham had come out of the Lincoln assassination trial with a chastened sense of the law of war powers he had exercised as a judge advocate. Now, on the floor of the House, Bingham emphasized that the bill instituted military rule "only until the people by a solemn vote at the polls, under the authority of the national law and the protection of the national Army, shall have assented to the constitutional amendment and set up a just and republican government." Once the Fourteenth Amendment was in place, the Congress would have a basis for legislating protections for the freedpeople and Unionists of the South without invoking the laws of war. Radicals like Thaddeus Stevens had taken to the war powers argument with fierce enthusiasm, in part because they believed that only the war power and the full authority of the U.S. Army could protect the freedpeople. In many respects, Stevens turned out to be right. But Bingham and the moderate wing of the Republican Party in Congress had come to see those same powers as a temporary and dangerous aberration in American law. The Reconstruction Act mobilized the laws of war precisely for the purpose of bringing the Civil War chapter of their history to a close.

O VER THE NEXT two years, the Congress, President Johnson, and the Supreme Court staged an elaborate dance around the authority asserted by the Military Reconstruction Act and its successors.

Two pieces of legislation enacted the same day as the Military Reconstruction Act aimed to insulate the War Department's military commissions from the president's control. The Tenure of Office Act limited Johnson's authority to remove cabinet officials like Stanton without Congress's consent. A rider to the annual appropriations act passed the same day required that all military orders pass through Stanton. Together, the measures sought to allow the War Department to function without Johnson's interference. Within a year, Johnson's attempt to circumvent the congressional limitations would lead the House to impeach him.

Congress also had to fend off the courts. More than 1,000 defendants were tried in military commissions during Reconstruction in the former rebel states. But the tribunals proceeded in the shadow of Lambdin Milligan. In November 1867, Mississippi newspaperman William McCardle was convicted in a military court of inciting insurrection and impeding Reconstruction by threatening to publish the names of anyone voting in elections held by the state's Reconstruction government. When McCardle sought to challenge his conviction in the Supreme Court, Congress pulled the rug out from under his suit by repealing the statute McCardle had relied on to get his case to the Court (a statute the Congress had enacted only a year before to provide access to the federal courts for freedpeople). The Court reluctantly upheld the repealer act and refused to review McCardle's conviction, but noted pointedly that an alternative path remained open to challenge military convictions in the courts via the Judiciary Act of 1789. A year later, another white southerner tested the alternative route. Edward Yerger, a Mississippi white man accused of killing a Union soldier, challenged his military commission conviction on the same grounds that McCardle, Milligan, and Vallandigham had raised before him. The Supreme Court seemed ready to entertain a challenge to the military commissions of Reconstruction. To avoid an adverse ruling, a new attorney general appointed by recently elected President Ulysses S. Grant arranged to have Yerger transferred to civil authorities and released.

B Y THE TIME of the *Yerger* case, the international law of war had largely run its course as a source of authority for the federal government in the postwar South. The customs and usages of war had offered Lincoln, the Congress, and the Bureau of Military Justice a way to direct the war effort, move forward with Emancipation, and organize Reconstruction in a constitutional system that was stingy with the powers it extended to the federal government. But precisely because of the broad authority it offered, many saw the law of war (not unreasonably) as a threat to the ordinary constitutional processes of peacetime, to the separation of powers, and to the guarantees of the Bill of Rights. Men like John Bingham had pressed the theory of the law of war's scope to extraordinary lengths when arguing before the Lincoln assassination commission. But as a congressman he had crafted the Fourteenth Amendment as a substitute and as a safer source of lawful authority.

For four long years following Lincoln's assassination, the laws of war had remained at the center of events. They had been the basis for the government's postwar prosecutions of war criminals and assassins. They had underwritten the Congress's Reconstruction efforts. But they had not punished Jefferson Davis.

Combatants in Open War

T HE FINAL DAYS of the war in early April 1865 found Francis Lieber fearful for the safety of Lincoln, who had traveled to the front lines in Virginia. "Induce . . . the President to return," he had implored his friend Charles Sumner. Lieber had not anticipated that the danger for the president would be as great in the nation's capital as it had been on the battlefields of Virginia. "My God!" he wrote Halleck on learning the terrible news. "That even this should befall us!" And Lieber knew what was to blame. "It is Slavery, Slavery!" he cried. Lincoln's assassination offered the final proof of slavery's barbarizing effects.

In the weeks that followed, Lieber became a prominent voice in the debate about justice for the Confederate leadership. Even before Lincoln's death, Lieber had come to think that the leaders of the rebellion—Jefferson Davis, Alexander Stephens, and others, even James Mason and John Slidell from the *Trent* affair of November 1861—ought to be tried for treason.

As controversy stirred over the postwar military tribunals, Lieber traveled to Washington to consult with President Johnson and the cabinet. Lieber met Attorney General James Speed and stayed overnight at his home in the capital. He sat down with Secretary of State William Seward, who was still recovering from the attempt on his life in April. He had an audience with Andrew Johnson, which to his dismay was interrupted by the crowds of southern pardon-seekers who thronged the White House day and night. He called on Edwin Stanton, and for the first time he met General Grant.

Since drafting the code for Lincoln and the Union, Lieber had bided his time while teaching his classes at Columbia College, always hoping for another opportunity to serve in the war effort. From New York, he had sent a steady stream of advice to Judge Advocate General Holt and his staff and had carried on a vast correspondence with Halleck, Sumner, and others. Now his legal expertise returned him to public attention. In May, he crafted what quickly became the leading statement of the law of postwar criminal justice. Published first in the *New York Independent* and then reprinted in the *Army and Navy Journal*, and read closely by members of the administration in Washington, Lieber's paper (like the code he had drafted while the war still raged) set out a fierce but law-bound vision of the law of armed conflict.

As Lieber explained, the tens of thousands of southern soldiers who had been paroled at the end of hostilities were prisoners of war. Any such man who had "committed crimes" by making "acts of injury not covered by the laws of war" was answerable to his captor for such crimes. That was the view of the code of 1863, Lieber pointed out, and the same rule applied in the postwar setting. Moreover, Lieber wrote, the laws of war only immunized paroled Confederate soldiers from treason prosecutions for the duration of the war. Once war was over, and once the legal regime of warfare (the "state of war") had given way to a state of peace, the immunity offered by military paroles fell away and rebels would be subject to criminal prosecution for treason unless they were pardoned by the president.

Yet what was permissible was not the same as what was advisable. As Lieber met with cabinet officials in July, he urged that the government not try Jefferson Davis by military commission, even if there proved to be sufficient evidence to convict him of participating in war crimes. In a private memorandum he summarized the reasons. He worried about the increased distrust of military commissions in the immediate wake of the Lincoln assassins' trial and the execution of Mary Surratt. He worried that such a trial would draw attention away from Davis's real crime, which to his mind was treason. To use a military commission, moreover, would "look like positive distrust in our law as it stands."

Within days of Lieber's visit, Johnson's cabinet met on a hot day in Washington and decided in favor of the approach laid out in Lieber's May paper and private memorandum. Stanton and Speed, the cabinet members with whom Lieber was closest, each voted in favor of a treason prosecution before a federal court. Seward preferred a military commission, but he was outvoted. Everyone agreed, however, that it would be "most calamitous," as Secretary of the Interior James Harlan put it, if Davis were acquitted.

*   *   *

THE BURDEN OF the Johnson administration's July decision was to build a case against Jefferson Davis. The president had already accused Davis of complicity in Lincoln's assassination in a May 2 proclamation offering a $100,000 reward for his arrest. In the trial of Booth's accomplices, Holt and Bingham had described Davis as standing at the head of the conspiracy. But accusations were one thing; proving them was another. And so, on the same day that the cabinet resolved to prosecute Davis in a federal court, Stanton asked Francis Lieber to go into the Confederate archives to link Davis definitively to wartime atrocities.

Lieber was appointed at the pay of a colonel of cavalry and given the travel allowance of a major general. In his first act, he appointed his son Norman, the former judge advocate under Holt, as his assistant. Along with a staff of six clerks, father and son faced 428 boxes, 69 barrels, 2 hogsheads, and 120 mailbags of rebel documents, many of them covered in dirt from the streets of Richmond. Henry Halleck, who oversaw the collection of rebel documents from late April onward, believed the collection would hold evidence of "plots of assassination, incendiaryism, treason, &c." The War Department assigned an armed guard to watch over the special bureau's work in a building on F Street in the capital. On Norman Lieber's strict orders, the guard was "to allow no person, not connected with the office, to enter the Building after office hours." The bureau operated in secrecy, and no one was allowed into the building without the written permission of Secretary Stanton.

Lieber had spent much of the second half of the war watching the conflict for violations in the customs and usages of war. He was certain the plot against Lincoln "emanated from or was countenanced by" Jefferson Davis in Richmond, and at the outset of his efforts in July and August he was confident that he would locate caches of documentary evidence on rebel war crimes. The bureau enjoyed some success in this regard. Lieber was able to send the judge advocate general's office documents for use in the trial of John Gee, the commander at the Salisbury prison camp. The documents failed to win a conviction in the case, but the bureau's work at least contributed to the effort.

Yet that was more than Lieber's bureau could claim in any other case, and in particular it was more than Lieber could do in the case of Jefferson Davis. Documents in the bureau's collection of Davis's papers established a connection between Davis and Confederate agents in Canada, but no one doubted such a connection. The real question was whether Davis had helped to plan the assassination, and here the documentary record was far weaker. In November, Lieber's team found a letter addressed to Davis proposing an assassination plot. Davis's handwritten endorsement referred the matter to Confederate secretary of war Seddon without comment. Lieber seized on the endorsement. But it was a slender thread, and letters like it had already been identified and made public in the trial of the Booth conspirators.

Strikingly, neither Lieber nor anyone else in the Johnson administration thought to make the Confederate policy toward black Union soldiers part of the postwar prosecution of Davis or the other Confederate leaders. Davis and the southern leadership had endorsed the policy of denying prisoner of war status to black soldiers. Indeed, they had publicly formulated it, and under its influence black soldiers had been enslaved and executed all across the South. The 1863 code had rejected Davis's position as a gross violaton of the customs and usages of warfare. And yet in 1865 and 1866, prosecuting high Confederate officials for crimes against black Union soldiers was so politically implausible that it did not even generate substantial internal debate among those directing the effort to prosecute Davis for his actions during the war.

Setting aside the Confederate policy on black soldiers, Lieber ultimately found almost nothing to connect the Confederate leadership to knowing violations of the laws of war. He confessed as much in a January 1866 report to Stanton, which the secretary hid in a drawer. Finally, in April, as the Congress grew restless at the continuing failure of the administration to try Jefferson Davis, Congressman George Boutwell of the House Judiciary Committee called on Lieber to report what he had found. As the credibility of witnesses like Sanford Conover collapsed, Lieber's work in the archives was thrust to the fore. But it fell short. Lieber was forced to go back to Stanton and admit that he had been unable to identify anything new of note. Boutwell's report, in turn, conceded that the Confederate archives had not been able to link Davis to Lincoln's death. Boutwell held out hope that "the capture of the rebel archives" would still produce such evidence, and Lieber shared Boutwell's optimism. In language that Lieber himself would have used, the congressman cited the South's "total disregard of inter-national law and of the usages of civilized war."

With Boutwell's encouragement, Lieber continued to pursue connections between the Confederate hierarchy and shadowy conspiracies among rebel agents in Canada and the North deep into 1866. Yet even Lieber was losing hope that anything could be done to charge the Confederate leadership. "The trial of Jeff. Davis," he wrote to Halleck soon after the Boutwell committee called him to testify, "will be a terrible thing. Volumes—a library—

of the most infernal treason will be brought to light. Davis will be found not guilty, and we shall stand there completely beaten. The time was lost and can never be recovered."

W HILE THE WAR Department searched for documents, Jefferson Davis languished ill and alone in Fort Monroe.

Johnson's cabinet had resolved to try Davis in a federal court for treason, but a series of maddening obstacles had prevented them from moving forward. Attorney General Speed concluded that the trial would have to take place in Virginia because of the constitutional requirement that trials be held in the same state in which the crimes took place. Because Virginia was in the fourth circuit, Chief Justice Salmon Chase in his capacity as circuit justice would have sat as one of the trial judges alongside District Judge John Curtiss Underwood. Chase, however, refused to sit in the circuit court until the war was formally over, citing the importance of judicial independence from the military. A prosecution could conceivably have moved forward without Chase, but Judge Underwood was an abolitionist judge from New York (a "carpetbagger," in the lingo of the white South), and administration officials feared that any conviction with Underwood presiding alone would be tainted by his political radicalism.

*Artist Alfred Waud sketched Jefferson Davis confined
at Fort Monroe in 1865.*

New problems arose in 1866 after President Johnson proclaimed the war over. A congressional reorganization of the federal judicial circuits in July failed to assign justices to the revised circuit courts. In Chase's view, he could not preside over Davis's case because no justice could serve on a circuit court until Congress's mistake had been fixed. By the time the problem had been remedied, however, Andrew Johnson's impeachment for firing Secretary Stanton in violation of the Tenure of Office Act required Chase's participation as the presiding officer in Johnson's trial before the Senate. At last, in late 1868, Chase was available for trial. But by then the government had lost whatever enthusiasm it originally had for bringing Davis to trial at all. On Christmas Day, Johnson issued one last amnesty proclamation pardoning Davis, Dr. Mudd, and the few remaining rebels he had not already pardoned.

Beneath the Union's posture toward Davis lay the widespread sentiment that punishing Davis as a criminal after the war's end was inconsistent with having treated him as a public enemy while the war was underway. Writing ten years after the end of the effort to prosecute Davis, the distinguished Maryland lawyer Bradley T. Johnson summed up the significance for postwar prosecutions of Lincoln's decision in the first year of the conflict to invoke the law of war tradition. Johnson had good reason to consider the subject, for he was the same Bradley Johnson who, after leaving his home state to serve the Confederacy as a brigadier general, had presided over the burning of Chambersburg and who late in the war had commanded the Confederate prison camp at Salisbury. Grant had insisted that the surrender terms at Appomattox barred Johnson's prosecution. Now, a decade later, Johnson keenly grasped the significance of the customs and usages of war for treason charges. When a rebellion grew so large and enduring as to compel "acceptance of the rules and usages which obtain in regular wars between independent nations," he wrote, then treason trials were beyond the pale. To be sure, he conceded, "when traitors and rebels oppose their government by open violence and are summarily put down, those not slain in the combat" could "fairly be tried for treason" as ordinary criminals. But to do so after a conflict rising to the level of the Civil War, Johnson thought, would be "inexpressibly revolting and contemptible." After four years of truce flags and prisoner exchanges (contentious though they were), four years of the "laws of chivalry," and four years in which "combatants in open war" had "recognized each other as soldiers and gentlemen engaged in a legitimate conflict," Johnson was convinced that honorable men could not go back and treat their enemies as criminals.

As a formal matter of legal doctrine, Johnson may have been wrong. Since 1861, Lincoln and Sumner had maintained that a nation's willingness to recognize the laws of armed conflict in a civil war did not displace the same nation's power to exercise the sovereign authority of its laws. "Our case is double," Sumner had said, and the Supreme Court had agreed, saying in *The Prize Cases* in 1863 that the United States could treat the rebels as enemies and criminals at one and the same time. Lieber's code, the United States' most systematic statement of the laws of war, had expressly reserved the right of a sovereign in a civil war to resort to treason prosecutions at war's end.

Yet when the time came to put Lieber's reserved treason charges to the test, treating the rebels as criminals proved to be a step too far. Adopting the laws of war had required commitments of fair treatment and reciprocal respect that were now difficult to square with prosecuting Davis for treason. Indeed, acceptance of the law of war framework made it hard to contemplate treason prosecutions for anyone who had taken up arms with the Confederacy. What the laws of war did was offer immunity from the criminal laws for the purpose of allowing the warring sides to come to a peaceful resolution of their conflict. And despite a powerful desire to move forward with prosecutions, the leadership of the Union understood this. The federal courts witnessed any number of indictments for treason during the course of the war, but not one execution followed. And though a flurry of new treason indictments came in the weeks and months after the war, prosecutors and courts universally dismissed the cases. It is one of the wonders of the war, as the mid-twentieth-century historian James Randall put it, that "no life was forfeited and no sentence of fine and imprisonment carried out in any judicial prosecution for treason arising out of the rebellion."

The laws of war had exerted considerable influence on the postwar military commissions as well. The postwar trials Joseph Holt orchestrated helped cement a conceptual innovation that had been working its way into the laws of war since the Mexican War in 1847 and 1848. Building on General Orders No. 100 and Lincoln's Emancipation, Holt had pursued a fierce conception of the laws of war, one that was importantly at odds with the Enlightenment model Francis Lieber loved to mock as so much namby-pambyism. Here was a law of war that reintroduced crime and punishment into the regulation of armed conflict. Francis Lieber even coined a new term to describe the new treatment that the United States had begun to deal out to those who violated the customs and usages of war. Writing to Stanton in 1865 on the question of postwar prosecutions, Lieber referred to such violations as a new species of offense, the "war-crime."

To be sure, the approach to the laws of war that Lincoln and Lieber crafted in 1862 and 1863 had fallen prey to Holt's erratic personality and poor judgment. It had given way to the desire in the Congress and in the Supreme Court for a restoration of constitutional normalcy. It had foundered on the orthodox doctrine that peace forgot all crimes of war. An uncooperative president had ensured that Holt's most expansive visions for postwar justice would be thwarted.

Yet the distinctive vision of the laws of war crafted by the Union in the Civil War had a future nonetheless. Even as Lieber was assisting in Holt's trouble-plagued prosecutions, the aging professor had begun to turn the code Lincoln commissioned into the beginnings of a next chapter for the laws of war around the globe.

PART III

The Howling Desert

All the means, not condemned as mean or cowardly (such as assassination or poisoning), which tend directly and adequately toward the destruction of the military power and resources of the enemy, must be regarded as legitimate. Such means cannot be condemned on the ground that they are terrible and sweeping in their destructive effect. On the contrary these are good reasons for their adoption, as tending to make the contest "short, sharp, and decisive," and still more, as tending to prevent nations from going to war upon slight provocation.

—Major General John M. Schofield, 1881

Chapter 11

Glenn's Brigade

———◆———

*No modern state . . . can sanction . . . a resort
to torture. . . . If it does, where is the line to
be drawn? If the "water cure" is ineffective,
what shall be the next step? Shall the victim
be suspended, head down, over the smoke of a
smouldering fire; shall he be tightly bound and
dropped from a distance of several feet; shall he
be beaten with rods; shall his shins be rubbed
with a broomstick until they bleed?*

—Judge Advocate General George B. Davis, 1902

*Terrible! Say you? Well, yes. War ought to be
terrible. The trouble is that it has ceased to be
terrible to altogether too many men.*

—Anonymous officer, U.S. Army, 1896

FRANCIS LIEBER DIED suddenly on October 2, 1872. He was seventy-four years old. Right up until his death, he had worked to expand the influence of the instructions he had written for Lincoln and the Union Army. Even as the Civil War raged, he launched General Orders No. 100 across the Atlantic. "Old Hundred," he began to call it. His longtime correspondent, the prominent Swiss-born jurist Johann Caspar Bluntschli at the University of Heidelberg, translated the code and added the terms of a treaty signed by twelve European nations at Geneva in 1864. The resulting book produced an influential German code just in time for Prussia's 1866 war with Austria. Lieber continued to develop the law of war back at home as well. When he died six years later, he left a sprawling unfinished manuscript charting a future for Old Hundred and its terms in the world.

It fell to Norman Lieber to carry on his father's efforts. Among the three Lieber boys, Norman alone had escaped the war unscathed, though he had fought in several of its terrible clashes. He had served as a judge advocate under Joseph Holt in the last year of the conflict. After the war, he had worked alongside his father in the rebel archives and then done a stint in the Department of Dakota in Minnesota, where the Army clashed with the Blackfeet and the Sioux Indians. By the late 1870s, he was back east teaching the laws of war at West Point. In 1884, Lieber became acting judge advocate general. In 1895, the War Department made his post permanent. By the time Lieber retired in 1901, he was the longest-serving head of the Judge Advocate corps in Army history, a distinction he still holds more than a century later.

With the younger Lieber presiding over the office of the Judge Advocate General, General Orders No. 100 began a new career. The code of 1863 took root in the inhospitable soil of the Indian wars in the American West. It shaped a new generation of lawmaking across the Atlantic. And it ventured gingerly into the Pacific. In 1862, the ideas that animated Lincoln's instructions to the Union Army had been decidedly unorthodox; they had embodied Clausewitz's fierce rejection of the rational Newtonianism of nineteenth-century military thought. Now Norman Lieber helped make such views the conventional wisdom of the Army officer corps.

But for all its success, one thing was certain. The code did not bring a stop to atrocities in combat. In that dismaying truth lay a clue to the nature of the law the Civil War had shaped.

Stay the Hand of Retribution

O N APRIL 11, 1873, two small groups of men, one Indian and one white, walked toward one another in the boulder-strewn lavabed moonscape on the south shore of Lake Tule in northern California. For six weeks the men had been meeting on and off again to try to craft a resolution to an intractable standoff. On one side stood the U.S. Army; on the other, a band of 150 Modoc Indians trying to repossess their old lands after their exile to an unsuitable reservation in Oregon.

For months, 600 soldiers under Major General Edward Canby had tried to capture the Modocs by force, only to be turned back time and again by 50 warriors led by the Modocs' chief, a man named Kintpuash, known to most as "Captain Jack." Canby enjoyed superior numbers, but Jack's men fought brilliantly from impenetrable positions in the fissures and caves of the lava-beds. And so, in early 1873, Canby resorted to peace negotiations. Captain Jack readily agreed to talk, in part because there seemed no prospect that he would be able to break out of the inhospitable rocky landscape without a negotiated peace. But unbeknownst to Canby, Captain Jack was locked in a struggle with dissident members of his own group who believed that peace negotiations were unwise. "You are like an old squaw," his critics jeered. They said he was "not fit to be chief" because he had never killed a white man. And on the night of April 10, the dissidents had finally gained a decisive victory in internal tribe deliberations. Jack agreed reluctantly that the next day he would kill Canby and the other peace commissioners.

As the two parties came together, Captain Jack drew his pistol and shot Canby dead. A frightful slaughter ensued. Two others in the U.S. delegation were killed almost instantly and a fourth white commissioner was badly wounded. The peace talks had come to a violent end.

With hopes of a peaceful resolution dashed, President Grant and General William Sherman (now the commanding general of the U.S. Army) authorized the "utter extermination" of the Modocs. Sherman called on General Jefferson C. Davis to root out the tribe. Davis (who was no relation to the Confederate president) had commanded one of Sherman's corps on the March to the Sea in 1864, and his conduct there suggested that he was unlikely to be held back by mawkish humanitarianism. In December 1864, Davis had ordered a pontoon bridge pulled up after him, leaving hundreds of freedpeople to the mercy of the Confederate forces trailing him. An unknown number of them drowned trying to swim across the river. Now Sherman ordered Davis to "shoot the leaders" of the Modoc band, to "hang the murderers," and to disperse the remaining tribe members so that the memory of the Modoc tribe would be erased within a generation.

Davis finally caught up to Captain Jack in June 1873 when the Modoc dissidents defected and led him to the Modoc chief's hideaway. With Jack in custody at last, Davis assumed he would simply execute the Indian as a killer without the formality of legal process. Newspapers around the country had called for no less as a response to Captain Jack's act of treachery. The *New York Herald* had predicted confidently that there would be "no desire to stay the hand of retribution." The *National Republican* in Washington, D.C., had urged that the Modocs should "be exterminated, root and branch." Even supporters of President Grant's recently inaugurated peace policy toward the Indians conceded that the Modocs should be killed.

Within hours of Captain Jack's capture, Davis issued orders for the Modoc chief's execution. He scheduled the hanging for the next day at sunset. But as Davis drew up a list of those he intended to execute along with the Modoc chief, news arrived from Washington. The president ordered Davis to hold the Modoc prisoners pending further instructions.

THE INDIAN WARS of the post–Civil War West threw American views of the laws of armed conflict into a vast confusion. After 1871, Congress moved away from treating Indian tribes as independent nations by announcing that the United States would no longer enter into treaties with Indian tribes. Strangely, the treatment of Indians in armed conflict drew ever more heavily on principles drawn from the laws of war—laws that had typically applied only in armed conflict among civilized states.

The instructions of 1863 seemed to have excluded Indians from their scope; international law, Lieber's text explained, protected only those who lived in modern organized sovereign states. Nonetheless, early signs of a turn toward the laws of war in Indian conflicts arose during the Civil War in the treatment of the Dakota Indians in Minnesota.

In August and September 1862, Dakota warriors associated with the Sioux Nation had launched a bloody series of assaults to reclaim land they had ceded to the United States. Disputes had arisen over payment for the land. The Dakota attacked white settler homesteads across the southwestern part of the state, killing 358 settlers in all, including women and children.

The American response was swift and ferocious. Major General John Pope, still smarting from his humiliating defeat at the Second Battle of Bull Run and now virtually exiled to the Military Department of the Northwest, ordered Colonel Henry Hastings Sibley to treat the Dakota "as maniacs or wild beasts," and declared his intent "utterly to exterminate" them. Pope's attitude was shared widely. "Nits," one soldier told Colonel Sibley, "make lice."

Yet in September and October, when he took into custody some 2,000 Dakota Indians, Colonel Sibley did not execute them summarily. Instead, he convened a five-officer military commission and tried the Dakota for

The log cabin behind these Dakota-Sioux Indian prisoners was the site
for military commission trials of 392 warriors, some 303
of whom were initially sentenced to death.

murder and related crimes. Minnesota settlers complained bitterly about the delayed retaliation against the Dakota. ("Daniel Boone," one newspaper editor protested, had "instituted no trial by jury when he caught a savage.") But the settlers did not have to wait long. The military trials began two days after Sibley had begun to take the Dakota into custody. On the first day, the commission tried sixteen men, sentencing ten to death by hanging and acquitting six others. When the trials concluded on November 3, the commission had heard charges against 392 Dakota for murder, rape, and robbery. The commission convicted 323 warriors, 303 of whom it sentenced to death.

Historians of the Dakota conflict have focused on the procedural shortcomings of the military commissions, which were considerable. Most trials were extremely short: some lasted no more than five minutes. Key evidence was often provided by cooperating witnesses who otherwise faced execution themselves. No defense counsel appeared.

But the more interesting question is not whether the military commission trials were paragons of civil libertarian virtue (they were not), or even whether they lived up to the already dubious standards of trials in nineteenth-century courts (they did not). The real question is why U.S. officials held trials at all.* Summary executions, after all, had been standard practice for American soldiers capturing Indians since the seventeenth century. In 1777, George Rogers Clark had executed Indians with an ax in full view of British forces at Fort Vincennes along the Wabash River. Forty years later, in the First Seminole War in Florida, Andrew Jackson executed Francis the Prophet and Homathlemico without even the pretense of a trial. In the Black Hawk War of 1832 in which Lincoln had played a small role, frontier volunteers had killed even Indian children without a second thought. "Kill the nits and you'll have no lice," said a member of the Illinois militia.

As recently as the 1850s, American armed forces in the West had been executing Indians summarily without compunction. In northern California, U.S. troops had trapped Indians on islands and killed them in what one officer described as natural slaughter pens. Colonel William S. Harney, known as "Squaw Killer," forced nearly 200 Nebraska Sioux into caves and killed 85 of them after a member of the tribe killed a white settler's cow. Even Ethan Allen Hitchcock, who was sharply critical of Harney and sympathized with many Indians, led an expedition along the Coquille River in Oregon that killed an entire Indian encampment in revenge for the killing of five white traders. Indeed, by 1862, some commanders in Missouri were applying the policy of summary execution not only to Indians but to Confederate guerrillas.

Yet even as summary executions continued, Indian campaigns after the Mexican War had begun little by little to adopt the trappings of a different approach. In the Oregon Territory in the 1850s, for example, Major Granville O. Haller, a veteran of the Mexican conflict, used hastily convened military commissions like those Winfield Scott had employed in Mexico to justify the execution of Wenneste Indian warriors accused of killing white settlers.

The military leadership in Minnesota had probably not learned about military commissions first-hand in Mexico. Henry Hastings Sibley had no military experience to speak of. But he may have heard talk of the Mexican commissions. He almost certainly got wind of the military commissions taking place in 1862 in Missouri under General Henry Halleck, who had just been promoted to general-in-chief of the Union Army. Only days before Sibley ordered the Minnesota trials, newspapers around the country had published Lincoln's September 24 proclamation authorizing military commission trials of rebel insurgents and "their aiders and abettors." By the last week

---

*A student of mine, Maeve Herbert Glass, makes this same point in a brilliant article on the Sioux military commissions of 1862: Maeve Herbert, "Explaining the Sioux Military Commission of 1862," *Columbia Human Rights Law Review* 40 (2009): 743.

of September 1862, military commissions were becoming standard practice in the U.S. armed forces. Sibley probably convened the commission for the Dakota simply because the idea of military commissions was in the air.

Once military commissions were in place in Minnesota, the laws of war began to shape the fate of the Dakota prisoners. Even though Francis Lieber had excluded Indians from the protections of the laws of war, he insisted that there were limits to what armies could do to them or any civilized enemy. Lieber thought that torture, for example, would clearly be beyond the pale, even if Indians inflicted it on U.S. soldiers first. Torture, he warned, would turn an army into a savage force like the one it was fighting. Now Secretary of the Navy Gideon Welles cautioned Lincoln against executing 300 Indians on similar grounds; it would, he warned, make the United States as much like "barbarians" as the Indians themselves. The Commissioner of Indian Affairs worried similarly that punishing men "who have laid down their arms and surrendered themselves as prisoners" would be "contrary to the spirit of the age." At a moment when the South had captured thousands of Union soldiers, when Lincoln's critics pilloried him for initiating a barbaric war of servile insurrection, the North could not afford to draw the charge of cruelly executing prisoners of war. And so, after agonizing over the cases for a month, Lincoln resolved them by applying a principle drawn from the laws of war. Distinguishing between those Indian warriors who had participated in massacres and those who had fought against soldiers and militia, he approved the death sentences of thirty-nine Dakota warriors and left the sentences of the others unresolved.

The implications of the formal framework of the laws of war became still clearer a year later when Sibley convened another military commission to try a sixteen-year-old Dakota named Wowinape, who had fled north to escape capture in 1862. The commission sentenced Wowinape to death by hanging for murders in the massacres of August 1862. But taking a cue from Lincoln's attention to the distinctions of the laws of war, General John Pope reversed the conviction on the basis of a legal technicality (a "technical difficulty," he called it) in the military commission that had convicted him.* Rarely if ever had U.S. military force against Indians been so closely regulated by law. But then, the United States had rarely been prepared to execute

---

*Sibley had both initiated the charges against Wowinape and reviewed them. Article 65 of the Articles of War prohibited officers from performing both these roles in courts-martial, and while the tribunal in question was technically not a court-martial but a military commission, Pope worried that the commissions were properly governed by the same rules. Judge Advocate General Holt agreed.

so many Indian warriors at once, by law or otherwise. The military commissions had served to restrain the use of sheer force. But commissions had also been a legitimating device, a way of moving forward with mass executions on an unprecedented scale.

THE DAKOTA TRIALS loomed in the background in June 1873 when General Jefferson C. Davis reluctantly called a halt to the swift execution of Captain Jack and the Modoc warriors in Oregon. General John M. Schofield of the Army's Division of the Pacific expressed grave concerns about the propriety of summary military executions under the laws of war. (Schofield had received a personalized copy of General Orders No. 100 from Henry Halleck ten years before.) Summary executions troubled William Tecumseh Sherman in Washington, too. But the military men were just as uncomfortable with Oregon governor LaFayette Grover's proposal to try Captain Jack and his confederates as ordinary criminals in state court. Neither path seemed right.

It fell to U.S. Attorney General George Henry Williams to craft a legal strategy for the Modoc case. As a senator from Oregon a few years before, Williams had been a core member of the radical wing of the Republican Party and an author of the 1867 Reconstruction Act with its broad reauthorization of military commissions. He had introduced the Tenure of Office Act, which aimed to seize congressional control of the War Department from Andrew Johnson, and he had been a principal advocate of Johnson's impeachment when the president tried to reclaim his authority. Now, building on his work in 1867, Williams advised President Grant that a military commission was the right way to proceed. Citing the prosecution of Henry Wirz and relying heavily on Attorney General Speed's opinion in the Lincoln assassination case, Williams argued that General Orders No. 100 from the Civil War established the legal authority of military commissions to try violations of the laws of war. Its Article 13, he said, recognized a "common law of war" between nations. Its Articles 40 and 41 rejected the existence of any other body of law between nations at war with one another. And its Article 59 expressly allowed the prosecution of a soldier for offenses against the laws of war.

On the ground in Oregon, Davis could barely believe that dealing with Indians warranted such legal care. "I thought to avoid an unnecessary expense and the farce of a trial," he told a reporter, "by doing the work myself." But to his disgust, Grant approved Williams's proposal for military commissions in the Modoc case. The United States charged Captain Jack and five other Modocs with murder in violation of the laws of war. After five days of trial at Fort Klamath in Oregon, the commission convicted them and sentenced each of them to death. Three months later, after the president commuted two sentences and approved the remaining four, the U.S. Army executed Captain Jack and three of his fellow Modocs on a gallows built especially for them. A newspaper correspondent at the scene reported that "Everything connected with the execution was in most perfect order and was performed in strict military precision." The "majesty of the laws," he added, had "been vindicated."

I N MOST INDIAN CONFLICTS, the majesty of the law more often gave way to a mix of tragedy and farce.

When General Nelson A. Miles captured the Apache leader Geronimo in 1886, chaos broke out at the highest reaches of the U.S. government because no one could understand the Apache renegade's legal status. President Grover Cleveland expressed the hope that Miles would simply hang him. The acting secretary of war contended that Geronimo should be tried and punished for murder by the civil authorities of the Territories of Arizona and New Mexico. General O. O. Howard objected that the terms of Geronimo's surrender ruled out both of these possibilities. But no one was sure exactly what those terms were, and no one had thought to write them down at the time. Weeks later, an embarrassed President Cleveland was forced to ask Geronimo what he had understood to be the terms of his own surrender.

Ultimately, the War Department shipped Geronimo and his small band of warriors off to Fort Pickens in Florida as prisoners of war. For the next twenty-five years, the band would live in captivity, first in Florida, then in Alabama and later Oklahoma, held as prisoners of war from a conflict that had long since ended. But this was a prisoner of war status like few others. Their ranks included not only men captured in arms with Geronimo, but also women and children (400 people in all). Dozens of children born into captivity became prisoners of war at birth. The adults moved freely around the towns in which they were confined from sunup until sundown. They raised cattle and grew crops. Until he drank himself to death in 1909, Geronimo traveled around the country to take part in Wild West exhibitions hawking cheap souvenir bows and authentic Geronimo autographs, all while formally a prisoner from the Indian wars of the 1880s.

The Apache case was especially prolonged, but it was not unique in its halfhearted incorporation of the laws of war. Indians were held in circumstances that would never have justified prisoner of war treatment of southern soldiers in the Civil War. The sixty-nine Dakota Sioux acquitted in the Minnesota trials of 1862 were not released. They were simply imprisoned in Fort Snelling along with all the other fighting-age male Dakotas, without regard to whether the war in which they had fought was over. In the 1870s, the startling inclusion of children among the Indian prisoners of war led to the establishment of a school in Carlisle, Pennsylvania, to educate child prisoners from conflicts with the Cheyenne and Comanche. In the early 1890s, Judge Advocate General Lieber sustained the indefinite detention of an Apache chief named Eskiminzin, who had been arrested for aiding his son-in-law, a renegade scout in the U.S. Cavalry named Apache Kid. Lieber approved Eskiminzin's captivity even though he could not say that there was a war and even though he could not identify a federal crime that the Apache might have committed.

Nor could the United States bring itself to enforce the laws of war strictly against its own soldiers in Indian conflicts. At Sand Creek in Colorado in 1864, the 3rd Colorado Volunteers slaughtered and mutilated some 200 Cheyenne and Arapaho Indians. Colonel John Chivington had ordered the deaths of men, women, and children alike. "Kill and scalp all, little and big," he told his men. "Nits," he scowled, echoing the now familiar refrain, "made lice." A court of inquiry recommended a formal denunciation of the massacre, but levied no punishments against anyone involved.*

None of this could be squared easily with the ordinary laws of war. One problem, as Attorney General Amos Akerman put it in 1871, was the peculiarity of the legal status of Indians more generally. Indians were at once independent nations capable of going to war and making peace, and domestic dependencies under the authority of the U.S. Congress and the president. Some critics chafed at such contradictions and puzzles and urged a more thoroughgoing adoption of the rules of war as the blueprint for American policy. Men like O. O. Howard thought the best way to spread "the blessing of a knowledge" of the European laws of war among the "savage races"

---

*Judge Advocate General Lieber later observed that the failure to punish Chivington stemmed in part from the fact that Chivington had already been mustered out of the Army by the time the court of inquiry concluded its business. See G. Norman Lieber to the Secretary of War, April 15, 1892, Letters Sent ("Record Books"), 1889–1895, Records of the Office of the Judge Advocate General (Army), 1792–2010, record group 153, National Archives and Records Administration.

would be to set a good example. Others like Chivington and Davis could not understand the new application of law of war principles to the Indian conflicts at all. Summary execution and simple massacre, in their view, had been the standard tools of Indian fighting.

In the end, however, the postwar Army's partial embrace of the laws of war in Indian conflicts fell somewhere between the two poles. This new ad hoc middle ground, between the virtually unbounded violence of the age of Jackson and the civilized limits of the Enlightenment laws of war, resembled Lincoln's pragmatic and partial adoption of the laws of war in the first year of the Civil War. Just as Lincoln had embraced the laws of war in the very months in which the Union was ratcheting up the destructiveness of its war effort, now officers learned to put the language of humanity and law to work as a justification for violence against Indians on the western frontier.

Some historians have argued that Sherman and the U.S. Army learned a form of total war in the conflict with the South and then applied it in the Indian campaigns of the West. Others object that the Army had employed brutally destructive tactics against the Indians long before the Civil War and that the Army's conduct at places like Sand Creek in 1864 and Wounded Knee in 1891 was far more indiscriminate and violent than anything directed against the South. Both positions misunderstand what the Civil War contributed to the postwar Indian campaigns. There was of course plenty of terrible violence used against Indians in the decades and centuries before the Civil War. What was new after the war—and what came out of it—was a confidence that the rules of civilized war no longer put undue restraints on the soldiers who sought to wage it. General Philip Sheridan (to whom the infamous phrase "the only good Indians I ever saw were dead" is usually attributed) justified violence in the Indian West in 1873 by asking whether it consisted of anything more than what the laws of war had been understood to permit in the South. "During the war, did any one hesitate to attack a village or town occupied by the enemy because women or children were within its limits? Did we cease to throw shells into Vicksburg or Atlanta because women or children were there?" Robert K. Evans, a recent graduate of the Military Academy at West Point and later a commander of the Army's Philippine Department, argued a few years later that anyone who actually sat down and read General Orders No. 100 would understand that the laws of war endorsed retaliation against savages. Only the mawkish humanitarians of the East, Evans complained, prevented the Army from vindicating the stern vision of the 1863 code Lincoln had approved.

Francis Lieber and Abraham Lincoln had helped make the laws of war safe for Indian fighting. Hostilities with Indians could now be brought under the umbrella of the laws of war because the United States' authoritative statement of those laws—a statement that carried with it the imprimaturs of Emancipation and Union victory—no longer interfered with the tactics employed in Indian conflicts. For some of the same reasons, many were beginning to ask whether the Civil War instructions might transform the international law of war in Europe as well.

The House in the Wood

IN JUNE 1859, a struggling Swiss banker named Henri Dunant caught up to the French army at the small town of Solferino in northern Italy. Dunant was seeking the French emperor, Napoleon III, in hopes of gaining the emperor's consent to water rights critical to Dunant's failing agricultural venture in French-controlled Algeria. Napoleon had marched from Paris with an army 120,000 strong to fight the Austrians on behalf of Italian unification, and Dunant had set off after him.

By chance, Dunant arrived at Solferino in the evening following a massive battle. Some 250,000 soldiers, French and Italian on one side, Austrian on the other, had fought in the heat of a blistering day. Now 30,000 wounded and 6,000 dead lay on the field. A late afternoon squall quickly turned the town's roads into impassable mud, hindering efforts to reach the injured, let alone move them off the field. Those among the wounded who were able to evacuate themselves seemed to fill every available space in the already crowded town. Overwhelmed doctors performed battlefield amputations by the hundreds. The groans of thirsty and desperate men filled the air. Wounded men on all sides begged passersby to put them out of their misery.

Like a good Swiss businessman, Dunant tried to organize the situation. He mobilized teams of local women to bring food to the injured and to wash their wounds. He dispatched others to collect linen for bandages. He drafted boys as water carriers. He conscripted tourists, journalists, and businessmen into his efforts. He extended aid to the wounded regardless of nationality. Injured soldiers, he said, had no country. They were all brothers. Dunant's efforts could hardly match the magnitude of the suffering on the field that evening, or the next day, or even the next day after that. But in a modest way, he had a made a difference.

Around Europe, men and women were having experiences startlingly like Dunant's. In Great Britain, Florence Nightingale organized British hospital services in the Crimea and captured the attention of English newspaper readers with her indictment of the treatment of the sick and wounded. In Naples in 1861, a doctor named Ferdinando Palasciano delivered lectures proposing that wounded soldiers be treated as neutrals outside of combat. In Paris, a French pharmacist named Henri Arrault proposed a system of military ambulances that all armies would agree to exempt from attack. In the United States, New Yorkers including the designer of Central Park, Frederick Law Olmsted, and the prominent lawyer and diarist George Templeton Strong founded a Sanitary Commission to deliver aid to the wounded in the Civil War.

Back in his hometown of Geneva, his Algerian enterprise now in ruins, Dunant marshaled these disparate efforts into an organized project. He started by writing a book about what he had seen. He called it *A Memory of Solferino*. The book was a stunning exposé of war's suffering. Behind the grand narrative of battle with its charges and countercharges, its heroic defenses and its sweeping assaults, Dunant revealed thousands of stories of extraordinary suffering: acts of brutality, smashed skulls, amputated limbs, and unendurable wounds. Suffering, Dunant forcefully insisted, was the real story of war. He distributed the book privately among friends in Geneva. His friends seemed to like it, so he printed more copies. Soon the book was being published in Leipzig, Paris, St. Petersburg, and Turin. Reform-minded men and women took up his work all across Europe. Dunant had touched a nerve. His powerful story did for the treatment of the wounded in Europe what Harriet Beecher Stowe's *Uncle Tom's Cabin* had done for slavery in the United States. But Dunant was more programmatic in his efforts than Stowe. His heartrending stories drew the reader ineluctably to a proposal at the book's end: a plan that would offer humanitarian care to the wounded on the field. Dunant proposed the creation of a new international organization that would formalize on a massive and far more effective scale the ad hoc volunteer efforts he had patched together in the aftermath of battle in 1859.

With the help of wealthy Swiss colleagues, Dunant convened conferences of European states at Geneva in 1863 and 1864 to craft terms for a treaty that would formalize the ad hoc system of volunteers he had put in place at Solferino. The first Geneva Convention followed. Twelve European states—including Belgium, Denmark, France, the Netherlands, Prussia, and Switzerland—took up one of the Enlightenment's great devices for limiting the destructive effects of war at sea and applied it to make new humanitarian progress in war on land. They agreed to treat ambulances and military hospitals not as enemies but as neutrals. The men and women employed in them, as well as inhabitants of the vicinity helping the wounded after a battle had finished, would be treated as neutrals, too. A distinctive arm badge—a red cross on a white ground—marked off its wearers as neutral humanitarian workers and thus exempt from the vicissitudes of combat.

D URING THE CIVIL WAR, Francis Lieber had lobbied his friends Henry Halleck and Charles Sumner to appoint him as the American delegate to the 1864 diplomatic conference in Geneva. "Am I not the man that ought to be sent?" he pleaded. But the pressing business of the Civil War, as well as the United States' long tradition of avoiding entanglements in European diplomacy, prevented Lincoln and Secretary of State Seward from officially participating in the Geneva conference. A skeletal delegation of the U.S. Sanitary Commission attended, but only for the limited purpose of sharing information about humanitarian work in the American conflict.

What Lieber had grasped was that new proposals for the laws of war were emerging all around the Atlantic world. "Our No. 100," Lieber told Halleck in 1864, had contributed its share to "the progress of our race," and now the advancement of civilization was continuing onward. Countless factors seemed to press in the same direction. War correspondents like William Howard Russell, who covered both the Crimean War and the Civil War for *The Times* of London, brought the face of battle into the homes of a burgeoning (and increasingly literate) middle class. The founder of the *New York Times*, Henry Raymond, reported from the field at Solferino, where he encountered Dunant wearing his trademark white suit in the midst of the carnage. War photographers like Roger Fenton in the Crimea and Mathew Brady and Alexander Gardner in America did in a few iconic pictures of death what the newspapers did in thousands of words. Armies themselves were changing. Eighteenth-century mercenary armies led by aristocratic officer corps had given way to vast mobilizations of citizen soldiers, imbued with the nationalistic spirit of the age. Even the weapons those soldiers used were different in ways that summoned a new legal architecture for combat. Improved rifling technology—the grooved barrels in infantry muskets—rendered obsolete the compact fighting formations of Napoleonic warfare and undid the tight boundaries of the eighteenth-century battlefield. The same technology that mowed down George Pickett's men at Gettysburg in 1863 also empowered irregulars ranging from Confederate guerrillas to the so-called *Franc-tireurs* of the war between France and Prussia in 1870–71. All these things—and more—prompted new initiatives in the laws of war.

Indeed, an entire generation of humanitarian reformers soon came to hope that the American code of 1863 and the Swiss convention of 1864 might be signs of a new epoch of moral progress, one that would not only ameliorate the horrors of war but one day even abolish it altogether. War had been a scourge of mankind since the beginnings of time, to be sure. But so had slavery. If the nineteenth century had managed to abolish the master's lash, why not the soldier's sword as well? In the United States, men such as the prominent Massachusetts pastor Richard Salter Storrs and Charles Loring Brace, the influential secretary of the New York Children's Aid Society, wrote best-selling books and delivered public lectures citing Lincoln's instructions for the Union armies as evidence of just such moral progress. The British jurist Sheldon Amos thought there was reason to believe that humanitarian reform would nurture "the very moral sentiment which, in time, will become the direct agency for the abolition of War itself." Many of the men behind the Geneva Convention in 1864 aimed one day to end the wars that for the time being they sought to humanize. Dunant signaled as much in his *Memory of Solferino*, where he echoed Sumner's early pacifism. War, Dunant said, turned men into murderers. Others, like the Swiss Gustave Moynier, who took over leadership of the International Committee of the Red Cross when Dunant proved too abidingly eccentric, told his fellow members of the organization that in the long run the brotherly sentiment nurtured by the Geneva Convention would make war itself seem as atavistic and barbaric as the acts of cruelty that the laws of war already prohibited. "*La civilisation de la guerre*—the humanizing of war—could end only in its abolition," Moynier declared.

Reformers' ambitions, however, ran ahead of the facts on the ground. Getting the states of late nineteenth-century Europe to agree to the Geneva Convention had proved relatively simple. Its terms dealt only with wounded men whose usefulness to any of the armies of Europe had, for all intents and purposes, come to an end. Indeed, it was not peacemakers who turned Dunant's Geneva principles of 1864 into a new body of international law, but rather some of the most uncompromising statesmen of the day. The militarists of Prussia (an army with a state, rather than a state with an army, the French revolutionary figure Mirabeau had quipped) took up the Geneva project of humanitarian aid to the wounded with more energy and enthusiasm than virtually any country in Europe, save perhaps Switzerland itself. When Prussia fought and decisively defeated Austria in 1866, it already had in place 120 different networks of volunteers to do the work of caring for the wounded under the Geneva rules. In the United States, which had not been formally represented in Geneva in 1864, the Senate finally ratified the convention only in 1882, when it acted at the behest of Secretary of State James "Jingo Jim" Blaine, whose central diplomatic legacy was to set the United States on a path toward more military interventions in Latin America.

Outside the relatively narrow issue of wounded soldiers, however, the leaders of powerful states were highly suspicious of any attempt to extend Dunant's humanitarian constraints into combat itself. Prussian military leaders objected vehemently to the barely concealed pacifist leanings of the humanitarian reformers. Field Marshal Helmuth von Moltke, the long-serving chief of staff of the Prussian army, spoke for many in Germany and elsewhere when he derided "perpetual peace" as "a dream," and "not even a beautiful dream" at that. War, he insisted, fostered "the noblest virtues of mankind"—courage, self-sacrifice, and fidelity to duty. And although civilization had brought with it a general "softening of manners," von Moltke warned that limiting the excesses of war was best left to the discipline of modern armies, not to the humanitarian efforts of lawyers and reformers. "The greatest kindness in war," von Moltke told the prominent European international lawyer Johann Caspar Bluntschli, "is to bring it to a speedy conclusion." Indeed, by the end of the century German officers worried that "it was impossible both to conduct a war successfully and observe the laws of war." Military necessity, they insisted, took "absolute precedence over any considerations for the law and customs of war."

Reaching consensus on rules of conduct was made even harder by the dense thicket of European rivalries. Proposals from the Russians immediately came under suspicion in Britain and Germany, where statesmen searched for ulterior motives. Suggestions from powerful states such as Prussia seemed to threaten small states such as Belgium, whose efforts in turn seemed designed to make hostile occupation as onerous as possible for strong occupiers and as gentle as possible for weaker occupied nations. Whenever the laws of war implicated the balance of power, diplomatic efforts came to a standstill. If international lawyers were to gain the consent of the states of Europe, they would need to accommodate themselves to the claims of powerful armies while finding a way to sidestep the rivalries of European politics.

T HE AMERICAN GENERAL ORDERS of 1863 arrived on the European stage as a kind of *deus ex machina* in the emerging drama of the European laws of war, one that offered a way to break the logjam that had blocked negotiations over the laws of war.

The document was instantly influential. As soon as Lincoln issued it, Lieber had sent copies to lawyers and statesmen in Berlin, Heidelberg, and Paris. European jurists understood exactly how useful the American contribution could be. Indeed, they sometimes seemed to claim American roots for their law of war projects whenever possible. Bluntschli dedicated his influential work to "Professor Dr. Franz Lieber in New-York" and credited "Präsidenten Lincoln" and "Professor Lieber" ("*mein lieber Freund!*") as his inspiration. He cited Lieber as inspiring the Institute of International Law, an important organization he founded with other international lawyers in Ghent in 1873. His *Modern Laws of War of Civilized States* (*Das moderne Kriegsrecht der civilisirten Staten*), which became the Germans' text on the laws of war in the Prussian wars with Austria and France, was little more than a translation of Lieber's "Old Hundred." Bluntschli's work was littered with references to the American Civil War code (the *Amerikanische Kriegsartikel*). Five years later, Bluntschli drew on Lieber's Code to put into print Lieber's new term in the laws of war: "war crime," or *Kriegsverbrechen* in the German. Lieber had used the term, though not in print. The idea had been implicit in the American experience from the Mexican War forward. Under the aegis of Lieber and Bluntschli, the idea of the war crime would shape the culture of warfare for at least the next century and a half.

General Orders No. 100 inspired imitators all across Europe. Bluntschli's work appeared in 1866 in Prussia. Military manuals on the laws of war followed in the Netherlands (1871), France (1877), Serbia (1879), Spain (1882), Portugal (1890), Great Britain (1894), and Italy (1896). Russia had a law of war manual in place by the time of the Russo-Turkish War of 1877–78. As the distinguished English jurist Henry Sumner Maine said, Lieber had set an example of "the formation of a practical Manual" that could be adapted to suit "the officers of each nation."

To harmonize the proliferating manuals on the international rules of warfare, members of the Russian foreign ministry developed Lieber's code into a proposal for a pan-European conference in 1874. When an ambitious midlevel civil servant in the Russian Ministry of Foreign Affairs named Fedor Fedorovich Martens first suggested the conference, he prepared a private draft for the Russian war minister that carefully cross-listed the articles of Lieber's code alongside the parallel provisions of his own proposed text. When the convention delegates assembled in Brussels in 1874, Martens introduced the initial draft convention as an amended version of Lieber's work in the Civil War.

Lieber's handiwork in 1862–63 was indeed apparent in the Russian proposal. Following Lieber's response to the 1862 prisoner parole controversies, Martens described the parole of prisoners as something permissible only with the consent of both the captor state and the captive's own government. Lieber had responded to the guerrilla problem and the threat of slave insurrection by providing that noncombatants who rose up in a territory already occupied by the enemy were not legitimate combatants and were liable to be treated as criminals; Martens followed suit. And like the code of 1863, the Martens draft left vast discretion to the doctrine of "military necessity." If necessity so demanded, even the execution of prisoners was permissible in Martens's initial draft, just as it had been under the terms of Lieber's code. Necessity, on Martens's account as in Lieber's, allowed the "seizure and destruction of everything that is necessary to the enemy in order to carry on the war," as well as everything that "hinders the success of warlike operations." As humanitarian critics noted at the time, even the gentlest provisions of texts like the Lieber code of 1863 and the Brussels Declaration of 1874 were shadowed by potentially eviscerating exceptions for the imperatives of military necessity.

Crucially, the American example offered an ingenious solution to the most difficult and contested issue in European law of war debates. The questions about guerrilla fighters that had arisen in Mexico in the 1840s and that Lieber had addressed in Missouri in 1862 turned out to be very much like the fast-emerging problem of irregular soldiers in European warfare. Were irregular combatants eligible for the privileges of prisoners of war? In 1871, when French farmers had fired on Prussian occupiers, the Prussians had required that any combatant be commissioned by a competent authority or otherwise be treated as a criminal. The Prussians had executed *Franc-tireurs* by the score. But the Prussian policy proved hotly controversial. And in the aftermath of the Franco-Prussian conflict, insiders thought that the hardest question to resolve in the laws of war would be "to whom does the right of combatant belong, in the case when a war is one of peoples, when the population, or a portion of it, has taken up arms?" The strong armies of Germany proposed a hard-and-fast rule favoring occupiers. After the eighth day of a conflict, they said, the privileges of lawful soldiers ought to be extended only to those wearing uniforms and acting "in direct subordination to a supreme commander-in-chief"; all other fighters would be simple criminals from that day forward. Smaller states, however, refused to go along, no doubt imagining with trepidation the risk of future German occupation. Belgium, which had good reason for concern, argued in favor of the opposite rule.

Populations rising in self-defense, the Belgians contended, ought to be given all the privileges of soldiers indefinitely.

Lieber's approach to the problem in 1862 cut through the knot of strong states and weak states. Martens, in particular, drew self-consciously on the functional strategy Lieber had crafted for defining soldiers and distinguishing them from criminal guerrillas. At Brussels in 1874, Martens adopted Lieber's functional redefinition of legitimate combatants, minimizing the significance of formal commissions and official uniforms, and emphasizing instead characteristics such as command control, distinctive insignia or marks, the open carrying of arms, and the observance of the laws and customs of war. By the end of the century, these four functional characteristics of soldiers had solidified into a widely accepted definition of the soldier, and indeed they have lasted as such into the twenty-first century.

The American instructions of 1863 also helped men like Bluntschli and Martens distinguish themselves and the laws of war they meant to promote from the efforts of the secret pacifists at Geneva. Lieber's personal views were far closer to those of the German von Moltke than they were to those of the Swiss Dunant. Bluntschli said of Lieber that he remained "fully aware that, in time of war . . . the harshest measures and most reckless exactions cannot be denied; and that tender-hearted sentimentality is here all the more out of place, because the greater the energy employed in carrying on the war, the sooner will it be brought to an end, and the normal condition of peace restored." The code Lieber had drafted was made up of rules that could appeal to the strong states of Europe and even to the most unsentimental of Europe's military men. Lincoln, after all, had adopted the code not to make peace but to make war. He had done so at just the moment when his nation's wartime fortunes seemed at their nadir. And Lincoln had won his war.

The American code had made the laws of war safe for the powerful states of late nineteenth-century Europe, just as it had for the Indian wars in the American West. In doing so, it touched off a battle over the meaning of international law in wartime. Would the laws of war be merely a tool for powerful armies? Or would accepting the idea of constraints slowly shape the conduct of strong states? Could a law of war that deferred to von Moltke also create meaningful moral limits on war's destructiveness?

IN A CONTEST for the soul of the law of war, Alfred Thayer Mahan would have played the Devil. An exceedingly tall man, with a bald pate, Mephistophelean beard, and baleful glare, Mahan was born on the campus of the

Military Academy at West Point in 1840, the oldest child of Dennis Hart Mahan, who was the academy's dominant figure for fifty years. From 1821 to 1871, the elder Mahan had adapted the axioms of French military strategy to instruct cadets in the conditions of American combat. He raised his children in a military spirit of rigorous and unquestioning adherence to rules. He gave his son the middle name Thayer in honor of Sylvanus Thayer, the superintendent of the Military Academy who had reorganized the school according to the professional standards of the French military model and defended its independence against Andrew Jackson's political meddling. As a boy, the younger Mahan grew up at West Point in a household that combined what Mahan's biographer calls "strict military obedience" with "a stern, literalist and fundamentalist form of Episcopalianism." His father's life was so bound up in the rigid order of the Military Academy that when Dennis Hart Mahan was at last forced out of the academy in 1871 at the age of sixty-nine, he stepped off the rear of a Hudson River steamboat into the vessel's churning wheels and killed himself.

It is too strong to describe Mahan's life as a rejection of his rulebound upbringing, though some biographers have been tempted to do so. His great act of defiance—signing up for the Naval Academy in Annapolis against his West Point father's wishes—looked more like thinly disguised emulation than rebellion. Yet one way or another, Mahan came to be known as a student not of rules but of power. Where his father had mastered the axioms of nineteenth-century tactics, Mahan became his generation's great prophet of power at a moment in history when an increasingly strong United States had begun to wield global authority.

In 1890, while serving as an instructor at the new Naval War College in Rhode Island, Mahan became a celebrity in the Atlantic world when he published a book entitled *The Influence of Sea Power Upon History*. Two years later, he published a sequel: *The Influence of Sea Power Upon the French Revolution and Empire*. Mahan's thesis was that the exercise of power—and in particular the use of navies—propelled modern history. Over the next twenty years, as the world's strongest states engaged in an arms race on the seas, Mahan became the voice of a new age of naval power. His work was translated widely and read around the world. Books and articles poured from his pen right up until his death in 1914. So great was Mahan's influence that more than three decades later, Henry Stimson, who served as U.S. secretary of war in World War II, would remember the Navy Department of Mahan's era as existing in "a dim religious world in which Neptune was God, Mahan his prophet, and the United States Navy the only true Church."

In virtually everything that he wrote, Mahan presented world history as the story of armed struggle. "Step by step," he wrote, "man has ascended by means of the sword." Mahan disavowed jingoism and wars of conquest. But he believed that just causes required powerful nations to use force to vindicate the right. "Power," he contended, was "a faculty of national life" given to particular peoples by God, and God expected those peoples to exercise it righteously.

Law was a thin reed in Mahan's stormy battles for justice and civilization. Laws were mankind's feeble attempt to codify universal moral imperatives. As a guide to moral action, he observed, they were often badly misleading. Some laws were simply unjust. In the pre–Civil War republic, Mahan liked to say, men of principle had defied fugitive slave laws. And rightly so. Nations, Mahan argued, had an even greater obligation to do justice in the face of misguided laws, for nations had a far greater capacity than individuals to use force in the name of righteousness, regardless of what the law said. Mahan conceded that it was dangerous to encourage lawbreaking. But he could come to no other conclusion than that it was a nation's inescapable duty to evaluate its moral obligations without undue deference to the dictates of the law.

Mahan's low regard for law made him a striking choice when, on the eve of a new century, Secretary of State John Hay selected Mahan as a delegate to a conference in The Hague convened by Czar Nicholas II to hammer out a new international law of war and peace. And yet for Hay, the choice was a natural one. Thirty-five years before, Hay had served as President Lincoln's private secretary. Now Hay chose a man very close to the ideas of war and law that Francis Lieber had infused into the code of 1863 and that Lincoln had developed over the course of his presidency. Lieber, too, had rebelled at elaborate legal schemes that sought to substitute themselves for first principles of justice. Now Mahan, by force of his ideas and his overpowering personality, became the dominant member of the American delegation at the conference that would turn the code Lincoln issued in 1863 into the founding document of the twentieth century's laws of war.

I N AUGUST 1898, the Russian foreign minister Count Muraviev surprised diplomats to the Romanov court by handing out a proposal for a conference on European disarmament and peace. (Ethan Allen Hitchcock, nephew and namesake of Civil War general Ethan Allen Hitchcock, accepted the message for the United States.) News of the czar's initiative quickly electrified resurgent peace movements around the world. In the United States, in particular, where pacifists were still recovering from the blow of the Civil War, the inheritors of the antebellum peace societies reacted with a special jolt of enthusiasm. Here at last, in a conference convening the great states of the world, might be a forum that could live up to the grandeur of their ambitions.

The enthusiasm of hopeful pacifists, however, was matched by the cynicism of diplomats and military men. Mahan saw the czar's call for the Hague conference as a defensive reaction to the new fact of U.S. power after the brief Spanish-American War of 1898. The American ambassador in St. Petersburg wrote to Secretary of State Hay warning that the United States should discount "the humanitarian aspect" of the Russian proposal. In "the ordinary Russian mind," he said, "the semi-oriental influences and traditions of the people have bred in them a slight regard for the value of human life." Others speculated that the czar's ministers were desperate to find a way to slow a European arms race with which the Russian treasury could no longer keep up. No wonder Andrew D. White, the longtime American diplomat chosen as the leader of the American delegation, expressed a "hopeless skepticism" about the conference's prospects.

In May 1899, delegations from twenty-six countries gathered in The Hague. They represented twenty European states, as well as four from Asia (China, Japan, Persia, and Siam), plus two from the Americas (Mexico and the United States). The delegates met at the House in the Wood, a seventeenth-century summer palace built just outside of town for the wife of the Dutch Stadholder, Prince Frederick Henry of Orange. It was a stately brick mansion with crisp white window frames and exquisite gardens. Over the door to the conference room hung an allegorical painting (by a protégé of the Flemish painter Rubens) of the Peace of Westphalia, the system of seventeenth-century treaties that had brought an end to the brutal Thirty Years' War and initiated the modern system of European states.

But not even a felicitous site could overcome the obstacles standing in the way of agreements on most of the conference's agenda items. When the delegates turned to the business at hand, it quickly became clear that arms agreements of the kind the czar's ministers seemed to desire would be impossible to attain. Any agreement to freeze in place an existing technology, or to reduce the growth of arms budgets, would create winners and

losers. No such agreement could gain the unanimous consent of the delegations. Secretary Hay, for one, had instructed the U.S. delegation flatly that
they were not to enter into any arms limitations discussions because the U.S.
level of armament was so low compared to European powers.

Proposals for the peaceful arbitration of national disputes fared only
slightly better. Arbitration was a favorite of the American peace movement,
which saw the United States as international arbitration's great champion.
Twice in the nineteenth century—once after the War of 1812 and then again
after the Civil War—the United States had successfully arbitrated disputes
over British conduct in wartime. But arbitration, too, faced high hurdles at
the conference. In particular, Germany opposed the idea of obligatory arbitration (Mahan did too), and the German position forced the Hague Peace
Conference to adopt a watered-down system of purely voluntary arbitration.
The English jurist Thomas Erskine Holland dismissed it as amounting "to
really nothing."

Russian statesmen thought it imperative for the czar's reputation that
something concrete come out of the conference. And so, facing inability
to get agreements on armaments or mandatory arbitration, the delegates
turned to the laws of war. Over the course of the summer of 1899, the delegations took the Geneva Convention's rules for wounded soldiers on land
and adapted them for naval warfare. They debated limits on the means and
methods of combat. And most important of all, they forged a general revision of the laws and customs of war. The Russian minister F. F. Martens,
who had initiated the Brussels talks a quarter century before and who now
headed the Hague committee charged with updating the laws of war, credited Lincoln and Lieber with creating a blueprint for the committee's work.
Martens adopted Lieber's functional evaluation of prisoner of war status. But
the Hague committee took the American example and built on it substantially. Even the American delegation described the work of the committee as
a distinct advance on the Civil War code of 1863. Where Lincoln's instructions had permitted the execution of prisoners when a commander found
himself in "great straits," the Hague Convention prohibited prisoner execution altogether and required humane treatment under all circumstances. (For
one thing, the signatory states of Europe and North America now all had the
administrative capacity to hold and maintain prisoners without being strate-
gically disadvantaged.) There was a difference in the spirit of the two documents as well, though it was not clear whether or how this translated into
differences in the law. In the 1863 rules, Lieber had set out a terrifying list of

the kinds of violence that war admitted and had admonished that sharp wars were shorter and thus more humane. He had written that, above all, saving the country was the paramount consideration. The Hague Conference's law of war convention, on the other hand, cautioned against destruction, observing in a clause usually attributed to Martens that even in the absence of a particular rule or prohibition, "populations and belligerents remain under the protection and empire of the principles of international law" in wartime.

Nonetheless, the delegates proved to be sharply divided on critical questions, including the core question for humanitarian law. Were limits on war's destructiveness really humanitarian at all? The conveners insisted that they were. The Russian president of a Second Hague Conference in 1907 would warn that while he had "heard the opinion expressed that it was an absolutely mistaken idea to seek to diminish the horrors of war," it seemed to him "an absolutely specious opinion." Yet that was precisely the opinion Mahan held. Indeed, the theorist of naval power held views closer to those of von Moltke and Lieber—and even Clausewitz—than to those of the humanitarian reformers. Mahan saw the world in bleak terms; Andrew White liked to say of Mahan that "when he speaks, the millennium fades." But Mahan was not alone in his skepticism of humanitarian reform. Secretary Hay's instructions to the American delegation approached legal limits for war with much the same caution. With respect to new forms of explosives, as well as to aerial projectiles launched from hot air balloons and new and more destructive technologies of naval warfare, Hay instructed the American delegates to the Hague Conference that it was "doubtful if wars are to be diminished by rendering them less destructive." To the contrary, Hay warned, the "plain lesson of history" was that "periods of peace have been longer protracted as the cost and destructiveness of war have increased." Moreover, as Hay saw it, limitations on new technologies of destruction were especially dangerous for the United States, since "the inventive genius" of entrepreneurial Americans was one of the nation's great strategic advantages.

Mahan ensured that the U.S. representatives would vindicate Hay's skeptical view. Andrew White, who headed the U.S. delegation, was no lightweight. He had been president of Cornell University and minister to Germany and Russia. He was the sitting ambassador to Germany when the conference began. But he was no match for the forcible Mahan.

The imposing Navy man also completely dominated Captain William R. Crozier, the American military delegate. Crozier was better known as an inventor of artillery devices than as a diplomat or strategist. He could claim credit for the Buffington-Crozier disappearing gun carriage, but he turned out to be out of his depth at the conference. Once Mahan got to him, however, Crozier served as a perfectly adequate mouthpiece for Mahan's views. In committees on which he represented the United States, Crozier first voted in favor of prohibitions on projectiles from hot air balloons and on so-called dumdum bullets that tumbled or expanded inside their target. But after Crozier consulted with Mahan, he changed his views on both questions. New technologies, Mahan admonished, might well improve navigation and make it possible for balloons to deliver decisive firepower to the battlefield without undue risk to noncombatants. In the long run, aerial warfare might thereby become the favored humanitarian way of war, reducing war's death toll and shortening its duration. In the right circumstances, the dumdum bullet might similarly turn out to be more humane than any alternative. British major general Sir John Ardagh, for example, contended that in combat in Africa or India, dumdum bullets could stop an onrushing savage when ordinary bullets would not. Crozier offered a substitute provision that would have prohibited the use of bullets inflicting "wounds of useless cruelty." When the conference rejected his substitute, Crozier and the British delegate cast the only two votes against the dumdum bullet ban. No other country joined them.*

Mahan himself took the lead role for the United States in discussing a proposed prohibition on the use of projectiles designed to spread asphyxiating gases, and here too he took a position against the weight of the conference. As White later recounted, Mahan believed that a ban on poison gas "would prove to be rather harmful than helpful to the cause of peace." Mahan announced that it was illogical and inhumane to be "tender about asphyxiating men with gas, when all were prepared to admit that it was allowable to blow the bottom out of an ironclad at midnight," thus causing 400 or 500 men to drown. Mahan's logic was the same with gas as it had been with balloons. Who was to say that under certain circumstances, gas might not be more humane than the gruesome destructive force of traditional military ordinance and explosive charges? It was the same logic, moreover, that Francis Lieber had brought to the laws of war and that had initially inclined him to oppose a ban on the use of poisons when he gave his public lectures on the laws of war at Columbia Law School in the winter

---

*Crozier also opposed efforts to limit the power of gunpowder in rifles. In addition, he cast votes against a ban on the use of mining shells in field artillery; a prohibition on new explosives for the bursting charge of projectiles; and a ban on the improvement of field guns. See James Brown Scott, ed., *Instructions to the American Delegates to the Hague Peace Conferences and Their Official Reports* (New York: Oxford University Press, 1916), 29.

of 1861–62. Though White initially opposed Mahan on the asphyxiating gas rule, he soon gave way to his colleague. At the end of the conference, the United States would vote against the prohibition on dumdum bullets, against the ban on asphyxiating gases, and would insist on a sunset provision limiting the prohibition on projectiles from hot air balloons to five years.

Even then, Mahan was not done. Secretary Hay had instructed White to push for the immunity of private property at sea. Few ideas were nearer to the heart of the American law of war tradition. Ben Franklin had promoted the idea in the 1770s and 1780s. So had John Quincy Adams in the 1820s. William Marcy and Franklin Pierce had advocated the immunity of private property as an alternative to the privateering prohibition of the Declaration of Paris in 1856. But privately Mahan was violently opposed to any attempt to exempt private property from seizure in wartime. Indeed, he even resisted the old American position that free ships made free goods, the rule under which neutral ships' cargoes were to be immune from seizure at sea. Stopping commerce on the high seas had been a critical factor in Britain's defeat of Napoleon, and the anglophilic Mahan was loath to let that power slip out of the hands of the American and British navies now. The Russian conveners kept the issue off the agenda in 1899; but when delegations returned to The Hague in 1907 for a follow-up conference, Mahan persuaded President Theodore Roosevelt, Secretary of State Elihu Root, and a new U.S. delegation to torpedo any movement to exempt private property, even though such an exemption was still officially part of the American program at the conference. Echoing Mahan, Secretary Root told the British foreign secretary Sir Edward Grey and the U.S. delegation that the threat of losing property in sharp wars at sea would incline the world toward peace. Indeed, the risk of losing their property would turn merchants around the world into a permanent lobby for peace. Grey agreed; "limited liability" wars, he said, were dangerous. The immunity of private property at sea would have to await another day.

F OR ALL THE Peace Conference's limits, the law of war convention at The Hague was a considerable success. Mahan may have helped to reign in the conference's most ambitious initiatives for controlling the means and methods of war. But relying in large part on American contributions from the Civil War onward, The Hague conference had produced a treaty for the law of war on which a large share of the world's sovereign states could agree. The Hague Convention even endorsed the form of the 1863 pamphlet.

It required its signatory states to issue instructions to their armed forces, instructions to be drawn up in the image of Lincoln's instruction manual for the Union armies.

Yet there was a difficulty haunting the laws of war even at the moment of their apparent success. Would the conduct that had once seemed morally permissible for the world-historic ends of abolition also prove justified in wars of empire? The conceit of the Enlightenment's customs and usages of warfare had been that the permissible means and methods of war could be understood independently of the justice of the cause in which they were deployed. The Civil War code had called that premise into question. But at the turn of the twentieth century, wars of empire sundered the connection between the new laws of war and the moral force of the antislavery effort that had precipitated their birth. Therein loomed a crisis for the law.

To the Philippines and Back Again

THE UNITED STATES went to war with Spain in 1898 deeply divided over its place in the world. A generation of aggressive imperialists, including Assistant Secretary of the Navy Theodore Roosevelt, saw the American overthrow of tottering Spanish imperial outposts in Cuba, Puerto Rico, Guam, and the Philippines as ratification of the kinds of global power that Mahan had imagined for the fast-growing republic. Missionary statesmen like the Congregationalist leader Josiah Strong thought that the United States was "divinely commissioned" to help the backward peoples of the world and to spread the blessings of American civilization. Roosevelt called the American campaign "a war for liberty and human rights." But many anti-imperialist critics worried that American traditions of liberty would be at risk in a republic turned into an empire. Others decried the incorporation of millions of nonwhite people into what they imagined was an Anglo-Saxon country. The controversy was especially acute with respect to the Philippines. Advocates of naval power longed for a coaling station and foothold in the western Pacific. Critics viewed the peoples of the Philippines as irredeemable savages whose annexation would degrade the American character and corrupt its institutions.

One result of the sharp domestic disagreements over the war was that no one really knew what would happen when the conflict arrived in the Pacific islands. For years, Filipino independence forces led by the handsome and charismatic Emilio Aguinaldo had been fighting against Spain and claiming (much as Washington and Jefferson had in the 1770s) the privileges of "a civilized" and "peace-loving" independent state. Now, in the summer of 1898, American forces under Commodore George Dewey, commander of the American fleet at Manila, forged an uneasy alliance with Aguinaldo's fighters in their common cause against Spain. Officials of the American State Department in the Pacific assured the Filipino leader of the United States' intent to cooperate with his independence efforts. But the truth of U.S. intentions was more ambiguous; and as President William McKinley dithered about whether to retain the Philippines after peace with Spain, tensions quickly heightened. For six months after Spain's defeat in August, the United States managed by a combination of untruths and misunderstandings to keep Aguinaldo guessing about American postwar plans for the archipelago. When it became clear that the United States had no intention of leaving, hostilities broke out in a war that proved far more difficult and deadly than the one Americans had fought with Spain.

The Philippine War of 1899–1902 produced a law of war crisis like none to that point in American history, though it bore an eerie resemblance to the controversies that would arise in Vietnam in the 1960s and in Afghanistan and Iraq in the early 2000s. After months of losing conventional battles against U.S. forces, Aguinaldo followed the Mexican example from 1847 and turned to guerrilla warfare. Among his advisers were men who admired the combat tactics of the American Indians; others adapted tactics drawn from the Cuban resistance to Spain and the Boer War against the British in South Africa. The violence of their campaign was often horrific. Corpses were mutilated; bodies were cut open and stuffed with food to attract voracious tropical ants. The insurgents executed prisoners, especially natives who collaborated with the American forces. Noncombatants were executed, too. The insurgents used poison and killed men under the protection of truce flags. American accounts of insurgent atrocities were often self-serving, but a Senate committee on the Philippines had no trouble filling reports with hundreds of credible episodes of brutal violence by insurgents.

Filipino leaders conceded that their tactics were harsh. But they also insisted that Americans unfairly tilted the standards in their favor. Aguinaldo's principal adviser Apolinario Mabini (widely known as "the brains of the revolution") told American general James Bell that the so-called rules of civilized combat that purported to require Filipinos to fight in uniforms in the open were designed simply to promote the power of strong armies at the expense of powerless peoples. Guerrilla warfare was the weapon of the weak, Mabini contended, and "when it comes to defending their homes and their freedoms against an invasion," Mabini made clear that he would be willing to resort to extraordinary means. In 1863, Francis Lieber had written that saving the country was paramount to all other considerations. Mabini now insisted that it was precisely a mark of the Filipinos' status as a civilized people that they would fight doggedly to save theirs.

The U.S. Army responded with a retaliatory campaign of startling violence and destruction. Reports of exceptionally harsh treatment of Filipino prisoners began to trickle back to the United States as early as May 1899. Over the next two years, American officers ordered or condoned dozens of prisoner executions, and perhaps more. Mass incarcerations put between 1,500 and 2,000 Filipinos in prison. Concentration camps moved civilians out of their homes and killed thousands when epidemics struck the overcrowded facilities. American troops destroyed large amounts of property and food supplies in the name of denying resources to the insurgents. In March 1901, when brigadier general and Congressional Medal of Honor winner Frederick Funston acquired evidence (possibly by torture) of Aguinaldo's whereabouts, he sent a band of American soldiers and Filipino scouts disguised as insurgents to capture him. President Roosevelt quietly asked the international law expert Theodore Woolsey of Yale University to defend the legality of the ruse in the pages of the popular press, but the use of enemy garb was clearly unlawful. Lieber's General Orders No. 100 had said so unequivocally, and in other contexts American officials said as much themselves. Funston's daring gambit was an impetuous breach of the basic laws of war.

Funston's ruse looked positively tame in comparison to some of the tactics American commanders were adopting. In the fall of 1901, General Jacob Smith reacted to the massacre of fifty-nine American soldiers in the town of Balangiga by ordering his men to retaliate against the entire island. Smith ordered his men "to kill and burn all persons who are capable of bearing arms in actual hostilities against the United States." Who was so capable? Any person over ten years old, Smith explained. The interior of the island of Samar, he instructed his men, "must be made a howling wilderness."

Most strikingly, American forces in the Philippines resorted to a systematic and widespread campaign of torture unlike anything in more than a century of American history. Officers hanged Filipino prisoners by the neck until they agreed to talk. They lowered prisoners headfirst in water to threaten drowning. The torture they employed most often was known as the water cure. The practice was designed to cause the perception—indeed, the reality—of drowning. While three or four soldiers held a man down, a carbine barrel would be shoved into his mouth making it impossible for him to close his jaws. With his head held back, water was poured into his mouth and nostrils until he became unconscious, at which point the torturers rolled him over or struck him in the stomach to expel the water. Sometimes American torturers used salt water, which made it worse, or a syringe to inject the water directly into the nostrils or throat. When a victim came to his senses, he was given the choice to divulge the wanted information about the location of insurrectionists or to endure the process again. In at least one well-established case, the water cure resulted in the death of its victim.

We can document with certainty fourteen instances in which United States forces administered the water cure. But that figure is almost surely a small fraction of the total. One enlisted man in 1902 said that he alone had administered the water cure to 160 Filipinos. Funston bitterly denied the man's claim, but when Lieutenant General Nelson A. Miles (the man who had captured Geronimo in 1886) toured the Philippines in late 1902, he heard complaints about torture from residents in the village of Lipa on the island of Cebu, from the people of Laoag on the island of Luzon, and from the inhabitants of Calbayog on Samar. Officers and enlisted men alike testified to having seen the water cure administered on multiple occasions. Cavalrymen composed songs celebrating torture and set them to the tune of the Battle Hymn of the Republic. ("Get the good old syringe boys and fill it to the brim / We've caught another nigger and we'll operate on him.") The future president William Howard Taft, who served as civilian governor of the Philippines beginning in 1900, conceded to a Senate committee investigating war atrocities that the "so called water cure" was employed "on some occasions to extract information," though Taft implausibly claimed to believe that prisoners asked to be tortured so as to avoid retaliation by Aguinaldo's insurgents for having divulged information to the Americans.

THE LEGALITY OF torture was a question to be decided by reference to the instructions of 1863, for at the outset of the Spanish-American War they were still the governing body of rules for the U.S. armed forces. As the war began, Judge Advocate General Norman Lieber had arranged to have his father's code reprinted and distributed by the thousands in a three-inch by five-inch blue pocket edition. Where Halleck and Judge Advocate General Joseph Holt had been obliged to build an entire system of military justice for the prosecution of law of war violations from scratch, the younger

Lieber presided over a new series of military commission trials made in the image of their Civil War predecessors. Lieber's military commissions tried crimes by Filipinos such as unlawfully furnishing supplies to the enemy and murder in violation of the laws of war. They tried more than 300 enlisted men in the U.S. Army, as well, for crimes ranging from petty theft and assault, to robbery and rape, to shooting and beating prisoners of war. In December 1900, Major General Arthur MacArthur commanding U.S. troops in the Philippines reissued selected sections of General Orders No. 100 to the armed forces under his command. Two years later, Secretary of War Elihu Root assured the Congress that all orders in the Philippines had conformed to the terms of Old Hundred.

Invocations of General Orders No. 100, however, disguised a transformation in military thought in the post–Civil War United States, one that had altered the delicate balance of humanity and necessity in the 1863 instructions. In 1892, Major General John Schofield, the commander of the U.S. Army from 1888 to 1895, had issued an order incorporating the terms of the 1864 Geneva Convention into Lieber's code, announcing that the Geneva rules would thenceforth "form part of the 'Instructions for the Government of the Armies in the Field.'" But Schofield argued openly for short and sharp wars that would avoid the quagmires all too often produced by what one like-minded officer called "squeamish humanity." Schofield, who served as superintendent of the Military Academy at West Point in the 1880s, who had helped shape the treatment of the Modoc Indians in 1873, and who had survived the guerrilla conflicts of Civil War Missouri, also explicitly rejected international law's formal moral symmetry for warring nations. He insisted instead that righteous causes licensed tougher methods.

Influential military strategists from the Army Officer Corps echoed Schofield's views, anticipating that the future of warfare would look more like Sherman's March to the Sea than like the set-piece battles of yesteryear. Leaders of the prominent U.S. Military Service Institution believed that modern wars would be campaigns with "no objective point, no lines of communication, no base of supplies." War would be fought by "armies of raiders." Everything from "railroads, telegraphs, factories, stores and store houses," to "shops, barns, roads, and bridges" would disappear before great devouring armies. "Giant famine and pestilence" would follow in their wake. Leading members of the turn-of-the-century officer corps did not shrink from this vision. They embraced it. "Terrible! Say you?" asked the editors of an influential strategy journal. They supplied their own answer: "Well, yes.

War ought to be terrible. The trouble is that it has ceased to be terrible to altogether too many men."

In the Philippines, the laws of war seemed to officers trained under Schofield's influence to be an inspiration for their fierce war strategy, not an obstacle to it. Some officers treated the Filipino resistance fighters as savages with no claim on the laws of war. (That had been Theodore Woolsey's ultimate defense of Funston's otherwise unlawful ruse to capture Aguinaldo.) But most embraced the laws of war and its terms, confident that they were adaptable to the irregular warfare of the Philippines. When MacArthur reissued the Civil War instructions in December 1900, he did so at the moment when the Army had decided to step up the aggressiveness of its campaign, just as Lincoln had in 1862. MacArthur's version of General Orders No. 100 was even tougher than Lincoln's, for MacArthur omitted the sections that imposed restraints on the soldiers and officers of the United States, while retaining the sections authorizing retaliatory violence for the savage conduct of Filipino independence fighters. MacArthur's reading of Old Hundred quickly became a pattern in American invocations of the Civil War instructions in the Philippines. General James Bell cited it to justify harsh measures against those who rose up against an occupation. "A short and severe war," he said, was better than "a benevolent war indefinitely prolonged." Bell announced that he would execute a prisoner for every American or friendly native murdered. On Samar, Jacob Smith cited General Orders No. 100 for the idea that the United States should "wage war in the sharpest and most decisive manner possible" because "short, severe wars" were "the most humane in the end." Smith's officers, in turn, believed that their policy of giving no quarter to prisoners was justified under the laws of war in general and General Orders No. 100 in particular. Newspaper editors and congressmen back home got into the act as well, urging critics of American soldiers to "study with advantage" the laws of war as embodied in Lincoln's Civil War instructions. Even Judge Advocate General Norman Lieber's office prepared a private defense of the Army's actions in the Philippines, finding support for its conduct in the code's articles.

S TILL, there seemed to be no getting around the question of torture. Torture was one of the few things that Old Hundred had ruled out as definitively unlawful. "Military necessity," stated Article 16, "does not admit of . . . torture to extort confessions." Article 80 provided further that it was unlawful to use "violence against prisoners in order to extort the desired information." It did not seem possible to justify torture by reference to the 1863 instructions. And when rumors of widespread torture began to leak back to the United States in early 1902, and when a politi cal firestorm seemed on the verge of engulfing the war effort, President Roosevelt and Secretary of War Root quickly ordered courts-martial for the worst offenders.

Army commanders initiated at least five trials of accused American torturers. The most prominent was that of Major Edwin F. Glenn, on charges of ordering the administration of the water cure in November 1900 on the island of Panay.

Born in North Carolina, Glenn was a member of the class of 1877 at West Point. He had a law degree from the University of Minnesota as well, and had served as a judge advocate beginning in the middle of the 1890s. In 1895, he had even published a book on international law designed for law students. The book discussed war at length and reprinted Lincoln's instructions of 1863 in their entirety. In 1898, Glenn led a pioneering expedition to southeastern Alaska, where his name still graces towns and highways. Now serving in the Philippines, he was the judge advocate for the island of Panay.

In 1900 and early 1901, while serving as the judge advocate, Glenn orchestrated a systematic campaign of arrests and torture. In the Philippine islands of Leyte and Samar, he led a mobile team of crack water cure experts who arrested community leaders (some called it kidnapping) to extract information about the insurgency. General Nelson Miles of Geronimo fame reported privately to Secretary of War Root that Glenn and his team had become notorious for moving around the islands and arresting men "for the purposes of extorting statements by means of torture." Glenn soon became so well known as the chief administrator of torture in the Philippines that the torture squad was called "Glenn's Brigade."

Members of Glenn's torture team did their work with little secrecy or shame. They thought their actions perfectly justifiable on the now familiar grounds that short wars were humanitarian wars. Glenn defended himself at his court-martial by conceding his acts and trying to justify them. "I am convinced that my action resulted in hastening the termination of hostilities and directly resulted in saving many human lives," he told the court. His actions, he claimed, were justified by military necessity. Water torture, insisted another officer prosecuted by court-martial, was the humane thing to do. "Without firing a shot or shedding blood," he had been able to uncover munitions stashes and, he believed, save lives.

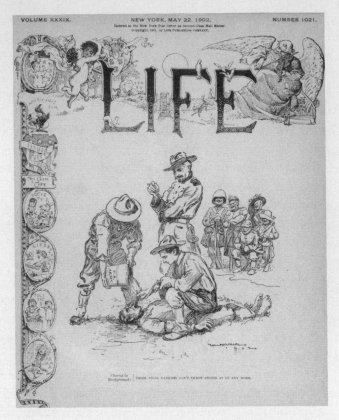

*Life magazine put the water cure on its cover in 1902,
showing American soldiers administering the "cure"
while European empires look on in delight.*

Judge Advocate General George B. Davis, Norman Lieber's successor, rejected Glenn's justifications. "No modern state," Davis concluded, could admit torture as a "usual practice" in wartime, even when "at war with a savage or semicivilized enemy." Here was a forceful refutation of Glenn's logic. Yet Davis's reasoning contained a surprising caveat. Lincoln's 1863 instructions had set torture outside the realm of necessity; it was never permitted. Davis, however, asked whether an emergency had existed that was "so instant and important as to justify the disobedience of the plain requirements of General Orders, No. 100." No such necessity had existed sufficient to justify torture, he concluded. But by asking whether torture was permitted under the circumstances, he seemed to have changed the law to allow it in at least some dire situations. Davis's recommendation to the president and the secretary of war urged approval of the conviction in Glenn's case but opened a door that Lieber had held shut.*

In the end, Glenn was convicted and his conviction affirmed by President Roosevelt. But his sentence barely amounted to a proverbial slap on the wrist. Citing Filipino provocations to which he was said to have been responding, the court sentenced Glenn merely to be suspended from his command for one month and fined a grand total of $50. The sentence was typical of other officers convicted at courts-martial for similar offenses. Some were simply reprimanded. Others were acquitted altogether. Of the fifteen officers prosecuted by general courts-martial in the Philippines for offenses of any kind, only one received a prison sentence, and that was for five years for killing a prisoner of war. Even then, President Roosevelt commuted the sentence to loss of half-pay for nine months and a loss of thirty-five places on the officer promotion list. Filipinos accused of law of war violations fared considerably less well. One man Glenn had tortured, Tobeniamo Ealdama, was convicted of being a war traitor under Articles 90 and 91 of the 1863 code. For the crime of rising against an occupying army, Ealdama, the torture victim, was sentenced to ten years imprisonment at hard labor.

Lincoln's fierce code seemed to have lost its way in the Philippines. A dubious war of empire had detached the code from the righteous cause that had produced it. It was as if questionable wars compelled the armies that fought them to go to ever more terrible lengths to defeat enemies whose own sense of righteousness drove them to ever stiffer forms of resistance. Senator George Frisbie Hoar of Massachusetts, the seventy-four-year-old lion of the anti-imperialist faction of Congress, believed that unscrupulous wars were precisely the kind of thing that empire would produce. Looking back on American conduct in the Philippine War, Hoar could only bemoan his country's new direction: "We have been brought to the unexampled dishonor of disregarding our own rules," he said, "for the conduct of armies in the field."

*   *   *

---

*Some otherwise excellent histories of the Glenn prosecution have missed the critical qualification in Davis's review of the Glenn conviction because they have focused on Davis's argument that the justification of necessity would lead quickly to a slippery slope: "[W]here is the line to be drawn?" Davis asked. "If the 'water cure' is ineffective, what shall be the next step?" Davis never tried to square his observations about the absence of stopping points with his case-by-case approach to deciding whether torture was warranted.

I N THE YEARS following the Philippine War, international lawyers, statesmen, and military men in the United States began to develop a law of war
that would no longer rest on the fifty-year-old rules that Francis Lieber had
drafted. William Tecumseh Sherman had praised General Orders No. 100
while serving as commander of the Army in the 1880s. As secretary of state
in 1913, Elihu Root celebrated the occasion of the code's fiftieth anniversary
with a public address praising Lincoln's order. The Army's chief of staff called
the code "almost sacred." Yet even as early as 1898, when Norman Lieber
had distributed his father's code at the outset of the Spanish-American War,
long sections of it must have struck him and his readers as odd. A dozen of
its articles dealt with questions arising out of slavery in wartime. There were
provisions for the status of captured and fugitive slaves, for slave insurrections in wartime, and for the enlistment of an enemy's slaves in the armed
forces. Lincoln's order prohibited the outlawry of black soldiers and declared
the sale of enemy prisoners of war unlawful. It was no wonder, then, that
when European lawyers like Bluntschli and Martens adapted Lieber's work
to their own conflicts, they quietly excised a number of irrelevant passages
that made no sense out of their original context.

The new conventions and treaties of the postwar period also left the Civil
War instructions badly incomplete. Privately published compilations stitched
together the 1863 rules with the Geneva Convention of 1864 and the Hague
Convention of 1899 to produce comprehensive but awkward treatments of
the rules of engagement. In the Judge Advocate General's office, an internal concordance literally constructed with scissors and glue tried to patch
together a reconciliation of the Lieber Code of 1863 with the Hague Convention. It was increasingly clear that a new departure was necessary.

But who was to produce such a document? Who would be the Francis
Lieber for the twentieth century? The task would be a delicate one; in 1904,
an ill-conceived code for naval warfare (designed, as Yale's Theodore Woolsey wrote in 1900, to be "comparable in all particulars with the land code of
thirty-seven years ago") had to be revoked when Navy men concluded it put
restraints on American conduct that were not likely to be reciprocated by the
country's future enemies. The job thus required someone with knowledge of
the international law questions at issue, ideally someone who also knew how
the Judge Advocate General's corps worked. Even better would be someone
who could bring to the task experience in wars of empire, which seemed
likely to be the kinds of wars that would occupy the U.S. military in the
twentieth century.

The man the Army chose was none other than Edwin F. Glenn. If not for the torture conviction, Glenn would have been a natural choice for the job. He had a law degree and had served as a judge advocate. He had published a treatise on international law. And he had considerable experience with courts-martial, though not all of it good. After his command of the torture squad in the Philippines, Glenn had been exiled for years to a series of backwater posts in upstate New York, Ohio, and Indiana. Having served a second stint in the Philippines in 1908, however, Glenn's sins had been forgotten. (The Army apparently viewed them as venal rather than mortal.) He was promoted to colonel in 1911. Two years later, he was detailed to the Army War College, then in Washington, D.C., which charged him with updating the old Civil War instructions.

In 1914, the War Department issued Glenn's field manual on the laws of war in a sturdy, yellow-bound, pocket-sized manual titled *Rules of Land Warfare*. The rules did not bear his name; they were ostensibly the product of the War Department as an institution, not of any one officer. But it was Glenn who was their primary author. Glenn described the new rules as retaining "everything vital" from Lincoln's *Instructions for the Government of Armies of the United States in the Field*, while shedding the anachronisms. Gone were the rules about slaves. But Glenn still filled his text with long passages taken verbatim from its 1863 predecessor. And Glenn's field manual would prove to have almost as long a life as Lieber's. After a few insignificant editorial alterations, Glenn's 1914 *Rules* accompanied American soldiers across the Atlantic to fight on the Western Front in World War I. A substantial update in 1934 retained the basic logic and structure of Glenn's text. With a few cosmetic changes in 1940, it was his manual that went to war again in Europe and the Pacific in 1941 and 1942. At the war crimes trials of Nazis in American-occupied Germany from 1946 to 1949, provisions of the laws of war that Glenn had written would be cited and argued about at length by prosecutors and defense lawyers alike. No one noted that they had been crafted by a convicted torturer, a man whom we would today (following Lieber and Bluntschli) call a war criminal.

S URELY HERE IS REASON to see the laws of war as shot through with hypocrisy. If the work of Lieber and Lincoln comes down to us through the dirty hands of a torturer, is this not irrefutable evidence that Cicero was right when he said that law was silent among arms? Or that Cervantes knew best when he said that all was fair in love and war? There is much to this view, of course. It would be feckless to dismiss it out of hand.

But the critics' view is too glib. For the most striking thing about Glenn's *Rules of Land Warfare* is not the identity of its author, but the restraint of its terms. The manual bore few traces of its author's terrible past. Judge Advocate General George B. Davis took to the pages of the official journal of the American Society of International Law to argue that the very man whose conviction for torture he had recommended the president uphold just twelve years before had "done his work exceedingly well." Reviewing the Philippines torture cases in 1902, Davis had condemned Glenn's necessity justification for torture in strong terms. Now, reviewing Glenn's *Rules of Land Warfare*, he wrote that Glenn's text could not "fail to be of the greatest assistance in following the course of the great war now in progress in continental Europe."

Indeed, the 1914 rules went considerably further than Mahan and the American delegates at The Hague had been willing to go in 1899. The new field manual prohibited the use of poisons, contagious diseases, and any weapon "of a nature to cause unnecessary injury," including "lances with barbed heads, irregular-shaped bullets, projectiles filled with glass," and "soft-nosed and explosive bullets." It banned the contamination of water supplies. Glenn gave the close reader a glimpse into his internal struggle when he observed Field Marshal von Moltke's bleak critique of the very idea of humanitarian limits ("the greatest kindness of war is to bring it to a speedy conclusion"). But *Rules of Land Warfare* also paid conspicuous homage to Fedor Fedorovich Martens's clause in the Hague Convention embracing the protections of the "laws of humanity." Glenn adopted Lieber's term "war crimes" for the first time in an official American document. And as for torture, Glenn faithfully reproduced precisely the section of the 1863 code that Judge Advocate General Davis had cited when he recommended that the president uphold Glenn's own conviction and sentence. "Military necessity," the *Rules of Land Warfare* stated, "does not admit of . . . torture to extort confessions." Following Lieber's Old Hundred, the *Rules* banned coercive means to obtain information from prisoners of war.

Glenn's 1914 *Rules of Land Warfare* marked a symbolic victory for a law that has often counted its successes in symbols. But symbols matter, and they matter because they shape the world in ways big and small. The laws of war have rarely if ever functioned like a beat cop or a stop sign. Rarely is there an impartial and stern judge standing at the ready to enforce them. Yet the laws of war shaped the way men talked about war. The entire Philippine controversy had played out in a moral vocabulary made up of terms from the laws of war. It was a venerable language, to be sure. It was one that spoke with tacit approval of terrifying acts of violence even as it denounced horrible cruelties. And it was a language that Abraham Lincoln, without quite knowing he was doing so, had transformed. Only a few years removed from the exclusion of non-European peoples from the law's protections, Secretary of War Root and President Roosevelt felt compelled in 1902 to initiate trials of the American officers accused of violating its terms. A controversy rooted in the laws of war had forced statesmen to spend valuable political capital. A decade later, Edwin Glenn—the man who had conducted a campaign of torture and expressed disdain for the law's core rules—would find himself speaking in the law's terms and extending its moral language to armed conflicts in the twentieth century and into the twenty-first.

The moral mandate of Lincoln's Civil War had crafted a common vocabulary, a way of talking about war's grave moral stakes that could be shared by war's fiercest defenders and its most uncompromising humanitarian critics alike. It was a language about the courage to act in a dangerous world and about the moral modesty that our weaknesses and frailties inevitably require. It was a language balanced, as Lincoln and Lieber had been, on a knife's edge between humility and justice.

———➤•◄———

Epilogue

———⟫•⟪———

E VERY GENERATION HAS its law of war crisis. Some have more than
one. The founding fathers confronted conflicts with Indians who fought
by different rules; they battled a British Empire that viewed them as traitors
instead of legitimate soldiers; and they grappled with the special dangers of a
slaveowners' republic in wartime. The first years of the early republic gave the
founders little respite from such debates. George Washington spent much of
his second term in office trying to secure a precarious position of neutrality
in the wars of the French Revolution.

The stakes involved and the novelty of the questions at issue ensure that
every new controversy in the law of armed conflict is fiercely contested. For
two decades after the founding, the U.S. Supreme Court and its chief justice,
John Marshall, managed an acrimonious diplomatic battle over the rights of
neutral states in wartime. More than once the dispute spilled over into actual
hostilities. In 1819, congressmen spent an entire month angrily debating
the lawfulness of Andrew Jackson's decision to execute two British subjects
captured among the Indians in Spanish Florida. Twenty years later, efforts
by New Yorkers to prosecute British soldiers on the Canadian border generated such tensions that war with Britain nearly broke out again. The same
decade saw American military officers invent a set of controversial military
commissions even as a sharp public debate broke out over whether the laws
of war were anything more than a legitimating device for the world's strongest states. A few years later, the first modern multilateral treaty on the laws
of war generated an angry backlash by statesmen who (with considerable
justification) saw the Declaration of Paris's prohibition on privateering as a
thinly veiled effort to disadvantage the United States.

In the Civil War, agonizing questions about the laws of war occupied
Lincoln's cabinet and his top military advisers from April 1861 onward.
From the blockade controversy to the question of the southern privateers,

from the irregular combatants who popped up across the Upper South and in border states like Missouri to slaves arriving at Union lines by the hundreds, the first year of the war posed an unending stream of problems for Lincoln and Seward and for commanders in the field. New difficulties arose throughout the war, and for months and even years after hostilities came to a close. In the decades that followed, the treatment of Indians, the atrocity-filled counterinsurgency in the Philippines, and the hammering out of a new generation of multilateral treaties in Europe all became central matters of concern for policymakers and soldiers, capturing widespread attention from the American public.

None of these episodes was more distinctive to the American experience of the laws of war than the epochal transformation of Emancipation. People around the world have experienced the moral tug-of-war between the pursuit of just ends and the adoption of humane means, for tensions between means and ends are endemic in human life and especially acute in wartime. That Americans have experienced such tensions hardly makes U.S. history exceptional. What was special about the American story, however, and what put Lincoln at its center, was the convulsive role of slavery.

For the first eighty-five years of the republic, slavery helped shape a distinctive approach to the law of war in a slave society that insisted it was also a civilized nation. The end of slavery was the quintessential event for the laws of war in American history. Emancipation seemed at the time to pose grave humanitarian risks—risks of a race war resembling the horrors of Haiti in the 1790s. And by the standards of the U.S. view of international law at the time, it was at best unclear whether the laws of war permitted it. Many thought the laws of civilized war flatly prohibited the freeing and arming of enemy slaves. Lincoln eventually moved ahead anyway. He did so rightly convinced of his cause's superior claims of justice. And in so doing he invoked a standard of military necessity that was at odds with the humanitarian limits of the age. But Lincoln did not dismiss the laws of war. To the contrary. He infused the proclamations of September 22, 1862, and January 1, 1863, with their spirit. The laws of war helped give shape to Emancipation's meaning, animating its ambitions and setting its limits.

What Lincoln came to understand in the summer and fall of 1862 was that the law of war asks the seemingly impossible. It presses upon us the obligations of human uncertainty at precisely our moment of maximum moral resolve. It was only because he was certain that the preservation of the Union was a worthy end that Lincoln was willing to go to war in the first place. It was only because he was certain that slavery was wrong that he was unwilling to compromise on it in the months between his election and his inauguration. Who but a madman would willingly cause 750,000 deaths without confidence in his purpose? But because Lincoln knew that white southerners prayed to the same God he did, because he knew they felt the same conviction in the righteousness of their cause that he did in his, he acted with an acute sense of his own fallibility. These were the core premises of the Enlightenment laws of war, and they were the ideas Lincoln worked through as he decided on Emancipation. In managing the fallout from Emancipation, his administration called forth a new blueprint for the international law of war, one that is with us to this day.

I n Lincoln's internal deliberations in the summer and fall of 1862, the laws of war provided a framework for ethical decision making. But from the Revolution to the Philippines, the laws of war served a number of additional functions, too, sometimes for good and sometimes for ill. The laws of war facilitated cooperation between the United States and the world. That was the role of the international law idea of neutrality, which helped harmonize the tense relations between a new nation and the warring states of Europe. That was the vital role of the laws of war in April 1861 as well, when Lincoln opted for a blockade so as to coordinate his efforts with the interests of Britain and France. The laws of war also served as a basis for the criminal punishment of individuals, as in the military commission prosecutions charging violations of the laws of war in the Civil War. The laws of war promoted the power of the executive branch in the U.S. constitutional system of checks and balances, as when Lincoln claimed the power of military emancipation for himself. They advanced the partisan interests of political factions aiming to mobilize public opinion. (Henry Clay used them thus, only to be disappointed that he could not turn them sufficiently to his advantage to keep Andrew Jackson out of the White House.) They promoted the military discipline of American soldiers, as in Winfield Scott's Mexico. They helped establish the professional identity of the legal and military professions, as among the Philadelphia lawyers and the West Point officers of the early republic. They promoted the interests of strong nation-states (witness Britain at the Declaration of Paris in 1856) and they offered shelter to the claims of weak nation-states (consider, for example, the United States in its fragile first years).

The laws of war do many things. And given the myriad uses to which they have been put, it ought to come as no surprise that the history of the laws of war in America has been one of repeated adaptations to fit the felt imperatives of the moment. Men like Jefferson and John Quincy Adams created (almost from whole cloth) a supposed rule against the freeing of enemy slaves. Winfield Scott stumbled upon the concept of the war crime in Mexico. The statesmen of the Civil War reversed the United States' positions on the rules governing blockades and on the permissibility of privateering. Emancipation impelled the administration to reverse a customary American position yet again. The laws of war were thus not an unchanging body of principles. Nor were they the exclusive province of learned jurists developing rules according to some autonomous internal logic of the law. To the contrary, statesmen and soldiers, lawyers and judges, critics and diplomats forged the laws of armed conflict to do battle in actual hostilities. To paraphrase Oliver Wendell Holmes, Jr., the life of the laws of war has not been logic. It has been experience.

American self-interest powerfully influenced specific adaptations of the laws of war. Indeed, alignment between the law and the interests of those who have aimed to deploy it has been a persistent theme in the history we have seen here. How else can we explain the Civil War reversals of long-standing U.S. policies on questions of neutrality and blockades? Only if we allow for a liberal dose of self-interest in the elaboration of the laws of war can we even begin to make sense of such episodes.

In this, the laws of war are much like the law in most other domains. Historians of the law of contracts, or automobile accidents, or antitrust, or constitutions do not expect the law to develop independent of its context or untethered from the needs and interests of the most concerned parties. How could it? What kind of law would this be? We no longer think of the law as something given to Moses on a mountaintop. We know that law is made by human beings for human beings. The law thus arises out of the very social phenomena it aims to regulate. That is a pervasive fact about law of all kinds. Its contours respond to external imperatives.

But as with other areas of the law, the laws of war are not constituted solely of self-interested revisions to suit the needs of the moment. The engagement with the laws of war that has been a hallmark of the American experience from the Revolution to the present has generated a tradition with powerful continuities. Even as it has taken on new content to suit the felt needs of new situations, it has retained a recognizable continuity with the past. If the law of war were nothing but the condensed interests of particular constituencies at particular moments, it could not do the work that it does— work in which American leaders since the founding have invested heavily.

The neutrality arguments of Washington and Marshall in the tenuous years of the early republic had weight to whatever extent they successfully mobilized Americans and appealed to principles thought to be shared across the Atlantic. Winfield Scott's military commissions, controversial though they were, gained legitimacy over summary executions by participating in and being shaped by the law. The Civil War blockade promoted coordination with Great Britain by adopting a set of terms and a framework that had international legitimacy. Indeed, the advancement of American interests through the laws of war today works when and if those laws retain some modicum of the same legitimacy. If the laws of war were utterly hollow, they would have fallen out of use long before now. Disillusionment ought to have led so many of us to disregard the law as hogwash that their invocation would be pointless. But the legal regulation of armed conflict has not fallen away. It has shown stunning durability.

Writing a half century ago, the eminent Civil War historian James G. Randall pronounced the history of the customs and laws of war "a disheartening business." It often is. But sometimes, just sometimes, there are glimmers of hope. In the end, the most remarkable feature of the history of the laws of war is the durability and persistence of efforts to make rules for the no-man's land of battle. For despite all the skeptics and critics, despite all the abuses and self-interested interpretations, very few of us are willing to do away altogether with the idea of a shared set of rules.

I N THE DECADE since 9/11, the laws of war have pushed their way to the fore once again. Thousands of American men and women now spend their professional lives working through the knotty problems of applying the laws of armed conflict to the wars of the twenty-first century. They work in the armed forces and in the State Department, in the White House and the U.S. Attorney General's office, in the U.S. Supreme Court and the Department of Defense. They come from nongovernmental watchdogs such as the Red Cross and human rights organizations, from private law practice and from law schools. They are soldiers, journalists, lawyers, and more. From personal experience, I can say that in universities across the country, students flock to courses on international armed conflict and its legal regulation in numbers unimagined a decade and a half ago.

Application of the international rules of armed conflict in twenty-first-century settings has yielded answers no more frequently or easily than it did in the days of Lieber and Lincoln. In trying to make sense of the controversies of our own day in light of the history of America's first century, however, we can do away with some dubious ideas that have come to occupy prominent places in debates about the laws of war. It is not true, as is often imagined by partisans on all sides, that the laws of war were once simpler than they are now, or that they were once less controversial. It is not the case that Americans in some time of yore did not worry themselves much about the laws of war. Nor is it the case that Americans simply adhered unquestioningly to those laws. Our history is far messier than that. It is hard even to say that the stakes are higher now, even if the weapons we and our enemies bring to bear are ever more powerful. Controversies over the laws of war and novel questions of great difficulty and grave significance are as old as the republic. And that alone is a vitally important insight, for once we have dispatched the myths of the left and the right, once we have dispelled the false versions of the American past, we can see a long history of soldiers and statesmen and lawyers who struggled with many of the same dilemmas we grapple with today.

Today, the laws of war serve at least as many functions as they did 150 years ago. They mark the outer boundaries of morally acceptable behavior. Just as they did in Lincoln's time, for example, they put torture beyond the pale. U.S. officials sometimes scoffed at such limits after 9/11, and the laws against torture did not prevent interrogation practices like the waterboarding that reprised Edwin Glenn's water cure of a century ago. But the laws of war played important roles in the torture controversy, even if they did not operate to prevent it or punish its principal perpetrators. What the laws of war accomplished was to help organize and galvanize the critics of torture. The international law that the United States helped to create more than a century ago added immeasurably to the costs America incurred by permitting such interrogation practices to go forward—costs measured in precious international reputation and credibility.

The case of torture barely begins to exhaust the many roles for the laws of war. International standards such as those in the Geneva Conventions serve to coordinate American actions with those of our allies. Adherence to the laws of armed conflict, to take another example, shapes U.S. targeting decisions, reducing civilian casualties and assisting American efforts to win over civilian hearts and minds. The laws of war here and elsewhere serve as a useful guide to the nation's long-term interests. And as in the nineteenth century, the laws of war have their domestic uses, too. Presidents—Republican and Democratic alike—have invoked the laws of war to bolster expansive conceptions of the power of the executive branch. The laws of war serve as the basis for the criminal prosecution of al-Qaeda members and associated forces in military commissions at Guantánamo Bay. At the same time, they function as a way of mobilizing opposition to the use of force, both domestically and abroad.

There is another, more abstract continuity with the past as well. For despite heated controversies and raging debates, it is the international laws of war that we are still arguing about. Andrew Jackson and his partisans often sneered with contempt at those they thought of as the self-appointed guardians of international morality. Sometimes they did so with considerable justification. But even Jackson's views of armed conflict were powerfully shaped by the law of war tradition. Much the same can be said of the lawyers and politicians who in the immediate aftermath of 9/11 sought to dismiss the laws of war as an anachronism. For they have found themselves enmeshed in arguments about those laws ever since.

It would of course be silly to deny the vast differences that separate the present day from the age that witnessed the rise of the modern laws of war. The sheer density of the relevant treaties, for example, is an utter novelty of the past sixty years. The Declaration of Paris of 1856 and the first Geneva Convention of 1864 made up a few thin reeds by comparison to the dense thickets of legal rules set forth in the four separate Geneva Conventions of 1949 and the two Additional Protocols to the Geneva Conventions negotiated (but not ratified) by the United States in 1977. If we add the 1985 Convention Against Torture, various human rights treaties of the post–World War II era, and the 1998 Rome Statute of the International Criminal Court, the picture becomes truly daunting. Even the Hague Convention of 1899 failed to create as dense a body of treaty law as is now standard in the field. Nor did the nineteenth century know anything like the twenty-four-hour news cycle and inexpensive video technology, or the presence of armed forces operating under the mandate of the United Nations.

One thing all this means is that statesmen like Washington, Marshall, John Quincy Adams, Winfield Scott, and Lincoln—even Francis Lieber— had what today would be unthinkable discretion to shape the laws of war as they saw fit. The laws of war are no longer subject to radical remaking in the same way they were in 1775 or 1847 or 1862 or 1899. American contributions have had much to do with this. The success of Lincoln's and Lieber's 1863 code, and its promulgation around the world, has in this sense helped constrain U.S. presidents a century and a half later, presidents who find themselves in a multilateral legal world even as the United States is (for now, anyway) the world's only military superpower.

Sharp breaks between past and present limit history's usefulness as a guide. History won't tell us what interrogation techniques are appropriate and permissible. It won't tell us whom we should prosecute in military commissions, or for what crimes. It won't tell us how many civilian casualties are permissible, or how much certainty we should require when issuing drone strikes against faraway people. But history does put us face-to-face with past generations' efforts to manage many of the same kinds of dilemmas we face today. And the tumultuous history of the laws of war offers a sense of what we can reasonably expect. Those who expect too much will be let down. How could regulating warfare be anything other than rife with unsatisfactory moral compromise and enduring controversy? On the other hand, those who expect too little threaten to undo the law's capacity to accomplish gravely important things on our behalf.

If there is one thing in this turbulent story that will not vary, if there is one firm rock on which we can rely, it is that to make our way through the next crisis will require deliberations on the nature of just wars: deliberations like those Lincoln engaged in during the summer and fall of 1862 as he prepared for Emancipation and set the stage for the code that followed. The laws of war require commitment to act on our best notions of justice in a world beset by violence and danger. Sometimes that commitment will require the use of force, notwithstanding all war's perils. But when we do use force, we will have to balance our ideas of justice with humility about our ends. This may be what President Barack Obama had in mind in his 2009 Nobel Peace Prize address when, in a speech praised as warmly by his critics as by his supporters, he defended the use of armed force but warned against those who would fight with the moral certainty of crusaders, convinced beyond the shadow of a doubt that they carry the will of God on their side. Lincoln proposed the same idea in his Second Inaugural Address, when he promised to win the war but confessed the sins of the North nonetheless. Lincoln's General Orders No. 100 aimed to establish a framework for making decisions in wartime that would make salient both of war's twin imperatives: resolve and humility. All too often Americans have failed to live up to the example Lincoln set. How could we not? But what is equally striking—what is remarkable and enduring—is that men and women have worked ever since to preserve the framework he helped to establish.

GENERAL ORDERS, ⎱   WAR DEPARTMENT,

No. 100. ⎰   Adjutant General's Office,

                               Washington, April 24, 1863.

The following "Instructions for the Government of Armies of the United States in the Field," prepared by Francis Lieber, LL.D., and revised by a Board of Officers, of which Major General E. A. Hitchcock is president, having been approved by the President of the United States, he commands that they be published for the information of all concerned.

By order of the Secretary of War:

                        E. D. TOWNSEND,

                          Assistant Adjutant General.

INSTRUCTIONS FOR THE GOVERNMENT OF ARMIES OF THE UNITED STATES IN THE FIELD.

SECTION I.

Martial law—Military jurisdiction—Military necessity—Retaliation.

1. A place, district, or country occupied by an enemy stands, in consequence of the occupation, under the Martial Law of the invading or occupying army, whether any proclamation declaring Martial Law, or any public warning to the inhabitants, has been issued or not. Martial Law is the immediate and direct effect and consequence of occupation or conquest.

The presence of a hostile army proclaims its Martial Law.

2. Martial Law does not cease during the hostile occupation, except by special proclamation, ordered by the commander-in-chief; or by special mention in the treaty of peace concluding the war, when the occupation of a place or territory continues beyond the conclusion of peace as one of the conditions of the same.

3. Martial Law in a hostile country consists in the suspension, by the occupying military authority, of the criminal and civil law, and of the domestic administration and government in the occupied place or territory, and in the substitution of military rule and force for the same, as well as in the dictation of general laws, as far as military necessity requires this suspension, substitution, or dictation.

The opening page of a rare original copy of General Orders No. 100. The corrected spelling of its drafter's name may be in Francis Lieber's own hand.

Appendix

————※•⊕•※————

GENERAL ORDERS, NO. 100.

WAR DEPARTMENT,
ADJUTANT GENERAL'S OFFICE,
Washington, April 24, 1863.

The following "Instructions for the Government of Armies of the United States in the Field," prepared by Francis Lieber, LL.D., and revised by a Board of Officers, of which Maj. Gen. E. A. Hitchcock is president, having been approved by the President of the United States, he commands that they be published for the information of all concerned.

By order of the Secretary of War:

E. D. TOWNSEND,
Assistant Adjutant-General.

————

INSTRUCTIONS FOR THE GOVERNMENT OF ARMIES OF THE UNITED STATES IN THE FIELD.

SECTION I.

Martial law—Military jurisdiction—Military necessity—Retaliation

1. A place, district, or country occupied by an enemy stands, in consequence of the occupation, under the Martial Law of the invading or occupying army, whether any proclamation declaring Martial Law, or any public warning to the inhabitants, has been issued or not. Martial Law is the immediate and direct effect and consequence of occupation or conquest.

The presence of a hostile army proclaims its Martial Law.

2. Martial Law does not cease during the hostile occupation, except by special proclamation, ordered by the commander-in-chief; or by special mention in the treaty of peace concluding the war, when the occupation of a place or territory continues beyond the conclusion of peace as one of the conditions of the same.

3. Martial Law in a hostile country consists in the suspension, by the occupying military authority, of the criminal and civil law, and of the domestic

administration and government in the occupied place or territory, and in the substitution of military rule and force for the same, as well as in the dictation of general laws, as far as military necessity requires this suspension, substitution, or dictation.

The commander of the forces may proclaim that the administration of all civil and penal law shall continue, either wholly or in part, as in times of peace, unless otherwise ordered by the military authority.

4. Martial Law is simply military authority exercised in accordance with the laws and usages of war. Military oppression is not Martial Law; it is the abuse of the power which that law confers. As Martial Law is executed by military force, it is incumbent upon those who administer it to be strictly guided by the principles of justice, honor, and humanity—virtues adorning a soldier even more than other men, for the very reason that he possesses the power of his arms against the unarmed.

5. Martial Law should be less stringent in places and countries fully occupied and fairly conquered. Much greater severity may be exercised in places or regions where actual hostilities exist, or are expected and must be prepared for. Its most complete sway is allowed—even in the commander's own country—when face to face with the enemy, because of the absolute necessities of the case, and of the paramount duty to defend the country against invasion.

To save the country is paramount to all other considerations.

6. All civil and penal law shall continue to take its usual course in the enemy's places and territories under Martial Law, unless interrupted or stopped by order of the occupying military power; but all the functions of the hostile government—legislative, executive, or administrative—whether of a general, provincial, or local character, cease under Martial Law, or continue only with the sanction, or if deemed necessary, the participation of the occupier or invader.

7. Martial Law extends to property, and to persons, whether they are subjects of the enemy or aliens to that government.

8. Consuls, among American and European nations, are not diplomatic agents. Nevertheless, their offices and persons will be subjected to Martial Law in cases of urgent necessity only: their property and business are not exempted. Any delinquency they commit against the established military rule may be punished as in the case of any other inhabitant, and such punishment furnishes no reasonable ground for international complaint.

9. The functions of Ambassadors, Ministers, or other diplomatic agents, accredited by neutral powers to the hostile government, cease, so far as regards the displaced government; but the conquering or occupying power usually recognizes them as temporarily accredited to itself.

10. Martial Law affects chiefly the police and collection of public revenue and taxes, whether imposed by the expelled government or by the invader, and refers mainly to the support and efficiency of the army, its safety, and the safety of its operations.

11. The law of war does not only disclaim all cruelty and bad faith concerning engagements concluded with the enemy during the war, but also the breaking

of stipulations solemnly contracted by the belligerents in time of peace, and avowedly intended to remain in force in case of war between the contracting powers.

It disclaims all extortions and other transactions for individual gain; all acts of private revenge, or connivance at such acts.

Offenses to the contrary shall be severely punished, and especially so if committed by officers.

12. Whenever feasible, Martial Law is carried out in cases of individual offenders by Military Courts; but sentences of death shall be executed only with the approval of the chief executive, provided the urgency of the case does not require a speedier execution, and then only with the approval of the chief commander.

13. Military jurisdiction is of two kinds: first, that which is conferred and defined by statute; second, that which is derived from the common law of war. Military offences under the statute law must be tried in the manner therein directed; but military offences which do not come within the statute must be tried and punished under the common law of war. The character of the courts which exercise these jurisdictions depends upon the local laws of each particular country.

In the armies of the United States the first is exercised by courts-martial; while cases which do not come within the "Rules and Articles of War," or the jurisdiction conferred by statute on courts-martial, are tried by military commissions.

14. Military necessity, as understood by modern civilized nations, consists in the necessity of those measures which are indispensable for securing the ends of the war, and which are lawful according to the modern law and usages of war.

15. Military necessity admits of all direct destruction of life or limb of *armed* enemies, and of other persons whose destruction is incidentally *unavoidable* in the armed contests of the war; it allows of the capturing of every armed enemy, and every enemy of importance to the hostile government, or of peculiar danger to the captor; it allows of all destruction of property, and obstruction of the ways and channels of traffic, travel, or communication, and of all withholding of sustenance or means of life from the enemy; of the appropriation of whatever an enemy's country affords necessary for the subsistence and safety of the army, and of such deception as does not involve the breaking of good faith either positively pledged, regarding agreements entered into during the war, or supposed by the modern law of war to exist. Men who take up arms against one another in public war do not cease on this account to be moral beings, responsible to one another, and to God.

16. Military necessity does not admit of cruelty, that is, the infliction of suffering for the sake of suffering or for revenge, nor of maiming or wounding except in fight, nor of torture to extort confessions. It does not admit of the use of poison in any way, nor of the wanton devastation of a district. It admits of deception, but disclaims acts of perfidy; and, in general, military necessity does not include any act of hostility which makes the return to peace unnecessarily difficult.

17. War is not carried on by arms alone. It is lawful to starve the hostile belligerent, armed or unarmed, so that it leads to the speedier subjection of the enemy.

18. When the commander of a besieged place expels the non-combatants, in order to lessen the number of those who consume his stock of provisions, it is lawful, though an extreme measure, to drive them back, so as to hasten on the surrender.

19. Commanders, whenever admissible, inform the enemy of their intention to bombard a place, so that the non-combatants, and especially the women and children, may be removed before the bombardment commences. But it is no infraction of the common law of war to omit thus to inform the enemy. Surprise may be a necessity.

20. Public war is a state of armed hostility between sovereign nations or governments. It is a law and requisite of civilized existence that men live in political, continuous societies, forming organized units, called states or nations, whose constituents bear, enjoy, and suffer, advance and retrograde together, in peace and in war.

21. The citizen or native of a hostile country is thus an enemy, as one of the constituents of the hostile state or nation, and as such is subjected to the hardships of the war.

22. Nevertheless, as civilization has advanced during the last centuries, so has likewise steadily advanced, especially in war on land, the distinction between the private individual belonging to a hostile country and the hostile country itself, with its men in arms. The principle has been more and more acknowledged that the unarmed citizen is to be spared in person, property, and honor as much as the exigencies of war will admit.

23. Private citizens are no longer murdered, enslaved, or carried off to distant parts, and the inoffensive individual is as little disturbed in his private relations as the commander of the hostile troops can afford to grant in the overruling demands of a vigorous war.

24. The almost universal rule in remote times was, and continues to be with barbarous armies, that the private individual of the hostile country is destined to suffer every privation of liberty and protection, and every disruption of family ties. Protection was, and still is with uncivilized people, the exception.

25. In modern regular wars of the Europeans, and their descendants in other portions of the globe, protection of the inoffensive citizen of the hostile country is the rule; privation and disturbance of private relations are the exceptions.

26. Commanding generals may cause the magistrates and civil officers of the hostile country to take the oath of temporary allegiance or an oath of fidelity to their own victorious government or rulers, and they may expel every one who declines to do so. But whether they do so or not, the people and their civil officers owe strict obedience to them as long as they hold sway over the district or country, at the peril of their lives.

27. The law of war can no more wholly dispense with retaliation than can the law of nations, of which it is a branch. Yet civilized nations acknowledge retaliation as the sternest feature of war. A reckless enemy often leaves to his opponent no other means of securing himself against the repetition of barbarous outrage.

28. Retaliation will, therefore, never be resorted to as a measure of mere revenge, but only as a means of protective retribution, and, moreover, cautiously and unavoidably; that is to say, retaliation shall only be resorted to after careful inquiry into the real occurrence, and the character of the misdeeds that may demand retribution.

Unjust or inconsiderate retaliation removes the belligerents farther and farther from the mitigating rules of a regular war, and by rapid steps leads them nearer to the internecine wars of savages.

29. Modern times are distinguished from earlier ages by the existence, at one and the same time, of many nations and great governments related to one another in close intercourse.

Peace is their normal condition; war is the exception. The ultimate object of all modern war is a renewed state of peace.

The more vigorously wars are pursued, the better it is for humanity. Sharp wars are brief.

30. Ever since the formation and co-existence of modern nations, and ever since wars have become great national wars, war has come to be acknowledged not to be its own end, but the means to obtain great ends of state, or to consist in defence against wrong; and no conventional restriction of the modes adopted to injure the enemy is any longer admitted; but the law of war imposes many limitations and restrictions on principles of justice, faith, and honor.

SECTION II.

Public and private property of the Enemy—Protection of persons, and especially women; of religion, the arts and sciences—Punishment of crimes against the inhabitants of hostile countries.

31. A victorious army appropriates all public money, seizes all public movable property until further direction by its government, and sequesters for its own benefit or of that of its government all the revenues of real property belonging to the hostile government or nation. The title to such real property remains in abeyance during military occupation, and until the conquest is made complete.

32. A victorious army, by the martial power inherent in the same, may suspend, change, or abolish, as far as the martial power extends, the relations which arise from the services due, according to the existing laws of the invaded country, from one citizen, subject, or native of the same to another.

The commander of the army must leave it to the ultimate treaty of peace to settle the permanency of this change.

33. It is no longer considered lawful—on the contrary, it is held to be a serious breach of the law of war—to force the subjects of the enemy into the service of the victorious government, except the latter should proclaim, after a fair and complete conquest of the hostile country or district, that it is resolved to keep the country, district, or place permanently as its own, and make it a portion of its own country.

34. As a general rule, the property belonging to churches, to hospitals, or other establishments of an exclusively charitable character, to establishments of education, or foundations for the promotion of knowledge, whether public schools, universities, academies of learning or observatories, museums of the fine arts, or of a scientific character—such property is not to be considered public property in the sense of paragraph 31; but it may be taxed or used when the public service may require it.

35. Classical works of art, libraries, scientific collections, or precious instruments, such as astronomical telescopes, as well as hospitals, must be secured against all avoidable injury, even when they are contained in fortified places whilst besieged or bombarded.

36. If such works of art, libraries, collections, or instruments belonging to a hostile nation or government, can be removed without injury, the ruler of the conquering state or nation may order them to be seized and removed for the benefit of the said nation. The ultimate ownership is to be settled by the ensuing treaty of peace.

In no case shall they be sold or given away, if captured by the armies of the United States, nor shall they ever be privately appropriated, or wantonly destroyed or injured.

37. The United States acknowledge and protect, in hostile countries occupied by them, religion and morality; strictly private property; the persons of the inhabitants, especially those of women; and the sacredness of domestic relations. Offenses to the contrary shall be rigorously punished.

This rule does not interfere with the right of the victorious invader to tax the people or their property, to levy forced loans, to billet soldiers, or to appropriate property, especially houses, lands, boats or ships, and churches, for temporary and military uses.

38. Private property, unless forfeited by crimes or by offences of the owner, can be seized only by way of military necessity, for the support or other benefit of the army of the United States.

If the owner has not fled, the commanding officer will cause receipts to be given, which may serve the spoliated owner to obtain indemnity.

39. The salaries of civil officers of the hostile government who remain in the invaded territory, and continue the work of their office, and can continue it according to the circumstances arising out of the war—such as judges, administrative or police officers, officers of city or communal governments—are paid from the public revenue of the invaded territory, until the military government has reason wholly or partially to discontinue it. Salaries or incomes connected with purely honorary titles are always stopped.

40. There exists no law or body of authoritative rules of action between hostile armies, except that branch of the law of nature and nations which is called the law and usages of war on land.

41. All municipal law of the ground on which the armies stand, or of the countries to which they belong, is silent and of no effect between armies in the field.

42. Slavery, complicating and confounding the ideas of property, (that is of a *thing*,) and of personality, (that is of *humanity*,) exists according to municipal law or local law only. The law of nature and nations has never acknowledged it. The digest of the Roman law enacts the early dictum of the pagan jurist, that "so far as the law of nature is concerned, all men are equal." Fugitives escaping from a country in which they were slaves, villains, or serfs, into another country, have, for centuries past, been held free and acknowledged free by judicial decisions of European countries, even though the municipal law of the country in which the slave had taken refuge acknowledged slavery within its own dominions.

43. Therefore, in a war between the United States and a belligerent which admits of slavery, if a person held in bondage by that belligerent be captured by or come as a fugitive under the protection of the military forces of the United States, such person is immediately entitled to the rights and privileges of a freeman. To return such person into slavery would amount to enslaving a free person, and neither the United States nor any officer under their authority can enslave any human being. Moreover, a person so made free by the law of war is under the shield of the law of nations, and the former owner or State can have, by the law of post-liminy, no belligerent lien or claim of service.

44. All wanton violence committed against persons in the invaded country, all destruction of property not commanded by the authorized officer, all robbery, all pillage or sacking, even after taking a place by main force, all rape, wounding, maiming, or killing of such inhabitants, are prohibited under the penalty of death, or such other severe punishment as may seem adequate for the gravity of the offense.

A soldier, officer or private, in the act of committing such violence, and disobeying a superior ordering him to abstain from it, may be lawfully killed on the spot by such superior.

45. All captures and booty belong, according to the modern law of war, primarily to the government of the captor.

Prize money, whether on sea or land, can now only be claimed under local law.

46. Neither officers nor soldiers are allowed to make use of their position or power in the hostile country for private gain, not even for commercial transactions otherwise legitimate. Offences to the contrary committed by commissioned officers will be punished with cashiering or such other punishment as the nature of the offence may require; if by soldiers, they shall be punished according to the nature of the offence.

47. Crimes punishable by all penal codes, such as arson, murder, maiming, assaults, highway robbery, theft, burglary, fraud, forgery, and rape, if committed by an American soldier in a hostile country against its inhabitants, are not only punishable as at home, but in all cases in which death is not inflicted, the severer punishment shall be preferred.

SECTION III.

Deserters—Prisoners of War—Hostages—Booty on the Battle-field.

48. Deserters from the American army, having entered the service of the enemy, suffer death if they fall again into the hands of the United States, whether by capture, or being delivered up to the American army; and if a deserter from the enemy, having taken service in the army of the United States, is captured by the enemy, and punished by them with death or otherwise, it is not a breach against the law and usages of war, requiring redress or retaliation.

49. A prisoner of war is a public enemy armed or attached to the hostile army for active aid, who has fallen into the hands of the captor, either fighting or wounded, on the field or in the hospital, by individual surrender or by capitulation.

All soldiers, of whatever species of arms; all men who belong to the rising *en masse* of the hostile country; all those who are attached to the army for its efficiency and promote directly the object of the war, except such as are hereinafter provided for; all disabled men or officers on the field or elsewhere, if captured; all enemies who have thrown away their arms and ask for quarter, are prisoners of war, and as such exposed to the inconveniences as well as entitled to the privileges of a prisoner of war.

50. Moreover, citizens who accompany an army for whatever purpose, such as sutlers, editors, or reporters of journals, or contractors, if captured, may be made prisoners of war, and be detained as such.

The monarch and members of the hostile reigning family, male or female, the chief, and chief officers of the hostile government, its diplomatic agents, and all persons who are of particular and singular use and benefit to the hostile army or its government, are, if captured on belligerent ground, and if unprovided with a safe conduct granted by the captor's government, prisoners of war.

51. If the people of that portion of an invaded country which is not yet occupied by the enemy, or of the whole country, at the approach of a hostile army, rise under a duly authorized levy, *en masse* to resist the invader, they are now treated as public enemies, and if captured, are prisoners of war.

52. No belligerent has the right to declare that he will treat every captured man in arms of a levy *en masse* as a brigand or bandit.

If, however, the people of a country, or any portion of the same, already occupied by an army, rise against it, they are violators of the laws of war, and are not entitled to their protection.

53. The enemy's chaplains, officers of the medical staff, apothecaries, hospital nurses and servants, if they fall into the hands of the American army, are not prisoners of war, unless the commander has reasons to retain them. In this latter case, or if, at their own desire, they are allowed to remain with their captured companions, they are treated as prisoners of war, and may be exchanged if the commander sees fit.

54. A hostage is a person accepted as a pledge for the fulfillment of an agreement concluded between belligerents during the war, or in consequence of a war. Hostages are rare in the present age.

55. If a hostage is accepted, he is treated like a prisoner of war, according to rank and condition, as circumstances may admit.

56. A prisoner of war is subject to no punishment for being a public enemy, nor is any revenge wreaked upon him by the intentional infliction of any suffering, or disgrace, by cruel imprisonment, want of food, by mutilation, death, or any other barbarity.

57. So soon as a man is armed by a sovereign government, and takes the soldier's oath of fidelity, he is a belligerent; his killing, wounding, or other warlike acts, are no individual crimes or offences. No belligerent has a right to declare that enemies of a certain class, color, or condition, when properly organized as soldiers, will not be treated by him as public enemies.

58. The law of nations knows of no distinction of color, and if an enemy of the United States should enslave and sell any captured persons of their army, it would be a case for the severest retaliation, if not redressed upon complaint.

The United States cannot retaliate by enslavement; therefore death must be the retaliation for this crime against the law of nations.

59. A prisoner of war remains answerable for his crimes committed against the captor's army or people, committed before he was captured, and for which he has not been punished by his own authorities.

All prisoners of war are liable to the infliction of retaliatory measures.

60. It is against the usage of modern war to resolve, in hatred and revenge, to give no quarter. No body of troops has the right to declare that it will not give, and therefore will not expect, quarter; but a commander is permitted to direct his troops to give no quarter, in great straits, when his own salvation makes it *impossible* to cumber himself with prisoners.

61. Troops that give no quarter have no right to kill enemies already disabled on the ground, or prisoners captured by other troops.

62. All troops of the enemy known or discovered to give no quarter in general, or to any portion of the army, receive none.

63. Troops who fight in the uniform of their enemies, without any plain, striking, and uniform mark of distinction of their own, can expect no quarter.

64. If American troops capture a train containing uniforms of the enemy, and the commander considers it advisable to distribute them for use among his men, some striking mark or sign must be adopted to distinguish the American soldier from the enemy.

65. The use of the enemy's national standard, flag, or other emblem of nationality, for the purpose of deceiving the enemy in battle, is an act of perfidy by which they lose all claim to the protection of the laws of war.

66. Quarter having been given to an enemy by American troops, under a misapprehension of his true character, he may, nevertheless, be ordered to suffer death if, within three days after the battle, it be discovered that he belongs to a corps which gives no quarter.

67. The law of nations allows every sovereign government to make war upon another sovereign state, and, therefore, admits of no rules or laws different from those of regular warfare, regarding the treatment of prisoners of war, although they may belong to the army of a government which the captor may consider as a wanton and unjust assailant.

68. Modern wars are not internecine wars, in which the killing of the enemy is the object. The destruction of the enemy in modern war, and, indeed, modern war itself, are means to obtain that object of the belligerent which lies beyond the war.

Unnecessary or revengeful destruction of life is not lawful.

69. Outposts, sentinels, or pickets are not to be fired upon, except to drive them in, or when a positive order, special or general, has been issued to that effect.

70. The use of poison in any manner, be it to poison wells, or food, or arms, is wholly excluded from modern warfare. He that uses it puts himself out of the pale of the law and usages of war.

71. Whoever intentionally inflicts additional wounds on an enemy already wholly disabled, or kills such an enemy, or who orders or encourages soldiers to do so, shall suffer death, if duly convicted, whether he belongs to the army of the United States, or is an enemy captured after having committed his misdeed.

72. Money and other valuables on the person of a prisoner, such as watches or jewelry, as well as extra clothing, are regarded by the American army as the private property of the prisoner, and the appropriation of such valuables or money is considered dishonorable, and is prohibited.

Nevertheless, if *large* sums are found upon the persons of prisoners, or in their possession, they shall be taken from them, and the surplus, after providing for their own support, appropriated for the use of the army, under the direction of the commander, unless otherwise ordered by the government. Nor can prisoners claim, as private property, large sums found and captured in their train, although they have been placed in the private luggage of the prisoners.

73. All officers, when captured, must surrender their side-arms to the captor. They may be restored to the prisoner in marked cases, by the commander, to signalize admiration of his distinguished bravery, or approbation of his humane treatment of prisoners before his capture. The captured officer to whom they may be restored cannot wear them during captivity.

74. A prisoner of war being a public enemy, is the prisoner of the government, and not of the captor. No ransom can be paid by a prisoner of war to his individual captor, or to any officer in command. The government alone releases captives, according to rules prescribed by itself.

75. Prisoners of war are subject to confinement or imprisonment such as may be deemed necessary on account of safety, but they are to be subjected to no other intentional suffering or indignity. The confinement and mode of treating a prisoner may be varied during his captivity according to the demands of safety.

76. Prisoners of war shall be fed upon plain and wholesome food whenever practicable, and treated with humanity.

They may be required to work for the benefit of the captor's government, according to their rank and condition.

77. A prisoner of war who escapes may be shot, or otherwise killed in his flight; but neither death nor any other punishment shall be inflicted upon him simply for his attempt to escape, which the law of war does not consider a crime. Stricter means of security shall be used after an unsuccessful attempt at escape.

If, however, a conspiracy is discovered, the purpose of which is a united or general escape, the conspirators may be rigorously punished, even with death; and capital punishment may also be inflicted upon prisoners of war discovered to have plotted rebellion against the authorities of the captors, whether in union with fellow-prisoners or other persons.

78. If prisoners of war, having given no pledge nor made any promise on their honor, forcibly or otherwise escape, and are captured again in battle, after having rejoined their own army, they shall not be punished for their escape, but shall be treated as simple prisoners of war, although they will be subjected to stricter confinement.

79. Every captured wounded enemy shall be medically treated, according to the ability of the medical staff.

80. Honorable men, when captured, will abstain from giving to the enemy information concerning their own army, and the modern law of war permits no longer the use of any violence against prisoners, in order to extort the desired information, or to punish them for having given false information.

SECTION IV.

Partisans—Armed enemies not belonging to the hostile army— Scouts—Armed prowlers—War-rebels.

81. Partisans are soldiers armed and wearing the uniform of their army, but belonging to a corps which acts detached from the main body for the purpose of making inroads into the territory occupied by the enemy. If captured, they are entitled to all the privileges of the prisoner of war.

82. Men, or squads of men, who commit hostilities, whether by fighting, or inroads for destruction or plunder, or by raids of any kind, without commission, without being part and portion of the organized hostile army, and without sharing continuously in the war, but who do so with intermitting returns to their homes and avocations, or with the occasional assumption of the semblance of peaceful pursuits, divesting themselves of the character or appearance of soldiers—such men, or squads of men, are not public enemies, and therefore, if captured, are not entitled to the privileges of prisoners of war, but shall be treated summarily as highway robbers or pirates.

83. Scouts, or single soldiers, if disguised in the dress of the country, or in the uniform of the army hostile to their own, employed in obtaining information, if found within or lurking about the lines of the captor, are treated as spies, and suffer death.

84. Armed prowlers, by whatever names they may be called, or persons of the enemy's territory, who steal within the lines of the hostile army, for the purpose of robbing, killing, or of destroying bridges, roads, or canals, or of robbing or destroying the mail, or of cutting the telegraph wires, are not entitled to the privileges of the prisoner of war.

85. War-rebels are persons within an occupied territory who rise in arms against the occupying or conquering army, or against the authorities established by the same. If captured, they may suffer death, whether they rise singly, in small or large bands, and whether called upon to do so by their own, but expelled, government or not. They are not prisoners of war; nor are they, if discovered and secured before their conspiracy has matured to an actual rising, or armed violence.

SECTION V.

Safe-conduct—Spies—War-traitors—Captured messengers— Abuse of the flag of truce.

86. All intercourse between the territories occupied by belligerent armies, whether by traffic, by letter, by travel, or in any other way, ceases. This is the general rule, to be observed without special proclamation.

Exceptions to this rule, whether by safe-conduct, or permission to trade on a small or large scale, or by exchanging mails, or by travel from one territory into the other, can take place only according to agreement approved by the government, or by the highest military authority.

Contraventions of this rule are highly punishable.

87. Ambassadors, and all other diplomatic agents of neutral powers, accredited to the enemy, may receive safe conducts through the territories occupied by the belligerents, unless there are military reasons to the contrary, and unless they may reach the place of their destination conveniently by another route. It implies no international affront if the safe conduct is declined. Such passes are usually given by the supreme authority of the state, and not by subordinate officers.

88. A spy is a person who secretly, in disguise or under false pretence, seeks information with the intention of communicating it to the enemy.

The spy is punishable with death by hanging by the neck, whether or not he succeed in obtaining the information or in conveying it to the enemy.

89. If a citizen of the United States obtains information in a legitimate manner, and betrays it to the enemy, be he a military or civil officer, or a private citizen, he shall suffer death.

90. A traitor under the law of war, or a war-traitor, is a person in a place or district under martial law who, unauthorized by the military commander, gives information of any kind to the enemy, or holds intercourse with him.

91. The war-traitor is always severely punished. If his offense consists in betraying to the enemy any thing concerning the condition, safety, operations or plans of the troops holding or occupying the place or district, his punishment is death.

92. If the citizen or subject of a country or place invaded or conquered gives information to his own government, from which he is separated by the hostile army, or to the army of his government, he is a war-traitor, and death is the penalty of his offence.

93. All armies in the field stand in need of guides, and impress them if they cannot obtain them otherwise.

94. No person having been forced by the enemy to serve as guide is punishable for having done so.

95. If a citizen of a hostile and invaded district voluntarily serves as a guide to the enemy, or offers to do so, he is deemed a war-traitor, and shall suffer death.

96. A citizen serving voluntarily as a guide against his own country commits treason, and will be dealt with according to the law of his country.

97. Guides, when it is clearly proved that they have misled intentionally, may be put to death.

98. All unauthorized or secret communication with the enemy is considered treasonable by the law of war.

Foreign residents in an invaded or occupied territory, or foreign visitors in the same, can claim no immunity from this law. They may communicate with foreign parts, or with the inhabitants of the hostile country, so far as the military authority permits, but no further. Instant expulsion from the occupied territory would be the very least punishment for the infraction of this rule.

99. A messenger carrying written dispatches or verbal messages from one portion of the army, or from a besieged place, to another portion of the same army, or its government, if armed, and in the uniform of his army, and if captured while doing so, in the territory occupied by the enemy, is treated by the captor as a prisoner of war. If not in uniform, nor a soldier, the circumstances connected with his capture must determine the disposition that shall be made of him.

100. A messenger or agent who attempts to steal through the territory occupied by the enemy, to further, in any manner, the interests of the enemy, if captured, is not entitled to the privileges of the prisoner of war, and may be dealt with according to the circumstances of the case.

101. While deception in war is admitted as a just and necessary means of hostility, and is consistent with honorable warfare, the common law of war allows even capital punishment for clandestine or treacherous attempts to injure an enemy, because they are so dangerous, and it is difficult to guard against them.

102. The law of war, like the criminal law regarding other offences, makes no difference on account of the difference of sexes, concerning the spy, the war-traitor, or the war-rebel.

103. Spies, war-traitors, and war-rebels, are not exchanged according to the common law of war. The exchange of such persons would require a special cartel, authorized by the government, or, at a great distance from it, by the chief commander of the army in the field.

104. A successful spy or war-traitor, safely returned to his own army, and afterwards captured as an enemy, is not subject to punishment for his acts as a spy or war-traitor, but he may be held in closer custody as a person individually dangerous.

SECTION VI.

Exchange of prisoners—Flags of truce—Flags of protection.

105. Exchanges of prisoners take place—number for number—rank for rank—wounded for wounded—with added condition for added condition—such, for instance, as not to serve for a certain period.

106. In exchanging prisoners of war, such numbers of persons of inferior rank may be substituted as an equivalent for one of superior rank as may be agreed upon by cartel, which requires the sanction of the government, or of the commander of the army in the field.

107. A prisoner of war is in honor bound truly to state to the captor his rank; and he is not to assume a lower rank than belongs to him, in order to cause a more advantageous exchange; nor a higher rank, for the purpose of obtaining better treatment.

Offenses to the contrary have been justly punished by the commanders of released prisoners, and may be good cause for refusing to release such prisoners.

108. The surplus number of prisoners of war remaining after an exchange has taken place is sometimes released either for the payment of a stipulated sum of money, or, in urgent cases, of provision, clothing, or other necessaries.

Such arrangement, however, requires the sanction of the highest authority.

109. The exchange of prisoners of war is an act of convenience to both belligerents. If no general cartel has been concluded, it cannot be demanded by either of them. No belligerent is obliged to exchange prisoners of war.

A cartel is voidable as soon as either party has violated it.

110. No exchange of prisoners shall be made except after complete capture, and after an accurate account of them, and a list of the captured officers, has been taken.

111. The bearer of a flag of truce cannot insist upon being admitted. He must always be admitted with great caution. Unnecessary frequency is carefully to be avoided.

112. If the bearer of a flag of truce offer himself during an engagement, he can be admitted as a very rare exception only. It is no breach of good faith to retain such a flag of truce, if admitted during the engagement. Firing is not required to cease on the appearance of a flag of truce in battle.

113. If the bearer of a flag of truce, presenting himself during an engagement, is killed or wounded, it furnishes no ground of complaint whatever.

114. If it be discovered, and fairly proved, that a flag of truce has been abused for surreptitiously obtaining military knowledge, the bearer of the flag thus abusing his sacred character is deemed a spy.

So sacred is the character of a flag of truce, and so necessary is its sacredness, that while its abuse is an especially heinous offense, great caution is requisite, on the other hand, in convicting the bearer of a flag of truce as a spy.

115. It is customary to designate by certain flags (usually yellow), the hospitals in places which are shelled, so that the besieging enemy may avoid firing on them. The same has been done in battles, when hospitals are situated within the field of the engagement.

116. Honorable belligerents often request that the hospitals within the territory of the enemy may be designated, so that they may be spared.

An honorable belligerent allows himself to be guided by flags or signals of protection as much as the contingencies and the necessities of the fight will permit.

117. It is justly considered an act of bad faith, of infamy or fiendishness, to deceive the enemy by flags of protection. Such act of bad faith may be good cause for refusing to respect such flags.

118. The besieging belligerent has sometimes requested the besieged to designate the buildings containing collections of works of art, scientific museums, astronomical observatories, or precious libraries, so that their destruction may be avoided as much as possible.

SECTION VII.

The Parole.

119. Prisoners of war may be released from captivity by exchange, and, under certain circumstances, also by parole.

120. The term *parole* designates the pledge of individual good faith and honor to do, or to omit doing, certain acts after he who gives his parole shall have been dismissed, wholly or partially, from the power of the captor.

121. The pledge of the parole is always an individual but not a private act.

122. The parole applies chiefly to prisoners of war whom the captor allows to return to their country, or to live in greater freedom within the captor's country or territory, on conditions stated in the parole.

123. Release of prisoners of war by exchange is the general rule; release by parole is the exception.

124. Breaking the parole is punished with death when the person breaking the parole is captured again.

Accurate lists, therefore, of the paroled persons must be kept by the belligerents.

125. When paroles are given and received, there must be an exchange of two written documents, in which the name and rank of the paroled individuals are accurately and truthfully stated.

126. Commissioned officers only are allowed to give their parole, and they can give it only with the permission of their superior, as long as a superior in rank is within reach.

127. No non-commissioned officer or private can give his parole except through an officer. Individual paroles not given through an officer are not only void, but subject the individual giving them to the punishment of death as deserters. The only admissible exception is where individuals, properly separated from their commands, have suffered long confinement without the possibility of being paroled through an officer.

128. No paroling on the battle-field, no paroling of entire bodies of troops after a battle, and no dismissal of large numbers of prisoners, with a general declaration that they are paroled, is permitted, or of any value.

129. In capitulations for the surrender of strong places or fortified camps, the commanding officer, in cases of urgent necessity, may agree that the troops under his command shall not fight again during the war, unless exchanged.

130. The usual pledge given in the parole is not to serve during the existing war, unless exchanged.

This pledge refers only to the active service in the field, against the paroling belligerent or his allies actively engaged in the same war. These cases of breaking the parole are patent acts, and can be visited with the punishment of death; but the pledge does not refer to internal service, such as recruiting or drilling the recruits, fortifying places not besieged, quelling civil commotions, fighting against belligerents unconnected with the paroling belligerents, or to civil or diplomatic service for which the paroled officer may be employed.

131. If the government does not approve of the parole, the paroled officer must return into captivity; and should the enemy refuse to receive him, he is free of his parole.

132. A belligerent government may declare, by a general order, whether it will allow paroling, and on what conditions it will allow it. Such order is communicated to the enemy.

133. No prisoner of war can be forced by the hostile government to parole himself, and no government is obliged to parole prisoners of war, or to parole all captured officers if it paroles any. As the pledging of the parole is an individual act, so is paroling, on the other hand, an act of choice on the part of the belligerent.

134. The commander of an occupying army may require of the civil officers of the enemy, and of its citizens, any pledge he may consider necessary for the safety or security of his army; and upon their failure to give it, he may arrest, confine, or detain them.

SECTION VIII.

Armistice—Capitulation.

135. An armistice is the cessation of active hostilities for a period agreed between belligerents. It must be agreed upon in writing, and duly ratified by the highest authorities of the contending parties.

136. If an armistice be declared, without conditions, it extends no further than to require a total cessation of hostilities along the front of both belligerents.

If conditions be agreed upon, they should be clearly expressed, and must be rigidly adhered to by both parties. If either party violates any express condition, the armistice may be declared null and void by the other.

137. An armistice may be general, and valid for all points and lines of the belligerents; or special—that is, referring to certain troops or certain localities only.

An armistice may be concluded for a definite time; or for an indefinite time, during which either belligerent may resume hostilities on giving the notice agreed upon to the other.

138. The motives which induce the one or the other belligerent to conclude an armistice, whether it be expected to be preliminary to a treaty of peace, or to prepare during the armistice for a more vigorous prosecution of the war, do in no way affect the character of the armistice itself.

139. An armistice is binding upon the belligerents from the day of the agreed commencement; but the officers of the armies are responsible from the day only when they receive official information of its existence.

140. Commanding officers have the right to conclude armistices binding on the district over which their command extends; but such armistice is subject to the ratification of the superior authority, and ceases so soon as it is made known to the enemy that the armistice is not ratified, even if a certain time for the elapsing between giving notice of cessation and the resumption of hostilities should have been stipulated for.

141. It is incumbent upon the contracting parties of an armistice to stipulate what intercourse of persons or traffic between the inhabitants of the territories occupied by the hostile armies shall be allowed, if any.

If nothing is stipulated, the intercourse remains suspended, as during actual hostilities.

142. An armistice is not a partial or a temporary peace; it is only the suspension of military operations to the extent agreed upon by the parties.

143. When an armistice is concluded between a fortified place and the army besieging it, it is agreed by all the authorities on this subject that the besieger must cease all extension, perfection, or advance of his attacking works, as much so as from attacks by main force.

But as there is a difference of opinion among martial jurists, whether the besieged have the right to repair breaches or to erect new works of defence within the place during an armistice, this point should be determined by express agreement between the parties.

144. So soon as a capitulation is signed, the capitulator has no right to demolish, destroy, or injure the works, arms, stores, or ammunition, in his possession, during the time which elapses between the signing and the execution of the capitulation, unless otherwise stipulated in the same.

145. When an armistice is clearly broken by one of the parties, the other party is released from all obligation to observe it.

146. Prisoners, taken in the act of breaking an armistice, must be treated as prisoners of war, the officer alone being responsible who gives the order for such a violation of an armistice. The highest authority of the belligerent aggrieved may demand redress for the infraction of an armistice.

147. Belligerents sometimes conclude an armistice while their plenipotentiaries are met to discuss the conditions of a treaty of peace; but plenipotentiaries may meet without a preliminary armistice; in the latter case, the war is carried on without any abatement.

SECTION IX.

Assassination.

148. The law of war does not allow proclaiming either an individual belonging to the hostile army, or a citizen, or a subject of the hostile government, an outlaw, who may be slain without trial by any captor, any more than the modern law of peace allows such international outlawry; on the contrary, it abhors such outrage. The sternest retaliation should follow the murder committed in consequence of such proclamation, made by whatever authority. Civilized nations look with horror upon offers of rewards for the assassination of enemies, as relapses into barbarism.

SECTION X.

Insurrection—Civil war—Rebellion.

149. Insurrection is the rising of people in arms against their government, or a portion of it, or against one or more of its laws, or against an officer or officers of the government. It may be confined to mere armed resistance, or it may have greater ends in view.

150. Civil war is war between two or more portions of a country or state, each contending for the mastery of the whole, and each claiming to be the legitimate government. The term is also sometimes applied to war of rebellion, when the rebellious provinces or portions of the state are contiguous to those containing the seat of government.

151. The term *rebellion* is applied to an insurrection of large extent, and is usually a war between the legitimate government of a country and portions or provinces of the same who seek to throw off their allegiance to it, and set up a government of their own.

152. When humanity induces the adoption of the rules of regular war toward rebels, whether the adoption is partial or entire, it does in no way whatever imply a partial or complete acknowledgment of their government, if they have set up one, or of them, as an independent or sovereign power. Neutrals have no right to make the adoption of the rules of war by the assailed government toward rebels the ground of their own acknowledgment of the revolted people as an independent power.

153. Treating captured rebels as prisoners of war, exchanging them, concluding of cartels, capitulations, or other warlike agreements with them; addressing officers of a rebel army by the rank they may have in the same; accepting flags of truce; or, on the other hand, proclaiming martial law in their territory, or levying war-taxes or forced loans, or doing any other act sanctioned or demanded by the law and usages of public war between sovereign belligerents, neither proves nor establishes an acknowledgment of the rebellious people, or of the government which they may have erected, as a public or sovereign power. Nor does the adoption of the rules of war toward rebels imply an engagement with them extending beyond the limits of these rules. It is victory in the field that ends the strife, and settles the future relations between the contending parties.

154. Treating, in the field, the rebellious enemy according to the law and usages of war, has never prevented the legitimate government from trying the leaders of the rebellion or chief rebels for high treason, and from treating them accordingly, unless they are included in a general amnesty.

155. All enemies in regular war are divided into two general classes; that is to say, into combatants and non-combatants, or unarmed citizens of the hostile government.

The military commander of the legitimate government, in a war of rebellion, distinguishes between the loyal citizen in the revolted portion of the country and the disloyal citizen. The disloyal citizens may further be classified into those citizens known to sympathize with the rebellion, without positively aiding it, and those who, without taking up arms, give positive aid and comfort to the rebellious enemy, without being bodily forced thereto.

156. Common justice and plain expediency require that the military commander protect the manifestly loyal citizens, in revolted territories, against the hardships of the war, as much as the common misfortune of all war admits.

The commander will throw the burden of the war, as much as lies within his power, on the disloyal citizens of the revolted portion or province, subjecting them to a stricter police than the non-combatant enemies have to suffer in regular war; and if he deems it appropriate, or if his government demands of him, that every citizen shall, by an oath of allegiance, or by some other manifest act, declare his fidelity to the legitimate government, he may expel, transfer, imprison, or fine the revolted citizens who refuse to pledge themselves anew as citizens obedient to the law, and loyal to the government.

Whether it is expedient to do so, and whether reliance can be placed upon such oaths, the commander or his government have the right to decide.

157. Armed or unarmed resistance by citizens of the United States against the lawful movements of their troops, is levying war against the United States, and is therefore treason.

Acknowledgments

------ ⋙ ◦ ⋘ ------

I T'S A GOOD thing for me that the law now discourages the use of armed force to collect unpaid debts, because in the course of writing this book I've amassed intellectual indebtedness on which I cannot imagine I'll ever be able to make good.

Two law school deans—Robert Post at Yale and David Schizer at Columbia—provided research support for a project that must sometimes have seemed unlikely ever to come to fruition. A fellowship from the John Simon Guggenheim Memorial Foundation in 2010–2011 gave me much-needed time to bring the book toward completion.

Collegial groups at law schools around the country read early drafts of parts of the book and provided invaluable feedback on the stories and arguments therein. At Columbia, George Fletcher and Lori Damrosch put together a workshop in 2007 in which I first rehearsed some of the ideas that gave shape to the project; almost five years later, Sarah Cleveland hosted another session at Columbia where I was able to hone some of the fine points as the book came together. Bernadette Meyler and the Cornell Law School Humanities Workshop helped me think more clearly about chapter 3. I'm grateful to the Harvard International Law Workshop, where Bill Alford and Ryan Goodman presided over a session on an early version of chapter 1. The Harvard Legal History Workshop, ably led by Jed Shugerman, read and commented on a version of chapters 7 and 8. Dan Hulsebosch, Bill Nelson, and John Reid hosted me with their usual aplomb at the NYU Golieb Legal History Colloquium and led me to substantially revise much of the material in chapter 2. David Golove and Rick Pildes at the NYU Public Law Colloquium did the same for chunks of Part I. Keith Whittington, Paul Frymer, Dirk Hartog, and the Princeton Public Law Workshop sharpened a number of the arguments of Part II. Bob Gordon and the Stanford Law School Legal History Workshop helped me think through much of the last part of the book. Barbara Fried, Dan Ho, Jenny Martinez, and the Stanford Legal Theory seminar pressed me on some of the hardest questions in chapter 8.

Chris Tomlins brought his characteristically sharp eye to a presentation on the book at the University of California at Irvine. Alison LaCroix hosted an afternoon session at the University of Chicago, where she, Adam Cox, Jake Gersen, Eric Posner, and others were terrific interlocutors. Steven Wilf gave me the opportunity to share some of the book's ideas at the University of Connecticut. Martha Jones and Rebecca Scott presided over an invaluable session at the University of Michigan that helped me impove the arguments in chapter 3. Bill Eskridge and Paul Gewirtz convened a session of the Yale Law School Faculty Workshop that hashed out some of the tricky puzzles of chapter 4.

The generosity of David Jones and the Yale Law School Class of 1960 made possible an inaugural lecture in which I presented some of the material on Lincoln and Lieber for the first time. Many thanks to the Duffy family— Lucy, Daniel, Sam, and Tim—for being a part of that occasion, which was held in honor of the late Allen Duffy. In Los Angeles, Gregory Rodriguez and the folks at Zócalo Public Square assembled a convivial audience to talk about the Mexican-American War of 1846–48. Many thanks to Bill Deverell and the Huntington-USC Institute on California and the West for arranging the Zócalo event, and to Bill and the Huntington Library's Jenny Watts for their magnificent hospitality. In Washington, the American Society of International Law and the American Red Cross hosted a stimulating session on the laws of war in the Civil War where Isabelle Daoust of the Red Cross, Dick Jackson of the Department of Defense, and Gary Solis of American University served as collegial fellow panelists for the day. Adam Tooze and Patrick Cohrs of the Yale History Department arranged a stimulating one-day session on war in the Atlantic world and graciously let me present material from chapters 9 and 11. A 2008 conference at Columbia University sponsored by Mark Mazower and the Center for International History allowed me to work out an early version of some of the ideas advanced here; many thanks to Philip Bobbitt, Sir Michael Howard, Jan-Werner Muller, W. Hays Parks, and Anders Stephanson for participating.

I have been fortunate to have the benefit of comments on parts of the manuscript from many friends and colleagues, including Bruce Ackerman, Mike Agger, Akhil Amar, Richard Bernstein, David Blight, Christina Burnett, Bo Burt, Chris Capozzola, Stephen Carter, David Brion Davis, Ariela Dubler, Noah Feldman, Willy Forbath, Charles Fried, Heather Gerken, David Glazier, Annette Gordon-Reed, Oona Hathaway, Isabel Hull, Paul Kahn, Marty Lederman, Tom Lee, Yair Listokin, Peter Maas, Trevor Morrison, Sam Moyn, Jens Ohlin, Nick Parrillo, Aziz Rana, Peter Reich, Judith Resnik, Jed Rubenfeld, Peter Schuck, Scott Shapiro, Mark Shulman, Ganesh

Sitaraman, Skip Stout, Adam Tooze, Matt Waxman, and Jim Whitman. I taught seminars on the history of the laws of war with Oona Hathaway, Sam Moyn, Jim Whitman; I am grateful to all three of them and to our students. Lori Damrosch generously sent along a Lieber letter from the University of South Carolina's Irvin Department of Rare Books and Special Collections. My one-time neighbor Jim Oakes of the City University of New York graciously shared an early draft of his terrific next book and offered incisive comments that significantly sharpened mine.

In the final months of completing the book, Burrus Carnahan, Gene Fidell, Jack Goldsmith, Dan Hulsebosch, Andrew Kent, Harold Koh, Craig Symonds, and Detlev Vagts each read and commented at length on the entire manuscript, for which I am eternally grateful.

A great number of superb librarians and archivists have helped me with one or another stage of the project. Kent McKeever at the Diamond Law Library at Columbia got me off to a flying start. Olga Tsapina at the Huntington Library helped me work with the library's Lieber materials. Roberta W. Goldblatt at the Library of Congress's Federal Research Division took time out from her busy schedule to give me access to the only partially cataloged collection of Lieber materials inherited by G. Norman Lieber and held on loan from the Judge Advocate General's Legal Center and School in Charlottesville, Virginia. A small army of manuscript specialists helped locate particularly valuable letters and other obscure items, including Nann J. Card at the Rutherford B. Hayes Presidential Center in Fremont, Ohio; Mary Person at the Harvard Law School Library; Michelle Gachette at the Harvard University Archives; Paul Harrison in the Archives Reference Section of the National Archives and Records Administration; and archivists at the Massachusetts Historical Society. Tom Lowry at the Index Project provided data from his massive database of Civil War courts-martial, a subset of which I was able to crosscheck. The reference librarian staff at the National Archives in Washington, D.C., is a constant reminder of what wondrous things a professional civil service is able to accomplish. At late stages in the process, James Tobias at the Historical Resources Branch of the U.S. Army Center of Military History and Dr. Andrew J. Birtle offered considerate responses to an out-of-the-blue inquiry, as did Shannon S. Schwaller of the U.S. Army Heritage and Education Center in Carlisle.

The Lillian Goldman Library at Yale Law School is one of the wonders of the known world. Blair Kauffman oversees a staff of indefatigable and super-smart librarians who tracked down endless leads (and often generated new leads all by themselves) in the search for materials for the book. I am especially grateful to John Nann for reference help and to Sarah Kraus and

Richard Hasbany for their good cheer and astounding speed. Fred Shapiro tracked down obscure quotations with the skill for which he is renowned.

I was also fortunate to have the benefit of heroic research assistants and students. At Columbia, Sameer Bajaj, John Eichlin, Gideon Hart, Dodi-Lee Hecht, Maeve Herbert, Matthew Podolsky, and Kamal Sidhu made the project their own for a time. (Gideon and Maeve published excellent scholarship of their own on the basis of research that began with what they did for me and then went far beyond.) At Yale, Kathryn Cahoy, Kellen Funk, Jeff Lingwall, and Dana Montalto put in more hours than I thought possible, and the book is better for it; Alyssa Briody, Marissa Doran, Adam Hockensmith, Gina Cabarcas Maciá, William Moon, David Rojas, and David Simons also helped collect and digest numerous sources. I am thankful for all their work, though they (like all those thanked here) are not responsible for any of the conclusions I reached or any errors I may have made.

With her usual good spirit, Alieta-Marie Lynch did yeoman's labor preparing the bibliography for the book (available on-line at the Yale Law School Library) and helping acquire images and permissions.

My agent, Andrew Wylie, has been unstintingly encouraging since the book's inception. Even better, he shared crucial Wylie family history relating to the assassination of Abraham Lincoln. Emily Loose at Free Press is as sympathetic an editor as I could possibly have hoped for; at every stage of the process, she understood exactly what the book was about. Thanks to her assistant Chloe Perkins, too, for excellent assistance in the final stages of the book's production, and to Ann Adelman for superb copyediting.

John C. Crowe, my great-great-grandfather, served in the Civil War as a drummer in the 74th New York Infantry and the 40th New York Infantry. While many of his neighbors and relatives in the Five Points neighborhood of New York City were protesting the draft and voting against Lincoln in the 1864 presidential election, he signed up to serve again when his three-year term expired. A little more than a century later, and under radically different circumstances, my father served as a conscientious objector during the Vietnam War. Each in his own way thought long and hard about justice in wartime.

Thanks most of all to my boys Gus and Teddy, for enthusiastically joining dinner table conversations about long-ago events, and to the incomparable Annie Murphy Paul, for being the ideal partner in all things big and small.

John Fabian Witt
New Haven, Connecticut
May 2012

Abbreviations Used in the Notes

LC   Library of Congress, Washington, DC

Malloy   William M. Malloy, ed., *Treaties, Conventions, International Acts, Protocols, and Agreements, 1776–1909* (Washington, DC: Government Printing Office, 1910), 2 vols.

Miller   Hunter Miller, ed., *Treaties and Other International Acts of the United States of America* (Washington, DC: Government Printing Office, 1931–48), 8 vols.

NARA   National Archives and Records Administration, Washington, DC

NYHS   New-York Historical Society Library, New York, NY

OR   *War of the Rebellion: A Compilation of the Official Records of the Union and Confederate Armies* (Washington, DC: Government Printing Office, 1880–1901), 70 vols.

ORN   *Official Records of the Union and Confederate Navies in the War of the Rebellion* (Washington, DC: Government Printing Office, 1894–1922), 30 vols.

PAH   Harold C. Syrett et al., eds., *The Papers of Alexander Hamilton* (New York: Columbia University Press, 1961–87), 27 vols.

PAJ   Sam B. Smith et al., eds., *The Papers of Andrew Jackson* (Knoxville, TN: University of Tennessee Press, 1980–2007), 8 vols.

PBF   Leonard W. Laboree et al., eds., *The Papers of Benjamin Franklin* (New Haven, CT: Yale University Press, 1957–), 40 vols.

PDW   Charles M. Wiltse, ed., *Papers of Daniel Webster* (Hanover, NH: University Press of New England, 1974–89), 14 vols.

PEMS   Papers of Edwin M. Stanton, Library of Congress, Washington, DC

PGW   W. W. Abbot et al., eds., *The Papers of George Washington* (Charlottesville, VA: University of Virginia Press, 1983–)

Pitman   *The Assassination of President Lincoln and the Trial of the Conspirators*, comp. & arr. Benn Pitman (New York: Moore, Wilstach & Baldwin, 1865)

PTJ   Julian P. Boyd et al., eds., *The Papers of Thomas Jefferson* (Princeton, NJ: Princeton University Press, 1950–), 37 vols.

Richardson   James D. Richardson, ed., *A Compilation of the Messages and Papers of the Presidents, 1789–1897* (Washington, DC: Government Printing Office, 1896–1899), 10 vols.

Stat.   *United States Statutes at Large* (Boston & Washington, DC, 1848–), 122 vols.

WGW   John C. Fitzpatrick, ed., *The Writings of George Washington: From the Original Manuscript Sources, 1745–1799* (Washington, DC: Government Printing Office, 1931–44), 39 vols.

Notes

A full bibliography of the sources used in writing this book
appears at the website of the Yale Law School Library.
See http://documents.law.yale.edu/lincolns-code.

Prologue

1 *Christmas Day:* Matilda Lieber to FL, December 24, 1862, box 34, FLP HL; FL to
Henry Halleck, December 16, 1862, box 27 FLP HL; FL to Matilda Lieber, December 18, 19, 20, 22, 24, 26, and 27, 1862, all in box 36, FLP HL; Photograph of Francis
Lieber, Columbia College Class of 1862 Album, Columbia University Archives, New
York, NY.

1 *At the request of:* FL to Halleck, December 7, 1862, & December 9, 1862, box 27, FLP
HL; FL to Benson J. Lossing, January 21, 1866, book 2, FLP LOC; Matthew J. Mancini, "Francis Lieber, Slavery, and the 'Genesis' of the Laws of War," *Journal of Southern
History* 77, no. 2 (May 2011): 325–48.

2 *President Lincoln will issue:* OR, 2: 5, 671.

2 *will soon cross the Atlantic:* G. I. A. D. Draper, "Implementation of International Law
in Armed Conflicts," *International Affairs* 48 (1972): 55; Peter Holquist, The Russian
Empire as a "Civilized State": International Law as Principle and Practice in Imperial
Russia, 1874–1878, The National Council for Eurasian and East European Research,
Washington, DC, 2006.

3 *"hard hand of war":* WTS to Henry Halleck, December 24, 1864, in Brooks D. Simpson & Jean V. Berlin, eds., *Sherman's Civil War: Selected Correspondence of William T.
Sherman, 1860–1865* (Chapel Hill: University of North Carolina Press, 1999), 776.

3 *more aggressive, not less:* Mark Grimsley, *The Hard Hand of War: Union Military Policy Toward Southern Civilians, 1861–1865* (New York: Cambridge University Press,
1995).

3 *"simpering sentimentalist":* FL to Charles Sumner, n.d. [January 1865?], LI 3763, box
45, FLP HL.

3–4 *His hero . . . Clausewitz:* Lieber, *Manual of Political Ethics*, 2: 631.

4 *urged blow after blow:* FL to Charles Sumner, January 20, 1865, box 45, FLP HL
("strike, strike and strike again").

4 *"The more vigorously wars": Instructions*, art. 29.

4 *civilian property:* Ibid., art. 15 & 38.

4 *forced return of civilians:* Ibid., art. 18.

4 *starving of noncombatants:* Ibid., art. 17.

4 *enemy guerrillas:* Ibid., art. 82.

4 *"To save the country":* Ibid., art. 5.

4 *"unrelenting and vindictive":* James A. Seddon to Robert Ould, June 24, 1863, OR, 2: 6,
46.

4 *"license for a man":* Robert Ould to Lt. Col. William Ludlow, June 5, 1863, OR, 2: 5,
744.

4   *Davis condemned the code . . . military necessity:* Davis's annual message to the Confederate Congress, December 7, 1863, *OR*, 4: 2, 1047–48.

4   *"securing the ends of the war": Instructions,* art. 14.

5   *a long American tradition of respect:* Good examples of this story in trade books include Jane Mayer, *The Dark Side: The Inside Story of How the War on Terror Turned into a War on American Ideals* (New York: Doubleday, 2008); Philippe Sands, *Torture Team: Rumsfeld's Memo and the Betrayal of American Values* (New York: Palgrave, 2008). Among historians, see Edwin Burrows, *Forgotten Patriots: The Untold Story of American Prisoners During the Revolutionary War* (New York: Basic Books, 2008); David Hackett Fischer, *Washington's Crossing* (New York: Oxford University Press, 2004); and Louis Fisher, *American Military Tribunals and Presidential Power: American Revolution to the War on Terrorism* (Lawrence: University of Kansas Press, 2005). For lawyers, see David Glazier, "Playing by the Rules: Combating Al Qaeda Within the Laws of War," *William & Mary Quarterly* 51 (2009): 980–82; and Jordan J. Paust, "In Their Own Words: Affirmations of the Founders, Framers, and Early Judiciary Concerning the Binding Nature of the Customary Law of Nations," *University of California Davis Journal of International Law & Policy* 14 (2008): 209. In journalism, see the editorial board of the *New York Times:* "Terrorism and the Law," July 17, 2011. In the political arena, see *Congressional Record,* vol. 150, pp. 12128–29 (2004) (comments of Senator Durbin).

5   *in historians' briefs:* Brief of Military Law Historians, Scholars, and Practitioners, *Hamdan v. Rumsfeld,* U.S. Supreme Court, No. 05–184 (2006).

5   *Supreme Court's cautious holdings: Hamdan v. Rumsfeld,* 548 U.S. 557, 595–98 (2006).

5   *international law has taken on:* Preeminent here is Jack Goldsmith, *The Terror Presidency: Law and Judgment Inside the Bush Administration* (New York: W. W. Norton Co., 2007). See also Samuel Moyn, "From Antiwar Politics to Antitorture Politics," Columbia University Working Paper, November 2011, available at http://papers.ssrn.com/sol3/papers.cfm?abstract_id=1966231. A variation of this view insists that even if there were older forms of international law, they are now "quaint" and impose newly impossible constraints on American statesmen and soldiers. See George Bush, "Memorandum for the Vice President," in Karen J. Greenberg & Joshua L. Dratel, eds., *The Torture Papers: The Road to Abu Ghraib* (New York: Cambridge University Press, 2006), 134.

6   *Making better sense of American history:* For a provocative recent example of the kind of history that goes beyond the mythmaking, see William Ranney Levi, "Interrogation's Law," *Yale Law Journal* 118 (2009): 1434, 1462–83.

6   *Carl Schmitt . . . thoroughly disingenuous:* Carl Schmitt, *The Nomos of the Earth in the International Law of Jus Publicum Europaeum* (New York: Telos, 2006); Jan-Werner Muller, *A Dangerous Mind* (New Haven, CT: Yale University Press, 2003), 26.

6   *to advance the authority of the world's:* See, e.g., Harold Pinter's 2005 Nobel Prize acceptance speech, available at http://nobelprize.org/nobel_prizes/literature/laureates/2005/pinter-lecture-e.html. See also Chris Jochnick & Roger Normand, "The Legitimation of Violence: Critical History of the Laws of War," *Harvard International Law Journal* 35 (1994): 49.

6   *Hawks in the United States and Israel:* Douglas J. Feith, "Law in the Service of Terror—The Strange Case of the Additional Protocol," *The National Interest* 1 (Fall 1985): 36–47.

7   *Hypocrisy . . . the tribute vice:* Michael Walzer, *Just and Unjust Wars* (New York: Basic Books, 1977), xxi.

7   *the conviction that their cause is right:* I will take up this problem in more detail in chapter 1; see also James Turner Johnson, *Ideology, Reason, and the Limitation of War: Religious and Secular Concepts, 1200–1740* (Princeton, NJ: Princeton University Press, 1975).

8   *almost half the defense spending:* Phillip Bobbitt, *Terror and Consent: The Wars for the Twenty-first Century* (New York: Alfred A. Knopf, 2008), 135; Stephen L. Carter, *The Violence of Peace: America's Wars in the Age of Obama* (New York: Beast Books, 2011), ix.

Part I You Have Brought Me into Hell!

11   *Epigraph:* Benjamin Franklin to Joseph Priestley, *PBF*, 37: 445.

Chapter 1. The Rights of Humanity

13   *The authorized maxims:* Alexander Hamilton to Col. John Laurens, October 11, 1780, in *PAH*, 2: 460, 467–68.

13   *went once again into the woods:* For a longer account of the episode, see Fred Anderson, *Crucible of War: The Seven Years War and the Fate of Empire in British North America, 1754–1766* (New York: Alfred A. Knopf, 2000), 50–59.

13   *In his official report:* GW to Robert Dinwiddie, May 29, 1754, in *PGW, Colonial Series*, 1: 107, 110–11.

13   *According to the French:* GW to Robert Dinwiddie, May 29, 1754, in ibid., 1: 116–17; Editorial Note, in *PGW, Diaries*, 1: 162–73.

14   *"You are not yet dead":* Richard White, *The Middle Ground: Indians, Empires, and Republics in the Great Lakes Region, 1650–1815* (New York: Cambridge University Press, 1991), 240–41.

14   *Fort Necessity:* Account by George Washington and James Mackay of the Capitulation of Fort Necessity, July 19, 1754, *PGW, Colonial Series*, 1: 159ff.

14   *an "assassination":* Articles of Capitulation, July 3, 1754, in ibid., 1: 165–68.

14   *He would blame:* GW to unknown, 1757, in ibid., 1: 168–72.

14   *Washington's diary . . . published: Mémoire Contenant le Précis des Faits avec Leurs Pieces Justificatives, Pour Servir de Réponse aux Observations Envoyés par les Ministres d'Angleterre, dans les Cours de l'Europe* (Paris: L'Imprimerie Royale, 1756). The French version of the diary circulated widely enough that Jefferson owned a copy in his library—see Sowerby, *Catalogue of the Library of Thomas Jefferson*, vol. 2, pp. 67, 86 (LC, 1952).

14   *"There is nothing more unworthy":* Duquesne to Contrecoeur, September 8, 1754, in *PGW, Colonial Series*, vol. 1, pp. 172–73.

14   *his long and storied career:* I have been influenced by Ron Chernow, *Washington: A Life* (New York: Penguin, 2010), and Joseph Ellis, *His Excellency: George Washington* (New York: Alfred A. Knopf, 2004).

15   *"plundered our Seas" . . . "an undistinguished Destruction":* Declaration of Independence, http://www.archives.gov/exhibits/charters/declaration_transcript.html.

15   *"You are to regulate": JCC*, 2: 96. In so instructing Washington, Congress undoubtedly intended for him to follow the Articles of War that it had just enacted. But those Articles picked up some features of the international laws of war. Moreover, if the Congress had wanted to limit the legal constraints on Washington to those Articles and exclude the international laws of war, it could easily have done so by limiting its instructions to the Articles.

15   *denouncing General Thomas Gage: JCC*, 2: 152 (July 6, 1775).

15   *"the happiness of modern times" . . . "in arms and in the field": JCC*, 4: 22 (Jan. 2, 1776).

15–16   *"execrable barbarity" . . . "Christianity may condemn": JCC*, 4: 21.

16   *exhausted and depopulated:* See, e.g., Peter H. Wilson, *The Thirty Years War: Europe's Tragedy* (Cambridge, MA: Harvard University Press, 2009); Geoffrey Parker, "Early Modern Europe," in Michael Howard, George J. Andreopulos, and Mark R. Shulman, eds., *The Laws of War* (New Haven, CT: Yale University Press, 1994), 53–55.

16   *elaborate (if deadly) games:* Michael Howard, *War in European History* (New York: Oxford University Press, 1976), 56–73; John Keegan, *A History of Warfare* (New York: Alfred A. Knopf, 1993), 342–45; Armstrong Starkey, *War in the Age of Enlightenment* (Westport, CT: Praeger, 2003).

16   *analogized war to chess:* Benjamin Franklin, *Franklin: The Autobiography and Other Writings on Politics, Economics, and Virtue*, ed. Alan Houston (1747; New York: Cambridge University Press, 2004).

16   *the metaphor of the gamble:* Matthew Smith Anderson, *War and Society in Europe of the Old Regime* (Buffalo: McGill-Queen's University Press, 1988), 189; see also Geoffrey Best, *Humanity in Warfare* (New York: Columbia University Press, 1980), 36.

16   *fancied himself a poet:* Coleman Phillipson, "Emerich De Vattel," in *Great Jurists of the World,* ed. John & Edward Manson MacDonell (Boston: Little, Brown, 1914), 479.

16   *most widely read:* Francis Stephen Ruddy, *International Law in the Enlightenment: The Background of Emmerich de Vattel's* Le Droit des Gens (New York: Oceana, 1975), 281–307.

16   *"The humanity":* Emmerich de Vattel, *Law of Nations,* ed. Joseph Chitty (Philadelphia: T & J. W. Johnson & Co., 1883), bk 2, §140, at 348.

17   *"with great moderation" . . . "extreme of politeness":* Ibid., bk 2, §158, at 363.

17   *St. Augustine:* Augustine, *Concerning the City of God Against the Pagans,* trans. Henry Bettenson (Harmondsworth, UK: Penguin Books, 1972), bk 1, ch. 21, & bk 19, chs. 7 & 12 (Bettenson trans., 1972); see also James Turner Johnson, *Ideology, Reason, and the Limitation of War: Religious and Secular Concepts, 1200–1740* (Princeton, NJ: Princeton University Press, 1975), 8–80; M. H. Keen, *The Laws of War in the Late Middle Ages* (Toronto: University of Toronto Press, 1965), 63–81; Stephen C. Neff, *War and the Law of Nations: A General History* (New York: Cambridge University Press, 2005).

17   *"A prince may do everything":* Francisco Vitoria, *Vitoria: Political Writings,* ed. Anthony Pagden & Jeremy Lawrance (New York: Cambridge University Press, 1991), 305.

17   *Such armies could lawfully:* Ibid., 317–18.

17   *sack entire cities:* Ibid., 322–23.

17   *to execute prisoners:* Ibid., 320–21.

17   *the grave passages of Deuteronomy:* See, esp., chap. 20, verses 12–20; also Vitoria, *Vitoria: Political Writings,* 316.

17–18   *"the first rule . . . on both sides"* and *"If people wish . . . return of peace":* Vattel, *Law of Nations,* bk 2, §189, 382.

18   *"quarter is to be given":* Ibid., bk 2, §140, 347–48.

18   *"Women, children":* Ibid., bk 2, §145, 351.

18   *"and other persons":* Ibid., 2, §146, 351.

18   *"to fear from":* Ibid., bk 2, §147, 352.

18   *"treacherous murder":* Ibid., bk 2, §155, 360.

18   *Even firing on an enemy's headquarters:* Ibid., bk 2, §158–59, 362–64.

18   *"to prefer the gentlest methods":* Ibid., bk 2, §178, 373.

18   *chivalric codes:* See Keen, *Laws of War in the Late Middle Ages;* Matthew Strickland, *War and Chivalry* (Cambridge: Cambridge University Press, 1996).

18   *Vitoria reasoned:* Vitoria, *Vitoria: Political Writings,* 237.

18   *Hugo Grotius had responded:* Hugo Grotius, *The Rights of War and Peace,* ed. Richard Tuck (Indianapolis, IN: Liberty Fund, 2005), bk 3, ch. 10, §1–3, 1411–13.

19   *"civilized powers" . . . "horrors of war":* G. F. Von Martens, *The Law of Nations: Being the Science of National Law . . . Founded Upon the Treaties and Customs of Modern Nations in Europe 1788 and 1829,* trans. William Cobbett (London: William Cobbett, 1829, 4th ed.), ch. 3, §1, 284.

19   *"an unjust enemy" . . . "a vast graveyard":* Immanuel Kant, *Kant: Political Writings,* ed. Hans Reiss (Cambridge: Cambridge University Press, 1991), 96.

19   *the balance of power:* Neff, *War and the Law of Nations,* 114.

19   *changes in military technology:* Keegan, *History of Warfare,* 342.

19   *newly professionalizing armies:* Howard, *War in European History,* 70–73.

19   *victory in pitched battle:* James Q. Whitman, *The Verdict of Battle: The Law of Victory and the Making of Modern War* (Cambridge, MA: Harvard University Press, 2012).

19   *"civility and decent behaviour":* Ellis, *His Excellency: George Washington,* 9.

19   *"I have a Gallows near 40 feet high":* Ibid., 27.

20   *rigid insistence on contract terms:* Ibid., 46–47.

20   *"from the noblest of all Principles" . . . "the rights of humanity":* GW to Lt. Gen. Thomas Gage, August 11, 1775, *PGW, Rev. War Series,* 1: 289–91.

20   *sign a copy of rules:* General Orders, August 9, 1775, ibid., 1: 278–79; GW to John Hancock, September 21, 1775, ibid., 2: 24.

20 *"be abused":* Instructions to Col. Benedict Arnold, September 14, 1775, ibid., 1: 458–60.
20 *He forbade pillage:* Ibid., 7: 458 (Boston, March 13, 1776); 7: 126 (New York, Aug. 25, 1776).
20 *"any person whatsoever"* . . . *"infamous mercenary ravagers":* General Orders, January 1, 1777, ibid., 7: 499.
21 *not prisoners of war:* Catherine M. Prelinger, "Benjamin Franklin and the American Prisoners of War," *William & Mary Quarterly* (3d series) 32, no. 2 (April 1975): 263–67.
21 *High-profile prisoners:* David Duncan Wallace, *The Life of Henry Laurens* (New York: G. P. Putnam's Sons, 1915).
21 *Ethan Allen:* Ethan Allen, *A Narrative of Colonel Ethan Allen's Captivity* (Philadelphia: Robert Bell, 1779).
21 *that 8,500 . . . died in captivity:* John E. Ferling, *Almost a Miracle: The American Victory in the War of Independence* (New York: Oxford University Press, 2007), 428. Edwin G. Burrows's *Forgotten Patriots: The Untold Story of American Prisoners During the Revolutionary War* (New York: Basic Books, 2008) argues that the number of deaths was far higher than even this, but I am skeptical of his reasoning. See my review in the online magazine *Slate*, December 9, 2008, http://www.slate.com/articles/news_and_politics/history_lesson/2008/12/ye_olde_gitmo.single.html.
21 *The grim prison ships:* Burrows, *Forgotten Patriots*, 53–65; Larry G. Bowman, *Captive Americans: Prisoners During the American Revolution* (Athens: Ohio University Press, 1976), 40–42.
21 *The smallpox epidemic:* Elizabeth A. Fenn, *Pox Americana: The Great Smallpox Epidemic of 1775–82* (New York: Hill & Wang, 2001), pp. 120–21, 267; Bowman, *Captive Americans*, 42–49.
21 *logistical shortcomings:* Charles H. Metzger, *The Prisoner in the American Revolution* (Chicago: Loyola University Press, 1971); Bowman, *Captive Americans*, 49; Richard H. Amerman, "Treatment of American Prisoners During the American Revolution," *Proceedings of the New Jersey Historical Society* 78 (1960).
21 *French prisoners were treated:* Olive Anderson, "The Treatment of Prisoners of War in Britain During the American War for Independence," *Bulletin of the Institute for Historical Research* 28 (1955), 72; Bowman, *Captive Americans*, 53–54; Prelinger, "Benjamin Franklin and the American Prisoners of War," 268 n. 23.
21 *the same medical attention:* Bowman, *Captive Americans*, 20–21.
21 *jails, old sugar warehouses:* David L. Sterling, "American Prisoners of War in New York: A Report," *William & Mary Quarterly* (3d series) 13 (1956), 380; Larry G. Bowman, "Military Parolees on Long Island, 1777–1782," *Journal of Long Island History* 18 (1982): 22.
21 *British officers extended:* Bowman, "Military Parolees on Long Island."
21 *privates were released on parole:* Bowman, *Captive Americans*, 12.
21 *prisoners were exchanged:* Paul J. Springer, *America's Captives: Treatment of POWs from the Revolutionary War to the War on Terror* (Lawrence: University Press of Kansas, 2010), 18–25.
22 *"Painful as it may be":* GW to Lt. Gen. Thomas Gage, August 11, 1775, *PGW, Rev. War Series*, 1: 289–91.
22 *"the unworthy Example":* GW to Maj. Christopher French, September 26, 1775, ibid., 2: 47–48.
22 *"his Excellency would rather":* Stephen Moylan to William Watson, November 16, 1775, ibid., 2: 322–23.
22 *refused to grant quarter . . . "rage and fury":* Harold E. Selesky, "Colonial America," in Howard et al., eds., *The Laws of War*, 84.
22 *convicted 194 soldiers for plundering:* James C. Neagles, *Summer Soldiers: A Survey and Index of Revolutionary War Courts-Martial* (Salt Lake City: Ancestry Inc., 1996), 34.
22 *"motives of . . . humanity":* Betsy Knight, "Prisoner Exchange and Parole in the American Revolution," *William & Mary Quarterly* (3d series) 48 (1991): 209.
22 *the Congress undermined:* Larry G. Bowman, "The Pennsylvania Prisoner Exchange Conferences," *Pennsylvania History* 45 (July 1978): 257–69.

23   *"motives of policy"*: GW to the President of Congress, July 10, 1780, *WGW*, 19: 147–48.
23   *conspired to find trumped-up reasons*: William M. Dabney, *After Saratoga: The Story of the Convention Army* (Albuquerque, NM: University of New Mexico Press, 1954), 16–25; Janet Beroth, "The Convention of Saratoga," *New York State Historical Association Quarterly Journal* 8 (1927): 257.
23   *He returned to British lines*: Knight, "Prisoner Exchange and Parole," 100–01.
23   *He released vessels*: Reginald Stuart, *War and American Thought* (Kent, OH: Kent State University Press, 1982), 32.
23   *ordered the humane treatment*: Stephen Moylan to William Bartlett, December 10, 1775, *PGW, Rev. War Series*, 2: 521–22; GW to John Hancock, November 8, 1775, ibid., 2: 330–33; Instructions to Col. Benedict Arnold, September 14, 1775, ibid., 1: 458–60.
23   *"I shall hold myself"*: GW to Gov. William Livingston, May 6, 1782, *WGW*, 24: 226–27.
24   *"Mercy! Mercy!"*: Ferling, *Almost a Miracle*, ch. 14.
24   *took 543 prisoners*: Armstrong Starkey, "Paoli to Stony Point: Military Ethics and Weaponry During the American Revolution," *Journal of Military History* 58 (1994), 22.
24   *"generosity and clemency"*: Ibid., 23.
24   *"You have established"*: Ibid., 20.
24   *"a man of real merit"*: Alexander Hamilton to John Laurens, October 11, 1780, *PAH*, 2: 467; see Sarah Knott, "Sensibility and the American War for Independence," *American Historical Review* 109 (2004): 19–40.
24   *"modesty and gentleness"*: Richard D. Loewenberg, "A Letter on Major John André in Germany," *American Historical Review* 49 (1944): 261.
25   *truce flag plan*: Robert Hatch, *Major John André: A Gallant in Spy's Clothing* (Boston: Houghton Mifflin, 1986), 259–63; Winthrop Sargent, *The Life and Career of Major John André, Adjutant-General of the British Army in America* (New York: William Abbat, 1902), 400–10.
25   *condemned the use of spies*: Vattel, *Law of Nations*, bk 2, §179, 375.
25   *executed a number of British spies: Ex parte Quirin*, 317 U.S. 1, 42 n. 14 (1942); John Marshall, *The Life of George Washington* (Philadelphia: C. P. Wayne, 1805), 4: 403; see also Roger Kaplan, "The Hidden War: British Intelligence Operations During the American Revolution," *William & Mary Quarterly* (3d series) 47 (1990): 131 & n. 44; Louis Fisher, "Military Commissions: Problems of Authority and Practice," *Boston University International Law Journal* 24 (2006): 19.
25   *Board of General Officers*: John Evangelist Walsh, *The Execution of Major André* (New York: Palgrave / St. Martin's Press, 2001), 16–18; Detlev Vagts, "Military Commissions: A Concise History," *American Journal of International Law* 101 (January 2007): 35, 37.
25   *condemned him as a spy*: Sargent, *Life and Career*, 400, 410.
25   *appealed for mercy . . . men of sensibility*: Knott, "Sensibility and the American War for Independence."
25   *"practice and usage of war"*: *WGW*, 8: 473.
25   *"Never . . . did any man suffer death"*: Hamilton to Laurens, 9/1780, in *Minutes of a Court of Inquiry, upon the Case of Major John André, with Accompanying Documents, Published in 1780 by Order of Congress* (Albany, NY: J. Munsell, 1865), 55.
25   *"more unfortunate than criminal"*: *WGW*, 7: 241.
26   *Mason Weems*: Lewis Leary, *The Book-Peddling Parson: An Account of the Life and Works of Mason Locke Weems, Patriot, Pitchman, Author and Purveyor of Morality to the Citizenry of the Early United States of America* (Chapel Hill, NC: Algonquin Books, 1984).
26   *"humanity, of zeal, interest and of honor"*: See, e.g., General Orders, September 4, 1777 (Wilmington, DE), *PGW, Rev. War Series*, 11: 141–43. Two contemporary orderly books recorded the order as referring not merely to "interest but to real interest."
27   *"wanton Cruelty" . . . "all good men"*: GW to Maj. Gen. Adam Stephen, April 20, 1777, *PGW, Rev. War Series*, 9: 223. Washington commended to Stephen the confluence of "Humanity & Policy."
27   *"open the eyes"*: Fischer, *Washington's Crossing*, 276.

27 *"No fact can be clearer":* Paul H. Smith et al., eds., *Letters of Delegates to Congress, 1774–1789* (Washington, DC: Library of Congress), 9: 244.

27 *"the authorized maxims":* Alexander Hamilton to Col. John Laurens, October 11, 1780, in *PAH*, 2: 460, 467–68.

27 *"little favourable to"*. . . *"usages of nations": PGW, Presidential Series,* 6: 441 (1790).

28 *alleged British atrocities:* Jefferson's preamble for the June 1776 Virginia Constitution is worth quoting at length. He accused the king of imposing tyranny

> by plundering our seas, ravaging our coasts, burning our towns and destroying the lives of our people;

> by inciting insurrections of our fellow subjects with the allurements of forfeiture & confiscation;

> by prompting our negroes to rise in arms among us; those very negroes whom, by an inhuman use of his negative, he hath refused permission to exclude by law;

> by endeavoring to bring on the inhabitants of our frontiers the merciless Indian savages, whose known rule of warfare is an undistinguished destruction of all ages, sexes, & conditions of existence;

> by transporting at this time a large army of foreign mercenaries *to complete* the works of death, desolation & tyranny already begun with *circumstances* of cruelty & perfidy so unworthy the head of a civilized nation. . . .

See Draft Constitution for Virginia 1776, at http://avalon.law.yale.edu/18th_century/jeffcons.asp.

28 *quoted Grotius:* E.g., TJ to George Hammond, May 29, 1792, *PTJ*, 23: 541.

28 *references to the Swiss-born diplomat Vattel:* E.g., TJ to James Madison, April 28, 1793, ibid., 25: 691.

28 *between noon and 2 p.m.:* TJ to John Garland Jefferson, June 11, 1790, ibid., 16: 481.

28 *van Bynkershoek . . . Burlamaqui:* Sowerby, *Catalogue of the Library of Thomas Jefferson,* 2: 67ff.; J. J. Burlamaqui, *The Principles of Natural and Politic Law,* trans. Thomas Nugent (Philadelphia: H. C. Carey & I. Lea, 1823), 2: 191.

28 *"opened his doors to them":* Merrill D. Peterson, *Thomas Jefferson and the New Nation: A Biography* (New York: Oxford University Press, 1970), 164.

28 *"great cause"* . . . *"individual animosities":* Ibid., 165.

29 *"to mitigate the horrors"* . . . *"foes and neutrals":* TJ to Patrick Henry, March 27, 1779, *PTJ*, 2: 237, 242.

29 *"other ordinary vocations"* . . . *"did not exist":* TJ to Thomas Pinkney, September 7, 1793, ibid., 27: 55, 56.

29 *Dunmore . . . threatened to free the slaves:* Maya Jasanoff, *Liberty's Exiles: American Loyalists in the Revolutionary World* (New York: Alfred A. Knopf, 2011), 48–49; Sylvia R. Frey, *Water from the Rock* (Princeton, NJ: Princeton University Press, 1991), 55; Simon Schama, *Rough Crossings: Britain, the Slaves, and the American Revolution* (New York: Ecco, 2006), 67.

29 *"All indentured Servants":* [Proclamation, Nov. 7, 1775], By His Excellency the Right Honourable John Earl of Dunmore, Evans Early American Imprint no. 14592.

29 *expanded Dunmore's proclamation:* Frey, *Water from the Rock,* 113; Schama, *Rough Crossings,* 100.

29 *some 20,000 slaves . . . twenty-three of Jefferson's two hundred:* Cassandra Pybus, "Jefferson's Faulty Math: The Question of Slave Defections in the American Revolution," *William & Mary Quarterly* (3d series) 62, no. 2 (2005): 243, 246. Pybus's article is an important revision downward of earlier estimates that were closer to 100,000. See, e.g., Schama, *Rough Crossings,* 8.

29 *partisan war against their former masters:* Schama, *Rough Crossings,* 125.

30 *A passage in Vattel's:* Vattel, *Law of Nations,* bk 2, §209, 394.

30 *Grotius observed that:* Grotius, *Rights of War and Peace,* bk 3, ch. 15, 1510.

30 *"nothing else but the state of war continued":* Quoted in David Brion Davis, Introduction to *Arming Slaves: From Classical Times to the Modern Age*, ed. Christopher Leslie & Philip D. Morgan Brown (New Haven, CT: Yale University Press, 2006), 3.

30 *"domestic enemies": JCC*, 2: 153 (July 6, 1775).

30 *Grotius had done nothing:* Martine Julia van Ittersum, *Profit and Principle: Hugo Grotius, Natural Rights Theories and the Rise of Dutch Power in the East Indies* (Boston: Brill, 2006).

30 *slavery had been justified:* Montesquieu, *The Spirit of the Law*, trans. Anne M. Cohler, Basia Carolyn Miller, & Harold Samuel Stone (Cambridge: Cambridge University Press, 1989), 247.

30 *"right of making slaves":* William Blackstone, *Commentaries on the Laws of England* (1768; Chicago: University of Chicago Press, 1979), 1: 411.

31 *from execution to enslavement:* David Brion Davis, *The Problem of Slavery in Western Culture* (Ithaca, NY: Cornell University Press, 1966), 425.

31 *"He has waged cruel war"* . . . *"execrable commerce": PTJ*, 1: 426.

31 *These lines were soon cut:* Pauline Maier, *American Scripture* (New York: Alfred A. Knopf, 1997), 146.

31 *"to give them freedom": PTJ*, 13: 363–64 (emphasis mine).

32 *"The known rule of warfare":* TJ to William Phillips, July 22, 1779, ibid., 3: 46.

32 *"to force them to respect":* Vattel, *Law of Nations*, bk 2, §141, 348.

32 *"coolly and deliberately":* Ibid., bk 2, §151, 355.

32 *"themselves the scourges and horror":* Ibid., bk 1, §56, 156–57.

32 *The "end proposed":* TJ to George Rogers Clark, January 1, 1779 [1780 new style], *PTJ*, 3: 259.

33 *a cultured aristocrat:* John D. Barnhart, *Henry Hamilton and George Rogers Clark in the American Revolution with the Unpublished Journal of Lieut. Gov. Henry Hamilton* (Crawfordsville, IN: R. E. Banta, 1951), 11.

33 *"well shaped":* Ibid., 12.

33 *Portrait sketches:* Henry Hamilton Drawings of North American Scenes and Native Americans (MS Eng 509.2), Houghton Library, Harvard University. Amazingly, one can now pull up the sketches online from the Houghton Library at Harvard. See http://oasis.lib.harvard.edu/oasis/deliver/~hou00125.

33 *from as early as 1774:* Barnhart, *Henry Hamilton and George Rogers Clark*, 24.

33 *"take up the hatchet":* Ibid., 25–29.

33 *an "uncommon humanity":* Ibid., 30.

33 *"an alarm upon the frontiers":* Ibid., 29.

33 *"The Hair-Buyer":* Bernard W. Sheehan, "The Famous Hair Buyer General: Henry Hamilton, George Rogers Clark, and the American Indian," *Indiana Magazine of History* 79 (1983): 1–28.

34 *"expected shortly to see":* Barnhart, *Henry Hamilton and George Rogers Clark*, 189.

34 *"made a vow":* Milo M. Quaife, *The Capture of Old Vincennes* (New York: Columbia University Press, 1927), 200.

34 *a daring and brilliantly executed:* James Alton James, *The Life of George Rogers Clark* (Chicago: University of Chicago Press, 1928), 137–38.

34 *"I told him":* James Alton James, ed., "George Rogers Clark Papers, 1771–1781," *Illinois Historical Library Collections* 8 (1912): 144.

34 *"to perpetrate"* . . . *"rewards for scalps": PTJ*, 2: 293–94.

34–35 *"conduct of British officers"* . . . *"publick jail":* Ibid.

35 *"fit subjects to begin":* Peterson, *Thomas Jefferson and the New Nation*, 180.

35 *badly exaggerated:* See, e.g., the view of the editors of *The Papers of George Washington, PGW, Rev. War Series*, 4: 390 n. 4, whose view is shared by virtually every historian since Barnhart published Hamilton's journals in 1952.

35 *killed a dozen Cherokee:* TJ to GW, June 19, 1779, *PTJ*, 3: 6.

35 *"ravages and enormities"* . . . *next breath:* TJ to John Jay, June 19, 1779, ibid., 3: 5.

35 *"ripping up her Belly":* Richard White, *The Middle Ground: Indians, Empires, and Republics in the Great Lakes Region, 1650–1815* (New York: Cambridge University Press, 1991), 388.

36 *"A young chief"*: Ibid., 377.

36 *encouraged the use of Indian warriors:* Colin G. Calloway, *The American Revolution in Indian Country: Crisis and Diversity in Native American Communities* (New York: Cambridge University Press, 1995), 46.

36 *"strike no small terror"*: James H. O'Donnell III, *Southern Indians in the American Revolution* (Knoxville: University of Tennessee Press, 1973), 71.

36 *"to any overture of peace"* . . . *"inspire them"*: GW to Maj. Gen. John Sullivan, May 31, 1779, *PGW, Rev. War Series*, 20: 718.

36 *scalp-buying:* James Axtell & William C. Sturtevant, "The Unkindest Cut, or Who Invented Scalping," *William & Mary Quarterly* (3d series) 37, no. 3 (1980): 451, 470.

36 *Pennsylvania . . . South Carolina . . . Indian graves:* Calloway, *American Revolution in Indian Country*, 49.

36 *"lend my hand to":* Joseph Ellis, *American Sphinx: The Character of Thomas Jefferson* (New York: Alfred A. Knopf, 1996), 40.

36 *"hallowed ark":* Robert W. Tucker & David C. Hendrickson, *Empire of Liberty* (New York: Oxford University Press, 1990), 7.

36 *"Interested men":* William Phillips to TJ, July 5, 1779, *PTJ*, 3: 25.

37 *British prison guards retaliated:* TJ to GW, October 2, 1779, ibid., 3: 99.

37 *"to pervert this":* TJ to George Matthews, October 8, 1779, ibid., 3: 102; see also 3: 44–46, 86–87, 245–46.

37 *"hard necessity":* TJ to GW, October 8, 1779, ibid., 3: 104.

37 *"On more mature consideration":* GW to TJ, August 6, 1779, ibid., 3: 61.

37 *"competition in cruelty":* GW to TJ, November 23, 1779, ibid., 3: 198.

37 *removed Hamilton's iron fetters:* TJ to GW, October 1, 1779, ibid., 3: 96; TJ to William Phillips, October 2, 1779, 3: 97–98.

37 *upstairs room . . . near Richmond:* Qaife, *Capture of Old Vincennes*, 214–15.

37 *paroled to British lines: PTJ*, 3: 24, 46–47.

37 *was exchanged . . . passage back:* Qaife, *Capture of Old Vincennes*, 219.

37 *"The bleeding Continent":* Cyrus Griffin to TJ, July 13, 1779, *PTJ*, 3: 34.

38 *"with as much relentless Fury":* John S. Pancake, *This Destructive War: The British Campaign in the Carolinas, 1780–1782* (Tuscaloosa: University of Alabama Press, 1985), 73.

38 *rumored to deny quarter:* Russell F. Weigley, *The Partisan War: The South Carolina Campaign of 1780–1782* (Columbia: University of South Carolina Press, 1970), 7.

38 *Benedict Arnold:* Pancake, *This Destructive War*, 146–48.

38 *just missed capturing Jefferson:* John Richard Alden, *The South in the Revolution, 1763–1789* (Baton Rouge: Louisiana State University Press, 1957), 294.

38 *smallpox-infected slaves:* Schama, *Rough Crossings*, 117.

38 *Isaac Hayne:* Bowman, *Captive Americans*, 101–03.

38 *"upwards of one thousand houses":* O'Donnell, *Southern Indians*, 107.

38 *executed and scalped:* John Grenier, *The First Way of War: American War Making on the Frontier* (New York: Cambridge University Press, 2005), 161.

38 *mission town of Gnadenhutten:* Peter Silver, *Our Savage Neighbors: How Indian War Transformed Early America* (New York: W. W. Norton & Co., 2008), 265–74; Grenier, *First Way of War*, 161 & 161 n. 50.

38 *"uncommon degree of restraint":* Charles Royster, *Light-Horse Harry Lee and the Legacy of the American Revolution* (New York: Alfred A. Knopf, 1981), 19.

39 *to give no quarter . . . burning the soles:* Ibid., 36–37.

39 *"extraordinary acts of brutality":* Don Higginbotham, *The War of American Independence: Military Attitudes, Policies, and Practice, 1763–1789* (New York: Macmillan, 1971), 362.

39 *"hunted them down":* Ibid., 362.

39 *"the milk of human kindness":* Metzger, *Prisoner in the American Revolution*, 185; see also pp. 161–62, 184.

39 *Simsbury copper mines:* Ibid., 185.

39 *widespread retaliation: JCC*, 21: 1017–18.

40 *"barbarity with which"* . . . *"humanity could suffer":* Irving Brant, *James Madison the Nationalist, 1780–1787* (Indianapolis, IN: Bobbs-Merrill, 1948), 159.

40 *"defenceless towns": JCC,* 21: 977.

40 *"strictly charge" . . . "to ashes":* Ibid., 21: 977–78.

40 *"to that God who searches" . . . "consigned to the flames":* Ibid., 21: 1017–18.

40–41 *"objects of our vengeance" . . . "put to instant death":* Ibid., 21: 1029–30.

41 *"the cause of heaven against hell":* Nathan O. Hatch, *The Sacred Cause of Liberty: Republican Thought and the Millennium in Revolutionary New England* (New Haven, CT: Yale University Press, 1977), 61.

41 *"the hand of God":* Benjamin Trumbull, Sermon, December 14, 1775, Benjamin Trumbull Papers, Manuscripts and Archives, Sterling Memorial Library, Yale University.

41 *"If this war be just":* Reginald Stuart, *War and American Thought: From the Revolution to the Monroe Doctrine* (Kent, OH: Kent State University Press, 1982), 23.

41 *"obedience to God" . . . "a cause of greater worth":* Merrill D. Peterson, *Thomas Jefferson and the New Nation: A Biography* (New York: Oxford University Press, 1970), 98 (quoting Franklin and Jefferson's 1782 motto for the republic and Thomas Paine, respectively).

42 *revolutionary millennialism broke out:* Ruth Bloch, *Visionary Republic: Millennial Themes in American Thought, 1756–1800* (New York: Cambridge University Press, 1985), 60.

42 *The violence of 1745:* Bruce Lenman, *The Jacobite Risings in Britain 1689–1746* (London: Eyre Methuen, 1980), 231–59.

42 *most midlevel British officers:* Stephen Conway, "British Army Officers and the Conduct of the Revolutionary War," *William & Mary Quarterly* (3rd series) 43 (1986): 400–07.

43 *"Oh God!":* Higginbotham, *War of American Independence,* 383.

43 *"according to the custom and usage of war":* 22 Geo 3, c. 10, p. 155 (March 25, 1782).

43 *"there hardly ever existed":* Gerald Stourzh, *Benjamin Franklin and American Foreign Policy* (Chicago: University of Chicago Press, 1969), 186.

43–44 *"very badly constructed" . . . "ashamed of a virtuous Action":* BF to Joseph Priestley, June 7, 1782, *PBF,* 37: 444.

44 *passed the book around:* Francis Wharton, ed., *The Revolutionary Diplomatic Correspondence of the United States* (Washington, DC: Government Printing Office, 1889), 2: 64.

44 *"for the interest of humanity":* Franklin's Thoughts on Privateering and the Sugar Islands: Two Essays, *PBF,* 37: 618.

44 *"Motives of general humanity":* BF to David Hartley, May 4, 1779, *PBF,* 29: 425.

44 *"since the foolish part of mankind":* Stourzh, *Benjamin Franklin and American Foreign Policy,* 186.

44 *the "plan of treaties":* Samuel Flagg Bemis, *The Diplomacy of the American Revolution* (New York: American Historical Association, 1935), 45.

44 *"the Ben Franklin program":* Best, *Humanity in Warfare,* 98.

44 *model treaty: JCC,* 5: 768–79.

45 *Peace of Utrecht:* Bemis, *Diplomacy of the American Revolution,* 46.

45 *adopted almost word for word:* Ibid., 61.

45 *"common benefit of mankind":* BF to Robert Morris, June 3, 1780, *PBF,* 32: 466–67.

45 *"farmers, fishermen & merchants":* BF to D. Wendorp & Thomas Hope Heylinger, June 8, 1781, ibid., 35: 134–35.

45 *"It is hardly necessary":* BF to Benjamin Vaughan, July 10, 1782, ibid., 37: 608, 610.

46 *"a few rich ships" . . . "even the undertakers":* Franklin's Thoughts on Privateering and the Sugar Islands, ibid., 37: 619.

46 *most respected Enlightenment sovereign . . . "age of Frederick":* Christopher Clark, *Iron Kingdom: The Rise and Downfall of Prussia* (Cambridge, MA: Belknap University Press, 2006), 252–53.

46 *a connection with Frederick:* Peterson, *Thomas Jefferson and the New Nation,* 306.

46 *"all women and children":* Malloy, 2: 1477, 1484.

46 *apparently inspired by Jefferson: PTJ,* 7: 476–78; see Burrus M. Carnahan, "Reason, Retaliation, and Rhetoric: Jefferson and the Quest for Humanity in War," *Military Law Review* 139 (1993): 83, 123–26.

46 *"a good Lesson to Mankind": PTJ,* 7: 465.

47 *The Netherlands and Sweden:* Malloy, 2: 1233, 1725.

47 *Morocco:* Ibid., 1: 1206.

47 *Great Britain:* Ibid., 1: 590, 605 (privilege of merchants).

47 *Spain:* Ibid., 2: 1640.

47 *Prussia:* Ibid., 2: 1486.

47 *France:* Ibid., 1: 496.

47 *Algiers:* Ibid., 1: 6.

47 *Central and South America:* Ibid., 1: 1117 (Treaty of Guadalupe Hidalgo with Mexico 1848, art. 22). For treaties influenced by the Franklin program in Central and South America, see ibid., 1: 164–68 (Central America 1825); 1: 174–78 (Chile 1832); 1: 1379–83 (Peru–Bolivia 1836); 2: 1836–39 (Venezuela 1836); 1: 425–29 (Ecuador 1839); 1: 865–68 (Guatemala 1849); 2: 1541–45 (Salvador 1850); 1: 345 (Costa Rica 1851); 2: 1395–98 (Peru 1851); 1: 18 (Argentina 1853); 2: 1402 (Peru 1856); 1: 119–22 (Bolivia 1858); 2: 1368 (Paraguay 1859); 2: 1849–53 (Venezuela 1860); 1: 956 (Honduras 1864); 1: 925–29 (Haiti 1864); 1: 408–11 (Dominican Republic 1867); 2: 1283–84 (Nicaragua 1867).

47 *Russia and Italy:* Ibid., 2: 1519; 1: 969.

47 *China:* Ibid., 1: 196.

48 *"happy in the confirmation of ":* Resignation Address, December 23, 1783, George Washington's Papers at the Library of Congress, http://memory.loc.gov/cgi-bin/ampage?collId=mgw3&fileName=mgw3a/gwpage007.db&recNum=161.

Chapter 2. The Rules of Civilized Warfare

49 *"Our object was the restoration":* Charles Francis Adams, ed., *Memoirs of John Quincy Adams, Comprising Portions of His Diary from 1795 to 1848* (Philadelphia: Lippincott, 1969), 3: 257.

49 *"It is among the evils of slavery":* Ibid., 1: 232.

49 *On the night of August 24, 1814:* J. C. A. Stagg, *Mr. Madison's War: Politics, Diplomacy, and Warfare in the Early American Republic, 1783–1830* (Princeton, NJ: Princeton University Press, 1983), 414–24; James Pack, *The Man Who Burned the White House: Admiral Sir George Cockburn, 1772–1853* (Emsworth, PA: Mason, 1987), 191–92.

49 *a battle-tested veteran:* Captain James Scott, R.N., *Recollections of a Naval Life* (London: Richard Bentley, 1834), 3: 298–99.

49 *Corps of Colonial Marines:* Christopher T. George, "Mirage of Freedom: African Americans in the War of 1812," *Maryland Historical Magazine* 91, no. 4 (1996): 427, 434–39.

50 *only after General Ross received no response:* Pack, *The Man Who Burned the White House,* 191–92.

50 *shot the horse out:* Scott, *Recollections of a Naval Life,* 3: 298.

50 *burned entire towns along the Canadian border:* Alan Taylor, *The Civil War of 1812: American Citizens, British Subjects, Irish Rebels & Indian Allies* (New York: Alfred A. Knopf, 2010), 215–17, 244–52; Jon Latimer, *1812: War with America* (Cambridge, MA: Harvard University Press, 2007), 223–24.

50 *"when necessity or the maxims of war":* Emmerich de Vattel, *The Law of Nations,* trans. Joseph Chitty (Philadelphia: T. & J. W. Johnson & Co., 1867), bk. 3, §168, p. 368.

50 *Napoleon had destroyed the Kremlin:* See Worthington Chauncey Ford, ed., *The Writings of John Quincy Adams* (New York: Macmillan, 1915), 5: 153–54.

50 *"wantonly destroyed":* James D. Richardson, ed., *A Compilation of the Messages and Papers of the Presidents 1789–1897* (Washington, DC: Government Printing Office, 1896), 1: 545.

51 *"most widely read geographical book":* Ralph H. Brown, "The American Geographies of Jedediah Morse," *Annals of the Association of American Geographers* 31, no. 3 (1941), 145, 148.

51–52 *"remarkable events" . . . "strict neutrality":* Jedediah Morse, *The American Universal Geography, or, a View of the Present State of All the Empires, Kingdoms, States, and Republics in the Known World, and of the United States of America in Particular* (Boston: Young & Etheridge, 1793), 2: 533, 548.

52 *"will regard his own country as a wife"*: PAH, 14: 267.
52 *neutrality as morally suspicious:* Stephen C. Neff, *The Rights and Duties of Neutrals: A General History* (New York: Cambridge University Press, 2000); Stephen C. Neff, *War and the Law of Nations: A General History* (New York: Cambridge University Press, 2005); Nicolas Politis, *Neutrality and Peace*, trans. Francis Crane Macken (Washington, DC: Carnegie Endowment for International Peace, 1935), 13–15; G. I. A. D. Draper, "Grotius's Place in the Development of Legal Ideas about War," in Hedley Bull et al., eds., *Hugo Grotius and International Relations* (Oxford: Clarendon Press, 1990), 177, 196.
52 *"the sorrowful state of souls unsure"*: *The Inferno of Dante: A New Verse Translation*, trans. Robert Pinsky (New York: Farrar, Straus & Giroux, 1994), 24–27, canto III, lines 30–53.
53 *"not to be countenanced"*: Vattel, *Law of Nations*, bk 3, §106, pp. 332–33.
53 *"The enemy of my friend"*: Cornelius van Bynkershoek, *On Questions of Public Law*, trans. Tenney Frank (1737; repr., Oxford: Clarendon Press, 1930), 2: 60.
53 *corrupt "jurisprudists"*: Harry Ammon, *The Genet Mission* (New York: W. W. Norton & Co., 1973), 76.
53 *Washington asked Chief Justice John Jay:* Stewart Jay, *Most Humble Servants: The Advisory Role of Early Judges* (New Haven, CT: Yale University Press, 1997), 113–48.
53 *issued through Jefferson a series of statements:* PTJ, 27: 328–73.
54 *Congress cemented:* An Act in Addition to the Act for the Punishment of Certain Crimes Against the United States, Stat., 1: 381–84. Even before the enactment of the neutrality legislation, the district attorney in Philadelphia indicted U.S. citizen Gideon Henfield for participating in a French privateering expedition aboard the *Citoyen Genet* in the summer of 1793. Associate Justice James Wilson charged the jury that Henfield's acts were a violation of "the law of nations" because he "committed an act of hostility against the subjects of a power with whom the United States are at peace." The jury acquitted Henfield, Wilson's charge notwithstanding.
54 *"the horrors of war in perfection"*: Jean Edward Smith, *John Marshall: Definer of a Nation* (New York: Henry Holt, 1996), 49.
54 *"Its destruction"*: Ibid., 51.
54 *"strangely woven"*: Albert J. Beveridge, *The Life of John Marshall* (Boston: Houghton Mifflin, 1919), 4: 1.
54 *never mustered out:* Smith, *John Marshall*, 69.
54 *a crucial diplomatic mission:* William Stinchcombe, *The XYZ Affair* (Westport, CT: Greenwood Press, 1980); Benjamin Munn Ziegler, *The International Law of John Marshall: A Study of First Principles* (Chapel Hill: University of North Carolina Press, 1939), 246–47.
55 *"uncommonly mild"*: Smith, *John Marshall*, 421–22.
55 *"unaffected modesty"*: Ibid., 291.
55 *"more use of his brains"*: Edward S. Corwin, *John Marshall and the Constitution: A Chronicle of the Supreme Court* (New Haven, CT: Yale University Press, 1919), 42.
55 *"The new world"*: George C. Herring, *From Colony to Superpower: U.S. Foreign Relations Since 1776* (New York: Oxford University Press, 2008), 69.
55 *British cruisers seized:* Jerald A. Combs, *The Jay Treaty: Political Battleground of the Founding Fathers* (Berkeley: University of California Press, 1970), 120; "Mission to France: Editorial Note," in Herbert A. Johnson et al., eds., *The Papers of John Marshall* (Chapel Hill: University of North Carolina Press, 1974), 3: 74.
55 *the French seized 316 American ships:* Alexander de Condé, *The Quasi-War: The Politics and Diplomacy of the Undeclared War with France, 1797–1801* (New York: Scribner, 1966), 9.
55 *Desperate for manpower:* Taylor, *Civil War of 1812*, 103–34.
55 *French commanders tortured:* de Condé, *Quasi-War*, 9.
56 Talbot v. Seeman: 5 U.S. (1 Cranch) 1 (1801).
56 *far less apparent when Marshall took the bench:* Harold Hongju Koh, "Transnational Public Law Litigation," *Yale Law Journal* 100 (1991): 2347, 2356; David Sloss, "Judi-

cial Foreign Policy: Lessons from the 1790s," *St. Louis University Law Journal* 53 (2008): 162–64.

57 *to recapture any vessel such as the* Amelia: An Act More Effectually to Protect the Commerce and Coasts of the United States, Stat., 1: 561 (May 28, 1798).

57 *authorized the collection of salvage fees:* An Act to Authorize the Defense of the Merchant-Vessels of the United States Against French Depredations, Stat., 1: 572 (June 25, 1798).

57 *"By this construction": Talbot,* 5 U.S. (1 Cranch) at 28.

57 *Marshall did his utmost:* R. Kent Newmeyer, *John Marshall and the Heroic Age of the Supreme Court* (Baton Rouge: Louisiana State University Press, 2001), 286.

57 *"to be construed to violate": Murray v. The Charming Betsy,* 6 U.S. (2 Cranch) 64, 118 (1804).

58 *The mere intention to go to a blockaded port: Fitzsimmons v. Newport Ins. Co.,* 8 U.S. 185 (1808).

58 *merely by inquiring: Maryland Ins. Co. v. Woods,* 10 U.S. 29 (1810).

58 *to undo the capture of a neutral: Little v. Barreme,* 6 U.S. (2 Cranch) 170 (1804).

58 *plausible but contested neutral status: The Charming Betsy,* 6 U.S. at 119–21; *Maley v. Shattuck,* 7 U.S. 458 (1806); *Sands v. Knox,* 7 U.S. 499 (1806).

58 *in an armed enemy convoy: The Nereide,* 13 U.S. (9 Cranch) 388, 419–23 (1815).

58 *"enlarges the sphere": The Nereide,* 13 U.S. at 419.

58 *the* Commercen: 14 U.S. (1 Wheat.) 382 (1816).

58 *The* Schooner Exchange: 7 U.S. 116, 126 (1812).

58 *routinely upheld the condemnation:* E.g., *The Hazard,* 13 U.S. 126 (1815); *The Fortuna,* 16 U.S. 236 (1818); *The Atalanta,* 18 U.S. 433 (1820).

59 *In case after case:* E.g., *The Gran Para,* 20 U.S. 471 (1822); *The Fanny,* 22 U.S. 658 (1824); *The Marianna Flora,* 24 U.S. 1 (1825).

59 *"The affairs of Europe":* Herring, *From Colony to Superpower,* 80.

59 *an identity as well as an interest:* David M. Golove & Daniel J. Hulsebosch, "A Civilized Nation: The Early American Constitution, the Law of Nations, and the Pursuit of International Recognition," *New York University Law Review* 85 (2010): 932; Daniel J. Hulsebosch, "Being Seen Like a State: The Constitution and Its International Audiences at the Founding," New York University School of Law, September 2011.

59 *neutral vessels were free to carry:* See, e.g., BF to Robert Morris, June 3, 1780, *PBF,* 32: 466–67; Samuel Flagg Bemis, *The Diplomacy of the American Revolution* (New York: American Historical Association, 1935), 131–34.

59 *two potentially gaping exceptions:* On the laws of war at sea, see Carlton Savage, *Policy of the United States Toward Maritime Commerce, 1776–1914,* 2 vols. (Washington, DC: Government Printing Office, 1934–36); Bryan Ranft, "Restraints on War at Sea Before 1945," in Michael Howard, ed., *Restraints on War* (Oxford: Oxford University Press, 1979), 39–56.

60 *Such goods were "contraband":* Philip C. Jessup, *American Neutrality and International Police* (Boston: World Peace Foundation Pamphlets, 1928), 111–12.

60 *Later the British declared:* Eli F. Hecksher, *The Continental System: An Economic Interpretation* (Oxford: Clarendon Press, 1922).

60 *food could not possibly be:* Thomas Pinckney to Thomas Jefferson, February 5, 1793, in *PTJ,* 25: 150; also Thomas Pinckney to Thomas Jefferson, February 5, 1793, and February 10, 1793, in *PTJ,* 25: 166.

60 *"actually besieged":* James Madison, *An Examination of the British Doctrine, Which Subjects to Capture a Neutral Trade, Not Open in Time of Peace* (Washington City: Samuel H. Smith, 1806), 6.

60 *"so manifestly contrary to the law":* Mr. Jefferson, Secretary of State, to Mr. Hammond, Minister Plenipotentiary of Great Britain, in *ASP: Foreign Affairs,* 1: 190.

60 *"a mass of contradictory decisions":* Henry Wheaton, *A Digest of the Law of Maritime Captures and Prizes* (New York: R. M'Dermut & D. D. Arden, 1815), v.

60 *"almost biblical elasticity":* Samuel Flagg Bemis, *Jay's Treaty: A Study in Commerce and Diplomacy* (New Haven, CT: Yale University Press, 1962), 185.

60   *so-called Rule of 1756:* Stephen C. Neff, *The Rights and Duties of Neutrals: A General History* (New York: Cambridge University Press, 2000), 66.

61   *"more unjust in itself":* Madison, *Examination of the British Doctrine*, 204.

61   *Madison was forced to distinguish:* Ibid., 19–23.

61   *determined in the* Essex *case:* Bradford Perkins, "Sir William Scott and the Essex," *William & Mary Quarterly* (3d series) 13, no. 2 (April 1966): 169, 179–80; Douglas J. Sylvester, "International Law as Sword or Shield? Early American Foreign Policy and the Law of Nations," *NYU Journal of International Law & Policy* 32 (1999): 52–53.

61   *reacted angrily to the* Essex *decision:* "The Case of the Essex," *Salem Register*, September 16, 1805; see also "An Interesting Case," *Alexandria Advertiser*, September 18, 1805; "Law Case," *Aurora General Advertiser*, October 21, 1805.

61   *"system of vexation and injury":* Bradford Perkins, *Prologue to War: England and the United States, 1805–1812* (Berkeley & Los Angeles: University of California Press, 1961), 79.

62   *shed little light on:* Cf. Madison, *Examination of the British Doctrine* (1806), and Tench Coxe [Juriscola], *An Examination of the Conduct of Great Britain, Respecting Neutrals, Since the Year 1791* (Boston: Oliver & Munroe, 1808), and William John Duane, *The Law of Nations, Investigated in a Popular Manner. Addressed to the Farmers of the United States* (Philadelphia: The Aurora, 1809), with James Stephen, *War in Disguise; or, the Frauds of the Neutral Flags* (New York: Hopkins & Seymour, 1806), and *An Examination of the British Doctrine Which Subjects to Capture a Neutral Trade Not Open in Time of Peace* (London: S. Gould, 2nd ed. 1806), and Alexander Croke, *Remarks on Mr. Schlegel's Work Upon the Visitation of Neutral Vessels Under Convoy* (London: J. White, 1801).

62   *the frigate USS* Chesapeake: Spencer C. Tucker & Frank T. Reuter, *Injured Honor: The Chesapeake-Leopard Affair, June 22, 1807* (Annapolis, MD: Naval Institute Press, 1996); Robert E. Cray, "Remembering the USS *Chesapeake*: The Politics of Maritime Death and Impressment," *Journal of the Early Republic* 25, no. 3 (2005): 445–74; Anthony Steel, "More Light on the *Chesapeake*," *Mariner's Mirror* 39, no. 4 (1953), 243–65.

63   *had not violated international law at all:* Tucker & Reuter, *Injured Honor*, 114.

63   *stripped itself of its neutrality:* Perkins, *Prologue to War*, 193.

63   *"inveigle away your troops":* Henry Adams, *History of the United States of America During the Second Administration of Thomas Jefferson* (New York: Charles Scribner & Co., 1890), 2: 44.

63   *"no impartial person":* Cray, "Remembering the USS *Chesapeake*," 465.

63   *"on no other grounds":* Canning to Monroe, August 3, 1807, in *ASP: Foreign Affairs*, 3: 188.

63   *"not because the lawyers":* Adams, *Second Administration of Thomas Jefferson*, 2: 78.

64   *Napoleon retaliated:* Neff, *Rights and Duties of Neutrals*, 76–85.

64   *"merely original and abstract":* Ibid., 82.

64   *were not contingent:* Perkins, *Prologue to War*, 257.

65   *"reason to believe":* Vattel, *Law of Nations*, bk. 2, §334, p. 280.

65   *"plausibly argued":* Reid quoted in Daniel J. Hulsebosch, *Constituting Empire: New York and the Transformation of Constitutionalism in the Atlantic World* (Chapel Hill: University of North Carolina Press, 2005), 32; see also James Parton, *The Life and Times of Aaron Burr* (New York: Mason Bros., 1858), 149 ("Law is whatever is boldly asserted and plausibly maintained'").

65   *"greatest curse of all":* Perkins, *Prologue to War*, 73.

65   *"sacred rights":* Cray, "Remembering the USS *Chesapeake*," 466.

65   *"a flagrant violation":* Ibid., 460.

65   *"Our rights are absolute":* Perkins, *Prologue to War*, 257.

65   *"We must strive for our rights":* Ibid., 298.

66   *"daring insult":* Cray, "Remembering the USS *Chesapeake*," 460.

66   *Crowds marched in the streets:* Robert E. Cray, Jr., "Commemorating the Prison Ship Dead: Revolutionary Memory and the Politics of Sepulture in the Early Republic, 1776–1808," *William & Mary Quarterly* (3d series) 56, no. 3 (1999): 565–90.

66   *at the Raisin River:* Donald R. Hickey, *The War of 1812: A Forgotten Conflict* (Urbana: University of Illinois Press, 1989), 86; Taylor, *Civil War of 1812*, 212–13.

67   *Along the Canadian border:* Latimer, *1812: War with America*, 225–26.

67   *retaliatory imprisonment:* Taylor, *Civil War of 1812*, 358–62.

67   *A congressional committee:* "Spirit and Manner in Which the War Is Waged by the Enemy," *ASP: Military Affairs*, 1: 339.

67   *torched the Canadian Parliament:* Taylor, *Civil War of 1812*, 215–17.

67   *burned more than 100 dwellings:* Ibid., 250–52.

67   *leave poisons in bottles:* Latimer, *1812: War with America*, 305.

67   *"No wars are so cruel":* Ford, *Writings of John Quincy Adams*, 5: 154.

67   *"the safe keeping":* An Act for the Safe Keeping and Accommodation of Prisoners of War, Stat., 2: 777 (1812).

67   *British merchants in American ports:* Stat. 2: 780, §§5–6; Anthony G. Dietz, *The Prisoner of War in the United States During the War of 1812*, Ph.D. diss., American University, 1964, 68.

67   *recognized flags of truce:* Ibid., 95.

67   *recognized the other's agents:* Ibid., 24, 39.

68   *released captured prisoners on parole:* Taylor, *Civil War of 1812*, 361–62.

68   *the exchange of all prisoners:* Miller, 2: 568–73.

68   *struck a more permanent deal:* Ibid., 2: 557–67; Latimer, *1812: War with America*, 190–91.

68   *"with humanity conformable":* Miller, 2: 557.

68   *exchanged more than 1,000 soldiers:* Dietz, *Prisoner of War*, 79.

68   *"downtown Mrs. Smith":* Ibid., 112.

68   *"sat down to tables":* Ibid., 113.

68   *received medical care:* Ibid., 101–02.

68   *The main complaint:* Ibid., 185–87.

69   *to escape too easily:* Ibid., 107–12.

69   *a cycle of retaliation:* Taylor, *Civil War of 1812*, 358–62.

69   *Francis Scott Key came to know:* Walter Lord, *The Dawn's Early Light* (New York: W. W. Norton & Co., 1972), 243.

70   *"We have a right":* Vattel, *Law of Nations*, bk. 3, §161, p. 364.

70   *"booty":* Ibid., bk. 3, §164, p. 365.

70   *"Every man in a just war":* J. J. Burlamaqui, *The Principles of Natural and Politic Law*, trans. Thomas Nugent (Philadelphia: H. C. Carey & I. Lea, 1823), 2: 203.

70   *"The conqueror has a right":* Georg Friedrich von Martens, *Summary of the Law of Nations*, trans. William Cobbett (Philadelphia: Thomas Bradford, 1795), 287–88.

70   *Benjamin Franklin's program:* PBF, 6: 608–10; PTJ, 7: 491–92.

70   *"softening and diminishing":* PTJ, 7: 490–91.

70   *"war gives the right to confiscate":* Brown v. United States, 12 U.S. 110, 125 (1814).

70   *"mitigations":* 12 U.S. at 123–24.

71   *"The Constitution of the United States":* 12 U.S. at 125.

71   *"the subjects of hostile nations":* 12 U.S. at 134 (J. Story dissenting).

71   *"there are great limitations"* ... *"without making compensation":* James Kent, *Commentaries on American Law* (New York: O. Halsted, 1826–30), 1: 86–87.

71   *made him a rich man:* John H. Langbein, "Chancellor Kent and the History of Legal Literature," *Columbia Law Review* 93 (1993): 565–66; Daniel J. Hulsebosch, "An Empire of Law: Chancellor Kent and the Revolution in Books in the Early Republic," *Alabama Law Review* 60 (2009): 377, 386.

71   *"Private property on land":* Henry Wheaton, *Elements of International Law: With a Sketch of the History of the Science* (Philadelphia: Carey, Lea & Blanchard, 1836), 252–54.

72   *"Horses, cattle":* Philo Camillus No. 2 [New York, Aug. 7, 1795], *PAH*, 19: 101.

72   *a provision protecting slave property:* Maya Jasanoff, *Liberty's Exiles: American Loyalists in the Revolutionary World* (New York: Alfred A. Knopf, 2011), 80; David Duncan Wallace, *The Life of Henry Laurens, with a Sketch of the Life of Lieutenant-Colonel John Laurens* (New York: G. P. Putnam's Sons, 1915), 402, 405.

72 *"carrying away any Negroes":* Malloy, 1: 586, 589.

72 *took at least 3,000 slaves:* Jasanoff, *Liberty's Exiles*, 89–90; Benjamin Quarles, *The Negro in the American Revolution* (Chapel Hill: University of North Carolina Press, 1961), 167–69; Simon Schama, *Rough Crossings: Britain, the Slaves, and the American Revolution* (New York: Ecco, 2006), 147.

72 *pressed the British for a return: ASP: Foreign Relations*, 1: 190–202.

72 *John Jay argued for compensation:* Combs, *The Jay Treaty*, 155; John Bassett Moore, *History and Digest of the International Arbitrations to Which the United States Has Been a Party* (Washington, DC: Government Printing Office, 1898), 1: 350–90; Walter Stahr, *John Jay: Founding Father* (New York: Hambledon, 2005), 204, 317–18.

73 *Cockburn began raiding:* Latimer, *1812: War with America*, 159–61; John Basset Moore, *A Digest of International Law* (Washington, DC: Government Printing Office, 1906), 7: 345–46.

73 *escaped from their masters:* Frank A. Cassell, "Slaves of the Chesapeake Bay Area and the War of 1812," *Journal of Negro History* 57, no. 2 (1972): 144–55; Christopher T. George, "Mirage of Freedom: African Americans in the War of 1812," *Maryland Historical Magazine* 91, no. 4 (1996): 427–50.

73 *to resell them in the West Indies:* See "Negro Stealing," *Palladium of Liberty* (Fauquier County, Va.), January 8, 1814; "Norfolk Public Ledger," *Daily National Intelligencer* (Washington, DC), April 12, 1815; "Editorial," *Raleigh Register*, April 7, 1815; "List of American Vessels Captured," *Commercial Advertiser* (Maryland), March 12, 1814.

73 *"enemy at home":* George, "Mirage of Freedom," 437.

73–74 *"flocking to the enemy" . . . "conflagration throughout these counties":* H. W. Flournoy, *Calendar of Virginia State Papers and Other Manuscripts* (Richmond, VA: R. F. Walker, 1892), 10: 367–68; see also 10: 337–38; Joseph Carrington Cabell to Hugh Nelson, February 17, 1814, Cabell Family Papers, University of Virginia.

74 *Haiti in the 1790s:* Alfred N. Hunt, *Haiti's Influence on Antebellum America: Slumbering Volcano in the Caribbean* (Baton Rouge: Louisiana State University Press, 1988).

74 *a slave named Gabriel:* See Douglas R. Egerton, *Gabriel's Rebellion: The Virginia Slave Conspiracies of 1800 and 1802* (Chapel Hill: University of North Carolina Press, 1993).

74 *executions and deportations:* George, "Mirage of Freedom," 436.

74 *"external enemies":* James Barbour to James Madison, February 17, 1814, James Madison Papers, LC.

74 *small vessels well-secured:* Cassell, "Slaves of the Chesapeake Bay Area," 147.

74 *"as free settlers":* Ibid., 150.

74 *creation of a Colonial Corps:* Latimer, *1812: War with America*, 249.

74 *3,000–5,000 slaves:* Cassel, "Slaves of the Chesapeake Bay Area," 154.

75 *"iniquitous scheme":* William Lee Miller, *Arguing About Slavery: The Great Battle in the United States Congress* (New York: Alfred A. Knopf, 1996), 162.

75 *"great and foul stain":* Alan Nevins, ed., *The Diary of John Quincy Adams, 1794–1845* (New York: Longmans, Green, 1928), 228–29.

75 *"seduction":* Adams, ed., *Memoirs of John Quincy Adams*, 3: 92.

75 *"Our object" . . . "from capture": ASP: Foreign Relations*, 4: 117.

75 *After much back-and-forth:* Ibid., 3: 733.

75 *"Slaves or other private property":* Malloy, 1: 613.

76 *In the British view:* Mary R. Bullard, *Black Liberation on Cumberland Island in 1815* (South Dartmouth, MA: M. R. Bullard, 1983), 86–87; *ASP: Foreign Relations*, 6: 339–55.

76 *"a violent and unnatural construction":* Adams, ed., *Memoirs of John Quincy Adams*, 5: 159.

76 *"dishonorable war":* Ibid., 5: 161.

76 *"deviations from the usages of war":* Ibid., 3: 257.

76 *"table or a chair":* Ibid.

76 *"There is something whimsical":* Ibid., 5: 160.

76 *slaveholder Henry Middleton:* Samuel Flagg Bemis, *John Quincy Adams and the Foundations of American Foreign Policy* (New York: Alfred A. Knopf, 1949), 263.

76   *unlawfully stealing slaves:* Adams, ed., *Memoirs of John Quincy Adams*, 5: 161.
76   *a mixed Anglo-American commission:* Bemis, *John Quincy Adams*, 293.
76   *to negotiate with the British: ASP: Foreign Relations*, 6: 346–55.
77   *rushed pell-mell to make claims:* See Don Fehrenbacher & Ward M. McAfee, *The Slave-holding Republic: An Account of the United States Government's Relations to Slavery* (New York: Oxford University Press, 2001), 96–97.
77   *"private property": ASP: Foreign Relations*, 4: 123.
77   *When Spain negotiated a treaty:* Ibid., 1: 278–79.

Chapter 3. A False Feeling of Mercy

79   *"The sovereign Editor":* American poet John Hunter Waddell, *Waddell to Coleman, Facts and Fancy—As You Like It—Go On, or Stop* (New York: n.p., 1819), 6.
79   *"I would barely remark": PAJ*, 4: 149.
79   *"a prisoner of war had a right":* John Reid & Henry Eaton, *The Life of Andrew Jackson: Major General in the Service of the United States* (Philadelphia: M. Carey & Son, 1817), 12.
80   *deep wound: PAJ*, 1: 9 n. 4.
80   *left him utterly alone:* Sean Wilentz, *Andrew Jackson* (New York: Times Books, 2005), 17.
81   *"We might have been taken":* Raymond Walters, Jr., *Alexander James Dallas: Lawyer—Politician—Financier* (Philadelphia: University of Pennsylvania Press, 1943), 160–61.
82   *"forbearance and urbanity":* G. Edward White, *The Marshall Court and Cultural Change, 1815–1835* (New York: Oxford University Press, 1991), 208.
82   *long vindication of American rights:* Robert Goodloe Harper, *Observations on the Dispute Between the United States and France, Addressed by Robert Goodloe Harper, of South Carolina, to His Constituents, in May, 1797* (Philadelphia: Philanthropic Press, 1798). Harper was also one of the strongest advocates of building a strong navy to protect American commercial rights. See Craig L. Symonds, *Navalists and Antinavalists: The Naval Policy Debate in the United States, 1785–1827* (Wilmington: University of Delaware Press, 1980), 77.
82   *immediately serialized: American Law Journal* (Philadelphia) 3, no. 2 (1810): i–218.
82   *foundational elements of the curriculum:* David Hoffman, *A Course of Legal Study: Respectfully Addressed to the Students of Law in the United States* (Baltimore: Coale & Maxwell, 1817), 242.
83   *"progress of civilization":* Henry Wheaton, *Elements of International Law: With a Sketch of the History of the Science* (Philadelphia: Carey, Lea & Blanchard, 1836), 254.
83   *"common standard of right and duty":* James Kent, *A Lecture, Introductory to a Course of Law Lectures in Columbia College, Delivered February 2, 1824* (New York: Clayton & Van Norden, 1824), 15.
83   *Story was doubtless the most learned justice:* See R. Kent Newmeyer, *Supreme Court Justice Joseph Story: Statesman of the Old Republic* (Chapel Hill: University of North Carolina Press, 1985).
83   *a technical book for lawyers:* Joseph Story, *A Selection of Pleadings in Civil Actions* (Salem, MA: Barnard B. Macanulty, 1805).
83   *two classic English law books:* Joseph Chitty, *A Practical Treatise on Bills of Exchange, Checks on Bankers, Promissory Notes, Bankers' Cash Notes, and Bank Notes*, ed. Joseph Story (Boston: Farrand, Mallory & Co., 1809); Charles Abbott, *A Treatise of the Law Relative to Merchant Ships and Seamen*, ed. Joseph Story (Newburyport, RI: Edward Little & Co., 1810).
83   *"of more transcendent dignity":* Joseph Story, *An Address Delivered Before the Members of the Suffolk Bar, at Their Anniversary: On the 4th of September, 1821, at Boston* (Boston: Freeman & Bowles, 1821), 30.
84   *a professional training ground:* James L. Morrison, Jr., *"The Best School in the World": West Point, the Pre–Civil War Years, 1833–1866* (Kent, OH: Kent State University Press, 1986); William B. Skelton, *An American Profession of Arms: The Army Officer Corps, 1784–1861* (Lawrence: University Press of Kansas, 1992), 103–72.

84 *in Vauban's conception:* Sebastien Le Prestre de Vauban, *The New Method of Fortification as practiced by Monsieur de Vauban, Engineer-General of France: Together with a new Treatise of Geometry* (6th edn.; London: C. Hitch & L. Hawes, 1762).

84 *"a small number of fundamental principles":* Baron de Jomini, *Summary of the Art of War, or a New Analytical Compendium of the Principal Combinations of Strategy, of Grand Tactics and of Military Policy* (New York: Putnam, 1854), 14.

84 *"ten positive maxims" . . . "natural genius" . . . "mechanism of determined wheelworks":* Jomini, *Summary of the Art of War*, 10, 14, 16.

85 *for 100 years:* "The New Infantry Tactics," *Army & Navy Chronicle* 1 (1835): 332–33.

85 *"rule and compass":* Skelton, *An American Profession of Arms*, 169.

85 *standard writings of Vattel:* Skelton, *American Profession of Arms*, 171.

85 *switched to Kent's* Commentaries: Skelton's *American Profession of Arms*, p. 171, gives the date 1825 for West Point's adoption of Kent's *Commentaries*, but Professor Daniel Hulsebosch of NYU, the leading authority on Kent's books, believes the adoption could not have happened before 1826. In 1829, the Military Academy's assignment of the book helped prompt a second print run—Hulsebosch, "An Empire of Law," 386–87 n. 28.

85 *the Army's Articles of War:* An Act for Establishing Rules and Articles for the Government of the Armies of the United States, Stat, 2: 359 (1806).

86 *"little exposure to":* Matthew Moten, *The Delafield Commission and the American Military Profession* (College Station: Texas A&M University Press, 2000), 36.

86 *a subject of ridicule:* Skelton, *An American Profession of Arms*, 171–72.

86 *the ubiquitous Vattel: General Regulations for the Army*; or, *Military Institutes* (Philadelphia: M. Carey & Sons, 1821), title page.

86 *"under the safeguard":* Ibid., 139.

86 *"a strict observance of good order":* Ibid., 147.

87 *"treaties, the laws of the United States": Marine Rules and Regulations* (Philadelphia: John Fenno, 1798), 27.

87 *Congress invoked:* Stat., 2: 45–53.

87 *ship chaplains were required:* John H. Schroeder, *Matthew Calbraith Perry: Antebellum Sailor and Diplomat* (Annapolis, MD: Naval Institute Press, 2001), 13.

87 *the new Naval Academy:* Peter Karsten, *The Naval Aristocracy: The Golden Age of Annapolis and the Emergence of Modern American Navalism* (New York: Free Press, 1972), 34–35.

87 *"judicious apprehension": Acts for the Government of the U.S. Navy Together with an Outline of the Course of Study in Political Science for the Graduating Class of the U.S. Naval Academy* (Newport, RI: Frederick A. Pratt, 1865), 5.

87–88 *often knew as much about the laws of war:* See generally David F. Long, *Gold Braid and Foreign Relations: Diplomatic Activities of U.S. Naval Officers, 1798–1883* (Annapolis, MD: Naval Institute Press, 1988).

88 *John Paul Jones:* Stephen Howarth, *To Shining Sea: A History of the United States Navy, 1775–1991* (New York: Random House, 1991), 41; Charles Óscar Paullin, *Diplomatic Negotiations of American Naval Officers, 1778–1883* (Gloucester, MA: Smith, 1967), 26–37.

88 *Latin American wars of independence:* John H. Schroeder, *Shaping a Maritime Empire: The Commercial and Diplomatic Role of the American Navy, 1829–1861* (Westport, CT: Greenwood Press, 1985), 16–17.

88 *"enlightened knowledge":* "U.S. Naval Lyceum," *The Naval Magazine* 1, no. 1 (1836): 15–16.

88 *A vast chasm:* See, e.g., Edward M. Coffman, *The Old Army: A Portrait of the American Army in Peacetime, 1784–1898* (New York: Oxford University Press, 1986), 77–102, 167–81; Skelton, *An American Profession of Arms*, 39.

88 *the Heart-of-the-Sky God:* Polly Schaafsma, "Head Trophies and Scalping: Images in Southwest Rock Art," in Richard J. Chacon & David H. Dye, eds., *The Taking and Displaying of Human Body Parts as Trophies by Amerindians* (New York: Springer, 2007), 109.

89   *In pre-contact California:* Patricia M. Lambert, "Ethnographic and Linguistic Evidence for Human Trophy Taking in California," in ibid., 66–67.

89   *cut the fingers and toes:* Jill Lepore, *The Name of War: King Philip's War and the Origins of American Identity* (New York: Alfred A. Knopf, 1998), 3.

89   *fed their male children:* Schaafsma, "Head Trophies," 113.

89   *necklaces from the fingertips:* Douglas Owsley et al., "Human Finger and Hand Bone Necklaces from the Plains and Great Basin," in Chacon & Dye, eds., *The Taking and Displaying of Human Body Parts*, 124–66.

89   *eating the hearts:* Daniel K. Richter, *The Ordeal of the Long-House: The Peoples of the Iroquois League in the Era of European Colonization* (Chapel Hill: University of North Carolina Press, 1992), 32–38; Barbara Graymont, *The Iroquois in the American Revolution* (New York: Syracuse University Press, 1972), 18.

89   *roasted the heads:* Nancy J. Curtin, *The United Irishmen: Popular Politics in Ulster and Dublin, 1791–1798* (Oxford: Clarendon Press, 1998), 217.

89   *heads impaled on spikes:* David A. Wilson, *United Irishmen, United States: Immigrant Radicals in the Early Republic* (Ithaca, NY: Cornell University Press, 1998), 32; Alan Taylor, *The Civil War of 1812: American Citizens, British Subjects, Irish Rebels, & Indian Allies* (New York: Alfred A. Knopf, 2010), 88.

89   *cut off the head:* John K. Mahon, *History of the Second Seminole War, 1835–1842* (Gainesville: University of Florida Press, 1967), 218.

89   *bounties for Indian scalps:* Nicholas Parrillo, *Against the Profit Motive* (New Haven, CT: Yale University Press, 2012).

89   *shipped the heads:* Robert M. Utley, *The Indian Frontier, 1846–1890* (Albuquerque: University of New Mexico Press, 2003), 170.

89   *"known rule of warfare":* Worthington Chauncey Ford, ed., *The Writings of John Quincy Adams* (New York: Macmillan, 1913–17), 5: 125–26.

90   *the "mourning war":* Richter, *The Ordeal of the Long-House*, 32–38.

90   *excruciating forms of torture killing:* Daniel K. Richter, "War and Culture: The Iroquois Experience," *William & Mary Quarterly* (3d series): 40 (no. 4): 540–44, 558–59.

90   *Colonel William Crawford:* Peter Silver, *Our Savage Neighbors: How Indian War Transformed Early America* (New York: W. W. Norton & Co., 2008), 281–82; Richard White, *The Middle Ground: Indians, Empires, and Republics in the Great Lakes Region, 1650–1815* (New York: Cambridge University Press, 1991), 395.

91   *"earned posthumous esteem":* Adam J. Hirsch, "The Collision of Military Cultures in Seventeenth-Century New England," *Journal of American History* 74 (1988): 1187, 1192.

91   *The logic of mourning war:* Richter, "War and Culture," 540–44; see also Wayne E. Lee, "Peace Chiefs and Blood Revenge: Patterns of Restraint in Native American Warfare, 1500–1800," *Journal of Military History* 71, no. 3 (2007): 701.

91   *"farre lesse bloudy":* Hirsch, "Collision of Military Cultures," 1191.

91   *"stamped and tore":* Ibid., 1202.

91   *the Wampanoag of New England:* Patrick Malone, *The Skulking Way of War: Technology and Tactics Among the New England Indians* (Lanham, MD: Madison Books, 1991).

91   *"hundreds of fields":* Don Higginbotham, *The War of American Independence: Military Attitudes, Policies, and Practices, 1763–1789* (New York: Macmillan, 1971), 326–27.

92   *"The reason":* John Winthrop, *Winthrop's Journal "History of New England," 1630–1649*, ed. James K. Hosmer (New York: Charles Scribner's Sons, 1908), 1: 218–19.

92   *"manage their warr fairly":* Hirsch, "Collision of Military Cultures," 1208.

92   *smallpox-infected blankets:* Colin G. Calloway, *The American Revolution in Indian Country: Crisis and Diversity in Native American Communities* (New York: Cambridge University Press, 1995), 5.

92   *"he would never spare":* John D. Barnhart, ed., *Henry Hamilton and George Rogers Clark in the American Revolution with the Unpublished Journal of Lieut. Gov. Henry Hamilton* (Crawfordsville, IN: R. E. Banta, 1951), 189; Gregory T. Knouff, "An 'Arduous Service': The Pennsylvania Backcountry Soldiers' Revolution," *Pennsylvania History* 61 (1994): 45, 64.

92   *"nothing less than a war"*: Skelton, *American Profession of Arms*, 320.
92   *"all the rights of war"*: Francisco Vitoria, *Vitoria: Political Writings*, ed. Anthony Pagden & Jeremy Lawrance (New York: Cambridge University Press, 1991), 283.
92   *"all men believe must be true"*: Hugo Grotius, *The Rights of War and Peace*, ed. Richard Tuck (Indianapolis, IN: Liberty Fund, 2005), 1: 161.
92   *"When we are at war"*: Emmerich de Vattel, *The Law of Nations*, trans. Joseph Chitty (Philadelphia: T. & J. W. Johnson & Co., 1867), bk 3, §141, p. 348.
93   *"the Christian nations of Europe"*: James Kent, *Commentaries on American Law* (New York: O. Halsted, 1826), 1: 3–4.
93   *"savage state"*: Ibid., 1: 52.
93   *"can only spring up among nations"*: Henry Wheaton, *Elements of International Law: With a Sketch of the History of the Science* (Philadelphia: Carey, Lea & Blanchard, 1836), 43.
93   *"entirely overlooked"*: Ibid., 140.
93   *"Why do we attempt"*: David S. Heidler & Jeanne T. Heidler, *Old Hickory's War: Andrew Jackson and the Quest for Empire* (Baton Rouge: Louisiana State University Press, 2003), 17.
93   *"cases of necessity"*: *PAJ*, 4: 149.
93   *Historians have been too quick:* For a recent example in an otherwise excellent article, see Deborah Rosen, "Wartime Prisoners and the Rule of Law: Andrew Jackson's Military Tribunals During the First Seminole War," *Journal of the Early Republic* 28, no. 4 (2008): 559, 593.
94   *In the just war tradition:* Stephen C. Neff, *War and the Law of Nations: A General History* (New York: Cambridge University Press, 2005).
94   *"rules that shall be more certain"*: Vattel, *Law of Nations*, bk 3, §189, p. 381.
94   *"sure and easy"*: Ibid., bk 3, §173, p. 369.
94   *"continual accusations"* ... *"utterly destroyed"*: Ibid., bk 3, §173, p. 369.
95   *"the so-called laws of war"*: Higginbotham, *War of American Independence*, 13.
95   *tiny fraction of the size:* David M. Kennedy, "War and the American Character," *The Nation*, May 3, 1975, p. 522.
95   *"free born sons"* ... *"national vengeance"*: Robert V. Remini, *Andrew Jackson: The Course of American Empire, 1767–1821* (New York: Harper & Row, 1977), 168–69—cited hereafter as Remini, *Andrew Jackson (I)*.
95   *executed captured Indian combatants:* J. C. A. Stagg, *Mr. Madison's War: Politics, Diplomacy, and Warfare in the Early American Republic, 1783–1830* (Princeton, NJ: Princeton University Press, 1983), 216, 220, 225.
95   *inside the stockade at Fort Mims:* Stagg, *Mr. Madison's War*, 354–55.
95   *"We shot them like dogs"*: Remini, *Andrew Jackson (I)*, 193.
95   *"Half-consumed human bodies"*: Ibid., 193.
96   *close to 2,000 Creek Indians:* Ibid., 206, 216.
96   *At Horseshoe Bend:* Armstrong Starkey, *European and Native American Warfare, 1675–1815* (Norman: University of Oklahoma Press, 1998), 159.
96   *bridle reins:* H. S. Halbert & T. H. Ball, *The Creek War of 1813 and 1814* (Chicago: Donohue & Henneberry, 1895), 275–78.
96   *cut the tips of the noses:* Ibid., 275–78.
96   *"unprovoked, inhuman"*: Stat., 7: 120.
96   *killing the more than forty men:* John K. Mahon, "The First Seminole War: November 21, 1817–May 24, 1818," *Florida Historical Quarterly* 77, no. 1 (1998): 62, 64.
96   *smashed their skulls:* Robert V. Remini, *Andrew Jackson and His Indian Wars* (New York: Viking, 2001), 133.
97   *"mildness and humanity"* ... *"impunity"*: Waldo S. Putnam, *Memoirs of Andrew Jackson, Major-General in the Army of the United States, and Commander in Chief of the Division of the South* (Hartford, CT: John Russell, Jr., 1818), 294.
97   *took them as prisoners:* Remini, *Andrew Jackson (I)*, 213.
97   *hundreds of scalps: ASP: Military Affairs*, 1: 704, 736.
98   *war poles festooned:* Ibid., 1: 699–700.

98   *luring them aboard:* Ibid., 1: 700; Remini, *Andrew Jackson (I)*, 354.
98   *"will end the Indian war": ASP: Military Affairs*, 1: 701.
98   *Arbuthnot and Ambrister on trial:* Frank L. Owsley, Jr., "Ambrister and Arbuthnot: Adventurers or Martyrs for British Honor," *Journal of the Early Republic* 5 (1985): 289.
98   *Jackson charged the two men: ASP: Military Affairs*, 1: 721, 731.
98   *cruel in the extreme:* Ibid., 1: 723–26.
98   *"as a nation more cruel":* Ibid., 1: 724.
98   *Witnesses with long-standing grudges:* Owsley, "Ambrister and Arbuthnot," 295, 303–04.
99   *"an established principle": ASP: Military Affairs*, 1: 734.
100 *Monroe submitted to Congress:* Richardson, 2: 42–43.
100 *condemning the executions: Annals of Congress*, 15th Cong., 2nd. sess., 584.
100 *Thomas Nelson of Virginia:* Ibid., 515–17.
100 *Richard Mentor Johnson:* Ibid., 518–27.
100 *John Marshall's Supreme Court:* Jean Edward Smith, *John Marshall: Definer of a Nation* (New York: Henry Holt & Co., 1996), 318–19.
100 *an outlaw of the Marquis de Lafayette: Annals of Congress*, 15th Cong., 2nd. sess., 517, 586.
100 *"Where was the absolute necessity":* Ibid., 516.
101 *"In one day":* Ibid., 588.
101 *"one of the best speeches":* Robert Remini, *Henry Clay: Statesman for the Union* (New York: W. W. Norton & Co., 1991), 163.
101 *"fair and open": Annals of Congress*, 15th Cong., 2nd. sess., 637.
101 *"the laws of civilized nations":* Ibid., 639.
101 *"most cheerfully":* Ibid., 647.
101 *"The eyes of the whole world":* Ibid., 654.
101 *"our principles":* Ibid., 640.
101 *"sat stony-faced":* Remini, *Henry Clay*, 163.
101 *"clear principle": Annals of Congress*, 15th Cong., 2nd. sess., 657.
101 *"banditti" or "pirates on land":* Ibid., 664.
102 *"an advocate of mercy":* Ibid., 668.
102 *"let no false feeling":* Ibid., 673.
102 *"all the proceedings of Gen. Jackson":* Ibid., 674.
102 *"tribe of savages":* Ibid., 687–88.
102 *"whatever degree of force":* Ibid., 689.
102 *"these vagrant savages":* Ibid., 706.
102 *James Barbour of Virginia:* Ibid., 764.
102 *"while we are searching our law books":* Ibid., 664.
102 *"General Jackson, in the wilds":* Ibid., 1039.
102 *"inflated appeals":* Ibid., 980.
102 *would cut off the ears:* Heidler & Heidler, *Old Hickory's War*, 218.
103 *"I was not prepared":* William Earl Weeks, *John Quincy Adams and American Global Empire* (Lexington: University Press of Kentucky, 1992), 144.
103 *"firebrands": ASP: Foreign Relations*, 539–46, esp. 541.
103 *appeared in the administration organ:* Weeks, *John Quincy Adams*, 159–68.
103 *"a desperate clan of outlaws":* Waldo, *Memoirs of Andrew Jackson*, 281, 294, 299.
103 *"delicate fastidiousness": Annals of Congress*, 15th Cong., 2nd. sess., 655.
103 *"for the first time in their lives":* Weeks, *John Quincy Adams*, 159.
103 *"Sir," he said indignantly: Annals of Congress*, 15th Cong., 2nd. sess., 716.
103 *approval of European diplomatic corps:* Ibid., 1094.
103 *"learned Puffendorffs":* John H. Schroeder, *Shaping a Maritime Empire: The Commercial and Diplomatic Role of the American Navy, 1829–1861* (Westport, CT: Greenwood Press, 1985), 28.
103 *"I, too," hate the "tomahawk": Annals of Congress*, 15th Cong., 2nd. sess., 638.
104 *"I have passed":* Heidler & Heidler, *Old Hickory's War*, 218.
104 *"to give no quarter":* Weeks, *John Quincy Adams*, 144.

104 *"an unnecessary act": ASP: Military Affairs*, 1: 743.
104 *"a strong advocate for neutral rights":* Ibid., 1: 742.
104 *"in direct opposition":* Ibid., 1: 742.
104 *"a wound":* Ibid., 1: 743.
105 *"among the most immediate":* Weeks, *John Quincy Adams*, 168.
105 *"gratitude" of the American people: PAJ*, 4: 294–96.
105 to thank Jackson for his great successes: *Journal of the House of Representatives of the State of New Hampshire, at Their Session, Begun . . . on the First Wednesday of June . . . 1819* (Concord, NH: Hill & Moore, 1819), 298.
105 *"have been with you": PAJ*, 4: 294–96.
105 *"the so-called rules of war":* Higginbotham, *War of American Independence*, 13.
106 *"the laws of civilized nations": Annals of Congress*, 15th Cong., 2nd. sess., 639.
106 *"our rule had been":* Ibid., 736.
106 *"technical niceties":* Ibid., 745.
107 *"that great general":* Ibid., 1115.
107 booty and plunder: John Missall & Mary Lou Missall, *The Seminole Wars: America's Longest Indian Conflict* (Gainesville: University Press of Florida, 2004), 132–33.
107 using flags of truce: John K. Mahon, *History of the Second Seminole War, 1835–1842* (Gainesville: University of Florida Press, 1967), 214–17.
107 *"unprecedented violation":* Missall & Missall, *The Seminole Wars*, 141.
107 *"another breach":* "Another Breach of National Honor," *The Philanthropist*, Jan. 30, 1838, p. 4.
107 Seminole named Coacoochee: Missall & Missall, *The Seminole Wars*, 141.
108 bloodhounds to track: Ibid., 171.

Chapter 4. Rules of Wrong

109 *"What is war":* Charles Sumner, *The True Grandeur of Nations: An Oration Before the Authorities of the City of Boston, July 4, 1845* (Boston: Lee & Shepard, 1893), 48.
109 Crisp uniforms: Anne-Marie Taylor, *Young Charles Sumner and the Legacy of the Enlightenment, 1811–1851* (Amherst: University of Massachusetts Press, 2001), 177.
109 local military academy: David Donald, *Charles Sumner and the Coming of the Civil War* (New York: Alfred A. Knopf, 1960), 11.
109 novels of Sir Walter Scott: Ibid., 16.
109 Supreme Court Justice Joseph Story: Ibid., 23.
110 took over Story's course: Ibid., 34.
110 the Continent's most distinguished: Ibid., 68.
110 *"trial of right":* Ibid., 16.
110 *"be ranked as crime":* Ibid., 17.
110 *"Laws of war" . . . "contradictory combination":* Charles Sumner, *The True Grandeur of Nations: An Oration Before the Authorities of the City of Boston, July 4, 1845* (Boston: J. H. Eastburn, 1845). Sumner edited the wording of this passage in subsequent editions. For the variation, see Sumner, *The True Grandeur* (Boston: Lee & Shepard, 1893), 28–29n.
110 *"Viewed in the unclouded":* Sumner, *The True Grandeur* (1893), 48.
110 *"comfort to wretchedness":* Ibid., 9.
110 *"absorbed in feats" . . . "Christian brotherhood":* Ibid., 10.
110 *"so many lions":* Taylor, *Young Charles Sumner*, 187–89.
110 *"criminal and impious custom":* Sumner, *The True Grandeur* (1893), 45.
111 *"Our country cannot":* Ibid., 128.
111 group of pacifists: Valerie H. Ziegler, *The Advocates of Peace in Antebellum America* (Bloomington: Indiana University Press, 1992).
111 using force in any way: Charles DeBenedetti, *The Peace Reform in American History* (Bloomington: Indiana University Press, 1980), 49.
111 The episode began in late 1837: Kenneth R. Stevens, *Border Diplomacy: The Caroline and McLeod Affairs in Anglo-American-Canadian Relations, 1837–1842* (Tuscaloosa: University of Alabama Press, 1989).
112 *"necessity of self-defence": PDW: Diplomatic Papers*, 1: 67.

112 *to conclude that Nazi Germany:* Yoram Dinstein, *War, Aggression, and Self-Defence* (Cambridge: Cambridge University Press, 4th ed., 2005), 249; Timothy Kearley, "Raising the Caroline," *Wisconsin International Law Journal* 17 (1999): 325.

113 *passenger named Amos Durfee:* R. Y. Jennings, "The Caroline and McLeod Cases," *American Journal of International Law* 32, no. 1 (1938): 82, 84.

113 *made Durfee a martyr:* Stevens, *Border Diplomacy*, 15–25.

113 *McLeod was notorious:* Ibid., 71–72.

113 *"aggravate beyond measure" . . . "long since banished":* PDW: *Diplomatic Papers*, 1: 43.

113 *"To hold the prisoner guilty":* People v. McLeod, 1 Hill. 377, 514 (N.Y. Sup. Ct. 1841).

114 *"under any obligation":* McLeod, 1 Hill. at 533.

114 *"a mistake":* McLeod, 1 Hill. at 592.

114 *New York's attorney general:* McLeod, 1 Hill. at 535–36.

114 *"informal and illegitimate":* Emmerich de Vattel, *The Law of Nations*, trans. Joseph Chitty (Philadelphia: T. & J. W. Johnson & Co., 1867), bk. §68, 320.

114 *"the hazards of war":* McLeod, 1 Hill. at 558.

114 *"outrage of our rights":* Stevens, *Border Diplomacy*, 97.

114–15 *Palmerston instructed Fox:* Howard Jones, *To the Webster–Ashburton Treaty: A Study in Anglo-American Relations* (Chapel Hill: University of North Carolina Press, 1977), 51.

115 *"war would be the inevitable":* Stevens, *Border Diplomacy*, 88.

115 *Peel was holding secret:* Jones, *To the Webster–Ashburton Treaty*, 62, 68.

115 *James Henry Hammond:* Robert V. Remini, *Daniel Webster: The Man and His Time* (Chapel Hill: University of North Carolina Press, 1997), 541.

115 *to sustain the country's honor:* Richard N. Current, "Webster's Propaganda and the Ashburton Treaty," *Mississippi Valley Historical Review* 34 (1947): 187–88.

115 *"the whole frontier":* Jennings, "Caroline and McLeod," 92 n. 37.

115 *to prepare for the impending conflict:* Stevens, *Border Diplomacy*, 87.

115 *"a principle of public law":* PDW: *Diplomatic Papers*, 1: 47.

115 *"would become a pirate":* Review, *North American Review* 142 (January 1849): 1, 30–31.

115 *dispatched Attorney General John Crittenden:* Stevens, *Border Diplomacy*, 95–97.

115 *pressed New York's governor:* Ibid., 93–95.

115–16 *asked the U.S. district attorney:* Ibid., 123.

116 *Governor William Henry Seward:* Jones, *To the Webster–Ashburton Treaty*, 55–56.

116 *"no musty volumes":* Cong. Globe, 27th Cong., 1st Sess., p. 43.

116 *a verdict of not guilty:* Marcus Tullius Cicero Gould, *The Trial of Alexander Mcleod, for the Murder of Amos Durfee* (New York: Gould's Stenographical Reporter, 1841), 358.

116 *arrested another alleged participant:* David Bederman, "The Cautionary Tale of Alexander Mcleod: Superior Orders and the American Writ of Habeas Corpus," *Emory Law Journal* 41 (1992): 515, 526.

117 *"Mexico":* Messages of the President of the United States, House Exec. Doc. no. 60, 30th Cong., 1st Sess. (Washington, DC: Government Printing Office, 1848), 8.

117 *"unjust, illegal":* House Exec. Doc. no. 60, p. 423.

118 *Taylor and his Mexican counterpart:* Ibid., p. 140.

118 *through white truce flags:* E.g., ibid., p. 346.

118 *formal capitulation agreements:* E.g., ibid., p. 346.

118 *readily exchanged prisoners:* K. Jack Bauer, *The Mexican War, 1846–1848* (New York: Macmillan, 1974), 81.

118 *routinely paroled captured Mexican:* Paul J. Springer, *America's Captives: Treatment of POWs from the Revolutionary War to the War on Terror* (Lawrence: University Press of Kansas, 2010), 75–77.

118 *"as prisoners of war":* House Exec. Doc. no. 60, p. 292.

118 *"kindness and attention":* Ibid., p. 292.

118 *"protected in their rights":* Ibid., pp. 166–68.

118 *"We come to make no war":* Ibid., p. 166.

118 *"within the rules":* Ibid., p. 2.

118 *known locally as the "Killers":* Paul Foos, *A Short, Offhand, Killing Affair: Soldiers and Social Conflict During the Mexican-American War* (Chapel Hill: University of North Carolina Press, 2002), 42.

118 *"a lawless set":* Felice Flannery Lewis, *Trailing Clouds of Glory: Zachary Taylor's Mexican War Campaign and His Emerging Civil War Leaders* (Tuscaloosa: University of Alabama, 2010), 93.

119 *"G-d d——d" thieves:* Foos, *A Short, Offhand, Killing Affair*, 123.

119 *"Goths and Vandals":* Justin H. Smith, "American Rule in Mexico," *American Historical Review* 23, no. 2 (January 1918): 287, 296.

119 *"like a body of hostile":* Marcus Cunliffe, *Soldiers and Civilians: The Martial Spirit in America, 1775–1865* (Boston: Little, Brown, 1968), 84.

119 *"to make Heaven weep":* Robert W. Johannsen, *To the Halls of the Montezumas: The Mexican War in the American Imagination* (New York: Oxford University Press, 1985), 35.

119 *"was everywhere marked":* Abiel Abbott Livermore, *War with Mexico Reviewed* (Boston: American Peace Society, 1850), 140.

119 *"inhumanities":* Mary R. Block, " 'The Stoutest Son': The Mexican-American War Journal of Henry Clay, Jr.," *Register of the Kentucky Historical Society* 160, no. 1 (2008): 5, 20.

119 *"had committed offenses":* Foos, *A Short, Offhand, Killing Affair*, 123.

119 *Taylor's popular quartermaster:* John S. D. Eisenhower, *So Far from God: The U.S. War with Mexico, 1846–1848* (New York: Random House, 1989), 65 n.

119 *"The weapon used":* George Wilkins Kendall, *Dispatches from the Mexican War*, ed. Lawrence Delbert Cress (Norman: University of Oklahoma Press, 1999), 413.

120 *switched their tactics:* Irving W. Levinson, *Wars Within Wars: Mexican Guerrillas, Domestic Elites, and the United States of America, 1846–1848* (Fort Worth: Texas Christian University Press, 2005), 34–35; Mark Saad Saka, *Peasant Nationalism and Social Unrest in the Mexican Huasteca, 1848–1884* (Houston: University of Houston Press, 1995), 176–85.

120 *"for the establishment of":* Levinson, *Wars Within Wars*, 34–35.

120 *stunning attack:* Bauer, *Mexican War*, 218.

120 *"an indiscriminate slaughter":* S. Compton Smith, M.D., *Chile Con Carne; or, The Camp and the Field* (New York: Miller & Curtis, 1857), 161–62.

120 *tied to a prickly pear:* Livermore, *War with Mexico Reviewed*, 145–46.

121 *"dreadfully wounded":* Smith, *Chile con Carne*, 107–09.

121 *"murder the soldiers":* J. Jacob Oswandel, *Notes on the Mexican War* (Philadelphia: J. Jacob Oswandel, 1885), 215–16.

121 *the guerrillas were heroes:* Albert C. Ramsay, ed., *The Other Side; or, Notes for the History of the War Between Mexico and the United States* (New York: John Wiley, 1850), 441.

121 *while they huddled inside:* Foos, *A Short, Offhand, Killing Affair*, 124.

121 *twenty-four Mexicans:* Bauer, *Mexican War*, 220; Joseph Wheelan, *Invading Mexico: America's Continental Dream and the Mexican War* (New York: Carroll & Graf, 2007), 293.

121 *"wave of vengeance" . . . "desolation and ruin":* Johannsen, *To the Halls of the Montezumas*, 36.

121 *"desolation and death":* Ramsay, ed., *The Other Side*, 442.

122 *captured by the British:* Allan Peskin, *Winfield Scott and the Profession of Arms* (Kent, OH: Kent State University Press, 2003), 27–29.

122 *In the decade thereafter:* Ibid., 63–67.

122 *the Napoleonic Wars of Europe:* Timothy D. Johnson, *Winfield Scott: The Quest for Military Glory* (Lawrence: University Press of Kansas, 1998), 166–69.

122 *Taylor had long complained:* House Exec. Doc. no. 60, p. 1138; Foos, *A Short, Offhand, Killing Affair*, 121–23.

123 *"to take cognizance":* House Exec. Doc. no. 60, pp. 369–70, 1265.

123 *Scott thought Marcy's advice:* Winfield Scott, *Memoirs of Lieut.-Gen. Winfield Scott* (New York: Sheldon & Co., 1864), 2: 392–93 n.

123 *no need for legislation:* Henry O. Whiteside, "Winfield Scott and the Mexican Occupation: Policy and Practice," *Mid-America* 52 (1970): 102, 106.

123 *"too explosive":* Scott, *Memoirs*, 2: 393.

123 *"the terrier mumbles":* Ibid., 2: 394.

123 *"military commissions":* General Orders No. 20, February 19, 1847, BL.

123 *He distributed the order widely:* General Orders No. 87, April 1, 1847, House Exec. Doc. No. 56, 30th Cong., 1st Sess., p. 104 (Vera Cruz); General Orders No. 190, June 26, 1847, NARA (Puebla); General Orders No. 287, September 17, 1847, NARA (Mexico City).

123 *303 Americans:* David Glazier, "Precedents Lost: The Neglected History of the Military Commission," *Virginia Journal of International Law* 46 (2005): 5, 37.

124 *"chivalric generosity":* Johannsen, *To the Halls of the Montezumas*, 32.

124 *"Mexican capital was not conquered":* Emma Willard, *Last Leaves of American History: Comprising a Separate History of California* (New York: George P. Putnam, 1849), 97–98.

124 *"It would be a blessing":* Ethan Allen Hitchcock, "Commentary on Winfield Scott's Campaign" (n.p., n.d.), 89–90, BL.

124 *"inhabitants of the hostile country":* House Exec. Doc. no. 60, p. 1266.

124 *a term of art that excluded soldiers:* See Charles James, *A Collection of the Charges, Opinions, and Sentences of General Courts Martial* (London: T. Egerten, 1820), 191, 569 (describing parties as either soldiers or "inhabitant[s]"); William Hough, *The Practice of Courts-Martial* (London: Kingsbury, Parbury & Allen, 2nd ed., 1825), 368, 796 (same as James, also listing names in index as "inhabitant" if not a soldier); Thomas Frederick Simmons, *Remarks on the Constitution and Practice of Courts Martial* (London: F. Pickney, 2nd ed., 1835), 27, 41–44 (describing parties as either soldiers or "inhabitant[s]").

124 *"injuries committed . . .":* Correspondence Between the Secretary of War and Generals Scott and Taylor, House Exec. Doc. 56, 30th Cong., 1st sess. (Washington, DC: Government Printing Office, 1848), 127.

124–25 *"hardly recognized as a legitimate":* House Exec. Doc. no. 60, p. 1007.

125 *attacks by "robbers":* Ibid., p. 1201.

125 *"guerrilla parties":* Levinson, *Wars Within Wars*, 67.

125 *"as many Mexicans":* Walter P. Lane, *The Adventures and Recollections of General Walter P. Lane, a San Jacinto Veteran* (Marshall, TX: Herald Print, 1887), 48.

125 *to execute the guerrilla leader: Message from the President of the United States to the Two Houses of Congress, at the Commencement of the Second Session of the Thirtieth Congress. December 5, 1848,* House Exec. Doc. no. 1, 30th Cong., 2nd Sess. (Washington, DC: Wendell & Van Benthuysen, 1848), 100.

125 *styled as "councils of war":* Erika Myers, "Conquering Peace: Military Commissions as a Lawfare Strategy in the Mexican War," *American Journal of Comparative Law* 35 (2008): 201, 229–30.

125 *Some 6,825 American soldiers:* John Whiteclay Chambers III et al., eds., *Oxford Companion to American Military History* (New York: Oxford University Press, 1999), 212.

125 *twenty-one accused recruiters:* Glazier, "Precedents Lost," 37.

125 *"almost always death":* Myers, "Conquering Peace," 230.

126 *"atrocious bands":* General Orders No. 372, Dec. 12, 1847, NARA.

126 *not a single surviving record:* Myers, "Conquering Peace," 230.

126 *"guerrilla warfare":* William Winthrop, *Military Law and Precedents* (Boston: Little, Brown, 2nd ed., 1896), 2: 1299.

126 *"without the sanction":* Myers, "Conquering Peace," 233.

127 *"of guarding against the mischief":* Vattel, *Law of Nations*, bk 3, §179, p. 375.

127 *by knights from around Europe:* M. H. Keen, *The Laws of War in the Late Middle Ages* (London: Routledge & Kegan Paul, 1965).

127 *dwindled into insignificance:* William Blackstone, *Commentaries on the Laws of England* (1768; Chicago: University of Chicago Press, 1979), 3: 68.

127 *charged him with treason:* Sidney B. Fay, "The Execution of the Duc D'Enghien (II)," *American Historical Review* 4, no. 1 (1898): 21, 26 (describing the charge that d'Enghien had "borne arms against the republic").

127 *"worse than a crime":* Ibid., 37.

127 *executed Don Giovanni Batista:* Raoul Guêze et al., *La Rivolta anti-Francese Delle Calabrie, 1806–1813* (Cosenza, Italy: Editoriale Progetto, 2000); Milton Finley, *The Most*

Monstrous of Wars: The Napoleonic Guerrilla War in Southern Italy, 1806–1811 (Columbia: University of South Carolina Press, 1994), 139.

128 *"to animadvert upon them":* Blackstone, *Commentaries,* 3: 68.

129 *elaborate taxonomies:* Vattel, *Law of Nations,* bk 2, §§339–54, pp. 281–89.

129 *"the established usages":* Henry Wheaton, *Elements of International Law: With a Sketch of the History of the Science* (Philadelphia: Carey, Lea & Blanchard, 1836), 253–54.

129 *"a Penal or Criminal Law":* Francis Lieber to Henry Halleck, October 3, 1863, FLP HL.

129 *"the cold steel of the bayonet":* Elbridge Colby, "War Crimes," *Michigan Law Review* 23 (1925): 482, 496.

129 *"soldiers who employ means":* G. F. von Martens, *Summary of the Law of Nations: Founded on the Treaties and Customs of the Modern Nations of Europe,* trans. William Cobbett (London: William Cobbett, 1795), bk 3, ch. 3, §6, pp. 284–85.

129 *"personally guilty":* Vattel, *Law of Nations,* bk 3, §150, p. 353.

129 *foreign military recruiters and assassins:* Vattel, *Law of Nations,* bk 3, §15, p. 298; bk 3 §155, 357–61.

129 *"not a relationship":* Jean-Jacques Rousseau, *Rousseau: The Social Contract and Other Later Political Writings,* ed. and trans. Victor Gourevitch (New York: Cambridge University Press, 1997), 46–47.

130 *"a universal right of war":* Scott, *Memoirs,* 575.

130 *"ought to be confined":* James Kent, *Commentaries on American Law* (New York: O. Halsted, 1826–30), 1: 88.

130 *"nothing wrong in the rule":* Thomas Maitland Marshall, "Diary and Memoranda of William L. Marcy," *American Historical Review* 24, no. 3 (1919): 444, 459 n. 23.

131 *"any of the guard":* William Jay, *A Review of the Causes and Consequences of the Mexican War* (Boston: American Peace Society, 1853), 206–07.

132 *more than a quarter of his troops:* Levinson, *Wars Within Wars,* 61.

132 *"the natural state of man":* William B. Skelton, *An American Profession of Arms: The Army Officer Corps, 1784–1861* (Lawrence: University Press of Kansas, 1992), 327.

132 *"moral distempers":* Peskin, *Winfield Scott,* 101.

133 *William Marcy:* Larry Gara, *The Presidency of Franklin Pierce* (Lawrence: University Press of Kansas, 1991), 138.

133 *The British government agreed:* Sir Francis Piggot, *The Declaration of Paris, 1856: A Study* (London: University of London Press, 1919), 13–18.

133 *"most auspicious":* House Exec. Doc. no. 103, 33d Cong., 1st Sess. (1854), 15.

133 *"a fair prospect":* Ibid., p. 12.

134 *For centuries, private vessels:* Mark Grimsley, "The Pirate and the State: Henry Morgan and Irregular Naval Warfare in the Early Modern World," in Jack Sweetman, ed., *New Interpretations in Naval History: Selected Papers from the Tenth Naval History Symposium* (Annapolis, MD: Naval Institute Press, 1993), 29–43.

134 *"responsible to":* Sir Robert Phillimore, *Commentaries Upon International Law* (Philadelphia: T. & J. W. Johnson, 1854–60), 1: 290.

134 *Benjamin Franklin argued: PBF,* 37: 618–19.

134 *The 1776 model treaty: JCC,* 5: 584.

134 *The 1785 treaty:* Malloy, 2: 1483.

134 *Jefferson's draft treaty with Austria:* Edmund C. Bennett, "Note on American Negotiations for Commercial Treaties, 1776–1786," *American Historical Review* 16, no. 3 (1911): 579, 587.

134 *a U.S. treaty with Spain:* Malloy, 2: 1645.

134 *"civilization and Christianity": ASP: Naval Affairs,* 1: 723.

134 *John Quincy Adams had advocated:* James E. Lewis, Jr., *John Quincy Adams: Policymaker for the Union* (Wilmington, DE: Scholarly Resources, 2001), 83–84.

134 *517 American privateering vessels:* David S. Heidler & Jeanne T. Heidler, *The Encyclopedia of the War of 1812* (Santa Barbara, CA: ABC-CLIO, 1997), 429; Jerome R. Garitee, *The Republic's Private Navy: The American Privateering Business as Practiced by Baltimore During the War of 1812* (Middletown, CT: Wesleyan University Press, 1977), xvi, 244.

134 *"from resorting to the merchant"*: House Exec. Doc. no. 103, p. 13.
135 *consisted of barely forty vessels*: John J. Lalor, ed., *Cyclopaedia of Political Science, Political Economy, and of the Political History of the United States* (Chicago: Melbert B. Care, 1883), 2: 408–10, 984–90.
135 *"was aimed exclusively"*: George Mifflin Dallas, *A Series of Letters from London Written During the Years 1856, '57, '58, '59, and '60* (Philadelphia: Lippincott, 1869), 1: 32–33, 75, 129–30.
135 *"catch brother Jonathan"*: Olive Anderson, "Some Further Light on the Inner History of the Declaration of Paris," *Law Quarterly Review* 76 (1960): 379, 384.
135 *no longer an effective mode*: Charles Francis Adams, *Seward and the Declaration of Paris: A Forgotten Diplomatic Episode, April–August, 1861* (Boston: Massachusetts Historical Society, 1912), 14, 53–55; John W. Coogan, *The End of Neutrality: The United States, Britain, and Maritime Rights, 1899–1915* (Ithaca. NY: Cornell University Press, 1981), 22–25; Edgar Stanton Maclay, *A History of American Privateers* (New York: D. Appleton, 1899), xxiii–xxiv; Bryan Ranft, "Restraints on War at Sea Before 1945," in Michael Howard, ed., *Restraints on War* (New York: Oxford University Press, 1979), 39–56; Theodore S. Woolsey, "The United States and the Declaration of Paris," *Yale Law Journal* 3, no. 3 (1894): 77, 80.
135 *learned to circumvent*: Adams, *Seward and the Declaration of Paris*, 53–55; *The Times* (London), May 26, 1856.
135 *"The capacity of carrying on"*: *The Times* (London), May 26, 1856.
136 *"to subserve their own interests"*: Senate Exec. Doc. no. 104, 34th Cong., 1st Sess. (1856), 12.
136 *"combined potentates"*: Dallas, *A Series of Letters from London*, 1: 130, 2: 171.
136 *"I am afraid"*: "Mr. Cobden on Maritime Law," *The Times* (London), December 11, 1856.

Part II A Few Things Barbarous or Cruel

139 *Epigraph*: AL to James C. Conkling, August 26, 1863, Basler, 6: 408.

Chapter 5. We Don't Practise the Law of Nations

141 *"I'm a good enough lawyer"*: Don E. Fehrenbacher & Virginia Fehrenbacher, eds., *Recollected Words of Abraham Lincoln* (Stanford, CA: Stanford University Press, 1996), 423.
141 *Lincoln himself bitterly opposed*: Cong. *Globe*, 30th Cong., 1st sess., appendix, p. 94.
141 *a brilliant battlefield tactician*: Joseph E. Chance, *Jefferson Davis's Mexican War Regiment* (Jackson: University Press of Mississippi, 1991), 98.
141–42 *"I had a good many"*: David Herbert Donald, *Lincoln* (New York: Simon & Schuster, 1995), 45.
142 *"knew absolutely nothing"*: Charles Francis Adams, *An Address on the Character and Services of William Henry Seward* (Albany, NY: Weed, Parson & Co., 1873), 2.
142 *the good sense to hide*: Dean B. Mahin, *One War at a Time: The International Dimensions of the American Civil War* (Washington, DC: Brassey's, 1999), 2.
142 *"know anything about diplomacy"*: Mahin, *One War at a Time*, 2.
142 *"We must not be enemies"*: Basler, 4: 271.
142 *"Acts of violence"*: Ibid., 4: 265.
142 *"be hospitable to a foe"*: Howard C. Perkins, ed., *Northern Editorials on Secession* (New York: D. Appleton-Century Co., 1942), 2: 785 (April 18, 1861).
142 *"entitled to the considerations"*: Ibid., 2: 1088 (May 30, 1861).
142 *"no quarters should be shown"*: Ibid., 2: 727 (April 13, 1861).
142 *"war of extermination"*: Ibid., 2: 746–47 (April 19, 1861).
142 *"refusing to lower"*: Elias B. Holmes to AL, April 20, 1861, ALP LC.
142–43 *"vindictive, fierce"*: "The Character of the Coming Campaign," *New York Herald*, April 28, 1861, 4.
143 *"Jeff. Davis & Co."*: Donald, *Lincoln*, 295.

143 *"if the U.S. determined"*: Lord Newton, *Lord Lyons: A Record of British Diplomacy* (London: Edward Arnold, 1913), 31, 33; see Craig L. Symonds, *Lincoln and His Admirals* (New York: Oxford University Press, 2008), 39–40.

144 *The bumper crop of 1860:* D. P. Crook, *Diplomacy During the American Civil War* (New York: John Wiley & Sons, 1975), 73–75.

144 *"vexations beyond bearing"*: Newton, *Lord Lyons*, 36.

144 *"a regular blockade"*: Ibid., 36.

145 *"to set on foot"*: Basler, 4: 339, 346–47.

145 *Lincoln understood all too well:* Theodore Calvin Peace & James G. Randall, eds., *The Diary of Orville Hickman Browning* (Springfield, IL: Illinois State Historical Library, 1925), 1: 489.

145 *"Our ships"*: Newton, *Lord Lyons*, 36.

145 *"A nation cannot blockade"*: Howard K. Beale, ed., *The Diary of Edward Bates, 1859–1866* (Washington, DC: Government Printing Office, 1933), 427; see also Edward Bates, "Memorandum, April 15, 1861," ALP LC.

145 *"the legal and straightforward"*: Montgomery Blair to AL, August 10, 1861, ALP LC.

145 *"preferred an embargo"* . . . *"quasi government"*: Gideon Welles, *Lincoln and Seward: Remarks Upon the Memorial Address of Chas. Francis Adams on the Late Wm. H. Seward* (New York: Sheldon & Co., 1874), 122–23.

145 *"If the interdiction is to be"*: Gideon Welles to AL, August 5, 1861, ALP LC.

145 *"the blockade of the Southern ports"*: William Howard Russell, *My Diary North and South* (New York: Harper & Bros., 1863), 177–78.

146 *"the law of Nations"*: Basler, 4: 339.

146 *"strange inconsistency"*: Welles, *Lincoln and Seward*, 128.

146 *"to avoid complications"* . . . *"on our hands at once"*: Ibid., 124.

146 *"to conduct the war"*: Charles M. Segal, *Conversations with Lincoln* (New York: G. P. Putnam, 1961), 114; see also Donald, *Lincoln*, 303.

147 *The Union blockading squadron's first capture:* Symonds, *Lincoln and His Admirals*, 37–38.

147 *captured a dozen: ORN*, series 1, 5: 637.

147 *the English bark* Hiawatha: Stuart L. Bernath, *Squall Across the Atlantic: American Civil War Prize Cases and Diplomacy* (Berkeley: University of California Press, 1970), 22.

147 *the schooner* Tropic Wind: *ORN*, series 1, 5: 667.

147 *intercepted more than 1,200 vessels: Prize Vessels: Letter from the Secretary of the Navy in answer to a resolution of the House of April 30, relative to prize vessels*, House Exec. Doc. no. 279, 40th Cong., 2d Sess. (1868).

147 *rail-thin and slightly stooped:* Russell, *My Diary North and South*, 34; Glyndon G. van Deusen, *William Henry Seward* (New York: Oxford University Press, 1967).

147 *"Seward is Weed"*: Welles, *Lincoln and Seward*, 23.

148 *Seward had been the favorite:* Doris Kearns Goodwin, *Team of Rivals: The Political Genius of Abraham Lincoln* (New York: Simon & Schuster, 2005), 11–16.

148 *"never given any particular"* . . . *"no lawyer and no statesman"*: Charles Francis Adams, *Seward and the Declaration of Paris: A Forgotten Diplomatic Episode, April–August, 1861* (Boston: Massachusetts Historical Society, 1912), 23–24.

148 *"His view of the relations"*: Newton, *Lord Lyons*, 30.

148 *merely sixty-seven ships:* Symonds, *Lincoln and His Admirals*, 49–50; John Niven, *Gideon Welles: Lincoln's Secretary of the Navy* (New York: Oxford University Press, 1973).

148 *a navy comprised of 588 vessels:* Basler, 7: 43.

148 *never a perfectly tight fit:* Bernath, *Squall Across the Atlantic*, 4–5, 11; Symonds, *Lincoln and His Admirals*, 38; cf. Stephen R. Wise, *Lifeline of the Confederacy: Blockade Running During the Civil War* (Columbia, SC: University of South Carolina Press, 1988); William N. Still, "A Naval Sieve: The Union Blockade in the Civil War," *U.S. Naval College Review* 36 (1983): 38–45.

148–49 *Yet the blockade deterred:* Craig L. Symonds, *The Civil War at Sea* (Santa Barbara, CA: ABC-CLIO, 2009), 54–58; Crook, *Diplomacy During the American Civil War*, 61–62.

149 *"the bold and vigorous mind"*: Welles, *Lincoln and Seward*, 123.

149 *"I am embarrassed"*: Gideon Welles to AL, August 5, 1861, ALP LC.

149 *"Every capture":* Ibid.

149 *would minimize the conflict:* Van Deusen, *William Henry Seward*, 300.

149 *"looked in [a] book":* Gideon Welles, *Diary of Gideon Welles, Secretary of the Navy Under Lincoln and Johnson* (Boston: Houghton Mifflin, 1911), 2: 232.

150 *denying Lincoln's authority to suspend:* See Carl B. Swisher, *History of the Supreme Court of the United States: The Taney Period, 1836–64* (New York: Macmillan, 1974), 844–54.

150 *"would end the war":* Samuel Shapiro, *Richard Henry Dana, Jr., 1815–1882* (East Lansing: Michigan State University Press, 1961), 121.

150 *"the foremost trial lawyer":* John D. Gordon III, "The Trial of the Officers and Crew of the Schooner 'Savannah,'" *Yearbook of the Supreme Court Historical Society* (1983): 31, 39.

150 *not to let the cases reach the Supreme Court:* Edward Bates to William M. Evarts, March 11, 1862, letterbook B-5, Attorney General Papers, record group 60, NARA; Swisher, *The Taney Period*, 881–82.

150 *adding a tenth seat:* An Act to Provide Circuit Courts for the Districts of California and Oregon, and for Other Purposes, Stat., 12: 794; David M. Silver, *Lincoln's Supreme Court* (Urbana: University of Illinois, 1998), 84. In the midst of a later court-packing controversy, Erwin Griswold of Harvard Law School explained the tenth circuit as an apolitical response to the founding of the Union Pacific Railroad, which made it possible for a justice to get to a new 10th circuit court based in California. See Hearings on S. 1392 Before the Senate Committee on the Judiciary, 75th Cong., 1st sess. (1937), 763. Dean Griswold wanted to find a neutral basis for the Civil War court packing in order to deny a historical precedent to Franklin Roosevelt's proposed New Deal court-packing plan.

150 *upholding the blockade: The Prize Cases*, 67 U.S. 635 (1863).

150 *take the slavery question out of politics:* Don E. Fehrenbacher, *Dred Scott: Its Significance in American Law and Politics* (New York: Oxford University Press, 1978), 311–14.

151 *"there must be war": The Prize Cases*, 67 U.S. at 644.

151 *"The law of nations": The Prize Cases*, 67 U.S. at 670.

151 *"may exercise both belligerent": The Prize Cases*, 67 U.S. at 673.

151 *"Our case is double":* Charles Sumner, *The Works of Charles Sumner* (Boston: Lee & Shepard, 1870–83), 7: 13.

152 *"To a long continuance":* Bernath, *Squall Across the Atlantic*, 4–5.

152 *a flotilla of 200 vessels: ORN*, series 1, 17: 403.

152 *"hope of crushing the rebellion": ORN*, series 1, 17: 192.

152 *The* Labuan *was a neutral vessel: ORN*, series 1, 17: 99–115; Bernath, *Squall Across the Atlantic*, 37–40.

153 *restored the vessel: The Labuan*, 14 F. Cas. 906 (D.C.N.Y. 1862).

153 *seized a parade of British vessels: ORN*, series 1, 18: 525 (*Will o' the Wisp*); Bernath, *Squall Across the Atlantic*, 52–60.

153 *ruled against U.S. Navy captors:* E.g., *The Dashing Wave*, 72 U.S. 170 (1866); *The Teresita*, 72 U.S. 180 (1866); *The Sir William Peel*, 72 U.S. 517 (1866).

153 *"large quantities of arms": ORN*, series 1, 1: 207.

153 *Welles ordered the Navy: ORN*, series 1, 1: 207–08.

154 *captured the English bark* Springbok*: ORN*, series 1, 2: 70.

154 *"the voyage from London": The Springbok*, 72 U.S. 1, 28 (1866).

155 *"when destined to the hostile country": The Peterhoff*, 72 U.S. 28, 59 (1866).

155 *"humane policy":* Montague Bernard, *A Historical Account of the Neutrality of Great Britain During the American Civil War* (London: Longmans, Green, Reader & Dyer, 1870), 153.

155 *"raised an inference":* Ibid., 503.

155 *"Old Abe":* Bradford Perkins, *The Cambridge History of American Foreign Relations. Vol. 1: The Creation of a Republican Empire, 1776–1865* (New York: Cambridge University Press, 1993), 223.

155 *"scarcely needs to be considered":* Basler, 4: 441 n. 47.

156 *facilitated the exit of foreign merchants:* Bernard, *Neutrality of Great Britain*, 101, 240.

156 *the status of foreign nationals:* Ibid., 324.
156 *subsequently seized the vessel back:* Ibid., 325–28.
156 *compensation of foreign nationals:* Basler, 7: 38, 40–41.
157 *sailed out of Charleston Harbor:* John Thomas Scharf, *History of the Confederate States Navy* (New York: Rogers & Sherwood, 1887), 84–85.
157 *Calvo had a wife: United States Census for 1850,* Town of Columbia, County of Richland, South Carolina, roll M432_858, p. 20A.
157 *a printer by trade:* John C. Ellen, Jr., "Political Newspapers of the South Carolina Up Country 1850–1859: A Compendium," *South Carolina Historical Magazine* 63 (1962): 158, 162.
157 *Along with thirty-four other men:* William Morrison Robinson, *The Confederate Privateers* (New Haven: Yale University Press, 1929), 89–92.
157 *the promise of huge profits:* Ibid., 30–46.
157 *eventually capturing the* Mary Alice *and its crew: ORN,* series 1, 6: 61–63, 68.
157 *imprisoned at Fort Hamilton: OR,* series 2, 3: 28.
158 *"a poor man"* . . . *"considered and treated the same":* J. P. M. Calvo to AL, November 12, 1861, ALP LC.
158 *"a good deal of joking":* Russell, *My Diary North and South,* 127.
158 *"an easy remedy for that":* Ibid., 175.
158 *"insane and blood-thirsty spirit":* "The *Charleston Mercury* on the Privateer *Savannah,*" *Christian Recorder* (Philadelphia), June 22, 1861.
158 *"A just regard to humanity":* James D. Richardson, *A Compilation of the Messages and Papers of the Confederacy* (Nashville, TN: United States Publ. Co., 1905), 2: 115.
159 *to accept belatedly the British invitation of 1856:* Van Deusen, *William Henry Seward,* 297.
160 *"only be because she is willing":* William Henry Seward to Charles Francis Adams, May 21, 1861, ALP LC.
160 *"inconsistencies of the Northern people":* Russell, *My Diary North and South,* 559.
160 *"Very well":* Jay Monaghan, *Diplomat in Carpet Slippers: Abraham Lincoln Deals with Foreign Affairs* (New York: Bobbs-Merrill, 1945), 82.
160 *"within the rules of modern civilized":* Perkins, *Creation of a Republican Empire,* 222.
161 *a federal grand jury in New York:* A. F. Warburton, *Trial of the Officers and Crew of the Privateer* Savannah, *on the Charge of Piracy, in the United States District Court for the Southern District of New York* (New York: Baker & Godwin, 1862); Mark A. Weitz, *The Confederacy on Trial: The Piracy and Sequestration Cases of 1861* (Lawrence: University Press of Kansas, 2005).
161 *a grand jury in Philadelphia:* D. F. Murphy, *The Jeff Davis Piracy Cases: Full Report of the Trial of William Smith for Piracy* (Philadelphia: King & Baird, 1861).
161 *verdict of guilty against William Smith:* Murphy, *Jeff Davis Piracy Cases,* 99–100.
161 *The New York trial:* Gordon, Warburton, "Trial of the Officers and Crew," 34–39.
162 *"as enemies, for the purpose":* Ibid., 124.
162 *remember that their fathers:* Ibid., 229.
162 *transferred from the Tombs:* Gordon, "Trial of the Officers and Crew," 43.
162 *At the end of May: OR,* series 2, 3: 611.
162 *the first great land battle of the war:* On the importance of Bull Run for the privateering cases, see Adams, *Seward and the Declaration of Paris,* 42.
163 *after an interview with Congressman Alfred Ely:* Scharf, *Confederate States Navy,* 78. Scharf puts the Ely meeting on February 2, 1862. Ely met with Lincoln on the evening of December 29, 1861—see "The War for the Union," *New York Tribune,* December 30, 1861, p. 5.
163 *to draw from a tin:* Alfred Ely, *The Journal of Alfred Ely, a Prisoner of War in Richmond* (New York: D. Appleton & Co., 1862), 212–14.
163 *commissioned only fifty-two privateers:* Spencer C. Tucker, *Blue and Gray Navies: The Civil War Afloat* (Annapolis, MD: Naval Institute Press, 2006), 74.
163 *lost interest in privateering:* Robinson, *Confederate Privateers,* 32, 38–40.
163 *a national celebrity:* Nathaniel Philbrick, *Sea of Glory: America's Voyage of Discovery, the U.S. Exploring Expedition, 1838–1842* (New York: Viking Penguin, 2003), xv, xix, 300.

164 *"the name of Wilkes":* Ibid., xxiv.

164 *Welles appointed Wilkes: ORN,* series 1, 1: 64–65.

164 *under Captain Samuel F. Du Pont:* Philbrick, *Sea of Glory,* 354.

164 *Violating his orders:* Norman B. Ferris, *The Trent Affair: A Diplomatic Crisis* (Knoxville: University of Tennessee Press, 1977), 18–19.

164 *Wilkes heard rumors: ORN,* series 1, 1: 143.

164 *fired shots across its bow:* Ferris, *The Trent Affair,* 21; Philbrick, *Sea of Glory,* 354; Symonds, *Lincoln and His Admirals,* 75.

165 *Wilkes had scoured the law books: OR,* series 2, 2: 1098.

165 *consideration for the passengers and crew: ORN,* series 1, 1: 184.

165 *"a storm of exultation":* Russell, *My Diary North and South,* 573–78; see also Charles Francis Adams, "The Trent Affair," *American Historical Review* 17 (April 1912): 540, 547–49.

165 *"conduct in seizing":* Bernard, *Neutrality of Great Britain,* 194.

165 *"such a burst of feeling":* Ferris, *The Trent Affair,* 179.

165 *"in very great haste":* Charles Wilson to William H. Seward, November 27, 1861, ALP LC.

165 *"England is exasperated":* Thurlow Weed to William H. Seward, December 4, 1861, ALP LC.

165 *"deliberately settled upon":* Thurlow Weed to William H. Seward, December 11, 1861, ALP LC.

166 *"The law of nations":* Beale, ed., *Diary of Edward Bates,* 202.

166 *"embodiment of dispatches":* Adams, "Trent Affair," 547.

166 *Former U.S. attorneys general and secretaries of state:* Ibid., 548 (Caleb Cushing and Edward Everett).

166 *law professors at Harvard:* Ibid., 548 (Theophilus Parsons).

166 *leading prize court lawyers:* Ibid., 549 (Richard Henry Dana).

166 *"superseded the authority":* Newton, *Lord Lyons,* 1: 64.

166 *But British lawyers and statesmen:* Adams, "Trent Affair," 554.

166 *"a suitable apology":* John Russell to Richard B. Pemell (Lord Lyons), November 30, 1861, ALP LC.

166 *Lyons was to request:* Newton, *Lord Lyons,* 1: 61.

166 *"timidly truckling":* Beale, ed., *Diary of Edward Bates,* 216.

167 *"Cuban Missile Crisis":* Symonds, *Lincoln and His Admirals,* 94.

167 *"taken into his own hands":* Newton, *Lord Lyons* , 1: 64.

168 *"was really defending":* George E. Baker, ed., *The Works of William H. Seward* (Boston: Houghton Mifflin, 1884), 5: 307.

168 *"carried before a legal tribunal":* Ibid., 5: 308.

168 *had hoped to arrange an arbitration:* Memorandum on the Trent Affair, December 1861, ALP LC.

168 *Lyons even forgave the absence:* Ferris, *The Trent Affair,* 196–98.

168 *"a technical wrong":* David Donald, ed., *Inside Lincoln's Cabinet: The Civil War Diaries of Salmon P. Chase* (New York: Longmans, Green, 1954), 55; see also Amanda Foreman, *A World on Fire: Britain's Role in the American Civil War* (New York: Randon House, 2010), 194.

168 *"bring law into contempt":* Adams, "Trent Affair," 555 and 555 n. 3.

169 *"every negro of every rebel":* John M. Palmer to Lyman Trumbull, December 28, 1861, ALP LC; see also Charles P. McIlvaine to AL, January 6, 1864, ALP LC; Crook, *Diplomacy During the American Civil War,* 58.

Chapter 6. Blood Is the Rich Dew of History

170 *The shorter war is:* Twenty-Seven Definitions and Elementary Positions Concerning the Law and Usages of War [1861], definition 19, folder 15, box 2, FLP JHU.

170 *Fort Donelson:* My account of the battle at Fort Donelson relies on *OR,* 1: 7, 174–78; Marion Morrison, *A History of the Ninth Regiment, Illinois Volunteer Infantry* (Monmouth, IL: J. S. Clark, 1864); Jack Hurst, *Men of Fire: Grant, Forrest, and the Campaign*

That Decided the Civil War (New York: Basic Books, 2007); Kendall B. Gott, *Where the South Lost the War* (Mechanicsburg, PA: Stackpole Books, 2003), 194–283; Benjamin Franklin Cooling, *Forts Henry and Donelson: The Key to the Confederate Heartland* (Knoxville: University of Tennessee Press, 1987); James O. Churchill, *A Letter Written During the Civil War, in Which Many St. Louis People Are Mentioned* (St. Louis: The Writer, 1909); John H. Brinton, *Personal Memoirs of John H. Brinton, Major and Surgeon U.S.V., 1861–1865* (New York: Neale Publishing, 1914), 91–92; *Medical and Surgical History of the Rebellion* (Washington, DC: Government Printing Office, 1870), appendix 26–28; and Frederick H. Dyer, *A Compendium of the War of Rebellion* (Des Moines: Dyer Publishing Co., 1908).

172 *the Naval Academy at Annapolis:* FL to Charles Sumner, February 4, 1853, box 42, FLP HL.

172 *a reputation for prodigious:* Hamilton Lieber to Guido Norman Lieber, March 24, 1862, box 55, FLP HL.

172 *tied a kerchief . . . smashed the elbow:* FL to Charles Sumner, March 23, 1862, box 42, FLP HL.

172 *"death storm":* J. S. Newberry, *A Visit to Fort Donelson, Tenn. for the Relief of the Wounded of Feb'y 15, 1862: A Letter* (New York: U.S. Sanitary Commission, 1862), 4.

172 *wounded . . . lay dead: Medical and Surgical History of the Rebellion,* appendix 28.

172 *8th Illinois and 18th Illinois:* Gott, *Where the South Lost the War,* 282–83.

172 *201 . . . especially gruesome:* Morrison, *History of the Ninth Regiment,* 17–24.

172 *makeshift field hospital:* Newberry, *A Visit to Fort Donelson,* 4–5.

173 *catch the attention:* Matilda Lieber to Hamilton Lieber, March 30, 1862, box 55, FLP HL.

173 *"unconditional and immediate": OR,* 1: 7, 161.

173 *"most disastrous":* Donald Stoker, *The Grand Design: Strategy and the U.S. Civil War* (New York: Oxford University Press, 2010), 116.

173 *decide the Civil War:* Gott, *Where the South Lost the War;* Stoker, *Grand Design,* 116.

173 *etch the date:* Hamilton's sword was put up for auction and sold by the auction house of James D. Julia in New Hampshire in 2005. See http://www.icollector.com/inscribed-us-model-1850-foot-officer-s-sword-with_i5323646, last visited November 24, 2011.

173 *born in Berlin:* The old but excellent biography of Lieber is Frank Freidel, *Francis Lieber: Nineteenth-Century Liberal* (Baton Rouge: Louisiana State University Press, 1947).

174 *assassinating Napoleon:* Ibid., 9.

174 *"able to expel the French":* Quoted in ibid., 19.

174 *"I suddenly experienced":* Thomas Sergent Perry, ed., *Life and Letters of Francis Lieber* (Boston: James R. Osgood, 1882), 16.

174 *fight for Greek independence:* Freidel, *Francis Lieber,* 30–33.

175 *"if there should not be":* Perry, *Life and Letters,* 38.

175 *"indelible horror":* Ibid., 12.

175 *a bewildered boy:* Ibid.

175 *"tremendous uproar and carnage":* Ibid.

175 *"over the mangled bodies":* Ibid.

175 *"I told my comrade":* Ibid., 14.

175 *stealing his watch:* Ibid., 18.

175 *Lieber was arrested and imprisoned:* Freidel, *Francis Lieber,* 23–30, 42–45.

175 *Matilda ("Matty") Oppenheim:* Matilda signed her letters as "Matty," and Francis (whom she called "Frank" in correspondence) addressed her the same way. See, e.g., FL to Matilda Lieber, August 5, 1854, box 36, FLP HL.

176 *President John Quincy Adams . . . William Marcy:* See Freidel, *Francis Lieber,* 58.

176 *President Jackson had a set:* Perry, *Life and Letters,* 92.

176 *Lincoln owned a set:* Joshua Wolf Schenk, *Lincoln's Melancholy: How Depression Challenged a President and Fueled His Greatness* (New York: Houghton Mifflin, 2005), 30; Freidel, *Francis Lieber,* 81 n. 44.

176 *a desultory teacher:* On Lieber as a teacher, see the student notes of Robert Bage Canfield from 1861 (Robert Bage Canfield Manuscripts, 1858–1862, Rare Books Room, Butler Library, Columbia University), as well as the lecture notes that Lieber made for himself in the margins of books he seems simply to have read out at great length in class, punctuated by lengthy digressions—see, e.g., Lieber's copy of [Thomas Arnold?], *History of Rome* (Philadelphia: Carey, Lea, & Blanchard, 1837), 195–97, in the Judge Advocate School Lieber Collection, Federal Research Division, LC.

176 *spoke in strange and idiosyncratic formulations:* Freidel, *Francis Lieber*, 199.

177 *"for want of a rapid":* Ibid., 140.

177 *"most fertile":* David Donald, *Charles Sumner and the Coming of the Civil War* (New York: Alfred A. Knopf, 1960), 81.

177 *"individual"* . . . *"lost more and more in the mass":* "Army," in *Encyclopaedia Americana*, ed. Francis Lieber (Philadelphia: Carey, Lea, & Blanchard, 1829), 1: 380.

177 *"by persons who have":* Francis Lieber, *Manual of Political Ethics* (Boston: Little, Brown, 1838–39), 2: 633.

177 *"energy and independence"* . . . *"moral electricity":* Ibid., 2: 632.

177 *"choicest pages":* Ibid., 2: 633.

177 *"Every single thread":* Law and Usages of War, No. II, 29 October 1861 [Notebook No. II], folder 16, box 2, FLP JHU.

177 *"Blood"* . . . *"vital juice":* FL to Fanny Longfellow, March 15, 1844, quoted in James F. Childress, "Francis Lieber's Interpretation of the Laws of War: General Orders No. 100 in the Context of His Life and Thought," *American Journal of Jurisprudence* 21 (1976): 34, 44 n. 33.

178 *"best and purest"* . . . *"degrading submissiveness":* Lieber, *Manual of Political Ethics*, 2: 646.

178 *"the nobleness of human nature"* . . . *"freedom of his children":* Ibid., 2: 633.

178 *"the greatest good":* Ibid., 2: 667.

178 *"that lively feeling":* Ibid., 2: 647.

178 *"not demoralizing":* Ibid., 2: 645.

178 *were morally responsible for their actions:* FL to Charles Sumner, April 1, 1841, May 20, 1841, and June 18, 1841, box 40, FLP HL; also FL to Senator Rufus Choate, December 25, 1841, in Perry, *Life and Letters*, 161.

178 *would have acquitted McLeod:* FL to Charles Sumner, May 20, 1841, box 40, FLP HL.

179 *"the worst advised":* Perry, *Life and Letters*, 198.

179 *"elevated intention":* The quotation comes from the marginalia on the cover of Lieber's copy of Sumner's *Oration at Union College* (July 25, 1848), FLP JHU.

179 *leaf from the field at Waterloo:* ML to Martin Russell Thayer, October, 1872, box 55, FLP HL.

179 *march of the cadets:* Perry, *Life and Letters*, 129.

179 *"spheres of action":* Freidel, *Francis Lieber*, 198.

179 *"shaping history in the field":* Perry, *Life and Letters*, 209–10.

179 *"I was born for action":* Ibid.

179 *"Would to God":* FL to Henry Halleck, February 8, 1862, box 27, FLP HL.

179 *"Oh! my poor life":* Freidel, *Francis Lieber*, 122.

180 *"a Slave State!":* Perry, *Life and Letters*, 104.

180 *enlisted in Hampton's Legion:* Freidel, *Francis Lieber*, 136 n. 38 & 306.

180 *"Behold in me":* Childress, "Francis Lieber's Interpretation," 43.

180 *"Strike, strike":* FL to Charles Sumner, January 20, 1865, box 44, FLP HL.

180 *"sledgehammer":* FL to Charles Sumner, February 13, 1865, box 45, FLP HL.

180 *"a death blow":* Edward Bates to FL, September 2 and 3, 1862, box 2, FLP HL.

180 *"Blow upon Blow":* FL to Alexander Dallas Bache, May 3, 1862, box 31, RC HL.

180 *"Hard, Harder":* FL to Alexander Dallas Bache, May 6, 1862, box 31, RC HL.

180 *"drive back":* Edward Bates to FL, September 2 and 3, 1862, box 2, FLP HL.

180 *arm-and-hammer sketch:* E.g., FL to Alexander Dallas Bache, May 12, 1862, box 31, RC HL.

180 *"I intended to do so":* FL to Matilda Lieber, July 26, 1861, box 36, FLP HL.

181 *"won't you give us at least":* Freidel, *Francis Lieber,* 308.

181 *"a peculiarly truthful":* FL to Henry Boynton Smith, August 15, 1861, box 39, FLP HL.

181 *"war does not absolve us":* Lieber, *Manual of Political Ethics,* 2: 658.

181 *"guided by no false sentimentality":* Lieber, "The Disposal of Prisoners," *New York Times,* August 19, 1861.

181 *around 100 people:* FL to Henry Halleck, October 28, 1863, box 28, FLP HL.

181 *an epic tour:* Lieber's lecture notes are available in box 2, folders 15–18, FLP JH.

181 *carried in the* New York Times *and reprinted:* E.g., "Lecture by Dr. Francis Lieber on the Laws and Usages of War—No. 1," *New York Times,* October 27, 1861; see also [clipping], *New York Evening Post,* in box 2, folder 18, FLP JH.

182 *"Father Namby Pamby":* FL to Henry Halleck, 10/3/1863, box 28, FLP HL. "Namby pamby" was Lieber's favorite insult. See the interleafed passages in his copy of his own *Manual of Political Ethics,* 2: 664–65, box 5, FLP JHU.

182 *"a period of peculiar martial character": Law and Usages of War,* No. I, 21 October 1861, folder 16, box 2, FLP JHU. All quotations from the lecture are from this source.

183 *"a rule of action":* Law and Usages of War, No. III, 3 December 1861 [Notebook No. III], folder 16, box 2, FLP JHU.

183 *"greater than necessary":* Law and Usages of War, No. IV, 17 December 1861 [Notebook No. IV], folder 16, box 2, FLP JHU.

183 *"unnecessary infliction of pain":* Law and Usages of War, No. III.

183 *"something fiendish"* . . . *"lawful to resort":* Law and Usages of War, No. IV.

184 *"No doubt"* . . . *"one of our own?":* Ibid.

184 *"those arms that do"* . . . *"peace and civilization":* Ibid.

184 "corte e grosse": Felix Gilbert, "Machiavelli: The Renaissance of the Art of War," in Peter Paret, ed. *Makers of Modern Strategy: From Machiavelli to the Nuclear Age* (Princeton, NJ: Princeton University Press, 1986), 11, 24 n. 26.

184 *"kurz und vives":* Jay Luvass, ed., *Frederick the Great on the Art of War* (New York: Free Press, 1966), 141.

184 *"but to make the calamity":* Montague Bernard, "The Growth of Laws and Usages of War," in *Oxford Essays* (London: Parker, 1856), 134–35.

184 *Carl von Clausewitz:* For Clausewitz's life, I have relied on the introductions in editors Michael Howard & Peter Paret's translation of Clausewitz's *On War* (Princeton, NJ: Princeton University Press, 1976); Peter Paret, *The Cognitive Challenge of War: Prussia, 1806* (Princeton, NJ: Princeton University Press, 2009); Peter Paret, *Understanding War: Essays on Clausewitz and the History of Military Power* (Princeton, NJ: Princeton University Press, 1992); Peter Paret, *Clausewitz and the State* (New York: Oxford University Press, 1976); and Roger Parkinson, *Clausewitz: A Biography* (New York: Stein & Day, 1971).

185 *"minutiae of service"* . . . *"fighting a battle":* Paret, *Cognitive Challenge,* 140.

185 *"hardly worth mentioning":* Clausewitz, *On War,* 75.

185 *"in the name of humanity"* . . . *"hack off our arms":* Ibid., 260.

185 *100 years after the Civil War:* Beatrice Heuser, *Reading Clausewitz* (London: Pimlico, 2002), 17; see also Christopher Bassford, *Clausewitz in English: The Reception of Clausewitz in Britain and America, 1815–1945* (New York: Oxford University Press, 1994), which notes that Clausewitz had some readers far earlier.

185 *"the continuation of politics":* Clausewitz, *On War,* 7, 69 ("war is nothing but a continuation of policy with other means"); 605 ("war is simply a continuation of political intercourse, with the addition of other means").

186 *"an act of force":* Ibid., 75.

186 *Clausewitz's definition:* Lieber, *Manual of Political Ethics,* 2: 631.

186 *"to compel him to peace"* . . . *"use all means":* Ibid., 2: 660 n. 3.

186 *"morality floats":* Law and Usages of War, No. IV.

186 *eschewed the quintessential strategy:* One twenty-first-century Clausewitz student puts it this way: "If the ends don't justify the means, I'd like to know what in the hell does!" See Phillip Bobbitt, *Terror and Consent: The Wars for the 21st Century* (New York: Alfred A. Knopf, 2007), 351.

186 *They rejoiced at the Union victory:* FL to Henry Halleck, February 8, 1862, box 27, FLP HL.

186 *bad tidings:* FL to Halleck, February 19, 1862, box 27, FLP HL.

187 *sought out his wounded son:* Oliver Wendell Holmes, "My Hunt After the Captain," *Atlantic Monthly* 10 (1862): 738–64; Stephen M. Frank, "Rendering Aid and Comfort: Images of Fatherhood in the Letters of Civil War Soldiers from Massachusetts and Michigan," *Journal of Social History* 21, no. 1 (1992): 15–17; Louis Menand, *The Metaphysical Club* (New York: Farrar, Straus & Giroux, 2001), 41.

187 *some 16,367 . . . half a million:* John Whiteclay Chambers et al., eds., *The Oxford Companion to American Military History* (New York: Oxford University Press, 1999), 50.

187 *Union wounded: Medical and Surgical History of the Rebellion,* appendix 27.

187 *he could not find him . . . "I knew war as [a] soldier":* FL to Charles Sumner, March 23, 1862, box 42, FLP HL.

187 *had dined regularly:* Henry Halleck to FL, February 3, 1862, box 9, FLP HL; FL to Henry Halleck, February 7, 1862, box 27, FLP HL.

188 *powerfully impressed:* Henry Halleck to FL, February 3, 1862, box 9, FLP HL; Henry W. Halleck, *Elements of Military Art and Science: Or, Course of Instruction in Strategy, Fortification, Tactics of Battles, Etc.* (New York: D. Appleton, 1862), 8–34, esp. 23–34.

188 *who directed Lieber:* Matilda Lieber to Guido Norman Lieber, February 27, 1862, box 55, FLP HL.

188 *"war is not" . . . "certain of success":* Halleck, *Elements of Military Art,* 145.

188 *"been rendered clear":* Henry W. Halleck, *International Law; Or, Rules Regulating the Intercourse of States in Peace and War* (New York: D. Van Nostrand, 1861), 30.

188 *"bound by rules":* Halleck, *Elements of Military Art,* 145.

188 *Instead, bands of irregular soldiers:* See Michael Fellman, *Inside War: The Guerrilla Conflict in Missouri During the American Civil War* (New York: Oxford University Press, 1989); Mark E. Neely, Jr., *The Civil War and the Limits of Destruction* (Cambridge, MA: Harvard University Press, 2007).

189 *"all fastidious notions":* Daniel E. Sutherland, ed., *A Savage Conflict: The Decisive Role of Guerrillas in the American Civil War* (Chapel Hill: University of North Carolina Press, 2009), 93.

190 *"bands of partisan rangers": OR,* series 4, 1: 1094–95.

190 *Arkansas:* Robert R. Mackey, *The Uncivil War: Irregular Warfare in the Upper South, 1861–1865* (Norman: University of Oklahoma Press, 2004), 30.

190 *Missouri:* Fellman, *Inside War,* 103.

190 *reluctant to adopt:* Sutherland, *Savage Conflict,* 53–54; Donald E. Sutherland. "Guerrilla Warfare, Democracy, and the Fate of the Confederacy," *Journal of Southern History* 68 (2002): 275–77.

190 *"might lay waste to Philadelphia":* Sutherland, *Savage Conflict,* 94.

190 *"plundering, devouring":* Mackey, *Uncivil War,* 39–40.

190 *"hurricane violence":* Silvana R. Siddali, ed., *Missouri's War: The Civil War in Documents* (Athens: Ohio University Press, 2009), 82.

191 *"principal occupation": OR,* series 1, 8: 641–42.

191 *Randolph was gone:* Brooks D. Simpson & Jean V. Berlin, eds., *Sherman's Civil War: Selected Correspondence of William T. Sherman, 1860–1865* (Chapel Hill: University of North Carolina Press, 1999), 306; see also Mark Grimsley, *The Hard Hand of War: Union Military Policy Toward Southern Civilians, 1861–1865* (New York: Cambridge University Press, 1995), 114–17.

191 *"all persons who shall be taken with arms": OR,* series 1, 3: 466–67.

191 *"not commissioned or enlisted":* Sutherland, *Savage Conflict,* 59.

191 *"duly enrolled" . . . "exempt them from punishment": OR,* series 1, 8: 822.

191 *"expressly authorized":* William Oke Manning, *Commentaries on the Law of Nations* (London: S. Sweet, 1839), 153.

191 *Martens had said the same:* G. F. von Martens, *Summary of the Law of Nations: Founded on the Treaties and Customs of the Modern Nations of Europe,* trans. William Cobbett (London: William Cobbett, 1795), bk 3, ch. 3, §6, pp. 284–85.

191 *"a commission from their sovereign":* Vattel, *Law of Nations,* bk 3, ch. 15, §226, p. 400.

192 *"without a sanction from their governments":* Theodore D. Woolsey, *Introduction to the Study of International Law, Designed as an Aid in Teaching, and in Historical Studies* (Boston: J. Munroe, 1860), 280.

192 *"partizan and guerrilla troops":* Halleck, *International Law*, 386.

192 *"You must be aware":* Sutherland, *Savage Conflict*, 64.

192 *"specially appointed":* Ibid., 63–64.

192 *"recognized by me":* Mackey, *Uncivil War*, 33.

192 *"We cannot be expected":* OR, series 1, 13: 726–28.

192–93 *"acting under the authority":* OR, series 2, 3: 885.

193 *fiercely defended the partisan rangers:* OR, series 2, 4: 907; Siddali, *Missouri's War*, 147–48.

193 *their oldest son:* FL to Alexander Dallas Bache, June 18, 1862, box 32, Bache Correspondence, Rhees Collection, HL.

193 *"has thus knocked":* FL to Henry Halleck, August 9, 1862, box 27, FLP HL.

193 *Behind the scenes in 1861:* Edward Bates to FL, August 13, 1861, December 19, 1861, May 6, 1862, May 9, 1862, and June 24, 1862, all in box 2, FLP HL; FL to Henry Halleck, January 30, 1862, box 27, FLP HL.

193 *call on Lieber to solicit:* Edward Bates to FL, June 10, 1862, box 2, FLP HL; FL to Matilda Lieber, August 7, 1862, box 36, FLP HL. Stanton requested, and Lieber wrote, a memorandum on the "military use of colored persons." FL to Henry Halleck, August 10, 1862, box 27, FLP HL.

193 *a formal memorandum:* FL to Henry Halleck, August 9, 1862, box 27, FLP HL.

193 *"I highly approve":* Henry Halleck to FL, August 20, 1862, box 9, FLP HL.

194 *"self-constituted":* Lieber, *Guerrilla Parties*, 8.

194 *"maintained in good faith":* Ibid., 17.

194 *verbose and rambling:* E.g., David Glazier, "Ignorance Is Not Bliss: The Law of Belligerent Occupation and the U.S. Invasion of Iraq," *Rutgers Law Review* 58 (2005): 154–55; Fellman, *Inside War*, 84.

194 *Clausewitz had described:* Clausewitz, *On War*, 76.

195 *"Whether the guerrillas":* William T. Sherman to Maj.-Gen. Thomas C. Hindman (C.S.A.), September 1862, in Mackey, *Uncivil War*, 35.

195 *summary field executions:* OR, series 1, 17: 97; OR, series 2, 4: 86–87; OR, series 2, 5: 411; Fellman, *Inside War*, 86–87; Clay Mountcastle, *Punitive War: Confederate Guerrillas and Union Reprisals* (Lawrence: University Press of Kansas, 2009), 39; Siddali, *Missouri's War*, 137–38.

195 *"The most disciplined soldiers":* Lieber, *Guerrilla Parties*, 17.

195 *death spiral of retaliation:* FL to Henry Halleck, June 2, 1863, box 27, FLP HL.

196 *precisely to avoid:* Robert R. Mackey, "Bushwackers, Provosts, and Tories: The Guerrilla War in Arkansas," in Daniel E. Sutherland, ed., *Guerrillas, Unionists, and Violence on the Confederate Homefront* (Fayetteville: University of Arkansas, 1999), 176–77.

196 *tablet on the mantelpiece:* Description of Francis Lieber's Library (n.d.), box 55, FLP HL.

196 *"war in earnest":* Clausewitz, *On War*, trans. J. J. Graham (London: N. Trubner, 1873), 149.

196 *"Blood":* Childress, "Francis Lieber's Interpretation," 44.

Chapter 7. Act of Justice

197 *The extraordinary spectacle:* Daniel Ruggles to Benjamin Franklin Butler, July 15, 1862, OR, series 1, 15: 520.

197 *a nineteenth-century celebrity:* Allan Nevins, *Frémont: Pathmarker of the West* (New York: D. Appleton Co., 1939).

198 *"Their slaves, if any they have":* OR, series 2, 3: 467.

198 *was inspiring outright terror:* Joseph Holt to AL, September 12, 1861, ALP LC.

198 *As protests from Kentucky:* Joshua Speed to AL, September 1, 1861, ALP LC; Green Adams and James Speed to AL, September 2, 1861, ALP LC.

198 *Missouri:* AL to David Hunter, September 9, 1861, ALP LC; Montgomery Blair to AL, September 14, 1861, ALP LC.

198 *"liberating [the] slaves":* Basler, 4: 506.

198 *"nearly the same as":* Ibid., 4: 532.

198 *"as long as the necessity lasts"* . . . *"their permanent future condition":* Ibid., 4: 531.

199 *"private property on land":* H. W. Halleck, *International Law, or, Rules Regulating the Intercourse of States in Peace and War* (San Francisco: H. H. Bancroft & Co., 1861).

199 *Roger Taney had endorsed:* See *United States v. Percheman*, 32 U.S. 51, 65 (1833).

199 *Henry Wheaton:* Henry Wheaton, *Elements of International Law: With a Sketch of the History of the Science* (Philadelphia: Carey, Lea & Blanchard, 1836), 252–54.

199 *"The just fame":* "The Rightful Power of Congress to Confiscate and Emancipate," *Monthly Law Reporter* 24 (1862): 469, 480.

199 *"double character":* Thomas R. R. Cobb, *An Inquiry into the Law of Negro Slavery in the United States of America* (Philadelphia: T. & J. W. Johnson & Co., 1858), 83.

200 *"the constant terrors":* "Histoire de l'Esclavage dans l'Antiquité," *North American Review* 91 (July 1860): 90, 94.

200 *slaves had massacred:* C. L. R. James, *The Black Jacobins: Toussaint L'Ouverture and the San Domingo Revolution* (New York: Vintage Books, 1963), 88–89. For a brilliant account of the memory of Haiti during the Civil War, see Matthew J. Clavin, *Toussaint Louverture and the American Civil War: The Promise and Peril of a Second Haitian Revolution* (Philadelphia: University of Pennsylvania Press, 2010).

200 *any "point of our immense coast":* George Mifflin Dallas, *A Series of Letters from London Written During the Years 1856, '57, '58, '59, and '60* (Philadelphia: Lippincott, 1869), 106.

200 *"You cannot fight!":* "Our Women in the War." The Lives They Lived; The Deaths They Died. From the Weekly News and Courier, Charleston, S.C.* (Charleston: News & Courier Book Presses, 1885), 340.

200 *a "private war":* Lysander Spooner, *A Plan for the Abolition of Slavery, and to the Non-Slaveholders of the South* (New York: Lysander Spooner, 1858).

200 *at the request of John Brown:* Herbert Aptheker, "Militant Abolitionism," *Journal of Negro History* 26, no. 4 (October 1941): 438, 468.

201 *"consequences attendant on":* Joel Parker, *The Character of the Rebellion and the Conduct of the War* (Cambridge: Welch, Bigelow & Co., 1862), 41.

201 *Buchanan blamed abolitionists:* Richardson, 5: 627.

201 *South Carolina listed northern incitement: Journal of the Convention of the People of South Carolina, Held in 1860, 1861, and 1862* (Columbia: R. W. Gibbes, 1862), 465.

201 *a "servile insurrection":* Thomas Jackson Arnold, ed., *Early Life and Letters of General Thomas J. Jackson, "Stonewall" Jackson* (New York: Fleming H. Revell, 1916), 294.

201 *whispered to one another:* C. Vann Woodward, *Mary Chesnut's Civil War* (New Haven, CT: Yale University Press, 1981), 43–44.

201 *Stories of secret caches:* Susan Dallas, ed., *Diary of George Mifflin Dallas, While United States Minister to Russia 1837 to 1839, and to England 1856 to 1861* (Philadelphia: J. B. Lippincott Co., 1892), 431–32.

201 *Suspicious arson in Texas:* See Allen C. Guelzo, *Lincoln's Emancipation Proclamation: The End of Slavery in America* (New York: Simon & Schuster, 2004), 17.

201 *slave conspiracy planned for March 4:* Armstead L. Robinson, "In the Shadow of Old John Brown: Insurrection Anxiety and Confederate Mobilization, 1861–1863," *Journal of Negro History* 65, no. 4 (Autumn 1980): 279, 287–88.

201 *"an insurrection"* . . . *the countryside near Huntsville, Alabama:* Robinson, "In the Shadow of Old John Brown," 288.

201 *"whole families":* "Imminent Peril of a Slave Insurrection [Correspondence of the *New York Tribune*]," *Liberator*, August 16, 1861, p. 130.

201 *letters poured into the offices:* Robinson, "In the Shadow of Old John Brown," 288.

201 *In the War of 1812:* See "Negro Stealing," *Palladium of Liberty* (Fauquier County, VA), January 8, 1814; "Norfolk Public Ledger," *Daily National Intelligencer* (Washington, DC), April 12, 1815; "Editorial," *Raleigh Register*, April 7, 1815.

201 *"in this, as in all other instances":* "Mobile Register [excerpt]," *Liberator*, June 14, 1861, p. 1.

202 *Southern state governors . . . 200,000 Confederate troops:* Robinson, "In the Shadow of Old John Brown," 283–88.

202 *"suppress servile insurrection": OR,* series 1, 2: 661–62.

202 *George Cadwalader of Philadelphia:* See "Speech of Wendell Phillips, Esq., at the Anti-Slavery Celebration at Framingham, July 4, 1861," *Liberator*, July 12, 1861.

202 *Union forces in western Virginia:* Stephen W. Sears, *George B. McClellan: The Young Napoleon* (New York: Ticknor & Fields, 1988), 79.

202 *the assistance of his Massachusetts forces: OR,* series 2, 1: 567.

202 *"contraband of war":* Adam Goodheart, *1861: Civil War Awakening* (New York: Alfred A. Knopf, 2011), 295–347.

202 *better suited to pistols:* Kate Masur, " 'A Rare Phenomenon of Philological Vegetation': The Word Contraband and the Meanings of Emancipation in the United States," *Journal of American History* 93 (March 2007): 1050, 1066.

202 *Butler was no abolitionist:* For Butler's life and career, see Hans L. Trefousse, *Benjamin Butler: The South Called Him Beast!* (New York: Twayne, 1957).

202 *at New Orleans, he would turn slaves away: OR,* series 1, 15: 439–40.

203 *Angry abolitionists:* "Repressing Slave Insurrections," *Liberator*, May 17, 1861, p. 79.

203 *"one of the inherent weaknesses":* "The Governor of Massachusetts on Slave Insurrections," *Lloyd's Weekly Newspaper* (London), June 2, 1861.

203 *"In what manner" . . . "honorable warfare":* "Interesting Correspondence: Repressing Slave Insurrections," *New York Times*, May 16, 1861.

204 *Sir Guy Carleton had:* Simon Schama, *Rough Crossings: Britain, the Slaves, and the American Revolution* (New York: Ecco, 2006), 151.

204 *Adams rediscovered his antislavery commitments:* William Lee Miller, *Arguing About Slavery: The Great Battle in the United States Congress* (New York: Alfred A. Knopf, 1996), 186–88; William Jerry MacLean, "Othello Scorned: The Racial Thought of John Quincy Adams," *Journal of the Early Republic* 4, no. 2 (1984): 143–60.

204 *Contesting the so-called gag rule: Cong. Globe,* 24th Cong., 1st sess., appendix 433–36.

204 *"laws and municipal institutions" . . . "slavery and emancipation":* Worthington Chauncey Ford & Charles Francis Adams, Jr., *John Quincy Adams: His Connection with the Monroe Doctrine (1843) and with Emancipation Under Martial Law (1819–1842)* (Cambridge: J. Wilson & Son, 1902), 75–77.

204 *"was fully warranted" . . . "why may he not negroes?":* Orville H. Browning to AL, September 30, 1861, ALP LC.

205 *from the day Fort Sumter was shelled:* David Donald, *Charles Sumner and the Coming of the Civil War* (New York: Alfred A. Knopf, 1960), 388.

205 *Sumner became convinced:* Charles Sumner, "Emancipation Our Best Weapon," in *The Works of Charles Sumner* (Boston: Lee & Shepard, 1870–83), 6: 31.

205 *Lincoln had abandoned:* Guelzo, *Lincoln's Emancipation Proclamation*, 57.

205 *an October speech:* Sumner, "Emancipation Our Best Weapon," 1–64.

205 *"horrid policy":* quoted in ibid., 42.

205 *"the slave property of rebels":* "The News," *Pacific Commercial Advertiser* (Honolulu), March 27, 1862, p. 2 (quoting *New York Journal of Commerce*).

205 *"nothing is truer":* "The Lounger," *Harper's Weekly*, October 19, 1861, pp. 658–59.

205 *"let slavery feel":* "Just and Sound," *Independent*, December 12, 1861, p. 4 (quoting *Christian Intelligencer*).

205 *defending a broad war power:* William Whiting, *The War Powers of the President and the Legislative Powers of Congress in Relation to Rebellion, Treason and Slavery* (Boston: J. L. Shorey, 1862).

205 *forty-three separate printings:* Mark E. Neely, Jr., *Lincoln and the Triumph of the Nation: Constitutional Conflict in the American Civil War* (Chapel Hill: University at North Carolina Press, 2012), 84.

205 *"like the letting loose":* Guelzo, *Lincoln's Emancipation Proclamation*, 48.

206 *"wild and lawless":* Sumner, "Emancipation Our Best Weapon," 27.

206 *"Servile insurrections":* "Selections," *Liberator*, December 7, 1860, p. 1.

206 *"What are these madmen":* Harriet Beecher Stowe, "The President's Message," *Independent,* December 20, 1860, p. 1.

206 *"Experiments of emancipation"* . . . *"must stand aghast!":* Charles Francis Adams, Jr., "Martial Law or Competition?" *Independent,* October 24, 1861, p. 1.

206 *Lincoln cast a losing vote:* Eric Foner, *The Fiery Trial: Abraham Lincoln and American Slavery* (New York: W. W. Norton & Co., 2010), 59–60. Don Fehrenbacher's excellent posthumous book uncharacteristically gets this episode in Lincoln's career wrong. See Don E. Fehrenbacher & Ward M. McAfee, *The Slaveholding Republic: An Account of the United States Government's Relations to Slavery* (New York: Oxford University Press, 2001), 369 n. 40.

206 *"Every civilized nation":* Foner, *Fiery Trial,* 60.

207 *from the day of his election:* Anonymous to AL, January 14, 1861, ALP LC; The Count Johannes [George Jones] to AL, April 28, 1861, ALP LC; James Hamilton to AL, May 3, 1861, ALP LC.

207 *Bates warned Lincoln repeatedly:* Edward Bates, "Memorandum, April 15, 1861," ALP LC; Howard K. Beale, ed., *The Diary of Edward Bates, 1859–1866* (Washington, DC: Government Printing Office, 1933), 179; Gideon Welles, *Lincoln and Seward: Remarks Upon the Memorial Address of Chas. Francis Adams on the Late Wm. H. Seward* (New York: Sheldon, 1874), 211–12.

207 *"All of us who live":* Joshua Speed to AL, September 1, 1861, ALP LC.

207 *He quietly approved Butler's:* Foner, *Fiery Trial,* 171.

207 *And when his beleaguered:* Ibid., 187–88.

207 *"Seven negroes":* Ibid., 9.

207 *Lincoln found himself wondering:* Guelzo, *Lincoln's Emancipation Proclamation,* 254–57.

207–208 *"military necessity"* . . . *"forever free":* OR, series 3, 2: 48.

208 *"Whether at any time":* Basler, 5: 222.

208 *"Rending or wrecking":* Ibid., 5: 223.

208 *on the peninsula between the Rappahannock:* On the Peninsula Campaign, see James M. McPherson, *The Battle Cry of Freedom: The Civil War Era* (New York: Oxford University Press, 1988), 426–90.

209 *"I have never written you":* Basler, 5: 185.

209 *"Our left is now":* George B. McClellan to Edwin M. Stanton, June 2, 1862, in Stephen W. Sears, ed., *The Civil War Correspondence of George B. McClellan: Selected Correspondence, 1860–1865* (New York: Ticknor & Fields, 1989), 286.

209 *"We ought instead of retreating":* McPherson, *Battle Cry of Freedom,* 470.

209 *warfare as a kind of chess match:* T. Harry Williams, *McClellan, Sherman, and Grant* (New Brunswick, NJ: Rutgers University Press, 1962), 23.

210 *"by pure military skill"* . . . *"brightest chapters":* George B. McClellan to Ambrose Burnside, May 21, 1862, in Sears, ed., *Civil War Correspondence,* 269.

210 *"tired of the sickening sight":* Williams, *McClellan, Sherman and Grant,* 24.

210 *"I confess":* Sears, *McClellan: The Young Napoleon,* 116.

210 *"an iron hand":* Ibid., 79.

210 *"sudden and general emancipation":* George B. McClellan, *McClellan's Own Story: The War for the Union, the Soldiers Who Fought It, the Civilians Who Directed It, and His Relations to Them* (New York: Charles L. Webster & Co., 1887), 33.

210 *"who assured the slaveholders":* "Gerrit Smith on McClellan's Nomination and Acceptance," *Liberator,* September 23, 1864, p. 155.

210–11 *"should be conducted"* . . . *"rapidly disintegrate our present armies":* OR, series I, 11 (part 1): 73–74.

211 *"come to the conclusion":* Gideon Welles, *Diary of Gideon Welles, Secretary of the Navy Under Lincoln and Johnson* (Boston: Houghton Mifflin, 1911), 1: 70–71.

211–12 *"as a fit and necessary"* . . . *"be free":* Basler, 5: 336–37.

212 *"The will of God"* . . . *"human instrumentalities":* Ibid., 5: 403–04.

213 *"I am almost ready":* Ibid., 5: 404.

213 *"certain that they represent"* . . . *"to favor their side":* Ibid., 5: 420.

213 *"Good men"* . . . *facts, principles, and arguments":* Ibid., 5: 421.

213 *"Do not misunderstand me":* Ibid., 5: 425.

214 *"depredation and massacre"... "arm the slaves":* John H. Niven, *The Salmon P. Chase Papers: Journals, 1829–1872* (Kent, OH: Kent State University Press, 1993–), 1: 351; also David Donald, ed., *Inside Lincoln's Cabinet: The Civil War Diaries of Salmon P. Chase* (New York: Longmans, Green, 1954), 99.

214 *Bates had long worried:* Gideon Welles, *Lincoln and Seward: Remarks Upon the Memorial Address of Chas. Francis Adams on the Late Wm. H. Seward* (New York: Sheldon, 1874), 211; Gideon Welles, "The History of Emancipation," *Galaxy* 14, no. 6 (1872): 838, 844.

214 *"stretching forth its hands"... "our last shriek":* F. B. Carpenter, *Six Months at the White House with Abraham Lincoln: The Story of a Picture* (New York: Hurd & Houghton, 1866), 20–22. Seward's comments echoed Psalm 68:31 ("Princes shall come out of Egypt; Ethiopia shall soon stretch out her hands unto God").

215 *"gave us the victory"... "in favor of the slaves":* Welles, *Diary of Gideon Welles*, 1: 143.

215 *"forever free"... "actual freedom":* Basler, 5: 434.

215 *"We say we are for"... "God must forever bless":* Ibid., 5: 537.

215 *"The dogmas"... "save our country":* Ibid., 5: 537.

216 *"inflict on the non-combatant population":* OR, series 4, 2: 211.

216 *"not only his approval":* OR, series 1, 15: 907.

216 *"seeking to bring upon us":* Francis Richard Lubbock, *Six Decades in Texas: or Memoirs of Francis Richard Lubbock, Governor of Texas in War Time, 1861–1863* (Austin, TX: Ben C. Jones & Co., 1900), 476.

216 *"that our homes should be burned":* Kate Mason Rowland and Agnes E. Croxall, eds., *The Journal of Julia LeGrand, New Orleans 1862–1863* (Richmond, VA: Everett Waddey Co., 1911), 132.

216 *"an invitation to servile war":* "Domestic Intelligence," *Harper's Weekly*, October 18, 1862, p. 659.

216 *"all rules of civilized warfare"... "suffer death":* "The Rebel Congress on the Emancipation Proclamation—The Rules of Civilized Warfare to Be Ignored," *Daily Evening Bulletin* (San Francisco), October 29, 1862.

216 *"inconsistent with the spirit":* OR, series 2, 5: 940–41.

216 *"fight for such an accursed doctrine":* Sears, ed., *Civil War Correspondence*, 481.

216 Louisville Journal *observed angrily: Weekly Mountain Democrat* (Placerville, CA), January 17, 1863 (quoting the *Louisville Journal*).

216 *"a servile war":* Thomas M. Monroe, "Slavery: Considered in Its Moral and Social Aspects," *Dubuque Herald*, March 19, 1863.

216 *"the lusts of freed negroes":* Allen C. Guelzo, "Defending Emancipation: Abraham Lincoln and the Conkling Letter, 1863," *Civil War History* 48, no. 4 (2002): 313, 320.

216 *"scenes of bloodshed":* Benjamin R. Curtis, *Executive Power* (Boston: Little, Brown, 1862), 13.

217 *Joel Parker:* Guelzo, *Lincoln's Emancipation Proclamation*, 211.

217 *the salons of Britain and France:* "Clip from London Paper," *Liberator*, November 21, 1862; "Louis Napoleon's Foreign Policy," *Independent*, December 11, 1862, p. 4.

217 *"inviting the negroes":* *Weekly Mountain Democrat* (Placerville, CA), November 29, 1862.

217 *"under no circumstances":* Report of the Secretary of War, House Exec. Doc. no. 1, 37th Cong., 3d sess., in *Executive Documents Printed by Order of the House of Representatives During the Third Session of the Thirty-Seventh Congress* (Washington, DC: Government Printing Office, 1863), 4: 19.

217 *"are, and henceforward"... "for reasonable wages":* Basler, 6: 29–30.

217 *"No servile insurrection":* Ibid., 7: 50.

218 *"as a fit and necessary"... "Almighty God":* Ibid., 6: 29–30.

218 *"merely a war measure":* John G. Whittier, *Letters of Lydia Maria Child* (Boston: Houghton Mifflin, 1883), 171.

218 *"all the moral grandeur":* Richard Hofstadter, *The American Political Tradition and the Men Who Made It* (New York: Alfred A. Knopf, 1948), 149.

219 *"vast and momentous":* Welles, *Diary of Gideon Welles*, 70.

Chapter 8. To Save the Country

220 *"To save the country": Instructions*, art. 5.

220 *As the moon sank low:* Stephen V. Ash, *Firebrand of Liberty: The Story of Two Black Regiments That Changed the Course of the Civil War* (New York: W. W. Norton & Co., 2008), 105–09.

220 *"not the phantom":* Thomas Wentworth Higginson, *Army Life in a Black Regiment* (Boston: Fields, Osgood, & Co., 1870), 99.

221 *admirer of John Brown:* Ibid., 4.

221 *Kansas jayhawker:* Mary Thacher Higginson, *Letters and Journals of Thomas Wentworth Higginson, 1846–1906* (Boston: Houghton Mifflin, 1921), 186. See also Keith Wilson, "In the Shadow of John Brown: The Military Service of Colonels Thomas Higginson, James Montgomery, and Robert Shaw in the Department of the South," in John David Smith, ed., *Black Soldiers in Blue: African-American Troops in the Civil War Era* (Chapel Hill: University of North Carolina Press, 2002), 306.

221 *arming Florida's freedmen: OR*, series 1, 14: 226.

221 *stunned residents: Milwaukee Daily Sentinel*, March 27, 1863.

221 *"in mortal dread":* "Interesting from Port Royal," *New York Times*, March 22, 1863.

221 *"a great volcano":* Higginson, *Army Life*, 99.

221–22 *"wretched business" . . . "force in the field":* "The Higginson Expeditions," *Newark Advocate* (Newark, OH), March 27, 1863 (reprinted from the *New York World*).

222 *Stanton . . . in August:* Higginson, 277–80.

222 *"consistent with the usages":* Ibid., 99.

222 *"partisan warfare":* Ibid., 167.

222 *"have none but civilized warfare":* Higgison, *Letters and Journals*, 207.

222 *Even before the announcement:* E.g., *OR*, series 2, 3: 898–99.

222 *made execution or re-enslavement: OR*, series 2, 5: 940–41.

222 *"Dere's no flags" . . . "he fight in earnest":* Higginson, *Army Life*, 151.

222 *with such speed and skill: OR*, series 1, 13: 227.

222 *"something far different":* *Boston Daily Advertiser*, March 31, 1863.

223 *The Confederacy had no need:* On the Confederacy's approach to law of war questions, see Daniel W. Hamilton, *The Limits of Sovereignty: Property Confiscation in the Union and the Confederacy During the Civil War* (Chicago: University of Chicago Press, 2007); Stephen C. Neff, *Justice in Blue and Gray: A Legal History of the Civil War* (Cambridge, MA: Harvard University Press, 2010); and William Morrison Robinson, *Justice in Grey: A History of the Judicial System of the Confederate States of America* (Cambridge, MA: Harvard University Press, 1941), 359–405.

223 *"the usages of civilized warfare":* Sequestration Act Passed by the Congress of the Confederate States, *Approved August 30, 1861* (Richmond, VA: Tyler, Wise, & Allegre, Printers, 1861), 3; James D. Richardson, ed., *A Compilation of the Messages and Papers of the Confederacy* (Nashville, TN: United States Publishing Co., 1905), 1: 104–05 ("usages of civilized nations").

223 *championed broad rights for neutral shipping:* Montague Bernard, *A Historical Account of the Neutrality of Great Britain During the American Civil War* (London: Longmans, Green, Reader & Dyer, 1870), 101; Richardson, ed., *Messages and Papers of the Confederacy*, 1: 104–12.

223 *an unlawful paper blockade:* "Blockade," *Daily Picayune* (New Orleans), July 14, 1861, 2.

223 *Declaration of Paris:* Bernard, *Historical Account*, 185.

223 *gleefully mocked:* Richardson, *Messages and Papers of the Confederacy*, 1: 281.

224 *"departed from the usages": Sequestration Act*, 3.

224 *retaliatory Sequestration Act:* Hamilton, *Limits of Sovereignty*, 89–139.

224 *"the desire of this Government":* Richardson, *Messages and Papers of the Confederacy*, 2: 115–16.

224 *deny prisoner of war status: OR*, series 2, 3: 898–99.

224 *"be no longer held and treated": OR*, series 1, 14: 599.

224 *bills that would have treated: Journal of the Congress of the Confederate States of America, 1861–1865* (Washington, DC: Government Printing Office, 1905), 5: 535–49; "The

Rebel Congress on the Emancipation Proclamation," *Daily Evening Bulletin* (San Francisco), October 29, 1862.

224 *"negro slaves": OR*, series 2, 5: 795–97.

225 *John Stuart Mill had forcefully observed:* John M. Robson, ed., *Collected Works of John Stuart Mill* (Toronto: University of Toronto Press, 1963–91), 21: 118.

225 *not the slaves but the slaveholders:* J. E. Cairnes, *The Slave Power: Its Character, Career, and Probable Designs* (New York: Carleton, 1862), 151–54.

225 *No state founded on:* Basler, 6: 176–77.

226 *"It is not the North that is against you":* Thomas Sergeant Perry, *Life and Letters of Francis Lieber* (Boston: J. R. Osgood & Co., 1882), 235.

226 *polygamy and concubinage:* Ibid., 243.

226 *"The whole movement of history":* Ibid., 267.

226 *spent $1,150 on two slaves:* Hartmut Keil, "Francis Lieber's Attitudes on Race, Slavery, and Abolition," *Journal of American Ethnic History* 28, no. 1 (2008): 13.

226 *"good looks":* Ibid.

226 *carefully checking their teeth:* Ibid., 21.

226 *"fully one thousand dollars":* Frank Freidel, *Francis Lieber: Nineteenth-Century Liberal* (Baton Rouge: Louisiana State University Press, 1947), 236.

227 *Lieber excused his ownership:* Keil, "Francis Lieber's Attitudes," 13–14.

227 *defended southern slaveowners' treatment:* FL to Charles Sumner, October 27, 1835, box 40, FLP HL.

227 *"a proslavery man":* Perry, *Life and Letters*, 297.

227 *an international congress of jurists:* FL to Charles Sumner, December 27, 1861, in ibid., 324–25.

227 *"a little book":* FL to Charles Sumner, August 19, 1861, box 42, FLP HL.

227 *Lieber took up the subject:* "The Disposal of Prisoners," *New York Times*, August 19, 1861.

227 *a creature of the laws:* Law and Usages of War, No. VIII, 6 February 1862 [Notebook No. 8], folder 16, box 2, FLP JHU.

227 *"not exist in conquered Territories":* Perry, *Life and Letters*, 250.

227 *Lieber visited Fort Monroe:* Matthew J. Mancini, "Francis Lieber, Slavery, and the 'Genesis' of the Laws of War," *Journal of Southern History* 77, no. 2 (2011): 333.

227 *"contraband" . . . "amazingly":* Francis Lieber to Benson J. Lossing, January 21, 1866, box 2, FLP LC.

227–28 *"must be, and are" . . . "difference of skin":* FL to Charles Sumner, December 19, 1861, box 42, FLP HL.

228 *"step back and fight":* Francis Lieber to Benson J. Lossing, January 21, 1866, box 2, FLP LC.

228 *Following Montesquieu and Blackstone:* Law and Usages of War, No. VII, 4 February 1862 [Notebook No. 7], folder 16, box 2, FLP JHU.

228 *"peculiar" laws:* Law and Usages of War, No. VIII, February 6, 1862 [Notebook No. 8], folder 16, box 2, FLP JHU.

228 *collecting notes for his friend:* FL to Charles Sumner, September 6, 1862, box 42, FLP HL.

228 *"men stand opposed" . . . "claiming our protection":* Francis Lieber, "The Duty of Provisional Governors," *New York Evening Post*, June 20, 1862.

228 *"acknowledged law of war":* "Memoir on the Military Use of Colored Persons," in FL to Henry Halleck, August 10, 1862, box 27, FLP HL.

228 *"one of the historic facts":* FL to Charles Sumner, June 10, 1863, FLP HL.

229 *armed "negro slaves": OR*, series 2, 5: 795–97.

229 *selling into slavery . . . begun to execute:* FL to Charles Sumner, November 28, 1862, box 42, FLP HL.

229 *The reports, it turned out, were true:* John David Smith, "Let Us All Be Grateful That We Have Colored Troops That Will Fight," in *Black Soldiers in Blue*, 44.

229 *Radicals in the Senate: OR*, series 2, 5: 9.

229 *The telegraph from Halleck:* FL to Henry Halleck, December 7, 1862, box 27, FLP HL.

229 *"a code of regulations": OR*, series 3, 2: 951.

229 *"the most urgent issues":* FL to Henry Halleck, November 13, 1862, box 27, FLP HL; see also FL to Charles Sumner, August 18, 1861, box 42, FLP HL.

229 *confusion over the status of slaves:* Francis Lieber to Benson J. Lossing, January 21, 1866, box 2, FLP LC; see Mancini, "Francis Lieber, Slavery, and the 'Genesis' of the Laws of War."

229 *John Pope issued a set:* James M. McPherson, *Battle Cry of Freedom: The Civil War Era* (New York: Oxford University Press, 1988), 501.

229 *A second Confiscation Act: United States Statutes at Large*, Vol. 12 (Washington, DC: Government Printing Office, 1863), 589–92.

230 *reached out to Lieber:* Joseph Holt to FL, February 20, 1863, box 11, FLP HL.

230 *a set of instructions for the treatment:* Ethan Allen Hitchcock, *Fifty Years in Camp and Field: Diary of Major-General Ethan Allen Hitchcock, U.S.A.* (New York: G. P. Putnam's Sons, 1909), 441.

230 *new instructions:* Paul J. Springer, *America's Captives: Treatment of POWs from the Revolutionary War to the War on Terror* (Lawrence: University Press of Kansas, 2010), 85.

230 *paroling thousands of U.S. troops:* A manuscript roll of battlefield paroles from the Gettysburg campaign survives in the Huntington Library. See Isaac Avery, "List of Prisoners Captured at York, Penn., June 28, 1863," box 2, Collection of James William Eldridge, 1797–1902.

230 *The Union protested:* Mancini, "Francis Lieber, Slavery, and the 'Genesis' of the Laws of War"; FL to Charles Sumner, August 20, 1861, box 42, FLP HL.

231 *The board gave him wide discretion:* R. R. Baxter, "The First Modern Codification of the Law of War," *International Review of the Red Cross* 3 (1963): 171, 180–85; Memorandum: General Orders No. 100 of 1863, file no. 4275, box 23, Office of the Judge Advocate General Document File, 1894–1912, NARA.

231 *"I had no guide":* FL to Henry Halleck, February 20, 1863, in Perry, *Life and Letters*, 331.

231 *proliferation of military manuals:* Peter Paret, *The Cognitive Challenge of War: Prussia, 1806* (Princeton, NJ: Princeton University Press, 2009), 88–91.

231 *in Lieber's private library:* George Friedrich Muller, *Das Krieges oder Soldatenrecht* (Berlin: Petit- and Schöneschen Bookshop, 1789), in box 7, Judge Advocate School Lieber Collection, Federal Research Division, LC.

231 *flags of truce and safe-conducts: Instructions*, art. 86–87, 111–14.

231 *"already wholly disabled":* Ibid., art. 71.

231 *It authorized the execution:* Ibid., art. 83, 88, 104.

232 *conscription of local guides:* Ibid., art. 93–97.

232 *rules for prisoner exchanges:* Ibid., art. 105–10.

232 *special yellow markings:* Ibid., art. 115.

232 *"an outlaw":* Ibid., art. 148.

232 *"peaceful pursuits" . . . "robbers or pirates":* Ibid., art. 82.

232 *only valid if approved:* Ibid., art. 128–30.

232 *"so plainly characterizes":* [A Note on] War [n.d.], box 19, FLP HL.

232 *"all soldiers": Instructions*, art. 49.

232 *"disgrace, by cruel imprisonment":* Ibid., art. 56.

232 *"plain and wholesome food":* Ibid., art. 76.

232 *No violence could be used:* Ibid., art. 80.

232 *"extort confessions":* Ibid., art. 16.

232 *"a man is armed":* Ibid., art. 57.

233 *was subject to retaliation:* Ibid., art. 59.

233 *"chief commander" could "permit":* A Code for the Government of Armies in the Field as Authorized by the Laws and Usages of War on Land, §35, p. 12, register no. 243077, Y Halleck II, HL.

233 *"permitted to direct his troops": Instructions*, art. 60.

233 *"known or discovered":* Ibid., art. 62.

233 *fought in enemy uniforms:* Ibid., art. 65 & 83.

233 *"without any plain":* Ibid., art. 63.

233 *"the unarmed citizen":* Ibid., art. 22.

233 *"not a relationship between":* Victor Gourevitch, ed., *Rousseau: The Social Contract and Other Later Political Writings* (New York: Cambridge University Press, 1997), 1: 46.
233 *"the citizen or native": Instructions,* art. 21.
233 *the starving of noncombatants:* Ibid., art. 17.
233 *bombard cities:* Ibid., art. 19.
233 *"throw the burden of the war":* Ibid., art. 156.
233 *"acknowledge and protect":* Ibid., art. 37.
233 *It gave special protections:* Ibid., art. 34.
234 *"seized and removed":* Ibid., art. 36.
234 *to tax the population or billet soldiers:* Ibid., art. 10, 37, 153.
234 *"for temporary and military uses":* Ibid., art. 37.
234 *"over-trained idea"* . . . *"nor ought it to be":* Law and Usages of War [1862], folder 18, box 2, FLP JHU.
234 *"useless destruction":* Francis Lieber, Law and Usages of War, unpublished MS [n.d.], folder 18, box 2, FLP JHU.
234 *"All captures and booty": Instructions,* art. 45.
234 *Neither "officers nor soldiers":* Ibid., art. 46.
234 *"lawful only as a means"* . . . *"civilized people":* [Francis Lieber], War and Peace: Destruction and Obstruction Characterize War; Production and Expanding Inter-Communication Distinguish Peace Among the Nations (1863), unpublished MS, box 19, FLP HL.
234 *"Unnecessary or revengeful": Instructions,* art. 68.
234 *"in great straits":* Ibid., art. 60.
234 *"as much as the contingencies":* Ibid., art. 116.
234 *"all cruelty and bad faith":* Ibid., art. 11.
235 *"admits of all direct destruction":* Ibid., art. 15.
235 *"Military necessity":* Ibid., art. 14.
236 *"When war is begun":* [Newspaper clipping], *New York Evening Post,* folder 18, box 2, FLP JHU.
236 *"The more vigorously wars": Instructions,* art. 29.
236 *"conventional restrictions of the modes":* Ibid., art. 30.
236 *"self-imposed, imperceptible":* Carl von Clausewitz, *On War,* trans. Michael Howard & Peter Paret (Princeton, NJ: Princeton University Press, 1989), 75.
236 *"To save the country": Instructions,* art. 5.
236 *"The law of war":* Ibid., art. 30.
236 *"torture to extort confessions":* Ibid., art. 16, 80.
236 *"If Indians slowly roast":* FL to Henry Halleck, December 21, 1864, box 28, FLP HU; see also Law and Usages of War, No. IV, December 17, 1861 [Notebook No. 4], folder 16, box 2, FLP JHU.
237 *"not admit of the use of poison": Instructions,* articles 16, 70.
237 *"military necessity does not include":* Ibid., art. 16.
237 *buried explosive shells:* Henry Halleck to FL, August 26, 1863, box 9, FLP HU.
237 *booby-trapped bodies:* Remarks on 'Incendiary Balls' or 'Rifle Bombs' Used by the Confederate Army—Also a Torpedo Device, unpublished MS, September 1 & 14, 1863, box 20, FLP HU.
237 *"the soldier within me"* . . . *"Quixotic tournaments":* FL to Henry Halleck, August 24, 1863, box 27, FLP HL.
237 *"Men who take up arms": Instructions,* art. 15.
237 *Halleck and Stanton handled that:* Halleck sent the telegraph asking Lieber to come to Washington. We know that Stanton was involved from the start because Lieber asked Halleck whether his travel plans would suit Stanton. See FL to Henry Halleck, December 9, 1862, box 27, FLP HL.
238 *"approved by the President":* OR, series 3, 3: 148.
238 *"liberty to use violence against":* Orville H. Browning to Abraham Lincoln, Sep. 31, 1861, ALP LC.
238 *"any available means"* . . . *"rose-water?":* AL to Cuthbert Bullitt, July 28, 1862, in Basler, 5: 346.

238 *"he was pretty well cured"*: Salmon P. Chase, *Inside Lincoln's Cabinet: The Civil War Diaries of Salmon P. Chase* (New York: Longmans, Green, 1954), 106.

238 *"mistaken deference"*: Horace Greeley to Abraham Lincoln, August 1, 1862, ALP LC.

238 *"If I could save the Union"*: AL to Horace Greeley, in Basler, 5: 388–89.

239 *"come to the conclusion"*: Gideon Welles, *Diary of Gideon Welles, Secretary of the Navy Under Lincoln and Johnson* (Boston: Houghton Mifflin, 1911), 1: 70.

239 *"Civilized belligerents"* . . . *"saving the Union"*: AL to James C. Conkling, August 26, 1863, Basler, 6: 406, 408.

239 *separated those who engaged in battles:* Carol Chomsky, "The United States—Dakota War Trials: A Study in Military Injustice," *Stanford Law Review* 43 (1990): 13; Maeve Herbert Glass, "Explaining the Sioux Military Commission of 1862," *Columbia Human Rights Law Review* 40 (2009): 743.

239 *"could not afford"*: Don E. Fehrenbacher & Virginia Fehrenbacher, eds., *Recollected Words of Abraham Lincoln* (Stanford, CA: Stanford University Press, 1996), 372.

239 *"where necessary for military"*: James Randall, *Constitutional Problems Under Lincoln* (Urbana: University of Illinois Press, 1951), 367.

240 *"Murders for old grudges"*: AL to Charles Drake, Oct. 5, 1863, Basler, 6: 500.

240 *"The colored population"*: James M. McPherson, *The Negro's Civil War: How American Negroes Felt and Acted During the War for the Union* (New York: Pantheon Books, 1965), 169.

240 *"important to the enemy"*: AL to David Hunter, April 1, 1863, Basler, 6: 158.

241 *Halleck asked Lieber to add:* Henry Halleck to FL, February 28, 1863, box 9, FLP HL; FL to Henry Halleck, March 4, 1863 and March 23, 1863, box 27, FLP HL; "For General Halleck: Insurrection. Rebellion. Civil War. Foreign Invasion of the United States" (1863), unpublished MS, box 18, FLP HL; Instructions for the Government of Armies of the United States in the Field, Section X. Insurrection.—Rebellion.—Civil War.—Foreign Invasion of the United States, unpublished MS, register no. 240460, HL.

241 *Lieber sent out a printed first draft:* E.g., FL to Henry Halleck, February 20, 1863, box 27, FLP HL.

241 *The passages he asked about:* FL to Charles Sumner, February 24, 1863, box 43, FLP HL.

241 *of which he was most proud:* FL to Charles Sumner, May 19, 1863, box 43, FLP HL.

241 *making important additions:* FL to HWH, June 18, 1863, box 27 (observing that Halleck drafted the last clause of s. 43 relating to belligerent liens and claims of service).

241 *omitting clauses he thought:* Code for the Government of Armies in the Field (register no. 243077, HL), §23, at p. 9, and §33, at 11.

241 *"better than the Emancipation Proclamation"*: Hamilton Fish to FL, March 10, 1863, box 7, FLP HL.

241 *"vast importance"*: Napoleon Bonaparte Buford to Francis Lieber, April 10, 1863, box 3, FLP HL.

242 *the more general idea in the law of nations that slavery could exist:* See James Oakes, *Freedom National: The Destruction of Slavery in the United States* (forthcoming). On *Somerset's Case*, see George van Cleve, "Somerset's Case and Its Antecedents in Imperial Perspective," *Law and History Review* 24 (2006): 645.

244 *had issued outlawry orders against the principal Union organizers:* OR, series 1, 14: 599.

244 *"African slaves"* . . . *"enemy of mankind"*: OR, series 1, 15: 906–08.

245 *issued early in the spring:* OR, series 2, 5: 306–07 (paroles).

245 *handed him a copy:* OR, series 2, 5: 690.

245 *"the boast of modern times"*: Cong. Globe, 29th Cong., 2nd sess. (1846), p. 23.

245 *"confused" and "undiscriminating"*: OR, series 2, 6: 41–47.

245 *"a license for a man"*: OR, series 2, 5: 744.

245 *"Christian warriors"*: OR, series 4, 3: 1048.

245 *"the most prominent of the matters"*: OR, series 2, 6: 47.

245 *"Discrimination among"*: OR, series 2, 6: 18.

246 *"The employment of a servile insurrection"*: OR, series 2, 6: 44.

246 Boston Herald: "New Military Instructions," *Boston Herald*, May 19, 1863, 4; see also "War Matters," *Boston Herald*, July 30, 1863, 2.

246 Daily National Intelligencer: "The Retaliatory Code," *Daily National Intelligencer*, June 5, 1863; see also "War Department has officially proclaimed the instructions," *Daily National Intelligencer*, May 26, 1863.

246 New York Times: "Our Militia Forces," *New York Times*, May 24, 1863. New York Herald: "News from Washington," *New York Herald*, May 19, 1863, 7.

246 Charleston Mercury: "Instructions of the Yankee War Department of the Government of Armies in the Field," *Charleston Mercury*, May 30, 1863, 1. Daily Picayune: "The New Code of Instruction for the United States Army," *Daily Picayune*, June 5, 1863, 2.

246 L'Union *in New Orleans:* "Instructions à l'Armée," *L'Union* (New Orleans), June 4, 1863, 1. Louisville Daily Journal: "The Policy of the War; Instructions for the Government of Armies of the United States in the Field," *Louisville Daily Journal*, May 23, 1863, 1.

246 *Extensive treatments soon came out:* "The New Code of Instruction for the United States Army," *Baltimore Sun*, May 21, 1863, 4; "Regulations for the Army," *New Haven Daily Palladium*, May 18, 1863; *Boston Daily Advertiser*, May 18, 1863; *Daily Cleveland Herald*, May 18, 1863; *Milwaukee Daily Sentinel*, May 19, 1863; *Daily Evening Bulletin* (San Francisco), June 13, 1863.

247 *"The President, by approving":* "Retaliatory Code," *Daily National Intelligencer*, June 5, 1863.

247 *"a complete fallacy":* "Instructions for the Government of the Army," *New York Herald*, May 20, 1863, 6.

247 *"employment of colored troops":* OR, series 1, 14: 466.

247 *joint resolution:* OR, series 2, 5: 940–41.

248 *the code was response enough:* "Retaliatory Code," *Daily National Intelligencer*, June 5, 1863.

248 *"not one person in a hundred"* . . . *"impress the rebels":* "Protection for Our Black Troops," *Boston Daily Advertiser*, June 11, 1863.

248 *"full conversation":* Henry Halleck to FL, August 4, 1863, box 9, FLP HL.

248 *in Stanton's War Department:* Basler, 6: 357 n. 1.

248 *"class, color, or condition":* Ibid., 6: 357.

248 *the Confederate government retreated:* Ira Berlin et al., eds., *Freedom: A Documentary History of Emancipation, 1861–1867—The Black Military Experience* (New York: Cambridge University Press, 1982), 580.

248 *"held like other captives":* Ibid.

248 *"in suggesting and building up":* Ethan Allen Hitchcock to FL, October 22, 1863, box 11, FLP HL.

249 *"that you may know":* OR, series 1, 32 (part 1): 601–02.

Chapter 9. Smashing Things to the Sea

250 *"The law of war imposes": Instructions*, art. 30.

250 *"War is simply power unrestrained":* OR, series 1, 32 (part 2): 280.

251 *On August 9 alone:* Stephen Davis, " 'Very Barbarous Mode of Carrying on War': Sherman's Artillery Bombardment of Atlanta, July 20–August 24, 1864," *Georgia Historical Quarterly* 79, no. 1 (1995): 57, 68.

251 *to single out particular homes:* Davis, " 'Very Barbarous Mode,' " 68 ("we can pick almost any house in the town").

251 *concentrate their fire at night:* Ibid., 68.

251 *killed a father and his daughter:* Marc Wortman, *The Bonfire: The Siege and Burning of Atlanta* (New York: Public Affairs, 2009), 294.

251 *"destroy Atlanta":* Davis, " 'A Very Barbarous Mode,' " 68.

251 *"make the inside":* W. T. Sherman, *Memoirs of William Tecumseh Sherman* (New York: Library of America, 1990) (1875), 575.

251 *killed around 20 noncombatants:* Wortman, *Bonfire*, 295; Stephen Davis, "How Many Civilians Died in Sherman's Bombardment of Atlanta?" *Atlanta History* 45, no. 4 (2003): 4, 19.

251 *"even if it result in":* Brooks D. Simpson & Jean V. Berlin, eds., *Sherman's Civil War: Selected Correspondence of William T. Sherman, 1860–1865* (Chapel Hill: University of North Carolina Press, 1999), 688.

251 *"no consideration":* B. H. Liddell Hart, *Sherman: Soldier, Realist, American* (New York: Dodd, Mead & Co., 1929), 309.

251 *"seeking the lives":* Simpson & Berlin, eds., *Sherman's Civil War*, 686.

251 *accused Hood of digging:* Ibid., 705–06.

251 *removed from the town by force:* Ibid., 327.

251 *"If the people raise a howl":* Simpson & Berlin, eds., *Sherman's Civil War*, 697.

251 *"in the name of God":* Sherman, *Memoirs*, 593.

251 *"the woe, the horrors":* Ibid., 599.

252 *"kindness"* . . . *"See the books":* Ibid., 594, 601.

252 *"moral cloak":* Harry Stout, *Upon the Altar of the Nation: A Moral History of the Civil War* (New York: Penguin, 2007), 193. Otherwise sophisticated observers often assert (wrongly) that Sherman's conduct in the war flatly violated the terms of Lieber's instructions. See Matthew Waxman, "Siegecraft and Surrender: The Law and Strategy of Cities as Targets," *Virginia Journal of International Law* 39 (1999): 353, 380; Thomas G. Robisch, "General William T. Sherman: Would the Georgia Campaigns of the First Commander of the Modern Era Comply with Current Law of War Standards?" *Emory International Law Review* 9 (1995): 459, 461. The more common form of historians' skepticism comes in simply ignoring Lieber altogether. Neither Lieber nor Lincoln's 1863 instructions are mentioned in James McPherson's magisterial *Battle Cry of Freedom* (New York: Oxford University Press, 1988).

253 *one of the great crusty characters:* Ethan Allen Hitchcock, *Fifty Years in Camp and Field*, (New York: G. P. Putnam's Sons, 1909), 60–69.

253 *"a picture of cruelty":* William B. Skelton, *An American Profession of Arms: The Army Officer Corps, 1784–1861* (New York: G. P. Putnam's Sons, 1992), 315.

253 *"as white men on this continent":* Hitchcock, *Fifty Years in Camp and Field*, 5.

253 *he read the political tracts:* Ibid., 121, 184–85, 207.

254 *a philosophical tract of his own:* Ethan Allen Hitchcock, *The Doctrines of Spinoza and Swedenborg Identified, So Far as They Claim a Scientific Ground* (Boston: Munroe & Francis, 1846).

254 *inspected Union prisoner of war camps:* Herman Hattaway & Eric B. Fair, "Ethan Allen Hitchcock," *American National Biography Online* February 2000, http://www.anb.org/articles/04/04-00506.html.

254 *Stanton appointed him:* Hitchcock, *Fifty Years in Camp and Field*, 444–45.

254 *Since July 1862:* OR, series 2, 4: 266–67.

254 *10,000 more prisoners:* Charles W. Sanders, Jr., *While in the Hands of the Enemy: Military Prisons of the Civil War* (Baton Rouge: Louisiana State University Press, 2005), 149.

254 *turned into breeding grounds:* OR, series 2, 5: 38; Sanders, *While in the Hands of the Enemy*, 136–42.

254 *never bothered to report:* OR, series 2, 5: 33.

254 *The parole of thousands:* Matthew J. Mancini, "Francis Lieber, Slavery, and the 'Genesis' of the Laws of War," *Journal of Southern History* 77, no. 2 (May 2011): 325, 339–40.

255 *battlefield paroles were of no legal effect:* OR, series 2, 5: 70 (Rosencrans); OR, series 2, 5: 191 (Rosencrans); OR, series 2, 5: 339–40.

255 *"not a private act":* Instructions, art. 121.

255 *James Seddon initially protested:* OR, series 2, 6: 45–47.

255 *captured Union soldiers by the thousands:* OR, series 2, 6: 60, 63, 77; Isaac Avery, "List of Prisoners Captured at York, Penn., June 28, 1863," [General Jubal Early's command], Collection of James William Eldridge, 1797–1902, HL.

255 *Stanton rushed out an order:* General Orders No. 207, OR, series 2, 6: 78–79.

255 *had not superseded the 1862 cartel:* OR, series 2, 6: 199; OR, series 2, 6: 471–73.

256 *Ould gleefully proposed:* OR, series 2, 6: 180–81.

256 *continued to treat them as fugitive:* Ira Berlin et al., eds., *Freedom: A Documentary History of Emancipation, 1861–1867—The Black Military Experience* (New York: Cambridge

University Press, 1982), 567–80 (cited hereafter as Berlin et al., eds., *Black Military Experience*).

256   *two free black boys: OR*, series 2, 5: 455, 484.

256   *"red handed on the field": OR*, series 1, 22 (part 2): 965.

256   *Newspapers listed:* Dudley Taylor Cornish, *The Sable Arm: Black Troops in the Union Army, 1861–1865* (Lawrence: University Press of Kansas, 1956), 178.

256   *sold into slavery: OR*, series 2, 5: 966–67.

256   *recommended summary execution:* Sanders, *While in the Hands of the Enemy*, 147.

256   *"no quarter": OR*, series 2, 6: 22–23.

256   *killed on the pretext: OR*, series 2, 6: 257–59.

256   *discouraged such practices: OR*, series 2, 6: 115; *OR*, series I, 22 (part 2): 964–65; Berlin et al., eds., *Black Military Experience*, 578–79.

256   *keeping the number of black prisoners: OR*, series 2, 7: 105.

256   *"the interest of the service": OR*, series 2, 6: 257–59.

257   *Ferguson and his men:* Thomas D. Mays, "The Battle of Saltville," in John David Smith, ed., *Blue: African-American Troops in the Civil War Era* (Chapel Hill: University of North Carolina Press, 2002), 200–26.

257   *"no orders, threats":* Cornish, *Sable Arm*, 177.

257   *"murdered on the spot": OR*, series 1, 34 (part 1): 746; Mike Fisher, "The First Kansas Colored—Massacre at Poison Springs," *Kansas History* (1979): 121–28.

257   *The most notorious race massacre:* John Cimprich & Robert C. Mainfort, Jr., "The Fort Pillow Massacre: A Statistical Note," *Journal of American History* 76, no. 3 (December 1989): 830–36; Noah Andre Trudeau, " 'Kill the Last Damn One of Them': The Fort Pillow Massacre," in Robert Cowley, ed., *With My Face to the Enemy: Perspectives on the Civil War* (New York: G. P. Putnam's Sons, 2001); Gregory J. Macaluso, *The Fort Pillow Massacre: The Reason Why* (New York: Vantage Press, 1989), 49.

257   *"the negroes were shown":* Cimprich & Mainfort, "Fort Pillow Massacre," 836.

257   *Two thirds of the 300 black:* Ibid., 835–36.

257   *Forrest would later deny:* Ronald K. Hutch, "Fort Pillow Massacre: The Aftermath of Paducah," *Journal of the Illinois State Historical Society* 66, no. 1 (1973): 60, 69.

258   *most historians now agree:* See John Cimprich, *Fort Pillow, a Civil War Massacre, and Public Memory* (Baton Rouge: Louisiana State University Press, 2005); John Cimprich, "The Fort Pillow Massacre," in Smith, ed., *Black Soldiers in Blue*, 15–68.

258   *as he would have treated slaves:* For a similar interpretation, see Macaluso, *Fort Pillow Massacre*, 49–51.

258–59   *"seldom imprisoned"* . . . *"Richmond and Charleston":* Robert Scott Davis, " 'Near Andersonville': An Historical Note on Civil War Legend and Reality," *Journal of African American History* 92 (2007): 96, 101.

259   *"ten or twelve thousand":* Sanders, *While in the Hands of the Enemy*, 156–57.

259   *"rest mainly upon the heads":* Walt Whitman, "The Prisoners" (Letter to the Editor), *New York Times*, December 27, 1864.

259   *was forbidden to withhold prisoner of war treatment: OR*, series 2, 6: 18.

259   *"protection to all persons": OR*, series 2, 6: 73.

259   *"irrespective of their color": OR*, series 2, 5: 711–12; Cornish, *Sable Arm*, 163.

259   *"bound to give the same": OR*, series 1, 24 (part 3): 425–26; see also 24 (part 3): 589.

259   *"the policy, dignity, nor honor": OR*, series 2, 7: 688.

259   *often to his own detriment:* E.g., Hitchcock, *Fifty Years in Camp and Field*, 66–67, 432.

259–60   *"extreme sufferings"* . . . *"warfare": OR*, series 2, 6: 594–600; see also Hitchcock's follow-up to the *Times*, *OR*, series 2, 6: 615–17.

260   *was merely a pretext for the real reason:* For a recent example, see Sanders, *While in the Hands of the Enemy*, 2 and passim.

260   *"a new army 40,000 strong": OR*, series 2, 6: 647.

260   *"the United States was prepared":* Berlin et al., eds., *Black Military Experience*, 88–89.

260   *"if the government employs":* Ethan Allen Hitchcock to FL, October 22, 1863, box 11, FLP HL.

260   *Hitchcock offered his resignation: OR*, series 2, 6: 639.

260–61 *"held on to their slaves" . . . "here in bondage":* William Marvel, *Andersonville: The Last Depot* (Chapel Hill: University of North Carolina Press, 1994), 147–48.

261 *Frederick Douglass had made clear:* John David Smith, "Let Us All Be Grateful That We Have Colored Troops That Will Fight," in Smith, ed., *Black Soldiers in Blue*, 47; Cornish, *Sable Arm*, 168; James M. McPherson, *The Negro's Civil War: How American Negroes Felt and Acted During the War for the Union* (New York: Vintage Books, 1965), 173–75.

261 *"it may as well disband":* Berlin et al., eds., *Black Military Experience*, 587.

261 *Grant agreed to resume:* James M. McPherson, *Ordeal by Fire: The Civil War and Reconstruction* (New York: McGraw-Hill, 1982), 456.

261 *The Union offered precisely:* E.g., *OR*, series 2, 6: 136; *OR*, series 2, 7: 687; *OR*, series 2, 8: 801.

261 *Grant himself offered:* McPherson, *Ordeal by Fire*, 456.

261 *"die in the last ditch":* *OR*, series 2, 6: 226.

262 *"They well know":* Kenneth W. Noe, " 'Alabama, We Will Fight for Thee': The Initial Motivations of Later-Enlisting Confederates," *Alabama Review* (July 2009): 163, 179.

262 *"the chief " and "insurmountable" obstacle:* *OR*, series 2, 7: 105.

263 *Some 55,000 men died:* Sanders, *While in the Hands of the Enemy*, 1.

263 *Joseph Holt was born . . . worked feverishly to bolster:* Elizabeth D. Leonard, *Lincoln's Avengers: Justice, Revenge, and Reunion After the Civil War* (New York: W. W. Norton & Co., 2004), 12–23; Mary Bernard Allen, *Joseph Holt, Judge Advocate General, 1862–1875: A Study in the Treatment of Political Prisoners by the United States Government During the Civil War*, Ph.D. diss., University of Chicago, 1927, 47–75.

263 *delivered to the new president:* Joshua E. Kastenberg, *Law in War, War as Law: Brigadier General Joseph Holt and the Judge Advocate General's Department in the Civil War and Early Reconstruction, 1861–1865* (Durham, NC.: Carolina Academic Press, 2011), 25–27.

263 *"went further in his hatred":* Ibid., 17.

263 *"the fallacy of neutrality":* Joseph Holt, *The Fallacy of Neutrality: An Address by the Hon. Joseph Holt, to the People of Kentucky, Delivered at Louisville, July 13, 1861* (New York: J. G. Gregory, 1861).

263 *he nearly chose Holt as Cameron's:* Leonard, *Lincoln's Avengers*, 25–26.

264 *From 1821 to 1849: The Army Lawyer: A History of the Judge Advocate General's Corps, 1775–1975* (Washington, DC: Judge Advocate General's Department, 1975), 35–40.

264 *John Fitzgerald Lee:* Kastenberg, *Law in War, War as Law*, 5, 38–52.

264 *He doubted military commissions' authority:* *OR*, series 2, 1: 373; Kastenberg, *Law in War, War as Law*, 49.

264 *"when not a legitimate belligerent" . . . "known to our laws":* Allen, *Joseph Holt, Judge Advocate General*, 37–39.

264 *recruited thirty-three men: The Army Lawyer*, 54; William McKee Dunn, *A Sketch of the History and Duties of the Judge Advocate General* (Washington, DC: Government Printing Office, 1876). Biographical information on the Civil War judge advocates is drawn mostly from Kastenberg, *Law in War, War as Law*, 117–58.

265 *affirmed the president's power:* Kastenberg, *Law in War, War as Law*, 27.

265 *"a most powerful and reliable":* Joseph Holt to Edwin M. Stanton, August 20, 1863, JHP LC.

265 *the self-defense rights of newly free:* Joseph Holt to AL, May 30, 1864, and Joseph Holt to AL, June 6, 1864, both in JHP LC; West Bogan, NN 1823, box 1689, record Group 153, NARA.

265 *"as occupying the status of freedmen":* Holt to AL, May 30, 1864.

265 *rumors that Confederate captors were quietly:* Kastenberg, *Law in War, War as Law*, 243.

266 *"barbarous avarice":* Joseph Holt to AL, May 24, 1864, JHP LC.

266 *"state or political prisoners":* Stat., 12: 755.

266 *"extremely difficult of construction":* Joseph Holt to Edwin M. Stanton, June 9, 1863, JHP LC.

267 *"the most common form of charge":* William Winthrop, *Digest of Opinions of the Judge Advocate General of the Army* (Washington, DC: Government Printing Office, 3d ed., 1868), 234.

267–68 *abusing prisoners of war . . . occasionally charged men:* See, e.g., Joseph J. Zabu, LL 561, record group 153, NARA; James Fitzgerald, LL 550, record group 153, NARA; John Flora, OO 1452, record group 153, NARA.

268 *lurking behind Union lines:* E.g., Thomas Laswell, LL 2638, box 762, record group 153, NARA; NN2732, record group 153, NARA.

268 *Breaking oaths of allegiance:* Winthrop, *Digest of Opinions,* 383.

268 *parole violation:* E.g., John A. Skaggs, MM 1303, box 990, record group 153, NARA.

268 *recruiting for the Confederacy behind Union lines:* John Thraikill, NN 1233, box 1638, record group 153, NARA; Joseph R. Mathews, LL 1902, record group 153, NARA; Edward A. Muir, LL 938, record group 153, NARA.

268 *constituted nearly 85 percent:* I made these calculations from Gideon Hart's research, which found military commissions charging law of war violations against 566 civilians, 32 guerrillas, 71 Confederate soldiers, and 13 Union soldiers. For examples, see James H. Smith, MM 1309, box 990, record group 153, NARA (violation of laws of war for being a guerrilla); Jesse Fassell, KK 121, record group 153, NARA (violation of the laws of war for being a marauder).

268 *suspected members of the notorious:* Jeremiah Hoy, KK 151, record group 153, NARA (violation of the laws of war for murdering with Quantrill's raiders).

268 *"using disloyal language" . . . Going into the South without a pass:* Winthrop, *Digest of Opinions,* 225–27, 230, 234, 288–89, 383–84, 386–87.

268 *trading with the enemy:* M. T. Wells, KK 833, record group 153, NARA (carrying a dispatch to a Confederate general); William J. Kribben, LL 534, LL 674, record group 153, NARA (carrying letters across Union lines to the South).

268 *after joining the rebel army:* Albert Johnson, II 999, record group 153, NARA; William Russell, LL 580, folder 1, record group 153, NARA; James Herron, LL 563, record group 153, NARA.

268 *evading service in the Union armed forces:* James C. Moore, LL 647, record group 153, NARA.

269 *One St. Louis woman:* Zaidee J. Bagwell, LL 548, record group 153, NARA.

269 *A Baltimore woman:* Winthrop, *Digest of Opinions,* 384.

269 *Horse-stealing could be a war crime:* Aroswell D. Severance, II 951, II 931, record group 153, NARA.

269 *Expressing anti-Union views:* J. S. Hyatt, KK 821, record group 153, NARA; Winthrop, *Digest of Opinions,* 225.

269 *Judge advocates sometimes charged:* E.g., Thomas Clark, KK 833, KK 818, record group 153, NARA; William Harding, KK 818, record group 153, NARA; A. Alexander, LL 289, folder 1, record group 153, NARA.

270 *Congress belatedly recognized this:* L. D. Ingersoll, *A History of the War Department of the United States: With Biographical Sketches of the Secretaries* (Washington, DC: Francis B. Mohun, 1879), 150.

270 *promoting the Judge Advocate General:* The Army Lawyer, 51.

270 *John Frémont in Missouri:* Gideon Hart, "Military Commissions and the Lieber Code: Toward a New Understanding of the Jurisdictional Foundations of Military Commissions," *Military Law Review* 203 (Spring 2010): 1, 9–12.

270 *So did Ulysses S. Grant:* Mark E. Neely, Jr., *The Fate of Liberty: Abraham Lincoln and Civil Liberties* (New York: Oxford University, 1991), 35, 39.

270 *to try civilians for treason:* Ibid., 42–43; Hart, "Military Commissions and the Lieber Code," 19.

270 *Halleck edited so heavily:* Halleck's markup of the committee print of Lieber's early draft code is in the Huntington Library. See "A Code for the Government of Armies in the Field as Authorized by the Laws and Usages of War on Land," HL, register no. 243077, Y Halleck II.

270 *cited particular code provisions:* E.g., James McGregory, NN 1234, box 1638, record group 153, NARA; Winthrop, *Digest of Opinions,* 382–83.

270   *relied on Lieber for advice:* Joseph Holt to FL, February 20, 1863, box 11, FLP HL; Joseph Holt to FL, February 26, 1863, box 11, FLP HL; Neely, *Fate of Liberty*, 160; Allen, *Joseph Holt*, 110; see also Elizabeth D. Leonard, *Lincoln's Forgotten Ally: Judge Advocate Joseph Holt of Kentucky* (Chapel Hill: University of North Carolina Press, 2011), 181.

270   *the prosecution and the defense:* E.g., Joseph Holt, "To Major General Summer, President and the Members of the Court," box 2, Joseph Holt Collection, HL.

270   *appointed Lieber's son Norman: The Army Lawyer*, 85–86.

270   *military commissions spread to military departments:* I rely here on the prodigious research done for me by Gideon Hart. See Hart, "Military Commissions and the Lieber Code," 41–42.

271   *"take cognizance of":* Ibid., 40.

271   *"War is not carried on": Instructions*, art. 17.

271   *"native of a hostile country":* Ibid., art. 21.

271   *"to property, and to persons":* Ibid., art. 7.

271   *"or rather must":* Neely, *Fate of Liberty*, 160.

271   *"careful trials of spies":* FL to Henry Halleck, March 18, 1865, box 28, FLP HL.

271   *"no person accused":* FL to Joseph Holt, June 12, 1863, JHP LC.

271   *arrested Vallandigham in his bedroom:* Frank L. Klement, *The Limits of Dissent: Clement Vallandigham & the Civil War* (New York: Fordham University Press, 1998), 157–58.

271   *"Lincoln and his minions": The Trial of Hon. Clement L. Vallandigham by a Military Commission and the Proceedings Under His Application for a Writ of Habeas Corpus* (Cincinnati: Rickey & Carroll, 1863), 11.

271–72   *"all persons found within":* General Orders No. 38, April 13, 1863, *OR*, series 1, 23 (part 2): 237. There is no direct evidence that Burnside drew on Lieber's text. Halleck told Lieber that Burnside had acted on his own without consulting Union authorities in Washington—Henry Halleck to FL, May 16, 1863, box 9, FLP HL. Early prints of the draft code had been distributed in March. Whether Burnside had patterned his order off Lieber's or not, Lieber thought that Burnside's order was dangerously aggressive—FL to Henry Halleck, May 15, 1863, box 27, FLP HL.

272   *he was not, he insisted: Trial of Hon. Clement L. Vallandigham*, 12, 29.

272   *Aaron Fyfe Perry: Biographical Directory of the United States Congress,* http://bioguide.congress.gov/scripts/biodisplay.pl?index=P000241.

272   *Flamen Ball:* "Obituary: Flamen Ball," *American Law Record* 13 (1885): 572.

272   *"laws of war" . . . "the women and children": Ex parte Vallandigham,* 28 F. Cas. 874, 894 (C.C.S.D. Ohio 1863) (argument of Aaron Perry).

272   *"Ohio . . . is at war":* 28 F. Cas. at 919 (argument of Flamen Ball).

273   *Sensing that he was in:* 28 F. Cas. at 922–23.

273   *pronounced Vallandigham guilty: Trial of Hon. Clement L. Vallandigham*, 33.

273   *Lincoln promptly reduced:* Ibid., 34.

273   *"in conformity with the instructions" . . . "common law of war": Ex parte Vallandigham*, 68 U.S. 243, 248–49 & nn.1–2 (1864).

273   *A small rebel office: The Army Lawyer*, 58–59.

273   *executed them by hanging: OR*, series 1, 10 (part 1): 630–38; William Pittenger, *Daring and Suffering: A History of the Andrews Railroad Raid into Georgia in 1862* (New York: War Publishing Co., 1887), supp. 50–51.

273   *refused to appoint a Judge Advocate General:* William Morrison Robinson, *Justice in Grey: A History of the Judicial System of the Confederate States of America* (Cambridge, MA: Harvard University Press, 1941), 378–80.

273   *martial law as anathema:* Ibid., 381.

273   *no military tribunal jurisdiction: OR*, series 2, 4: 894–97.

274   *"irksome, uncongenial":* Henry G. Connor, *John Archibald Campbell: Associate Justice of the United States Supreme Court, 1853–1861* (Boston: Houghton Mifflin, 1920), 159.

274   *under the state criminal laws:* Berlin et al., eds., *Black Military Experience*, 567–68.

274   *Athens, Georgia, in 1862:* Mark Grimsley, *The Hard Hand of War: Union Military Policy Toward Southern Civilians, 1861–1865* (New York: Cambridge University Press, 1995), 81–84; Earnest E. East, "Lincoln's Russian General," *Illinois State Historical*

Society 52, no. 1 (Spring 1959): 106, 108–12; George C. Bradley & Richard L. Dahlen, *From Conciliation to Conquest: The Sack of Athens and the Court-Martial of Colonel John B. Turchin* (Tuscaloosa: University of Alabama Press, 2006).

274 *the events at Chambersburg:* Harry Stout, *Upon the Altar of the Nation: A Moral History of the Civil War* (New York: Penguin Books, 2005), 375–76.

274 *taken out and shot by firing squad:* Lonnie R. Speer, *War of Vengeance: Acts of Retaliation Against Civil War POWs* (Mechanicsburg, PA: Stackpole Books, 2002), 29–41.

275 *the population had provided:* Burrus M. Carnahan, *Lincoln on Trial: Southern Civilians and the Law of War* (Lexington, KY: University Press of Kentucky, 2010), 63–64.

275 *internecine guerrilla actions across the Upper South:* See, e.g., Richard R. Duncan, *Beleaguered Winchester: A Virginia Community at War, 1861–1865* (Baton Rouge: Louisiana State University Press, 2007), 177–91; Robert R. Mackey, *The Uncivil War: Irregular Warfare in the Upper South, 1861–1865* (Norman: University of Oklahoma Press, 2004), 33–40.

275 *Rumors of exploding bullets:* "Greek Fire," from the *New York Evening Post*, September [1?], 1863, in box 20, FLP HL.

275 *old vessels in the mouth of the harbor:* Clippings on "Stone Blockade," folder 18, box 2, FLP JHU.

275 *booby-trapped bodies: Harper's Weekly*, September 19, 1863, box 20, FLP HL.

275 *Sherman's background:* John F. Marszalek, *Sherman: A Soldier's Passion for Order* (New York: Free Press, 1993).

275 *"standard of conduct was":* Charles Royster, *The Destructive War: William Tecumseh Sherman, Stonewall Jackson, and the Americans* (New York: Alfred A. Knopf, 1991), 95.

276 *"Goths or Vandals":* James M. McPherson, "Two Strategies of Victory: William T. Sherman in the Civil War," *Atlanta History* 33, no. 4 (Winter 1989–90): 5, 12.

276 *"fugitive slaves must be delivered": OR*, series 2, 1: 749.

276 *"all in the South are enemies":* McPherson, "Two Strategies of Victory," 15.

276 *"not only fighting hostile armies":* Simpson & Berlin, eds., *Sherman's Civil War*, 776.

276 *"all the damage you can":* McPherson, "Two Strategies of Victory," 6.

276 *"destroy every mill":* Sherman, *Memoirs*, 603.

276 *"make a wreck of the road": OR*, series 1, 36 (part I): 39.

276 *"the utter destruction": OR*, series 1, 39 (part 3): 162.

277 *"If a little salt":* Sherman, *Memoirs*, 700.

277 *"I propose":* Joseph T. Glatthaar, *The March to the Sea and Beyond: Sherman's Troops in the Savannah and Carolina Campaigns* (New York: New York University Press, 1985), 6.

277 *"I can make the march":* Hart, *Sherman: Soldier, Realist, American,* 320.

277 *"desolating the land":* Sherman, *Memoirs*, 614.

277 *"all idea of the establishment":* Ibid., 364.

277 *"I would not coax them":* Ibid., 365.

277 *managed to limit the violence:* See Glatthaar, *March to the Sea*, 73–74, 87; Grimsley, *The Hard Hand of War*, 199 and *passim*; Mark E. Neely, Jr., *The Civil War and the Limits of Destruction* (Cambridge, MA: Harvard University Press, 2007); and James M. McPherson, "The Hard Hand of War," in James M. McPherson, *This Mighty Scourge: Perspectives on the Civil War* (New York: Oxford University Press, 2007), 123–29.

277 *"anything of any military value":* Glatthaar, *March to the Sea*, 8.

277 *90,000 bales of cotton:* Statistics of destruction come from ibid., 130–36.

277 *"The remainder": OR*, series 1, 44: 13.

277 *"spare nothing":* Sherman, *Memoirs*, 662.

278 *the "whole army":* Grimsley, *Hard Hand of War*, 201.

278 *The capital itself:* Royster, *Destructive War*, 3–33.

278 *"hypocritical appeals":* Simpson & Berlin, eds., *Sherman's Civil War*, 706.

278 *"outrages, cruelty, [and] barbarity" . . . "can whip":* Ibid., 694.

278 *"crowds of idlers":* Ibid., 689.

278 *"slow the progress of his army":* Paul J. Springer, *America's Captives: Treatment of POWs from the Revolutionary War to the War on Terror* (Lawrence, KS: University Press of Kansas, 2010), 89.

278 *"At times"*: Major S. H. M. Byers, *With Fire and Sword* (New York: Neale Publishing Co., 1911), 177.

278 *"To secure the navigation"*: *OR*, series 1, 31 (part 3): 459.

278 *mass relocation of the southern population:* E.g., *OR*, series 1, 32 (part 2): 278; Simpson & Berlin, eds., *Sherman's Civil War*, 183.

279 *cotton works at Roswell:* Mary Deborah Petite, *"The Women Will Howl": The Union Army Capture of Roswell and New Manchester, Georgia, and the Forced Relocation of Mill Workers* (Jefferson, NC: McFarland Publishing Co., 2008).

279 *then again at Atlanta:* Grimsley, *Hard Hand of War*, 186–90.

279 *"the humanities of the case"*: McPherson, "Two Strategies of Victory," 15.

279 *the way to end the suffering of his people:* Simpson & Berlin, eds., *Sherman's Civil War*, 707–09.

279 *"the more awful you can make"*: Byers, *With Fire and Sword*, 177.

279 *One officer under his command later remembered:* Ibid.

279 *could not recall the occasion:* Marszalek, *Sherman: A Soldier's Passion*, 477.

279 *"War is barbarism"*: Hart, *Sherman: Soldier, Realist, American*, 310.

279 *"war is simply power"*: *OR*, series 1, 32 (part 2): 280.

279 *"war is cruelty"*: Simpson & Berlin, eds., *Sherman's Civil War*, 708.

279 *"Boys, it is all hell"*: Fred R. Shapiro, ed., *The Yale Book of Quotations* (New Haven, CT: Yale University Press, 2006), 708.

280 *"barbarous cruelty"* . . . *"Thirty Years' War"*: Jefferson Davis, *The Rise and Fall of the Confederate Government* (New York: D. Appleton & Co., 1881), 2: 564, 629.

280 *Lincoln followed Sherman's campaign:* Henry Hitchcock to FL, January 15, 1865, box 11, FLP HL.

280 *taken care of the injured Hamilton:* FL to Henry Halleck, March 18, 1862, box 27, FLP HL; FL to Charles Sumner, March 23, 1862, box 42, FLP HL.

280 *"Sherman moves his army better than"*: FL to Henry Halleck, February 24, 1865, box 28, FLP HL.

280 *"Assuredly my name is"* . . . *"ruthless revenge"*: FL to Henry Halleck, February 11, 1865, box 28, FLP HL.

280 *Napoleon's rise from popular general:* See, e.g., FL to [Alexander Dallas Bache], December 14, 1861, box 23, FLP HL; FL to Charles Sumner, March 28, 1865, box 44, FLP HL; see also Francis Lieber, "Washington and Napoleon," in Daniel C. Gilman, ed., *The Miscellaneous Writings of Francis Lieber* (Philadelphia: J. B. Lippincott, 1881), 1: 413–41.

281 *"forage liberally"* . . . *"discreet officers"*: Sherman, *Memoirs*, 652.

281 *"most important"*: Ibid., 651.

281 *"soldier passed me with a ham"*: Ibid., 658.

281 *to vacuum all the usable goods:* Glatthaar, *March to the Sea*, 121–55.

281 *Bummers hanged:* Ibid., 72–73.

281 *pistols to the heads:* Ibid., 126.

281 *Executions sometimes followed:* Ibid., 72–73, 126.

282 *Confederate home guards:* Ibid., 128.

282 *counted 173 of its men:* Ibid., 128.

282 *booby-trapped false caches:* Ibid., 126.

282 *ordered the execution of Confederate prisoners:* Ibid., 152–53.

282 *only "corps commanders" were authorized:* Sherman, *Memoirs*, 652.

282 *burned some 5,000 homes:* Glatthaar, *March to the Sea*, 139.

282 *"almost as though there was a Secret"*: Ibid., 140.

282 *"inexcusable and wanton"*: James Reston, Jr., *Sherman's March and Vietnam* (New York: Macmillan, 1984), 70.

282 *"I never ordered"* . . . *"Jeff Davis burnt them"*: Ibid., 31.

282 *"the soldiers will take"*: Royster, *Destructive War*, 344.

282 *"many acts of pillage"*: Sherman, *Memoirs*, 659.

282 *cited Sherman's approval in his defense:* Royster, *Destructive War*, 343.

283 *"in particular places":* Frank Freidel, "General Orders 100 and Military Government,"
      Mississippi Valley Historical Review 32, no. 4 (March 1947): 541, 552–53 (Halleck to
      Hurlbut); see also *OR,* series 1, 22 (part 2): 292 (Halleck to Schofield).
283 *"War is an uncivil game":* Glatthaar, *March to the Sea,* 136.
283 *"Truly":* Grimsley, *Hard Hand of War,* 185.
283 *"Boys, this is old South Carolina":* Ibid., 201.
283 *"country behind us":* Glatthaar, *March to the Sea,* 142.

Chapter 10. Soldiers and Gentlemen

285 *With malice toward none:* Basler, 8: 333.
285 *"one of the worst for which":* Ulysses S. Grant, *Personal Memoirs of U.S. Grant* (1885–86);
      ed. James M. McPherson, New York: Penguin Books, 1999, 601.
285 *"the great mass":* Ibid., 603.
285 *Grant promised that:* Ibid., 604.
286 *"a general oblivion":* See, e.g., Article I of the Treaty of Paris in 1763 at the end of the
      Seven Years' War, available at http://avalon.law.yale.edu/18th_century/paris763.asp;
      see generally Lassa Oppenheim, *International Law: A Treatise* (New York: Longmans,
      Green, 1912), 2: 334–35.
286 *"forgetting and amnesty":* George Friedrich Muller, *Das Krieges oder Soldatenrecht* (Ber-
      lin: Petit- and Schöneschen Bookshop, 1789), §9, in box 7, Judge Advocate School
      Lieber Collection, Federal Research Division, LC.
286 *Sherman and General Joseph Johnston:* OR, series 1, 47 (part 3): 243–45.
286 *the president issued an amnesty:* Richardson, 6: 310–12; *OR,* series 2, 8: 578–60.
286 *"general amnesty of all past offences":* Kappler, 2: 920.
286 *the English Civil War:* Barbara Donagan, *War in England, 1642–1649* (Oxford: Oxford
      University Press, 2008); Geoffrey Parker, "Early Modern Europe," in Michael How-
      ard, George J. Andreopulos, & Mark R. Shulman, eds., *The Laws of War: Constraints on
      Warfare in the Western World* (New Haven, CT: Yale University Press, 1994), 50–51.
286 *the uprising in Scotland:* Bruce Lenman, *The Jacobite Risings in Britain 1689–1746*
      (London: Eyre/Methuen, 1980).
286 *executed thousands of defeated Irish:* Alan Taylor, *The Civil War of 1812: American Citi-
      zens, British Subjects, Irish Rebels, & Indian Allies* (New York: Alfred A. Knopf, 2010),
      80.
286 *Napoleon imposed:* Milton Finley, *The Most Monstrous of Wars: The Napoleonic Guer-
      rilla War in Southern Italy, 1806–1811* (Columbia: University of South Carolina Press,
      1994), 139–40; Charles J. Esdaile, *Fighting Napoleon: Guerrillas, Bandits, and Adven-
      turers in Spain, 1808–1814* (New Haven, CT: Yale University Press, 2004).
286 *it authorized treason prosecutions: Instructions,* art. 154 & 157.
287 *cast Jefferson Davis:* William J. Cooper, *Jefferson Davis, American* (New York: Alfred A.
      Knopf, 2000), 536–38.
287 *held his vice president:* Thomas E. Schott, *Alexander H. Stephens of Georgia: A Biography*
      (Baton Rouge: Louisiana State University Press, 1988), 451.
287 *Union forces arrested: OR,* series 2, 8: 529 (Ould), 539 (Vance), 550 (Hunter), 551
      (Campbell and Stephens), 553–57 (Wirz), 560 (Cobb, Toombs, and Brown), 566–
      68 (Campbell, Reagan, and Seddon), 577 (Hill), 639 (Wirz), 658 (Allison), 662–64
      (Trenholm and Mallory), 690 (Davis), 812–14 (Clay).
288 *"read the same Bible" . . . "with all nations":* Basler, 8: 333.
288 *"had been gentle & forgiving":* Charles Sumner to Elizabeth Georgiana Campbell,
      Duchess of Argyll, April 24, 1865, HM 51929, Charles Sumner Collection, HL.
      Sumner took Lincoln's paraphrase of Matthew 7:1 and unconsciously reverted to the
      text of the King James Bible.
288 *he offered full pardons:* Basler, 7: 53–56.
288 *"otherwise than lawfully":* Ibid., 7: 55.
288 *the offer remained open:* Ibid., 8: 152.
288 *"reaccept the Union":* Ibid., 8: 151.

288   *Privately he hoped Davis:* David Herbert Donald, *Lincoln* (New York: Simon & Schuster, 1995), 583.

288   *In February 1865, Lincoln even:* Basler, 8: 260–61.

289   *"If you go to war":* Cong. *Globe,* 38th Cong., 2nd sess., 364; see also Bruce Tap, *Over Lincoln's Shoulder: The Committee on the Conduct of the War* (Lawrence: University Press of Kansas, 1998), 207; H. L. Trefousse, *Benjamin Franklin Wade* (New York: Twayne, 1963), 237; Harry Williams, "Benjamin F. Wade and the Atrocity Propaganda of the Civil War," *Ohio State Archaeological and Historical Quarterly* 68 (1939): 33–43.

289   *Sumner disagreed: Cong. Globe,* 38th Cong., 2nd sess., 381–82.

289   *"If they take a tooth": Cong. Globe,* 38th Cong., 2nd sess., 517.

289   *he aimed to adapt:* On Holt, see Elizabeth D. Leonard, *Lincoln's Forgotten Ally: Judge Advocate General Joseph Holt of Kentucky* (Chapel Hill: University of North Carolina Press, 2011); Elizabeth D. Leonard, *Lincoln's Avengers: Justice, Revenge, and Reunion After the Civil War* (New York: W. W. Norton & Co., 2004).

289   *Stanton personally launched:* Leonard, *Lincoln's Avengers,* 8–11.

290   *The new attorney general . . . agreed:* For the cabinet discussion, which appears to have been cursory, see Gideon Welles, *Diary of Gideon Welles, Secretary of the Navy Under Lincoln and Johnson* (Boston: Houghton Mifflin, 1911), 2: 303–04. Only Welles and Benjamin McCulloch, the new secretary of the Treasury, disagreed with the decision to use a military commission.

290   *"one of the feeblest men":* Charles Fairman, *Mr. Justice Miller and the Supreme Court, 1862–1890* (Cambridge, MA: Harvard University Press, 1939), 118.

290   *"If the persons charged": AG Opinions,* 11: 297, 317.

290   *reached his conclusion by May 1:* Edward Steers, Jr., *The Trial: The Assassination of President Lincoln and the Trial of the Conspirators* (Lexington, KY: University Press of Kentucky, 2003), 17.

291   *They were dressed in black:* Leonard, *Lincoln's Avengers,* 69.

291   *spared the indignity of the hood:* Edward Steers, Jr., & Harold Holzer, *The Lincoln Assassination Conspirators: Their Confinement and Execution, As Recorded in the Letterbook of John Frederick Hartranft* (Baton Rouge: Louisiana State University Press, 2009), 88–90 (pp. 19–21 of the MS letterbook). Precisely who among the accused were wearing hoods and shackles has long been a source of minor controversy. John Hartranft, who commanded the military prison where the prisoners were held and who wrote letters contemporaneous with the events, denied that Mudd or Surratt wore hoods. On the other hand, commission member August Kautz recalled that all the accused conspirators wore hoods. See August V. Kautz, "Reminiscences of the Civil War: Transcribed from the Original Manuscripts and Presented to the Army War College Library," unpublished MS, NYHS.

291   *"I was quite impressed":* Leonard, *Lincoln's Avengers,* 69.

291   *The secrecy rule was lifted:* Ibid., 71.

291   *George Atzerodt . . . weapons and a bankbook:* Pitman, 144.

291   *Lewis Powell . . . was identified:* Ibid., 155–56.

291   *convincingly connected:* Ibid., 235.

291   *Edman Spangler:* Ibid., 75–76, 79–80.

291   *had sought medical assistance:* Ibid., 168.

292   *Weichman further testified that he had spent time together with Mudd and Booth:* Ibid., 114.

292   *all frequented the Surratt boardinghouse:* Ibid., 113–15.

292   *left guns and ammunition:* Ibid., 85.

292   *The charges named:* Ibid., 18.

292   *had jurisdiction only over soldiers:* Ibid., 22, 251–63.

293   *Thomas Ewing, Jr. . . . argued:* Ibid., 245–47.

293   *"By what law":* Ibid., 352.

293   *"the civil courts have no more right": AG Opinions,* 315.

294   *"the common law of war": Instructions for Armies of the United States,* art. 13; *Ex parte Vallandigham,* 68 U.S. 243, 249 (1864).

294 By *"what code or system of laws":* Pitman, 246.

294 *"the common law of war":* Ibid., 247.

294 *he offered into evidence:* Ibid., 243–44. The leading publisher of the trial proceedings included the entire text of Lincoln's 1863 instructions as an appendix to the trial transcript. See ibid., 410–19.

294 *returned guilty verdicts for all eight:* Ibid., 247–49.

294 *Judge Andrew Wylie: The Trial of the Assassins and Conspirators at Washington, D.C., May and June, 1865, for the Murder of President Abraham Lincoln* (Philadelphia: T. B. Peterson & Brothers, 1865), 209–10; see also Pitman, 250, which (though usually superior to the Peterson edition of the transcript) is less useful on this point. I am grateful to Andrew Wylie, great-grandson of Judge Wylie, for helping me with the family history here.

295 *The commission heard about surreptitious:* Pitman, 53–54 (burn the North's major cities); 47–49 (destroy civilian steamboats); 50–51 (Union supply lines at City Point); 54–57 (introduce infectious diseases); 57–62 (starve captured Union soldiers); 53 (St. Albans, Vermont).

295 *Holt relied on a man:* Ibid., 28–33.

295 *"the plot to assassinate":* Ibid., 28.

295 *For Conover, whose real name:* Leonard, *Lincoln's Avengers,* 86, 103–04, 215–36, 266–70.

295 Toronto Globe *published:* "General News," *New York Times,* June 26, 1865.

295 New York Times *reported:* "Sanford Conover," *New York Times,* June 18, 1865.

295 *warned Holt that Conover was a notorious character:* Leonard, *Lincoln's Avengers,* 85.

296 *"Everybody":* Pitman, 239.

296 *"simply because they were Trojans":* Ibid., 267.

296 *"all the people of the United States":* Ibid., 266.

296 *to set fire to Chicago: OR,* series 2, 8: 54; Stephen Z. Starr, *Colonel Grenfell's Wars: The Life of a Soldier of Fortune* (Baton Rouge: Louisiana State University Press, 1971).

296 *John Yates Beall at Fort Lafayette: The Trial of John Yates Beall as a Spy and Guerrillero, by Military Commission* (New York: D. Appleton & Co., 1865).

297 *"It is a murder": Memoir of John Yates Beall: His Life; Trial; Correspondence; Diary; and Private Manuscript Found Among His Papers* (Montreal: John Lovell, 1865), 87.

297 *Booth had hoped to avenge:* James G. Randall, ed., *The Diary of Orville Hickman Browning* (Springfield, IL: Illinois State Historical Library, 1933), 2: 19.

297 *to set a great fire in Manhattan:* Nat Brandt, *The Man Who Tried to Burn New York* (Syracuse, NY: Syracuse University Press, 1986).

297 *P. T. Barnum's museum:* "Barnum's American Museum" [advertisement], *Frank Leslie's Illustrated Newspaper* (New York), April 22, 1865, p. 66.

297 *in the Department of the Cumberland:* E.g., Lewis C. Adams, General Court-Martial Order 17, General Court-Martial Orders: Department of the Cumberland, 1861–1865, Library of Congress Rare Book and Special Collections.

298 *in the Department of the East:* E.g., Joseph V. Smedley and John P. Roberts, General Orders No. 5, Military Trials: Department of the East, 1865–1866, LC.

298 *in Virginia and North Carolina:* E.g., Samuel Etheridge, James White, and Charles Bullock, General Court-Martial Order No. 7, General Orders: Department of Virginia and North Carolina, 1864–1865, U.S. Military Academy Library at West Point, Special Collections.

298 *in the Department of the Gulf:* Charles Cavanac and S. U. Birt, General Orders No. 12, General Orders: Department of the Gulf, 1865, LC.

298 *and in Missouri:* E.g., Joseph T. Weldon and George M. Tye, General Orders No. 40, General Orders: Department of Missouri, 1865, New-York Historical Society.

298 *tried and convicted Champ Ferguson:* Thomas D. Mays, *Cumberland Blood: Champ Ferguson's Civil War* (Carbondale, IL: Southern Illinois University Press, 2008).

298 *another commission in Wilmington:* Letter of the Secretary of War, Senate Exec. Doc. No. 11, 39th Cong.. 1st sess. (1866).

298 *a bleak seventeen-acre camp:* Ovid L. Futch, *History of Andersonville Prison* (Gainesville:

University Press of Florida, 1968); Charles W. Sanders, Jr., *While in the Hands of the Enemy: Military Prisons of the Civil War* (Baton Rouge: Louisiana State University Press, 2005), 198–317; J. H. Segars, *Andersonville: The Southern Perspective* (Atlanta: Southern Heritage Press, 1995).

298 *took in between 41,000 and 45,000:* William Marvel, *Andersonville: The Last Depot* (Chapel Hill: University of North Carolina Press, 1994), ix (41,000); Paul J. Springer, *America's Captives: Treatment of POWs from the Revolutionary War to the War on Terror* (Lawrence: University Press of Kansas, 2010), 96 (45,000).

298 *As many as 32,899:* Dora L. Costa & Matthew E. Kahn, *Heroes & Cowards: The Social Face of War* (Princeton, NJ: Princeton University Press, 2008), 126.

298 *Three quarters of the patients . . . 12,912 men:* Springer, *America's Captives*, 96.

299 *"when the animal is excited":* Norton Parker Chipman, *The Tragedy of Andersonville: Trial of Captain Henry Wirz, the Prison Keeper* (San Francisco: Blair Murdock Co., 2nd ed., 1911), 106.

299 *the trial got off to:* Ibid., 28–30; Lewis L. Laska & James M. Smith, " 'Hell and the Devil': Andersonville and the Trial of Capt. Henry Wirz, CSA, 1865," *Military Law Review* 68 (Spring 1975): 77, 101.

299 *But Wirz's two lawyers both:* Trial of Henry Wirz, House Exec. Doc. no. 23, 40th Cong., 2nd sess., p. 9 (1866).

299 *threatened to walk off the case:* "The Trial of Captain Henry Wirz," *American State Trials* (St. Louis: F. H. Thomas Law Book Co., 1917), 8: 657, 691, 744.

299 *arrested James Duncan: American State Trials*, 8: 730; Joshua E. Kastenberg, *Law in War, War as Law: Brigadier General Joseph Holt and the Judge Advocate General's Department in the Civil War and Early Reconstruction, 1861–1865* (Durham, NC: Carolina Academic Press, 2011), 258–59.

299 *sought to call Robert Ould:* Kastenberg, *Law in War, War as Law*, 259.

299 *A court reporter delivered: American State Trials*, 8: 741 & n.

299 *instances of abuse by Wirz:* E.g., ibid., 8: 704–05, 718–19, 729–30, 734.

300 *to the attention of Richmond officials: OR*, series 2, 8: 111 *American State Trials*, 8: 713, 732, 739.

300 *to improve the camp bakery . . . improve the water quality:* Chipman, *The Tragedy of Andersonville*, 115–16; William Best Hesseltine, *Civil War Prisons: A Study in War Psychology* (Columbus: Ohio State University Press, 1930), 139–40; Marvel, *Andersonville: The Last Depot*, 80; see also *OR*, series 2, 7: 167–68, 207, 521.

300 *"a servant and instrument": American State Trials*, 8: 682.

300 *"tool of monsters": OR*, series 2, 8: 793.

300 *"in their present condition": American State Trials*, 8: 717; Chipman, *The Tragedy of Andersonville*, 115.

300 *Even Winder:* Futch, *History of Andersonville*, 75.

300 *died of a heart attack:* Arch Frederic Blakey, *General John H. Winder, C.S.A.* (Gainesville: University of Florida Press, 1990), 201.

300 *Death rates in northern camps:* See Roger Pickenpaugh, *Captives in Gray: The Civil War Prisons of the Union* (Tuscaloosa, AL: University of Alabama Press, 2009).

301 *worked to turn the attention back: The Demon of Andersonville or, the Trial of Wirz for the Cruel Treatment and Brutal Murder of Helpless Union Prisoners in His Hands* (Philadelphia: Barclay & Co., 1865), 107.

301 *"where the responsibility rested": American State Trials*, 8: 749.

301 *"rather as a demon": OR*, series 2, 8: 781.

301–302 *expanding the use of military commissions: OR*, series 2, 8: 782–83; Mary Bernard Allen, *Joseph Holt, Judge Advocate General, 1862–1875: A Study in the Treatment of Political Prisoners by the United States Government During the Civil War.* PhD diss., University of Chicago, 1927, 146–47; Leonard, *Lincoln's Avengers*, 161.

302 *"Where do you make the distinction": The Trial of John Yates Beall as a Spy and Guerrillero*, 65.

302 *it lacked jurisdiction to prosecute:* Kastenberg, *Law in War, War as Law*, 262–64.

302 *acquitted Confederate general Hugh W. Mercer: OR*, series 2, 8: 871.

302 *Major John H. Gee:* "Major John H. Gee," *Daily National Intelligencer* (Washington, DC), June 27, 1866.

302 *worse even than at Andersonville:* Costa & Kahn, *Heroes & Cowards*, 149.

303 *James Duncan . . . a commission: OR*, series 2, 8: 926–28.

303 *When Duncan escaped:* Robert Scott Davis, "An Historical Note on 'The Devil's Advocate': O. S. Baker and the Henry Wirz/Andersonville Military Tribunal," *Journal of Southern Legal History* 10 (2002): 25, 55 n. 46.

303 *Grant insisted:* Kastenberg, *Law in War, War as Law*, 265.

303 *Wirz's lawyers had made: American State Trials*, 8: 681.

303 *Grant successfully prevented:* Kastenberg, *Law in War, War as Law*, 266–67.

303 *"the terms of the parole":* Ibid.

303 *the formal end of the insurrection:* Richardson, 6: 429–32.

303 *"seemed like skipping":* Kastenberg, *Law in War, War as Law*, 261.

303 *"no responsibility":* "The Acquittal of Major Gee," *Boston Daily Advertiser*, September 4, 1866.

304 *President Johnson had been appointing:* Richardson, 6: 312–14; Eric Foner, *Reconstruction: America's Unfinished Revolution, 1863–1877* (New York: Harper & Row, 1988), 183–216.

304 *"Siamese twins": Cong. Globe*, 39th Cong., 1st sess., 523; Foner, *Reconstruction*, 243–47.

305 *"status of the rebel States": Cong. Globe*, 39th Cong., 1st sess., 24.

305 *"Unless the law of nations":* Ibid., 73.

305 *"views on this point coincide":* Ibid., 117.

305 *would preclude prosecuting any:* Ibid., 121.

305 *would characterize:* Ibid., 121.

305 *Yet the most commonly cited alternative:* William M. Wiecek, *The Guarantee Clause of the U.S. Constitution* (Ithaca, NY: Cornell University Press, 1972); Bruce Ackerman, *We The People 2: Transformations* (Cambridge, MA: Belknap Press, 1998), 168.

306 *President Johnson had relied on the clause:* Richardson, 6: 312.

306 *open-ended federal government intervention:* Michael Les Benedict, *A Compromise of Principle: Congressional Republicans and Reconstruction 1863–1869* (New York: W. W. Norton & Co., 1974), 215, 413 n. 29; Michael Les Benedict, "Preserving the Constitution: The Conservative Basis of Radical Reconstruction," *Journal of American History* 61 (1974): 65, 66–76.

306 *"hold the other in the grasp":* Benedict, *Compromise of Principle*, 125.

307 *"the sovereign may exercise":* Samuel Shapiro, *Richard Henry Dana, Jr., 1815–1882* (East Lansing: Michigan State University Press, 1961), 119.

307 *"the same national authority": The Works of Charles Sumner* (Boston: Lee & Shepard, 1870–83), 9: 425.

307 *"null and void": Cong. Globe*, 39th Cong., 1st sess., 39, 41.

307 *"The men who went into rebellion":* Benedict, "Preserving the Constitution," 76.

307 *an early champion:* Herman Belz, *Reconstructing the Union: Theory and Policy During the Civil War* (Ithaca, NY: Cornell University Press, 1969), 10.

308 *prosecution of Confederate naval officer: Diary of Gideon Welles*, 2: 471–77.

308 *"wished to put no more in Holt's control":* Ibid., 2: 423.

308 *"dupe of his own imaginings":* Ibid., 2: 423.

308 *"arbitrary tribunals":* Richardson, 6: 399.

308 *"are in time of peace dangerous":* Ibid., 6: 432.

308 *prosecution of rebel captain Richard B. Winder: OR*, series 2, 8: 887–88.

308 *Holt confidently insisted: OR*, series 2, 8: 890–92.

308 *a citizen of Indiana named Lambdin Milligan:* Samuel Klaus, ed., *The Milligan Case* (London: George Routledge & Sons, 1929), 27–35.

309 *for conspiring against . . . and violating the laws of war:* Ibid., 74–81.

309 *"an inhabitant, resident":* Ibid., 66.

309 *"in full exercise of their functions":* Ibid., 122.

309 *"the laws of war":* Ibid., 140.

310 *"take and kill":* Ibid., 124.

310 *"dark and bloody machinery":* Ibid., 146.
310 *"all peace provisions"* . . . *"by civilized nations":* Ibid., 91, 90.
310 *"all municipal institutions":* Ibid., 215.
310 *"all the powers incident"* . . . *"liberty, property, and life":* Ibid., 222.
310 *Observers of the case:* See, e.g., Professor Curtis A. Bradley's excellent "The Story of *Ex parte Milligan*: Military Trials, Enemy Combatants, and Congressional Authorization," in Christopher H. Schroeder & Curtis A. Bradley, eds., *Presidential Power Stories* (New York: Thomson Reuters / Foundation Press, 2009), 93, 120.
311 *a judge in Florida ruled: Ex parte Mudd,* 17 F. Cas. 954 (S. D. Fla. 1868).
311 *grandson's challenge to the accuracy: Mudd v. Caldera,* 134 F. Supp. 2d 138 (D.D.C. 2001).
312 *claimed (wrongly) that Lincoln never:* Willard L. King, *Lincoln's Manager: David Davis* (Cambridge, MA: Harvard University Press, 1960), 254. As president, Lincoln anticipated that commissions would try civilians in his September 1862 suspension of the writ of habeas corpus (Basler, 5: 436–37), and reaffirmed the practice just two weeks before he died (ibid., 8: 359–60). He defended the practice in a long letter on the *Vallandigham* case (ibid., 6: 303). And he routinely reviewed civilians' convictions by military commission without apparent objection to the practice (e.g., ibid., 8: 180, 198, 211, 224, 251, 270, 303, and 326). See Mark E. Neely, Jr., *The Fate of Liberty: Abraham Lincoln and Civil Liberties* (New York: Oxford University Press, 1991), 165–66.
312 *"equally in war and in peace": Ex parte Milligan,* 71 U.S. 2, 120 (1865).
312 *"If he cannot enjoy": Milligan,* 71 U.S. at 131.
313 *"the locality of actual war": Milligan,* 71 U.S. at 127.
313 *likened the ruling to the* Dred Scott *decision:* Charles Fairman, *History of the Supreme Court of the United States, Vol. 6: Reconstruction and Reunion, 1864–88* (New York: Macmillan, 1971), 1: 213–14, 232.
313 Milligan *was worse:* Hans L. Trefousse, *Thaddeus Stevens: Nineteenth-Century Egalitarian* (Chapel Hill: University of North Carolina Press, 1997), 205.
313 *"assailed the Union":* Bradley, "Story of *Ex parte Milligan*," 117.
313 *"the revolutionary proceedings":* Fairman, *Reconstruction and Reunion,* 1: 215.
313 *"scenes of bloodshed":* Benjamin R. Curtis, *Executive Power* (Boston: Little, Brown, 1862), 13.
313 *Now it was Curtis to whom:* Fairman, *Reconstruction and Reunion,* 235–36. An aging Curtis pleaded illness and overwork and declined to take up Davis's suggestion.
313 *the Joint Committee on Reconstruction:* Foner, *Reconstruction,* 253.
313 *the House and the Senate proposed:* Stat., 14: 358–59.
313–14 *all but one of the white southern:* Joseph B. James, *The Ratification of the Fourteenth Amendment* (Macon, GA: Mercer University Press, 1984), 19–24; David E. Kyvig, *Explicit & Authentic Acts: Amending the U.S. Constitution, 1776–1995* (Lawrence: University Press of Kansas, 1995), 170–71.
314 *Race riots:* Foner, *Reconstruction,* 261–63.
314 *Military Reconstruction Act:* Stat., 14: 428–29.
314 *his theory of the power of conquerors: Cong. Globe,* 39th Cong., 2nd sess., 1076.
314 *"unlimited power for the common defense":* Ibid., 1082.
314 *Zachariah Chandler:* Ibid., 1135.
314 *William D. Kelley:* Ibid., 1177.
314 *expressly authorized military commissions:* Stat., 14: 428, §3.
315 *In a blistering opinion: AG Opinions,* 12: 182, 198–200 (June 12, 1867).
315 *"only until the people": Cong. Globe,* 39th Cong., 2nd sess., 1212.
315 *Tenure of Office Act: Act Regulating the Tenure of Certain Civil Officers,* Stat., 14: 430–32.
315 *A rider to the annual appropriations act: An Act Making Appropriations for the Support of the Army,* Stat., 14: 485, 486–87 §2.
316 *More than 1,000 defendants:* Neely, *Fate of Liberty,* 176–77.
316 *under the shadow of Lambdin Milligan:* At least two lower federal courts discharged men convicted by military commissions—see Detlev Vagts, "Military Commissions: A Concise History," *American Journal of International Law* 101 (January 2007): 35, 40 n. 35.

316 *William McCardle:* Daniel Meltzer, "The Story of *Ex parte McCardle:* The Power of Congress to Limit the Supreme Court's Appellate Jurisdiction," in Vicki C. Jackson & Judith Resnik, eds., *Federal Court Stories* (New York: Foundation Press, 2010), 57–86.

316 *by repealing the statute: An Act to Amend an Act Entitled "An Act to Amend the Judiciary Act Passed the Twenty-Fourth of September, Seventeen Hundred and Eighty-Nine,"* Stat., 15: 44 (repealing Stat., 14: 385).

316 *The Court reluctantly upheld: Ex parte McCardle,* 74 U.S. 506, 514–15 (1868).

316 *Edward Yerger:* Fairman, *Reconstruction and Reunion,* 1: 558–91.

317 *"Induce . . . the President to return":* FL to Charles Sumner, April 4, 1865, box 45, FLP HL.

317 *"My God!":* FL to Henry Halleck, April 15, 1865, box 28, FLP HL.

317 *ought to be tried for treason:* FL to Charles Sumner, April 1, 1865, box 45, FLP HL.

317 *Lieber traveled to Washington:* Frank Freidel, *Francis Lieber: Nineteenth-Century Liberal* (Baton Rouge: Louisiana State University Press, 1947), 369–70.

318 *the leading statement of the law:* "The Status of Rebel Prisoners of War," in *The Miscellaneous Writings of Francis Lieber* (Philadelphia: J. B. Lippincott, 1881), 293–97; see also The Civil Status of Paroled Rebels After the Pacification of the Country, folder 30, box 2, FLP JHU.

318 *"committed crimes":* Lieber, "Status of Rebel Prisoners of War," 294.

318 *"look like positive distrust":* A Memorandum: Reasons Why Jefferson Davis Ought Not to Be Tried by Military Commission for Complicity in the Unlawful Raiding, Burning, Etc. (July 1865), folder 33, box 2, FLP JHU.

318 *"most calamitous": Diary of Gideon Welles,* 2: 337–40.

318 *a May 2 proclamation:* Richardson, 6: 307–08.

319 *to go into the Confederate archives: OR,* series 3, 5: 95.

319 *428 boxes, 69 barrels:* Dallas Irvine, "The Archive Office of the War Department: Repository of Captured Confederate Archives, 1865–1881," *Military Affairs* 10, no. 1 (Spring 1946): 93, 98.

319 *"plots of assassination":* Carl L. Lokke, "The Captured Confederate Records Under Francis Lieber," *American Archivist* 9, no. 4 (1946): 277, 279.

319 *"to allow no person":* Ibid., 292–93, 305.

319 *"emanated from or was countenanced by":* FL to Henry Halleck, April 26, 1865, box 28, FLP HL.

319 *for use in the trial of John Gee:* Lokke, "Captured Confederate Records," 305.

319 *between Davis and Confederate agents:* E.g., FL to Joseph Holt, September 15, 1865, JHP LC.

319 *proposing an assassination plot:* House Report No. 104, 39th Cong., 1st sess. (1866), pp. 24–25; Lokke, "Captured Confederate Records," 310.

320 *a January 1866 report to Stanton:* Lokke, "Captured Confederate Records," 302 n. 109.

320 *unable to identify anything:* Leonard, *Lincoln's Avengers,* 216; also Francis Lieber, Report of the Chief of the Archive Office, MSS 17,814, PEMS LC.

320 *Boutwell's report:* House Report No. 104, 39th Cong., 1st sess. (1866), p. 1.

320 *"The trial of Jeff. Davis":* FL to Henry Halleck, May 19, 1866, box 28, FLP HL.

320 *would have to take place in Virginia: AG Opinions,* 11: 411–13.

320 *refused to sit in the Circuit Court:* Roy Franklin Nichols, "United States vs. Jefferson Davis, 1865–1869," *American Historical Review* 31, no. 2 (January 1926), 266, 267–68.

321 *an abolitionist judge:* Nichols, "*United States vs. Jefferson Davis,*" 268 & 268 n. 7.

321 *had failed to assign justices:* Fairman, *Reconstruction and Reunion,* 1: 608.

321 *one last amnesty proclamation:* Richardson, 6: 708.

322 *"acceptance of the rules" . . . "legitimate conflict":* Bradley T. Johnson, ed., *Reports of Cases Decided by Chief Justice Chase in the Circuit Court of the United States for the Fourth Circuit During the Years 1865 to 1869* (New York: Diossy & Co., 1876), 13–14.

322 *"Our case is double": The Works of Charles Sumner* (Boston: Lee & Shepard, 1870–83), 7: 13.

323 *"no life was forfeited":* James G. Randall, *Constitutional Problems Under Lincoln* (New York: D. Appleton & Co., 1926), 91.

323 *a new species of offense:* Francis Lieber, Memorandum, folder 33, box 2, FLP JHU.

Part III The Howling Desert

325 *Epigraph:* John M. Schofield, "Notes on 'The Legitimate' in War," *Journal of the Military Service Institution of the United States* 2 (1881): 1, 3.

Chapter 11. Glenn's Brigade

327 *"No modern state":* Trials or Courts-Martial in the Philippine Islands in Consequence of Certain Instructions, Senate Doc. no. 213, 57th Cong., 2nd sess. (1903), 42.

327 *"Terrible!":* "Impending Changes in the Character of War," *Journal of the Military Service Institution of the United States* 19 (1896): 83, 88.

327 *died suddenly:* Thomas Sergeant Perry, *The Life and Letters of Francis Lieber* (Boston: James R. Osgood & Co., 1882), 430.

327 *launched General Orders No. 100:* E.g., FL to Henry Halleck, October 4, 1863, box 28, FLP HL.

327 *"Old Hundred":* E.g., FL to Henry Halleck, May 28, 1866, box 28, FLP HL

327 *Bluntschli . . . translated the code:* Dr. Bluntschli, *Das moderne Kriegsrecht der civilisirten Staten als Rechtsbuch dargestellt* (Nördligen: C. H. Beck'schen Buchhandlung, 1866).

328 *influential German code:* Betsy Baker Röben, *Johann Caspar Bluntschli, Francis Lieber und das moderne Völkerrecht 1861–1881* (Baden-Baden: NOMOS Verlagsgesellschaft, 2003); Theodor Meron, "Francis Lieber's Code and Principles of Humanity," *Columbia Journal of Transnational Law* 36 (1997): 269; Betsy Baker Roben, "The Method Behind Bluntschli's 'Modern' International Law," *Journal of the History of International Law* 4 (2002): 249–92.

328 *unfinished manuscript:* Untitled MS, box 3, Papers of Brig. General Norman Lieber, 1867–1898, Records of the Office of the Judge Advocate General, record group 153, NARA.

328 *stint in the Department of Dakota: Report of the Secretary of War,* House Exec. Doc. no. 1, 41st Cong., 2nd sess., part 2, vol. 1 (1870), p. 41.

328 *teaching the laws of war:* Robert Wolfe, "Francis Lieber's Role as Archivist of the Confederate Records," in Charles R. Mack & Henry H. Lesesne, eds., *Francis Lieber and the Culture of the Mind* (Columbia, SC: University of South Carolina Press, 2005), 42, 46.

328 *became acting judge advocate general: The Army Lawyer: A History of the Judge Advocate General's Corps, 1775–1975* (Washington, DC: U.S. Judge Advocate General's Department, 1975), 83–86; William Fratcher, "History of the Judge Advocate General's Corps, United States Army," *Military Law Review* 4 (1959): 88, 98–99.

328 *On April 11, 1873:* For my account of the Modoc episode, I have relied on Keith A. Murray, *The Modocs and Their War* (Norman, OK: University of Oklahoma Press, 1959); Robert M. Utley, *The Indian Frontier, 1846–1890* (Albuquerque: University of New Mexico Press, 2003); and the documents and scholarship cited below.

329 *600 soldiers under:* J. F. Santee, "Edward R. S. Canby, Modoc War, 1873," *Oregon Historical Quarterly* 33 (1932): 70, 74.

329 *"You are like an old squaw":* Francis S. Landrum, *Guardhouse, Gallows, and Graves: The Trial and Execution of Indian Prisoners of the Modoc Indian War by the U.S. Army, 1873* (Klamath Falls, OR: Klamath County Museum, 1998), 128.

329 *"utter extermination":* "The Modoc Massacre: Extermination of the Tribe Justified," *Philadelphia Inquirer*, April 15, 1873.

329 *ordered a pontoon bridge:* Joseph T. Glatthaar, *The March to the Sea and Beyond: Sherman's Troops in the Savannah and Carolina Campaigns* (New York: New York University Press, 1985), 64.

329 *"shoot the leaders":* Murray, *Modocs and Their War*, 276.

330 *"no desire to stay the hand":* "New York Press Comments on the Modoc Massacre," *Augusta Chronicle*, April 16, 1873.

330 *"be exterminated":* "New York Press Comments on the Modoc Massacre," *Augusta Chronicle,* April 16, 1873.

330 *But as Davis drew up:* Jefferson Davis to HQ, S.F.P. [San Francisco Presidio], June 5, 1873, vol. 3, #217, part 1, entry 706: Letters and Telegrams Sent, 1870–1902, Department of the Columbia, record group 393, NARA; Landrum, *Guardhouse, Gallows, and Graves,* 21–22.

330 *would no longer enter into treaties:* Nell Jessup Newton et al., *Cohen's Handbook of Federal Indian Law* (Newark, NJ: LexisNexis, 2005), §1.03, p. 75.

330 *in modern organized sovereign states: Instructions,* art. 20; see also art. 25, 29, and 30.

330 *the Dakota Indians in Minnesota:* My account of the Dakota Sioux episode of 1862 relies on Carol Chomsky, "The United States–Dakota War Trials: A Study in Military Injustice," *Stanford Law Review* 43, no. 1 (1990): 13–98; and Maeve Herbert, "Explaining the Sioux Military Commission of 1862," *Columbia Human Rights Law Review* 40 (2009): 743–98.

330 *"as maniacs or wild beasts":* Chomsky, "Dakota War Trials," 23.

330 *"Nits":* Herbert, "Sioux Military Commission," 767.

331 *"Daniel Boone":* Ibid., 791.

331 *On the first day . . . it sentenced to death:* Chomsky, "Dakota War Trials," 25–28.

332 *executed Indians with an ax:* See chapter 1.

332 *without even the pretense:* See chapter 3.

332 *"Kill the nits":* John W. Hall, *Uncommon Defense: Indian Allies in the Black Hawk War* (Cambridge, MA: Harvard University Press, 2009), 1.

332 *As recently as the 1850s:* Herbert, "Sioux Military Commission," 755–56.

332 *some commanders in Missouri:* Michael Fellman, *Inside War: The Guerrilla Conflict in Missouri During the American Civil War* (New York: Oxford University Press, 1989), 86–87; Daniel E. Sutherland, *A Savage Conflict: The Decisive Role of Guerrillas in the American Civil War* (Chapel Hill: University of North Carolina Press, 2009), 123.

332 *In the Oregon Territory:* Herbert, "Sioux Military Commission," 756–57.

333 *"their aiders and abettors":* Basler, 5: 436–37.

333 *even if Indians inflicted it:* FL to Henry Halleck, April 19, 1864, box 28, FLP HL; Law and Usages of War, No. IV, 17 December 1861 [Notebook No. 4], folder 16, box 2, FLP JHU.

333 *as much like "barbarians":* Herbert, "Sioux Military Commission," 778 n. 178.

333 *"who have laid down":* Ibid., 779–80 n. 180.

333 *by applying a principle drawn:* Basler, 5: 542–43; Chomsky, "Dakota War Trials," 32, 89.

333 *named Wowinape:* Chomsky, "Dakota War Trials," 41–43.

334 *"technical difficulty":* Ibid., 42.

334 *General John M. Schofield:* Murray, *Modocs and Their War,* 272–73.

334 *personalized copy of General Orders: OR,* series 1, 22 (part 2): 292.

334 *Attorney General George Henry Williams:* Leonard Schlup, "George Henry Williams," *American National Biography Online,* February 2000.

334 *established legal authority for military commissions: Modoc War: Message from the President of the United States, Transmitting Copies of the Correspondence and Papers Relative to the War with the Modoc Indians in Southern Oregon and Northern California, During the Years 1872 and 1873, February 10, 1874,* House Exec. Doc. no. 122, 43d Cong., 1st sess. (1874), pp. 88–90.

335 *"I thought to avoid":* Landrum, *Guardhouse, Gallows, and Graves,* 18.

335 *murder in violation . . . each of them to death: Modoc War,* House Exec. Doc. no. 122, pp. 133–35, 181–83.

335 *"Everything connected with the execution":* Ludlow, *Guardhouse, Gallows, and Graves,* 74–75.

335 *President Grover Cleveland expressed the hope: Letter from the Secretary of War, Transmitting, In response to Resolution of February 11, 1887, Correspondence with General Miles Relative to the Surrender of Geronimo,* Senate Exec. Doc. no. 117, 49th Cong., 2nd sess. (1887), p. 4.

335 *should be tried and punished:* Letter from the Secretary of War, Senate Exec. Doc. no. 117, p. 10.

335 *General O. O. Howard objected:* Ibid., p. 12.

335 *forced to ask Geronimo himself:* Ibid., pp. 21–22.

336 *a prisoner of war status like few others:* John Anthony Turcheneske, Jr., *The Chirica-hua Apache Prisoners of War: Fort Sill 1894–1914* (Niwot, CO.: University Press of Colorado, 1997); H. Henrietta Stockel, *Survival of the Spirit: Chiricahua Apaches in Captivity* (Reno: University of Nevada Press, 1993); Peter Aleshire, *The Fox and the Whirlwind: General George Crook and Geronimo* (New York: John Wiley & Sons, 2000); Odie B. Faulk, *The Geronimo Campaign* (New York: Oxford University Press, 1969), 210–12; Frederick Turner, ed., *Geronimo: His Own Story, as Told to S. M. Barrett* (New York: Meridian, 1970).

336 *The sixty-nine Dakota Sioux acquitted:* Chomsky, "Dakota War Trials," 28.

336 *establishment of a school in Carlisle:* Richard H. Pratt, "Violated Principles the Cause of Failure in Indian Civilization," *Journal of the Military Service Institution of the United States* 7 (1886): 46, 58–60.

336 *the indefinite detention:* G. Norman Lieber to Adjutant General, August 26, 1893, Letters Sent ("Record Books"), 1889–1895, Records of the Office of the Judge Advocate General (Army), 1792–2010, record group 153, NARA.

336 *"Kill and scalp all":* Katie Kane, "Nits Make Lice: Drogheda, Sand Creek, and the Poetics of Colonial Extermination," *Cultural Critique* 42 (1999): 81, 82–84; see also Stan Hoig, *The Sand Creek Massacre* (Norman, OK: Oklahoma University Press, 1961).

337 *the peculiarity of the legal status: AG Opinions,* 13: 470, 472.

337 *"the blessing of a knowledge":* "Laws of War in Ashantee," *New York Times,* April 20, 1884; see also *Sunday Oregonian* (Portland), July 6, 1884. On Howard, see Richard N. Ellis, "The Humanitarian Generals," *Western Historical Quarterly* 3, no. 2 (1972): 169, 169–72.

337 *Some historians have argued:* See Lance Janda, "Shutting the Gates of Mercy: The American Origins of Total War, 1860–1880," *Journal of Military History* 59, no. 1 (1995): 7–26; and Harry Stout, *Upon the Altar of the Nation: A Moral History of the Civil War* (New York: Penguin Books, 2007), 460.

337 *Others object:* Mark E. Neely, Jr., *The Civil War and the Limits of Destruction* (Cambridge, MA: Harvard University Press, 2007); Mark Grimsley, *The Hard Hand of War: Union Military Policy Toward Southern Civilians, 1861–1865* (New York: Cambridge University Press, 1995).

337 *"only good Indians":* Wolfgang Mieder, " 'The Only Good Indian Is a Dead Indian': History and Meaning of a Proverbial Stereotype," *Journal of American Folklore* 106, no. 419 (Winter 1993): 38, 45–46.

337 *"During the war":* Letter from the Secretary of War in Answer to a Resolution of the House, of March 3, 1870, in Relation to the Late Expedition Against the Piegan Indians, in the Territory of Montana, House Ex. Doc. no. 269, 41st Cong., 2nd sess., p. 70.

338 *Robert K. Evans . . . stern vision of the 1863 code:* Robert K. Evans, "The Indian Question in Arizona," *Atlantic Monthly* (August 1886): 171–73.

338 *banker named Henri Dunant:* Caroline Moorehead, *Dunant's Dream: War, Switzerland, and the History of the Red Cross* (London: HarperCollins, 1998), 2–7.

339 *In Great Britain:* Mark Bostridge, *Florence Nightingale: The Making of an Icon* (New York: Farrar, Straus & Giroux, 2008).

339 *Ferdinando Palasciano:* Moorehead, *Dunant's Dream,* 27.

339 *Henri Arrault:* Ibid., 26.

339 *founded a Sanitary Commission:* Charles J. Stillé, *History of the United States Sanitary Commission: Being the General Report of Its Work During the War of the Rebellion* (Philadelphia: J. B. Lippincott, 1866).

339 *a stunning exposé:* J. Henry Dunant, *A Memory of Solferino* (Washington, DC: American Red Cross, 1939), (trans. of the 1862 French original).

340 *The first Geneva Convention:* Bevans, 1: 7–11; see Martha Finnemore, *National Interests in International Society* (Ithaca, NY: Cornell University Press, 1996), 69–88.

340 *"Am I not the man":* FL to Charles Sumner, June 20 & 21, 1864, box 44, FLP HL; see also FL to Charles Sumner, June 24, 1864, box 44, FLP HL; FL to Henry Halleck, June 18, 1864, and June 25, 1864, box 28, FLP HL.

340 *A skeletal delegation: Report of Charles S. P. Bowles, Foreign Agent of the United States Sanitary Commission Upon the International Congress of Geneva* (London: R. Clay, Son, & Taylor, 1864).

340 *"Our No. 100":* FL to Henry Halleck, June 18, 1864, box 28, FLP HL.

340 *Henry Raymond:* Francis Brown, *Raymond of the Times* (New York: W. W. Norton & Co., 1951), 167–79. On the press and humanitarianism, see Gary J. Bass, *Freedom's Battle: The Origins of Humanitarian Intervention* (New York: Alfred A. Knopf, 2008), 35–37.

340 *War photographers:* Susan Sontag, *Regarding the Pain of Others* (New York: Farrar, Straus & Giroux, 2003), 48–58.

340 *given way to vast mobilizations:* David A. Bell, *The First Total War: Napoleon's Europe and the Birth of Warfare as We Know It* (Boston: Houghton Mifflin, 2007).

341 *Improved rifling technology:* Compare John Keegan, *A History of Warfare* (New York: Alfred A. Knopf, 1993), 342–43, describing the tight formations of eighteenth-century musket tactics, with Max Boot, *War Made New: Weapons, Warriors, and the Making of the Modern World* (New York: Gotham Books, 2007), 127–28, describing the rise of rifled barrels and the dispersion of troops that followed, though only after terrible lessons were inflicted on hundreds of thousands of soldiers.

341 *as evidence of just such moral progress:* Charles Loring Brace, *Gesta Christi: or, A History of Humane Progress Under Christianity* (New York: A. C. Armstrong & Son, 1883), 335; Richard S. Storrs, *The Divine Origin of Christianity, Indicated by Its Historical Effects* (New York: Anson D. F. Randolph & Co., 1884), 204, 521.

341 *"the very moral sentiment":* Sheldon Amos, *Political and Legal Remedies for War* (London: Cassell, Petter, Galpin & Co., 1880), 336.

341 *turned men into murderers:* Dunant, *Memory of Solferino*, 28.

341 *"La civilisation de la guerre":* Geoffrey Best, *Humanity in Warfare* (New York: Columbia University Press, 1980), 10.

341 *The militarists of Prussia:* Geoffrey Wawro, *War and Society in Europe, 1792–1914* (London: Routledge, 2000), 77.

342 *120 different networks:* Moorehead, *Dunant's Dream*, 53.

342 *James "Jingo Jim" Blaine:* Clara Barton, *The Red Cross: A History of This Remarkable International Movement in the Interest of Humanity* (Washington, DC: American National Red Cross, 1898), 36–45.

342 *"perpetual peace" . . . "speedy conclusion":* Count von Moltke to Johan Caspar Bluntschli, December 11, 1880, reprinted in Thomas Erskine Holland, ed., *Letters to The Times Upon War and Neutrality, 1881–1909* (New York: Longmans Green, 2nd ed., 1914), 25–26.

342 *"it was impossible both":* Peter Holquist, *The Russian Empire as a "Civilized State": International Law as Principle and Practice in Imperial Russia, 1874–1878.* National Council for Eurasian and East European Research Working Paper, July 14, 2006, pp. 13–14 (available at http://www.nceer.org/papers).

342 *the dense thicket of European rivalries:* Papers Relating to the Foreign Relations of the United States, Transmitted to Congress with the Annual Message of the President, December 6, 1875, House Exec. Doc. no. 1, part 1, vol. 2, 44th Cong., 1st sess., pp. 1014–46; [Brussels Conference], *New York Herald*, July 28, 1874; Martin Aust, "Western European and German Perceptions of Fedor Martens and Russian Developments in the Field of International Law (1870s to 1900s)." Paper presented to the American Historical Association Conference, New York, New York, January 2009; Geoffrey Best, "Restraints on War by Land Before 1945," in Michael Howard, ed., *Restraints on War* (New York: Oxford University Press, 1977), 33–34; Calvin deArmond Davis, *The United States and the First Hague Peace Conference* (Ithaca, NY: Cornell University, 1962), 38–44.

343 *Berlin:* FL to Henry Halleck, October 4, 1863, box 28, FLP HL (Heffter); Frank Freidel, *Francis Lieber: Nineteenth-Century Liberal* (Baton Rouge: Louisiana State University Press, 1947), 402.

343 *"Professor Dr. Franz Lieber in New-York":* Dr. J. C. Bluntschli, *Das moderne Völkerrecht der civilisirten Staaten als Rechtsbuch dargestellt* (Nördlingen: C. H. Beck'schen Buch-

handlung, 1878), iii–iv; see also Bluntschli, *Moderne Kriegsrecht*, iii ("Professor Lieber in New-York ... und ... Präsident Lincoln).

343 *He cited Lieber as inspiring:* Martti Koskenniemi, *The Gentle Civilizer of Nations: The Rise and Fall of International Law, 1870–1960* (New York: Cambridge University Press, 2001), 42.

343 *"war crime," or* Kriegsverbrechen: Bluntschli, *Moderne Völkerrecht*, §643a, p. 360.

343 *Netherlands (1871) ... Italy (1896):* G. I. A. D. Draper, "Implementation of International Law in Armed Conflicts," *International Affairs* 48 (1972): 46, 55; War Office, *Manual of Military Law* (London: Her Majesty's Stationery Office, 1894), 303–20; see also Thomas Erskine Holland, *Studies in International Law* (Oxford: Clarendon Press, 1989), 87 n. 1.

343 *by the time of the Russo-Turkish War:* Holquist, *Russian Empire as a "Civilized State,"* 14.

343 *"the formation of a practical Manual":* Henry Sumner Maine, *International Law: A Series of Lectures Delivered Before the University of Cambridge, 1887* (London: John Murray, 1888), 129.

344 *prepared a private draft:* V. V. Pustogarov, *Our Martens: F. F. Martens International Lawyer and Architect of Peace*, ed. & trans W. E. Butler (London: Simmonds & Hill, 2000), 108–09; Holquist, *Russian Empire as a "Civilized State,"* 12–13 n. 37.

344 *as an amended version of Lieber's work:* Holquist, *Russian Empire as a "Civilized State,"* 12–13.

344 *Martens described the parole: Project for an International Convention on the Laws and Customs of War Presented by the Russian Government, in Documents Relating to the Program of the First Hague Peace Conference* (Oxford: Clarendon Press, 1921), §35–36, p. 44.

344 *noncombatants who rose up in a territory:* Ibid., §45, p. 45.

344 *even the execution of prisoners:* Ibid., §12 (c), p. 45.

344 *"seizure and destruction":* Ibid., §13(b) & (c), p. 45.

344 *As humanitarian critics noted:* Foreign Relations of the United States, House Exec. Doc. no. 1, part 1, vol. 2, 44th Cong., 1st sess., pp. 1027–29.

344 *"to whom does the right":* Holquist, *Russian Empire as a "Civilized State,"* 13.

345 *"in direct subordination":* Ibid., 14–15.

345 *Martens adopted Lieber's functional: Project of an International Declaration Concerning the Laws and Customs of War*, Brussels, 27 August 1874, art. 9, available at http://www.icrc.org/ihl.nsf/FULL/135?OpenDocument.

345 *it has lasted as such:* Convention (III) Relative to the Treatment of Prisoners of War, Geneva, 12 August 1949, art. 4(A)(2), available at http://www.icrc.org/ihl.nsf/FULL/375.

345 *"fully aware that":* Meron, "Francis Lieber's Code," 271.

346 *"strict military obedience":* Robert Seager II, "Alfred Thayer Mahan," *American National Biography Online*, http://www.anb.org/articles/05/05-00466.html; Robert Seager II, "Alfred Thayer Mahan: Christian Expansionist, Navalist, and Historian," in James C. Bradford, ed., *Admirals of the New Steel Navy: Makers of the American Naval Tradition, 1880–1930* (Annapolis, MD: Naval Institute Press, 1990), 24–72.

347 *"a dim religious world":* Philip A. Crowl, "Alfred Thayer Mahan: The Naval Historian," in Peter Parat, ed., *The Makers of Modern Strategy: From Machiavelli to the Nuclear Age* (Princeton, NJ: Princeton University Press, 1986), 444.

347 *"Step by step":* Alfred Thayer Mahan, *Some Neglected Aspects of War* (London: Sampson Low, Marston, & Co., 1899), 45.

347 *"Power":* Mahan, *Some Neglected Aspects*, 46; see also p. 107.

347 *without undue deference:* Ibid., 37–42.

348 *Ethan Allen Hitchcock ... accepted the message:* Davis, *First Hague Peace Conference*, 37–38.

348 *electrified peace movements:* Ibid., 61; James J. Sheehan, *Where Have All the Soldiers Gone? The Transformation of Modern Europe* (Boston: Houghton Mifflin, 2008), 22–34.

348 *Mahan saw the czar's call:* Davis, *First Hague Peace Conference*, 38.

348 *"the humanitarian":* Ibid., 42.

348 *to slow a European arms race:* Ibid., 43–44.

348 *"hopeless skepticism":* Andrew D. White, *The First Hague Conference* (Boston: World Peace Foundation, 1912), 8.

348 *seventeenth-century summer palace:* Barbara W. Tuchman, *The Proud Tower: A Portrait of the World Before the War, 1890–1914* (New York: Macmillan, 1966), 257; Davis, *First Hague Peace Conference,* 92; Stephen Barcroft, "The Hague Peace Conference of 1899," *Irish Studies in International Affairs* 3, no. 1 (1989): 55, 62.

349 *they were not to enter into any:* James Brown Scott, ed., *The Hague Peace Conferences of 1899 and 1907: A Series of Lectures Delivered Before the Johns Hopkins University in the Year 1908* (Baltimore: Johns Hopkins University Press, 1909), 2: 7.

349 *Mahan did too:* Davis, *First Hague Peace Conference,* 187; Mahan, *Some Neglected Aspects,* 25.

349 *"to really nothing":* Davis, *First Hague Peace Conference,* 188.

349 *generously credited Lincoln:* William I. Hull, *The Two Hague Conferences and Their Contributions to International Law* (Boston: International School of Peace, 1908), 214–15.

349 *distinct advance on the Civil War code:* James Brown Scott, ed., *Instructions to the American Delegates to the Hague Peace Conferences and Their Official Reports* (New York: Oxford University Press, 1916), 46.

350 *prohibited prisoner execution: Regulations Concerning the Laws and Customs of War on Land.* The Hague, 29 July 1899, art. 4 & 23(c), available at http://www.icrc.org/ihl.nsf/FULL/150?.

350 *"populations and belligerents":* Convention (II) with Respect to the Laws and Customs of War on Land, [preamble], available at http://www.icrc.org/ihl.nsf/FULL/150.

350 *"heard the opinion expressed":* "Session Is Brief," *Dallas Morning News,* June 16, 1907.

350 *"when he speaks":* Tuchman, *Proud Tower,* 267.

350 *"doubtful if wars" . . . "inventive genius":* Scott, ed., *Instructions to the American Delegates,* 7.

351 *White was no lightweight:* See Andrew D. White, *The Autobiography of Andrew Dickson White* (New York: Century, 1905).

351 *an inventor of artillery devices:* Davis, *First Hague Peace Conference,* 75.

351 *he had to order copies:* Ibid., 132.

351 *New technologies:* Tuchman, *Proud Tower,* 262.

351 *dumdum bullets could stop:* Davis, *First Hague Peace Conference,* 121.

351 *"wounds of useless cruelty":* Scott, ed., *Hague Peace Conferences,* 2: 33–35; Scott, ed., *Instructions to the American Delegates,* 29.

352 *"would prove to be rather harmful":* White, *First Hague Conference,* 40.

352 *"tender about asphyxiating":* Scott, ed., *Hague Peace Conferences,* 2: 37; see also Robert Seager II & Doris D. Maguire, eds., *Letters and Papers of Alfred Thayer Mahan* (Annapolis, MD: Naval Institute Press, 1975), 2: 642, 650–51.

352 *Though White initially opposed:* Davis, *First Hague Peace Conference,* 119.

352 *to push for the immunity of private property at sea:* Scott, ed., *Instructions to the American Delegates,* 9.

352 *Mahan was violently opposed:* Alfred T. Mahan, *The Influence of Sea Power Upon History, 1660–1783* (Boston: Little, Brown, 1890), 539–40; Seager & Maguire, eds., *Letters and Papers of Alfred Thayer Mahan,* 3: 112–13, 157, and also 2: 638.

352 *even resisted the old American position:* Seager, *Alfred Thayer Mahan,* 28.

352 *persuaded President Theodore Roosevelt:* Richard W. Turk, *The Ambiguous Relationship: Theodore Roosevelt and Alfred Thayer Mahan* (New York: Greenwood Press, 1987), 135–36.

353 *"limited liability":* Calvin DeArmond Davis, *The United States and the Second Hague Peace Conference: American Diplomacy and International Organization, 1899–1914* (Durham, NC: Duke University Press, 1975), 140, 171.

353 *it required its signatory states:* Convention (II) with Respect to the Laws and Customs of War on Land, art. 1.

353 *as ratification of the kinds of global power:* Stuart Creighton Miller, *"Benevolent Assimilation": The American Conquest of the Philippines, 1899–1903* (New Haven, CT: Yale University Press, 1982), 7; also Gail Bederman, *Manliness and Civilization: A Cultural*

History of Gender and Race in the United States, 1880–1917 (Chicago: University of Chicago Press, 1995), 170–216.

353   *"divinely commissioned":* Stanley Karnow, *In Our Image: America's Empire in the Philippines* (New York: Random House, 1989), 81.

354   *"a war for liberty":* Miller, *"Benevolent Assimilation,"* 102.

354   *millions of nonwhite people:* Christina Burnett & Burke Marshall, eds., *Foreign in a Domestic Sense: Puerto Rico, American Expansion, and the Constitution* (Durham, NC: Duke University Press, 2001).

354   *longed for a coaling station:* Turk, *Ambiguous Relationship*, 36.

354   *irredeemable savages:* Miller, *"Benevolent Assimilation,"* 124–28.

354   *"a civilized":* Paul A. Kramer, "Race-Making and Colonial Violence in the U.S. Empire: The Philippine-American War as Race War," *Diplomatic History* 30, no. 2 (April 2006): 169, 181.

354   *the United States' intent to cooperate:* Paul A. Kramer, *The Blood of Government: Race, Empire, the United States, & the Philippines* (Chapel Hill: University of North Carolina Press, 2006), 94–96.

354   *a combination of untruths:* Ibid., 94–111.

354   *who admired the combat tactics:* Ibid., 76.

354   *resistance to Spain and the Boer War against the British:* Ibid., 131.

354   *often horrific:* E.g., Karnow, *In Our Own Image*, 190–91.

355   *used poison and killed:* Trials or Courts-Martial in the Philippine Islands in Consequence of Certain Instructions, Senate Doc. no. 213, 57th Cong., 2nd sess. (1903), 9.

355   *filling reports with hundreds:* Charges of cruelty, etc., to the natives of the Philippines. Letter from the Secretary of War relative to the reports and charges in the public press of cruelty and oppression exercised by our soldiers toward natives of the Philippines. February 19, 1902, Senate Doc. no. 205, 57th Cong., 1st sess.

355   *"the brains of the revolution":* Karnow, *In Our Own Image*, 116.

355   *"when it comes to defending":* Kramer, "Race-Making and Colonial Violence," 199; see also Kramer, *The Blood of Government*, 134–36.

355   *began to trickle back:* Miller, *"Benevolent Assimilation,"* 88.

355   *between 1,500 and 2,000 Filipinos:* Ibid., 154.

355   *epidemics struck:* Kramer, *Blood of Government*, 157.

355   *disguised in the uniforms:* Miller, *"Benevolent Assimilation,"* 167–70.

356   *"to kill and burn":* Kramer, *Blood of Government*, 145.

356   *"must be made":* Trials or Courts-Martial in the Philippine Islands, Doc. no. 213, 57th Cong., 2nd sess., pp. 6–7.

356   *hanged Filipino prisoners by the neck:* Affairs in the Philippine Islands. Hearings Before the Committee on the Philippines of the United States Senate. Senate Doc. no. 331, 57th Cong., 1st sess., part 2 (Washington, DC: Government Printing Office, 1902), 901–02.

356   *known as the water cure:* See Paul A. Kramer's brilliant article, "The Water Cure," *The New Yorker*, January 25, 2008.

356   *While three or four soldiers:* Richard E. Welch, Jr., "American Atrocities in the Philippines: The Indictment and the Response," *Pacific Historical Review* 43, no. 2 (1974): 233, 235.

356   *salt water . . . or a syringe:* Miller, *"Benevolent Assimilation,"* 251; Kramer, *The Blood of Government*, 201.

356   *resulted in the death of the victim:* Judge Advocate General George B. Davis to Secretary of War Elihu Root, Nov. 17, 1902, file 12291, box 63, Office of the Judge Advocate General Document File, 1894–1912, record group 153, NARA.

356   *fourteen instances:* Welch, "American Atrocities in the Philippines," 234.

356   *administered the water cure:* Affairs in the Philippine Islands. Hearings Before the Committee on the Philippines of the United States Senate. Senate Doc. no. 331, 57th Cong., 1st sess., part 2 (Washington, DC: Government Printing Office, 1902), 951.

356   *Nelson A. Miles . . . heard complaints:* Welch, "American Atrocities in the Philippines," 236–37.

356 *seen the water cure administered:* E.g., Trials or Courts-Martial in the Philippine Islands, Senate Doc. no. 213, 57th Cong., 1st sess., 114, 119.

356 *"Get the good old syringe":* Kramer, *The Blood of Government,* 141.

357 *"so called water cure":* Miller, *"Benevolent Assimilation,"* 213.

357 *Norman Lieber had arranged: Instructions for the Government of Armies of the United States in the Field* (Washington, DC: Government Printing Office, 1898), in box 2, Papers of Brig. General Norman Lieber, 1867–1898, Records of the Office of the Judge Advocate General, record group 153, NARA.

357 *presided over a new series:* See A Complete List of Prisoners Under the Control of the Civil Government of the Philippine Islands, Who were tried and sentenced by General Courts-Martial, Provost Courts and by Military Commissions and Who were in Confinement in Bilibid Prison on the 1st Day of January, 1904, file no. 17546, box 90, Office of the Judge Advocate General Document File, 1894–1912, record group 153, NARA.

357 *unlawfully furnishing supplies . . . and murder:* Memorandum in regard to Trials of Filipinos by Military Commissions for cruelty against soldiers, January 1, 1900 to December 31, 1901, file 12291, box 63, Office of the Judge Advocate General Document File, 1894–1912, record group 153, NARA.

357 *more than 300 enlisted men:* Memorandum in regard to trials by courts-martial and military commissions of persons in or connected with the Army in the Philippine Islands for offenses against natives, file 12291, box 63, Office of the Judge Advocate General Document File, 1894–1912, record group 153, NARA.

357 *Arthur MacArthur:* Annual Report of Maj. Gen. Arthur MacArthur . . . Military Governor in the Philippine Islands, in *Annual Reports of the War Department for the Fiscal Year Ended June 30, 1901, Report of the Lieutenant-General Commanding the Army,* House Doc. no. 2, 57th Cong., 1st sess., part 2 (Washington, DC: Government Printing Office, 1901), 91–92.

357 *conformed to the terms of Old Hundred:* Orders and Instructions Issued to Military Officers in the Philippines, House Doc. no. 596, 57th Cong., 1st sess. (1902), 1.

357 *"form part of the 'Instructions'":* William E. Birkhimer, *Military Government and Martial Law* (Kansas City: Franklin Hudson Publishing Co., 1914), 614.

357 *Schofield argued openly:* John M. Schofield, "Notes on 'The Legitimate' in War," *Journal of the Military Service Institution of the United States* 2 (1881): 1, 1.

357 *"squeamish humanity":* "What War Means," *Journal of the Military Service Institution of the United States* 20 (1897); 34, 36.

357 *international law's formal moral symmetry:* Schofield, "Notes on 'The Legitimate,'" 5–6.

358 *"no objective point" . . . "too many men":* "Impending Changes in the Character of War," *Journal of the Military Service Institution of the United States* 19 (1896): 83, 88.

358 *no claims on the laws of war:* Kramer, *The Blood of Government,* 146–47.

358 *even tougher than Lincoln's:* Annual Report of Maj. Gen. Arthur MacArthur, 91–92; Kramer, *The Blood of Government,* 136.

358 *"A short and severe war":* Kramer, *The Blood of Government,* 154.

358 *"wage war in the sharpest":* Annual Reports of the War Department for the Fiscal Year Ended June 30, 1902 (Washington, DC: Government Printing Office, 1902), 9: 208–09.

359 *giving no quarter to prisoners:* Trials or Courts-Martial in the Philippine Islands in Consequence of Certain Instructions, Senate Doc. no. 213, 57th Cong., 2nd sess. (1903), p. 11.

359 *"study with advantage":* "General Orders No. 100," *Duluth News-Tribune,* April 29, 1902.

359 *prepared a private defense:* Memorandum for the Judge Advocate General, July 8, 1904, file no. 4275, box 23, Office of the Judge Advocate General Document File, 1894–1912, record group 153, NARA.

359 *immediately ordered courts-martial:* Philip C. Jessup, *Elihu Root* (New York: Dodd, Mead, 1938), 1: 342.

359 *Glenn was a member:* "Maj. Gen. E. F. Glenn Will Retire Dec. 31," *New York Times,* December 21, 1919.

359 *even published a book:* Captain Edwin F. Glenn, *Hand-Book of International Law* (St. Paul, MN: West Publishing Co., 1895).

359 *expedition to southeastern Alaska:* Gregg Jones, *Honor in the Dust: Theodore Roosevelt, War in the Philippines, and the Rise and Fall of America's Imperial Dream* (New York: New American Library, 2012), 210; *Guide to the Edwin F. Glenn Papers*, Collection no. HMC-0116, University of Alaska.

359 *judge advocate for the island of Panay:* Moorfield Storey & Julian Codman, *Marked Severities in Philippine Warfare: Secretary Root's Record—An Analysis of the Law and Facts Bearing on the Action and Utterances of President Roosevelt and Secretary Root* (Boston: Geo. H. Ellis Co., 1902), 62.

359 *a mobile team of crack:* Andrew J. Birtle, *U.S. Army Counterinsurgency and Contingency Operations Doctrine, 1860–1941* (Washington, DC: Center of Military History, 1998), 118; Brian McAllister Linn, *The Philippine War, 1899–1902* (Lawrence, KA: University Press of Kansas, 2000), 253, 315, 319; Kramer, "Water Cure."

360 *"for the purposes of extorting":* Welch, "American Atrocities in the Philippines," 237.

360 *"I am convinced":* "Defended the Water Cure," *New York Times,* July 25, 1902.

360 *justified by military necessity:* Trials or Courts-Martial in the Philippine Islands in Consequence of Certain Instructions, Senate Doc. no. 213, 57th Cong., 2nd sess. (1903), p. 26.

360 *"Without firing a shot":* Ibid., p. 85.

361 *"No modern state":* Ibid., pp. 27, 42, 70.

361 *"so instant and important":* Ibid., pp. 26–27.

361 *Roosevelt commuted the sentence:* Miller, "Benevolent Assimilation," 218.

361 *Ealdama:* Trials or Courts-Martial in the Philippine Islands in Consequence of Certain Instructions, Senate Doc. no. 213, 57th Cong., 2nd sess. (1903), p. 25.

362 *"We have been brought":* Congressional Record 35: 5795 (May 22, 1902).

362 *Sherman had praised:* William Tecumseh Sherman, "Military Law," *Journal of the Military Service Institution of the United States* 1 (1880): 385, 437.

362 *Elihu Root celebrated:* Elihu Root, "Francis Lieber," *American Journal of International Law* 7, no. 3 (1913): 453–69. Root's address was delivered by James Brown Scott after Root had to rush home because of the death of a grandchild. See "Plea for Equality of Tolls Is Made," *Oregonian* (Portland), April 25, 1913.

362 *"almost sacred":* Lt. Col. [Kerr?], General Staff, Acting Chief, First Division, July 8, 1904, file no. 4275, box 23, Office of the Judge Advocate General Document File, 1894–1912, record group 153, NARA.

362 *Privately published compilations:* Birkhimer, *Military Government,* 584–614.

362 *literally constructed with scissors and glue:* Memorandum for the Judge Advocate General, July 8, 1904, file no. 4275, box 23, Office of the Judge Advocate General Document File, 1894–1912, record group 153, NARA.

363 *"comparable in all particulars":* Theodore S. Woolsey, "The Naval War Code," *Columbia Law Review* 1 (1901): 298.

363 *had to be revoked:* U.S. Naval War College, *International Law Discussions, 1903: The United States Naval War Code of 1900* (Washington, DC: Government Printing Office, 1904).

363 *The man the Army chose:* Donald A. Wells, *The Laws of Land Warfare: A Guide to the U.S. Army Manuals* (Westport, CT: Greenwood Press, 1992), 4; Geo. B. Davis, [untitled], *American Journal of International Law* 8, no. 4 (1914): 950–51. As far as I can tell, the only other person to make the connection between the Glenn of the water cure and the Glenn of the 1914 field manual is Dr. Andrew J. Birtle in his *U.S. Army Counterinsurgency and Contingency Operations Doctrine,* at p. 179. I am grateful to Dr Birtle for helping me confirm that the two references to Edwin F. Glenn were to one and the same man.

363 *exiled for years to a series:* I have used Glenn's manuscript service records available in the research library edition of www.ancestry.com.

363 64 *cited and argued about at length by prosecutors and defense lawyers alike:* Trials of War Criminals Before the Nuernberg Military Tribunals Under Control Council Law No. 10, Nuernberg, October 1946–April 1949, 15 vols. (Washington, DC: Government Printing Office, 1949–53).

364 *"done his work exceedingly well"* . . . *"continental Europe":* Davis, [untitled], 951.
364 *poisons . . . contamination of water supplies: Rules of Land Warfare* (1917), §176–85, at pp. 56–58.
364 *"the greatest kindness of war":* Ibid., §10, at p. 14.
364 *"laws of humanity":* Ibid., §4, at pp. 12–13.
364 *"war crimes":* Ibid., §366, at p. 129.
364 *"Military necessity":* Ibid., §13, at p. 14; see also §57, at p. 27.

Epilogue

368 *willingly cause 750,000 deaths:* For the new, higher death toll from the Civil War, see J. David Hacker, "A Census-Based Count of the Civil War Dead," *Civil War History* 57, no. 4 (2011): 307, which raises the figure from older estimates of 620,000 deaths.
369 *the life of the laws of war:* Paraphrasing Oliver Wendell Holmes, Jr., *The Common Law* (Boston: Little, Brown, 1881), 1.
370 *"a disheartening business":* James G. Randall, *Constitutional Problems Under Lincoln,* rev. ed. (Urbana: University of Illinois Press, 1951), p. xxx.

Illustration Credits

Illustrations from the text

262 Alfred R. Waud, *Returned prisoners of war exchanging their rags for new clothing on board Flag of Truce boat New York,* 1864. Library of Congress Prints and Photographs Division.

297 *[Photo of Champ Ferguson, rebel guerrilla, during his trial, with a guard of the 9th Michigan Infantry],* 1865. Louis E. Springsteen Photograph Collection, Bentley Historical Library, University of Michigan.

321 Alfred R. Waud, *The casemate, Fortress Monroe, Jeff Davis in prison,* 1865. Library of Congress Prints and Photographs Division.

331 Adrian J. Ebell, *Indian jail for Sioux uprising captives,* 1862. Minnesota Historical Society.

360 *The Water Cure,* from *Life Magazine,* May 22, 1902. Courtesy of the Sterling Memorial Library, Yale University.

374 *General Orders No. 100,* 1863. Courtesy of the Rare Book & Manuscript Library, Columbia University.

Illustrations from the insert

Number

1. John Trumbull, *General George Washington at Trenton,* 1792. Yale University Art Gallery, Gift of the Society of the Cincinnati of Connecticut.

2. George Munger, *[U.S. Capitol after burning by the British],* c. 1814. Library of Congress, Prints & Photographs Division.

3. C. W. Peale, *John Quincy Adams,* 1819. Courtesy of the Philadelphia History Museum at the Atwater Kent, the Historical Society of Pennsylvania Collection.

4. Albert Sands Southworth and Josiah Johnson Hawes, *John Quincy Adams,* c. 1850. Image copyright © The Metropolitan Museum of Art. Image source: Art Resource, NY.

5. George Cruikshank, *American Justice!! Or the Ferocious Yankee Genl. Jack's Reward for Butchering Two British Subjects!!,* 1819. Courtesy of the Tennessee State Museum.

6. *Hon. Charles Sumner of Mass.,* c. 1855–1865. Brady-Handy Photograph Collection, Library of Congress Prints and Photographs Division.

7. Mathew Brady, *[Abraham Lincoln, seated next to small table, in a reflective pose, May 16, 1861],* 1861. Library of Congress Prints and Photographs Division.

8. William J. Baker, *[The Secretary of State and the diplomatic corps at Trenton Falls, New York],* 1863. Library of Congress Prints and Photographs Division.

9. Alfred R. Waud, *[Incident in the blockade],* c. 1860–1865. Library of Congress Prints and Photographs Division.

10. *"Policeman Wilkes,"* from *Harper's Weekly,* November 30, 1861. Library of Congress Prints and Photographs Division.

11. Francis Lieber, c. 1859. Courtesy of the University Archives, Columbia University in the City of New York.

12. John A. Scholten, *[Portrait of Maj. Gen. Henry W. Halleck, officer of the Federal Army],* c. 1860–1865. Library of Congress Prints and Photographs Division.

13. David B. Woodbury, *A Negro family coming into the Union Lines,* 1863. Library of Congress Prints and Photographs Division.

14. *Revenge taken by the Black Army*, 1805. Library of Congress Prints and Photographs Division.

15. Alexander Gardner, *[Abraham Lincoln on battlefield at Antietam, Maryland]*, 1862. Library of Congress Prints and Photographs Division.

16. Adalbert John Volck, *Worship of the North*, c. 1861–1863. Photograph © Museum of Fine Arts, Boston, Gift of Maxim Karolik for the M. and M. Karolik Collection of American Watercolors and Drawings, 1800–1875.

17. Henry Louis Stephens, *The Lash*, c. 1863. Library of Congress Prints and Photographs Division.

18. Henry Louis Stephens, *Blow for Blow*, c. 1863. Library of Congress Prints and Photographs Division.

19. Francis Lieber, *Class of 1862 class photograph*, 1862. Courtesy of the University Archives, Columbia University in the City of New York.

20. Samuel A. Cooley, *[Beaufort, South Carolina. 29th Regiment from Connecticut]*, 1864. Library of Congress Prints and Photographs Division.

21. Henry Louis Stephens, *Make Way for Liberty!*, c. 1863. Library of Congress Prints and Photographs Division.

22. Alfred R. Waud, *[Black Soldier]*, c. 1862–1865. Library of Congress Prints and Photographs Division.

23. George N. Barnard, *[Atlanta, Ga. Gen. William T. Sherman on horseback at Federal Fort No. 7]*, 1864. Selected Civil War photographs, 1861–1865, Library of Congress.

24. George N. Barnard, *[Atlanta, Ga. The shell-damaged Ponder House]*, 1864. Selected Civil War photographs, 1861–1865, Library of Congress.

25. Mathew B. Brady, *[Ethan Allen Hitchcock, head-and-shoulders portrait, facing front]*, c. 1853–1859. Library of Congress Prints and Photographs Division.

26. *[A Federal prisoner, returned from prison, full-length, seated, nude, facing front]*, c. 1861–1865. Library of Congress Prints and Photographs Division.

27. *Confederate prisoners at Belle Plain Landing, Va., captured with Johnson's Division, May 12, 1864.* Library of Congress Prints and Photographs Division.

28. Alexander Gardner, *[Abraham Lincoln, full-length portrait, seated, facing slightly right]*, 1863. Library of Congress Prints and Photographs Division.

29. *[General Nathan B. Forrest]*, c. 1861–1865. Brady-Handy Photograph Collection, Library of Congress.

30. Alexander Gardner, *[Washington, D.C. Hanging hooded bodies of the four conspirators; crowd departing]*, 1865. Selected Civil War photographs, 1861–1865, Library of Congress.

31. *Drawing rations; view from main gate. Andersonville Prison, Georgia, August 17, 1864.* National Archives and Records Administration, Record Group 162, 165-A-445.

32. Alexander Gardner, *[Washington, D.C. Reading the death warrant to Wirz on the scaffold]*, 1865. Library of Congress Prints and Photographs Division.

33. Thomas Nast, *Union soldiers in Andersonville prison / The rebel leader, Jeff Davis, at Fortress Monroe*, 1865. Library of Congress Prints and Photographs Division.

34. Harris & Ewing, photographer, *General G. Norman Lieber*, c. 1905. Library of Congress Prints and Photographs Division.

35. *Te-he-do-ne-cha. (One who forbids his house.) Sioux warrior, executed at Mankato, for taking part in Indian Massacre of 1862,* c. 1857–1863. Yale Collection of Western Americana, Beinecke Rare Book and Manuscript Library.

36. *Modocs scalping and torturing prisoners,* from *Harper's Weekly,* 1873. Library of Congress Prints and Photographs Division.

37. Lewis Herman Heller & Carleton E. Watkins, *Schonchin and Jack,* 1873. Yale Collection of Western Americana, Beinecke Rare Book and Manuscript Library.

38. *Chiricahua Prisoners, including Geronimo,* 1886. National Archives and Records Administration, 111-SC-82320.

39. *Francs-tireurs Arronssohn, tirailleurs des ternes : ils en ont vu bien d'autres,* from *Souvenirs du siége de Paris : les défenseurs de la capitale* (Paris: Bureau de l' Eclipse, 1871). Mid-Manhattan Library, Picture Collection, New York Public Library.

40. *Johann Caspar Bluntschli,* from *Zürich: Geschichte, Kultur, Wirtschaft* (Zürich: Gebr. Fretz, 1933), courtesy Sterling Memorial Library, Yale University.

41. *Alfred Thayer Mahan,* c. 1900. LC-USZ62–3124, Library of Congress Prints and Photographs Division.

42. *[Water Cure],* 1899–1902. 111-SC-98202, National Archives and Records Administration.

43. Harris & Ewing, photographer, *Plattsburg Reserve Officers Training Camp. Major Edwin F. Glenn, U.S.A.,* 1916. Library of Congress Prints and Photographs Division.

Index

Page numbers in *italics* refer to illustrations.

About the Author

John Fabian Witt is the Allen H. Duffy Class of 1960 Professor of Law at Yale Law School. He has taught at Columbia University, Harvard Law School, the University of Leiden in The Netherlands, and the University of Tokyo. His work has appeared in the *New York Times*, *Slate*, the *Harvard Law Review*, the *Yale Law Journal*, and numerous other scholarly journals. He is the author of two books published by Harvard University Press: *Patriots and Cosmopolitans: Hidden Histories of American Law* (2007), and *The Accidental Republic: Crippled Workingmen, Destitute Widows, and the Remaking of American Law* (2004). In 2010, Witt was awarded a Guggenheim Fellowship for his work on the history of the laws of war. He lives with his wife and children in New Haven, Connecticut.